Carrying on the Anatomical Studies

Left to right: Thorstein Veblen, Joseph Schumpeter, John Maynard Keynes, and Alfred Marshall.

The
Economic Problem

The Economic Problem

REVISED 8TH EDITION

ROBERT L. HEILBRONER

JAMES K. GALBRAITH

Prentice-Hall, Inc., Englewood Cliffs, NJ 07632

Library of Congress Cataloging-in-Publication Data

Heilbroner, Robert L.
  The economic problem.

  Includes index.
  1. Economics. I. Galbraith, James K. II. Title.
HB171.5.H39 1987   330   86-18747
ISBN 0-13-233081-4

Editorial/production supervision: Susan Fisher
Interior design: Jules Perlmutter and Judith A. Matz-Coniglio
Cover design: Judith A. Matz-Coniglio
Cover photo: Michel Tcherevkoff
Manufacturing buyer: Ed O'Dougherty

Endpaper drawings by Bernarda Bryson. The "Colloquy" illustrated "Economic Psychology" by George Katona, and is copyrighted © 1954 by Scientific American, Inc. All rights reserved.

Printed in the United States of America

10 9 8 7 6 5 4 3 2 1

ISBN 0-13-233081-4   01

Prentice-Hall International (UK) Limited, *London*
Prentice-Hall of Australia Pty. Limited, *Sydney*
Prentice-Hall Canada Inc., *Toronto*
Prentice-Hall Hispanoamericana, S.A., *Mexico*
Prentice-Hall of India Private Limited, *New Delhi*
Prentice-Hall of Japan, Inc., *Tokyo*
Prentice-Hall of Southeast Asia Pte. Ltd., *Singapore*
Editora Prentice-Hall do Brasil, Ltda., *Rio de Janeiro*

Contents

CHAPTER 1
What This Book Is All About   *1*

The Economic Mystique Mystery of Money Language of Economics
The "Difficulty" of Economics **Organizing the Subject**
The First Part: Economic Background **Next: From Fact to Theory**
Part Three: The Macro Economy Macro in Four Sections
The Microeconomic Side: Part Four **The Rest of the World: Part Five**
How Should You Study Economics? Vocabulary Diagrams Key Ideas
Questions and Extra Words Analysis and Abstraction

PART ONE
The Economic Background

CHAPTER 2
The Evolution of Capitalism   *13*

Where Did Capitalism Come From? The Elements of Capitalism
The Economic Revolution Freedom and Necessity **The Unleashing of Technology**
Precapitalist Technology Why Technology Slumbered The Incentive of Capitalism
The Industrial Revolutions The Effects of Technology **The Political Dimension**
Political Freedom Laissez-Faire vs. Political Intervention

v

PART TWO
Some Basic Economics

CHAPTER 7
Economic Science *123*

Maximizing vs. Constraints **Hypotheses about Behavior** Maximizing Utilities
Satiable and Insatiable Wants Rationality The Economist's View of Humankind
Hypotheses about Constraints Constraints of Nature Opportunity Cost
Constraints and Costs Constraints of Society **Basic Hypotheses**
Economics as a Social Science

CHAPTER 8
Supply and Demand *135*

Prices and Behavior **Demand** Taste and Income Diminishing Marginal Utility
Demand Curves The Puzzle of Bread and Diamonds **Supply** Supply and Demand
Balancing Supply and Demand **Emergence of the Equilibrium Price**
Interplay of Supply and Demand The Market Clears
Characteristics of Equilibrium Prices Does "Demand Equal Supply"?
The Role of Competition **Shifts in Demand and Supply**
Shifts in Curves vs. Movements Along Curves Price Changes Long and Short Run
A Last Word on Maximizing

CHAPTER 9
Why Economists Disagree *155*

Economics and Forecasting Beyond Meteorology **From Prediction to Understanding**
Commonsense Prediction Prediction vs. Expectations **From Understanding to Advocacy**
Values Producer vs. Consumer Well-Being Concentrated Pains, Diffuse Benefits
Values and Interests **From Values to Conceptions** Is Capitalism Inherently Workable?
A Last Look at Disagreement

CHAPTER 10
An Economist's Kit of Tools *167*

**Ceteris Paribus Functional Relationships Identities Schedules Graphs Equations
Economic Techniques Reviewed Economic Fallacies
An Extra Word About Graphs and Economic Causation**

Section Two: The Sectors in Action

CHAPTER 15
Household Demand   *245*

CHAPTER 16
Business Investment   *265*

CHAPTER 17
Public Spending and Deficits   *291*

CHAPTER 18
Aggregate Demand   *315*

Section Three: Microeconomic Challenges

CHAPTER 32
The Control of Market Power   585

CHAPTER 33
The Distribution of Income — In Theory   601

CHAPTER 34
How Incomes Are Distributed — In Fact   623

CHAPTER 35
Unemployment and Poverty   643

Foreword

Over the past decade I have thoroughly enjoyed writing *The Economic Problem* with Robert Heilbroner. Jointly authored works often make for conflicts over what to emphasize, add, or subtract, but in this case the difficulties did not exist. The work flowed fluidly and easily.

Given this reality, one might ask 'Why not continue as a co-author?' The answer is simple. As difficult as students will find it to believe, writing or rewriting an introductory textbook is more work than reading and mastering the material in it. It is a job that takes a lot of time if it is to be done well.

After spending a decade shepherding *The Economic Problem,* there are other activities to which I wish to devote more of my time. I hope to work out economic theories that will be more compatible with reasonable behavioral hypotheses than those commonly used today.

It is not without regret that I leave *The Economic Problem,* but I am sure that Bob Heilbroner and James Galbraith will write a textbook that is even better than it has been in the past. I wish both them and the students that read their new textbook great success.

Lester C. Thurow

To the Instructor

Here is the eighth edition of *The Economic Problem,* which makes this text older than many of its readers. It is in many ways the recognizable descendant of its first edition, but in other ways it is very different. Times change and textbooks change with them—especially in a field such as ours, where the subject matter simply refuses to stand still.

The first big change in the current edition is the name of James Galbraith. Lester Thurow, co-author for the previous four editions, has decided to devote his writing time entirely to his own books. The senior author will miss him sorely, but has been recompensed by the acquisition of a new partner who brings the same interest and expertise in policy questions as did his predecessor. James Galbraith, son of John Kenneth Galbraith, is known to many users of this book for his work as executive director of the Joint Economic Committee, Congress of the United States, in the early 1980s. He is now associate professor at the Lyndon B. Johnson School of Public Affairs, University of Texas at Austin.

TEXTUAL CHANGES

How is this edition different from previous ones? Perhaps the most important change is its much greater international focus. Beginning in Part One, we introduce the student to the question of America in the world economy, in our opinion the most significant economic issue confronting us today. This international exposure, continuing in Parts Three and Four, Macro- and Microeconomics, is one of the main themes of the text.

We recognize, of course, that international economics is intrinsically more complicated than the economics of a closed system and correspondingly more difficult to teach. We have tried to give the student a working grasp of the issues, even though considerations of space and time have forced us to postpone a formal consideration of comparative advantage and exchange rates until Part Five, The Rest of the World.

Next, organization. In this edition there are more "sections"—sequences of chapters that fit together to make a study unit. They are laid out in the contents and explained again in the introduction, "What This Book Is All About." We think the sections will simplify the problem of presentation. In addition, in the previous edition we put all the Great Unresolved Questions—the Challenges—into one part. We are persuaded that a consideration of these central issues more naturally lies where they arise from the preceding material. Hence, there is a section on Challenges at the end of both macro and micro parts. As before, we have tried to make these chapters provocative without being one-sided. They are intended to open discussions, not to close them off.

Instructors who have used the text before will find a good deal of new material in it, beginning with Chapter 6, "America in the World Economy." There is a new Chapter 9 in Part Two, "Why Economists Disagree." That ought to provide a lively class! There are new approaches to the deficit problem in Chapter 19 and to monetary issues in Chapters 21 through 23. Finally, the reader will find considerable changes in the challenge chapters at the end of the macro part.

The micro part is not much altered in its expositional sections, but there is a new consideration of the issues of welfare, poverty, and regulation—the focal micro issues for the Reagan administration—in Chapters 34 and 35. We have tried to present a balanced assessment of these issues without hiding our own judgments where these seemed appropriate.

PEDAGOGY

And then of course there is the usual updating; correcting of egregious errors that have a way of slipping into texts when the authors aren't looking; improving as best we could each word, sentence, graph, and chapter.* In the "Guide to Chapters and Extra Words," we have established three categories intended to help the instructor select chapters best suited to his or her teaching purposes. The chapters labeled "Basic" cover the standard essentials of micro and macro, plus three chapters of historical background—Chapters 4 through 6—that we think every student ought to read for background's sake.

Chapters and extra words listed under "Institutional and Historical" include those that stress empirical matters rather than analytics. We have separated them from the "Basic" category for two reasons: first, they are chapters that can readily be assigned to students without class coverage; and second, they stress the kind of material that may be of special value for students interested in grasping the workaday aspects of the economy, rather than its theoretical representation.

The chapters or extra words under the heading of "Supplemental" are intended to identify material that is relatively advanced, or of secondary empirical

---

* We would like to thank Robin King for her devoted labors in the cause of accuracy.

importance—in a word, material that can most easily be postponed to a later course, or omitted if the press of time requires.

The usual expositional aids will be found before and after each chapter—*A Look Ahead* and *Looking Back, Key Concepts,* the *Economic Vocabulary,* and a small battery of questions, all designed to help put across the ideas of the chapter in a way that will stick, even after the last exam is done. A new workbook, the *Student Companion,* is available to supplement the text, as are tests for the basic parts, together with their answers, in the *Instructor's Manual.* There is also a set of transparency masters.

In the end of course, we know that the real test of this text, like all others, is its clarity, its cogency, and its ability to communicate to students. We also know that no matter how carefully planned, its success hinges largely on the enthusiasm and expertise of instructors. We are grateful for your support and would welcome any criticisms and suggestions that you might wish to send.

Robert L. Heilbroner and
(except for the second paragraph)
James Galbraith

A Guide
to Chapters
and
Extra Words

BASIC

About the Authors

Robert Heilbroner began his studies in economics at Harvard University, from which he graduated, summa cum laude, in 1940; and went on to complete his graduate work at the New School for Social Research in New York City. While still a graduate student, he published his first book *The Worldly Philosophers* which quickly became a standard introduction to economics in hundreds of colleges. Later books, including *The Making of Economic Society* and *An Inquiry into the Human Prospect,* together with a wide variety of articles in both scholarly and popular journals, won for him a wide audience as both economic historian and social philosopher. Dr. Heilbroner has been the recipient of numerous awards and honors, including election as Vice President of the American Economic Association. He teaches at his graduate alma mater as Normal Thomas Professor, specializing in the history of economic thought. He is married and lives in New York City.

James K. Galbraith is Associate Professor at the Lyndon B. Johnson School of Public Affairs, University of Texas at Austin, where he teaches economics. Before becoming a Texan, he served on the staff of the U.S. Congress, including as executive director of the Joint Economic Committee, where he was responsible for congressional oversight of monetary policy and of the Reagan economic program. He has been a Visiting Scholar at the Brookings Institution and a Marshall Scholar at King's College, University of Cambridge. He holds an A.B. from Harvard College and a Ph.D. in economics from Yale University. He is married to Lucy Ferguson Galbraith, a microeconomist. They have a son Douglas and daughter Margaret, who shares her birthday (June 5) with Adam Smith and John Maynard Keynes.

Photo by Waring Abbott

Photo by Michael Lyon

The
Economic Problem

CHAPTER 1
What This Book Is All About

a look ahead

This is the chapter in which to get your bearings. As you read, keep in mind these objectives:

1 to get a feel for what is to come;
2 to learn how the book is organized; and
3 most important of all, to pick up a few study hints — you really want to pay attention to these.

THE ECONOMIC MYSTIQUE

M̲ost students begin a first course in economics with mixed feelings. On the one hand, everyone knows that economics is terribly important. On the other hand, everyone has the uneasy feeling that it is terribly difficult. It may reassure you to learn that you are not alone in this frame of mind. Every year, national pollsters report that economic problems, such as inflation or unemployment or taxes, rank high on the public's agenda of worries. But every year the pollsters also discover that the economics and business pages of newspapers and magazines are those that are *least* read. It seems that we all worry about economic matters, but we all throw up our hands at the idea of trying to understand what worries us.

Why does economics have this curious mystique? Three reasons suggest themselves.

1. Mystery of Money

The first is that economics is inextricably involved with money, and money is certainly perplexing. Why is a piece of paper worth anything at all? What do banks do with the money we put into them? Why isn't there enough money to go around at some times, "too much" money at others — to repeat the baffling opinions we hear?

Money is surely one reason for the economic mystique. But the problem with money is not just its inherent complexity. It is that we all use money, talk about money, worry about money, without ever having been educated about it. One purpose of learning economics is to repair that serious omission in our knowledge.

2. Language of Economics

A second reason why economics is generally regarded with unease is that it speaks in a tongue we don't quite understand. "Prices are up because of rising demand," says the TV commentator, and we nod our heads. But exactly what is "demand"? What makes it "rise"? What are those other words that the news commentators use with such assurance — gross national product, consumption, investment? What do they really mean? Because we do not "speak" economics we wonder whether or not we are being bamboozled; and when we ourselves use the words of economics, we often know that we are partly bluffing.

Therefore another purpose of this book is to introduce you to the language of economics. Like all disciplines, it has a fair number of specialized terms, but it is certainly no more difficult to speak or to understand than any of a dozen familiar subjects. By the end of the course, you should speak it pretty fluently.

3. The "Difficulty" of Economics

Last, there is the matter of the mystique itself, the reputation for difficulty that economics has acquired. It may come as a surprise to learn that there was a time when economics was reputed to be a rather easy subject, especially suited to the education of proper young ladies (this was in the 1830s). Later—indeed, up to the Great Crash of 1929—economics was still widely regarded as little more than common sense, instantly comprehensible by all right-thinking persons, especially if they thought along Solid Business Principles.

The aura of mystery that clings to economics today is mainly a product of the past generation or so, when economics itself came into national prominence. The aura is undoubtedly mixed up with the increased use of government powers in the economy, especially the use of spending and taxing to affect the level of national well-being. Here *is* something to be learned that is different from Solid Business Principles. But as you will discover, it is still nothing but logical thought, although applied from a national perspective, rather than from that of an individual enterprise.

Thus the overriding aim of our book is to demystify economics. Of course this does not mean that we can give you answers to all the problems of the economy. We don't know them. But we hope that when you finish the book, you will never again throw up your hands at the idea of *thinking* about economic problems. Once and for all, that should have lost its terror.

ORGANIZING THE SUBJECT

Economics is a very large subject with many aspects—economic history, economic statistics, economic theory, economic policy, and still others. We cannot study all these aspects in an introductory text, but it will help you grasp the larger subject of economics itself if we outline very generally what lies ahead.

We have organized our book into five major *parts,* each one of which has groups of related chapters or *sections.* The five major parts are these:

1. Economic history and background
2. Economic science
3. The study of the macro system of economic growth
4. The market mechanism, or microeconomics
5. International economics

Different instructors will have different inclinations about what parts to stress, and we have written the text to allow as much flexibility as possible in planning a coherent course. Even if there is no time to study all the parts of the text, you ought to glance at them to round out your understanding of what the dimensions of the subject embrace.

THE FIRST PART: ECONOMIC BACKGROUND

Many students would like to jump right into the midst of our current economic problems, and some instructors like to teach their courses that way. In fact, our book is organized so that a direct approach to major issues is possible by starting in macroeconomics or microeconomics.

But ideally we ought to acquire some perspective on our subject before getting embroiled in how things work. We ought, for example, to have a good working idea of economic history — of how our economy got where it is. We should know at least the rudiments of what some great economists of the past have said about how the economic system works. And we should be familiar with the economy in the same sense that we are familiar with the size and shape of the United States and where its great rivers and mountain ranges are.

That is what Part One is about. Its initial chapter will give you a jet-speed voyage through economic history. The next chapter takes you rapidly down the gallery of the world's great economists — the "worldly philosophers." Then, in three successive chapters we fly you over the economic continent and then over the economic planet. *Try to read these chapters as background, even if your instructor doesn't have time to assign them as classwork.*

NEXT: FROM FACT TO THEORY

In Part Two we turn to a very different subject — the core elements of economic "science." We put the word in quotes because, as you will discover, our subject both is and is not a science like the natural sciences. It has aspects that very much resemble sciences like physics, and aspects that are much more akin to studies like government or morality.

The science-like aspect has to do with the fact that the economic world, for all its variety and complexity, can often be understood in a highly generalized, abstract way. As a result, economists do not consider their task to be only that of describing phenomena, such as we have done in Part One. They also seek to find similar characteristics hidden within seemingly different problems or institutions, much as a doctor first takes a patient's life history and then examines him or her for signs of a general condition called a "disease."

In Chapter 7 we tell you something about the basis on which this capacity for generalization and abstraction rests. It is our introduction to the idea of *economic theory*. Then in Chapter 8 we go on to apply theory to the single most widely used generalization about economic life — supply and demand. Thereafter, to balance the picture, we look at another side of economics in a chapter whose subject matter you must surely have wondered about: "Why Economists Disagree." Finally, in Chapter 10 we add a kind of appendix to Part Two in a "Kit of Tools." Here is a brief introduction to the basic technical elements you will have to know, from reading a chart to saying some easy but powerful things in mathematical sentences. Many students will not need this chapter at all; others may find it a lifesaver.

PART THREE: THE MACRO ECONOMY

The subject we cover in the next 14 chapters is the issue of macroeconomics — the study of how the economy grows (and sometimes fails to grow), and of how and why it develops inflationary tendencies or unemployment. Note that there are very important issues which are not included in the macro point of view — for example, pollution or the problem of riches and poverty. These problems are best examined from the micro perspective that we will take up in the second major portion of the text.

Macro in Four Sections

It will help us organize the macro problem if we tackle it in four separate sections. In the first of these, covering Chapters 11 through 14, we learn about gross national product and the process of saving and investing that underlies growth. The second section, from Chapter 15 to Chapter 19, takes up the sectors of the economy in action, so that we become familiar with the workings of the household or consumption sector, the business or investment sector, and the government or public sector. At the end of this part we should understand how the level of GNP is determined.

The next section, comprising Chapters 20 to 23, fleshes out the macro picture by introducing us to the question of money — how it is "created," how its supply is regulated, how it affects the activity of the sectors and therefore the level of GNP itself.

Last but not least, in Chapters 23 and 24 we turn to the central challenges of macroeconomics — inflation and stagnation. We have put these chapters into a special section of their own. There is a reason for this. Up to this point we have mainly been explaining things about which there is a great deal of agreement. But when it comes to the big macroeconomic issues, disagreements are more readily noted than agreement. We have tried to point out the basis for these disagreements, as well as where our own judgment inclines us. But the unsettled nature of these questions seemed to us best emphasized by setting them apart.

THE MICROECONOMIC SIDE: PART FOUR

Microeconomics is every bit as interesting and important as macro—some economists would say more interesting and more important. It certainly offers a clearer perspective on some kinds of issues than can be gained from the macroeconomic vantage point.

Like macro, we have organized the micro portion of our text into a series of sections—chapters that fit together to make a unit of study. The first of these, Chapters 25 through 28, takes us through the workings of the market system itself, just as the first part of macro took us through the basic mechanisms of growth. The next section, Chapters 29 to 32, brings a new subject to our attention—the unit of business enterprise that economists call "the firm." Unless we understand how the firm operates, we can't really understand how the market system works.

The third micro section, Chapters 33 through 35, brings us to the counterpart of the challenges confronting macroeconomics. Here we look into poverty, welfare, regulation, and other questions, all as unsettled as their macro sisters. Once again we have tried to show both sides of these issues, as well as our own diagnosis.

THE REST OF THE WORLD: PART FIVE

Traditionally, there has been a terrible parochialism to American economics. It has tended to assume that learning about domestic issues, macro and micro, was really all a student—especially a beginning student—had to do. The rest of the world was relegated to the back pages of texts, and to the second and third years of economic studies.

As our text illustrates, this indifference to international economic problems is no longer the rule (although it *was*, as recently as the last edition). Already in Chapter 6 we have looked into the ways in which the American economy is entangled with the economies of other nations, and an international theme has surfaced again and again in our studies of both macro- and microeconomics.

Nevertheless, there are aspects and elements of international economics that do have to be postponed until a student has some working grasp of the fundamentals. These are the matters we take up in this part, where the mysteries of the exchange rate and of international competition are examined.

HOW SHOULD YOU STUDY ECONOMICS?

Vocabulary

We have already stressed the importance of acquiring a new economic vocabulary. **To become economists, you will have to learn at least a dozen words and phrases that have meanings somewhat different from those of everyday usage:** *capital, investment, demand,* **for example.** You will have to master another dozen phrases that come awkwardly to the tongue (and sometimes not at all to the mind): *marginal propensity to consume* is a good example.

In economics, as in French, some people acquire new words and phrases easily, some do not; and in economics, as in French, until you can say things correctly, you are apt to say them very wrongly. So when the text says *gross private domestic investment* those are the words to be learned, not just any combination of three of them because they seem to mean the same thing. Fortunately, the necessary economic vocabulary has far fewer words than French has, and the long and awkward phrases seem shorter and easier after you've said them a few times.

Diagrams

Associated with learning the vocabulary of economics is learning how to draw a few diagrams. Diagrams are an immensely powerful way of presenting many economic ideas. Far from complicating things, they simplify them enormously. A supply and demand diagram makes things immediately clear in a way that a dozen pages could not.

So you must learn to draw a few diagrams. There is a great temptation to do so hastily, without thinking about the problem that the diagram is trying to make clear. A little care in labeling your axes (how else can anyone know what the diagram is about?) or in making lines tangent where they are supposed to touch, or cross where they are supposed to intersect, will not only make the difference between a poor grade and a better one, but will demonstrate that you truly understand the matter being illustrated.

You will also note that throughout the book, with each figure and most tables, a sentence or a paragraph highlights the point being made. This should help you in reviewing the material.

Key Ideas

Studying a vast subject requires organization. This means putting first things first and keeping details and secondary material in the background.

We've tried to simplify the task of learning by putting a highly abbreviated and goal-oriented "A Look Ahead" and "Looking Back" at the beginning and at the end of each chapter. These sections do not necessarily embrace all the vocabulary or ideas in each chapter; instead, they try to give you objectives to bear in mind before starting, and summaries to collect your thoughts when you're done.

At the end of each chapter, first read the general review. Then look only at Key Concepts to see if you can reproduce that review. Last, a glance at Economic Vocabulary will serve as a final test. Page numbers follow each word for easy reference.

Questions and Extra Words

Next, take time to answer all the questions at the ends of chapters. We have tried to make them few and central. If your instructor assigns the Student Guide that accompanies this text, do those problems too. There is no substitute for working out an example or for jotting down three reasons for this, four reasons for that. Learning is a process about which we know very little, but we do know that the physical and intellectual act of writing (or mumbling to yourself) is much more effective than merely thinking. Practice, as they say, makes perfect. You might reflect on the story of the sailor on a sinking ship. When asked if he knew how to swim, he answered, "Well, I understand the theory of it. . . ."

Economics has to be learned by arguing about it. Therefore after many chapters you will find a few additional pages — sometimes to add to your historical, statistical, or analytic knowledge, more often to open for your consideration problems of public policy that are related to the issues we have studied. The policy issues are often controversial. We hope you will worry about them — not just read them. They are there to open debate, not close it.

Analysis and Abstraction

The idea of arguing brings us to our last word of counsel. Economics, as we have been at pains to say, is really not a hard language to learn. The key words and concepts are not too many or too demanding; the diagrams are no more difficult than those of elementary geometry. It is economic *thinking* that is hard, in a way that may have something to do with the aura of mystery we are out to dispel.

The hardness is not the sheer mental ability that is required. The reason lies, rather, in a **special attribute of economic thought:** *its abstract, analytic character.* Abstractness does not mean an indifference to the problems of the real world. Economics is about things as real as being without work. Nevertheless, as economists we do not study unemployment to learn firsthand about the miseries and sufferings that joblessness inflicts. We study unemployment to understand and analyze the causes of this malfunction of the economic system. Similarly, we do not study monopoly to fulminate against the profiteering of greedy capitalists, or labor unions to deplore the abuse of power by labor leaders, or government spending to declaim against politicians. We study these matters to shed light on their mechanisms, their reasons for being, their consequences.

There is nothing unusual in this abstract, analytic approach. All disciplines necessarily abstract from the immediate realities of their subject matters so that they may make broader generalizations or develop theories. What makes abstraction so difficult in economics is that the problems of the discipline are things that affect us deeply in our lives. It is difficult, even unnatural, to suppress our feelings of approval or anger when we study the operations of the economic system and the main actors in it. The necessary act of analysis thus becomes mixed up with feelings of economic concern or even partisanship. **Yet, unless we make an effort to think analytically and abstractly in a detached way, we can be no more than slaves to our unexamined emotions.** Someone who *knows* that corporations or labor unions or governments are "good" or "bad" does not have to study economics, for the subject has nothing to teach such a person.

You must therefore make an effort to put aside your natural partisanship and prejudice while you study the problems of economics from its abstract, analytic, detached perspective. After you are done, your feelings will assuredly come back to you. No one has ever lost a sense of social outrage or social justice by taking a course in economics. But many students have changed or modified their preconceived judgments in one way or another. There is no escape, after all, from living in the world as economic citizens. But there is the option of living in it as intelligent and effective economic citizens. That is the prize we hope you carry away from this course.

PART ONE

the economic background

CHAPTER 2
The Evolution of Capitalism

a look ahead

There is one central idea this chapter will present—a very simple but exceedingly important idea. It is that capitalism—our Western economic society—represents a dramatic change in the way that humankind has grappled with its economic problems. In this chapter we will trace three main aspects of this change.

1 The emergence of a market system.
2 The development of a powerful industrial technology.
3 The assertion of political limits on the economic machinery.

The purpose of this chapter is not only to review these critical elements of economic history, but to make you think about the subject of economics itself in a historical, evolutionary way.

WHERE DID CAPITALISM COME FROM?

The economic system we are going to study in this book is called **capitalism,** or sometimes the *free enterprise system.* In a way, we all know about capitalism because it surrounds us. It is the world we live in. But the question we are going to start with is far removed from our daily experience: Where did capitalism come from? How did the free enterprise system come to be?

People sometimes talk about capitalism as if it were as old as the hills, as ancient as the Bible. Yet this is clearly not the case. Nobody ever called the Egyptian pharaohs "capitalists." The Greeks about whom Homer wrote were not a business society, even though there were merchants and traders in Greece; neither was imperial Rome a capitalist system. Medieval Europe was certainly not capitalist. Nor would anyone use the word *capitalist* to describe the brilliant civilizations of India or China, about which Marco Polo wrote, or the great empires of ancient Africa or the Islamic economies of which we catch glimpses in *The Arabian Nights.*

We will make explicit why these were not capitalist economies in a moment. But we must begin by realizing that capitalism is a modern economic system — and furthermore, a geographically limited one. **Most of the people in the world's history have never had any direct contact with it; Even today, less than half of the world's population lives in a system that we would call capitalist.**

The Elements of Capitalism

What is capitalism? The fact that the system appears in history only after many thousands of years suggests that we would do well to search for its identifying characteristics in historic changes, rather than in specific institutions that exist today. Here are three of the changes that help us recognize capitalism as a unique socioeconomic organization of human affairs.

1. Capitalism Becomes Visible When Economic Activity Becomes Detached from the Activity of the State. Economic activity refers to all the tasks carried on in society to produce and distribute wealth. Before capitalism, those activities were inextricably mixed with the exercise of rulership itself. Typically, precapitalist societies were large, imperial kingdoms or small domains ruled by local lords. In all these societies, large or small, production and distribution were carried on under the direct supervision of the ruler. The peasant working in the field and the artisan in his workshop were not working as they wished, for their own account. They were directly or indirectly carrying out orders from above, for whose power and glory their labors would be used. Such societies have been described as "tributary" systems — a telling phrase that emphasizes the subordination of economic activity to the benefit of its political elites.

Merchants, who *did* carry on economic activity for their own account, also existed in these societies. But they were at the fringes of society, not at its center. Certainly the provision of the essentials of state power and continuity — basic foodstuffs, for example — were not entrusted to the pull and tug of mercantile activity. So a decisive change that marks the emergence of capitalism as a new mode of social organization was the spread of market activity into every area of economic life.

Shortly we shall see how this took place. But here we need to note a crucially important consequence of that spread. As the importance of buying and selling expanded, the authority of the state shrank. Within the state a new entity appeared — an *economy* whose function was to carry on the production and distribution of wealth for society. The economy thus appears as a kind of state within a state, a realm of society in which were contained vital activities formerly carried on as part of the overall exercise of authority from above. **Thus capitalism brings into being a new sphere of private economic activity — activity conducted for the self-interest of its actors, not for the glorification of the state.**

This new private sphere is the root of one of the most important political accomplishments of capitalism, the establishment of economic freedom. This is a theme to which we will often revert. But it is crucial to guard against thinking of capitalism as consisting only of private economic activity. The state remains under capitalism, not merely to carry on its traditional functions of war and peace and internal order, but also to provide essential services to the private sphere of activity — roads and ports, public works needed for health and safety, courts and coinage, to name only a few. Thus the public sphere shrinks as capitalism emerges, but it does not disappear. The state is indispensable for the operation of a market economy, in ways we will talk about many times in the pages to follow.

It is also clear, however, that there is a deep tension between the economic and political activities of a capitalist state. This tension is not just a passing "political" issue, but comes from the very nature of the system, which creates two realms of authority where formerly there was only one.

2. CAPITALISM IS MARKED BY ITS DYNAMIC SEARCH FOR THE ACCUMULATION OF MATERIAL WEALTH. The next historic change follows from the first. It is the extraordinary dynamism developed by capitalism, a dynamism that takes the form of an unprecedented piling up of wealth in a new form — not for consumption and display, but as capital.

Here a glance backward serves to illustrate the point. Precapitalist societies were certainly capable of accumulating staggering displays of wealth. No single creation of capitalism is likely to endure as long as the pyramids of Egypt, the Great Wall of China, the monuments of the Incas, or the stupendous cathedrals of medieval Europe.

Yet when we look back over the societies that built these empires and monuments, what strikes us is how slow was their normal rate of change, how changeless was the tenor of their daily lives. The boundaries of empires might expand or contract, great works might take shape over a ruler's lifetime, but the level of mass existence varied little from period to period. It is sobering to consider that the diet, the housing, the clothing and material possessions of the Egyptian peasants at the time of Napoleon's invasion of Egypt were little different from those of the time when Cheops built his gigantic pyramids. The level of material life of the French peasants who witnessed the building of the cathedral of Chartres was not substantially different from that of their ancestors who helped the Roman legions construct the aqueducts through Gaul.

It is this basically static quality of life that capitalism removes. Economic historian W. W. Rostow has estimated that between the age of the American Revolution and our own times, the volume of manufactured goods increased by *seventeen hundred times*.* This is a display of expansion and accumulation beside which the achievements of prior civilizations pale into insignificance. Nothing resembling such a force for the creation of material wealth had ever existed before.

What was the source of this accumulative thrust? Essentially it was the very change we have just noted — namely, the emergence of a realm of economic life separated from the state itself. In the previous "tributary" mode of organizing economic life, the surplus of society's production was devoted to the glorification of its rulers through the construction of monuments intended to last through history, or for arms to protect the kingdom, or simply to provide the luxury by which imperial majesty displayed itself to the world.

For the new mercantile groups, however, economic activity had a different aim — not to display wealth, but to accumulate it as a route to power and prestige. This required that wealth take the form of capital. What is capital? It is wealth that can be used to create still more wealth. The humblest commodities can be capital as well as the most dazzling jewels, as long as they can be sold to gain still more wealth. **This use of wealth as capital rather than as a means of display or of luxury consumption was the vital difference brought about by the detachment of the economic sphere of life from the state.**

The consequences of the drive for the accumulation of capital are immense — indeed, capitalism derives its name from a recognition of the central importance of this propulsive force. One of these consequences is the instability of the system, bursting with energy when the accumulation of wealth goes smoothly, wracked with economic and social troubles when it does not. A major theme of economics is the investigation of the sequence of fast and slow accumulation — of growth and stagnation, boom and bust, prosperity and depression — that capitalism brings. That theme will occupy us throughout much of this book.

But another consequence deserves special attention at this initial stage of our inquiry: It is the encouragement given by capitalism to the development of technology as the principal means from which the expansive tendency of the system gains its momentum and through which it exerts its impact on daily life. At the end of this chapter we will look more closely into technology and its special significance for capitalism.

3. CAPITALISM DEVELOPS A NEW MECHANISM FOR ITS INTERNAL GUIDANCE. The mechanism was the market system — not just individual markets, but a network of interconnected markets that would guide the production and distribution of economic activity as a whole. We will spend much of this book learning how such a market system serves as a guidance mechanism for capitalism. Here we want once

---

* W. W. Rostow, *The World Economy* (Austin, TX: University of Texas Press, 1978), p. 48.

again to see the rise of such a system in a manner that helps us identify, and therefore understand, the larger historic change itself.

How did the market system come into being? The answer is that a vast revolution undermined an older world of tradition and command, and brought into existence a hitherto unknown world in which not only goods, but the services of labor, land, and capital were offered for sale. We have a name for the services of labor, land, and capital that are hired or fired in a market society. They are called the **factors of production,** and a great deal of economics is about how the market combines their essential contributions to production. But just because they *are* essential, a question must be answered. How were the factors of production put to use prior to the market system? The answer tells us a great deal.

There were no factors of production before capitalism. Of course, human labor, nature's gift of land and natural resources, and the artifacts of society have always existed. But labor, land, and capital were not commodities for sale. Labor was performed as part of the social duties of serfs or slaves, who were not paid "wages" for doing their work. Indeed, the serf paid fees to his lord for the use of the lord's equipment, and he never expected to be remunerated when he turned over a portion of his crop as the lord's due. Land was regarded as the basis for military power or civil administration, just as a state is regarded today — not as real estate to be bought and sold. And capital was thought of as "treasure" or as the necessary equipment of an artisan, not as an abstract sum of wealth with a market value. The idea of liquid, fluid capital would have been as strange in medieval life as we would find it strange to think of stocks and bonds as heirlooms never to be sold.

The Economic Revolution

How did wageless labor, unrentable land, and private treasures become "factors of production"; that is, homogeneous commodities to be bought and sold like so many yards of cloth or bushels of wheat? Beginning roughly in the sixteenth century — although with roots that can be traced much further back — a process of change, sometimes gradual, sometimes violent, broke the bonds and customs of the medieval world of Europe and ushered in the market society we know.

We can only touch on that long, tortuous, and sometimes bloody revolution here. In England the process bore with particular severity on the peasants, who were expelled from their lands through the "enclosure" of common grazing lands. This enclosure took place to make private pasturage for the lord's sheep, whose wool had become a profitable commodity. As late as 1820, the Duchess of Sutherland evicted 15,000 tenants from 794,000 acres, replacing them with 131,000 sheep. The tenants, deprived of their traditional access to the fields, drifted into the towns, where they were forced to sell their services as a factor of production: *labor.*

In France, the creation of factors of production bore painfully on land. When prices began to rise in sixteenth-century Europe as gold from the New World flowed in, feudal lords found themselves in a terrible squeeze. Like everything in medieval life, the rents and dues they received from their serfs were fixed and unchangeable. But the prices of merchandise were not fixed. Although more and more of the serfs' obligations were changed from "kind" to cash, and from physical duties to money dues, prices kept rising so fast that the feudal lords found it impossible to meet their bills.

Hence we begin to find a new economic individual, the *impoverished aristocrat.* In the year 1530, in the Gévaudan region of France, the richest manorial lord had an income of 5,000 livres; but in towns, some merchants had incomes of 65,000 livres. Thus the balance of power turned against the landed aristocracy, reducing many to shabby gentility. The upstart merchants lost no time in acquiring lands that they soon came to regard not as ancestral estates, but as potential capital.

This brief glance at economic history brings home an important point. **The factors of production, without which a market society could not exist, are not eternal attributes of a natural order. They are the creations of a process of historic change, a change that divorced labor from social life, that created real estate out of ancestral land, and that made treasure into capital. Capitalism is the outcome of a revolutionary change — a change in laws, attitudes, and social relationships as deep and far-reaching as any in history.** *

Freedom and Necessity

The revolutionary aspect of capitalism lies in the fact that an older, feudal way of life had to be dismantled before the market system could come into being. This brings us to think again about the economic freedom that accompanies the rise of a private sector of economic life, detached from the state. For we can now see that economic freedom did not arise just because men and women directly sought to shake off the bonds of custom and command. It was also thrust upon them, often as a very painful and unwelcome change.

For feudalism, with all its cruelties and injustices, did provide a modicum of economic security. However mean a serf's life, he could not be arbitrarily thrown off the lord's land, and in bad times he was guaranteed a small dole from his lord's granary. However exploited a medieval journeyman, at least he knew that he could not be summarily thrown out of work under the rules of his master's guild. And however squeezed a lord, he too knew that his rents and dues were secured by law and custom and would be coming in, weather permitting.

The eruption of the market system destroyed all of that. The creation of factors of production meant the end of assured livelihoods. If a landless laborer could not find work, that was not the responsibility of his lord, for he no longer *had* a lord. Nor was it the lookout of any former employer, who had no obligation to pay anyone who was not an employee. If a worker in the market system was fired, he or she could not complain to the guild, because there *was* no guild. For that matter,

---

* One of the many fascinating questions that surround the origins of capitalism is why it arose only in Europe, and never in any other part of the world. The probable explanation is that the collapse of the Roman Empire left many towns without an allegiance to anyone. In time, these towns, which were naturally centers of trading and artisan work, grew powerful and managed to bargain for privileges with kings and lords. Capitalism thus grew up in the interstices of the medieval system. A similar opportunity and stimulus did not present itself elsewhere.

neither could an employer protest to the guild about some intruder who was "stealing" trade. And if a landlord's rents declined in a bad year, that was no one's worry but his own; there were no more "customary" rents to rely on.

Economic freedom therefore meant that each person was thrown on the marketplace to sink or swim. This freedom could be a precious achievement for individuals who had formerly been deprived of the right to enter into legal contracts. For many, it meant the chance to rise out of a station in life from which, in earlier times, there was no exit. But economic freedom had another equally important aspect. This was the necessity to stay afloat by one's own efforts in rough waters where all were struggling to survive, and where no one much cared when a laborer, a landowner, or a capitalist disappeared from view.

The market system was thus the cause of unrest, insecurity, and individual suffering, just as it was also the source of progress, opportunity, and fulfillment. In this contest between the costs and benefits of economic freedom lies a theme that is still a crucial issue for capitalism.

THE UNLEASHING OF TECHNOLOGY

As we have already noted, the creation of a market society paved the way for a change of profound significance in bringing about modern economic life. This was the incorporation of science and technology into the very midst of daily life.

Precapitalist Technology

Technology is not, of course, a modern phenomenon. The gigantic stones that form prehistoric Stonehenge, the precision and delicacy of the monumental Egyptian pyramids, the Incan stone walls fitted so exactly that a knife blade cannot be put between adjoining blocks, the Chinese Great Wall, and the Mayan observatories attest to mankind's long possession of the ability to transport and hoist staggering weights, to cut and shape hard surfaces, and to calculate complex problems. Indeed, many of these works would challenge our present-day engineering capabilities.

Nonetheless, although precapitalist technology reached great heights, it had a very restricted base. The basic tools of agriculture and artisan crafts remained little changed over millennia. So "simple" an invention as a horse collar shaped to prevent a straining animal from pressing against its windpipe did not appear during all the glories of Greece and triumphs of Rome. Not until the Middle Ages was there a switch from the ox to the draft horse as a ploughing animal (a change that improved efficiency by an estimated 30 percent), or was the traditional two-field system of crop rotation improved by adopting a three-field system (see box).

Thus precapitalist technology was lavished on the needs of rulers, priests, warriors; its application to common everyday work was virtually ignored.

ECONOMIC LIFE IN THE MIDDLE AGES, ILLUSTRATED IN THE BREVIARIUM GRIMANI

(The Bettmann Archive, Inc.)

THE DIFFERENCE TECHNOLOGY MAKES: THREE FIELDS VS. TWO

Until the Middle Ages, the prevailing system of cultivation was to plant half of a lord's arable land in a winter crop, leaving the other half fallow. The second year, the two fields simply changed functions.

Under the three-field plan, the arable land was divided into thirds. One section was planted with a winter crop, one section with a summer crop, and one was left fallow. The second year, the first section was put into summer crops, the second left fallow, and the third put into winter grains. In the third year, the first field was left fallow, the second used for winter crops, the third for spring planting.

Therefore, under the three-field system only one-third, not one-half, of the arable land was fallow in any year. Suppose that the field as a whole yielded 600 bushels of output. Under the two-field system, it would give an annual crop of 300 bushels. Under the three-field system the annual crop would be two-thirds of the area, or 400 bushels — an increase of one-third. Further, in those days it was customary to plough fallow land twice, and cultivated land only once. By cutting down the ratio of fallow to cultivated land, plowing time was greatly reduced, and peasant productivity even more significantly improved. For more on this and other fascinating advances in precapitalist technology, see Lynn White, *Medieval Technology and Social Change* (Oxford: Clarendon Press, 1962).

Why Technology Slumbered

There were, of course, good reasons why the technology of daily life was ignored. The primary effect of technological change in daily activity is to increase output, to enhance the productivity of the working person. But in a society still regulated by tradition and command, where production was mainly carried on by serfs and slaves and custom-bound artisans, there was little incentive to look for increases in output. The bulk of any increase in agricultural yields would only go to the lord in higher rents, not to the serf or the slave who produced them. To be sure, a lord would benefit greatly from increases in agricultural output. But how could a great noble be expected to know about, or to concern himself with, the dirty business of sowing and reaping?

So too, any artisan who altered the techniques of his trade would be expected, as a matter of course, to share these advances with his brethren. And how could his brethren, accustomed over the years to disposing of a certain quantity of pots or pans or cloth in the village market, expect to find buyers for more output? Would not the extra production simply go begging?

Thus productive technology in precapitalist societies slumbered because there was no incentive to search for change. Indeed, because technological change could only introduce an unsettling element into the world, powerful social forces were ranged against it. How could a society whose whole way of life rested on the reproduction of established patterns of life even imagine a world where the technology of production was constantly in flux, and where limits were no longer recognized in any endeavor?

The Incentive of Capitalism

These inhibiting forces were ruthlessly swept away by the currents of the emerging markets for labor, land, and capital. Serfs were uprooted to become workers forced to sell their labor power for wages; aristocratic landlords were rudely shouldered aside by money-minded parvenus; guild masters and artisans watched commercial enterprises take away their accustomed livelihood; a new sense of necessity, of urgency, altered economic life. What had been a more or less unchanging routine of life became increasingly a scramble for existence.

The growing importance of the market, where a producer had to win a place for himself every day, radically altered the place of technology, especially in the small workshops and minuscule factories that were the staging areas of the capitalist revolution. Here the free-for-all brought a need to find toeholds in the struggle for a livelihood. And one toehold available to any aspiring capitalist with an inquiring mind and a knowledge of the actual processes of production was technology itself — some invention or improvement that would lower costs or change a product to give it an edge on its competitors.

This is where the appearance of wealth as *capital* made an enormous difference. It brought into being a wholly new personage in economic history — the *industrial capitalist* who made his wealth in pursuits that would never have led to riches in another age.*

For example there was John Wilkinson, son of an iron producer who became a driving force for technical change in his trade. Wilkinson insisted that everything

---

* This is not a text in economic history, and therefore we must pass too quickly over a change of great importance in the evolution of the system. It is the leap from the earliest form of *merchant capitalism* into *industrial capitalism,* the form of the system on which we will henceforth concentrate our attention.

The crucial change is the rise of industrial activity, with its key institution of labor working for wages in factories. As a consequence of that new institution, the focus of profit-seeking turned away from mercantile trading to the production process itself. That is, the main source of profits was no longer sought in profitable exchange but in profitable production, brought about by driving and disciplining labor and developing its productivity through machinery.

That change did not occur everywhere. For instance, the shift from mercantile to industrial capitalism was not made in early eighteenth-century Holland, so that the Dutch — formidable rivals of the English in the seventeenth century — were bypassed when England became an industrial society and the Dutch remained a trading one. Anyone interested in this chapter of the history of capitalism should look into Jan de Vries' marvellously interesting book, *The Economy of Europe in an Age of Crisis: 1600 – 1750* (New York: Cambridge University Press, 1976).

be built of iron — pipes and bridges, bellows and cylinders (one of which powered the newfangled steam engine of John Watt). He even constructed a much derided iron ship — later much admired. There was Richard Arkwright, barber by trade, who made his fortune by inventing (or perhaps by stealing) the first effective spinning machine, becoming in time a great mill owner. There were Peter Onions, an obscure foreman who originated the puddling process for making wrought iron; Benjamin Huntsman, a clockmaker who improved the method of making steel; and a score more. A few, like Sir Jethro Tull, a pioneer in the technology of agriculture, were great gentlemen, but on the whole the technological leaders in industry were men of humble origin.

The Industrial Revolutions

The new dynamism revealed itself in a series of technological "revolutions" — periods in which the basic ways of making things suddenly underwent startling changes, and in which new kinds of goods and services entered, and radically changed, daily life.

The first of these periods is often called *the* Industrial Revolution, although actually it was only the initial rush of a long, multiphase process. Beginning in the late eighteenth century and continuing for over twenty-five years, the first industrial revolution mechanized spinning and weaving, enormously improved and expanded iron production, brought the all-important gift of power in the form of the steam engine, and introduced a crucial change in the application of technology to production — the large, controlled workplace we call the factory.

The second industrial revolution followed in the mid-nineteenth century, bringing railroads and steamships, cheap steel, agricultural machinery, and the first mass-produced chemicals. Then in the early years of the twentieth century, a third burst came with the development of the automobile, electrical power, and consumer durable goods; and in our own day we are witnessing a fourth — the revolution of computers, air transportation, perhaps nuclear power.

The Effects of Technology

Many profound changes have followed in the wake of capitalism — no other socio-economic upheaval has so fundamentally altered life in its every aspect. But of the changes wrought, none was more dramatic than the industrial revolutions. The new technology literally remade life, and we should take a few moments to clarify some of the ways in which it did so.

1. OUTPUT INCREASED ENORMOUSLY, RAISING LIVING STANDARDS. First a few figures. Between 1701 and 1802, as the technology of spinning and weaving was gradually perfected, the use of cotton in England expanded by 6,000 percent. Between 1788 and 1839, when the process of iron manufacture passed through its first technological upheaval, the output of pig iron jumped from 68,000 to

1,347,000 tons. In France, in the thirty years after 1815, iron output quintupled, coal output grew sevenfold, and transportation tonnage mounted ten times.

But these figures do not convey a sense of the effect of technology on daily life. *Things* became more common — and more commonplace. As late as the seventeenth century, what we would consider the most ordinary possessions were scarce. A peasant counted his worldly wealth in terms of a few utensils, a table, perhaps one complete change of clothes. Shakespeare left Ann Hathaway his "second best bed." Iron nails were so scarce that pioneers in America burned down their cottages to retrieve them. In the wilder parts of Scotland in Adam Smith's time, nails even served as money.

Technology brought a widening and deepening and ever faster flowing river of things. Shoes, coats, paper, window glass, chairs, buckles — objects of solicitous respect in precapitalist times for all but the privileged few — became everyday articles. **Gradually, capitalism gave rise to what we call a "rising standard of living" — a steady, regular, systematic increase in the number, variety, and quality of material goods enjoyed by the great bulk of society. No such process had ever occurred before.**

2. The Scale of Economic Organization Grew Vastly Larger. A second change wrought by technology was a striking increase in the size of society's productive apparatus.

The increase began with the enlargement of the equipment used in production — an enlargement that stemmed mostly from advances in the technology of iron and later steel. The typical furnace used in extracting iron ore increased from 10 feet in height in the 1770s to over 100 feet a century later; during the same period the crucibles in which steel was made grew from cauldrons hardly larger than an oversized jug to converters literally as big as a house. The looms used by weavers expanded from small machines that fitted into the cottages of artisan-weavers to monstrous mechanisms housed in mills that still impress us by their size. Perhaps the thrust to bigness in machinery was best symbolized in the great Corliss engine (see illustration) that dominated the Philadelphia Exposition of 1876, perfectly illustrating the technological imperative for power and strength.

Equally remarkable was the expansion in the social scale of production. The new technology almost immediately outstripped the administrative capability of the small-sized business establishment. As the apparatus of production increased in size, it also increased in speed. As outputs grew from rivulets to rivers, a much larger organization was needed to manage production — to arrange for the steady arrival of raw materials, to supervise the work process, and to find a market for its end product.

Thus we find the size of the typical business enterprise steadily increasing as its technological basis became more complex. In the last quarter of the eighteenth century, a factory of ten persons was worthy of note by Adam Smith, as we shall see in the next chapter. By the first quarter of the nineteenth century, an ordinary textile mill employed several hundred men and women. Fifty years later, many railways employed as many individuals as constituted the armies of respectable monarchs in Adam Smith's time. And in still another fifty years, by the 1920s,

THE CORLISS ENGINE

many large manufacturing companies had almost as many employees as the populations of respectable eighteenth-century cities. The Ford Motor Company, for example, had 174,000 employees in 1929.

3. THE DIVISION OF LABOR CHANGED THE NATURE OF WORK. Technology also played a decisive role in changing the nature of that most basic of all human activities, work. **It did so by breaking down the complicated tasks of productive activity into much smaller subtasks, many of which could then be duplicated, or at least greatly assisted, by mechanical contrivances. This process was called the division of labor.** Adam Smith was soon to explain that the division of labor was mainly responsible for the increase in productivity of the average worker.

The division of labor altered social life in other ways as well. Work became more fragmented, monotonous, tedious, "alienated." And the self-sufficiency of individuals was greatly curtailed. In precapitalist days, most people produced their own subsistence or made some article that could be exchanged for subsistence: peasants grew crops; artisans produced cloth, shoes, implements. But as work became more and more finely divided, the products of work became ever smaller pieces in the total jigsaw puzzle. Individuals did not spin thread or weave cloth, but manipulated levers and fed the machinery that did the actual spinning or weaving. A worker in a shoe plant made uppers or lowers or heels, but not shoes. No one of these products, by itself, would have sustained its performer for a single day; and no one of these products could have been exchanged for another product except through a complicated network of exchange. **Technology freed men and women from much material want, but it bound them to the workings of a market mechanism.**

4. A New Form of Economic Insecurity Arose. Not least of the mighty impacts of technology was its exposure of men and women to an unprecedented degree of change. Some of this was welcome, for change literally opened new horizons of material life: travel, for instance, once the prerogative of the wealthy, became a possibility for the masses.

However, the changes introduced by technology had their negative side as well. Already buffeted by market forces that could mysteriously dry up the need for work or just as mysteriously create it, society now discovered that entire occupations, skills acquired over a lifetime, companies laboriously built up over generations, age-old industries could be threatened by the appearance of technological change. **For the first time in history, machinery appeared as the enemy, as well as the ally, of humankind.** No wonder that the textile weavers, whose cottage industry was gradually destroyed by competition from the mills, banded together as Luddites to burn down the hated buildings.*

These aspects of change do not begin to exhaust the ways in which technology, coupled with the market system, altered the very meaning of existence. But in considering them, we begin to see how profound and how wrenching was the revolution capitalism introduced. Technology was a genie that capitalism let out of the bottle; it has ever since refused to go back in.

THE POLITICAL DIMENSION

The disturbing, upsetting, revolutionary nature of the market and of technology sets the stage for one last aspect of capitalism that we want to note. This is the political currents of change that capitalism brought — political currents that are as much a part of the history of capitalism as the emergence of the market or the dismantling of the barriers against technical change.

Political Freedom

One of these political currents was the rise of democratic, or parliamentary, institutions. Democratic political institutions far predate capitalism, as the history of ancient Athens or the Icelandic medieval parliamentary system shows. Nonetheless, the rise of the mercantile classes was closely tied to the struggle against the privileges and legal institutions of medieval European feudalism. The historic

---

* The word *Luddite* comes from a mythical General Ludd who supposedly led these raids of anger and desperation. The term has come to mean an "antimachine" attitude.

movement that eventually swept aside the precapitalist economic order also swept aside its political order. **Along with the emergence of the market system we find a parallel and supporting emergence of more open, libertarian political ways of life.**

We should be cautious, however, in maintaining that capitalism either guarantees, or is necessary for, political freedom. We have seen some capitalist nations, such as pre-Hitler Germany, descend into nightmarish dictatorship. We have seen other capitalisms, such as Sweden, move toward a kind of socialism without impairing democratic liberties. Moreover, the exercise of political democracy was very limited in early capitalism: Adam Smith, for example, although comfortably off, did not possess enough property to allow him to vote!

Therefore we cannot claim a hard and fast tie between capitalism and political freedom. It is true nonetheless that political liberties do not exist or scarcely exist in nations that have deliberately sought to remove the market system. This suggests, although it does not prove, that some vital connection exists between democratic privileges as we know them and an open society of economic contract, whether it be formally capitalist or not.

Laissez-Faire vs. Political Intervention

Because of the economic freedom on which the market system rested, the basic philosophy of capitalism from Adam Smith's day forward has been laissez-faire —a French phrase, difficult to translate exactly, that means "leaving things alone."* But within a few years of Adam Smith's time, the idea of leaving things alone was already being breached. In England, the Factory Act of 1833 established a system of inspectors to prevent child and female labor from being abused. The Ten Hour Act (1847) set limits to the number of hours an employer might demand of his work force. In the United States, the Sherman Antitrust Act (1890) made illegal the banding together of large companies to create "trusts." In the 1930s, the Social Security Act established a system of old-age pensions; unemployment insurance assured unemployed workers of incomes; the Securities and Exchange Act imposed restrictions on the issuance of new securities. And in our time, a long roster of legislation imposes government regulations with respect to the environment, occupational safety, and nuclear power, to mention only a very few instances.

The effects of these interventions into the market process have become central questions for economics itself. As we study micro- and macroeconomics, we will be studying not only how the market system works, but how various efforts to interfere with the market system exert their influence. Needless to say, intervention into the market is one of the most controversial aspects of economics. But we are

---

* It is said that a group of merchants called on the great Colbert, French finance minister from 1661 to 1683, who congratulated them on their contribution to the French economy and asked what he could do for them. The answer was *Laissez-nous faire*— "leave us alone." Since Colbert was a strong proponent of the complex regulations and red tape that tied up industry in France at this time—a system we call *mercantilism*—we can imagine how gladly he received this advice.

not interested at this juncture in taking sides, pro and con. Rather, we should understand that from the first Factory Acts, intervention has largely arisen from a desire to impose corrective limits on the way in which the market system worked or on the unwanted effects produced by technology.

Thus, if capitalism has brought a strong impetus for laissez-faire, it has also brought a strong impetus for political intervention. Indeed, the very democratic liberties that capitalism has encouraged have been a main source of demands for political action to curb or change the manner in which the economic system worked. The political economy of capitalism has always revealed a tension between laissez-faire and intervention—a tension rooted in the tug of war between the equal distribution of voting power and the unequal distribution of buying power. That tension continues today, a deeply embedded part of the historic momentum of the capitalist system.

looking back

KEY CONCEPTS

The purpose of this chapter is to set our economic system into historic perspective. We have highlighted a few central ideas to give structure to this perspective.

Capitalism brings three historic changes:
- a private sphere
- accumulation of wealth as capital
- a market system

1 Capitalism is a complex system to define or describe. We have sought to emphasize three striking changes that it introduces into economic history. First, it creates a realm of production and distribution that is no longer under state authority. This is the genesis of economic freedom. Second, the new economic sphere accumulates capital, wealth used to create more wealth, not luxurious consumption or public monuments. Third, the new manner of organizing economic life develops a new internal guidance mechanism—the market.

The market creates factors of production

2 The market creates "factors of production"—workers who own and sell their laboring power, landlords who own and freely sell land, capitalists who own and sell capital. This means that labor, land, and capital have become commodities offered for hire in a vast market system where their owners are paid wages, salaries, rents, or interest. This way of bringing the services of these forces of production into social use contrasts sharply with the older means of tradition or command. Capitalism relies on economic freedom and its linked aspect, economic necessity.

3 Capitalism is closely entwined with technology. The market system encouraged the introduction of technology into everyday productive use by removing the inhibitions of serf- and slave-

The market contrasts with tradition and command Capitalism encourages technology, which has come in waves—industrial revolutions	based modes of production and by thrusting responsibility for economic success or failure on the shoulders of each person. Technological advance has come in a series of great bursts or waves called industrial revolutions, beginning with *the* Industrial Revolution (spinning, ironmaking, steam power) of the late eighteenth and early nineteenth centuries.
Technology affects output, scale, and the division of labor	4 Technology has profoundly affected economic and social life. It is responsible for the beginning of the rise in standard of living associated with capitalism. It is the main factor in the vast growth in size of business organizations. It is the source of a much greater division of labor and of a highly intensified interdependence of individuals.
The rise of capitalism is associated with political liberty; this has created tension between laissez-faire and intervention	5 Capitalism is closely connected with political movements. One of these is the association with parliamentary democracy, arising from the struggle to break the hold of feudalism. Another has been the underlying belief in laissez-faire as the main principle of economic policy. A third has been the effort to intervene against the workings of the market and technology, when these powerful forces have disrupted or endangered social life.

ECONOMIC VOCABULARY

Factors of production 17	Division of labor 25
Industrial revolution 23	Laissez-faire 27

QUESTIONS

1. Are there elements of tradition and command still visible in our market system? How important do you think they are? Can you imagine a system in which there was *no* guiding force of tradition and *no* exercise of command (government) at all?

2. What reasons do you think are plausible in explaining why it took so long before capitalism finally burst on the scene; and how do you explain the fact that it emerged only in Europe, not in Africa, Asia, or South America? *Note:* The question is far from settled. If you devise a really persuasive answer, you will be well on your way to becoming a world-famous historian.

3. Profit-making is certainly as old as biblical man. Why are not the institutions of capitalism equally old?

4. Describe the social, political, and economic repercussions of the following: the typewriter, the jet plane, TV, penicillin. Is the economic impact always greater than the social or political impact? Is the economic impact always favorable?

5. Do you think capitalism is necessary for political freedom? First frame your answer, and then test it against these facts: (a) There has been no political freedom in any modern nation that has decisively rejected capitalism (that lets out Sweden which does not actively oppose capitalism). (b) The Union of South Africa is certainly capitalist, and is not a politically free nation, especially if you are not white. *Note:* These facts suggest that there are *no* open-and-shut answers to this question. The issue is a complicated one — more complicated than one would expect.

CHAPTER 3
The Great Economists

a look ahead

The rise of the market system brought with it a great puzzle: to explain how such a system "worked"—what kept it together and in what direction it was headed. The name of this puzzle is economics.

In this chapter we learn more about the background of economics by looking into the ideas of three great economists whose thoughts still dominate our understanding of capitalism: Adam Smith, Karl Marx, and John Maynard Keynes. As we study them, a few central questions come to the fore.

1 What holds the system together and gives it "micro" order?
2 Where is the system headed, giving it "macro" motion?
3 What should we do to improve the system's operations, or what policies should we pursue?

THE INVENTION OF ECONOMICS

T he emergence of capitalism brought an extraordinary puzzle into being. The puzzle was to explain how a society could hang together when the time-honored mechanisms of tradition and command no longer played their accustomed roles. How could economic life unfold in an orderly and reliable fashion when each actor on the marketplace was out for himself, devil take the hindmost; and when it was already clear that change, not inertia, was to be the order of the day?

Mercantilism

Capitalism needed a philosophy—a reasoned explanation of how it worked. But the philosophy was a long time in emerging. All during the seventeenth and eighteenth centuries, for example, the understanding of market society was very imperfect. One group of British pamphleteers, whom we call the Mercantilists, tried to explain its workings in terms of a struggle among nations to gather "treasure"—gold and silver bullion. In this struggle, the Mercantilists saw merchants (hence *Mercant*—ilism) playing a central role because they exported goods that were paid for in treasure.

Early mercantilist policy was very simple: Let England sell as much and buy as little abroad as possible. In that way, its national wealth would steadily pile up. Later mercantilist theory was a good deal more sophisticated. Can you see why the earlier idea of amassing treasure could not successfully serve as a policy for *all* nations?

Physiocracy

In France during the eighteenth century an entirely different and equally inadequate explanation was called physiocracy. In many ways the French school of ideas was the opposite of the British school. Physiocracy taught that the real wealth of economic life lay in production, not in exchange—an important step in the right direction. But the Physiocrats believed that production was essentially a gift of nature (*physiocracy* means the order of nature), and that therefore only labor working with nature was truly productive. Thus, whereas the Mercantilists extolled the merchants as active agents in creating national wealth, the Physiocrats regarded them as a "sterile" class that did no more than handle the wealth produced by the agriculturalist.

Mercantilism and physiocracy are both indispensable steppingstones on the road to modern economics. Each yielded useful insights into the still unfinished economic revolution. But neither made the crucial breakthrough of seeing that the market was a *system*. That is, neither Mercantilists nor Physiocrats saw that the market network possessed an internal guidance mechanism to keep it on a steady course and that a society powered by the market was headed toward a visible destination.

These crucial insights came with Adam Smith, patron saint of our discipline and a figure of towering intellectual stature.

ADAM SMITH (1723–1790)

Adam Smith's fame resides in his masterpiece, *The Wealth of Nations*, published in 1776, the year of the Declaration of Independence. All things considered, it is not easy to say which document is of greater historic importance. The Declaration sounded a new call for a society dedicated to "Life, Liberty, and the pursuit of Happiness." The *Wealth* explained how such a society worked.

The Role of Competition

Smith set himself two main problems, one on the micro, and one on the macro level (although you will not find these terms used in his great, rambling, discursive tract). The first problem was to elucidate how a market-run economic system was articulated, how it achieved what we would call micro order.

Here Smith begins by resolving a perplexing question. The actors in the market, as we know, are all driven by the desire to make money for themselves — to "better their condition," as Smith puts it. The question is obvious: How does a market society prevent self-interested, profit-hungry individuals from holding up their fellow citizens for ransom? How can a socially workable arrangement arise from such a dangerously unsocial motivation as self-betterment?

PORTRAIT OF AN ABSENT-MINDED PROFESSOR

"I am a beau in nothing but my books" was the way that Adam Smith once described himself. Indeed, the famous medallion profile shows us a homely face. In addition, Smith had a curious stumbling gait that one friend called "vermicular," and was given to notorious fits of absent-mindedness. On one occasion, absorbed in discussion, he fell into a tanning pit.

Few other adventures befell Smith in the course of his scholarly, rather retiring, life. Perhaps the high point was reached at age four when he was kidnapped by a band of gypsies passing near Kirkaldy, his native hamlet in Scotland. His captors held him only a few hours; they may have sensed what a biographer later wrote: "He would have made, I fear, a poor gypsy."

Marked out early as a student of promise, at 16 Smith won a scholarship that sent him to Oxford. But Oxford was not then the center of learning that it is today. Little or no systematic teaching took place, the students being free to educate themselves, provided they did not read dangerous books. Smith was nearly expelled for owning a copy of David Hume's *Treatise of Human Nature,* a work we now regard as one of the philosophic masterpieces of the eighteenth century.

After Oxford, Smith returned to Scotland, where he obtained an appointment as Professor of Moral Philosophy at the University of Glasgow. Moral philosophy covered a large territory in Smith's time: We have notes of his lectures in which he talked about jurisprudence, military organization, taxation, and "police"—the last word meaning the administration of domestic affairs that we would call economic policy.

In 1759 Smith published *The Theory of Moral Sentiments,* a remarkable inquiry into morality and psychology. The book attracted widespread attention and brought Smith to the notice of Lord Townshend, one day to be the Chancellor of the Exchequer, responsible for the notorious tax on American tea. Townshend engaged Smith to serve as tutor to his stepson, and Smith resigned his professorial post to set off on the Grand Tour with his charge. In France he met Voltaire, Rousseau, and François Quesnay, the brilliant doctor who had originated the ideas of physiocracy. Smith would have dedicated *The Wealth of Nations* to him, had Quesnay not died.

Returning to Scotland in 1766, Smith lived out the remainder of his life largely in scholarly retirement. It was during these years that the *Wealth* was slowly and carefully composed. When it was done, Smith sent a copy to David Hume, by then his dear friend. Hume wrote: "Euge!* Belle! Dear Mr. Smith: I am much pleased with your Performance. . . ." Hume knew, as did virtually everyone who read the book, that Smith had written a work that would permanently change society's understanding of itself.

* Greek for "Well done!"

The answer introduces us to a central mechanism of a market system, the mechanism of competition. For each person, out for self-betterment, with no thought of others, is faced with a host of similarly motivated persons. As a result, each market actor is forced to meet the prices offered by competitors.

In the kind of competition that Smith assumes, a manufacturer who tries to charge more than other manufacturers will not be able to find any buyers. A job seeker who asks more than the going wage will not be able to find work. And an employer who tries to pay *less* than competitors pay will not find anyone to fill the jobs.

In this way, the market mechanism imposes a discipline on its participants—buyers must bid against other buyers and therefore cannot gang up against sellers. Sellers must contend against other sellers and therefore cannot impose their will on buyers.

The Invisible Hand

But the market has a second, equally important function. Smith shows that the market will arrange for the production of the goods that society wants, in the quantities society wants—without anyone ever issuing an order of any kind! Suppose that consumers want more pots and fewer pans than are being turned out. The public will buy up the existing stock of pots, and as a result the price of pots will rise. Contrariwise, the pan business will be dull; as pan-makers try to get rid of their inventories, pan prices will fall.

Now a restorative force comes into play. As pot prices rise, so will profits in the business of pot making; and as pan prices fall, so will profits in that business. Once again, the drive for self-betterment will go to work. Employers in the favored pot business will seek to expand, hiring more factors of production—more workers, more space, more capital equipment; and employers in the disfavored pan business will reduce their use of the factors of production, letting workers go, giving up leases on space, cutting down on capital investment.

Hence the output of pots will rise and that of pans will fall. And this is what the public wanted in the first place.**Thus the pressures of the marketplace direct the selfish activities of individuals as if by an Invisible Hand (to use Smith's wonderful phrase) into socially responsible paths. The Invisible Hand transmutes private, self-regarding motives into public, socially oriented behavior. The market becomes a mechanism for the allocation of resources into the channels desired by society.**

The Self-Regulating System

Smith's demonstration of how a market performs its social functions has never ceased to be of interest. Much of microeconomics, as we shall see, consists of learning again, or of examining more closely, how the Invisible Hand works. Not that it does always work. There are areas of economic life where the Invisible Hand does not exert its influence at all. In every market system, for instance, tradition continues to play a role in nonmarket methods of remuneration such as tipping or the sharing of incomes within a family. So too, command is always in evidence within organizations or in the exercise of government powers such as taxation. Further, the market system has no way of providing certain public goods—goods that cannot be privately marketed, such as national defense or public law and order. Smith knew about these and recognized that such goods would have to be supplied by the government, not by the market.

Then too, the market does not always meet the ethical or esthetic criteria of society, or it may produce goods that are profitable to make, but harmful to consume. We shall look into these problems in due course. At this juncture, however, we had better stand in considerable awe of Smith's basic insight, for he showed his generation and all succeeding ones that a market system is a responsive and reliable force for basic social provisioning.

He also showed that it was self-regulating. The beautiful consequence of the market is that it is its own guardian. If anyone's prices, wages, or profits stray from levels that are set for everyone, the force of competition will drive them back. Thus a curious paradox exists. The market, which is the acme of economic freedom, turns out to be the strictest of economic taskmasters.

Smith's Philosophy

Because the market is its own regulator, Smith is vehemently opposed to government intervention that will interfere with the workings of self-interest and competition. Therefore, laissez-faire becomes his fundamental philosophy — not because Smith is opposed to the idea of social responsibility, but because he thinks it will be most effectively provided by the Invisible Hand, not by the efforts of government.

His commitment to laissez-faire does not make Smith a conventional conservative. The *Wealth of Nations* is shot through with biting remarks about the "mean and rapacious" ways of the manufacturing class (Smith does not use the word *capitalist*), and the book is openly sympathetic with, and concerned about, the lot of the workingman, hardly a popular position in Smith's day. If Smith is passionately in favor of the "system of natural liberty"—the system founded on economic freedom — the reason is that he believed it would benefit the general public, not the interests of any single class.

Economic Growth

Smith's discovery of the self-regulating properties of a market system was his great "micro" insight (remember that is our phrase, not his). But his vision of an internally coherent market system was matched in importance by a second, "macro" vision. **Smith saw that the market system, left entirely to its own devices, would grow, that the wealth of a nation under a system of "natural liberty" would steadily increase.**

What brought about this growth? As before, the motive force was the drive for self-betterment, the thirst for profits, the wish to make money. This meant that every employer was constantly seeking to accumulate more capital, to expand the wealth of the enterprise. In turn, this led each employer to seek to increase sales in the hope of gaining a larger profit.

The Division of Labor Again

But how to enlarge sales at a time long before advertising existed as we know it? Smith's answer was to improve productivity: Increase the output of the work force. And the road to increasing productivity was very clear: **Increase the division of labor.**

In Smith's conception of the growing *wealth* (we would say the growing *production*) *of nations*, the division of labor therefore plays a central role, as this famous description of a pin factory makes unforgettably clear:

> *One man draws out the wire, another straits it, a third cuts it, a fourth points it, a fifth grinds it at the top for receiving the head; to make the head requires two or three distinct operations; to put it on is a peculiar business; to whiten it another; it is even a trade by itself to put them into paper.*
>
> *. . . . I have seen a small manufactory of this kind where ten men only were employed and where some of them consequently performed two or three distinct operations. But though they were poor, and therefore but indifferently accommodated with the necessary machinery, they could when they exerted themselves make among them about twelve pounds of pins in a day. There are in a pound upwards of four thousand pins of middling size. These ten persons, therefore, could make among them upward of forty-eight thousand pins in a day. . . . But if they had all wrought separately and independently . . . they could certainly not each of them make twenty, perhaps not one pin in a day.* *

Capital and Growth

But how is the division of labor to be enhanced? Smith places principal importance on the manner already announced in his description of the process of making pins: *Machinery is the key.* The division of labor—and therefore the productivity of labor—is increased when the tasks of production can be taken over, or aided and assisted, by the capacities of machinery. In this way, each firm seeking to expand is naturally led to introduce more machinery as a way of improving the productivity of its workers. **The market system thus becomes an immense force for the accumulation of capital, mainly in the form of machinery and equipment.** Moreover, Smith showed something remarkable about the self-regulating properties of the market system as a growth-producing institution. We recall that growth occurred because employers installed machinery that improved the division of labor. But as they added to their work force, would not wages rise as all employers competed to hire labor? And would that not squeeze profits and dry up the funds by which machinery could be bought?

Once again, however, the market was its own regulator. For Smith showed that the increased demand for labor would be matched by an increased supply of labor, so that wages would not rise or would rise only moderately. The reason was plausible. In Smith's day, infant and child mortality rates were horrendous: "It is

* Adam Smith, *The Wealth of Nations* (New York: Modern Library, 1937), pp. 4, 5.

not uncommon," wrote Smith, ". . . in the Highlands of Scotland for a mother who has borne twenty children not to have two alive." As wages rose and better food was provided for the household, infant and child mortality would decline. Soon there would be a larger work force available for hire: Ten was the working age in Smith's day. The larger work force would hold back the rise in wages — and so the accumulation of capital could go on. Just as the system assured internal micro order, it also provided an overall macro dependability.

Smith Today

Of course, Smith wrote about a world that is long since vanished — a world in which a factory of ten people, although small, was still significant enough to play a central illustrative role; in which remnants of mercantilist, and even feudal, restrictions determined how many apprentices an employer could hire in many trades; in which labor unions were largely illegal; in which almost no social legislation existed; and above all, where the great majority of people were very poor.

Yet Smith saw two essential attributes in the economic system that was not yet fully born in his time:

1. A society of competitive profit-seeking individuals can assure its orderly material provisioning through the self-regulating market mechanism.
2. Such a society tends to accumulate capital, and in so doing enhances its productivity and wealth.

These insights are not the last word. We have already mentioned that the market mechanism does not always work successfully, and our next two economists will demonstrate that the growth process is not without serious defects. But the insights themselves are still germane. Micro- and macroeconomics are about internal order and growth, even though we may come to different conclusions than those of Smith. What is surprising after two centuries is not how mistaken Smith was, but how deeply he saw. In a real sense, as economists we are still his pupils.

KARL MARX (1818 – 1883)

Every economist is roughly familiar with the ideas and influence of Adam Smith. Not so many recognize the degree to which economics also owes a debt to Karl Marx — not as the founder of a political movement that has troubled the world ever since, but as an economist whose dissection of capitalism has much to teach us.

Class Struggle

Adam Smith was the architect of capitalism's orderliness and progress: Marx, the diagnostician of its disorders and eventual demise. Their differences are rooted in the fundamentally opposite way each saw history. In Smith's view, history was a succession of stages through which humankind traveled, climbing from the "early and rude" society of hunters and fisherfolk to the final stage of commercial society. **Marx saw history as a continuing struggle among social classes, ruling classes contending with ruled classes in every era.**

PROFILE OF A REVOLUTIONARY

A great, bearded, dark-skinned man, Karl Marx was the picture of a revolutionary. And he was one—engaged, mind and heart, in the effort to overthrow the system of capitalism that he spent his whole life studying. As a political revolutionary, Marx was not very successful, although with his lifelong friend Friedrich Engels, he formed an international working class "movement" that frightened a good many conservative governments. But as an intellectual revolutionary Marx was probably the most successful disturber of thought who ever lived. The only persons who rival his influence are the great religious leaders, Christ, Mohammed, and Buddha.

Marx led as turbulent and active a life as Smith's was secluded and academic. Born to middle-class parents in Trier, Germany, Marx was early marked as a student of prodigious abilities, but not temperamentally cut out to be a professor. Soon after getting his doctoral degree (in philosophy) Marx became editor of a crusading newspaper, which rapidly earned the distrust of the reactionary Prussian government. It closed down the paper. Typically, Marx printed the last edition in red. With his wife Jenny (and Jenny's family maid, Lenchen, who remained with them, unpaid, all her life), Marx thereupon began life as a political exile in Paris, Brussels, and finally in London. There, in 1848, together with Engels, he published the pamphlet that was to become his best known, but certainly not most important work: *The Communist Manifesto.*

The remainder of Marx's life was lived in London. Terribly poor, largely as a consequence of his hopeless inability to manage his own finances, Marx's life was spent in the reading room of the British Museum, laboriously composing the great, never finished opus, *Capital.* No economist has ever read so widely or so deeply as Marx. Before even beginning *Capital,* he wrote a profound three-volume commentary on all the existing economists, eventually published as *Theories of Surplus Value,* and filled 37 notebooks on subjects that would be included in *Capital*—these notes, published as the *Grundrisse* (Foundations) did not appear in print until 1953! *Capital* itself was written backwards, first Volumes II and III, in very rough draft form, then Volume I, the only part of the great opus that appeared in Marx's lifetime, in 1867.

Marx was assuredly a genius, a man who altered every aspect of thinking about society—historical and sociological as well as economic—as decisively as Plato altered the cast of philosophic thought, and Freud that of psychology.

Very few economists today work their way through the immense body of Marx's work; but in one way or another his influence affects most of us, even if we are unaware of it. We owe to Marx the basic idea that capitalism is an *evolving* system, deriving from a specific historic past and moving slowly and irregularly toward a dimly discernible, different form of society. That is an idea accepted by many social scientists who may or may not approve of socialism, and who are on the whole vehemently "anti-Marxist"!

Moreover, Smith believed that commercial society would bring about a harmonious, mutually acceptable solution to the problem of individual interest in a social setting that would go on forever—or at least for a very long time. Marx saw tension and antagonism as the outcome of the class struggle, and the setting of capitalist society as anything but permanent. Indeed, the class struggle itself, expressed as the contest over wages and profits, would be the main force for changing capitalism and eventually undoing it.

Capitalist Growth: Using M

A great deal of interest in Marx's work focuses on that revolutionary perspective and purpose. But Marx the economist interests us for a different reason: Marx also saw the market as a powerful force in the cumulation of capital and wealth. From his conflict-laden point of view, however, he traces out the process—mainly in Volume II of *Capital*—quite differently than Smith does. As we have seen, Smith's conception of the growth process stressed its self-regulatory nature, its steady, hitch-free path. Marx's conception is just the opposite. To him, growth is a process full of pitfalls, a process in which crisis or malfunction lurks at every turn.

Marx starts with a view of the accumulation process that is much like that of a businessman. The problem is how to make a given sum of capital—money sitting in a bank or invested in a firm—yield a profit. As Marx puts it, how does M (a sum of money) become M', a *larger* sum?

Marx's answer begins with capitalists using their money to buy commodities and labor power. Thereby they ready the process of production, obtaining needed raw or semi-finished materials, and hiring the work capabilities of a labor force. Here the possibility for crisis lies in the difficulty that capitalists may have in getting their materials or their labor force at the right price. If that should happen—if labor is too expensive, for instance—M stays put, and the accumulation process never gets started at all.

The Labor Process

But suppose the first stage of accumulation takes place smoothly. Now money capital, M, has been transformed into a hired work force and a stock of physical goods. These have next to be combined in the labor process; that is, actual work

KARL MARX
(Courtesy of the Library of Congress)

must be expended on the materials and the raw or semi-finished goods transformed into their next stage of production.

It is here, on the factory floor, that Marx sees the genesis of profit. **In his view, profit lies in the ability of capitalists to pay less for labor power — for the working abilities of their work force — than the actual value workers will impart to the commodities they help to produce.** This theory of *surplus value* as the source of profit is very important in Marx's analysis of capitalism. But it is not central to our purpose here. Instead, we stop only to note that the labor process is another place where accumulation can be disrupted. If there is a strike, or if production encounters resistances, the *M* that is invested in goods and labor power will not move along toward its objective, *M'*.

Completing the Circuit

But once again suppose that all goes well and workers transform steel sheets, rubber casings, and bolts of cloth into automobiles. The automobiles are not yet money. They have to be sold — and here, of course, lie the familiar problems of the marketplace: bad guesses as to the public's taste; mismatches between supply and demand; recessions that diminish the spending power of society.

If all goes well, the commodities *will* be sold—and sold for M', which is bigger than M. In that case, the circuit of accumulation is complete, and the capitalists will have a new sum M', which they will want to send on another round, hoping to win M''. But unlike Adam Smith's smooth growth model, we can see that Marx's conception of accumulation is riddled with pitfalls and dangers. Crisis is possible at every stage. Indeed, in the complex theory Marx unfolds in *Capital*, the inherent tendency of the system is to generate crisis, not to avoid it.

We will not trace Marx's theory of capitalism further except to note that at its core lies a complicated analysis of the manner in which surplus value (the unpaid labor that is the source of profit) is squeezed out through mechanization. A student who wants to learn about Marx's analysis must turn to other books, of which there are many.*

Instability and Breakdown

Our interest lies in Marx as the first theorist to stress the *instability* of capitalism. Adam Smith originated the idea that growth is an inherent characteristic of capitalism, but to Marx we owe the idea that that growth is wavering and uncertain, far from the assured process Smith described. Marx makes it clear that capital accumulation must overcome the uncertainty inherent in the market system and the tension of the opposing demands of labor and capital. The accumulation of wealth, although certainly the objective of business, may not always be within its power to achieve.

In *Capital,* Marx sees instability increasing until finally the system comes tumbling down. His reasoning involves two further, very important prognoses for the system. The first is that the size of business firms will steadily increase as the consequence of the recurrent crises that wrack the economy. With each crisis, small firms go bankrupt and their assets are bought up by surviving firms. A trend toward big business is therefore an integral part of capitalism.

Second, Marx expects an intensification of the class struggle as the result of the "proletarianization" of the labor force. More and more small businesspeople and independent artisans will be squeezed out in the crisis-ridden process of growth. Thus the social structure will be reduced to two classes—a small group of capitalist magnates and a large mass of proletarianized, embittered workers.

In the end, this situation proves impossible to maintain. In Marx's words:

> *Along with the constant decrease in the number of capitalist magnates, who usurp and monopolize all the advantages of this process of transformation, the mass of misery, oppression, slavery, degradation and exploitation grows; but with this there also grows the revolt of the working class, a class constantly increasing in numbers, and trained, united and organized by the very mechanism of the capitalist process of production. The monopoly of capital becomes a fetter upon the mode of production*

* At the risk of appearing self-serving, a good first reader is R. L. Heilbroner, *Marxism: For and Against* (New York: Norton, 1980).

which has flourished alongside and under it. The centralization of the means of production and the socialization of labour reach a point at which they become incompatible with their capitalist integument. This integument is burst asunder. The knell of capitalist private property sounds. The expropriators are expropriated.*

Was Marx Right?

Much of the economic controversy Marx generated has been focused on the questions: Will capitalism ultimately undo itself? Will its internal tensions, its "contradictions," as Marx calls them, finally become too much for its market mechanism to handle?

There are no simple answers to these questions. Critics of Marx insist that capitalism has *not* collapsed, that the working class has *not* become more and more "miserable," and that a number of predictions that Marx made, such as that the rate of profit would tend to decline, have not been verified.

Supporters of Marx argue the opposite case. They stress that capitalism almost did collapse in the 1930s. They note that more and more people have been reduced to a "proletarian" status, working for a capitalist firm rather than for themselves; in 1800, for example, 80 percent of Americans were self-employed; today the figure is 10 percent. They stress that the size of businesses has constantly grown, and that Marx did correctly foresee that the capitalist system itself would expand, pushing into noncapitalist areas such as Asia, South America, and Africa.

Marx's Socioanalysis

It is doubtful that Marx's contribution as a social analyst will ultimately be determined by this kind of scorecard. Certainly he made many remarkably penetrating statements, and equally certainly, he said things about the prospects for capitalism that seem to have been wrong. **What Marx's reputation rests on is something else. It rests on his vision of capitalism as a system under tension, and in a process of continuous evolution as a consequence of that tension.** Many economists do not accept Marx's diagnosis of class struggle as the great motor of change in capitalist and precapitalist societies or his prognosis of the inevitable arrival of socialism, but few would deny the validity of that vision.

There is much more to Marx than the few economic ideas sketched here suggest. Indeed, Marx should not be thought of primarily as an economist, but as a pioneer in a new kind of critical social thought: It is significant that the subtitle of *Capital* is *A Critique of Political Economy.*

In the gallery of the world's great thinkers, where Marx certainly belongs, his statue would be centrally placed, overlooking many corridors of thought—sociological analysis, philosophic inquiry, and of course, economics. For Marx's

---

* Karl Marx, *Capital*, Vol. I (New York: Vintage, 1977), p. 929.

lasting contribution was a penetration of the *appearances* of our social system and of the ways in which we think about that system, in an effort to arrive at buried essences deep below the surface. That most searching aspect of Marx's work is not one that we will pursue here; but bear it in mind, because it accounts for the persisting interest of Marx's thought.*

JOHN MAYNARD KEYNES (1883–1946)

Marx was the intellectual prophet of capitalism as a self-destructive system; John Maynard Keynes (the name should be pronounced "canes," not "keens") was the engineer of capitalism repaired. Today, that is not an uncontested statement. To some people, Keynes's doctrines are as dangerous and subversive as those of Marx —a curious irony, since Keynes himself was totally opposed to Marxist thought and wholly in favor of sustaining and improving the capitalist system.

The reason for the continuing distrust of Keynes is that more than any other economist he is the father of the idea of a "mixed economy" in which the government plays a crucial role. To many people these days, all government activities are suspicious at best and downright injurious at worst. Thus, in some quarters Keynes's name is under a cloud. Nonetheless, he remains one of the great innovators of our discipline, a mind to be ranked with Smith and Marx as one of the most influential our profession has brought forth. As Nobelist Milton Friedman, a famous conservative economist, has declared: "We are all Keynesians now."

The Great Depression

The great economists were all products of their times: Smith, the voice of optimistic, nascent capitalism; Marx, the spokesman for the victims of its bleakest industrial period; Keynes, the product of a still later time, the Great Depression.

The Great Depression hit the world like a typhoon. In America one-half the value of all production simply disappeared. One-quarter of the working force lost its jobs. Over a million urban families found their mortgages foreclosed, their houses lost to them. Nine million savings accounts went down the drain when banks closed, never to reopen.

Against this terrible reality of joblessness and loss of income, the economics profession, like the business world or government advisers, had nothing to offer.

---

* What about the relation of Marx to present-day communism? That is a subject for a book about the politics, not the economics, of Marxism. Marx himself was a fervid democrat—but also a very intolerant man. Perhaps his system of ideas has encouraged intolerance in revolutionary parties that have based their ideas on his thought. Marx himself died long before present-day communism came into being. We cannot know what he would have made of it—probably he would have been horrified at its excesses, but still hopeful for its future.

PORTRAIT OF A MANY-SIDED MAN

Keynes was certainly a man of many talents. Unlike Smith or Marx, he was at home in the world of business affairs, a shrewd dealer and financier. Every morning, abed, he would scan the newspaper and make his commitments for the day on the most treacherous of all markets, foreign exchange. An hour or so a day sufficed to make him a very rich man; only the great English economist David Ricardo (1772–1823) could match him in financial acumen. Like Ricardo, Keynes was a speculator by temperament. During World War I, when he was at the Treasury office running England's foreign currency operations, he reported with glee to his chief that he had got together a fair amount of Spanish pesetas. The chief was relieved that England had a supply of *that* currency for a while. "Oh no," said Keynes. "I've sold them all. I'm going to break the market." And he did. Later during the war, when the Germans were shelling Paris, he went to France to negotiate for the English government; on the side, he bought some marvelous French masterpieces at much reduced prices for the National Gallery—along with a Cezanne for himself!

More than an economist and speculator, he was a brilliant mathematician; a businessman who very successfully ran a great investment trust; a ballet lover who married a famous ballerina; a superb stylist and an editor of consummate skill; a man of huge kindness when he wanted to exert it, and of ferocious wit when (more often) he chose to exert that. On one occasion, banker Sir Harry Goshen criticized Keynes for not "letting things take their natural course." "Is it more appropriate to smile or rage at these artless sentiments?" wrote Keynes. "Best, perhaps, to let Sir Harry take *his* natural course."

Keynes's greatest fame lay in his economic inventiveness. He came by this talent naturally enough as the son of a distinguished economist, John Neville Keynes. As an undergraduate, Keynes had already attracted the attention of Alfred Marshall, the commanding figure at Cambridge University for three decades. After graduation, Keynes soon won notice with a brilliant little book on Indian finance; he then became an adviser to the English government in the negotiations at the end of World War I. Dismayed and disheartened by the vengeful terms of the Versailles Treaty, Keynes wrote a brilliant polemic, *The Economic Consequences of the Peace,* that won him international renown.

Almost thirty years later, Keynes would himself be a chief negotiator for the English government, first in securing the necessary loans during World War II, then as one of the architects of the Bretton Woods agreement that opened a new system of international currency relations after that war. On his return from one trip to Washington, reporters crowded around to ask if England had been sold out and would soon be another American state. Keynes's reply was succinct: "No such luck."

Economists were as perplexed at the behavior of the economy as were the American people themselves. In many ways, the situation reminds us of the uncertainty that the public and the economics profession share in the face of inflation or international competition today.

The *General Theory*

It was against this setting of dismay and near-panic that Keynes's great book appeared: *The General Theory of Employment Interest and Money*. A complicated book — much more technical than the *Wealth of Nations* or *Capital* — the *General Theory* nevertheless had a central message that was simple enough to grasp. The overall level of economic activity in a capitalist system, said Keynes (and both Marx and Adam Smith would have agreed with him) was determined by the willingness of its entrepreneurs to make capital investments. From time to time, this willingness was blocked by considerations that made capital accumulation difficult or impossible: In Smith's model we saw the possibility of wages rising too fast, and Marx's theory pointed out difficulties at every stage of the process.

But all the previous economists, even Marx to a certain extent, believed that a failure to accumulate capital would be a temporary, self-curing setback. In Smith's scheme, the rising supply of young workers would keep wages in check. In Marx's conception, each crisis (up to the last) would present the surviving entrepreneurs with fresh opportunities to resume their quest for profits. For Keynes, however, the diagnosis was more severe. **He showed that a market system could reach a position of "underemployment equilibrium" — a kind of steady, stagnant state — despite the presence of unemployed workers and unused industrial equipment. The revolutionary implication of Keynes's theory was that there was no self-righting property in the market system to keep capitalism growing.**

The Role of Government

We will not understand the nature of Keynes's diagnosis until we get into our study of macroeconomics, but we can easily see the conclusion to which his diagnosis drove him. If there was nothing that would automatically provide for capital accumulation, a badly depressed economy could remain in the doldrums — unless some substitute were found for business spending. And there was only one such possible source of stimulation: the government. **The crux of Keynes's message was therefore that government spending might be an essential economic policy for a depressed capitalism trying to recover its vitality.**

Whether or not Keynes's remedy works and what consequences government spending may have for a market system have become major topics for contemporary economics — topics we will deal with later at length. But we can see the

JOHN MAYNARD KEYNES
(The Bettmann Archive, Inc.)

significance of his work in changing the very conception of the economic system in which we live. Adam Smith's view of the market system led to the philosophy of laissez-faire, allowing the system to generate its own natural propensity for growth and internal order. Marx had stressed a very different view in which instability and crisis lurked at every stage, but of course Marx was not interested in policies to maintain capitalism. Keynes propounded a philosophy as far removed from Marx as from Smith. For if Keynes was right, laissez-faire was not the appropriate policy for capitalism — certainly not for capitalism in depression. And if Keynes was right about his remedy, the gloomy prognostications of Marx were also incorrect — or at least could be rendered incorrect.

But was Keynes right? Was Smith right? Was Marx right? To a very large degree these questions frame the subject matter of economics today. That is why, even if their theories are part of our history, the "worldly philosophers" are also contemporary. A young writer once remarked impatiently to T. S. Eliot that it seemed so pointless to study the thinkers of the past, because we knew so much more than they. "Yes," replied Eliot. "They are what we know."

looking back

This chapter has tried to give us a conception of capitalism as seen by the three greatest economists—conceptions that still powerfully affect our understanding of the system. Let us go over the main ideas that have emerged from this survey:

Mercantilists and Physiocrats extolled treasure and land

1 Economics itself is a modern intellectual invention that awaited the advent of market society. Prior to Adam Smith, the main attempts to understand and explain the system were those of the Mercantilists, who stressed the importance of foreign trade as a means of gaining gold or treasure; and those of the French Physiocrats, who extolled the wealth-generating powers of the land and who dismissed the merchant class as sterile.

Adam Smith's Invisible Hand—competition plus self-interest

2 Adam Smith contributed two immensely important ideas to economic understanding. The first was the idea of an Invisible Hand by which the market system converted the selfish drives of individuals to a coordinated mechanism for social provisioning. Smith showed how this fortunate outcome arose from the workings of competition, which prevented the drive for profits or selfish interest from simply gouging the consumer or the worker.

Capital accumulation and division of labor bring growth

3 Smith was also the first economist to explain how the market provided a powerful mechanism for accumulating capital. Smith's theory of economic growth hinged on the steady improvement in productivity that occurred when machinery was added to production, making possible a finer division of labor.

Class struggle

4 Marx was the great prophet of capitalism's doom. The essential cause of its demise would be the class struggle between workers and capitalists.

The unstable process of production

5 Marx also saw the market mechanism as inherently unstable—as tending toward crisis or disruption in the accumulation of capital. He analyzed this instability by tracing the obstacles faced by a firm as it sought to convert M, a sum of capital, into M', a larger sum. This was done in three stages: first by using M to buy labor power and materials, then by combining labor power with materials, and finally by selling the finished goods. At each stage, the accumulation process was subject to disruption of various sorts.

Growth of monopolies and proletarians lead to revolution

6 In Marx's view the process of capitalist accumulation lead to the growth of big business and an "immiserated" proletariat. As successive crises wracked the system, the working class would

eventually revolt, and a transition would be made from capitalism to socialism.

Marxism as a system of thought

7 Marx's system of thought was much larger than an effort to analyze the economic tensions of capitalism. Essentially it embraced a mixture of philosophy, historical analysis, and a critique of economic beliefs and forms.

Keynes's *General Theory* with its idea of underemployment equilibrium, ushered in the mixed economy

8 John Maynard Keynes's *General Theory* (as it is widely called) was an attempt to explain how capitalism could have a *lasting* depression. In technical terms, Keynes's breakthrough was the explanation of underemployment equilibrium.

9 Equally important was Keynes's work in paving the way for the mixed economy in which government plays a crucial role in maintaining the economic growth of capitalism. Mixed economies are found in every capitalist system today; we will be studying them in depth in the pages to come.

ECONOMIC VOCABULARY

QUESTIONS

1. Why does Smith's model of the economy require *two* elements — the motivation of self-betterment and the restraining institution of competition? Explain why the system would not work with only one of the two.

2. From your own experience, think of how the division of labor can increase productivity. Choose one example from agriculture, one from manufacturing, and one from a service industry, such as hotel management, transportation, or retailing.

3. Is the accumulation of capital needed for the improvement of productivity today? In what ways could additional capital — more machines, buildings, roads, etc. — improve the amount of production a typical farmer or worker could create?

4. Take any business you know about and see if you think that Marx's description of the circuit *M*-into-*M ′* describes the way in which that business tries to accu-

mulate capital. Which of Marx's three phases of the accumulation process is most likely to lead to trouble, in your opinion?

5. How do you feel about the idea of a mixed economy? Do you think it means an economy in which the government does a lot of interfering? Could a government simply spend money—for example, for social security—and not interfere in the market system at all? Could it interfere extensively, but not spend much money? Which of the two functions—interfering (regulating) or spending—is basic to Keynes's theory? Is it possible, do you think, to have a basically laissez-faire policy with respect to the market, and yet have government spending to cure a depression?

AN EXTRA WORD ABOUT

Paradigms

How does science advance? The prevailing view used to be that it grew by accretion, gradually adding new knowledge and better established hypotheses while shedding error and disproved hypotheses. That view has now been seriously challenged by the influential book, *The Structure of Scientific Revolutions,* by Thomas Kuhn, published in 1962.

Kuhn's view is that the growth of science is not a continuous, seamless extension of knowledge. Rather, science grows in discontinuous leaps, in which one prevailing paradigm is displaced by another. *A paradigm is a set of premises, views, rules, conventions, and beliefs that form the kinds of questions that a science asks.* For example, the Ptolemaic paradigm, with its view of the earth as the center of the universe, was replaced by the Copernican paradigm, which based its questions on the premise that the planets revolve around the sun. In cosmology the Newtonian paradigm was displaced by the Einsteinian, in biology the biblical paradigm by the Darwinian.

Paradigms change, says Kuhn, when the puzzles encountered by scientists become more and more difficult to answer within the existing set of ground rules. Then, usually in a short space of time, a new view of things comes to the fore, explaining the puzzles of the earlier paradigm and reorienting the questions for scientists who will work within the new rules.

PRECLASSICAL AND CLASSICAL ECONOMICS

Kuhn's short, provocative book is worth reading by anyone interested in science or social science. The question it raises for us is whether economics also has paradigms. The answer seems to be both yes and no.

First the yes answer. We can easily separate the history of economic thought into paradigm-like divisions that resemble the bounded inquiries of science. *One of the first such paradigms was the economics of the medieval schoolmen who argued and worried about the moral problems raised by the emerging market process.* For example, one of their main concerns was whether lending money at interest (usury) was in fact a sin (remember, in the early Middle Ages it had been considered a *mortal* sin); and they endlessly discussed the criteria for the "just" prices at which commodities should sell.

That view of the economic world was displaced by the Classical economists, whose most brilliant achievements were expressed in the works of Adam Smith and David Ricardo (1772–1823). The Classical economists had no interest whatever in "just" prices or in the sinfulness of usury. For them the great question was *how to understand, not evaluate, economic processes, in particular the accumulation and distribution of national wealth.* Smith, as we have seen, wrote an extraordinary exposition of how the members of society, although engaged in a search for their individual betterment, were nonetheless guided by an Invisible Hand (the market) to expand the wealth of nations. Ricardo wrote with equal force about the course of national economic growth, arguing that a growing population, pressing against limited fertile acreage, would drive up crop prices and divert the wealth of the country into the hands of the landlords.

MARGINALIST ECONOMICS

The Classical paradigm concerned large issues of national growth and dealt boldly with the fate of social classes. The Marxian paradigm, in turn, grew out of the Classical, differing from it in its much more critical approach to society and to thinking about society. Then, around the 1870s, a new angle of vision abruptly displaced the older one. The new view had numerous European originators, preeminent among them W. Stanley Jevons and Leon Walras. As a group they are referred to as the Marginalists, for *they turned the focus of economic inquiry away from growth and class conflict into a study of the interactions of individuals.*

The new paradigm explained many things that the older one did not, above all the finer workings of the price system. But just as the Classical or Marxian paradigms had dropped all interest in the just prices of the medievalists, so the Marginalists paid little attention to the questions of growth and class fortune that had so preoccupied the Classicists and Marxists.

KEYNESIAN ECONOMICS

Inherent in the Marginalist view of the world, with its extreme emphasis on interacting individuals rather than on classes, was a micro approach to economic problems. The next radical shift in view came from the work of John Maynard Keynes, whose perception of the economic system brought into focus a macro perspective on *total* income, *total* employment, *total* output. *The most striking result of Keynes's shift from a micro to a macro perspective was his discovery that an economy that worked well at the micro level did not necessarily work well at the macro level.* From the perspective of the Marginalists, such an economic state of affairs could hardly be envisioned.

PARADIGMS OR NOT?

Hence we can certainly discern sharp changes in the views and visions of economics. The very definition of the economic problem itself alters as we go from the medieval school-men to the Keynesians. Classical economists, as we have said, forgot about economic justice; Marginalist economists, about growth or classes; Keynesian economists, about the inner working of the market.

These shifts in economic concerns resemble those of natural science. According to

Kuhn, new paradigms bring new problems into focus, rather than resolving old ones within a new encompassing view. The camera of science is aimed, as it were, at a new subject and the former subject is relegated to the background, or drops out of the picture entirely.

Now the "no" part of the answer. Where economics differs from its resemblance to these paradigmatic jumps of science is that we can relate its changes in focus to a changing backdrop of social organization. Each "school" of economic thought reflects to some degree the historical characteristics and problems of its time; whereas a change in social structures generally plays a small role in causing one scientific perspective to replace another.

What "paradigm" rules economics today? A mixture of Marginalist and Keynesian thought lies behind most contemporary micro- and macroeconomics. A Marxian view underlies much of the radical critique of our time. Perhaps it is fair to say that no paradigm is firmly ensconced today. We live in a period in which much of the conventional wisdom of the past has been tried and found wanting. Economics is in a state of self-scrutiny, dissatisfied with its established premises, not yet ready to formulate new ones. Indeed, perhaps the search for a new vision of economics, a vision that will highlight new elements of reality and suggest new modes of analysis, is the most pressing economic task of our time.

CHAPTER 4
A Bird's Eye View of the Economy

a look ahead

Before we begin our study of economics as a subject, we ought to know something about the economy. In this chapter we take a high altitude pass over the terrain.

Things to watch for are

1 The general dimensions of the two worlds of business—big business and small business.
2 The way in which income is divided up among households.
3 The size of the various government sectors. Note the plural—there is more than one meaning to "the government."

W e can't begin to study economics without knowing something about the economy. But what is "the economy"? When we turn to the economics section of *Time* or *Newsweek* or pick up a business magazine, a jumble of things meets the eye: stock market ups and downs, reports on company fortunes and mishaps, accounts of incomprehensible "fluctuations in the exchange market," columns by business pundits, stories about unemployment or inflation.

How much of this is relevant? How are we to make our way through this barrage of reporting to something that we can identify as the economy?

BUSINESS

Of course we know where to start. Business enterprise is the very heart of an economic system of private property and market relationships. Let us begin, then, with a look at the world of business.

The first thing we notice is the enormous number of business enterprises — over sixteen million in all. If we divide them into proprietorships (businesses owned by a single person), partnerships, and corporations, the world of business is classified in Table 1.

Small Business

Just looking at Table 1 makes one conclusion immediately clear: **There are at least two worlds of business.** One of them is the world of small business. It embraces nearly all proprietorships and partnerships, as well as a large percentage of corporations. Here are the vast bulk of the firms we find in the Yellow Pages of the phone book, the great preponderance of the country's farms, myriad mom-and-pop stores, restaurants, motels, movie houses, dry cleaners, druggists, retailers — in short, perhaps 95 percent of all the business firms in the nation.

Table 1
DIMENSIONS OF BUSINESS, 1981

Note that corporations are overwhelmingly the most important, but by no means the most numerous, form of business organization.

	Total Number of Firms (000s)	Total Sales (Billions)	Average Sales per Firm
Proprietorships	12,185	$ 523	$ 42,922
Partnerships	1,461	272	186,174
Corporations	2,812	7,026	2,498,578

Source: *Statistical Abstract of the United States,* 1985.

Small business is the part of the business world with which we are all most familiar. We understand how a hardware store operates, whereas we have only vague ideas about how General Motors operates. But the world of small business warrants our attention for two other reasons.

First, small business is the employer of a substantial fraction—about half—of the nation's labor force. Second, the world of small business is the source of much "middle-class" opinion. Of the 15 million small businesses in the country, two-thirds have sales (not profits) of less than $50,000 a year. These are tiny enterprises, but they certainly give a small business point of view to at least 10 million households—one out of every seven households.

We should know something about what life is like in this world, and indeed, a considerable amount of economics is concerned with the problems of operating a small business. Later, when we reach microeconomics, we will study how small business fits into the economic picture.

Big Business

We have already glimpsed another business world, mainly to be found in the corporate enterprises of the nation. Compare the average size of the sales of corporations (Table 1) with those of proprietorships and partnerships. But even these figures hide the extraordinary difference between very big business and small business. Within the world of corporations, for example, 85 percent do less than $1 million worth of business a year. But the 10 percent that do more than $1 million worth of sales a year take in 93 percent of the receipts of all corporations.

Thus, counterposed to a world of very numerous small businesses, there is the world of much less numerous big businesses. How large a world is it? Suppose we count as a big business any corporation with assets of $250 million or more. There are roughly 3,000 such businesses in America. Half of them are in finance, mainly insurance and banking. A quarter are in manufacturing. The rest are to be found in transportation, utilities, communication, trade. Just to get an idea of scale, the largest enterprise in the nation in 1985 was Exxon, with assets of $69 billion and sales of $87 billion.

THE INDUSTRIAL SECTOR

Big business is to be found in all sectors; but its special place is the industrial sector, in which manufacturing plays the predominant role.

The figures in Table 2 show once again the twofold division of the business world. If we subtract the 500 biggest industrial corporations and their sales from the total of all manufacturing firms and their sales, we see that the top 500 firms—not even one tenth of one percent of the total number—accounted for about 70 percent of all sales. **Indeed, if we take only the biggest 100 firms, we find that they are the source of almost half the sales of the entire industrial sector.**

Table 2
INDUSTRIAL SECTOR, 1983

The 500 biggest firms—about .003% of all firms—account for seven-tenths of all industrial sales.

	$ Billion
Total sales of all industrial firms	$2,452
Total sales of the 500 biggest industrial corporations	1,687

Source: *Statistical Abstract of the United States,* 1985, Fortune 500.

Big Employers

Big business obviously dominates many areas of the marketplace. Is big business also a big employer? That varies from one field to another. In manufacturing enterprises, the top 500 firms employ about 45 percent of all persons in manufacturing. In transportation and public utilities, about half the work force is hired by a giant utility or airline or railway (most of the rest work for small trucking firms). In finance, insurance, and real estate, the top 150 companies employ about 45 percent of the persons working in that area. In retail trade, the top 50 companies hire about 20 percent of the total.

In all, about a fifth of the nation's work force is employed by a firm that we would call a "big business."* To put it differently, 1,000 leading firms in manufacturing, transportation, utilities, finance, and retailing employ roughly as many persons as the remaining 15 million proprietorships, partnerships, and smaller corporations.

HOUSEHOLDS

Business is not the only institutional feature we need to inspect in this introduction to the economy. How could business operate without a work force? Let us look at this work force as a collection of "households," as shown in Table 4.

The Work Force

Our table shows us an interesting fact about the household "sector." There are more individual workers than there are households. This means that a typical household must have more than one member in the labor market.

---

* There is no official designation of a "big" business. We have used the *Fortune* magazine list of the top 500 industrial firms, plus its list of the top 50 firms in banking, insurance, finance, transportation, utilities, and retailing.

SECTORS

Economists are always talking about sectors. Sometimes, as is frequently the case in this book, they mean a part of the economy in which *motivations* are similar. For example, we talk of a private sector, made up of households and firms, and a public sector comprised of local, state, and federal agencies. The key difference here is motive. The private sector is driven by the desire for income or wealth. The public sector is directed by the aims and ambitions of people in political life. Private enhancement may be among these aims and ambitions, but usually much larger and more "public" issues motivate the lawmakers and administrators.

Sometimes, however, economists mean a *functional* division of the economy's activities. Then they typically speak of three sectors: (1) an agricultural sector that grows and harvests natural products, (2) an industrial sector that extracts and alters and assembles raw materials, and (3) a service sector that performs a miscellany of tasks: providing power and transportation, performing the tasks of storage and selling, and furnishing the thousand ministrations of personal service—legal services, maids' services, doctors' services, various governmental services.

There are many problems associated with this functional grouping. But because it is commonly used, we should have a general idea of the way in which employment and output is distributed among the three main functional sectors (Table 3).

Table 3

EMPLOYMENT AND GNP BY SECTORS, 1985

Most of the labor force works in stores or offices. Note how this ties into occupations, shown in Table 6.

	Employment	*GNP*
Agriculture	3%	2%
Industry	27	48
Services	70	50

Sources: Survey of Current Business; Bureau of Labor Statistics *Employment and Earnings.*

Notice that roughly two-thirds of all employment and half of all output takes place in the service sector. This does *not* mean that industry and agriculture are therefore unimportant. Try to imagine the consequences of a six-month shutdown in our smallest sector, farming!

Table 4
HOUSEHOLD CHARACTERISTICS, 1985
There are more workers than households.

	Millions
Total population	240
Number of households	87
Families	63
Non-family households	24
Individuals in work force	117

Sources: Census Bureau Reports *P–25* (Sept. 1985), and *P–60* (March 1985); *Economic Indicators*, (Sept. 1985).

But what is a typical household? The answer is not easy, because there are many kinds of households: young or elderly households with only one individual in them; young married households without children; families with young children; families with offspring who are no longer young.

Economists look at the relation between households and work in terms of a **participation rate,** showing the percentage of various groups who are working or looking for work. In the formal language of the statistician, they are "in the labor market." Table 5 shows how considerable is the variation of these rates.

Occupations

The table also shows us that sex is still a decisive element in determining the characteristics of the labor force. This has changed significantly and will probably change still further in the years to come: Women were only 31 percent of all workers in 1950; today they are roughly 50 percent.

What sort of work does our labor force perform? Table 6 tells us.

Later we will be looking more carefully into problems of occupations. Here we might note in passing that "white collar" jobs — professional, managerial, sales, and clerical — include over half the working force. Here is another strong root of the American middle-class mentality.

Table 5
PARTICIPATION RATES, 1985
Participation rates vary greatly.

	Percent of Group in Labor Market
Males, 20 years and older	78
Females, 20 years and older	55
Both sexes, 16–19	55
Males, 65 and older	16
Females, 65 and older	7

Source: Bureau of Labor Statistics *Employment and Earnings.*

Table 6
OCCUPATIONAL DISTRIBUTION OF THE
LABOR FORCE, 1985
Over half the work force is white collar.

		Percent
Professional ⎤		15 ⎤
Managerial ⎟ White	11 ⎟
Sales ⎟ collar	12 ⎟ 54
Clerical ⎦		16 ⎦
Craftsmen ⎤		13 ⎤
Operatives ⎟ Blue	11 ⎟
Nonfarm laborers ⎟ collar	4 ⎟ 30
Farm workers ⎦		4 ⎦
Service workers	Both	14

Source: Bureau of Labor Statistics *Employment and Earnings.*

Distribution of Income

Households interest us not only because they are the source of our labor power, but also because they are the focus of our income and our wealth. Much of the buying that powers the economic machine is cycled through the household, where purchasing power is collected as wages, salaries, dividends, interest, and rents, to be pumped out again as a flow of spending for consumers' goods. Consumer buying, as we will see later, is a strong force in the momentum of our economy, although we should emphasize right away that household buying is not the only force. Business and government are also buyers in their own right and strong influences in maintaining the flow of purchasing power.

If we focus on households at this stage of our inquiry, it is because their function as buyers leads us naturally to inquire into the distribution of purchasing power among families. This is a subject about which many people are very sensitive. **A persistent stress on *political* equality leads us to ignore or play down the facts of economic inequality.** We even lack adequate statistics about wealth, largely because of an unwillingness to give official recognition to this aspect of our economic realities.

There are many ways of describing income distribution. We will use a method that will divide the country into five equal layers, like a great cake. The layers will help us give dollars-and-cents definitions of what we usually have in mind when we speak of the poor, the working class, the middle class, and so on. As we will see, the amounts are not at all what most of us imagine.

The Poor

We begin with the bottom layer, the poor. By our definition, this will include all the households in the bottom 20 percent of the nation. From data gathered by the Census Bureau, we know that the highest income of a family in this bottom slice of

A PARADE OF BUSINESS FIRMS

We shall have a good deal to investigate in later chapters about the world of big business. But it might be useful to end this initial survey with a dramatization of the problem. Suppose that we lined up our roughly 16 million businesses in order of size, starting with the smallest, along an imaginary road from San Francisco to New York. There will be 4,000 businesses to the mile, or a little less than one per foot. Suppose further that we planted a flag for each business. The height of the flagpole represents the volume of sales: each $10,000 in sales is shown by one foot of pole.

The line of flagpoles is a very interesting sight. From San Francisco to about Reno, Nevada, it is almost unnoticeable, a row of poles about a foot high. From Reno eastward the poles increase in height until, near Columbus, Ohio—about four-fifths of the way across the nation—flags fly about 10 feet in the air, symbolizing $100,000 in sales. Looking backward from Columbus, we can see that 11 million out of 16 million firms have sales of less than that amount.

But as we approach the eastern terminus, the poles suddenly begin to mount. There are about 900,000 firms in the country with sales over $500,000. These corporations occupy the last 75 miles of the 3,000-mile road. There are 512,000 firms with sales of over $1 million. They occupy the last 50 miles of the road, with poles at least 100 feet high. Then there are 1,500 firms with sales of $50,000,000 or more. They take up the last quarter mile before the city limits, flags flying at skyscraper heights, 500 feet up.

But this is still not the climax. At the very gates of New York, on the last 100 feet of the last mile, we find the 100 largest industrial firms. They have sales of at least $10 billion, so that their flags are already miles high, far above the clouds. Along the last 10 feet of the road, there are the ten largest companies. Their sales are roughly $25 billion and up: astronauts are the only ones who ever get a chance to see these flags.

the five-layered cake was $12,500 in 1984. The official "poverty line" is somewhat lower and includes fewer people: 14.4% of the total population was below the Census Bureau's poverty level of $10,609 for a family of four in 1984.

The box headed "Poverty" on p. 63 shows some of the characteristics of poor families, but there are two additional facts about poverty that we should note.

First, not all families who are below the poverty line in any given census remain poor in the next one. About one-fifth of all poor households are young people, just starting their careers. Some of these low-income beginners will escape from pov-

UNIONS

How many members of the labor force offer their services through labor unions? In 1982 there were 20 million. That was 19 percent of the labor force. The figures do not convey the power of labor unions, because they do not point out the strengths of unions in the industrial sector. Table 7 shows more accurately how labor unions fit into the overall work picture.

Like corporations, unions show great disparity of size and strength. In 1983 there were some 50,000 local unions. Many of these small unions had memberships of 50 persons or fewer and were confined to a single enterprise. At the other end of the scale we find 210 large "national" unions, including such giants as the Teamsters (1.8 million members in 1982) or the United Auto Workers (1.1 million members in the same year). In fact, the 10 biggest unions in the country account for 55 percent of all union membership. Thus unions, like corporations, divide into a world of small and large operations, although the contrast in the unions is not quite so dramatic as in the corporations.

Table 7
PERCENT OF UNIONIZATION, 1980
Unionization is very unevenly distributed by sectors.

Sector	Employment (Millions)	Unionized
Agriculture	1.5	3.5%
Industry (mfg. and mining)	26.9	32.3
Services and other	63.2	18.8
Government	5.4	33.8

Source: AFL–CIO *Directory of Labor Organizations 1982–83.*

erty. In addition, about a quarter of the members of the poverty class are older people. Many of these were not poor in an earlier, more productive stage of their economic lives. At the same time, this also means that some families that are not poor when a census is taken will fall into poverty at a later stage of their lives. The moral of this is that poverty is not entirely static. At any moment, some families are escaping from poverty, some entering it. What counts, of course, is whether the net movement is in or out. This is important with regard to welfare, a problem we will take up in Chapter 30.

A second characteristic is that one quarter of the families below the poverty line have at least one wage earner in the labor force. Thus their poverty reflects inadequate earnings. A considerable amount of poverty, in other words, reflects the fact that some jobs do not pay enough to lift a jobholder above the low-income level. In some regions, certain jobs pay so little that even two jobholders in a family (especially if one works only seasonally) will not suffice to bring the family out of poverty. This is often the case, for example, with migrant farm workers, or with immigrants who must take the least desirable jobs.

The Working Class

We usually define the working class in terms of certain occupations. We call a factory operative — but not a salesclerk — working class, even though the factory employee may make more than a salesclerk.

For our purposes, however, we will just take the next two layers of the income cake and call them working class. This will include the 40 percent of the population that is above the poor. We choose this method to find out how large an income a family can make and still remain in the working class, as we have defined it. The answer is just under $31,500. To put it differently, 40 percent of the families in the country earn more than $12,500 but less than $31,500 a year.

The Rich and the Upper Class

With the bottom three-fifths of the nation tagged — one-fifth poor, two-fifths working class — we are ready to look into the income levels of upper echelons.

First the rich. Where do riches begin? A realistic answer is probably around $100,000 a year, the magic six-figure income that goes with significant corporate responsibility. There are at least 500,000 such rich families in America. They are the icing on the cake.

But under the truly rich is a considerably larger group that we will call the upper class. This is the top 5 percent of the nation, its average doctors, airline pilots, managers, lawyers — even some economists. Some 3.1 million families are in this top 5 percent.

How much income does it take to get there? In 1984 a family made it into the 95th percentile with an income of $73,000. These numbers have a certain shock value. It takes more money to be rich, but less to be upper class, than we ordinarily think.

The Middle Class

This leaves us with the middle class — the class to which we all think we belong. By our method of cutting the cake, the middle class includes 35 percent of the nation — everyone above the 31,500 top working-class income and below the $73,000

Chapter 4 / A Bird's Eye View of the Economy   **63**

POVERTY

What characteristics distinguish poor families? Old age is one: almost a third of the low-income group consists of retirees. Curiously, youth is also characteristic. A household (married or single) headed by someone under age 25 is much more likely to be a low-income family than one headed by an older person. Color counts. About 12 percent of the white population is poor; about one-third of the black population. Sex enters the picture. Households headed by a female are twice as likely to be poor as one headed by a male. Schooling is an attribute. Almost half of all poor families have only grade school educations. Occupation is another: one-third of all the nation's farmers are poor.

Many of the characteristics overlap: poor families are often old and black and poorly educated. No one characteristic is decisive in "making" a family poor. The poor are not poor just because they have no education, but often have no education because they have come from poor households themselves.

threshold of upper-class income. In 1984 an average white married couple, both working, earned about $33,000—just enough to enter middle class economic territory. No wonder that a middle-class feeling pervades American society, regardless of the occupation or social milieu from which families come.*

WEALTH

It is obvious that there are great extremes of income distribution in the United States. The economist Paul Samuelson has made the observation that if we built an income pyramid out of children's blocks, with each layer representing $1,000 of income, the peak would be far higher than the Eiffel Tower—but most of us would be within a yard of the ground.

Even more striking than the inequality of income, however, is the inequality of wealth—that is the ownership of assets of all kinds. A 1983 survey by the Federal

* Maybe you wonder how an "average white married couple" could enter an income group that we have defined as being not average. The answer is that not every household in our national layer cake is white or married, with both husband and wife working. Don't forget that these figures apply to 1984. To bring them up to date, increase them by the change in average prices since 1984. That won't be precisely accurate, but close enough.

A PARADE OF INCOMES

Suppose that like our parade of flags across the nation representing the sales of business firms, we lined up the population in order of its income. Assume the height of the middle family to be 6 feet, representing a median income of $26,500 in 1984. This will be our height, as observers. What would our parade look like?*

It would begin with a few families *below* the ground, for there are some households with negative incomes; that is, they report losses for the year. Mainly these are families with business losses, and their negative incomes are not matched by general poverty. Following close on their heels comes a long line of grotesque dwarfs who comprise about one-fifth of all families, people less than 3 feet tall. Some are shorter than 1 foot.

Only after the parade is half over do we reach people whose faces are at our level. Then come the giants. When we reach the last 5 percent of the parade — incomes around $73,000 — people are 17 feet tall. At the end of the parade, people tower 600 to 6,000 feet into the air — 100 to 1,000 times taller than the middle height. What is the largest income in the country? We do not know: Probably our ten to fifteen billionaires have incomes of over $100 million.

* Adapted from the brilliant description of an "income parade" by Jan Pen, *Income Distribution*, trans. Trevor S. Preston (New York: Praeger, 1971), pp. 48–59.

Reserve Board gives us the overall distribution of wealth which we show in Table 8. This shows us that four out of ten American families have little or no wealth. Their average holdings probably include a small bank account, a mortgaged home, perhaps some life insurance or pension rights. The next third of all families have modest assets — a larger bank account, a better home less encumbered with a mortgage, more insurance coverage. It is not until we reach the upper quarter (actually the upper 28 percent) that we begin to find considerable personal assets, and not until we have entered the top group that we encounter substantial holdings. Here is where the millionaire category begins.

Millionaires

How many U.S. families are millionaires — that is, own net assets worth $1 million or more? The Federal Reserve study shows that the number is considerably larger than was the case 20 years ago (allowing for inflation, of course). Four percent of all American families are estimated to be worth $500,000, and 2 percent of all families (an estimated 1,310,000) had a net worth of $1 million in 1983. If we exclude

Table 8

THE DISTRIBUTION OF WEALTH, 1983

We can see that wealth is much more unevenly distributed than income

Net Worth	Percentage of All Families
Less than $16,000	40
16,001 to 82,000	33
82,001 to 327,000	21
327,001 to 655,000	4
655,000 or more	3

Source: *Federal Reserve Bulletin,* March 1986, p. 167. All figures have been rounded for convenience sake.

the direct ownership of a home or personal business, about 320,000 families — one half of one percent of all families — were worth $1 million or more in financial assets alone — stocks and bonds of publicly owned companies, mutual funds, insurance, bank deposits, and the like. This is about twice as large a percentage of all families as in 1962.*

America's millionaires own a very large proportion of the nation's financial assets. The Federal Reserve study shows that in 1983 the top one half of one percent of families owned 56 percent of the nation's municipal (tax-exempt) bonds, 43 percent of all publicly traded stock, 69 percent of all trust accounts. The top *ten* percent of all families owned 92 percent of all municipal bonds, 85 percent of all traded stock, and 88 percent of all trust funds, as well as about 40 percent of all checking accounts, almost three quarters of all money market mutual funds, and almost two thirds of all retirement or Keogh accounts.

There is no doubt, in other words, that the ownership of wealth is heavily concentrated. The *value* of this wealth can fluctuate considerably, however. Someone who was a millionaire in 1970, and who invested his or her wealth in common stocks, would have lost about one half the value of this wealth by early 1982, because the cost of living doubled, but the stock market stubbornly refused to budge. Then came a great stock market boom in 1982 and a second, even more dramatic one, in late 1985 and early 1986. As a result of those booms, our millionaire's wealth would have caught up with the cost of living by the end of 1982, and gone out ahead of it in 1985–1986. So we can see that the value of the wealth held by the top wealth-holders can change dramatically, even though the actual holdings of assets hardly changes at all.

GOVERNMENT

We have almost completed our first overview of the economy, but there remains one institution with which we must gain an acquaintance: the government. How shall we size up so vast and complex an institution? Let us begin with the question of size: How big is the government within the overall economy?

* "Financial Characteristics of High-Income Families," *Federal Reserve Bulletin,* March 1986, pp. 163–177.

Table 9
SIZE OF GOVERNMENT SECTOR, 1985
Note that the size of the sector varies, depending on what function of government we emphasize.

	Percent of Total
Employment by government	16%
GNP bought by government	21
Household income paid by government	26

The Size of the Public Sector

The question can be answered in several ways, as Table 9 shows.

The table shows that there are at least three different measures of the government's bulk within the economy.**In round numbers it employs about one-sixth of the labor force; it buys about one-fifth of our total output (GNP); and it pays out about one-quarter of all incomes.** This is obviously big government. Is it too big? That is not a question that can easily be answered yes or no. The following facts bear on our answer.

State and Local vs. Federal

When economists speak of "government" or the "public sector," they refer to *all* government activities, not just those of the federal government. For example, as Table 10 shows, state and local government play a considerably larger role than federal government when it comes to our first measure — public employment.

Table 10
KINDS OF DIRECT PUBLIC OUTPUT, AS SHOWN BY PUBLIC EMPLOYMENT, 1983
Most public employees work for states and localities, not for the federal government. The figure for national defense includes civilian employment only. It does not cover some two million in the armed forces.

	Federal	State	Local
	(Number of Employees) in Thousands		
National defense	1,042	—	—
Postal service	669	—	—
Education	16	1,666	5,125
Highways	5	243	284
Health	281	846	951
Police	64	76	595
Fire protection	—	—	310
Sanitation	—	1	215
Resources and recreation	244	188	257
Financial administration	108	119	187
Other	449	676	1,420
Total	2,878	3,815	9,344

Source: *Statistical Abstract of the United States,* 1985.

Indeed, if we take away national defense, as a special kind of activity, state and local government becomes about *seven times larger* than the federal government as an employer.

Government as a Buyer of GNP

Next let us consider the size of government as a buyer of GNP — that is, as a direct purchaser of the goods and services counted within GNP. Here two considerations should be borne in mind: (1) About 40 percent of the GNP bought by the public sector is purchased by the federal government. Three-quarters of this is for defense. Sixty percent of GNP purchases are bought by state and local governments for the kinds of purposes outlined in Table 8. (2) The fraction of GNP bought by the total government sector is roughly the same in this country as in other Western capitalisms, as Table 11 shows.

Transfers vs. Purchases

Finally, we have to consider the size of government measured by its contribution to income. The reason that the contribution of government to total incomes is larger than the value of public output is that government pays out more money to households than the wages and salaries earned in creating public goods and services. The additional incomes are called *transfer payments*, because they transfer incomes from some members of the community (usually taxpayers) to others — retirees, handicapped persons, disadvantaged citizens.

Transfers are almost entirely paid by the federal government. Of the many kinds of transfer payments, social security is by far the most important. Together with Medicare, this absorbs about a third of all expenditures made by the public sector for all purposes. A quite different form of transfer is interest payments on the

Table 11

SIZE OF THE PUBLIC SECTOR IN WESTERN CAPITALISMS, 1983

Measured by employment or expenditure, the United States public sector is well within the range of the public sectors in other major capitalist countries.

Country	Gov't Employment as Percent of Total Employment	Gov't Outlays as Percent of Total GDP*
United States	16.5	38.1
Japan	6.5	34.8
West Germany	15.9	48.6
United Kingdom	22.0	47.2

* GDP is Gross Domestic Product (GNP less net factor payments to foreigners).
Source: *OECD Historical Statistics* (OECD 1985).

national debt, or subsidies to farmers or businesses. Still another form of transfers are unemployment benefits or out-and-out welfare programs of one kind or another.

Welfare programs are a bone of contention among economists, as they are among politicians. We will look into the welfare question in Chapter 35. But while we are still taking the measure of the public sector, we ought to note that the relation of all transfer payments to GNP tends to be smaller in the United States than in other capitalisms. We are not carrying a transfer burden that is heavier than that of, say, Canada or West Germany or Italy.

Government Waste

Finally, in considering the size of the public sector we have to consider its weight on our backs. Does government spending retard economic growth? Is it wasteful? That is a question we will meet many times as we go along. But in view of the heat it generates, we ought to state our own position now. **We believe that government can be a source of vitality and growth to the economy as well as a drag and a drain.** Everyone is acutely aware of the wasteful nature of many public projects, local as well as federal. On the other side of the coin, anyone who has ever gone to a public school, been treated in a public hospital, traveled on a public road, or flown in a plane guided by a public beacon system knows how useful public output can be. No simple judgment about the public sector can be an intelligent one.

looking back

KEY CONCEPTS

The purpose of this chapter is not to load you with facts and figures, but to give you a sense of economic geography—a feeling for the terrain we call The Economy. The central ideas that we ought to have clearly in mind are these:

Business institutions:
corporations
partnerships
proprietorships

1 Business is the most distinctive and important institution in a capitalist system. There are a very large number of private business organizations, but by far the most important of them are corporations, not partnerships or proprietorships. If you are not sure of the difference, read the important "Extra Word" following this.

Big business accounts for the preponderance of sales; small business is a substantial source of employment

2 In the world of corporations there are clearly visible two sub-worlds of business—big business and little business. There is no official dividing line between the two. But if we take the top 500 corporations, we find that we account for 70 percent of all industrial sales, 45 percent of all industrial employment, and

about 20 percent of all employment. Small business is important because it is a big employer of nonindustrial workers—retail or service workers—and because it is an important source of political sentiment.

Households are the source of labor

3 Households are the source of the nation's labor force. Most households supply more than one worker, but participation rates vary widely among age and sex groups.

Income distribution: about one-fifth poor; about one-third middle class; about 5 percent affluent

4 Household income distribution shows us that roughly one-fifth of all families and individuals can be classified as poor; about two-fifths as working class; about one-third as middle class, and about 5 percent as upper class. These are arbitrary dividing lines that serve only to give us some idea as to what family incomes are like in the different layers of the national income cake. We should note that the distribution of wealth is much more lopsided than the distribution of income.

The government sector varies in size, depending on what you measure

There are many measures of government's size, depending on its function

5 Government is a very important but confusing institution to study. Its size depends on whether we assess its contribution to employment (about one-sixth); to GNP (about one-fifth); or to total household incomes (about one-quarter). Facts to remember: (1) state and local government is the main source of government employment and buys more of GNP than the federal government, whose purchases are mainly for defense; (2) transfer payments, largely for social security, swell the total of income payments above that of purchases of goods and services; and (3) the overall size of government in GNP, on any measure, is much like that of other Western capitalist systems.

ECONOMIC VOCABULARY

Sector   57   Participation rate   58

QUESTIONS

1. How would you explain the fact that big business has made so much headway in industrial production, but not in farming or retailing?
2. Do the facts of income and wealth distribution surprise you? Please you? Shock you? With what arguments would you defend the existing distribution: Fairness and equity? Efficiency? Natural differences among individuals?

3. When we say that the government is "too big" in this country, do we mean as a producer, employer, or payer of incomes? Is it possible to argue that the government is too *small* a producer, employer, or income payer? Suppose you wanted to increase our defense budget. Would you not be arguing just that?

AN EXTRA WORD ABOUT

Business Organization

Business is a central institution in our economic system, and all of us ought to know something about how business, especially the corporation, is legally organized. Although corporations are the dominant form of business property, too few people are well informed about them. Here is a brief introduction to the main forms of business organization.

PROPRIETORSHIPS

A proprietorship is the simplest kind of business organization. Usually it can be set up without any legal fuss at all, simply by opening a place of business. Sometimes one has to register or get a license, for instance, to open a liquor store or to set up practice as a physician or lawyer. But proprietorships are the easiest to understand of all forms of business.

They are also, as we have seen, the most widespread form (see Table 1). Why are not all businesses proprietorships? The answer lies in certain problems that proprietorships have.

1. A proprietorship has difficulty growing because its ability to borrow money is limited to the amount of credit its owner-proprietor can raise. Only a very rich man can borrow very much.

2. A proprietor is personally liable for all losses that his business may incur (he also gets all its profits). A rich man is not likely to open a proprietary business, because if an unexpected loss is incurred — if his business is sued by an irate customer and loses the case — *the proprietor must pay from his own funds any obligations that the business cannot pay from its funds.* In fact, there is really no division between the property of the owner and that of the business.

3. When a proprietor dies, the business comes to an end. All debts must be paid, and a new business established to take over the old. This is hard on the spouse of the proprietor, the employees, and the creditors.

PARTNERSHIPS

Partnerships remedy many of these difficulties. Basically, a partnership is a combination of proprietors who have agreed, usually by legal formalities, to share a certain proportion of the profits and the losses of their business. The fact that there are now several people associated in the business obviously makes it easier to raise additional capital. Very large businesses have been partnerships, at least until recent days.

Nonetheless, there are still problems for partnerships.

1. Partners are together responsible for all the losses or debts of the business. Jointly they have, like proprietors, "unlimited" liability, although some partners may have limited liability.

2. The death of each partner requires the business to be legally reconstituted. When a partner of a firm dies, the firm usually has to undergo a reorganization. This is expensive and bothersome and often creates frictions.

CORPORATIONS

The corporation, as we have seen, is the most powerful although not the most prevalent form of business organization. Let us be sure that we understand exactly what a corporation is.

1. A corporation is a legal entity created by the state. Unlike a proprietorship or a partnership, all corporations must apply to their states for a charter allowing them to carry on business. The charter specifies in general terms the kinds of business they will carry on and the general financial structures they will have. Charters cost money, which is one reason that all proprietorships are not corporations. Another reason is that corporations pay income taxes on their income, before it goes to stockholders.

2. Once a corporation is chartered, it exists as a "person." That is, the corporation itself—not the individuals who own it or work for it—can bring suit, be sued, or own property. This has an immediate advantage. It is that the liability of an owner of a corporation is limited to the money he has put into the corporation. If the corporation is sued for more funds than the business possesses, the corporation will declare bankruptcy and the suer has no recourse to the private funds of the persons who own it.

3. Because the corporation is a "person," it does not go out of business when its owners die. The corporation is "immortal." It goes on until it fails as a business organization or voluntarily goes out of business, or until its charter is revoked by the state.

CORPORATE ORGANIZATION

Clearly, the corporation has substantial advantages over proprietorships and partnerships. But how does it run? Who owns it?

A corporation is owned by the individuals who buy shares in it. Suppose that a corporation is granted a charter to carry on a business in retail trade. The charter also specifies how many shares of stock this business enterprise is allowed to issue. For example, a corporation may be formed with the right to issue 100,000 shares. If these shares are sold to individuals at a price of $10 each, the original shareholders (also called stockholders) will have put $1 million into the corporation. In return each will receive stock certificates indicating how many shares that person has bought.

These stock certificates are somewhat like a partnership agreement, although there are noteworthy differences. If you buy 1,000 shares in our imaginary corporation, you will own 1 percent of the corporation. You will have the right to receive 1 percent of all income that it pays out as dividends on its stock. You will also be entitled to cast 1,000 votes—one vote per share — at the meetings of shareholders that all corporations must hold. In this way, a shareholder is very much like a junior partner who was given a one percent interest in a business.

ADVANTAGES OF SHARE OWNERSHIP

But here are the critical differences between corporations and partnerships.

1. As we have already said, a stockholder is not personally liable for any debts that the corporation cannot pay.   If the company goes bankrupt, the shareholder will lose his investment of $10,000 (1,000 shares @ $10) but cannot be sued for any further money. *Liability is thereby limited to the amount the shareholder has invested.*

2. Unlike partnership shares, which are usually very difficult to sell, corporation shares are generally easy to sell if one owns the stock of a company that is listed (bought and sold) on one of the nation's several stock markets.   (The shares of a very small corporation are not, of course, so easy to sell, although they are less difficult to dispose of than a partnership.) Moreover, a stockholder may sell shares to anyone, at any price. If our imaginary corporation prospers, its shares may sell for $20 each. A stockholder is perfectly free to sell his or her shares at that price. As we have just mentioned, marketplaces for stocks and bonds have developed along with the corporation, to facilitate such sales of stock. The most important of these markets, the New York Stock Exchange, was organized in 1817. Today over 30 billion shares a year are bought and sold on the stock exchange. Thus, with the corporation comes the advantage of a much greater "liquidity" of personal wealth — that is, greater ease of turning assets into cash.

3. Shares of stock entitle the stockholder to the dividends that the directors of the corporation (see below) may decide to pay out for each share.   But a shareholder is not entitled to any fixed amount of profit. If the corporation prospers, the directors may vote to pay a large dividend. But they are under no obligation to do so. They may wish to use the earnings of the corporation for other purposes, such as the purchase of new equipment or land. If the corporation suffers losses, ordinarily the directors will vote to pay no dividend or only a small one to be paid from past earnings. Thus, as an owner of ordinary common stock, the stockholder must take the risk of having dividends rise or fall.

4. Corporations are also allowed to issue bonds, as well as stock.   A bond is different from a share of stock in two ways. First, a bond has a *stated value* printed on its face, whereas a share of stock does not. A $1,000 bond issued by a corporation is a certificate for a debt of $1,000. The bondholder is not a sharer in the profits of the company but a creditor of the corporation — someone to whom the corporation is in debt for $1,000. In case of corporate bankruptcy, the claims of bondholders take precedence over those of shareholders.

Second, a bond also states on its face the *amount of income* it will pay to bondholders. A $1,000 bond may declare that it will pay $80 a year as interest. Unlike dividends, this interest payment will not rise if the corporation makes money, nor will it fall if it does not. Thus there is no element of profit sharing in bonds, as there is in stocks.

There is a compensation for this, however. The risk of owning a bond is usually less than that of owning a stock. A bond is a legal obligation of the corporation, which *must* pay interest, and which *must* buy back the bond itself when a fixed term of years has expired and the bond becomes "due." If it fails to meet either of these obligations, the courts will declare the firm bankrupt, and all its assets will be turned over to the bondholders to satisfy their debts. If the firm's assets are not enough to repay the bondholders, they will suffer a degree of loss; but the shareholders will lose *all* of their equity, for a share of stock has no such obligations attached to it and never becomes due. No shareholder can sue a corporation if it fails to pay a dividend.

OWNERSHIP AND CONTROL

One last matter is also of significance in discussing the organization of the corporation. The new mode of structuring enterprise has made possible a development of great importance: the separation of ownership and control.

As we have seen, stockholders are the actual owners of a corporation, but it is obviously impossible for large numbers of stockholders to meet regularly and run a company. A.T.&T. has well over 1,000,000 stockholders. Where could they meet? How could they possibly decide what the company should do?

All corporations, small or large, therefore, are run by boards of directors (who may or may not own stock in the company), and who are elected by the stockholders. At regular intervals, all stockholders are asked to elect or reelect members of the board, each casting as many votes as the number of shares that he owns. In turn, the board of directors appoints the "management" — main officials of the corporation; for example, its chief executive officer. Management hires the rest of the employees. As the number of share-owners grows, it is not surprising that power drifts into the hands of the management. (The extent to which managers can operate independently of, or even contrary to, the interests of stockholders is one of the hotly debated questions in economics.)

STOCK EXCHANGES

We have mentioned stock exchanges as the organized markets in which shares are traded. *An important thing to realize is that buying a share of stock does not put money into a corporation, unless the stock is newly issued by the company.*

Most of the shares bought and sold on the stock exchanges are old shares, issued years ago. When you buy a share of General Motors, the money you pay does *not* go to General Motors. It goes to the individual who sold you the shares. If you own shares in a company that produces cigarettes, and you want to get out of this business because you disapprove of smoking, you sell your shares. *But doing so does not take any money out of the cigarette business.* It simply transfers your shares to another person who will pay you for your stock certificates.

Does it then make no difference to a cigarette company whether you buy its shares or not? Not quite. Corporations like to have their shares well regarded by the public, because from time to time they *do* issue new shares, and they want an eager market for these shares. So, too, if their shares are in general disfavor, they will sell for lower prices, and at a lower price a company is easier to "take over" than at a higher price.* Finally, managers usually own shares in their own companies. As the shares go up, they become richer. So companies are far from indifferent to the fate of their shares. Nonetheless, we should clearly understand that we do not put money into businesses when we buy their outstanding shares.

---

* A "takeover" is a concerted effort, usually by a small group of individuals who own a considerable amount of the company's stock, to round up enough proxies (votes) to oust an incumbent management and to install a management of its own. Takeovers are dramatic when they occur. They are not frequent, but they happen often enough so that corporations keep an eye out for "raiding" interests. If the price of the stock falls, it is often an invitation to be taken over, simply because it is cheaper to buy the votes (shares) when the price is depressed.

CHAPTER 5
The Trend of Things

a look ahead

The last chapter was an aerial photo of the economy, giving us the lay of the land. Now we want to take a series of pictures over time to give us a sense of change in the economic landscape. This will fit into our first historic conception of capitalism, gained in Chapter 2, and will also give us a chance to test some of the theories about capitalism we covered in Chapter 3.

In particular we are going to examine four major trends of modern times.

1 The growth of production measured by GNP—gross national product.
2 Trends in income distribution.
3 The drift toward big business.
4 The rapid rise in government.

Warning before you begin: Don't get bogged down in facts and figures. Keep your eye out for trends and for explanations of trends. The facts are there to illustrate these trends and to test explanations, not to be learned for themselves.

THE PROCESS OF GROWTH

Imagine that we have had a camera trained on the U.S. economy over the last eighty years or so. What would be the most striking changes to meet our eye?

There is no doubt about the first impression: It would be a sense of growth. Everything would be getting larger. Business firms would be growing in size. Labor unions would be bigger. There would be many more households, and each household would be richer. Government would be much larger. And underlying all of this, the extent of the market system itself—the great ongoing flow of inputs and outputs—would be steadily increasing in size.

Growth is not, of course, the only thing we would notice. Businesses are different as well as bigger when we compare 1980 and 1900: There are far more corporations now than in the old days, far more diversified businesses, fewer family firms. Households are different because more women work outside the home. Labor unions today are no longer mainly craft unions, limited to one occupation. Government is not only bigger but has a different philosophy.

Total Output

Nonetheless, it is growth that first commands our attention. The camera vision of the economy gives us a picture that keeps widening. It *has* to widen to encompass the increase in the sheer mass of output. Hence the first institution whose growth we must examine is that of the market system itself.

More specifically, we must trace the tremendous growth in our total output. The technical name for this flow of output is gross national product (GNP), a term we will use many times in the future and which we will later define more carefully. Here we only note that it is the dollar value of our annual flow of final output. Figure 1 gives us a graphic representation of this increase in yearly output.

Correcting for Inflation

As we can see, the dollar value of all output from 1900 to 1985 has grown by a factor of over 180. But perhaps a cautionary thought will have already struck you. If we measure the growth of output by comparing the dollar value of production over time, what seems to be growth in actual economic activity may be no more than a rise in prices. If the economy in 1985 produced no more actual tons of grain than the economy in 1900 but grain prices were double those of 1900, our GNP figures would show growth where there was really nothing but inflation.

To arrive at a measure of real growth, we have to correct for changes in prices. To do so, we take one year as a *base* and use the prices of that year to evaluate output in all succeeding years.

Here is an elementary example. Suppose our grain economy produced 1 million tons in 1900 and 2 million in 1985, but wheat sold for $1 in 1900 and $4 in 1985. Our GNP in the current prices of 1900 and 1985 is $1 million for 1900 and $8

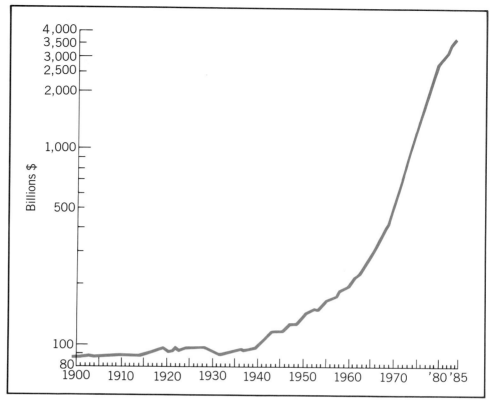

Figure 1

VALUE OF GNP 1900 – 1985

Gross National Product (GNP) has increased 180 fold in three quarters of a century, measured in the prices of each year's production.

million 85 years later. But if we evaluate the GNP *using only the 1900 prices* (i.e., $1 per bushel), our GNP is reduced to $2 million in 1985. This constant dollar GNP is often referred to as the**real GNP,** while the current dollar GNP is called the **nominal GNP.** We can use the prices of any year as the base. The important thing is that all outputs must be evaluated with only one set of prices.

Figure 2 shows us the much-reduced growth of output when output is measured in 1982 dollars, a year frequently used as a base.

Per Capita Growth

As we can see, growth in real (or constant dollar) terms is much less dramatic than growth in current dollars that make no allowance for rising prices. Nonetheless, the value of 1982 output, compared to that of 1900, with price changes eliminated as best we can, still shows a growth factor of almost 40.

VOLUME AND VALUE

You should be warned that there is no entirely satisfactory way of wringing price increases out of the hodgepodge of goods and services called GNP, because different items in this collection of goods rise or fall in price in different degrees. There is always a certain element of arbitrariness in correcting GNP for price changes. Different methods, each perfectly defensible, will yield somewhat different measures of "corrected" GNP.

Isn't there some way of getting around the problem of dollar values when we compare GNPs? One way is to measure actual physical volumes. When certain kinds of outputs, such as foodstuffs, bulk very large in GNP as they do in India or China, we sometimes measure growth just by adding up the tonnages of food production. The problem, of course, is that the composition of these tonnages may change—more wheat one year, more rice another—which gets us into another comparison problem. And then such a measure ignores entirely the outputs of nonagricultural goods. (We meet the same problem if we try to measure growth by tonnages of freight, metal production, etc.)

A more defensible way might be to consider GNP as a sum total of labor time, the embodiment of so many million hours of work. Even this does not get us around the measurement and comparison problem, for we use different kinds of labor as time goes on. Therefore, we have to make the difficult assumption that all kinds of labor, skilled and unskilled, trained and untrained, can be "reduced" to multiples of one "basic" kind. That basic labor, in turn, would have to boil down to some constant unit of "effort." But does the unit of "effort"—of human energy—remain constant over time?

In the end, the task of measuring an aggregate of different things can never be solved to our complete satisfaction. Any concept of GNP always has an element of unmeasurableness about it. Growth is a concept we constantly use, but it remains tantalizingly beyond precise definition.

But there still remains one last adjustment to be made. The growth of output is a massive assemblage of goods and services to be distributed among the nation's households, and the number of those households has increased. In 1900, United States population was 76 million; in 1985 it was about 240 million. To bring our constant GNP down to life size, we have to divide it by population to get GNP per person, or per capita.

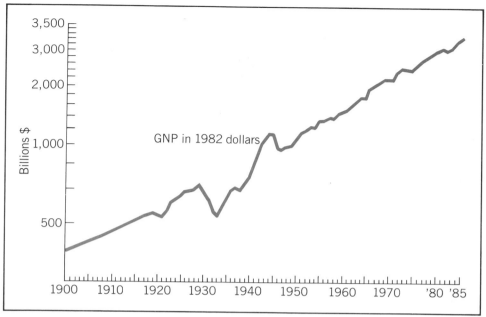

Figure 2
GNP IN CONSTANT (1982) DOLLARS

Measured in real terms, GNP has increased only about 35 times, not 180+ times. In this graph we use a semi log scale because it shows more clearly the rate of growth *rather than the absolute dollar growth of GNP.*
Source: *Economic Report of the President,* 1986.

Historical Record

In Figure 3 we see the American experience from the middle of the nineteenth century in terms of real per capita GNP, this time in 1929 prices.* Viewed from the long perspective of history, our average rate of growth has been astonishingly consistent. This holds true for an average over the past thirty-odd years since the Great Depression or back to the 1870s (or even 1830s). As the chart shows, the swings are almost all contained within a range of 10 percent above or below the trend. The trend itself comes to about 3.5 percent a year in real terms, or a little over 1.5 percent a year per capita. Although 1.5 percent a year may not sound like much, remember that this figure allows us to double our real per capita living standards every 47 years. This is Adam Smith's growth model come to life!

* Why do we use 1929 as a base here and 1982 as a base in Figure 2? We do it to accustom you to the idea that different years can serve as the basis for comparison.

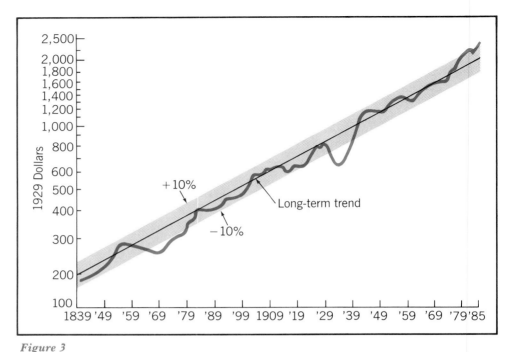

Figure 3
REAL GNP PER CAPITA (1929 DOLLARS)
Real GNP per capita has shown a long, irregular, but fairly steady upward trend.

Sources of Growth

How do we explain this long upward trend? Here we can give only a brief summary of the causes we will study more systematically later. Essentially, we grew for two reasons:

1. THE QUANTITY OF INPUTS GOING INTO THE ECONOMIC PROCESS INCREASED. In 1900 our civilian labor force was 27 million. In 1985 it was about 117 million. Obviously, larger inputs of labor produce larger outputs of goods and services. (Whether they may even produce *proportionally* larger outputs is another question we will investigate later.)

Land and capital in use also increased. Land is easier to measure. In 1900, there were 839 million acres of land used for cultivation, and over 1,000 million acres for other purposes such as grazing. By 1985, land in cultivation had increased to over 1,000 million acres, and land in grazing use had also increased: We had reclaimed virgin land and made it economically productive.

2. THE QUALITY OF INPUTS IMPROVED. The population working in 1985 was not only more numerous than in 1900, it was better trained and better schooled. The best overall gauge of this is the amount of education stored up in the work force. In

1900, when only 6.4 percent of the working population had gone beyond grade school, there were 223 million man-years of schooling embodied in the population. In 1985, when over two-thirds of the population had finished high school, the stock of education embodied in the population had grown to over a billion man-years.

The quality of capital has also increased, along with its quantity. As an indication of the importance of the changing quality of capital, consider the contribution made to our output by the availability of surfaced roads. In 1900 there were about 150,000 miles of such roads. In 1985, there were almost 4 million miles. That is an increase in the quantity of roads of over 25 times. But that increase does not begin to measure the difference in the transport capability of the two road systems, one of them gravelled, narrow, built for traffic that averaged 10 to 20 miles per hour; the other, concrete or asphalt, multilane, fast-paced.

Productivity

There are still other sources of growth, such as shifts in occupations and efficiencies of large-scale operation, but the main ones are the increase in the quantity and the quality of inputs. Of the two, **improvements in the quality of inputs — in human skills, in improved designs of capital equipment — have been far more important than mere increases in quantity.** Better skills and technology enable the labor force to increase its productivity, the amount of goods and services it can turn out in a given time.

Figure 4 shows the trend in productivity during recent years. As you can see, the growth has been fairly steady up to the early 1970s, despite occasional dips. After 1972 the trend seems to shift downward, and in 1979 and 1980 it actually turns negative — we grew less productive! This may have been a short-lived phenomenon, having to do with the inefficient (unproductive) use of labor in a recession.

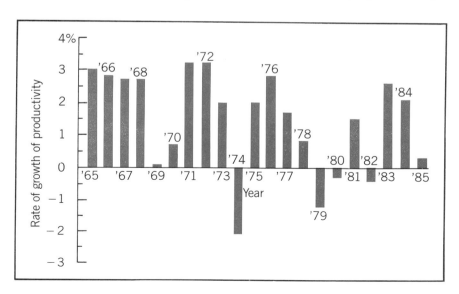

Figure 4
THE PRODUCTIVITY PICTURE

These data show that our increases in productivity have fallen precipitously in recent years. The causes for this productivity decline will interest us later in our book.
Source: *Economic Indicators.*

Here we want to emphasize the contribution made to long-term growth by our normal steady improvement in our ability to grow and extract and handle and shape and transport goods.

THE DIFFERENCE GROWTH RATES MAKE

The normal range in growth rates for capitalist economies does not seem to be very great. How much difference does it make, after all, if output grows at 1.7 or 2.7 percent?

The answer is: an amazing difference. This is because growth is an *exponential* phenomenon involving a percentage rate of growth on a steadily rising base. At 1.7 percent, per capita real income will double in about 40 years. At 2.7 percent, it will double in 26 years.

Professor Kenneth Boulding has pointed out that before World War II no country sustained more than 2.3 percent per capita growth of GNP. Since World War II, Japan has achieved a per capita growth rate of 8 percent. Boulding writes: "The difference between 2.3 and 8 percent may be dramatically illustrated by pointing out that [at 2.3 percent] children are twice as rich as their parents—i.e., per capita income approximately doubles every generation —while at 8 percent per annum, children are six times as rich as their parents."

CHANGES IN DISTRIBUTION

We have seen how striking was the increase in output in the twentieth century. But what happened to the division of this output among the various classes of society? Have the rich gotten richer and the poor poorer? Has the trend been in the direction of greater equality?

Changes in Dollar Incomes vs. Changes in Shares

The question is not easy to answer. Remember, we are interested in the changes in *shares* going to different groups, not just in absolute amounts. There has certainly been a tremendous change in the dollar amounts that we have used to define different social classes, as Figure 5 shows.*

The figures show that growth has helped boost all income classes. But has the *proportion* of income going to the various classes also changed? That is not what we

* Social class has been defined, for illustrative purposes, by income. See discussion pages 61–63.

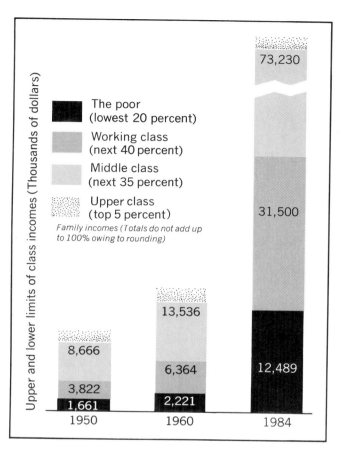

The poor
(lowest 20 percent)

Working class
(next 40 percent)

Middle class
(next 35 percent)

Upper class
(top 5 percent)

Family incomes (Totals do not add up to 100% owing to rounding)

Figure 5

UPPER AND LOWER DOLLAR LIMITS OF SOCIAL CLASSES

The dollar incomes of all social classes have increased markedly. (Notice there is no upper bound to the topmost class. Do you understand why?)
Source: Census Bureau *P–60,* 149.

find. Figure 6 shows that sharing-out of incomes among social groups has been remarkably steady.

Thus the distribution of total income among those at the top, in the middle, and on the bottom has not shifted very much. The poor have a little larger share of the income cake; the well-to-do, a little smaller. Only if we go back to the 1920s do we see a marked change. In those days, the share of the top 5 percent was perhaps twice as large as it is today. In addition, various social programs, such as Medicare or state-supported higher education, have probably raised the *real income* of the poorest 20 percent somewhat more than Figure 6 shows.*

> * A more detailed study of changes in income distribution would have to take into account some facts that are not included in the figures above. For technical reasons, the Census Bureau does not include most forms of capital income (such as capital gains on stocks or real estate) in its computation of incomes. If it did, the share of the top 1 percent would be larger. The Census Bureau also does not fully take into account cash and noncash payments to the poor, such as food stamps or welfare aid. This would add to the share of the poor. In other words, the Census figures are mainly derived from earnings, not returns on capital or "transfers" that may benefit high- or low-income groups. It is extremely difficult to net out the effects of all these flows of money. The "real" result is probably more favorable to lower income groups, but it is not possible to say by exactly how much. In all likelihood, the net change is not very great.

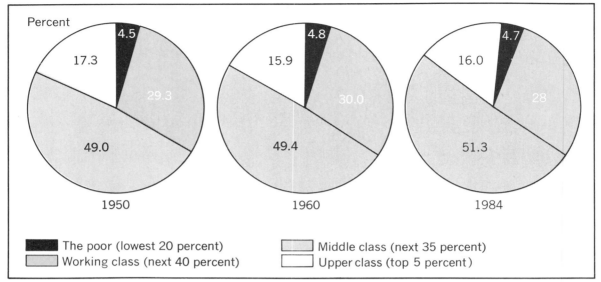

Figure 6
SHARES OF TOTAL INCOME GOING TO DIFFERENT SOCIAL CLASSES
The distribution of income among different social classes has shown very little change.
Source: Census Bureau P–60.

The Elimination of Poverty?

Does this mean that poverty is being eliminated from the United States? Until recently the number of persons below the designated low-income level has been dropping, both absolutely and relative to the larger population, even though the threshold of an officially defined "poverty" income has been steadily adjusted upward to allow for inflation. We can see this gradual shrinkage in Table 1, where poverty drops markedly from 1959 until 1969. Then in 1975 the decline stops, due to a sharp recession. Thereafter poverty rises and falls with economic condition: down in the recovery of 1976–78, up sharply in the deep recession and cutbacks in antipoverty programs of 1980–82, followed by a slight fall with the recovery of the mid-1980s.

Even the dramatic fall between 1959 and 1979 does not tell us, however, whether poverty simply melts away as a result of overall growth or whether we

Table 1
PERSONS BELOW LOW-INCOME LEVEL

	1959	*1965*	*1969*	*1975*	*1981*	*1984*
All persons (millions)	39.5	33.2	24.1	25.9	31.8	33.7
Percent of population	22.4	17.3	12.1	12.3	14.0	14.4

Source: Census Bureau P–60.

eliminate certain kinds of poverty (such as poverty from low wages), while leaving other kinds relatively untouched. We do know, however, that the decline in poverty has been heavily concentrated among one section of the population — the elderly — and is due primarily to a rise in the coverage and real value of social security benefits. By the mid-1980s, poverty among older people had declined to historically low levels. On the other hand, conditions for single women with children and for minorities had not gotten better, and had perhaps even deteriorated. This makes it difficult to say that the "poverty problem" in the nation as a whole has gotten better.

Such considerations also make it difficult to pass judgment on Marx's expectations of "increasing misery." Many people have argued that this is the least justified of Marx's expectations about capitalism. Others have claimed that by "misery" Marx did not mean money income, but the quality of life. Perhaps a fair judgment is that misery measured in money has probably decreased much more than Marx ever imagined, but that misery measured in the experience of social life may not have disappeared nearly as much as Marx's critics expected.*

TRENDS IN BUSINESS

We have examined the main trends in personal income. Now let us turn to business. Here one change immediately strikes the eye. There is a marked decline of the independent, small business — with its self-employed worker — as a main form of enterprise.

In 1900 there were about 8 million independent enterprises, including 5.7 million farms. By 1985, as we saw in the last chapter, the number of proprietorships had grown to over 12 million, a figure that included some 2.4 million farms. Meanwhile, the labor force itself more than tripled. Thus as a percentage of all persons working, the proportion of self-employed has fallen from about 30 percent in 1900 to under 10 percent today.

Rise of Big Business

With the decline of the self-employed worker has come the rise of the giant firm. Back in 1900, the giant corporation was just arriving on the scene. In 1901, financier J. P. Morgan created the first billion-dollar company when he formed the United States Steel Corporation out of a dozen smaller enterprises. In that year, the total capitalization of all corporations valued at more than $1 million was $5 billion. By 1904 it was $20 billion. In 1985 it was over $8 trillion.

---

* It is worth remarking that Adam Smith also expected "misery" to increase, despite a rise in income, because commercial society (as he called it) exposed the working population to the dulling influence of monotonous work. A capitalist society, Smith believed, was rich, but its working classes were likely to be made less alert and intelligent because of the labor they performed. See *Wealth of Nations* (1937), p. 734.

POVERTY AGAIN

In a box on page 63 we took a quick look at some of the characteristics of the poor. Here is a second, more systematic glance. It puts all households — families and individuals — into various categories and shows us the chance that someone in a given category will be a member of a low-income (poor) household.

But we must always be very careful before we impute poverty to any single source. One of the authors, sitting in a Ph.D. exam, was questioning a candidate about a dissertation on poverty. It seemed there were many causes for poverty, all impressively substantiated with evidence.

Chances of Being Poor (1985)	
	%
All families	14.4
Single persons	23.5
White families	9.1
Black families	30.9
Families headed by females	
White	27.1
Black	51.7

Source: Census Bureau *P–60.*

"But if you had to single out one cause as the *most* important," asked the examiner, "which would it be?"

The candidate hemmed and hawed. There was skill. There was health. There was culture. There was native ability. But if he *had* to choose, he would say that education — or rather, the lack of it — was the greatest contributory factor in poverty. Most poor people simply didn't have the knowledge to enable them to get high-paying jobs.

"And why didn't they have the education?" asked the examiner.

That was easy. Education was expensive. Poor people couldn't afford private schools. The need for income was so great that they dropped out of school early to earn money.

"I see," said the examiner. "People are poor because they are uneducated. They are uneducated because they haven't the money to buy education. So *poverty causes poverty.*"

Table 2
LARGEST MANUFACTURERS SHARE OF ASSETS (%)
The share of the biggest corporations grew rapidly during the fifties and sixties and stabilized in the seventies and may have risen since then.

	1948	1960	1970	1981	1982	1983
100 largest corporations	40.2	46.4	48.5	46.8	47.7	48.3
200 largest corporations	48.2	56.3	60.4	60.0	60.8	60.8

Source: *Statistical Abstract of the United States,* Table #866.

It hardly comes as a surprise that the main trend of the past 80 years has been the emergence of big business. More interesting is the question of whether big business is continuing to grow. This is a more difficult question to answer, for it depends on what we mean by "growth."

Certainly the place of the biggest companies within the world of corporations has been rising. Marx was indubitably right in predicting this trend. Indeed, as Table 2 shows, the top 100 companies in 1970 held approximately as large a share of total corporate wealth as the top 200 companies in 1948.

Merger Mania

Until recently, economists generally believed that the concentration movement had leveled off. Between 1960 and the early 1980s, the percentage of assets held by the top one hundred corporations remained fairly steady, and the concentration of sales likewise showed no signs of significant change.

Beginning in the early 1980s, however, this condition of overall stability changed suddenly and dramatically. A new merger wave broke out — a wave of such immense proportions as to dwarf all earlier periods of corporate acquisition. During the quiet years before this wave, the annual number of mergers in the ranks of the nation's larger corporations averaged less than one hundred, and the total amount of assets involved in all mergers amounted to something like $5 billion per year. Then merger mania began. In 1984, 2,999 "big" mergers took place, involving $124 billion in total assets. In 1985 the number was higher, and **in that year there were at least five mergers whose individual values were larger than the total value of all mergers in the pre-merger decades.** (See box for details).

Behind the Merger Wave

What brought about this extraordinary and quite unforeseen merger frenzy? Two factors seem to underline the boom — one financial, the other legal. The financial impetus resulted from the combination of high interest rates and high inflation, which together depressed the price of corporation shares to the point where the value of the actual assets of many corporations, such as the oil reserves of the big oil

1985's BILLION DOLLAR CLUB

TRANSACTIONS COMPLETED IN 1985 VALUED AT $1 BILLION OR MORE

Value (billions)	Buyer	Company Bought
$6.3	General Electric	RCA
6.2	Kohlberg, Kravis, Roberts	Beatrice Company
5.8	Philip Morris	General Foods
5.1	General Motors	Hughes Aircraft
5.0	Allied Corporation	Signal Companies
4.9	R. J. Reynolds	Nabisco
3.8	Baxter Travenol	American Hospital Supply
3.7	U.S. Steel	Texas Oil and Gas
3.5	Capital Cities Communications	American Broadcasting Companies
2.8	Monsanto	G. D. Searle
2.5	Coastal Corporation	American Natural Resources
2.5	Kohlberg, Kravis, Roberts	Storer Communications
2.3	Internorth	Houston Natural Gas
1.8	Pantry Pride (buyout)	Revlon
1.7	Kohlberg, Kravis, Roberts	50% of Union Texas Petroleum (Allied-Signal subsidiary)
1.7	Rockwell International	Allen-Bradley
1.6	Procter & Gamble	Richardson-Vicks
1.4	Rupert Murdoch	Seven Metromedia television stations
1.3	Farley Industries	Northwest Industries
1.3	Chesebrough-Pond's	Stauffer Chemical
1.2	Midcon Corporation	United Energy Resources
1.1	Haas family (buyout)	Levi Strauss
1.0	BASF	Inmont Corporation (United Technologies subsidiary)
1.0	Wickes Companies	Consumer/Industrial Products (Gulf and Western subsidiary)

companies, were worth substantially more than the stock market's appraisal of the corporations as going concerns. This presented opportunities to aggressive companies or shrewd financiers to buy out undervalued corporations, and to realize large profits by disposing of their assets at much higher values than those of the stock market.

The legal cause of the merger mania was a change in the attitude of government. The deregulation of a number of industries, such as oil or transportation, set the stage for a general competitive consolidation within those industries. And a more benign attitude of the Justice Department toward mergers themselves, especially where it was felt that the new corporations might fare better against the pressure of international competition, removed an obstacle that had formerly dampened merger enthusiasm.

Hostile Mergers

In addition to two new sources of merger initiative, the merger wave differed from earlier waves in another respect. Previous merger waves generally resulted from the desires of all parties to the merger to consolidate their companies. By way of contrast, the merger wave of the mid-1980s was often the result of "hostile" takeovers — purchases of one company by another, or by a financier, despite the objections of the first. Here the impetus was supplied by two factors. One was the anonymity of most managements, whose names were not known to their stockholders, as were once the names of manager-owners like Henry Ford and Andrew Carnegie. When shareowners received bids to buy their shares at lucrative prices, there was little concern for the appeals of the existing management, to whom shareowners felt no loyalty. A second was that hostile takeovers were made possible because banks were willing to lend "raiders" very large amounts of money, often on frail security. The merger deals were then financed by buying out shareowners with the bank's money, after which the raider typically unloaded his debt on the company he had acquired, causing it to issue bonds whose proceeds then reimbursed the bank. Some of these free-and-easy financing methods have recently been stopped by the action of Federal Reserve Board.*

Consequences of the Merger Wave

The effects of the merger wave cannot be described as clearly as its causes. It will be some time before we know to what degree the overall concentration of assets will be affected, or whether the domination of big companies in individual markets has changed. In the meanwhile the most important effect of the merger wave is likely to be on corporate profitability. Interest on the $200-odd billion of new debt that has been issued comes as an *expense* that must be met before profits can be realized. If this expense is not met — and in the case of ill-secured "junk bonds" it may not be — any adverse turn of events, either in a single strategic company or in the overall economy, might well precipitate a "panic" comparable to those that shook the financial world in earlier periods of financial wheeling and dealing.

* For a fuller discussion of the merger phenomenon, with its strange language of "white knights" (friendly acquirers who forestall hostile takeovers), "golden parachutes," "greenmail" and the like, see Peter Drucker, "Corporate Takeovers — What Is To Be Done?" in *The Public Interest,* Winter 1986.

Is it possible that the merger wave may turn out to be a good thing, not a bad one? Its supporters claim that the effect will be the creation of larger, wealthier, and more efficient institutions, capable of better meeting massive competition from abroad. Its detractors worry about financial instability and about the wholesale elimination of jobs—including middle management jobs—when companies merge. And in the background there is always the troublesome issue of the concentration of economic power. Perhaps by the next edition of this book these issues will be clearer. All we can say now is that we are still in the midst of a remarkable transformation of the corporate scene whose dimensions have already altered the configuration of the American economy.

Explaining the Trend to Business Size

Can we explain the long-term trend toward the concentration of business assets, as we did the trend toward growth in GNP? By and large, economists would stress three main reasons for the appearance of giant enterprise.

1. Advances in Technology Have Made Possible the Mass Production of Goods or Services at Falling Costs. The rise of bigness in business is very much a result of technology. Without the steam engine, the lathe, the railroad, it is difficult to imagine how big business would have emerged.

But technology went on to do more than make large-scale production possible. Typically it also brought an economic effect that we call **economies of scale.** That is, technology not only enlarged, it also cheapened the process of production. Costs per unit fell as output rose. The process is perfectly exemplified in the huge reduction of cost in producing automobiles on an assembly line rather than one car at a time (see box).

Economies of scale provided further powerful impetus toward a growth in size. **The firm that pioneered in the introduction of mass production technology usually secured a competitive selling advantage over its competitors, enabling it to grow in size and thereby to increase its advantage still further.** These cost-reducing advantages were important causes of the initial emergence of giant companies in many industries. Similarly, the absence of such technologies explains why corporate giants did not emerge in all fields.

2. Concentration Is Also a Result of Corporate Mergers. We have just looked into the merger wave of the mid-1980s. But ever since J. P. Morgan assembled U.S. Steel, mergers have been a major source of corporate growth. At the very end of the nineteenth century there was the first great merger wave, out of which came the first huge companies, including U.S. Steel. In 1890 most industries were competitive, without a single company dominating the field. By 1904 one or two giant firms, usually created by mergers, had arisen to control at least half the output in 78 different industries.

Again, between 1951 and 1960 one-fifth of the top 1,000 corporations disappeared — not because they failed, but because they were bought up by other corporations. **In all, mergers have accounted for about two-fifths of the increase in concentration between 1950 and 1970; internal growth accounts for the rest.**

3. **DEPRESSIONS OR RECESSIONS PLUNGE MANY SMALLER FIRMS INTO BANKRUPTCY AND MAKE IT POSSIBLE FOR LARGER, MORE FINANCIALLY SECURE FIRMS TO BUY THEM UP VERY CHEAPLY.** This is once more as Marx anticipated. Certainly the process of concentration is abetted by economic distress. When industries are threatened, the weak producers go under; the stronger ones emerge relatively stronger than before. Consider, for example, that three once-prominent American automobile producers succumbed to the mild recessions of the 1950s and 1960s, and to the pressure of foreign competition: Studebaker, Packard, Kaiser Motors; more recently, Chrysler only escaped by congressional bailout.

HOW BIG IS BIG?

Just to get an idea of scale, the 36th largest industrial corporation in 1984 ranked by sales was Beatrice Foods. Its sales that year were $9.3 billion. It was not the 36th largest in terms of assets, which were $4.5 billion. The 36th largest firm in assets was Avco, with assets of $6.9 billion. However, its sales of $2.1 billion ranked it only 176th in terms of sales.

Thus it makes a difference whether we rank companies in size by sales or assets. At the very top of the heap, the top 13 firms in terms of sales are the top 13 in terms of assets. Nine of the first 10 firms in sales are also among the top 10 in assets. This coincidence weakens as we move down the list. Some examples: Chrysler was 14th in sales, 31st in assets; General Dynamics was 44th in sales, 31st in assets; Deere was 86th in sales, 49th in assets; Pennzoil was 176th in sales, 36th in assets.

Which is more important, sales or assets? Sales measure the dominance of a company within its field; assets measure its overall financial strength. Actually both sales and assets measure size, but what counts in the marketplace is profitability. Here the correct measure is the net rate of return — the rate of profit earned per dollar of capital. The average big business earns two to three times the return of the average small business, but really spectacular rates of return are usually found in smaller businesses on their way to stardom.

Last rule of thumb: To make it into the top 500 companies, your sales have to be about $400 million; your assets, $150 million.

FROM PIN FACTORY TO ASSEMBLY LINE

We recall Adam Smith's pin factory. Here is a later version of that division of labor, in the early Ford assembly lines.

> *Just how were the main assembly lines and lines of component production and supply kept in harmony? For the chassis alone, from 1,000 to 4,000 pieces of each component had to be furnished each day at just the right point and right minute: a single failure, and the whole mechanism would come to a jarring standstill. . . . Superintendents had to know every hour just how many components were being produced and how many were in stock. Whenever danger of shortage appeared, the shortage chaser—a familiar figure in all automobile factories—flung himself into the breach. Counters and checkers reported to him. Verifying in person any ominous news, he mobilized the foreman concerned to repair deficiencies. Three times a day he made typed reports in manifold to the factory clearing-house, at the same time chalking on blackboards in the clearing-house office a statement of results in each factory-production department and each assembling department.* *

Such systemizing in itself resulted in astonishing increases in productivity. With each operation analyzed and subdivided into its simplest components, with a steady stream of work passing before stationary men, with a relentless but manageable pace of work, the total time required to assemble a car dropped astonishingly. Within a single year, the time required to assemble a motor fell from 600 minutes to 226 minutes: to build a chassis, from 12 hours and 28 minutes to 1 hour and 33 minutes. A stopwatch man was told to observe a 3-minute assembly in which men assembled rods and pistons, a simple operation. The job was divided into three jobs, and half the men turned out the same output as before.

As the example of the assembly line illustrates, the technology behind economies of scale often reduced the act of labor to robot-like movements. A brilliant account of this fragmentation of work will be found in Harry Braverman's *Labor and Monopoly Capital* (New York: Monthly Review Press, 1974).

* Allan Nevins, *Ford, the Times, the Man, the Company* (New York: Scribner's, 1954), pp. 1, 507.

Labor Unions

What about labor unions? Have they also shown trends comparable to the big corporation? Their history is parallel in many ways. Over the last 75 years, the percent of the labor force belonging to a union has increased from 3.2 to 19

Table 3
LABOR FORCE IN UNIONS
The importance of unions in the labor force has been falling, although unions remain powerful in key sectors.

	1940	1950	1960	1970	1980	1983
Percent unionized	27.2	31.9	31.4	27.3	22.0	19.0

Source: AFL-CIO *Directory of Labor Organizations.*

percent. Thus, the twentieth century has seen the emergence of big labor alongside big business. Yet, as Table 3 shows, the peak came in the 1960s and the percent of unionized nonagricultural workers has actually declined since then.

This does not mean, of course, that all unions today are diminishing. The last two decades have brought a boom in unions for white-collar workers, such as teachers or office workers; in unions for municipal employees, such as police, firefighters, transit workers; in diversified union organization, such as the powerful Teamsters. The declines have come where industries are declining, such as among railwaymen, clothing trades workers, or auto workers. Unions are certain to remain a major force in crucial areas of the economy, particularly insofar as union wage settlements in industries such as steel, autos, and chemicals tend to establish wage levels in other industries.

THE TREND IN GOVERNMENT

We pass now to a consideration of the last great trend in the economy — the trend in government, whose end result has been the emergence of the modern public sector. This is a matter where tempers tend to run ahead of judgments. Hence we must be careful not to confuse our diagnosis of what happened with our judgments about whether this has been a good or bad development.

From Small to Large Government

First we must try to explain the rise of the government sector from its relative insignificance at the beginning of the century to the general magnitude and importance it enjoys today. What follows is an analysis of the historic trend that we believe most economic historians, conservative or liberal, would agree on.

1. THE GROWING SIZE OF BUSINESS EVOKED A NEED FOR GOVERNMENT SUPERVISION. As business firms increased in size, private decisions became fraught with much larger social consequences. As business increased in size, the social impact of its activities steadily widened. Building or not building a plant came to spell prosperity or decline for a town, even for a state. Cutthroat competition came to mean ruin for an industry. Thus, one important reason for the long-term growth of government has been its efforts to prevent or to cope with problems that arose from the sheer increase in business size.

2. TECHNOLOGY BROUGHT A NEED FOR PUBLIC SUPERVISION. Much of the long-term growth of government stems from the impact of technology. Examples: As the automobile came to be a commonplace object, it created a need for traffic authorities to deal with it—some ten percent of state and local government employment exists to deal with the automobile. The same effect followed the appearance of the airplane and the radio (how would access to "channels" be determined, what would stations be permitted to broadcast?). And of course in our own day we have seen the same effect from atomic energy, new drugs, space, and weaponry.

3. URBANIZATION INCREASED THE NEED FOR GOVERNMENT. City life has its appeals, but it also has its perils. People cannot live in crowded quarters without police, public health and other facilities far more complex than those needed in a rural setting. Government has always been an urban phenomenon, and as every nation has urbanized, its reach of government has increased.

4. UNIFICATION OF THE ECONOMY GAVE RISE TO ADDITIONAL PROBLEMS. Industrialization knits an economy together into a kind of vast, interlocked machinery. An unindustrialized, localized economy is like a pile of sand: If you poke a finger into one side of it, some businesses and individuals will be affected, but those on the other side of the pile will remain undisturbed. The growing scale and specialization of industrial operations unifies the sandpile. You poke one side of it, and the entire pile shakes. Problems can no longer be localized. The difficulties of the economy grow in extent: There is a need for a national, not a local, energy program, for national transportation, urban and educational programs. Government—largely federal government—is the principal means by which such problems have been handled.

5. ECONOMIC MALFUNCTION BROUGHT PUBLIC INTERVENTION. Fifty or seventy-five years ago, the prevailing attitude toward the economy was a kind of awed respect. People felt that the economy was best left alone, that it was fruitless as well as ill-advised to try to change its normal workings. That attitude changed with the advent of the Great Depression. In the ensuing collapse, the role of government greatly enlarged, to restore the economy to working order. The trauma of the Depression and the determination to prevent its recurrence were a watershed in the trend of government spending and government intervention. Keynes's thinking played a very important part in this transition.

6. A NEW PHILOSOPHY OF "ENTITLEMENT" REPLACED THE OLDER ONE OF "RUGGED INDIVIDUALISM." Largely, but not wholly as a consequence of the experience of the Depression, a profound change has been registered in public attitudes toward the appropriate role of government. We no longer live in a society in which old-age retirement, medical expenses, and income during periods of unemployment are felt to be properly the sole responsibility of the individuals concerned. For better or worse, these and similar responsibilities have been gradually assumed by governments in all capitalist nations. In fact, the United States is a laggard in these matters compared with many European capitalist states. Here lie crucial reasons for the swelling volume of state, local, and federal production and purchase that have steadily enlarged the place of government within the economy.

The Trend in Recent Years

What has happened to the trend toward big government in recent years? In most people's minds, the trend of the past has continued or accelerated. The years since 1950 are popularly regarded as a time when the reach of government has vastly increased.

Figure 7

GOVERNMENT BUYING OR SPENDING SINCE 1950

Government trends are much more stable, as a percentage of GNP, than is apparent in the nominal data.

Source: Economic Report of the President, 1985.

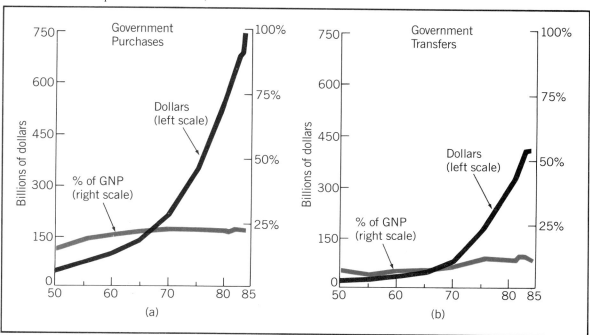

Has it? In Figure 7(a) we trace the evolution of the public sector over the last thirty-five years. The first thing that strikes us is the tremendous increase in government purchases, shown by the black line. This surely seems evidence of an unprecedented growth of government in modern times. But the upward sweeping line is not corrected for inflation or real growth. In the colored line below it we show the same dollar figures as a percentage of GNP. A completely different picture now emerges. **As a share of the economy, there has been no appreciable growth at all in government spending for goods and services over the last thirty-five years.**

The Trend in Transfers

The picture is somewhat different when we look at Figure 7(b), which shows the growth of government transfers. Here we find a rise not only in the dollar totals, but in the size of transfers compared to GNP. In 1950 transfer payments of all kinds amounted to about 6.3 percent of GNP; in 1984 they had grown to about 11 percent of GNP.

But now we must distinguish between the growth of *programs* and the growth of *expenditures*. The number of welfare programs has not increased, particularly since the Reagan administration's effort to reduce the government's role to that of providing a relatively small "safety net." Expenditures have only grown because the expansion of a few large entitlement programs has far outweighed the savings from the abandonment of numerous smaller ones. Primary among these increases in expenditure have been growth of social security payments, "indexed" to the cost of living, and the very rapid rise in Medicare costs. Together these two transfer programs have increased from $150 billion in 1980 to over $250 billion in 1985. An additional factor has been the mushrooming growth of interest payments on the national debt, up from $52 billion to $141 billion over the same five years.

Growth in Intervention?

Last comes a question that is not so readily answerable by graphs and figures. Has government intervention into the workings of the system followed the rising trend that marked the period from the late nineteenth century to the present?

That is a question we cannot answer because we are still in the midst of a history-making experiment. A great many regulatory efforts of the past have been undone — for example, the regulation of airline routes and trucking rates and the safety and environmental aspects of enterprise. The United States is passing through a period of impatience with government intervention, together with a willingness to let the market mechanism itself serve as the great regulator of the system. It is too early to know how far this movement will go, or how permanent will be the changes it has already brought. This is an issue to which we will return.

looking back

This chapter has been concerned with the economy in movement —not in quick, month-to-month fluctuations of the kind that will concern us when we study macroeconomics, but in longer-run, year-to-year, or decade-to-decade changes. Here are the most important of them.

Real vs. nominal growth

1 There is a long-term growth pattern to GNP—a pattern that is much more striking in nominal GNP than in real GNP (that is, in figures uncorrected for inflation than in corrected figures), but remarkable even with all adjustments for rising prices. The source of this growth can be attributed mainly to two factors: an increase in the quantity of inputs as our labor force and our stock of wealth grows, and an increase in the quality and effectiveness of inputs as our productivity grows. Here is Adam Smith's growth projection in reality.

More inputs and more productive inputs

Rise in incomes but little change in distribution

2 A second main trend is directly connected with the rise in output. It is the rise in dollar incomes for all levels of households —a rise that is, of course, much greater before we adjust for inflation than after. The distribution of income among classes changes only very slowly, however. Poverty has been gradually eroded, but remains a stubborn problem, recently worsened.

Big business share of assets has grown, but not its share of individual markets

3 The share of total assets belonging to the biggest corporations showed a startling increase in the decades of the 1950s and 1960s. However, the increase in the share of sales in different markets going to the biggest firms has shown no significant change. Big firms get bigger by absorbing assets of companies in *different* branches of business, so that their degree of monopoly control within markets shows little change. The main sources of business growth have been technology (recall Chapter 2) and mergers.

Reasons for a growing public sector are linked to the attributes of evolving capitalism

4 The public sector has grown dramatically since the late nineteenth century. Here is a list of the most important causes:

the growing size of business
the disruptive effects of technology
urbanization
the unification of the economy
a Keynesian remedy for economic malfunction
a new philosophy of entitlement

A new merger wave in the mid-1980s may disrupt the corporate scene	5 Starting in the mid-1980s, an unprecedented merger wave has brought enormous changes to the corporate world. The concentration of overall assets has certainly increased, but it is less certain that market concentrations have also increased. The merger wave has created a considerable threat of financial instability because mergers have often taken place through the issuance of ill-secured new bonds to finance company takeovers.
For the last 35 years we have seen stability in the public sector, except for a few big entitlement programs	6 There has been a striking stability in the trend of the public sector since 1950. The ratio of government spending to GNP has been virtually unchanged, although the dollar amounts are of course much larger. Transfer payments have risen as a fraction of GNP, but this is the result of indexing social security, the growth of Medicare, and higher interest payments on the national debt, not because of a growing number of transfer programs.
Can the trend be reversed?	7 We are now in the midst of an effort mounted by the Reagan Administration to curtail further government growth, and to cut back certain government programs. It is too early yet to tell whether this effort will succeed.

ECONOMIC VOCABULARY

Gross national product	76	Productivity	81
Real and nominal GNP	77	Economies of scale	90

QUESTIONS

1. Here are some raw data:

	GNP (Current $Billions)	Price Index	Population (Millions)
1970	$ 977	100	204
1975	1,549	138	216
1980	2,633	195	227
1982	3,058	227	232
1985	3,966	280	240

What is real GNP per capita in 1980 and 1985 in 1970 dollars? In 1975 dollars? Hint: You will need a new price index with 1975 = 100.

2. If there were no change whatsoever in technology, do you think that a larger quantity of labor might result in GNP growing faster or slower than the sheer increase of man-hour input? *Hint:* Can people organize their activities better as their numbers change? Does this continue indefinitely?

3. Do you think it might be possible to construct a theory to explain why the pretax, pretransfer shares of income are so fixed? Could there be a kind of pecking order in society? Could different groups establish economic distances that satisfy them? Would they then strive only to retain, not to increase, those differences?

4. Can you imagine an invention that would result in rapid concentration in a very unconcentrated industry, say the restaurant business? Or the laundry business? Can you imagine an invention that could radically deconcentrate an industry? How might a watch-sized CB radio affect the telephone industry? What invention could do the same for Exxon? U.S. Steel?

5. Do you think the rise of government within the economy is "socialistic"? "Capitalistic"? What do you mean by either term?

AN EXTRA WORD ABOUT

The Military Subsector

No description of the trend of things would be complete without some consideration of the role of military spending in the American economy and in the world. Here is a brief overview of that economy-within-an-economy.

THE DOD

The Department of Defense (DOD) is the largest planned economy outside the Soviet Union. Its property — plant and equipment, land, inventories of war and other commodities — amounts to about 7 percent of the assets of the entire American economy. It owns 39 million acres of land, roughly an area the size of Hawaii. It rules over a population of more than 3 million — direct employees or soldiers — and spends an "official" budget of over $150 billion, a budget 40 percent as large as the entire gross national product of Great Britain.

This makes the DOD richer than any small nation in the world and, of course, incomparably more powerful. That part of its assets represented by nuclear explosives alone gives it the equivalent of 6 tons of TNT for every living inhabitant of the globe, to which must be added the awesome military power of its conventional weapons.

The DOD system embraces both people and industry. In 1982 the people included, first, some 2 million soldiers deployed in more than 5,000 bases or locations abroad and at home, plus another 1 million civilian employees located within the United States and abroad. No less important are about 2 million civilian workers who are directly employed on war production, in addition to a much larger number employed in the secondary echelon of defense-related output. This does not include still further millions who owe their livelihood to the civilian services they render to the military.

THE WEB OF MILITARY SPENDING

The web of DOD expenditures extends to more areas of the economy than one might think. All in all, some twenty-odd thousand firms are prime contractors with the DOD, although the widespread practice of subcontracting means that a much larger number of enterprises look to defense spending for a portion of their income. Within the main constituency, however, a very few firms are the bastion of the DOD economy. The hundred largest defense contractors supply about two-thirds of the $50 odd billion of manufactured deliveries; and within this group, an inner group of 10 firms by themselves account for one third of the total.

Meanwhile, the establishment has a powerful political arm as well. In the early 1970s the DOD employed more than 300 lobbyists on Capitol Hill and (a conservative estimate) some 2,700 public relations people in the United States and abroad. This close political relationship undoubtedly has some bearing on the Pentagon's requests for funds being given, until recently, only the most cursory congressional inspection, leading among other things to $10 to $30 billion of annual waste, according to President Reagan's former budget director, David Stockman.

This is not to say, of course, that the United States does not need a strong defense capability today. But there is no question that the Pentagon subeconomy has become a major element in, and a major problem for, American capitalism. Indeed, the questions it raises are central: How important is this subeconomy to our economic vitality? How difficult would it be to reduce? Could our economy get along without a military subsector?

MILITARY DEPENDENCY

Let us begin by reviewing a few important facts. At the height of the Vietnam war in 1968, more than 10 percent of our labor force was employed in defense-related work. As the Vietnam War gradually decelerated, this percentage fell to about 5.5 percent. Defense expenditures, however, rose to about $277 billion in 1985 and are slated to rise more over the next few years.

These global figures do not, however, give a clear picture of the strategic position of defense spending within the economy. War-related spending and employment are not distributed evenly across the system but are bunched in special areas and industries. In a survey made in 1967, the Defense Department found that 72 employment areas depended on war output for 12 percent or more of their employment and that four-fifths of these areas were communities with labor forces of less than 50,000. This concentration of defense activity is still a fact of economic life in the 1980s. The impact of a cutback on these middle-sized communities can be devastating.

In addition, defense-employment is concentrated among special skills as well as in a nucleus of defense-oriented companies. In the late 1960s, about one scientist or engineer out of every five in private industry was employed on a defense-related job. Thirty-eight percent of all physicists depended on war-work. Twenty-five percent of all sheet metal workers, the same proportion of pattern-makers, and 54 percent of all airplane mechanics worked on defense projects. These proportions have declined, but defense is still a major employer of these skills. And as we have already remarked, there is a core of companies dependent on military spending for their very existence. These are not usually the largest companies in the economy (for whom, on the average, defense receipts amount to about 10 percent of total revenues) but the second echelon of corporations: Of 30 companies with assets in the $250 million to $1 billion range, 6 depended on war spending for half their incomes, and 7 depended on it for a quarter of theirs.

Thus a cutback in defense spending is always felt very sharply in particular areas, where there may be no other jobs available, or among occupational groups who have no alternative employment at equivalent pay, or in companies that are "captives" of the DOD. Such companies and areas naturally lobby hard for the defense expenditure on which their livelihood depends. So do their representatives in Congress. It is this interweaving of economic and political interests that makes the problem of defense cutbacks so difficult.

CONVERSION POSSIBILITIES

Yet a cutback is not economically impossible. *What is crucial, economically, is that the decline in war-related spending be offset by increases in peace-related spending, to be sure that the overall level of demand would remain high enough to act as a magnet, attracting the displaced workers to other jobs.* Unless we were willing to undertake an ambitious program of public spending or tax cuts, the conversion would certainly generate severe unemployment—and consequent political pressures to maintaining military spending.

Meanwhile, it is clear that the armaments economy is not only costing us a vast sum of money, but is also weighing heavily on the Russians. The annual military expenditure of the United States and the USSR together amounts to about two-thirds of the entire output of the billion people of Latin America, Southeast Asia, and the Middle East. Not only is this an opportunity cost of tragically large dimensions, if we consider the uses to which those resources might otherwise be applied, but even in terms of a strictly military calculus, much of it is *total waste, since neither side has been able to gain a decisive advantage despite its enormous expenditures.* Plausibly, the same military balance could be achieved with lower expenditures on both sides.

PRISONERS' DILEMMA

How does such a senseless course commend itself to national governments? Needless to say, the answers lie deep in the web of political, economic, and social forces of our times. Analytical reasoning can nonetheless throw some light on the matter by unraveling the peculiar situation involving two prisoners, each of whom knows something about the other and who are being interrogated separately. If *both* prisoners remain silent, both will get very light terms since the evidence against each is not conclusive. If one prisoner squeals on the other, he will get off scot-free as a reward for turning state's evidence, while the other prisoner will get a heavy term. If both prisoners squeal, both will get severe terms, convicted by each other's testimony.

Now, if the two prisoners could confer—and if they trusted each other absolutely—they would obviously agree that the strategy of shared silence was the best for each. But if the prisoners are separated or unsure of each other's trustworthiness, each will be powerfully tempted to rat on the other in order to reduce his own sentence. As a result, since the two are equally tempted, the outcome is likely to end in *both* sides ratting—and in *both* sides getting heavy punishment. Thus the pursuit of individual self-interest lures the two prisoners into a strategy that penalizes them both.

Something very like the prisoners' dilemma afflicts the nations of the world, especially the two superpowers, America and Russia. Although a policy of limited arms spending would clearly be to their mutual best advantage, their distrust of each other leads each to try to get ahead of the other. This state of mutual suspicion is then worsened when special interest groups in each nation deliberately play on the fears of the public. The end result is that both spend vast sums on armaments that yield them no advantage, while the world (including themselves) suffers an opportunity cost on an enormous scale. Only with a frank and candid exploration of shared gains and losses can both prisoners hope to get out of their dilemma. Prospects for a conversion of the U.S. arms economy may hinge on our understanding of this central military and political reality of our time.

CHAPTER 6
America in the World Economy

a look ahead

With a rude shock, Americans have realized that our national economic health depends on events in the wider world. The United States is a trading nation. We have a need for foreign raw materials and a taste for foreign goods. We rely on foreign markets for the products of our agriculture, our aerospace, our capital equipment, and much else. We are affected by drought in the Soviet Union, by war in the Middle East, by depression in Latin America. It used to be said that when America sneezed, Europe caught pneumonia; now it is at least true that when the world economy catches cold, we sneeze.

This chapter is a first look at a problem that will occupy us many times as we move through our studies. It focuses our attention on three main problems:

1 What is the position of the United States in the world economy today?
2 What has happened to our traditional competitive advantages?
3 What challenges lie ahead?

THE WORLD ECONOMY

Not many years ago, problems of international economics were largely relegated to the backs of almost all textbooks, including this one, and it was understood that the busy instructor and the overworked student were both to be forgiven for letting them go by. There were two main reasons for this deliberate downplaying of the international side. The first was that America was still generally thought of as a **closed economy,** one that was able to get along quite well without worrying too much about the rest of the world. The second reason was that international economics introduced a new, seemingly unnecessary complication into the economic problem. It necessitated thinking about two kinds of money — ours and theirs.

For better or worse, the closed economy has become wide open. The rest of the world has moved from the backs of textbooks to the front pages of every newspaper. One does not have to be an economist to become aware of the "invasion" of foreign goods into American markets, an invasion that has not been forced on us, but that we have brought about freely by choosing to buy foreign cars and TV sets and shoes and machine tools. All of us, economists and noneconomists alike, became aware of another aspect of America's international economic problems in August 1982, when Mexico nearly defaulted on its almost $100 billion debt to U.S. and foreign banks. Then we realized for the first time the extent of our financial involvement with the rest of the world — over $400 billion of loans, many of them very shaky.

So the era of the closed economy — it was never *really* closed — is over. Students and instructors, indeed all American citizens, must henceforth learn to think about a world where America's problems are tied into foreign problems, and where even the American dollar has to be understood as just one currency among many. That is what this chapter is about.

A SPECTRUM OF NATIONS

Let us begin by taking a look at the world economy, as it might appear to an economist traveling at a planet-encompassing height. The first thing to be noted is that the United States is still the world's wealthiest economy. Our gross national product is about equal, each year, to that of *all* of Western Europe. We produce only a little more per capita than Japan, but more than twice as much overall, since Japan has only half of our population. We are twice as productive, both absolutely and on a per person basis, as our major strategic rival, the Soviet Union. We are sixty times more productive per worker than China, and twelve times more productive overall, since we have only one-fifth of its population. All in all, as Table 1 shows, we still possess the richest and most productive large industrial economy in the world.

Table 1
POPULATION, GNP, AND GNP PER CAPITA—SOME COMPARATIVE FIGURES.

Country	Population (Millions)	GNP (Millions of $)	GNP Per Capita (Actual $)
Ethiopia	40.9	$ 4,270	$ 120
Bangladesh	95.5	10,640	130
Indonesia	155.7	78,320	560
El Salvador	5.2	3,700	710
Nicaragua	3.0	2,700	880
Mexico	75.0	145,130	2,240
Poland	36.6	186,800	5,160
Israel	4.1	20,660	5,370
USSR	272.5	1,715,000	6,352
Italy	56.8	352,840	6,400
Hungary	10.7	65,200	6,901
United Kingdom	56.3	455,100	9,200
Japan	119.3	1,062,870	10,120
Germany	61.4	653,080	11,430
Saudi Arabia	10.4	120,560	12,230
Canada	24.9	324,000	12,310
U.S.	234.5	3,275,701	14,110
Switzerland	6.5	97,120	16,290

Sources: *World Development Report, 1985* (1983 data) and CIA *1984 Fact Book* (1982 data).

Other Advanced Nations

Although we are the world's wealthiest nation, we are certainly not the world's only wealthy nation. Japan, for example, has made tremendous strides over the last forty years, up from poverty, defeat, and underdevelopment to the point where its average income is three-quarters of our own. Its best manufacturing industries are second to none in efficiency. Its high rates of household saving and of investment are the envy of the world, and its economic growth rates have for decades averaged over twice our own. If Japan were not a crowded island chain with few natural resources, dependent on the Middle East and Indonesia for energy, on Australia and the Americas for food, and on the United States and Europe to provide markets for its manufacturing production, probably Japan would today be richer than we are.

Europe is not short of land or resources, but it has lacked the political and cultural unity that has so favored the development of Japan. Until the twentieth century, Europe was by far the most developed part of the world, dominant in world politics and in world trade. Then nationalism, warfare, political upheaval, loss of empire, economic depression, and an inability to integrate narrow national markets into a single economy brought a loss of Europe's competitive edge. But since World War II Europe has begun to overcome these obstacles, and to build a stable, modern, integrated multinational economy. Today Europe is rich, peaceful, and self-sufficient, although plagued by high unemployment and worried about whether it can keep up with the Americans and the Japanese.

Among the advanced nations and areas of the world, the Soviet Union should by no means be overlooked. It has come up from extreme backwardness in the nineteenth and early twentieth centuries, and from the devastation of World War II, to the point where its population enjoys a standard of living today that would not have been dreamed of forty years ago. But Russia is still far from catching up with any of the economies of the West. Many specialists believe that it has reached the limits of development possible under a centrally planned system, and will be forced to undertake major reforms of that system to avoid falling even further behind.

The Third World

Beyond these giants there is the vast diversity of the Third World, where more than 3 billion of the world's people now live. The Third World encompasses every kind of economic experience, as well as every standard of living. Average living standards range from near-starvation (the per capita GNP of Ethiopia is $120 per year), to "middling" (Brazil, Chile, and Mexico have per capita incomes around $2,000 per year), but these averages are the result of lumping together the incomes of the affluent few and the indigent many. On this basis of averaging rich and poor, a few tiny principalities and sheikhdoms enjoy the highest living standards on the planet—the "average" per capita (not per household) income in the United Arab Emirates was $23,370, almost twice that of the United States.

Collectively, Third World nations have demonstrated their importance in two ways. The first was their ability to extract an enormous flow of wealth from the West when the Organization of Petroleum Exporting Countries (OPEC) boosted oil prices from $2.59 to $11.59 per barrel in 1973 and again from $13.34 to $24.00 in 1979. The oil transfer amounted to over $377 billion. It gave a tremendous boost to inflation in the West and produced some economic development in a few countries of the East and South. It set into motion a spiral of lending, partly to help finance oil imports into countries like Brazil that had few domestic supplies, partly to finance industrialization in oil-exporting countries like Venezuela and Mexico. This lending spree ended in a vast overextension of credit that still hangs over the world. Perhaps most significant of all, OPEC made abundantly clear the vulnerability of all Western economies to any long-lasting interruption of oil supplies. Until the price of oil collapsed in 1986, the political geography of the planet was profoundly changed.

A second impact was less dramatic but no less significant. It was a demonstration that the underdeveloped areas could combine low wage labor with high technology to create export industries capable of challenging the Western nations themselves. New techniques of transportation and communication made it possible to make circuit boards in Hong Kong, TV sets in Taiwan, automobiles in South Korea — achievements utterly impossible only a few years before. These countries soon became principal suppliers for their European and American markets. So far only a few of the underdeveloped countries have achieved this capability, but the more successful among them have become new and, to some, worrisome entrants to the advanced capitalist world.

FITTING INTO THE WORLD ECONOMY

How does the United States fit into this array of national economies? The United States has long been the largest trader in the world. In 1985 we imported $428.5 billion worth of goods, about as much as the entire gross domestic product of Great Britain! (We exported $364.3 billion, about the same as the whole GNP of Canada.) What's more, the American presence is felt in world trade even where the United States is not a direct party. The American dollar has been the unit of account for world trade since the end of World War II. Today, it is estimated that up to a trillion dollars are held by foreigners who use them to finance world trade. Oil moving all over the world is priced in dollars, and the same is true of many other commodities traded on the international markets.

Nonetheless, until recently most Americans were not aware of the role the rest of the world played in their economic lives. That is because our participation in world trade and finance, vast though it was, was still small in comparison with the business we did internally, with ourselves.

Rising U.S. Involvement

But over the past twenty-five years that has changed. The change seems fairly modest when viewed against *total* GNP. In 1960, exports and imports amounted to only 5 percent of the total value of goods and services produced in the United States. By 1985, exports had risen to 9 percent of GNP and imports to 11 percent.

But look at manufacturing: Today, one dollar in every five earned from the sale of U.S. manufactures come from an export; 1 dollar in every three spent by Americans on manufactured products is spent on an import. These figures hit home harder when they are made more specific. One out of every 5 American-made jet planes, about 1 out of every 5 welding tools, approximately 1 of every 3 computers is destined for sales overseas. Taken together, exports are responsible for the jobs of 13 million Americans. At the same time, American consumers have acquired an even greater taste for imported manufactured goods, from automobiles to umbrellas, and American companies have come to rely more and more on raw materials, and intermediate goods such as steel, that are produced abroad. In 1960, foreign cars held only 4 percent of the U.S. market; in 1985 their share was 26 percent. In certain parts of the country, such as California, all the top-selling automobiles are imported. In steel, the share of imports in U.S. production has

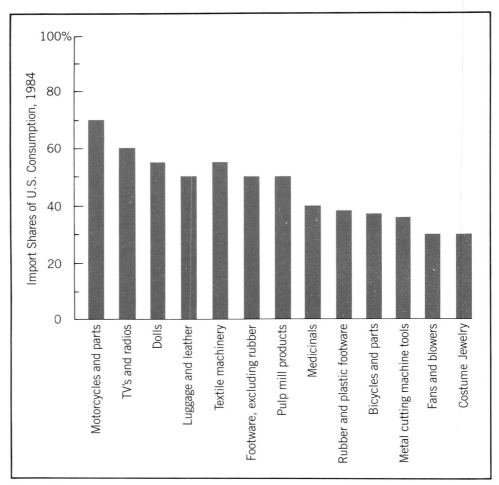

Figure 1
Americans Buy Many Foreign-made Goods
Source: Department of Commerce.

risen from 4.2 percent to 30 percent since 1960. Similar statistics could be cited for a host of other products — radios, televisions, bicycles and motorcycles, textiles, leather goods, and much more. We get a sense of this by looking at Figure 1.

The Trade Deficit

If our rising involvement in the world economy meant only a greater interweaving of American production and American consumption with world demand and world supply, we might still be able to put the international economy at the back of our textbooks. But something has happened in addition to a globalization of Amer-

Table 2

U.S. EXPORTS AND IMPORTS

Starting in 1983 there is a striking change in our balance of foreign trade.

Period	*Exports and Imports of Goods and Services*		
	Exports	*Imports*	*Net Exports*
1974	146.2	132.8	13.4
1975	154.9	128.1	26.8
1976	170.9	157.1	13.8
1977	182.7	186.7	−4.0
1978	218.7	219.8	−1.1
1979	281.4	268.1	13.2
1980	338.8	314.8	23.9
1981	369.9	341.9	28.0
1982	348.4	329.4	19.0
1983	336.2	344.4	−8.3
1984	364.3	428.5	−64.2
1985	347.7	441.6	−94.0

Source: *Economic Report of the President*, 1986.

ican economic activity. The globalization has taken place unevenly, with our imports rising much more rapidly than our exports.

We can see this in Table 2. Note that up to 1982 our exports were generally larger than our imports, so the *trade balance*—the net difference between what foreigners paid us for American goods and services and what we paid them—showed a sum in America's favor. In 1982, for example, the balance was $19 billion. If we think of the United States economy as a kind of national "firm" trading with (and competing against) other national "firms," that is the net amount we earned that year. Now look at the years since then. Our purchases have far outrun our sales, so we have run up a very substantial deficit. In effect, we are no longer paying our way.

A Word about Trade Deficits

Here we come to one of those complications that we used to skip: A nation is not a firm; and although individual businesses make or lose money in international trade, the nation runs no such profit and loss account. Instead, **a nation earns or loses claims against other countries from its exports and imports.** When we sell American goods abroad, we are paid in dollars by foreigners. Where do they get those dollars? Either from selling goods and services to us, or by borrowing from American lenders, such as investors who will buy their bonds or banks (probably American banks) who will extend them credit in dollars, or by spending any stores of previously earned dollars, called **reserves.**

If Americans buy more than we sell, we must also find the **foreign exchange**—the needed foreign currencies—to pay for what they have not earned. Where do we get that exchange? Exactly like foreigners, we have no choice but to spend any reserves we have accumulated or to borrow the money from banks who will lend us exchange, or from investors who will buy our bonds.

What Table 2 shows is that in three years, we have had to pay almost $200 billion more to foreigners than we have earned from them. This means that we have had to borrow that much from foreign banks and other lenders, mainly by selling them United States bonds. For a nation as large and wealthy as the United States, a debt of $200 billion to foreigners is not a serious problem, particularly because we have large investments abroad. But even a nation as wealthy as the United States cannot go on piling up such debts indefinitely. At some point the American debt would seem so large that foreigners would no longer consider the United States a good risk. They would no longer be willing to buy our bonds or to extend credit for their currencies against IOUs in dollars.

A Trade Crunch

At that point America would have to bring its imports into line with its exports. America would have to "pay its way" because there would be no other source of foreign currencies with which to buy the foreign goods it wanted. We would then experience the same trade crunch that has been felt by countries such as Mexico or Brazil, whose economic plight has made them very poor credit risks.

Because Mexicans or Brazilians cannot borrow foreign currencies, they are forced to limit their imports to the amount that they can sell abroad — minus a very large fraction of those export earnings that must be paid to foreigners as interest on past debts. **The result is a severe fall in the standard of living.** The same result would be felt by this country if, let us say, our foreign debt was not $200 billion, but $2 trillion, and our ability to get foreign credits vanished. We would then have to bring our imports down to the value of our exports — minus the huge interest payments we would owe on our $2 trillion debt.

It remains unlikely that the United States, with its vast strength, will ever have to experience a trade crunch like that of Mexico or Brazil. But it is not a scenario to be dismissed as "impossible," for that is the direction in which events are moving unless we bring order into our international economic relationships — an order that is not there as we write these words.

Behind the Trade Deficit

Why did the richest nation in the world become a debtor in the world economy? There is no single or simple answer, but we should become familiar with two main explanations.

1. THE DOLLAR WAS TOO HIGH. In the international economy, currencies of different countries are constantly being exchanged for one another, and their prices often move dramatically. In the case of the United States, the rate of exchange of the dollar against other main currencies fell in the 1970s, and then moved sharply up after the turn of the decade. In 1980, for example, it cost $2.33 to purchase a British pound. In early 1985 the price of dollars had risen — and the price of pounds had correspondingly fallen — to the point at which you could buy a pound for $1.24. Over the same five-year period, the **exchange rate** for dollars against French francs had risen from 4.22 francs to the dollar to over 10 francs, and from 1.82 German marks to 3.1 marks.

Why was the dollar so high? As with the prices of commodities, we explain movements of currencies in terms of supply and demand. A high price for dollars meant that foreigners were seeking to acquire dollars more than Americans were seeking to acquire other moneys. The main reason foreigners wanted dollars so strongly is that American interest rates became higher, and American inflation rates lower, than in many European countries. Investors in those countries, or big international companies looking for a place to park their funds, bought dollars in order to purchase U.S. bonds or other investments. As this "portfolio" demand grew, the price of dollars rose.*

What is the effect of a high dollar? Now we put ourselves first into the shoes of an American importer, then into those of an American exporter. Suppose we are a department store buyer shopping for sweaters in England. The English manufacturer doesn't quote us a price in dollars; he gives us a price in English pounds — don't forget that he probably sells the greater part of his sweaters to English stores, not American ones. Say that his price is £30. The high dollar becomes a wonderful break for our department store buyer. The higher the dollar goes, the fewer dollars she has to pay to acquire the pounds she needs. In 1980, for example, a £30 sweater would have cost $69.90. By early 1985, the same £30 sweater cost her only $37.20.

So high dollars mean cheap imports. Can you see that for the same reasons high dollars mean expensive exports? A French buyer of computers will be much less eager to pay $1,000 for an American computer when the dollar is high than when it is low, because it will cost him more francs to purchase that thousand dollars.

We have to leave a deeper examination of the exchange rate for Chapter 37. But we have seen one very important reason for the American trade deficit. A high dollar has priced us out of a competitive position in exports, and lured us into a vast import boom. Most experts believe that the dollar in 1985 was at least 30 percent over its normal relationship to other currencies. Will the dollar come down — helping make our exports more competitive and making imports less so? Yes. When will that happen? No one knows. Much depends on things that simply cannot be predicted: shifts in U.S. monetary policy, turbulence in the banking system, changes of government and policy in Europe and Japan. Possibly some of these changes will have occurred between the time we write these words and the time you read them.

2. PRODUCTIVITY GROWTH WAS TOO LOW. The high dollar is a big factor in the adverse American trade balance, but it is not the only reason for concern about America's position in the world economy. A second type of apprehension stresses real, not monetary, factors.

---

* Later on we will find that American interest rates have been high because of American monetary policy. That is a twist to the story which we must postpone for the moment.

Table 3
MANUFACTURING PRODUCTIVITY
The United States is no longer a world leader in productivity.

	Output per Hour (1983)	Rate of Growth (%) 1977–82
United States	$18.21	0.6%
Germany	20.22	2.1
France	19.80	3.0
Italy	17.72	3.6
Japan	17.61	3.4
Canada	17.03	−0.3
U.K.	11.34	2.7

Source: Lester Thurow, *The Zero Sum Solution* (New York: Simon & Schuster, Inc., 1985), p. 49.

Behind the Productivity Lag

The data in Table 3 show that U.S. manufacturing productivity has already been bettered by Germany, France, and Italy. It has also probably been surpassed by a number of smaller European countries such as Sweden, the Netherlands, Switzerland, Austria, and others. Thus we are no longer the undisputed leader in productivity, at least not in the manufacturing sector that is so crucial for overall economic growth. Even more disturbing are the data that show our rate of growth to be slower than that of our main competitors. We may recall from Chapter 5 how important growth rates are (look back for a moment to the box on page 82). Our performance during the five years shown in Table 3 reveals that we have been one of the worst performers in the advanced industrial world.

A country whose productivity is growing more slowly than that of its competitors will slowly find itself priced out of the market, exactly the same as a company whose efficiency is improving less rapidly than its competition. Although high exchange rates make our competitive position very difficult in the short run, low productivity growth makes it difficult in the long run.

Too Many Services?

What lies behind this laggard performance? Few important phenomena are less well understood. Some economists believe the reason lies in the failure of the American economy to save and invest as large a fraction of its GNP as its major competitor nations—Japan, for example, invests 28 percent of its GNP, Germany 31 percent, France 20 percent—against our 17 percent.

This relatively low investment share in GNP reflects another big change in the U.S. economy—toward a lower share of manufacturing in total employment. We are shifting workers, in effect, from high-productivity-growth manufacturing jobs into lower-productivity-growth service jobs. In Chapter 4 we have already seen that seven out of every ten Americans today work in service occupations. These occupations range from highly skilled tasks such as architect and engineer to low-skilled jobs in fast food operations, but on the average, services produce less GNP per worker per year than either agriculture or manufacturing.

Hence the sheer movement into services pulls down our productivity average. This drift is visible in all advanced countries, but nowhere has it developed to the extent of the United States — in Italy, the service sector absorbs only 44 percent of the labor force. Moreover, the distribution of the labor force *within* the service sector is not helpful to the United States. Consider this comparison: for every 10,000 U.S. working people, there are 20 lawyers, 40 accountants, and 70 engineers. In Japan the numbers are 1 lawyer, 3 accountants, and 400 engineers.*

Is the service shift an unalloyed social "bad?" Not all economists think so. Economist Robert Z. Lawrence† has pointed out that the share of manufacturing in *output* has not fallen since the 1950s; hence manufacturing investment has pretty well kept place with the growth of GNP. So the shift to services may be nothing more than a shift in the structure of demand as incomes have risen (more vacation resorts and security guards, fewer automobiles and toasters), and the economy's corresponding efforts to find useful work for people who are no longer needed in advanced manufacturing processes. After all, who would have thought, a century ago, that the work of 3 percent of the population would more than suffice to feed us? Why should we be surprised now that the work of 20 percent more than suffices to supply us with material goods?

So long as external trade was in approximate balance, as was true up until the early 1980s, it was relatively easy to accept the benign view of U.S. productivity performance. But the trade deficits that have emerged since make this harder. If the dollar stays high (and who is to say it will not?), then improving U.S. productivity growth to overcome our trade disadvantages will certainly become an issue of paramount importance.

Other Explanations

Another explanation calls attention to our educational system. Much as with our relatively poor showing in capital formation, the United States shows up poorly in its formation of human capital. We do not place the same importance on education as many other nations. In 19 international tests of educational achievement, Americans never scored at the top, and in 7 tests scored at the bottom.‡

And there are still other explanations — adversarial rather than cooperative relations between American management and labor; the absence of a workable consensus on the role of government in the economy; inflexible management styles and failure to take full advantage of the flexible production techniques high technology makes possible; a decline of the old-fashioned work ethic; and more besides.

* *The New York Times*, December 19, 1982, Sec. 12.
† *Can America Compete?* (Washington: The Brookings Institution, 1984).
‡ Barbara Lerner, "American Education: How Are We Doing?" *Public Interest*, Fall 1982, p. 64.

Productivity and Policy

Although the diagnoses of the productivity problem differ, in one way all point to a different conclusion than the problem of the high dollar. If the dollar is truly "out of equilibrium," as some economists believe, then market forces alone will eventually restore its proper value. At the very worst, all that is required is a change of monetary and fiscal policies, put into effect by the actions of the Federal Reserve, the President, and Congress.

But the productivity problem does not lend itself to so tidy a solution. The cure will not come by itself, and no simple change in the gross parameters of macroeconomic policy will bring it about. On the contrary, no matter what the root of the problem — capital formation, our occupational mix, our educational system, labor-management structure — the cure involves our whole society, at every level and in every public and private dimension. **Some form of national policy will be needed to change the underlying configuration of American society in ways that encourage rather than discourage national productivity growth.**

FINDING OUR PLACE

As we move through macro and micro economies and into international trade, we will have a chance to consider policies that may help us find a viable place in a world. In this introduction to the problem, let us end as we began, by trying to see the problem as a whole.

A DEBTOR NATION?

In the summer of 1985, the Commerce Department announced that the United States had become a debtor nation for the first time since 1914. By a debtor nation, we mean that the value of U.S. assets held by foreigners — real plant and equipment, real estate, stocks and bonds, CDs, or just bank balances — exceeded the value of foreign assets of similar kinds held by Americans. Moreover, this net external debt was growing rapidly. By the end of 1985, it had already exceeded $100 billion, making us one of the world's largest net debtors. At the rate it was growing, our debt would reach $1 trillion by 1990. The *New York Times* called this "the most dramatic transformation in [the United States] financial position since World War I."*

* As we will see when we look into multinational corporations (Chapter 30), the way we measure our international indebtedness is not altogether reliable. But there is no denying the trend.

The basic cause of the startling turnaround lies in our adverse balance of trade. As we know, the only way any nation can import more than it exports is to borrow the foreign exchange needed to pay for its import surplus. Our own borrowing took the form of selling many kinds of United States obligations to foreigners from Treasury bonds to mutual funds or CDs. All these transactions made foreign currencies available to Americans because foreigners had to sell their own currencies in order to buy U.S assets. The foreign funds they sold then became available through the banking system to U.S. importers.

Is the net U.S. debt a worrisome thing? There is no simple answer to this question. Insofar as our import surplus stimulates foreign production, our growing debt makes a sizable contribution to world economic growth, from which we benefit as well as others. In addition, the sale of Treasury bonds or bills and other securities to foreigners makes it possible for the United States to incur its own domestic debts, both private and public, without relying exclusively on its own savings. This eases the pressure on interest rates and helps growth at home.

The main danger is that the growth of foreign debt will eventually imperil America's international creditworthiness—its ability to borrow more foreign funds. That depends not so much on the size of our foreign borrowings as on the use to which we put them. In the nineteenth century we borrowed heavily from Europe to build a vast transcontinental railway system. But because foreign savings were put to such productive use, American international credit remained good despite the occasional bankruptcies of the railroads themselves. If our present and future international debt were put to equally productive use, the same optimistic forecast would seem appropriate today. Alas, that does not seem to be the case. Our foreign borrowings have not been earmarked for the creation of productive assets, public or private. Even though our borrowings have helped world economic recovery and have stimulated American growth, there is no reason for foreigners to feel that the value of their American assets is secure because those assets are "real wealth," like railways. The danger is that foreign lenders will appraise the soundness of their investments in the United States by the general condition of the American economy—*including its ability to make its exports pay for its imports.* If that test of success is not met, foreigners may change their minds about lending to America and may sell their U.S. assets in a rush to get out. We will look into these matters again when we study the workings of the Federal Reserve in Chapter 20.

An Interdependent World

As we have seen, the importance of the rest of the world for the U.S. economy has risen sharply. Curiously, the importance of the U.S. economy *within* the rest of the world has not. In 1960 it was estimated that the United States accounted for 40 percent of all the production in the world. By 1984 this fraction had fallen to 24 percent. This is even more striking on an industrial basis. In 1960, U.S. steel companies produced 26 percent of the world's steel. In 1984 they produced only 14 percent. In 1960 we produced 52 percent of the world's automobiles; in 1984 only 26 percent.

Up to now we have considered this global shift from America's point of view, where it appears as a formidable problem. But there is also the view of the rest of the world. From this perspective, the relative decline in U.S. importance appears as an opportunity, not a problem. It reflects the success of other nations — some left behind in the nineteenth century, some still in the ninth century — in finding a place in the world economy necessary for their own well-being. American policies in both Europe and the underdeveloped world have tried to stimulate growth in these areas. Thus America's relative decline in the world economy represents a political success, even though it comes as an economic challenge.

We do not know at all what a truly integrated and well-functioning world economy would look like. Would it be knit together solely by market forces, or would there have to be a political framework of constraint over the whole? Would there be a single world monetary unit, or would each nation, as today, insist on its inviolable right to coin its own money? Would nations continue to define the boundaries of what we call "economies," or would there be such an intermingling of markets that national boundaries would have very little economic significance?

We cannot begin to answer these questions yet. Indeed, we hardly know whether they are the right questions to ask. But they give us some sense of the real significance of the relation between what we call the economy of the United States and the economy of the world.

looking back

KEY CONCEPTS

The U.S. is no longer a closed economy

1 The United States economy is still the richest and most productive economic entity in the world. But it is certainly not a "closed" economy. Both in trade and finance, it is enmeshed in a world economy.

A spectrum of economies from rich to poor

2 The world economy is made up of a wide range of nations, from the Euro-Japanese group of "Western" economies through the underdeveloped, or Third World, where live most of the world's population. The Third World nations have made a significant impact through OPEC and as the location of new high-tech, low-wage industry.

Rising U.S trade involvement

3 United States involvement in the world economy has been rising steadily in recent years until exports plus imports come

to one-fifth of GNP. More important is the very high ratio of manufacturing exports and imports: 20 percent of manufactures exported; 29 percent of manufactures imported.

The growing trade deficit

4 The United States has normally exported more goods and services than it has imported. During the last several years, however, it has incurred a very large and growing deficit in its balance of trade.

Deficits require using reserves or borrowing from abroad

5 A deficit means that a nation has not earned enough from exports to pay for its imports. It must finance the deficit either by using its reserves of foreign exchange or by borrowing from abroad. If deficits become too large, a nation may no longer be able to borrow and will be forced to reduce its exports to the level of its imports—less any payments of interest on its debt abroad.

A basic explanation for our trade deficits is the high dollar, which cheapens imports into the U.S. and makes U.S. goods expensive to foreigners

6 A basic general explanation for our trade deficit is that the dollar is too high. When the dollar is high, imports become cheap because we can buy many units of a foreign currency with each dollar; when the dollar falls, it takes more dollars to buy the same amount of foreign currency, and the price of imports goes up. By the same token, a high dollar makes our goods expensive for foreigners, while a lower dollar cheapens our goods in foreign money. The dollar has been extremely high in the 1980s, because of attractive U.S. interest rates. If it declines, the trade deficit will be eased.

Lagging productivity has weakened the U.S. competitive position

7 A second general explanation for U.S. trade difficulties, especially in manufacturing, is lagging productivity. Numerous reasons have been offered for this lag, among them inadequate capital formation, a shift to low-productivity occupations in the service sector, and a comparatively poor education system.

National policy will be needed to correct lagging productivity

8 The high dollar may decline by market forces, but policy changes affecting our whole society will be needed to bring about a shift in these (or other) causes of our low rate of productivity improvement.

A debtor nation

9 Largely because of our chronic trade deficit, the United States has suddenly become a net debtor to the world. If our trade deficit continues at the present level, we will owe the rest of the world huge amounts within a few years. International debts are not necessarily bad—indeed, they can be very useful, when the borrowed money is put to productive use, as in the building of the railways. The worry about the present rise of international debt is that it has not been productively used, and that it might end in a panicky flight from U.S. banks.

An interdependent world is emerging

10 The United States economy no longer bulks so large in the world economy. This is due to the rise of Europe, Japan, and now some parts of the underdeveloped world to a position of greater well-being. This represents a political gain, even though it poses an economic challenge. What a fully interdependent world would look like we do not know.

ECONOMIC VOCABULARY

Closed economy   104
Reserves   109
Trade deficit   108

Foreign exchange   109
High and low dollar   110
Exchange rate   111

QUESTIONS

1. What do you think are the advantages of an open economy? The disadvantages?
2. Describe what is meant by a trade "deficit." What is a trade "surplus"? If one nation runs a deficit, must another run a surplus?
3. How does the United States manage to buy $100 billion more than it sells? Why cannot a country like Israel run up as large a deficit as the United States?
4. Suppose that it costs 50 francs to produce a bottle of French wine, and that the dollar buys 5 francs. What is the price of wine, ignoring transportation costs, to a New York retailer of wine? Now suppose that the dollar buys 10 francs instead of 5. Do we say that the dollar has gone up or down? Does a higher dollar make French goods cheaper or dearer? Will that increase imports or decrease them? Now put yourself in the shoes of a French importer of American wheat, which sells for $5 a bushel. Again forgetting transportation costs, what will the wheat sell for in Paris if 1 franc buys 20 cents? If 1 franc buys 5 cents? Can you see that a high dollar must mean a low franc? Are high dollars good for American grain exporters? High francs? Try to see international transactions as always involving two *differing* points of view.
5. Let us suppose you were convinced that the long-run cause of our trade deficit was a failure to build up our capital. What measures might help remedy this situation? Suppose you thought the trouble lay essentially in our education system. Now what would you recommend to make our performance as good as that of our main competitors?

6. Do you think economic relations tend to unite nations or divide them? Think about the effect on global living standards if there were no trade — and then think about the quarrels and wars that have been fought over economic spoils. Do you think it is possible that economic interrelations serves both to unite and to separate the world?

PART TWO

some basic economics

CHAPTER 7
Economic Science

a look ahead

Now that we have some background in the field, we are ready to take the next step toward becoming economists by learning something of the ways economists think. Here we are dealing with the abstract and analytic aspects of the field that we mentioned in Chapter 1.

Essentially this short chapter tells you that economic theory is about maximizing behavior that takes place against constraints. Acquisitiveness is a good first approximation of the meaning of "maximizing," and "constraints" implies limits, boundaries, or costs.

Economic reasoning consists of puzzling out what happens when rational acquisitors face constraints imposed by nature or society. Keep that in mind and the chapter will unfold step by step.

What is it that we are trying to understand as economists? Certainly it is not the economic attributes of *all* societies. Our first chapters focus on the United States not merely because we are naturally interested in the economic aspects of our own country, but also because the United States is a kind of society that lends itself to economic analysis. Economic reasoning, we should note at the outset, applies most cogently to market societies, to capitalism.

Equally to be noted, economic reasoning will not try to come to grips with all of society. Our earlier survey paid little attention to vast areas of social life that we call sociological or political, much less religious or artistic. Economics mainly is concerned with the facts that bear on only one aspect of our social life: our efforts to produce and to distribute wealth. Boom and bust, inflation and depression, poverty and riches, growth or no growth — all can be described in terms of the production of wealth and its distribution.

MAXIMIZING VS. CONSTRAINTS

Our task, then, is to find some way of explaining production and distribution. Therefore, economists observe the *human* universe, much as natural scientists observe the physical universe, in search of data and orderly relationships that may permit them to construct hypotheses.

What do economists see when they scrutinize the world of economic activity? Two attributes of a market society attract their attention:

1. Individuals in such a society display a particular behavior pattern when they participate in economic activities, as consumers or businesspeople. They behave in acquisitive, money-searching, "maximizing" ways. (See box, p. 125.)
2. A series of obstacles or constraints stands between the acquisitive drive of marketers and their realization of economic gain. Some are the constraints of nature; some are the obstacles of social institutions.

Thus an extraordinary conclusion begins to dawn. A great deal of the activity of a market society can be explained as the outcome of two interacting forces. One is the force of maximizing behavior — a force we have described in terms of the acquisitive behavior of men and women in a market society. The other is the constraining counterforce of nature or of social institutions — a series of obstacles that holds back or channels or directs the acquisitive drive. This suggests the daring scientific task that economics sets for itself. It is to explain the events of economic reality — even to predict some of the events of future economic reality — by reasoning based on fundamental hypotheses about maximizing behavior and its constraints.

HYPOTHESES ABOUT BEHAVIOR

Let us start with the economist's assumption about behavior. We can sum it up in a sentence: People are maximizers.

Maximizing Utilities

What does that hypothesis mean? Essentially, it means that people in market societies seek to gain as much pleasurable wealth from their economic activity as they can. **We call this pleasurable wealth "utility." Thus we hypothesize that men and women are *utility maximizers*.**

Note that we define utility as *pleasurable* wealth. Economists do not argue that people try to accumulate the largest amount of wealth possible, regardless of its pleasures. We all know that after a certain point, wealth-producing work brings fatigue, or even pain. Therefore we assume that as people work to maximize their wealth, they take into account the pains (or disutilities) of achieving it.

It is impossible to *prove* that people maximize in this fashion. But it seems plausible that most of us do seek wealth both as wage earners or as businesspeople, and that we take account of the nuisances and difficulties of achieving it.

Satiable and Insatiable Wants

Economics not only assumes that men and women are maximizers, but it also has a hypothesis about why they behave so acquisitively. **The hypothesis is that peoples' wants are insatiable; that human desires for utility can never be filled.**

Are our wants, in fact, insatiable? Does human nature keep us on a treadmill of striving that can never bring us to a point of contentment? As with maximizing, there is a prima facie plausibility about the assumption. For if we include leisure as well as goods among our aims, more time to enjoy ourselves as well as more income to be enjoyed, it seems true enough that something very much like insatiability

ACQUISITIVENESS

Remember that we are talking about the kind of behavior that we find in a market society. Perhaps in a different society of the future, another hypothesis about behavior would have to serve as our starting point. People might then be driven by the desire to better the condition of others rather than of themselves.

A story about heaven and hell is to the point. Hell has been described as a place where people sit at tables laden with sumptuous food, unable to eat because they have three-foot long forks and spoons strapped to their hands. Heaven is described as the very same place. There, people feed one another.

afflicts most people. At least this seems true in societies that encourage striving for status and success and that set high value on consumption and recreation.

For example, surveys regularly show that men and women at all economic levels express a desire for more income (usually about 10 percent more than they actually have), and *this drive for more does not seem to diminish as we move up the economic scale.* If it did, we would be hard put to explain why people who are generally in the upper echelons of the distribution of wealth and income work just as hard as, or even harder than, those on the lower rungs of the economic ladder.

There is, however, a very important qualification to the assumption that wants are insatiable for all wealth, including leisure. **The qualification is that economists assume human wants for** *particular kinds* **of wealth, including leisure, are indeed capable of being satisfied.** This idea of the satiability of *particular* wants will play a key role in our next chapter, when we see how we can derive the concept of demand and demand "curves" from our hypotheses concerning behavior.

Rationality

Equally important is an assumption about the way individuals think and act as they go about striving to fulfill their insatiable wants-in-general or their satiable wants-in-particular. **This assumption is that people are** *rational* **maximizers.** Economists mean by this that people in a market milieu stop to consider the various courses of action open to them and to calculate in some fashion the means that will best suit their maximizing aims. There may be two different ways of producing a good. As rational actors, people will choose the method that will yield them the good for the smallest effort or cost.

This concept of rational maximizing does not mean that human beings may not wish, on some occasions, to go to more trouble than necessary. After all, people could worship God in very simple buildings or out-of-doors, but they go to extraordinary lengths to erect magnificent churches and decorate them with sculpture and paintings. It is meaningless to apply the word *rational* to pursuits such as these, which may have vast importance for society.

But when people are engaged in producing the goods and services of ordinary life, seeking to achieve the largest possible incomes or the most satisfaction-yielding patterns of consumption, the economist assumes that they *will* stop to think about the differing ways of attaining a given end and will then choose the way that is least costly. This is particularly true of businesspeople, whose activities are vital for a capitalist society.

The Economist's View of Humankind

Of course, economists do not believe that men and women, even in business life, are solely rational, acquisitive creatures. They are fully aware that a hundred motivations impel people: aesthetic, political, religious. If economists concentrate on the rational and acquisitive elements in people, it is because they believe these to be decisive for most economic behavior; that is, for the explanation of our ordinary productive and distributive activities.

Economic theory is therefore a study of the effects of one aspect of human behavior as it motivates people to undertake their worldly activities. Very often, as economists well know, other aspects will override or blunt the acquisitive, maximizing orientation. To the extent that this is so, economic theory loses its clarity or may even suggest outcomes different from those that we find in fact. **But economists think that rational maximizing—the calculated pursuit of pleasurable wealth—is universal and strong enough to serve as a good working hypothesis on which to build their complicated theories.** To put it differently, economists do *not* think that political or religious or other such motives regularly overwhelm maximizing behavior. If that were so, economic theory would be of little avail.

A final point. Economists regard maximizing as a potentially useful mode of behavior. Of course economists understand that there is a lot more to life than making as much money as possible. But economics allows us to see that maximizing can be a beneficial activity. Business schools exist, in part, to teach people to be better maximizers—that is, more efficient and productive, and therefore more socially useful managers.

HYPOTHESES ABOUT CONSTRAINTS

So far, we have traced the basic assumptions of economic reasoning about behavior. What about constraints? As we have seen, people do not maximize in a vacuum or, to speak in more economic terms, in a world where all goods are free, available effortlessly in infinite amounts. Instead, people exert their maximizing efforts in a world where nature, technical limitations, and social institutions oppose those efforts. Goods and services are not free; they must be won by working with the elements of the physical world. Land, resources, and artifacts inherited from past generations are not boundlessly abundant. Laws and social organizations constantly impede our maximizing impulses.

Another way of putting it is that maximizing describes what we *want* to do while constraints describe what we *cannot* do. Economics thus studies the problems, and sometimes the impossibility, of achieving what we want. That is why economics is often characterized as *maximizing subject to constraints.*

Constraints of Nature

Constraints are obviously very important. But we cannot sum them up as simply as we can sum up the idea of maximizing.

Let us first think about three constraints on our maximizing desires that are imposed by nature. Later we will study these constraints in greater detail, but this is a good time to become generally familiar with them.

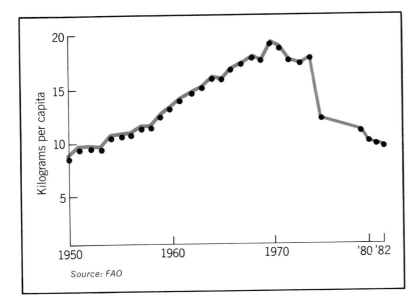

Figure 1
WORLD FISH CATCH PER
CAPITA, 1950–82

*Despite steadily increasing inputs
of capital (ships), the output of
fish has dwindled.*

1. DIMINISHING RETURNS. It's quite apparent that we cannot grow all the world's food requirements in a flowerpot. But why not? Why can't we go on adding seeds and getting more and more output?

The answer has to do with the physical and chemical properties of nature. If you go on adding more and more of any single input to a fixed amount of other inputs, after a time you will run up against obstacles imposed by the structure of things. Add more and more labor to a factory, and after a time it will be so crowded that output will fall. Add more and more ships to the earth's fishing fleet, and after a time the increase in the catch will diminish; in fact, as Figure 1 shows, that seems to be exactly what has been happening.

The same effect of a diminishing increment of production per constant increments of input seems to be taking place in world grain production. According to the Food and Agriculture Organization, in the mid-1930s an additional ton of fertilizer produced almost 15 tons of grain. Decade by decade this has been falling, until the latest figures for the mid-1970s show that world grain output rose only by 5.8 tons for each additional ton of fertilizer applied.

Thus nature imposes limits or constraints because we have to expect, and allow for, diminishing returns. **We can't usually count on twice as much output just by doubling one input.**

2. ECONOMIES OF SCALE. A second constraint has to do with sheer size, or scale. It describes the fact that size matters — also a consequence of the physical world.

You can't mass-produce automobiles in a garage. Why not? Because mass production requires giant presses and an organized flow of assembly, and those require a big scale of production.

This constraint means that small might be more beautiful, but big is often more economical. It means we can expect that production will become more efficient, and that each additional unit will become cheaper, as we move from small-scale to large-scale production — at least up to a point.

3. INCREASING COST. The last constraint is the least familiar. It looks like diminishing returns, but it is different. It has to do with the fact that not all land or labor or resources are alike, so that **as we move from one kind of production to another, we are likely to find it more and more costly to produce more and more of the new output.**

Here a diagram can help us visualize the problem. In Figure 2 we see a community that can produce two kinds of output — milk and grain. If it puts all its labor and all its land into milk production, it can produce an amount of milk that we'll represent by the distance *OA* on the milk axis. If it puts all its land and labor into grain, it will produce *OB* of grain, as represented on that axis.

Now suppose that our community is producing nothing but milk and that it decides to balance its output. It cuts milk production in half (to *OX*), moving land and labor into grain. We can see that it thereby gains *OY* amount of grain. Now notice what happens if the community moves the remaining half of its land and labor into grain. Output rises only a small amount, *YB*. Why is the second half of the community investment in land and labor less productive than the first half? Because we have already plowed the best fields and availed ourselves of the most skilled farmers. The last bushels of grain are much harder to win than the first. And of course the same result would take place in reverse if we started from all grain, at *B*, and switched over into milk. **The constraint means that the more of any one product that we want, the more of some other product we have to give up to get it.**

How much of one thing do we have to surrender to get something else? That depends on a host of things — the resources available, the technology we can call on, the energy we can muster. The curve in Figure 2 shows us the grain-milk tradeoff in our hypothetical community on some imaginary date, but a new invention, a change in climate, even a new economic system could change the efficiency with which we use our wealth. Thus the curve in Figure 2, which we call a **production possibilities curve,** can move — loosening our constraints, as the dotted line shows, or possibly tightening them. We will come back to study this when we take up the subject of economic growth.

Opportunity Cost

Here is a good place to make a very important point about the constraint of cost: **Cost constrains us because it means that we have to give something up to gain wealth.** The cost of the grain in Figure 2 is the milk we had to give up to get it, and the cost of the milk is the grain we had to forego. That is why economists say "There is no such thing as a free lunch." Even if you did not pay money for it, someone had

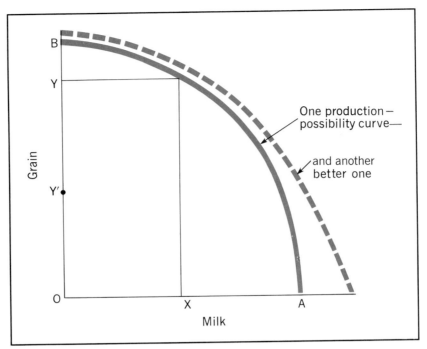

Figure 2
INCREASING COST

*The curve **AB** is called a production possibility curve. It is an imaginary curve here, but it is meant to depict a real-life situation, in which we see how many tons of outputs, like milk or grain, a society could produce by using its resources in various combinations. The dotted line shows how better technology, for instance, could move such a curve out. What would an earthquake do to it? Draw in such a reduced production possibility curve. The curve bows because of the law of increasing cost—that is, because it becomes less and less efficient to move labor and resources from one use to another. Compare how much grain we get (**OY**) as we cut milk production in half (moving from **OA** to **OX**), with how little we get (**BY**) as we move the remaining half (**OX**). Use a pencil to see if it works the other way around. Start from all grain (**OB**) and zero milk. First chart how much milk you get if you move the economy out of grain (from **OB** to **OY**'). Now eliminate all grain production. How much additional milk do you get?*

to produce that lunch, and the actual labor and materials that were used to make it can never be retrieved to make something else.

All costs, to economists, are opportunity costs. They are the utilities we must do without because we have chosen to devote our energies and wealth to creating the utilities we have. Later on, we will be talking about costs in dollars and cents, which is the way we usually think of cost. But when we say that something costs $10, what we really mean is that it costs us whatever utilities we might have enjoyed if we had spent the $10 on something else. Have you ever hesitated over whether to buy this *or* that? Then you know what opportunity cost means.

Constraints and Costs

All these properties of nature set the stage for maximizing behavior. People seek wealth through the production and exchange of goods and services, but they do not maximize in a world where goods can be limitlessly and effortlessly obtained. Nature and our given technology offer us their services easily or reluctantly, depending on whether we are trying to maximize output by adding more and more of one kind of input (when we encounter diminishing returns); whether we are seeking to organize our production in accordance with the technological characteristics of the agencies of production (economies of scale); or whether we are trying to increase the output of one good or service at the expense of others (when the law of increasing cost comes into play).

Needless to say, different societies enjoy different settings in nature — rich or poor soils, cold or warm climates, easily available or scarce mineral deposits. These gifts of nature help establish the limits of our productive activities, our national budget of annual output.

Thus constraints will play a basic role in establishing costs or supplies. We return to these considerations in the next chapter, where we encounter a *supply curve,* the counterpart of the demand curve, about which we first heard a few pages back.

Constraints of Society

Perhaps we can already see the makings of a powerful analytic device in the interplay of maximizing drives and constraining influences. Before we move on, however, it is necessary to recognize that nature is not the only constraint on the maximizing force of behavior.

Society's constraints on our behavior are just as effective as nature's. The *law* is a major constraining factor on our acquisitive propensities. *Competition* also limits freedom of action, preventing us from charging as much as we would like for goods or services. The banking system, labor unions, the legal underpinnings of private property are all *institutions* that operate like the constraints of nature in curbing the unhampered exercise of our maximizing impulse. So is the constraint of our available resources, our *budget.* Like technology, this is partly a constraint imposed by nature, partly one that is the consequence of man.

Not least, constraints affect us by our choice of the *social organization* of our productive efforts, as well as by their technical efficiency. The very same factory may have high or low output depending on whether employees' morale is good or bad.

BASIC HYPOTHESES

Let us briefly review the basic propositions in this first look into economic analysis. They can be summed up very simply.

Because economics generalizes about human behavior and the behavior of nature, it can theorize about, and to some extent predict, the operations of a market society. If we were not able to make such generalizations, if we could not begin with the plausible hypothesis that people are maximizers and that nature (and social institutions) constrain their behavior in clearly defined ways, we could not hazard the simplest predictive statement about economic society. We could not explain why a store that wants to sell more goods marks its prices down rather than up or why copper costs will probably rise if we try to double copper production in a short period of time.

Economics as a Social Science

Perhaps these simple generalizations about behavior and nature do not seem to be an impressive foundation for a social science. Ask yourself, though, whether we can match these economic generalizations when we think in political or sociological terms. Are there political or social laws of behavior that we can count on with the same degree of certainty we find in laws of economics? Are there constraints of nature, comparable to the laws of production, discoverable in the political and social areas of life? There are not. That is why we are so much less able to predict political or sociological events than to predict economic events.

Although economic prediction has sharp limitations, its underlying structure of behavioral and natural laws gives it unique strength. Its capabilities we must now explore. The place to begin must be obvious from our look into economic reality and our first acquaintance with supply and demand. It is the market mechanism.

looking back

KEY CONCEPTS	This chapter covers quite a few technical ideas, such as diminishing returns or increasing costs. Don't try to master them yet. Instead, be sure that you have the following simple conception of economic reasoning firmly in mind.
Economics is about production and distribution	1 Economic reasoning is about production and distribution of wealth, and only about those things. Economics has nothing to say about politics, religion, or anything other than material wealth.

Economics theorizes from two premises: utility maximizing and constraints	**2** Economics constructs hypotheses—or, much the same thing, economics theorizes—about the production and distribution of wealth. In doing so, it begins from two premises: (a) Men and women are maximizers of utility, and (b) they maximize in the face of well-defined obstacles or constraints.
Maximizing means insatiable desire for utility in general, not for any one kind of utility	**3** Maximizing behavior means that individuals seek as much pleasurable wealth as possible. This pleasurable wealth is called utility. Economists believe that in a market society such as ours, there is an insatiable desire for pleasurable wealth in general, although not for each particular kind of pleasurable wealth; after a certain point, more food makes us sick, more leisure is a bore.
Maximizing is guided by rational choice	**4** Economists also assume that individuals pursue their maximizing goals rationally—not in a haphazard, thoughtless way, but by making the best choices they can. Maximizing can therefore be socially useful.
Nature's constraints are three	**5** Maximizing behavior has to contend with the obstacles set by nature and by society. Nature and technology together establish three important kinds of constraints:
• Diminishing returns	The law of diminishing returns puts limits on the amount of output we can get from adding any one input—we can't grow all the world's food in a flowerpot.
• Increasing costs	The law of increasing costs limits our attempts to maximize because not all resources can be applied efficiently to any given purpose: We can't raise dairy cattle in Nevada. We can graph this in a production possibility curve.
• Scale	Returns to scale inhibit maximizing, because it is not efficient to produce all kinds of goods on a very small (or a very large) scale. Small may be beautiful, but it is also very expensive if you are thinking about making steel.
Institutional and social constraints	**6** Society also imposes constraints on maximizing—laws, institutional barriers, competition, and the like. Other important limits are imposed by budget considerations, and by morale.
Costs are missed opportunities	**7** Costs are basically missed opportunities. The term *opportunity cost* makes it clear that costs are not just sums of money, but possibilities for making wealth of various kinds that are forever missed because we have chosen to make wealth of one kind.
Maximizing subject to constraints is the analytic basis for much economics	**8** A powerful social science has been derived from the idea of interplay between maximizing and constraining forces. We shall see a demonstration of this power as we enter into a discussion of supply and demand in the next chapter.

ECONOMIC VOCABULARY

QUESTIONS

1. Do you feel like a maximizer? Are you content with your income? If you are not, do you expect that some day you will be satisfied?

2. Do you act rationally when you spend money? Do you consciously try to weigh the various advantages of buying this instead of that, and to spend your money for the item that will give you the greatest pleasure? Consciously or not, do you generally act as a rational maximizer?

3. How valid do you think the laws of economic behavior are? If they are *not* valid, why does economic society function and not collapse? If they *are* valid, why can't economists predict more accurately?

4. In what way is competition an institution? Are people naturally competitive? Would there be competition in a society that denied spatial or social mobility to labor, as under feudalism?

5. Can you think of any political activities or limits comparable to economic maximizing or constraints? Are there constraints of national size? Might it be possible to devise an economics of politics? For example, do you think politicians seek to maximize votes?

6. Suppose that you had a very large flowerpot and extraordinary chemicals and seeds. Could you conceivably grow all the world's food in it? Why would you still get diminishing returns?

7. Describe the economies of scale that might be anticipated if you were opening a department store. What economies might be expected as the store grew larger? Do you think you would eventually reach a ceiling on these economies?

8. What is the opportunity cost of undertaking a program such as space exploration? Of mounting a vast slum clearance program? Suppose the two cost the same amount of money? Does that mean the opportunity cost is the same?

CHAPTER 8
Supply and Demand

a look ahead

Here is your first real encounter with economics. In it you come to grips with the most important and powerful tool that economic reasoning gives us. The tool is an understanding of supply and demand and how they drive the market system.

It will help you to go through this chapter if you keep the following four steps in mind:

1 You are going to learn exactly what the word *demand* means, and what a "demand curve" represents.

2 You will learn the same thing about supply — what the word *supply* means and what a "supply curve" represents.

3 You will put the two together and see how demand and supply give rise to the idea of an equilibrium price.

4 We begin to distinguish shifts of supply and demand curves from movements along those curves. It is the shifts of the curves themselves that are the causes of price change.

What impresses us first when we study the market as a solution to the economic problem? The striking fact is that the market uses only one means of persuasion to induce people to engage in production or to undertake the tasks of distribution. It is neither time-honored tradition nor the edict of any authority that tells the members of a market society what to do. *It is price.*

Prices and Behavior

Thus the first attribute of a market system that we must examine is how prices take the place of tradition or command to become the guide to economic behavior.

The key lies in maximization. Through prices, acquisitive individuals learn what course of action will maximize their incomes or minimize their expenditures. This means that in the word *price* we include prices of labor or capital or resources that we call wages, profits, interest, or rent. Of course, within the category of prices we also include those ordinary prices that we pay for the goods and services we consume and the materials we purchase in order to build a home or to operate a store or factory. In each case, the only way that we can tell how to maximize our receipts and minimize our costs is by reading the signals of price that the market gives us.*

Therefore, if we are to understand how the market works as a mechanism — that is, how it acts as a guide to the solution of the economic problem — we must first understand how the market sets prices. When we say "the market," we mean the activity of buying and selling, or in more precise economic language, *demand and supply*. Let us discover how demand and supply interact to establish prices.

DEMAND

Taste and Income

When you enter the market for goods and services (almost every time you walk along a shopping street), two factors determine whether or not you will actually become a buyer and not just a window shopper. The first factor is your desire for the good. Economists call this "taste." It is your taste that determines in large degree whether a good offers you pleasure or utility, and if so, how much. The windows of shops are crammed with things you could afford to buy but which you simply do not wish to own, because they do not offer you sufficient utility. Perhaps if some of these were cheaper, you might wish to own them; but some goods you would not want even if they were free. For such goods, for which your tastes are too

---

* In the real world, reading prices can be very complicated, for it involves not only how much we know about the market, but how much we *think* we know about it. Here we simplify matters and assume, to begin with, that we all have perfect knowledge.

weak to motivate you, your demand is zero. **Thus taste determines your willingness to buy.**

On the other hand, taste is by no means the only component of demand. Shop windows are also full of goods that you might very much like to own but cannot afford to buy. Your demand for Rolls Royces is also apt to be zero. **In other words, demand also hinges on your ability to buy — on your possession of sufficient wealth or income as well as on your taste.** If demand did not hinge on ability as well as willingness to buy, the poor, whose wants are always very large, would constitute a great source of demand.

Diminishing Marginal Utility

Note that your demand for goods depends on your willingness and ability to buy goods or services *at their going price.* From this it follows that the amounts of goods you demand will change as their prices change, just as it also follows that the amounts you will demand change as your wealth or income changes. There is no difficulty understanding why changing prices should change our ability to buy: Our wealth simply stretches further or less far. **In economic language, our budget constraint is loosened when prices fall and tightened when they rise.**

But why should our *willingness* to buy be related to price? The answer lies in the nature of utility. People are maximizing creatures, but they do not want ever more of the *same* commodity. On the contrary, as we saw, economists take as a plausible generalization that additional increments of the same good or service, within some stated period of time, will yield smaller and smaller increments of pleasure. **These increments of pleasure are called marginal utility, and the general tendency of marginal utility to diminish is called the law of** *diminishing marginal utility.* Remember: Diminishing marginal utility refers strictly to behavior and not to nature. The units of goods we continue to buy are not smaller — it is the pleasure associated with each additional unit that is smaller.

Demand Curves*

In the bar chart on the left of Figure 1, we show the ever smaller amounts of money we are willing to pay for additional units of some good or service, simply because each additional unit gives us less utility than its predecessor. In the graph on the right, we have drawn a *demand curve* to generalize this basic relationship between the quantity of a good we are interested in acquiring and the price we are willing to pay for it.

Figure 1 deserves a careful look. Note that each *additional* unit affords us less utility, so we are not willing to pay as much for the next unit as for the one we just bought. This does not mean that the *total utility* we derive from all 3 or 4 units is less

* Anyone unfamiliar with graphs should turn right now to p. 171 and learn how to read them and use them. Look as well into the Extra Word on graphs on pp. 178–179.

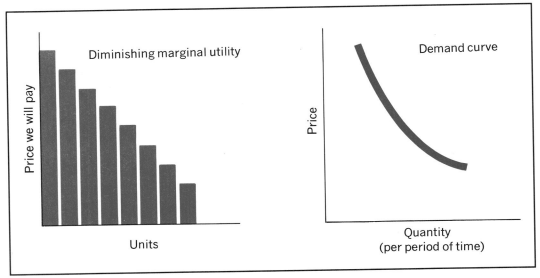

Figure 1
DIMINISHING MARGINAL UTILITY AND A DEMAND CURVE
Notice, on the left, how the marginal utility of each additional unit of a good diminishes. The curve on the right simply generalizes the fact that each additional unit yields less pleasure than the one before it, and will therefore command a smaller price.

than that derived from the first. Far from it. It is the *addition* to our utility from the last unit that is much lower than the *addition* of the first or second.

The Puzzle of Bread and Diamonds

The notion of diminishing marginal utility also clears up an old puzzle of economic life. This is why we are willing to pay so little for bread, which is a necessity for life, and so much for diamonds, which are not. The answer is that we have so much bread that the marginal utility of any loaf we are thinking of buying is very little, whereas we have so few diamonds that each carat has a very high marginal utility. If we were locked inside Tiffany's over a long holiday, the prices we would pay for bread and diamonds, after a few days, would be very different from those we would have paid when we entered.

SUPPLY

What about the supply side? Here too, willingness and ability enter into the seller's actions. As we would expect, they bring about reactions different from those in the case of demand.

UTILITIES AND DEMAND

Does diminishing marginal utility really determine how much we buy? The idea seems far removed from common sense, but is it? Suppose we decide to buy a cake of fancy soap. In commonsense language, we'll do so only "if it's not too expensive." In the language of the economist this means we'll only do so if the utilities we expect from the soap are greater than the utilities we derive from the money we have to spend to get the soap.

If we buy one or two cakes, doesn't this demonstrate that the pleasure of the soap is greater than the pleasure of holding onto the money or spending it for something else? In that case, why don't we buy a year's supply of the soap? The commonsense answer is that we don't want *that much* soap. It would be a nuisance. We wouldn't use it all for months and months, etc. In the language of the economist, the utilities of the cakes of soap after the first few would be less than the utilities of the money they would cost.

In the accompanying diagram we show these diminishing marginal utilities of successive cakes over some fixed period of time — that is, the pleasures yielded by successive cakes. The unchanging price of soap represents the utility of the money we have to pay. As you can see, if soap costs *OA*, we'll buy three cakes; no more. This is because the marginal utility of the fourth cake is less than that of the money we would have to pay for it.

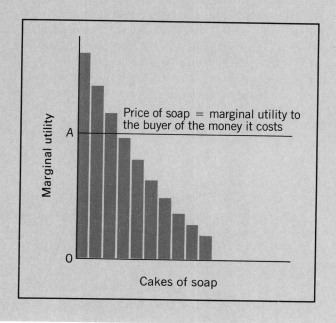

Price of soap = marginal utility to the buyer of the money it costs

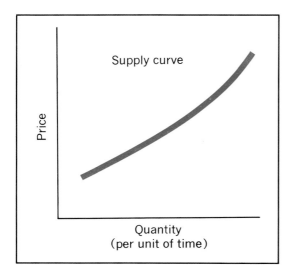

Price

Supply curve

**Quantity
(per unit of time)**

Figure 2
THE SHORT-RUN SUPPLY CURVE
*A typical supply curve slopes upward
because each additional unit tends to be
more difficult or expensive to make, at
least in the short run.*

At high prices, sellers are much more *willing* to supply goods and services because they will take in more money. They will also be much more easily *able* to offer
more goods because higher prices will enable less efficient suppliers to enter the
market, or will cover the higher costs of production that may result from increasing
their outputs.

Therefore, we depict normal supply curves as rising. These rising curves present
a contrast to the falling curves of demanders: sellers eagerly respond to high prices;
buyers respond negatively. Figure 2 shows such a typical supply curve. Note that a
supply curve, like its demand counterpart, represents a functional relationship:
how much we will offer at different prices. Presumably time does not enter into this
curve—it does not show changes that would require time-consuming activity,
such as changing our scale of operation. That is why it is called a *short-run* supply
curve.

Supply and Demand

The idea that buyers welcome low prices and sellers welcome high prices is hardly
apt to come as a surprise. What is surprising is that the meaning of the words *supply*
and *demand* differs from the one we ordinarily carry about in our heads. It is very
important to understand that when we speak of demand as economists, we do not
refer to a single purchase at a given price. **Demand in its proper economic sense
refers to the various quantities of goods or services that we are willing and able
to buy at different prices at a given time. That relationship is shown by our
demand curve.**

The same relationship between price and quantity enters into the word *supply.* When we *supply,* we do not mean the amount a seller puts on the market at a given price. We mean the *differing* amounts offered at *different* prices. Thus our supply curves, like our demand curves, portray the relationship between willingness and ability to enter into transactions at different prices.

Balancing Supply and Demand

We are now ready to see how the market mechanism works. Undoubtedly you have already grasped the crucial point on which the mechanism depends. **This is the opposing behavior that a change in prices brings about for buyers and sellers. Rising prices will be matched by an increase in the willingness and ability of sellers to offer goods, but by a decrease in the willingness and ability of buyers to take goods.**

It is through these opposing reactions that the market mechanism works. Let us examine the process in an imaginary market for shoes in a small city. In Table 1 we show the price-quantity relationships of buyers and of sellers: How many thousand pairs will be offered for sale or sought for purchase at a range of prices from $50 to $5. We call such an array of price-quantity relationships a **schedule** of supply and demand.

As before, the schedules tell us that buyers and sellers react differently to prices. At high prices, buyers are either not willing or unable to purchase more than small quantities of shoes, whereas sellers would be only too willing and able to flood the city with them. At very low prices, the quantity of shoes demanded would be very great, but few shoe manufacturers would be willing or able to gratify buyers at such low prices.

Table 1

DEMAND AND SUPPLY SCHEDULES

Go down the price schedule and notice that quantities demanded do not equal quantities supplied—until you get to $25. Below $25 they are also unequal. $25 is the equilibrium price.

Price	Quantity Demanded (1,000 PR)	Quantity Supplied (1,000 PR)
$50	1	125
$45	5	90
$40	10	70
$35	20	50
$30	25	35
$25	30	30
$20	40	20
$15	50	10
$10	75	5
$ 5	100	0

If we now look at *both* schedules at *each* price level, we discover an interesting thing. **There is one price at which the quantity demanded is exactly the same as the quantity supplied.** This price is $25 in our example. At every other price, one schedule or the other is larger, but at $25 the amounts in both columns are the same: 30,000 pairs of shoes. We call this balancing price the **equilibrium price.** We shall soon see that it *is* the price which emerges spontaneously in an actual market where supply and demand contend.*

EMERGENCE OF THE EQUILIBRIUM PRICE

How do we know that an equilibrium price will be brought about by the interaction of supply and demand? The process is one of the most important in all of economics, so we should understand it very clearly.

Interplay of Supply and Demand

Suppose in our example above that for some reason or other the shoe retailers put a price tag on their shoes not of $25 but of $45. What would happen? Our schedules show us that at this price shoe manufacturers will be pouring out shoes at a rate of 90,000 pairs a year, whereas customers would be buying them at the rate of only 5,000 pairs a year. Shortly, the shoe factories would be bulging with unsold merchandise. It is plain what the outcome of this situation must be. In order to realize some revenue, shoe manufacturers will begin to unload their stocks at lower prices. They do so because this is their rational course as competitive maximizers.

As they reduce the price, the situation will begin to improve. At $40, demand picks up from 5,000 to 10,000, while at the same time the slightly lower price discourages some producers, so that output falls from 90,000 pairs to 70,000. Shoe manufacturers are still turning out more shoes than the market can absorb at the going prices, although the difference between the quantities supplied and the quantities demanded is smaller than it was before.

Let us suppose that the competitive pressure continues to reduce prices so that shoes sell at $30. Now a much more satisfactory state of affairs exists. Producers will be turning out 35,000 pairs of shoes. Consumers will be buying them at a rate of 25,000 a year. Still there is an imbalance. Some shoes will still be piling up, unsold, at the factory or in stores. Prices will therefore continue to fall, eventually to $25. At this point, the quantity of shoes supplied by the manufacturers — 30,000 pairs — is exactly that demanded by customers. There is no longer a surplus of unsold shoes hanging over the market and acting to press prices down.

---

* Of course we have made up our schedules so that the quantities demanded and supplied would be equal at $25. The price that actually brought about such a balancing of supply and demand might be some odd number such as $24.98.

The Market Clears

Now let us quickly trace the interplay of supply and demand from the other direction. Suppose that prices were originally $5. Our schedules tell us that customers would be standing in line at the shoestores, but producers would be largely shut down, unwilling or unable to make shoes at those prices. We can easily imagine that customers, many of whom would gladly pay more than $5, let it be known that they would welcome a supply of shoes at $10 or even more. They too are trying to maximize their utilities. If enough customers bid $10, a trickle of shoe output begins. Nevertheless, the quantity of shoes demanded at $10 far exceeds the available supply. Customers snap up the few pairs around and tell shoe stores they would gladly pay $20 a pair. Prices rise accordingly. Now we are getting closer to a balance of quantities offered and bid for. At $20 there will be a demand for 40,000 pairs of shoes, and output will have risen to 20,000 pairs. Still the pressure of unsatisfied demand raises prices further. Finally a price of $25 is tried. Now, once again, the quantities supplied and demanded are exactly in balance. There is no further pressure from unsatisfied customers to force the price up further, because at $25 no customer who can afford the going price will remain unsatisfied. The market "clears."

Characteristics of Equilibrium Prices

Thus we can see how the interaction of supply and demand brings about the establishment of a price at which both suppliers and demanders are willing and able to sell or buy the same quantity of goods. We can visualize the equilibrating process more easily if we now transfer our supply and demand schedules to graph paper. Figure 3 is the representation of the shoe market we have been dealing with.

The graph shows us at a glance the situation we have analyzed in detail. At the price of $25, the quantities demanded and supplied are equal: 30,000 pairs of

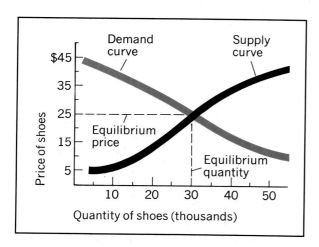

Figure 3
DETERMINATION OF AN EQUILIBRIUM PRICE
Demand and supply curves only show what the schedule has already revealed: There is one price at which the two quantities are equal. This is the equilibrium price.

shoes. The graph also shows more vividly than the schedules why this is an *equilibrium* price.

Suppose that the price were temporarily lifted above $25. If you will draw a horizontal pencil line from any point on the vertical axis above the $25 mark to represent this price, you will find that it intersects the demand curve before it reaches the supply curve. In other words, **the quantity demanded is less than the quantity supplied at any price above the equilibrium price, and the excess of the quantity supplied means that there will be a downward pressure on prices, back toward the equilibrium point.**

The situation is exactly reversed if prices should fall below the equilibrium point. Now the quantity demanded is greater than that supplied, and the pressure of buyers will push the price up to the equilibrium point.

Thus equilibrium prices have two important characteristics:

1. They are the prices that will spontaneously establish themselves through the free play of the forces of supply and demand.
2. Once established, they will persist unless the forces of supply and demand themselves change.

Does "Demand" Equal "Supply"?

There is one last thing to be noted carefully about equilibrium prices. They are the prices that bring about an equality in the *quantities demanded* and the *quantities supplied*. They are not the prices that bring about an equality of "supply and demand."

Probably the most common beginning mistake in economics is to say that supply and demand are equal when prices are in equilibrium. If we remember that both supply and demand mean the *relationships* between quantities and prices, we can see that an equality of supply and demand would mean that the demand schedule and the supply schedule for a commodity were alike, so that the curves would lie one on top of the other. In turn, this would mean that at a price of $50, buyers of shoes would be willing and able to buy the same number of shoes that suppliers would be willing to offer at that price, and the same for buyers at $5. If such were the case, prices would be wholly indeterminate and could race high and low with no tension of opposing interests to bring them to a stable resting place.

Hence we must take care to use the words *supply* or *demand* to refer only to relationships or schedules. When we want to speak of the effect of a particular price on our willingness or ability either to buy or sell, we use the longer phrase *quantity demanded* or *quantity supplied*.

The Role of Competition

We have seen how stable, lasting prices may spontaneously emerge from the flux of the marketplace, but we have silently passed over a basic condition for the formation of these prices. This is the role played by competition in the operation of the market mechanism.

SUPPLY AND DEMAND, AGAIN

Here is one of the oldest "puzzles" in economics. Suppose that the price of A.T.&T. stock rises. Because the price rises, the demand for the stock falls. Therefore the price of A.T.&T. must decline. It follows that the price of A.T.&T. should never vary or at least should quickly return to the starting point.

Tell that to your broker. Better, tell it to your instructor and show him — and yourself — with a graph of supply and demand, where the fallacy of this puzzle lies. *Hint:* When the price rises, does the *demand* for A.T.&T. stock fall or does the *quantity demanded* fall? Will the price fall again?

Competition is often discussed as a somewhat unpleasant attribute of economic man. Now, however, we can see that it is an attribute that is indispensable if we are to have socially acceptable outcomes for a market process.

Competition is the regulator that "supervises" the orderly working of the market. But economic competition (unlike the competition for prizes outside economic life) is not a single contest. It is a *continuing process*. It monitors a race that no one ever wins, a race where all must go on endlessly trying to stay in front, to avoid the economic penalties of falling behind.

Moreover, unlike the contests of ordinary life, economic competition involves not just a single struggle among rivals, but two struggles. One is between the two sides of the markets; the other is among the marketers on each side. **The competitive marketplace is not only where the clash of interest between buyer and seller is worked out by the opposition of supply and demand, but also where buyers contend against buyers and sellers against sellers.**

SHIFTS IN DEMAND AND SUPPLY

Equilibrium prices, emerging from the wholly unsupervised interaction of competing buyers and sellers, are now a part of our understanding. These prices, once formed, silently and efficiently perform the necessary social task of allocating goods among buyers and sellers. Yet our analysis is still too static to resemble the actual play of the marketplace, for one of the attributes of an equilibrium price, we remember, is its lasting quality, its persistence. Things are different in the real world around us, where prices are often in movement. How can we introduce this element of change into our analysis of microeconomic relations?

The answer is that the word *equilibrium* does not imply changelessness. Equilibrium prices last only as long as the forces that produce them do not change. To put it differently, if we want to explain why any price changes, we must always look for changes in the forces of supply and demand that produced the price in the first place.

What makes supply and demand change? If we recall the definition of those words, we are asking: What might change our willingness or ability to buy or sell something at any given price? Having asked the question, it is not difficult to answer it. If our *incomes* rise or fall, that will clearly alter our *ability* to buy. Similarly, a change in the price of *other* commodities will alter our real income and thus our ability to buy. When food goes up, we go to the movies less often. Finally, a change in *tastes* will change our willingness to buy.

On the seller's side, things are a bit more complicated. If we are owners of the factors of production (labor, land, or capital), changes in incomes or tastes will also change our ability and willingness to offer these factors on the market. If we are making decisions for firms, changes in *cost* will be the main determinant.

Shifts in Curves vs. Movements along Curves

Thus changes in tastes or prices or in income or wealth will shift our whole demand schedule. The same changes, plus any change in costs, will shift our whole supply schedule.

Note that this is very different from a change in the quantity we buy or sell when *prices* change. **In the first case, as our willingness and ability to buy or sell is increased or diminished, the whole demand and supply schedule (or curve) shifts bodily. In the second place, when our basic willingness and ability is unchanged, but prices change, our schedule (or curve) is unchanged, but we move back or forth along it.**

Here are the two cases to be studied carefully in Figure 4. Note that when our demand schedule shifts, we buy a *different amount at the same price*. If our willingness and ability to buy is enhanced, we will buy a larger amount; if they are diminished, a smaller amount. Similarly, the quantity a seller will offer will vary as his willingness and ability are altered. Thus demand and supply curves can shift about, rightward and leftward, up and down, as the economic circumstances they represent change. In reality, these schedules are continuously in change, since tastes and incomes and attitudes and technical capabilities (which affect costs and therefore sellers' actions) are also continuously in flux.

Price Changes

How do changes in supply and demand affect prices? We have already seen the underlying process at work for shoes. Changes in supply and demand will alter the *quantities* that will be sought or offered on the market at a given price. An increase

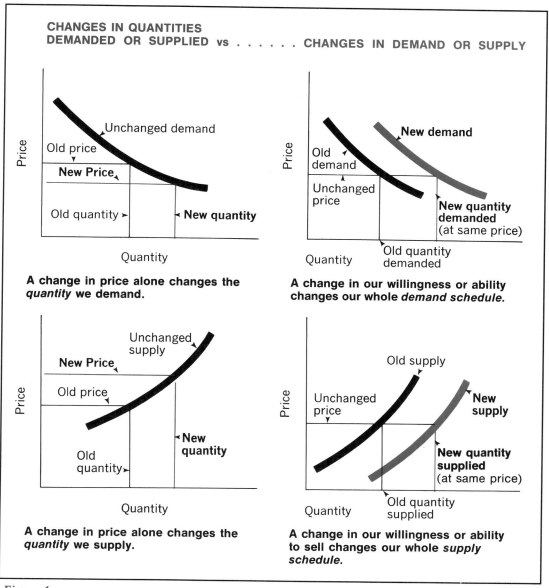

CHANGES IN QUANTITIES DEMANDED OR SUPPLIED vs . . . . . . **CHANGES IN DEMAND OR SUPPLY**

Price / Quantity

Unchanged demand
Old price
New Price
Old quantity ► ◄ New quantity

A change in price alone changes the *quantity* we demand.

New demand
Old demand
Unchanged price
New quantity demanded (at same price)
Old quantity demanded

A change in our willingness or ability changes our whole *demand schedule.*

Unchanged supply
New Price
Old price
Old quantity ►
◄ New quantity

A change in price alone changes the *quantity* we supply.

Old supply
Unchanged price
New supply
New quantity supplied (at same price)
Old quantity supplied

A change in our willingness or ability to sell changes our whole *supply schedule.*

Figure 4

Here is where we can see the difference between a change in demand or supply, and a change in the quantity demanded or supplied. This is a graph that should be studied until you fully understand it.

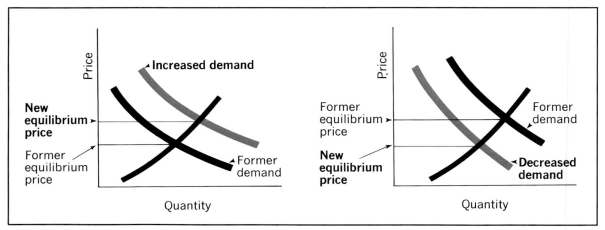

Figure 5
SHIFTS IN DEMAND

An increase or decrease in our demand schedule changes the equilibrium price, raising it in the first case, lowering it in the second.

in demand, for instance, will raise the quantity sought. Since there are not enough goods offered to match this quantity, prices will be bid up by unsatisfied buyers to a new level. At that level, quantities offered and sought will again balance. Similarly, if supply shifts, there will be too much or too little put on the market in relation to the existing quantity of demand, and competition among sellers will push prices up or down to a new level at which quantities sought and offered again clear.

Figure 6
SHIFTS IN SUPPLY

Shifts in supply also change equilibrium prices. Increased supplies lower them; decreased supplies raise them.

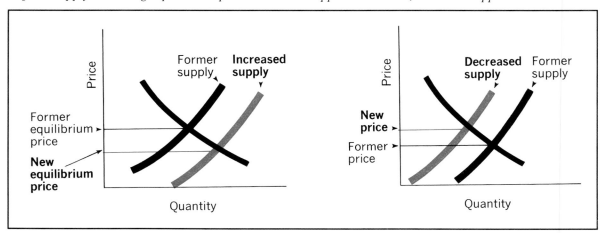

In Figure 5, we show what happens to the equilibrium price in two cases: first, when demand increases (perhaps owing to a sudden craze for the good in question); second, when demand decreases (when the craze is over). Quite obviously, a rise in demand, other things being equal, will cause prices to rise; a fall will cause them to fall.

We can depict the same process from the supply side. In Figure 6, we show the impact on price of a sudden rise in supply and the impact of a fall. Again the diagram makes clear what is intuitively obvious: An increased supply (given an unchanging demand) leads to lower prices; a decreased supply to higher prices.

And if supply and demand *both* change? Then the result will be higher or lower prices, depending on the shapes and new positions of the two curves; that is, depending on the relative changes in the willingness and ability of both sides.

Figure 7 shows a few possibilities, where *S* and *D* are the original supply and demand curves, and *S'* and *D'* the new curves.

Figure 7

SHIFTS IN BOTH SUPPLY AND DEMAND

When both supply and demand change, prices may rise, fall, or remain unchanged. The outcome is determined by the intersection of both *curves, so that we can never tell what will happen to price if we only know what has happened to one curve, but not to the other. It will help greatly if you try different combinations.*

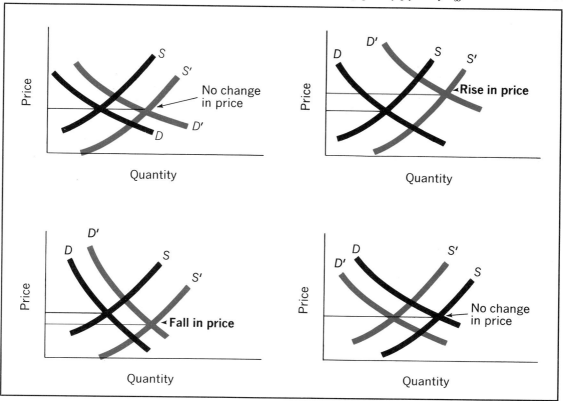

Long and Short Run

There is one point we should add to conclude our discussion of supply and demand. Students often wonder which "really" sets the price—supply or demand. Alfred Marshall, the great late-nineteenth-century economist, gave the right answer: *both do,* just as both blades of scissors do the cutting.

Yet, whereas prices are always determined by the intersection of supply and demand schedules, we can differentiate between the *short run,* when demand tends to be the more dynamic force, and the *long run,* when supply is the more important force. In Figure 8 we see (on the left) short-run fixed supply, as in the instance of fishermen bringing a catch to a dock. Since the size of the catch cannot be changed, the supply curve is fixed in place, and the demand curve is the only possible dynamic influence. Broken lines show that changes in demand alone will set the price.

Now let us shift to the long run and draw a horizontal supply curve representing the average cost of production of fish (and thus the supply price of fish) in the long run. Fluctuations in demand now have no effect on price, whereas a change in fishing costs that would raise or lower the supply curve would immediately affect the price.

Figure 8
SHORT- AND LONG-RUN SUPPLY CURVES

Short-run supply is represented by a vertical curve since the same amount is offered no matter what the price. Here, demand "sets" the price, although without the supply curve there would be no price. In the long run, supply is horizontal, and demand has no effect on price. Yet without a demand curve there would be no sales of fish—and therefore no price at all! Both supply and demand are essential for all prices.

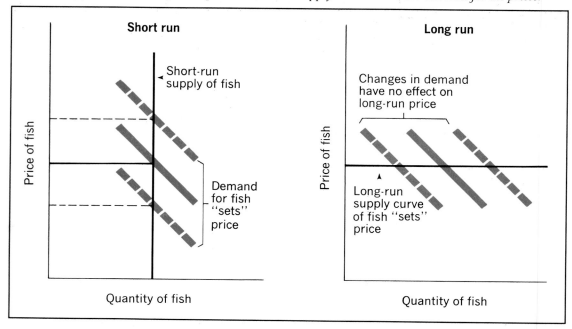

In all cases, do not forget, *both* demand and supply enter into the formation of price. In the short run, as a rule, changes in demand are more likely to affect changes in prices. In the long run, changes in supply are apt to be the predominant cause of changes in price, as when technology lowers the cost of commercial fishing.

A Last Word on Maximizing

Does the market mechanism bear a relation to the general notion of maximizing? Indeed it does. Buyers and sellers both are *willing* to respond to price signals because they wish to maximize their incomes or utilities. But neither can maximize at will. Buyers are *constrained* by their budgets, and sellers are *constrained* by their costs. Thus the *ability* of buyers or sellers to respond to price signals is limited by obstacles of budgets or cost.

In addition, buyers and sellers are both constrained by the operation of the market. A seller might like to sell his goods above the market price, and a buyer might like to buy goods below the market price; but the presence of competitors means that a seller who quotes a price above the market will be unable to find a buyer, and a buyer who makes a bid below the market will be unable to find a seller.

Thus the market mechanism is a very important example of what economists call "maximizing subject to constraints." We will learn more about this in Part Four. But already we can see that it is the very interaction of the maximizing drives and the constraining obstacles that leads the market to the establishment of equilibrium prices. We can also see that if we could know these maximizing forces and constraints beforehand, we would know the supply and demand curves of a market and could actually predict what its equilibrium price would be! In actual fact, our knowledge falls far short of such omniscience, but the imaginary example nonetheless begins to open up for us the analytical possibilities of economics.

looking back

KEY CONCEPTS

You can now see that the purpose of this chapter is to show how maximizing subject to constraints works in terms of demand and supply. Here are the main points that you should carry away from what you have read:

Demand is the willingness and ability to buy at a given price

1 Demand is a central idea of economics. It means the willingness and ability of any person or group of persons to buy a good or service at a particular price. Your demand schedule reflects your desire to maximize your utilities for that good, within the constraint of your budget.

Marginal utility typically falls	2 Our willingness or ability to buy more of any kind of good reflects the marginal utility that another unit of that good will yield. The marginal utility means the additional utility—the pleasures of the *next* movie, the *next* pair of shoes, the *next* dollar of income—within a given period of time. A basic assumption of economic reasoning is that the marginal utility of any one thing diminishes: The second movie, pair of shoes, or dollar will not give as much pleasure as the first one.
Therefore typical demand curves fall	3 This gives rise to normal, downward-sloping demand curves, showing that we are only willing to buy more units of the same goods at cheaper prices. These curves represent our schedules in simplified form.
Supply curves typically rise	4 Supply curves typically rise, because suppliers are not able (or willing) to offer more and more goods within a given period of time, except at higher prices.
Supply and demand vs. quantities supplied or demanded	5 Supply and demand refer to the range of goods or services that sellers or buyers will offer at differing prices. At any given price we should refer to the *quantity supplied* or the *quantity demanded*. When we say supply or demand, we mean the whole schedule or the curve that represents that schedule.
The idea of equilibrium where quantities offered are equal to quantities demanded	6 When we compare schedules, or plot two supply and demand curves, we can find out if there is an equilibrium price. This is a price where the quantities offered or supplied are equal to the quantities demanded. Economists are often careless and say that at an equilibrium price "supply equals demand," but students should watch their language! In an equilibrium price, the *quantities demanded* equal the *quantities supplied*, and the market clears.
How equilibrium prices emerge and persist	7 Equilibrium prices are spontaneously established through the interplay of supply and demand, and they will persist unless the willingness or abilities of buyers and sellers change.
There is a two-sided aspect of competition	8 There is a double-edged aspect to competition. Competition not only means that buyers oppose sellers, each trying to get the better of the other, but also that buyers have to win out against other buyers and that sellers have to outdo—or do as well as—other sellers.
Changes in supply or demand mean shifts in the entire curves, not movements along them	9 Changes in price occur when there are shifts in supply and demand—that is, when the quantities that people are willing and able to buy or sell change at a given price. These changes are characterized by shifts in the supply and demand curves rather than by movements along these curves. Thus an increase (decrease) in demand means that we buy more (less) *at the same price*.
The price system	10 Last, bear in mind that you are learning the remarkable way in which an economic mechanism coordinates the very different

objectives and activities of buyers and sellers through only one means—the signal of price. Prices inform people how to maximize rationally, given their constraints. The Invisible Hand does the rest!

ECONOMIC VOCABULARY

Demand   136
Taste   136
Diminishing marginal utility   137
Supply   139
Schedules   141
Equilibrium prices   142

Demand and supply curves   141, 142, 145
Competition, two aspects   145
Shifts in curves versus movements along curves   146

QUESTIONS

1. Fill out the schedule below by supplying reasonable numbers to show the quantities demanded and supplied for T-shirts in a small town, at prices ranging from $1 to $10, over a period of, say, one year. (You might assume that there are about 10,000 potential buyers in your market.) Now graph the schedule in the graph space provided. Be sure to indicate the quantities on the horizontal axis.
2. Choose any arbitrary price above equilibrium. How will maximizing behavior change this higher price back toward equilibrium? Does it require a contest among buyers? Sellers? Both? Either?
3. Now do the same thing with a price below the equilibrium.

SCHEDULE OF SUPPLY AND DEMAND FOR T-SHIRTS, PER YEAR

Price of T-Shirts	Quantity Demanded	Quantity Supplied
$10		
9		
8		
7		
6		
5		
4		
3		
2		
1		

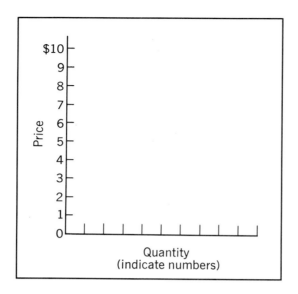

4. Subtract the quantities in your supply schedule from those in your demand schedule. There will be a plus or minus at all prices except one. Why is that? Does that help explain why an equilibrium price clears a market?

5. Whatever quantity is sold must be bought; whatever is bought must be sold. Then how can we say that only one price will clear the market? *Hint:* Look again at your answer to question 2.

6. What changes in your economic condition would increase your demand for clothes? Draw a diagram to illustrate such a change. Show on it whether you would buy more or less clothes at the prices you formerly paid. If you wanted to buy the same quantity as before, would you be willing and able to pay prices different from those you paid earlier?

7. Suppose that you are a seller of costume jewelry. What changes in your economic condition would decrease your supply curve? Suppose that costs dropped. If demand were unchanged, what would happen to the price in a competitive market?

8. Draw a diagram that shows what we mean by an increase in the quantity supplied; another diagram to show what is meant by an increase in supply. Now do the same for a decrease in quantity supplied and in supply. (*Warning:* It is very easy to get these wrong. Check yourself by seeing if the decreased supply curve shows the seller offering less goods at the same prices.) Now do the same exercise for demand.

CHAPTER 9
Why Economists Disagree

a look ahead

We have just seen that economics has many science-like aspects. Yet we all know that no two economists ever seem to agree. Why is this the case? This chapter talks about the inherent difficulties of forecasting; about the reasons why predictions concerning human behavior can never have the same degree of accuracy as predictions about natural processes; and about the ways in which our values color our perceptions and lead us to different expectations concerning economic events.

This is certainly not a difficult chapter to read or understand. But it is exceedingly difficult to apply. Indeed, the whole secret of being a good economist lies in the lessons it tries to teach.

Economists are notorious for disagreeing. No two forecasts for the economy are alike. Liberal and conservative economists often seem to be looking at two entirely separate worlds. Different economists will recommend different, and sometimes diametrically opposed, policies as fervidly on one side as on the other. If economics is as analytic a study as we have made it out to be, why don't economists agree more?

Of course there is a quick rejoinder. Scientists disagree. Lawyers disagree. Even mathematicians disagree. Evidently there is nothing in the nature of science, or argument, or even abstract logic that forces unanimity of thought on all its practitioners. So an easy response to the question of this chapter is simply that disagreement is a common attribute of human discourse. If economists didn't disagree, they would be a world apart — supermen.

But that is not a wholly satisfactory answer because it does not tell us anything about the *reasons* why economists (or scientists or lawyers or mathematicians) differ. The reasons are interesting because they make us think about the foundations of economics.

ECONOMICS AND FORECASTING

Perhaps the first place where we ordinarily notice the differences among economic opinions is in the general field of forecasting. We are all familiar with the clash of forecasts put out by the economists of the administration (any administration) and of Congress, or the divergences of views of well-known private economists in banks or industry or foundations.

Why do forecasts vary so frequently and so much? A good answer is that economists' forecasts differ for exactly the same kinds of reasons as meteorologists'. Meteorologists typically differ as to their predictions, and even the most reliable of them make terrible mistakes. Asking why meteorological forecasting is so often mistaken or at odds with itself deepens our understanding of why economic forecasting is also often wrong. Here are two reasons that apply in both cases: the problem of data and the problem of complexity.

1. THE PROBLEM OF DATA. The meteorologist is often wrong because he or she doesn't have enough data. Moreover, no meteorologist can ever have enough data. That would require him or her to know everything about the weather at any moment — the temperatures at every point in the country, the direction and intensity of each and every wind current. Thus, every meteorologist is forced to make forecasts on the basis of partial information; and, that which has been left out may turn out to have been decisive. "Ah! If I'd only known about *that*," says the weather person, asked why his "sunny day tomorrow" turned out to be a flood.

The same is true for the economist. No economic forecaster can know the complete state of the economy at any moment. *Indeed, no one knows it.* Of necessity this introduces an element of uncertainty into every forecast. Something is always left out. If it is important, the forecast will be wrong.

2. THE PROBLEM OF COMPLEXITY. The second problem is closely allied with the first. Even if the weather person knows each and every fact about today's meteorological conditions, there is no way to combine the data to yield tomorrow's weather with absolute certainty. This is because the "systems" that constitute weather are too complex to be reduced to exact models. For example, atmospheric turbulence cannot be described except in very general terms. Therefore it is impossible to know exactly in what direction a storm will veer. The best meteorologists can do is to say that usually storms move in such and such a way, and that therefore *probably* the storm they are tracking will move that way too.

The same problem applies to economics. Even if some gigantic computer had stored within it every bit of data concerning individual incomes and tastes, and every last iota of technical information about production techniques, and all the other facts that impinge on economic activity, there still exists no way of putting these billions of items into a precise model of the actual economy. It is not surprising, then, that economists' forecasts will differ, because different economists will combine the data at hand in different ways.

BEYOND METEOROLOGY

These are obvious reasons why economic forecasting, like weather forecasting, cannot be an exact science. But there are other reasons why economists disagree —reasons that are not to be found in meteorology, or for that matter in any other natural science.

1. WILL AND INTENTION. One of these is that the elements of the social world differ from those of the natural world in a very important respect: They possess wills and intentions. When the astronomer predicts the eclipses of the moon, he or she does not have to worry about how the moon feels about going into eclipse: if astronomers did, astronomy would be a much less reliable science than it is.

But that is very much part of what economists must constantly worry about. An economist who predicts that prices or GNP will rise has to make assumptions about the behavior of human beings, not of inanimate objects. Because no one can ascertain how the members of a society think or feel at any moment, an economist is forced to assume that human beings will act in the way economic theory assumes to be their normal behavior—as rational, maximizing beings.

But suppose that they do not. Suppose that whims or fads, or patriotic or revolutionary sentiments sweep the country. Then prices may not behave in textbook fashion because consumers rush into or shun the commodity in question for no "good" reason at all; or GNP may fall because workers go on strike—perhaps "against their best interests." Such kinds of behavior are not an ordinary part of social life — if they were, we would not be able to talk about rational, maximizing behavior as the norm. But as long as individuals have wills and purposes, unexpected behavior will occur. Of course, when it does forecasts will go wrong.

2. EXPECTATIONS. But let us suppose that behavior *is* normal. Can forecasts still go askew?

They can and will if the forecaster does not correctly assess the frame of mind of the economic agents with respect to the future. Forecasting depends critically on *correctly assessing the expectations* of the actors on the marketplace.

This is such an important aspect of economic prediction that we must take a moment to illustrate it. Let us look at the operation of a simple market, when the price of a commodity rises (perhaps because of a rise in the cost of producing it). In Figure 1 we see the result. Price moves from *OA* to *OB*; the quantity bought declines from *OX* to *OY*; and that is that. A new stable equilibrium has been reached.

But now let us introduce the matter of expectations. Suppose that consumers interpret the rise in the price of the commodity as indicating a further rise to come. They think: "This is only the beginning. Prices will be soon be worse." **Because of these changed expectations, a rational, maximizing pattern of behavior will lead to a different course of action.** Instead of buying less, consumers will buy more to stock up on the item before its price goes higher. In that case, the same increase in prices will lead to a shift in the demand curve, from *DD* to *D'D*. The quantity demanded will not fall, but will actually rise, as Figure 2 shows.

Hence a major element in all economic forecasting involves assumptions about the way actors in the market think about the future. Car manufacturers cut prices. Will that lead to a rise in sales? It will, if households expect that prices will rise again in the future, or will at least stay at their new levels. But if buyers read the cut in prices as a forerunner of future cuts, their rational maximizing behavior will lead

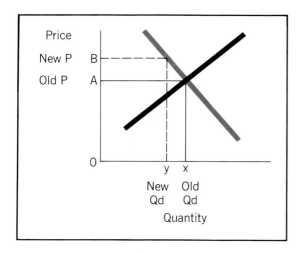

Figure 1

A NORMAL PRICE RESPONSE

A normal response to higher prices is a fall *in the quantity demanded (Q_d).*

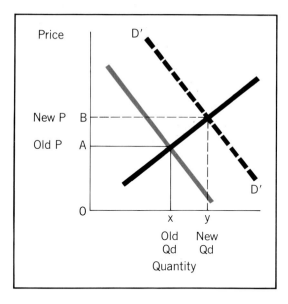

Figure 2
HOW EXPECTATIONS CHANGE
MARKET BEHAVIOR
*If expectations move the demand curve
out to D'D', higher prices will result in
an* increase *in* Q_d.

them to hold back and wait for bigger bargains to come. In that case, the price cut
will result in a drop in auto sales, not an increase.

One last complication. Expectations not only play a critical role in determining
how markets behave, but they are beyond direct observation. There is no way of
knowing what consumers think about the future because expectations are subject
to lightning changes. We all know the biggest difficulty in political polling is that
voters change their minds in the voting booth. The same problem complicates the
"polling" of economic expectations — a complication magnified by the fact that we
cast our economic votes much more frequently than our political ones.

3. THE SPEED OF ECONOMIC ADJUSTMENT. A third problem that plagues economic
forecasting involves the speed at which economic changes take place. When scientists predict the outcome of natural processes, they often know very clearly how
long it will take for the process under observation to reach its expected conclusion.
We know how rapidly the earth spins, the speed at which light travels, and a
number of other such constants that involve time. Even then, natural scientists
cannot always predict how rapidly changes will occur — the rain predicted for
today may arrive tomorrow.

Economists are in a much worse fix because they have no constants that involve
time. There are no regularities in economic life by which we can set our clocks. We
do not spend our incomes, or respond to price changes, or even work with clocklike
regularity. As a result, economic processes can take place slowly or rapidly. Markets, disturbed by some outside shock like a bad harvest, may restore order in a
matter of days or hours, or may fluctuate irregularly for weeks. Workers who have
been thrown out of their jobs may rapidly find new work, or may suffer unemploy-

ment for long periods of time. Businesspeople may respond to optimistic news quickly or slowly.

The speed at which the economy adjusts to changes — including the very important changes of government policy — profoundly affects forecasting. How many times have we not heard an economist whose predictions have failed to come true say: "Wait!" The difficulty is, of course, that no one can say how long to wait. Yet we can see that the pace of economic adjustment is bound to affect the rightness or wrongness of our economic pronouncements.

FROM PREDICTION TO UNDERSTANDING

It is clear that economic prediction is inherently fraught with problems. No one can foresee with 20-20 vision tomorrow's price of apples or next week's Dow Jones average, or next month's GNP. Indeed, we can see that exact prediction is beyond the capabilities of the science.

Commonsense Prediction

Is all prediction therefore illegitimate for economists? That is certainly not our conclusion. **In a powerful sense, it is impossible not to predict.** When we declare ourselves in favor of, or opposed to, any form of policy — a tax increase or decrease, high tariffs or no tariffs, it is because we are predicting the effect of such a policy on our nation's fortunes. On a smaller scale, when we decide to buy more or less of an item when its price changes, it is because we are predicting that the given change will or will not be followed by further changes in the same direction.

But how can we predict when we have just declared that prediction is beyond the reach of economics? Part of the answer lies in the degree of precision we expect of prediction. Exact prediction is impossible, but not workable predictions on which we can rely with a fair degree of certainty. A good many economic processes display a kind of stability that makes it possible to forecast their course within boundaries that are fairly narrow; others have no such built-in stabilizing properties. No one has yet invented a system for predicting the stock market, which can — and sometimes does — show tremendous jumps or declines. On the other hand, the day-to-day course of GNP cannot fluctuate like the stock market, as long as 100 million Americans get up in the morning and go to work (as economist Herbert Stein has put it).

Thus we can make much more reliable forecasts about the course of GNP than about that of the stock market. By the same token, however, our demands for accuracy rise, so that a forecast for GNP a year from now that is 10 percent off is deemed a failure, whereas such a forecast for the stock market would be a triumph.

Prediction vs. Expectations

A second approach to the problem draws a distinction between precise prediction and a general state of reasoned expectations. Even if we cannot predict the movements of the economy with a high degree of accuracy and a strictly fixed time schedule, **we can have informed anticipations of economic developments.** To the degree that we grasp the underlying forces and constraints of economic life, we can understand economic events as parts of a "system." The workings of the economy do not appear as inexplicable events sent by the gods, but as happenings that reveal—however deep below the surface—the presence and influence of economic regularities.

Not prediction, but reasoned expectations based on understanding is therefore the goal of economic science. These reasoned expectations can never attain the precision of an astronomer's calculations, so that two economists, telling us what tomorrow's economic weather will be, are as likely to disagree as to agree. Indeed, as long as observers differ in their assessments of such noneconomic factors as the nation's frame of mind, or its adaptability to change, or its stability of purpose and intention, they *must* come to different answers about the economic future.

Nevertheless, they will each try to reach reasoned conclusions about the shape of things to come, based on the application of economic laws (such as supply and demand or diminishing return) to the situation as they perceive it. They will talk about the future as emerging from the working out of a set of forces and constraints, not as mere chance.

FROM UNDERSTANDING TO ADVOCACY

A great deal of economic prediction is, in fact, economic advocacy. Or to put it the other way around, we often advocate economic policies, such as higher or lower taxes, because we predict that the effect of these changes will be favorable for the system. This introduces the question of values into the question of why economists disagree.

Values

Values are an inextricable part of all social thinking. We are "for" or "against" such matters as economic equality among citizens or among nations in much the same way that we are for or against political equality. One can argue endlessly about such matters, but there is no final court of appeal. In the end, values remain —values. They are social arrangements that we prefer, sometimes mildly, sometimes passionately. They are not conclusions that are irrefutably thrust upon us by logic.

Value judgments permeate many of our economic determinations. They deeply affect the manner in which economists perceive the social world, and as a result, they also affect the ways in which economists tell us that the economy will behave. Here are a few examples.

Producer vs. Consumer Well-Being

Many economic events affect us in two different ways—for instance, as producers and as consumers. When prices go up, they favor us if we are producers of that commodity, but not if we are consumers of it. When imports are taxed or otherwise restrained, we are grateful if we are workers in an industry whose existence is threatened by foreign competition, but resentful if we want to buy those goods as inexpensively as possible.

Which side of this clash of interests is entitled to preference—workers in American automobile plants or would-be buyers of Nissans and Hondas? As we will see when we study microeconomics and again when we look into foreign trade, that is a very hard question to answer. To a large degree it depends on the assumptions we make about how quickly and easily our economy will adjust to imports. If we think the adjustment will be quick and relatively painless, we will favor the consumer side. If not, we are likely to be more sympathetic to the producer side. Since some economists feel one way and some the other, they will disagree as to the policy we ought to follow—and as to the consequences of doing one thing or another.

Concentrated Pains, Diffuse Benefits

Another common case in which economists differ involves situations in which a given policy, or course of economic events, inflicts considerable pain on a few individuals, but benefits the general public. An instance in point might be a reduction in welfare payments that hurts poor families but lightens general taxes, or the lifting of rent controls that penalizes occupants of those apartments but stimulates the construction of new dwellings.

Once again, values come to the forefront. There is no cut and dried way of comparing the cost to those individuals who are adversely affected by the events or policies in question with the benefits for those who will gain. Much as with the opposed interests of producers and consumers, different economists will judge the situation differently, in part depending on their values—their "affinity" for those on each side; in part on their appraisal of how quickly and easily individuals and firms will respond to one set of arrangements or the other. The result is that one economist will be all for reducing welfare payments and easing our tax burdens, while another will be against it; one economist will seek to protect rent control and another will urge getting rid of it.

Values and Interests

Of course values enter here, too. There is no purely objective criterion that guides us when we decide whether the pains of unemployment or of relocation are justified by the gains to society. Our value judgments reign in these matters, although they may be buttressed by facts and figures. Yet, as we know from our own experience, there are often facts and figures on the other side too.

In this difficult question, we can often rely on one guide.**Our values are frequently, although not always, affected by our interests.** We learn to look with skepticism on the "disinterested" opinion of someone who stands to gain from one side or another of a dispute. The same applies, of course, to economic disputes. It would be a true cynic who declared that our judgments always reflect our selfish interests, but it would be a fool who declared that there was no connection between them. The fact that values normally and naturally incline us to one side or another of issues adds another degree of clarification to economic disagreements. Does the advocate of a policy stand to gain from its adoption? Do two economists in debate have affiliations with opposing economic groups? To the extent that that is the case, of course they will disagree. The only disreputable aspect of such a disagreement is to conceal one's interest, or pretend that it plays no role in one's judgment.

FROM VALUES TO CONCEPTIONS

Beneath values lies a still more deeply buried substratum on which differences are also based. There are fundamental perceptions about the nature of the economic system itself. We have already seen how differently capitalism looked to Adam Smith and Marx and Keynes. Those deeply divided perceptions continue to the present day, giving rise to many of the differences in economic pronouncements.

What are some of these ground-level disagreements? One of them is of special importance: the inherent stability or instability, self-correcting or self-destroying property of capitalism.

Is Capitalism Inherently Workable?

Adam Smith certainly believed in the workability of the system. Its success derived, in his view, from the inherent tendency of a market society to grow because of the driving force of its thrust for accumulation, and to adapt to change because of the mobility of its market institutions. Marx believed it was not workable because the very process of expansion, in the absence of any plan, would lead to crises of one sort or another. Keynes thought that capitalism might be workable, provided that government intervened to prevent it from long-lasting unemployment.

Many economists today strongly believe that Smith was essentially right, and that capitalism will work — if it is left alone. Obviously such economists predict a different outcome for the system than those who believe, along with Keynes, that the economy tends to settle down into a condition of persisting unemployment, unless the government steps in to remedy this state of affairs. And neither the Smith nor the Keynes-oriented economist will expect or predict the same outcome as someone influenced by Marx.

Which view of capitalism is correct? Economists have debated these matters for a long time, and have not come to any agreement. **Moreover, as we see it, one can legitimately perceive the economy from each of these (and perhaps still other) perspectives. There are aspects of the system that are strongly self-stabilizing and corrective, other aspects that are powerfully self-destabilizing and destructive, and still others in which the workability of the system appears to depend on the policies we undertake.**

At any rate, that is the point of view that will appear in this book, which adheres to no single school of thought. Recognizing the existence — and in our view, the validity — of multiple perspectives sheds still more light on the question of why economists disagree.

A Last Look at Disagreement

So it is clear that economists will continue to disagree. But it should also be clear that what they disagree about is not the nature of economic inquiry itself. Economists of all schools use the same basic tools of inquiry, talk about supply and demand and constraints of various kinds, rely on the idea of "maximizing" as the force that drives the system, and of "rationality" as the mind set that guides its actors. **There is, in other words, a language of economics common to all economists — the language we have set out to learn in this introduction to the subject.**

To speak the same language, however, is not to say the same thing. Economists disagree about matters that are fundamentally political or social, matters that are fraught with value suppositions and deeply held views about the economic world that are neither provable nor disprovable. From this point of view, being a good economist requires more than merely speaking its language well. One also has to have a keen sense of what the world is all about. That is a matter for which no introductory texts exist — nor any advanced ones, either.

looking back

KEY CONCEPTS

Disagreement is common among scientists

1 The fact that economics has science-like aspects does not exempt economists from disagreement. Scientists also disagree, as do philosophers and other scholars.

Forecasters often rely on different facts

2 Economic forecasters often differ for exactly the same reasons as do meteorologists. The data of the economic universe are too

numerous to be completely gathered, and too complex to be understandably ordered.

Humans possess wills and intentions and form expectations concerning the future. That also often makes their behavior unpredictable

3 In addition, economists deal with human beings, whose actions are influenced by wills and intentions and by expectations concerning the future. Expectations can turn our actions around 180°, because our rational maximizing impulse will cause us to hold back when prices fall and to rush in when prices rise — if we expect the fall or rise to worsen. If we expect the price change to be shortlived, our behavior will be just the opposite.

Uneven speeds of adjustment also cloud economic predictions

4 Further, accurate predictions are made more difficult because there are no constant speeds of behavioral adjustment in economic processes. Markets may move quickly or slowly — making predictions right or wrong, depending on the time frame of the predictor.

Workable predictions are made on the basis of inertia

5 Nonetheless, we all "predict" economic outcomes, both in our daily lives and as practicing economists. Often we do so on the basis of the natural stability or inertia of social processes. The question then is how accurately we can speak of their future course.

Reasoned explanation is the economists' goal, not exact prediction

6 Because exact predictions are impossible, the goal of economics might better be described as its ability to form reasoned explanations. These enable us to speak about the future as determined, however inexactly, by the kinds of regularities and processes we have previously looked into.

We often base advocacy on prediction. Values usually enter these decisions, as well as interests

7 Economic advocacy often involves prediction — we favor certain policies because we expect certain consequences to follow from their adoption. Advocacy also involves value judgments — deep-seated preferences concerning the desirability of various economic (or social) outcomes. Very often these values are revealed in our preferences for one side or another when economic processes benefit some but not all. In turn, our values are often determined by our interests.

Preconceptions about the workings of capitalism also affect our judgment

8 As deep as our values are basic conceptions about the nature of the economic system itself, in particular about the inherent tendencies of a capitalist system. There is no general agreement among economists as to whether the system has stabilizing, destructive, or correctible aspects. Our own belief is that it contains all three, so that different conceptions are legitimate concerning different aspects of its workings. This too introduces a reason for the disagreement among economists.

Despite these disagreements, economics provides a language of discourse

9 Disagreements are therefore built into the nature of economic understanding. Nonetheless, economists have devised a language that enables them to speak in widely shared meanings about the properties of their subject. This language is economics.

ECONOMIC VOCABULARY

QUESTIONS

1. What is the difference between the "behavior" of an atomic particle and that of a buyer or seller?
2. Describe a scenario in which expectations make prices rise instead of fall, as we would normally expect. And vice versa.
3. What characteristics would we have to expect of stock traders to give us the grounds for a reliable prediction of stock prices?
4. Can you suggest some general attributes of our economic system that seem to have self-stabilizing tendencies? Self-destabilizing ones? How about sales of commodities like salt for one, and runs on banks for another?
5. Are you aware of value preconceptions in yourself? For example, do you think that men and women are entitled to equal pay for equal work? That economic inequality is acceptable, but not political inequality?

CHAPTER 10
An Economist's Kit of Tools

a look ahead

This is a chapter about concepts and techniques. It isn't about "economics," but about some ideas, simple statistical devices, and other tools with which every economist must be familiar. There is no single, large idea to keep in mind as you go through this chapter. We suspect that for most students it will be very easy; easy or hard, it has to be mastered. Keep a list of the six ideas as they come, and check them off against the review in "Looking Back" after you have finished.

This chapter will give us a series of concepts and techniques that we will use in thinking clearly about economics. Some of them seem very simple but are more subtle than they appear at first. Others look demanding at first, even though they are actually very simple. There are six of these intellectual tools. Try to master them, for we will be using them continuously from now on.

CETERIS PARIBUS

The first concept is the need to eliminate outside influences that might invalidate our efforts to make scientific statements about economic behavior. If we were physicists trying to arrive at the formula for gravitation, for instance, we would have to make allowances for wind or air resistance in calculating the force that gravity really exerts. So in economics we have to eliminate disturbing influences from our observations. We do so by making the assumption that "other things" remain constant while we focus on the particular relationships we're interested in.

This assumption of holding "other things equal" is called by its Latin name, *ceteris paribus.* It is extremely easy to apply in theory and extremely difficult in practice. In our examination of the demand curve, for example, we assume that the *income* and *tastes* of the person (or of the collection of persons) are unchanged while we examine the influence of price on the quantities of shoes they are willing and able to buy. The reason is obvious. If we allow their incomes or tastes to change, both their willingness *and* their ability would also change. If prices doubled but a fad for shoes developed, or if prices tripled but income quadrupled, we would not find that demand decreased as prices rose.

Ceteris paribus is applied every time we speak of supply and demand and on many other occasions as well. Since we know that in reality prices, tastes, incomes, population size, technology, moods, and many other elements of society are continually changing, we can see why this is a heroic assumption. It is one that is almost impossible to trace in actual life or to correct for fully by special statistical techniques.

Yet we can also see that unless we apply *ceteris paribus*, **at least in our minds, we cannot isolate the particular interactions and causal sequences that we want to investigate.** The economic world then becomes a vast Chinese puzzle. Every piece interlocks with every other, and no one can tell what the effect of any one thing is on any other. If economics is to be useful, it must be able to tell us something about the effect of changing *only* price or *only* income or *only* taste or any *one* of a number of other things. We can do so only by assuming that other things are equal and by holding them unchanged in our minds while we perform the intellectual experiment in whose outcome we are interested.

STATICS AND DYNAMICS: THE IMPORTANCE OF TIME

Of all the sources of difficulty that creep into economic analysis, none is more vexing than *time*. The reason is that time changes all manner of things and makes it virtually impossible to apply *ceteris paribus*. That is why, for example, we always mean "within a fixed period of time" when we speak of something like diminishing marginal utility. There is no reason for the marginal utility of a meal tomorrow to be less than one today, but good reason to think that a second lunch on top of the first will bring a sharp decline in utilities.

So too, supply and demand curves presumably describe activities that take place within a short period of time, ideally within an instant. The longer the time period covered, the less is *ceteris* apt to be *paribus*.

This poses many difficult problems for economic analysis, because it means that we must use a "static" (or timeless) set of theoretical ideas to solve "dynamic" (or time-consuming) questions. The method we will use to cope with this problem is called *comparative statics*. We compare an economic situation at one period with an economic situation at a later period, without investigating in much detail the path we travel from the first situation to the second. To inquire into the path requires calculus and advanced economic analysis. We'll leave that for another course.

FUNCTIONAL RELATIONSHIPS

Economics, it is already very clear, is about relationships — relationships of human beings and nature, and relationships of individuals to one another. The laws of diminishing marginal utility or diminishing returns or supply and demand are all statements of those relationships, which we can use to explain or predict economic matters.

We call relationships that portray the effect of one thing on another *functional relationships.* Functional relationships may relate the effect of price on the quantities offered or bought, or the effect of successive inputs of the same factor on outputs of a given product, or the effect of population growth on economic growth, or whatever.

One important point: Functional relationships are not logical relationships of the kind we find in geometry or arithmetic, such as the square of the hypotenuse of a right triangle being equal to the sum of the squares of the other two sides, or the number 6 being the product of 2 times 3 or 3 times 2. Functional relationships cannot be discovered by deductive reasoning. They are descriptions of real events that we can discover only by empirical investigation. We then search for ways of expressing these relationships in graphs or mathematical terms. In economics, the technique used for discovering these relationships is called *econometrics*.

IDENTITIES

Before going on, we must clarify an important distinction between functional relationships and another kind of relationship called an *identity*. We need this distinction because both relationships use the word *equals*, although the word has different meanings in the two cases.

A few pages ahead we shall meet the expression

$$Q_d = f(P)$$

which we read "Quantity demanded (Q_d) *equals* or *is* a function of price ($= f(P)$)." This refers to the kind of relationship we have been talking about. We shall also find another kind of "equals," typified by the statement $P \equiv S$ or purchases equals sales. $P \equiv S$ is *not* a functional relationship, because purchases do not "depend" on sales. They are *the same thing* as sales, viewed from the vantage point of the buyer instead of the seller. P and S are identities: Q and P are not. The identity sign is $\equiv$.

Identities are true by definition. They cannot be "proved" true or false, because there is nothing to be proved. On the other hand, when we say that the quantity purchased will depend on price, there is a great deal to be proved. Empirical investigation may disclose that the suggested relationship is not true. It may show that a relationship exists but that the nature of the relationship is not always the same. Identities are changeless as well as true. They are logical statements that require no investigations of human action. The signs $\equiv$ and $=$ do not mean the same thing.

Sometimes identities and behavioral equations are written in the same manner with an equal sign ($=$). Technically, identities should be written with an identity sign ($\equiv$). Unfortunately, the sign also reads "equals." Since it is important to know the difference between definitions, which do not need proof, and hypotheses, which *always* need demonstration or proof, we shall carefully differentiate between the equal sign ($=$) and the identity sign ($\equiv$). **Whenever you see an equal sign, you will know that a behavioral relationship is being hypothesized. When you see the identity sign, you will know that a definition is being offered, not a statement about behavior.**

Identities, being definitions, deserve our attention because they are the way we establish a precise working language. Learning this language, with its special vocabulary, is essential to being able to speak economics accurately.

SCHEDULES

We are familiar with the next item in our kit of intellectual tools. It is one of the techniques used to establish functional relationships: the technique of drawing up *schedules* or lists of the different values of elements.

We met such schedules in Chapter 7, in our lists of the quantities of shoes supplied or demanded at various prices. **Schedules are thus the empirical or hypothetical data whose functional interconnection we wish to investigate.** As working economists, we would experience many problems in drawing up such schedules in real life. We often use them, however, in economic analysis, as examples of typical economic behavior.

GRAPHS

The depiction of functional relationships through schedules is simple enough, but economists usually prefer to represent these relationships by graphs or equations. This is so because schedules show the relationship only between *specific* quantities and prices or specific data of any kind. **Graphs and equations show *generalized* relationships, relationships that cover all quantities and prices or all values of any two things we are interested in.**

The simplest and most intuitively obvious method of showing a functional relationship in its general form is through a graph. Everyone is familiar with graphs of one kind or another, but not all graphs show functional relationships. A graph of stock prices over time, as in Figure 1, shows us the level of prices in different periods. It does not show a behavioral connection between a date and a price. Such a graph merely describes and summarizes history. No one would maintain that such and such a date *caused* stock market prices to take such and such a level.

UPWARD-SLOPING DEMAND CURVES

Although most demand curves slope downward, in three interesting cases they do not. The first concerns certain *luxury* goods in which the price itself becomes part of the "utility" of the good. The perfume Joy used to be extensively advertised as "the world's most expensive perfume." Do you think its sales would have increased if the price had been lowered and the advertisement changed to read "the world's second-most expensive perfume"?

The other case affects just the opposite kind of good: certain basic staples. Here the classic case is potatoes. In nineteenth-century Ireland, potatoes formed the main diet for very poor farmers. As potato prices rose, Irish peasants were forced to cut back on their purchases of other foods to devote more of their incomes to buying this necessity of life. More potatoes were purchased, even though prices were rising, because potatoes were still the cheapest thing to eat.

Such goods have upward-sloping demand curves. The higher the price, the more you (are forced to) buy. Of course, when potatoes reach price levels that compete with, say, wheat, any further price rises will result in a fall in the quantity demanded, since buyers will shift to wheat.

Figure 1
STOCK MARKET PRICES
Some graphs, like this one, just show how a given variable behaves over time. **Source:** *Moody's Handbook of Common Stocks.* (Summer 1985).

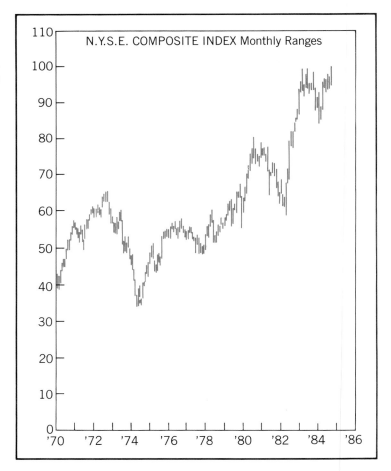

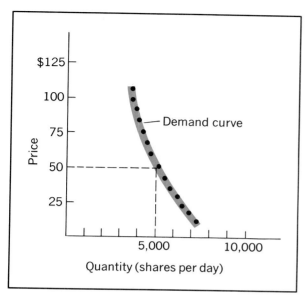

Figure 2

PRICE-QUANTITY RELATIONSHIP OF A GIVEN SHARE
Other graphs, like this one, depict relationships. There is more about this in the extra word following this chapter.

On the other hand, a graph that related the price of a stock and the quantities that we are willing and able to buy *at that price, ceteris paribus,* is indeed a graphic depiction of a functional relation. If we look at the hypothetical graph below, we can note the dots that show us the particular price-quantity relationships. Now we can tell the quantity that would be demanded at any price, simply by going up the price axis, over to the demand curve, and down to the quantity axis. In Figure 2, for example, at a price of $50 the quantity demanded is 5,000 shares per day.*

EQUATIONS

A third way of representing functional relationships is often used for its simplicity and brevity. **Equations are very convenient means of expressing functional relationships, since they allow us to consider the impact of more than one factor at a time.** A typical equation for demand might look like this:

$$Q_d = f(P)$$

Most of us are familiar with equations but may have forgotten their vocabulary. There are three terms in the equation above: Q_d, f, and P. Each has a name. We are

* Technically we would need a schedule of survey results showing the quantities demanded for every conceivable price in order to draw a graph. In fact, we obtain results for a variety of prices and assume that the relationship between the unmeasured points is like that of the measured points. The process of sketching in unmeasured points is called *interpolation.*

interested in seeing how our quantity demanded (Q_d) is affected by changes in price (P). In other words, our "demand" is dependent on changes in price. Therefore the term Q_d is called the **dependent variable**: "variable" because it changes; "dependent" because it depends on changes in P. As we would imagine, the name for P is the **independent variable.**

Now for the term f. The definition of f is simply **function** or "function of," so that we read $Q_d = f(P)$ as "quantity demanded is a function of price." If we knew that the quantity demanded was a function of both price *and* income (Y), we would write $Q_d = f(P,Y)$. Such equations tell us what independent variables affect what dependent variables, but they do not tell us *how* Q_d changes with changes in P or Y.

The "how" depends on our actual analysis of actual market behavior. Let us take a very simple case for illustrative purposes. Suppose that a survey of consumer purchasing intentions tells us that consumers would take 100 units of a product if its price were zero — that is, if it were given away free — and that they would buy one-half unit less each time the price went up by \$1. The demand equation would then be:

$$Q_d = 100 - .5(P)$$

Thus, if price were \$10, buyers would take $100 - .5 \times 10$, or 95 units.*

We should stop to note one important property of ordinary price-quantity demand or supply functions. It is that they have opposite "signs." A normal demand function is negative, showing the quantities demanded *fall* as prices rise. A supply function is usually positive, showing that quantities supplied *rise* as prices rise. A survey of producers might tell us that the quantity supplied would go up by 2 units for every \$1 increase in price, or

$$Q_s = 2(P)$$

Note that the sign of the function 2 is positive, whereas the sign of the demand function was negative, $-.5$.

ECONOMIC TECHNIQUES REVIEWED

The basic assumptions that economics makes regarding economic society can be summed up in two sets of general propositions or laws — laws about behavior and laws about production. What we have been learning in this chapter are the *techniques* of economic analysis — the ways in which economics uses its basic premises.

* Suppose we wanted an equation that would measure the effect on quantity demanded of both price and income (see box p. 176). Such an equation might be:

$$Q_d = 100 - .5(P) + .1(Y)$$
$$\text{where } Y = \text{income}$$

In this equation the quantity demanded goes *up* by 100 units whenever incomes rise by \$1,000. As before, it goes *down* by ½ unit as prices rise by \$1. If incomes were \$2,000 and P were \$10, the quantity demanded would be $(100 - .5 \times 10 + .1 \times 2,000) = 295$ units.

These techniques, as we have seen, revolve around the central idea of functional relationships. Because behavior or production is sufficiently regular, functions enable us to explain or predict economic activity. Their relationships are presented in the form of graphs or equations derived from the underlying schedules of data.

As we have seen, the ability to establish functional relationships depends critically on the *ceteris paribus* assumption. Unless we hold other things equal, either by econometric means or simply in our heads, we cannot isolate the effect of one variable on another.

ECONOMIC FALLACIES

No chapter on the mode of economic thought would be complete without reference to *economic fallacies*. **Actually there is no special class of fallacies that is called economic. The mistakes we find in economic thought are only examples of a larger class of mistaken ways of thinking that we call fallacies.** But they are serious enough to justify a warning in general and some attention to one fallacy in particular.

The general warning can do no more than ask us to be on guard against the sloppy thinking that can make fools of us in any area. It is easy to fall into errors of false syllogisms,* of trying to prove an argument *post hoc, ergo propter hoc* ("after the fact, therefore because of the fact"). An example would be "proving" that government spending must be inflationary by pointing out that the government spent large sums during periods when inflation was present, ignoring other factors that may have been at work.

The gallery of such mistaken conclusions is all too large in all fields. One fallacy that has a special relevance to economics is called the **fallacy of composition.** Suppose we had an island community in which all farmers sold their produce to one another. Suppose further that one farmer was able to get rich by cheating: selling his produce at the same price as everyone else, but putting fewer vegetables into his bushel baskets. Does it not follow that all farmers could get rich if all cheated?

We can see that there is a fallacy here. Where does it arise? In the first example, when our cheating farmer got rich, we ignored a small side effect of his action. The side effect was that a loss in real income was inflicted on the community. To ignore that side effect was proper so long as our focus of attention was what happened to the one farmer. When we broaden our inquiry to the entire community, the loss of income becomes a consideration. Everyone loses as much by being shortchanged as he gains by shortchanging. The side effects have become central effects. What was true for one turns out not to be true for all. Later on, in macroeconomics, we will find a very important example of exactly such a fallacy when we encounter what is called the Paradox of Thrift.

---

* See the questions at the end of this chapter.

EQUILIBRIUM IN EQUATIONS

It is very easy to see the equilibrium point when we have a supply curve and a demand curve that cross. But since equations are only another way of representing the information that curves show, we must be able to demonstrate equilibrium in equations. Here is a simple example:

Suppose the demand function, as before, is:

$Q_d = 100 - .5 (P)$, and that the supply function is:
$Q_s = 2(P)$

The question is, then, what value for P will make Q_d equal to Q_s? The answer follows:

If $Q_d = Q_s$, then $100 - .5(P) = 2(P)$.

Putting all the P's on one side
$2(P) + .5(P) = 100$, or $2.5p = 100$. Solving, $P = 40$.

Substituting a price of 40 into the demand equation we get a quantity of 80. In the supply equation we also get 80. Thus 40 must be the equilibrium price.

looking back

KEY CONCEPTS	This is a chapter about the concepts and techniques of economic analysis, not about the basic assumptions underlying economic theory. We should become familiar with a few of these ideas, or tools.
Ceteris paribus	1 *Ceteris paribus* is the assumption that everything other than the two variables whose relationship is being investigated is kept equal. Without *ceteris paribus* we cannot discern functional relationships.
Functional relationships	2 Functional relationships showing that X depends on Y lie at the very center of economic analysis. They are not logical or deductive relationships but relationships that we discover by *empirical investigation*.

Identities	**3** Identities are purely definitional, therefore not subject to proof or to empirical investigation. Such definitions can, however, be very important.
Schedules, graphs, and equations	**4** The three techniques used to present functional relationships are: **a.** Schedules, or lists of data **b.** Graphs, or visual representations **c.** Equations
Independent and dependent variables functions	**5** You should know the meaning of three equational terms: the *independent variable*, the causative element that interests us; the *dependent variable*, the element whose behavior is affected by the independent variable; and the *function*, a mathematical statement of the relation between the two. Read the sentence $x = f(y)$ as "*x* is a function of *y*." Here, *x* is the dependent variable; *y* is the independent variable.
Fallacy of composition	**6** Finally, learn to be on guard against economic fallacies, especially against the fallacy of composition.

ECONOMIC VOCABULARY

QUESTIONS

1. Suppose you would acquire 52 books a year if books were free, but that your acquisitions would drop by 5 books for every $5 that you had to pay. Can you write a demand function for books?

2. Can you write a hypothetical function that might relate your demand for food and the price of food, assuming *ceteris paribus*?

3. "The quantity of food bought equals the quantity sold." Is this statement a functional relationship? If not, why not? Is it an identity?

4. Here is a schedule of supply and demand:

Price	Units Supplied	Units Demanded
$1	0	50
2	5	40
3	10	30
4	20	25
5	30	20
6	50	10

Does the schedule show an equilibrium price? Can you draw a graph and approximate the equilibrium price? What is it?

5. How do we read aloud the following? $C = f(Y)$ where C = consumption and Y = income. Which is the independent variable? The dependent?

6. Which of the following statements is a fallacy?

All X is Y

  Z is Y

Therefore Z is X

All X is Y

  Z is X

Therefore Z is Y

Try substituting classes of objects for the Xs and Y, and individual objects for the Zs. Example: All planets (Xs) are heavenly bodies (Y). The sun (Z) is a heavenly body (Y). Therefore the sun (Z) is a planet (X). Clearly, a false syllogism. *Other fallacies:*

If I can move to the head of the line, all individuals can move to the head of the line.

If I can save more by spending less, all individuals should be able to save more by spending less. *Hint:* If all spend less, what will happen to our incomes?

The fact that Lenin called inflation a major weapon that could destroy the bourgeoisie indicates that inflations are part of the communist strategy for the overthrow of capitalism.

AN EXTRA WORD ABOUT

Graphs and Economic Causation

Many students worry a great deal about drawing graphs and worry very little about what graphs show. They are wrong on both counts. The technique of graphing is essentially simple. What graphs show is not.

USES OF GRAPHS

Some graphs show the movement of a variable over time — for example, stock market prices. No one is perplexed by graphs of this kind. But other graphs show relationships. These are the graphs that worry students. Here are some hints to help you to draw these kinds of graphs.

1. Always begin by labeling the axes of a graph. Even the most common supply and demand type of graph should have one label identified as price (or *P*) and another as quantity (or *Q*). No mistake is as frequent as omitting *P*s and *Q*s or whatever identifying symbols are called for on a graph.

2. Each point on a graph represents two variables. Each point shows what value of *X* is related to a given value of *Y* — e.g., what quantity is offered (or bought) at a given price. Therefore every point must always be referred to *both* axes. In the figure at the bottom of the page for example, point *H* shows *five* units of quantity offered at a price of *six* dollars. Five units and six dollars are called the *coordinates* of point *H*.

3. Curves show how relationships vary. A given dot shows the relation of only one pair of coordinates, such as five units and six dollars. A curve shows the relationship of many pairs of coordinates for the function we are interested in. The upward curve *FGH* shows how *P* and *Q* vary for sellers, for instance. Another curve, *ABC*, shows a relationship with a

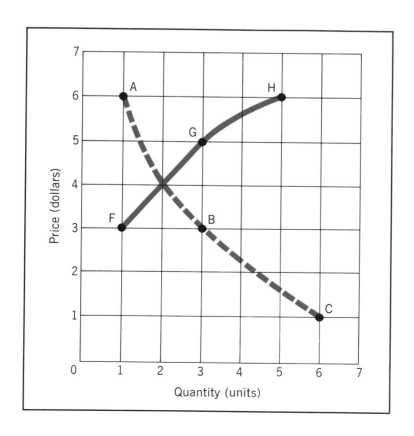

downward slope, perhaps for buyers. What are the actual values of *P* and *Q* at points *A*, *B*, and *C*? What, if any, coordinates are shared by both curves?

4. Graphs should be carefully drawn.   Very often a graph represents an important idea visually. It may show that a pair of coordinates lies on *two* curves, as does the equilibrium point in the standard supply-demand graph. Or it may show that one curve touches another at just one point, which also means that the two curves have one pair of coordinates in common. When you draw a curve, you are *describing* a relationship: Be sure you describe it right. On p. 181 are two freehand examples for you to study.

5.   Professor Edwin Dolan writes in *Basic Economics,* ''When you come to a chapter in this book that is full of graphs, how should you study it? The first and most important rule is do *not ever memorize graphs.*'' Professor Dolan is so right! Graphs come last, to capsulize what you know. They never come first, to tell you what you *should* know. Graphs are a pictorial shorthand for ideas, usually ideas about functional relationships (curves) and their interconnections. Learn the economics and the graphs will follow. Learn the graphs — and you will know only geometry.

CORRELATION

That was the easy part of understanding graphs. Now for the hard part. Most students think that graphs ''explain'' things. They look at a graph of a demand curve and say ''The lower price *causes* us to buy more.'' They look at a graph showing a nice regular pattern between variable *A* and variable *B*, and they assume that this pattern of ''correlation'' implies an explanation.

Here's an example. On the left, p. 182, we have plotted the shoe size and the IQs of a group of seniors. No pattern — no ''correlation'' — is visible.

Hence no one assumes that large shoe sizes cause high IQs. In the graph on the right, we correlate a sample of the heights and the IQs of a number of individuals. There is a clearly visible pattern or correlation.

Does this mean that height causes IQ to increase? Certainly not. Height is associated with age. Our graph happens to cover a population that includes both infants and adults, and so of course there is a correlation, but it is not a causal one. Height does not *cause* IQ. It is associated with IQ through the mediating factor of age and maturity. Lesson: **Be very, very careful of jumping to conclusions about causes just from the evidence of associations, or correlations.**

Here are a few examples for you to think about.

1. Wrong-way causation.   It is a statistical fact that there is a positive correlation between the number of babies born in various cities of northwestern Europe and the number of storks' nests in those cities. Is this evidence that storks really do bring babies? The answer is that we are using a correlation to establish a causal connection the wrong way. The true line of causation lies in the opposite direction. Cities that have more children tend to have more houses, which offer storks more chimneys to build their nests in!

2. Spurious causation.   Suppose there was a positive correlation all during the 1970s between the cost of living in Paris and the numbers of Americans visiting there. Does that imply that American visitors were the cause of price increases in that city?

Here at least there is little danger of getting the causal links back to front. Few people would argue that more Americans visited Paris *because* its prices were going up. It would be equally difficult to argue that American tourists were the cause of rising Parisian prices,

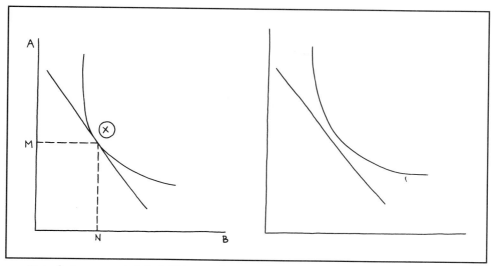

Note that axes are labeled. This graph shows that there is one point (X), where there is a common pair of coordinates, M and N, for two functions or curves.

Note axes are not labeled. The graph shows that there is no point where one pair of coordinates relates to both curves. Is that what you want to show?

simply because the total amount of American spending was small in relation to the total amount of expenditure in Paris.

The answer, then, is that the correlation is spurious in terms of causality, although it is real in terms of sheer statistics. The true explanation for the correlation is that the rising numbers of American visitors and the rising costs of living in Paris were both aspects of a worldwide expansion in incomes and prices. Neither was the "cause" of the other. Both were the results of more fundamental, broader-ranging phenomena.

***3. The problem of* ceteris paribus.**   Finally, we must consider again the now familiar problem of "other things being equal." Suppose we correlate prices and sales, in order to test the hypothesis that lower prices "cause" us to increase the quantities we buy. Now suppose that the correlation turns out to be very poor. Does that disprove the hypothesis? Not necessarily. First we have to find out what happened to income during this period. We also have to find out what, if anything, happened to our tastes. We might also have to consider changes in the prices of other, competitive goods.

As we know, this problem affects all scientific tests, not just those of economics. Scientists cannot test the law of gravitation unless "other things" are equal, such as an absence of air that would cause a feather to fall much more slowly than Galileo predicted. The trouble with the social sciences is that the "other things" are often more difficult to spot—or just to think of—than they are in the laboratory.

WHAT CAN CORRELATION TELL US?

These (and still other) pitfalls make economists extremely cautious about using correlations to "prove" causal hypotheses. ***Even the closest correlation may not show in which direction the causal influences are working.***

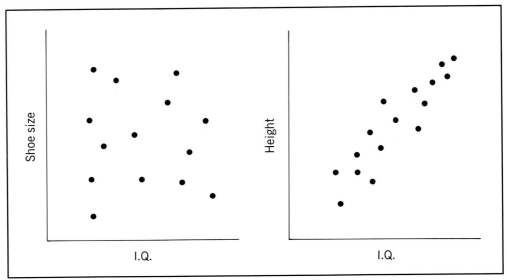

No pattern or correlation exists here.   *A clear pattern or correlation is visible.*

So too, the interconnectedness of the economic process often causes many series of data to move together. In inflationary periods, for example, most prices tend to rise, or in depression many indexes tend to fall, without establishing that any of these series was directly responsible for a movement in another particular series.

Finally, economists are constantly on the lookout for factors that have not been held constant during correlation, so that ceteris paribus conditions were not in fact maintained.

Is there an answer to such puzzling problems of correlation and causation? There is a partial answer. We cannot claim that a correlation is proof that a causal relationship exists. But every valid hypothesis — economic or other — *must* show a high and "significant" correlation coefficient between "cause" and "effect," provided that we are reasonably certain that our statistical test has rigorously excluded spurious correlations and unsuspected "other things."

This exclusion is often very difficult, sometimes impossible to achieve with real data. A physicist can hold "other things equal" in his laboratory, but the world will not stand still just so an economist can test his theories. ***The net result is that correlations are a more powerful device for disproving hypotheses than for proving them.*** All we can say on the positive side is that a causal relationship is likely to exist (or at least has not been shown *not* to exist) when we can demonstrate a strong correlation backed by solid reasoning.

PART THREE

macroeconomics

CHAPTER 11
GNP — The Nation's Output

a look ahead

Here we begin a section of four chapters whose overall purpose is to give us a first working knowledge of how the macroeconomy works. We are going to gain this knowledge in four steps. In Chapter 11, immediately ahead, we learn what GNP consists of, how economists describe and define it. In Chapter 12, we move to the question of how GNP is "sustained"—that is, where the purchasing power comes from that enables production to go on year after year. In Chapter 13, we go from sustaining GNP to increasing it, as we look more deeply than before into the sources of economic growth. And finally, in the last chapter of our section, we investigate the savings-investment relationship, the critical link in the macroeconomic system of a capitalist economy.

Chapter 11 presents us with two tasks.

1 We learn the vocabulary that economists use in describing GNP and its components. These definitions should be learned by heart—you cannot "speak economics" unless you know these words and phrases and their meaning.

2 We look into the question of the degree to which GNP is a reliable indicator of our well-being. This is a more reflective, less exact part of our introduction to GNP, but certainly not a less important one.

What is *macroeconomics*? The word derives from the Greek *macro* meaning "big," and the implication is therefore that it is concerned with bigger problems than is microeconomics (*micro* = small). Yet microeconomics wrestles with problems that are quite as large as those of macroeconomics. The difference is really not one of scale; it is one of approach, of original angle of incidence. **Macroeconomics begins from a viewpoint that initially draws our attention to aggregate economic phenomena and processes, such as the growth of total output.** Microeconomics begins from a vantage point that first directs our analysis to the workings of the marketplace. Both views are needed to comprehend the economy as a whole, just as it takes two different lenses to make a stereophoto jump into the round. Since we can learn only one view at a time, we now turn to the spectacle of the entire national economy as it unfolds to the macroscopic gaze.

The Macro Perspective

What does the economy look like from the macro perspective? We look down on the economy as from a plane, to see it as a vast landscape stretching from one horizon to the other. We know that this landscape is populated by business firms, households, and government agencies, but from the macro perspective, as from an airplane, it is not these individual features that stand out. Instead, the focus is on a process of central and crucial importance that is more easily perceived from above than from ground level. This is the ceaseless activity of production on a national scale, the never-ending creation and re-creation of wealth by which the country replenishes and renews and expands its material life.

OUTPUT

How does this flow of production arise? Later, in microeconomics, we investigate motives that lead factors of production to offer their services to business firms, and motives that lead entrepreneurs to hire factors. A macro perspective, however, studies the market process from a somewhat different standpoint, one that focuses on the stream of output as a whole, rather than tracing it back to its individual springs and rivulets.

It may help us picture the flow as a whole if we imagine that each and every good and service that is produced — each loaf of bread, each nut and bolt, each doctor's service, each theatrical performance, each car, ship, lathe, or bolt of cloth — can be identified and followed as a radioactive isotope allows us to follow the circulation of certain kinds of cells through the body. Then if we look down on the economic panorama, we can see the continuous combination of land, labor, and capital giving off a continuous flow of "lights" as goods and services emerge in their salable form.

Intermediate Goods

Where do these lights go? Many are soon extinguished. **The goods or services they represent are *intermediate* goods that are incorporated into other products to form more fully finished items of output.** Thus, from our aerial perspective we can follow a product such as cotton from the fields to the spinning mill, where its light is extinguished, for there the cotton disappears into a new product—yarn. In turn, the light of the yarn traces a path as it leaves the spinning mill by way of sale to the textile mill, there to be doused as the yarn disappears into a new good—cloth. Again, cloth leaving the textile mill lights a way to the factory where it will become part of an article of clothing.

A First "Final" Good: Consumption

And what of the clothing? **Here at last we have what the economist calls a *final* good. Why "final"? Because once in the possession of its ultimate owner, the clothing passes out of the active economic flow.** As a good in the hands of a consumer, it is no longer an object on the marketplace. Its light is now extinguished permanently; or if we wish to complete our image, we can imagine it fading gradually as the clothing disappears into the utility of the consumer. In the case of consumer goods like food or of consumer services like recreation, the light goes out faster, for these items are "consumed" as soon as they reach their final destination.* We call the expenditures that are made for private household consumption —not for public consumption, such as education— **personal consumption expenditures.**

We shall have a good deal to learn in later chapters about the macroeconomic behavior of consumers. What we should notice in this first view is the supreme importance of this flow of production into consumers' hands. By this vital process, the population replenishes or increases its energies and ministers to its wants and needs. If the process were halted very long, society would perish. That is why we speak of *consumption* as the ultimate end and aim of all economic activity.

A Second Final Good: Investment

Nevertheless, for all the importance of consumption, if we look down on the illuminated flow of output we see a surprising thing. Whereas the greater portion of the final goods and services of the economy is bought by the human agents of

---

* In fact, of course, they are not *really* consumed but remain behind as garbage, junk, wastes, and so on. Economics used to ignore these residuals, but it does so no longer.

production for their consumption, we also find that a lesser but still considerable flow of final products is not. What happens to it?

If we follow an appropriate good, we may find out. Watch the destination of steel leaving a Pittsburgh mill. Some of it, like our cotton cloth, will become incorporated into consumer goods, ending up as cans, automobiles, or household articles. But some will not find its way to a consumer at all. Instead, it will end up as part of a machine or an office building or a railroad track.

Now in a way these goods are not "final," for they are used to produce still further goods or services. The machine produces output of some kind; the building produces office space, the rail track produces transportation. Yet there is a difference between such goods, used for production, and consumer goods, like clothing. The difference is that the machine, the office building, and the track are goods that are used by business enterprises as part of their permanent productive equipment. In terms of our image, these goods slowly lose their light-giving powers as their services pass into flows of production, but usually they are replaced with new goods before their light is extinguished.

That is why we call them *capital goods* or *investment goods*, as distinguished from consumer goods. As part of our capital, they will be preserved, maintained, and renewed, perhaps indefinitely. Hence the stock of capital, like consumers, constitutes a final destination for output.

Gross and Net Investment

We call the great stream of output that goes to capital *gross investment*. The very word *gross* suggests that it conceals a finer breakdown; and looking more closely, we can see that the flow of output going to capital does indeed serve two distinct purposes. Part of it is used to replace the capital — machines, buildings, track, or whatever — that has been used up in the process of production. Just as the human agents of production have to be replenished by a flow of consumption goods, so the material agents of production need to be maintained and renewed if their contribution to output is to remain undiminished. We call the part of gross investment whose purpose is to keep society's stock of capital intact replacement investment, or simply **replacement.**

Sometimes the total flow of output going to capital is not large enough to maintain the existing stock, as for example when we allow inventories (a form of capital) to become depleted, or when we simply fail to replace worn-out equipment or plant. This running down of capital we call **disinvestment,** meaning the very opposite of investment. Instead of maintaining or building up capital, we are literally consuming it.

Not all gross investment is used for replacement purposes, however. Some of the flow may *increase* the stock of capital by adding buildings, machines, track, inventory, and so on. **If the total output consigned to capital is sufficiently great not only to make up for wear and tear but to increase the capital stock, we say there has been new or net investment, or net capital formation.**

A Third Final Good: Government Purchases

While consumption by private households and investment by private firms constitute by far the greater part of the final disposition of goods and services, government also plays a role in the composition of output. Rather, it plays two roles. A small part of final output is *directly produced* by government activity — for example, the clean water produced by a local sewage treatment plant, or the services produced by firefighters, teachers, or the armed forces. Another part is not directly produced by government but is *bought* by it. Thus, the bulk of the equipment used by the armed forces is produced by private contractors. Roads and school buildings are generally built by private firms, with local, state or federal agencies playing the role of buyer, not producer.

In either event — whether the government itself produces output or buys it from a private producer — we treat these *government purchases of goods and services* as a category of final output. Taken in their entirety, these public goods and services come to about a quarter of our total final production.

Two Oddities

There are two odd aspects of this government part of final demand. The first is that our system of national accounting does not indicate whether a government purchase is for consumption or investment. Whether government spends its income for such purposes as to provide weather information (it is hard to think of a more fleeting service) or for a vast dam (it is hard to think of a more durable good), it is all one and the same to the statisticians who tot up the national accounts. Both items are lumped under a single category — government purchases — rather than being classified as government investment or government consumption. Later we will see that this has considerable consequences in assessing the national deficit.

The second odd aspect to government is that a very large flow of government spending does not show up in our final output at all! This is the flow we call *transfer payments,* the most important of which are social security. Why do we not count social security in GNP? The answer is that transfer payments show up in other categories of final demand. When a household spends its social security check, that is counted as part of personal consumption expenditures. When a firm, such as a farm, spends a government subsidy (also a transfer payment), that too shows up somewhere in the flow of output, perhaps as the payment for an intermediate good. To count the social security or the subsidy check as a direct part of final output would be to include it twice — once when it was paid out, and once when it was spent.

Transfer payments are an extremely important form of government policy by which it seeks to redistribute incomes. We will be looking into the use — and abuse — of transfer payments, especially those for welfare purposes, as we move further into macroeconomic policy. In the meantime, it is important to understand why we do not include welfare, or subsidies, or any other form of transfer as part of our flow of production.

A *Final* Final Good: Net Exports

Finally, let us pay heed to a small flow of production that has previously escaped our notice. This is the net flow of goods and services that leaves the country; that is, the total flow going abroad minus the flow that enters. This international branch of our economy has been playing an increasingly important role in recent years; you have already learned something about it in Chapter 6. It will crop up again and again as our analysis unfolds, and then be treated in detail in Part Five. We must give it its proper name, *net exports.* Because these net exports are a kind of investment (they are goods we produce but do not consume), we must now rename the great bulk of investment, other than government investment, that remains in this country: We will henceforth call it **gross private domestic investment.**

Figure 1
THE CIRCULAR FLOW VIEW I

The first view of the circular flow shows that output divides into two main streams, consumption and investment—consumption replenishing our human capital, investment replenishing our material capital. Note that there are public and private flows in both consumption and investment output.

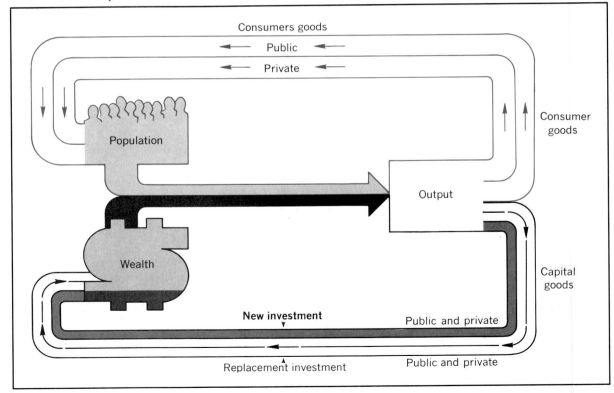

The Circular Flow

A simple diagram may help us picture the flow of final output we have been discussing. Figure 1 calls our attention to these paramount attributes of the output process:

1. **The flow of output is self-renewing, self-feeding.** This circularity is one of the dominant elements in the macroeconomic processes we will study. Consumption output returns to restore or increase our human capital—our ability to work. Investment output restores or increases our material capital.

2. **Societies must make a choice between consumption and investment.** At any given level of output, consumption and investment uses are rivals for the current output of society. Furthermore, we can see that society can add to its capital only the output that it refrains from consuming. Even if it increases its output, it cannot invest the increase except by not consuming it.

3. **Both consumption and investment flows are split between public and private use.** Like consumption and investment, these are also rival uses for output. A society can devote whatever portion of output it pleases to public consumption or public investment, but only by refraining from using that portion for private consumption or investment.

4. **Output is the nation's budget constraint.** Our output is the total quantity of goods and services available for all public and private uses (unless we want to use up our past wealth). More goods and services may be desired, but if output is not large enough, they cannot be had.

GROSS NATIONAL PRODUCT

We have had a first view of the overall flow of national output that will play so large a role in our macroeconomic studies. Now we want to look into the flow more closely. Here we can begin by defining gross national product, a term that is already familiar to us from Chapter 5. **We call the dollar value of the total annual output of final goods and services in the nation its gross national product.** The gross national product (or GNP as it is usually abbreviated) is thus nothing but the dollar value of the total output of all consumption goods and of all investment goods produced in a year. We are already familiar with this general meaning; now we must move on to a more precise definition.

Reminder: GNP Measures Final Goods

Remember that we are interested, through the concept of GNP, in measuring the value of the *ultimate* production of the economic system; that is, the total value of all goods and services enjoyed by its consumers or accumulated as new or replacement capital.

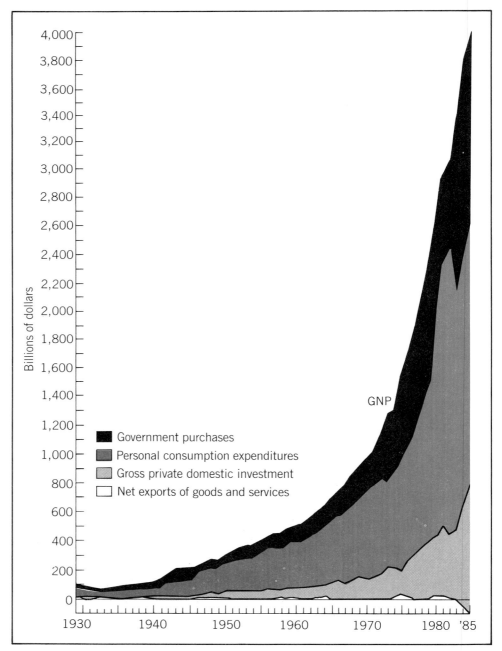

Figure 2
GNP AND COMPONENTS, 1929–1985

Here we see the historical record of GNP (a graph we have already met), this time with its component parts added.

Hence we do not count the intermediate goods we have already noted in our economic panorama. We do not add up the value of the cotton *and* the yarn *and* the cloth *and* the final clothing when we compute the value of GNP. That kind of multiple counting might be very useful if we wanted certain information about our total economic activity, but it would not tell us accurately about the final value of output. When we buy a shirt, the price we pay includes the cost of the cloth to the shirtmaker. In turn, the amount the shirtmaker paid for cloth included the cost of the yarn. In turn again, the seller of yarn included in its price the amount paid for raw cotton. Embodied in the price of the shirt, therefore, is the value of all the intermediate products that went into it.

Thus in figuring the value for GNP, we add only the values of all final goods, both for consumption and for investment purposes. Note as well that GNP includes only a given year's production of goods and services. Therefore sales of used car dealers, antique dealers, etc., are not included, because the value of these goods was picked up in GNP the year they were produced. However, the service provided by the used car dealer *is* included, valued as the dealer's income.

Four Streams of Final Output

We now have four streams of final output, each going to a final purchaser of economic output. **Therefore we can speak of gross national product as being the sum of personal consumption expenditure (*C*), gross private domestic investment (*I*), government purchases (*G*), and net exports (*X*), or (to abbreviate a long sentence) we can write that**

$$GNP \equiv C + I + G + X$$

This is a descriptive identity that should be remembered.

It helps, at this juncture, to look at GNP over the past decades. In Figure 2 we show the long irregular upward flow of GNP from 1929 to the present, with the four component streams of expenditure visible. Later we will be talking at length about the behavior of each stream, but first we need to be introduced to the overall flow itself.

GNP AS A MEASURE

GNP is an indispensable concept in dealing with the performance of our economy, but it is well to understand the weaknesses as well as the strengths of this most important single economic indicator.

1. GNP DEALS IN DOLLAR VALUES, NOT IN PHYSICAL UNITS; WE HAVE TO CORRECT IT FOR INFLATION. Trouble arises when we compare the GNP of one year with that of another to determine whether or not the nation is better off. If prices in

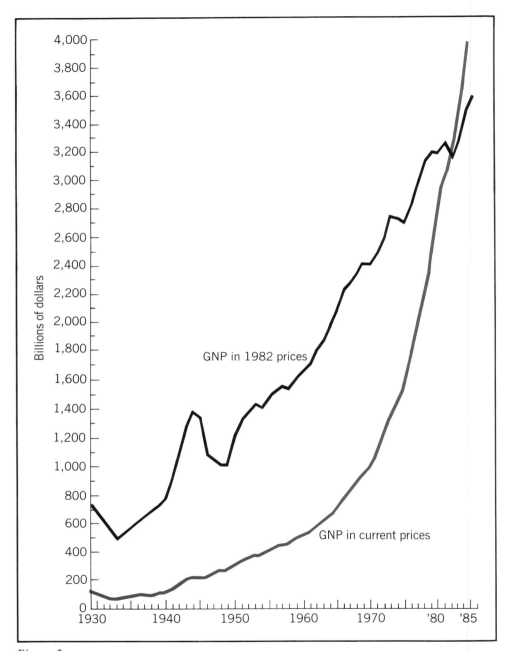

Figure 3

GNP IN CONSTANT AND CURRENT PRICES, 1929–1985

We reduce nominal or current GNP — output measured at existing prices — to real GNP by using a price index. Because relative prices change, it matters which year we use as our base. There is no correct year, but our choice affects our results. Here we use 1982 as the base.

the second year are higher, GNP will appear higher, even though the actual volume of output is unchanged or even lower!

We could correct for this price change easily if all prices moved in the same direction or proportion. We would then choose any year as a "base year," and we could easily establish an index to show whether GNP in another year was really higher or lower than in the base year, and by how much.

Problems arise, however, when there are changes in relative prices, with some prices rising more rapidly than others. Then the choice of a base year will affect our calculations. There is no correct way of choosing a base year. We just have to be aware that our choice affects our results. In Figure 3 we have used 1982 as our base. **Notice the enormous difference between nominal and real GNP!**

2. Changes in Quality of Output Will Not Show in GNP. The second weakness of GNP also involves its inaccuracy as an indicator of "real" trends over time. The difficulty revolves around changes in the utility of goods and services. In a technologically advancing society, goods are usually improved from one decade to the next or even more rapidly, and new goods are constantly being introduced. In an urbanizing, increasingly high-density society, the utility of other goods may be lessened over time. An airplane trip today, for example, is certainly preferable to one 30 years ago; a subway ride is not. This year's car costs more than last year's car, but it also gets better gas mileage.

REAL AND CURRENT GNP

It's worth a moment to review the ideas on pp. 193–194.

How do we arrive at a figure for "real" GNP? *The answer is that we "correct" the value of GNP (or any other magnitude measured in dollars) for the price changes that affect the value of our dollars but not the real quantities of goods and services our dollars buy.*

We make this correction by applying a *price index.* Such an index is a series of numbers showing the variation in prices year to year, from a starting or *base year* for which the price level is set at 100. Thus if prices go up 5 percent a year, a price index starting in year one will read 105 for year two, 110.25 + for year three (105 × 1.05), 115.8 for year four, and so on.

In correcting GNP we use a very complex price index called a GNP *price deflator.* This index, constructed by the Department of Commerce, allows for the fact that different parts of GNP, such as consumer goods and investment goods, may change in price at different rates. The present price deflator uses GNP price levels in 1982 as a base. In 1985, the value of the deflator was 111.7. That is, the price index was up 11.7% from 1982.

Now let us work out an actual example. *To arrive at a corrected GNP, we divide the current GNP by the deflator and then multiply by 100.* For example, GNP in current figures was $3,305 billion for 1983; $3,663 for 1984; and $3,993 billion for 1985. The deflators for those years were 215, 223, and 231. Here are the results:

$$\frac{\$3402}{104} = 32.71 \times 100 = 3271 \text{ billion}$$

$$\frac{\$3775}{108} = 34.95 \times 100 = 3495 \text{ billion}$$

$$\frac{\$3993}{112} = 35.65 \times 100 = 3565 \text{ billion}$$

Thus the "real value" of GNP in 1985 was $3,565 billion, *in terms of 1982 prices,* rather than the $3,993 billion of its current value. Two things should be noted in this process of correction. First, the real value of any series will differ, depending on the base year that is chosen. For instance, if we started a series in 1985, the real value of GNP for that year would be $3,993 billion, the same as its money value.

Second, the process of constructing a GNP deflator is enormously difficult. In fact there is no single, accurate way of constructing an index that will reflect all the variations of prices of the goods within GNP. To put it differently, we can construct different kinds of indexes, with different "weights" for different sectors, and these will give us differing results. The point then is to be cautious in using corrected figures. Be sure you know what the base year is. And remember that complex indexes, such as the GNP deflator, are only approximations of a change that defies wholly accurate measurement.

How much of the increase in price reflects that improvement in quality and how much of the increase is simply an increase in price? It is difficult for anyone to know, but government statisticians try to adjust GNP statistics for just such changes in quality. Generally speaking, the longer the time period over which comparisons of real GNP are being made, the larger is the quality factor, and therefore the more tentative the results become.

3. GNP DOES NOT REFLECT THE PURPOSE OF PRODUCTION. A third difficulty with GNP lies in its blindness to the ultimate use of production. If in one year GNP rises by a billion dollars owing to an increase in expenditure on education, and in another year it rises by the same amount because of a rise in cigarette production, the figures in each case show the same amount of growth of GNP. Even output that turns out to be wide of the mark or totally wasteful—such as military weapons that are obsolete from the moment they appear—all are counted as part of GNP.

The problem of environmental deterioration adds another difficulty. Some types of GNP growth directly contribute to pollution—cars, paper or steel production, for example. Other types of GNP growth are necessary to stop pollution—sewage disposal plants or the production of cleaner internal combustion engines. Still other types of GNP have little direct impact on the environment. Most personal services fall into this category.

Our conventional measure of GNP makes no distinction among the uses of outputs. For instance, the cleaning bills we pay to undo damage caused by smoke from the neighborhood factory become part of GNP, although cleaning our clothes does not increase our well-being. It only brings it back to what it was in the first place.

4. GNP DOES NOT INCLUDE MOST GOODS AND SERVICES THAT ARE NOT FOR SALE. Presumably GNP tells us how large our final output is. Yet it does not include one of the most useful kinds of work and chief sources of consumer pleasure—the labor of women in maintaining their households. Yet, curiously, if this labor were paid for—that is, if we engaged cooks and maids and babysitters instead of depending on wives for these services, GNP *would* include their services as final output, since they would be purchased on the market. The labor of wives, being unpaid, is excluded from GNP.*

A related problem is that some parts of GNP are paid for by some members of the population and not by others. Rent, for example, measures the services of landlords for homeowners and is therefore included in GNP. But what of the homeowner who pays no rent? Similarly, what of the family that grows part of its food at home and therefore does not pay for it?

There is no entirely satisfactory solution to such problems. Because no one has devised a way of valuing housewives' services in a manner that appears fair and objective, we just leave the value of these services out of GNP. On the other hand, when it is possible to impute a value to unpaid services, statisticians at the Department of Commerce do so. For instance, they include in GNP an estimate of the value of the rentals of owner-occupied homes and of food grown at home.

5. GNP DOES NOT INDICATE ANYTHING ABOUT THE DISTRIBUTION OF GOODS AND SERVICES AMONG THE POPULATION. Societies differ widely in how they allocate their production of purchasable goods and services among their populations. A pure egalitarian society might allocate everyone the same quantity of goods and services. Many societies establish minimum consumption standards for individuals and families. Few deliberately decide to let someone starve if they have the economic resources to prevent such a possibility. **Yet to know a nation's GNP, or even to know its average (per capita) GNP, is to know nothing about how broadly or how narrowly this output is shared.** A wealthy country can have many poor families. A poor country can have some very wealthy families.

---

* An added difficulty here is that we are constantly moving toward purchasing "outside" services in place of home services. Laundries, bakeries, restaurants all perform work that used to be performed at home. Thus the process of "commoditizing" activity gives an upward trend to GNP statistics that is not fully mirrored in actual output.

GNP and Welfare

All these doubts and reservations should instill in us a permanent caution against using GNP as if it were a clear-cut measure of social contentment or happiness. Economist Edward Denison once remarked that perhaps nothing affects national economic welfare so much as the weather, which certainly does not get into the GNP accounts! Hence, because the United States may have a GNP per capita that is higher than that of say, Holland, it does not mean that life is better here. It may be worse. In fact, by the indices of health care or quality of environment, it probably *is* worse.

Yet, with all its shortcomings, GNP is still the simplest way we possess of summarizing the overall level of market activity of the economy. If we want to examine its welfare, we had better turn to specific social indicators of how long we live, how healthy we are, how cheaply we provide good medical care, how varied and abundant is our diet, etc. — none of which we can tell from GNP figures alone. But we are not always interested in welfare, partly because it is too complex to be summed up in a single measure. For better or worse, therefore, GNP has become the yardstick used by most nations in the world. Although other yardsticks are sure to become more important, GNP will be a central term in the economic lexicon for a long time to come.

looking back

KEY CONCEPTS

The macro perspective

1 Our introduction to macroeconomics involves a special perspective on the economy, one that emphasizes total output rather than behavior in the marketplace.

Intermediate vs. final goods: consumption and investment

2 Observing the flow of total output, we discover that it can be divided into intermediate goods and final goods. Intermediate goods go *into* final goods. Final goods are those used for consumption or for investment.

Gross investment comprises net investment and replacement

3 Investment can be further divided into gross and net investment. Gross investment is the sum of output not used for consumption. Part of it is for replacement of worn out capital goods. The remainder is net investment.

Government purchases have the characteristics of both consumption and investment, but are treated as one category

4 Government also enters into final output, when it produces public goods such as education, or when it buys them from private contractors or producers. Although these government purchases may have the characteristics of consumption goods or investment goods, they are conventionally added together as a

single category of final output called *government purchases*. Note that these purchases do not include transfer payments, which are picked up as part of consumption or investment or as intermediate flows.

Exports minus imports gives us a last category: net exports

5 A final category of final demand consists of those goods that we produce at home but ship abroad — our exports — less goods produced abroad and shipped here for final use — imports. These net exports are actually a category of investment, but they are shown as a separate part of final output. Gross investment, less net exports, is properly called *gross private domestic investment*. The "domestic" calls attention to the fact that exports have been excluded.

Output is a circular flow

6 The flow of output has four major characteristics: It is circular, replenishing our human or material wealth; it is used for consumption or investment, but the same item cannot be used for both simultaneously; it has public and private uses, both as consumption and as investment; and it constitutes the budget constraint of the nation.

Gross national product is the value of final output

7 The annual flow of final output, valued at its market price, is called the *gross national product*, or *GNP*. Note that it includes only final, not intermediate, output.

GNP ≡ C + I + G + X

8 The annual output can be described as comprising four distinct flows:

a consumption flow
a net export flow
a flow of domestic gross private investment
a public flow

Together they give us the identity $GNP \equiv C + I + G + X$.

Real GNP is a widely used measure of performance. But GNP does not show quality, usefulness, or nonmarket output, and it ignores income distribution

9 Gross national product is widely used as a measure of economic performance. However, it suffers a number of deficiencies as such a measure. It has even more difficulty as an indicator of welfare or well-being because:

Real GNP is not easy to calculate from nominal GNP. And even real GNP (GNP corrected for price changes) does not tell us about the quality, or purpose, or distribution of income. It also ignores nonmarketed output.

GNP gives a very imperfect indication of the quality of output. The size of GNP does not inform us of its purpose or usefulness.

GNP does not include (or imprecisely includes) any output that is not sold.

GNP gives us no clue as to the distribution of income.

ECONOMIC VOCABULARY

QUESTIONS

1. Explain how the circularity of the economic process means that the outputs of the system are returned as fresh inputs.
2. What is meant by net investment? How is it different from gross investment? Does the idea of "net consumption" mean anything? (Suppose there is a minimum amount of consumption needed to keep body and soul together?)
3. Why are investment goods considered final goods and not intermediate ones?
4. Do you think that education is a consumption service — or an investment? What about military expenditure? Can you see one might classify many such expenditures in more than one way?
5. Write the basic formula for GNP.
6. Do you think we should develop measures other than GNP to measure our performance? What sorts of measures?

CHAPTER 12
Buying the National Product

a look ahead

So far we have looked only into one side of the national income "accounts ledger," the side concerned with *output*. Now we move to the other side, which is concerned with *income*. We begin our analysis of a central question: How can an economy sustain itself? How can it buy back all its own production?

We will attack the problem by seeing how every item of cost incurred in production becomes someone's income. That is a key part of the answer. Costs are also incomes. But it is not the whole answer: Incomes must thereafter be spent if they are to become demand. And if they are not spent? Then we have trouble, recession, slowdowns in production.

This chapter is the basis on which rests a great deal of what follows in the study of the macroeconomy. We suggest you read it twice—once quickly to get the point, once very slowly to master each link in the argument.

I n the last chapter we talked about gross national product from the supply point
of view. That is, we learned to see the great stream of final output as a river that
feeds four sectors—a sector of private households that require consumption
goods, a sector of firms that need investment goods of various kinds, a sector of
government agencies concerned with public goods, and a sector made up of individuals and firms and governments of other countries—the export or foreign
sector.

FROM SUPPLY TO DEMAND

Now we must look at that same stream of production from another perspective,
that of demand. This brings us to a question whose answer we will soon discover is
both simple and surprisingly complex. **The question is where the economy finds
the necessary purchasing power to buy the output it has produced.** Specifically,
where will households get the money to buy the consumer goods that have been
produced? Where will businesses get the funds to buy the investment goods they
seek? Where will government find the wherewithal to purchase public goods?*

The question leads us to seek a link between the supply of output and the
demand for output. The link is not hard to find. Anyone in business will tell you
that the crucial factor in determining the supply of output is the demand for
it—that is, the presence of buyers who are willing and able to buy goods or services
at prices that sellers are willing to accept.

So demand is necessary to assure supply. But where does demand come from?
Here is the surprising twist. **Demand is produced by supply!** Ask any buyers in the
marketplace where their incomes come from, and the answer you will get is that
their incomes come directly or indirectly from production itself—from the wages
or rents or profits or interest that have been received because these buyers have
entered the economy on the supply side as factors of production.

Thus output is generated by demand—and demand is generated by output!
Our quest for the motive force behind the flow of production therefore leads us to
discover a great *circular flow* within the economy.

The Circular Flow

At the top of the circle in Figure 1 we see payments flowing from households to
firms or government units (cities, states, federal agencies), thereby creating the
demand that brings forth production. At the bottom of the circle we see more
payments, this time flowing from firms or governments back to households, as

---

* We will not look into the question of where foreigners get the money they need because we are not
yet ready to step into the world of international trade and finance. So we confine our investigation to an
economy that is "closed"—that is, an economy that buys and sells nothing abroad. Later we will make
the corrections necessary to bring the foreign sector into the picture.

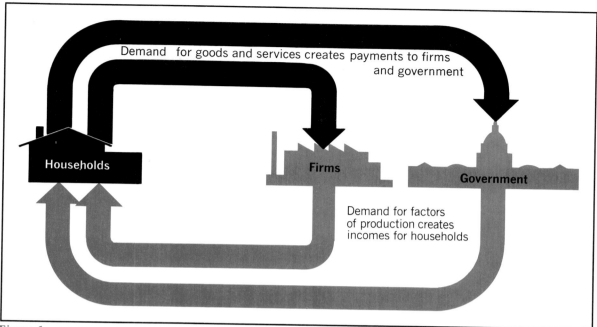

Figure 1

THE CIRCULAR FLOW OF SUPPLY AND DEMAND

This is the same circular flow concept that we encountered in Figure 1, Chapter 11. Here we use it to emphasize that the demand for output is itself generated by output.

businesses or government agencies hire the services of the various factors in order to carry out production. **Thus we can see that there is a constant regeneration of demand as money is first spent by the public on the output of firms and governments, and then in turn spent by firms and governments for the services of the public. That is how an economy that has produced a given GNP is able to buy it back.**

This is by no means a self-evident matter. Indeed, one of the most common anxieties about the flow of economic activity is that there will not be enough purchasing power to buy everything we have produced—that somehow we are unable to buy enough to keep up with the output of our factories. So it is well to understand once and for all how an economy can sustain a given level of production through its purchases on the market.

We start, then, with an imaginary economy in full operation. We can, if we wish, imagine ourselves as having collected a year's output, which is now sitting on the economic front doorstep looking for a buyer. What we must now see is whether it will be possible to *sell* this gross national product to the people who have been engaged in producing it. We must ask whether enough income or receipts have been generated in the process of production to buy back all the products themselves.

COSTS AND INCOMES

How does production create income? Businesspeople do not think about "incomes" when they assemble the factors of production to meet the demand for their product. They worry about *cost.* All the money they pay out during the production process is paid under the heading of *cost,* whether it be wage or salary cost, cost of materials, depreciation cost, tax cost, or whatever. Thus the concept of cost offers us a point of entry into the economic chain. **If we can show how all costs become incomes, we will have taken a major step toward understanding whether our gross national product can in fact be sold to those who produced it.**

It may help us if we begin by looking at the kinds of costs incurred by business firms in real life. Since governments also produce goods and services, this hypothetical firm should be taken to represent government agencies as well as business firms. Both incur the same kinds of costs; only the labels differ.

Table 1, a hypothetical expense summary of General Output Company, will serve as an example typical of all business firms, large or small, and all government agencies. (If you examine the year-end statements of any business, you will find that costs all fall into one or more of the cost categories shown.)

Factor Costs

Some of these costs we recognize immediately as payments to factors of production. The item for wages and salaries is obviously a payment to the factor *labor.* The item for interest (perhaps not so obviously) is a payment to the factor *capital;* that is, to those who have lent the company money in order to help it carry on its productive operation. The item for rent is, of course, a payment for the rental of *land* or natural resources from their owners.

Note that we have included profits with rent and interest. In actual accounting practice, profits are not shown as a cost. For our purposes, however, it will be quite legitimate and very helpful to regard profits as a special kind of factor cost going to businesspeople for their risk-taking function. Later we shall go more thoroughly into the matter of profits.

Table 1
GENERAL OUTPUT COMPANY COST SUMMARY

Wages, salaries, and employee benefits	$100,000,000
Rental, interest, and profit payments	5,000,000
Materials, supplies, etc.	60,000,000
Taxes other than income	25,000,000
Depreciation	20,000,000
Total	$210,000,000

Factor Costs and Value of Output

Two things strike us about these factor costs. *First, it is clear that they represent payments that have been made to secure production.* In more technical language, they are payments for factor inputs that result in commodity outputs. All the useful activity actually carried on within the company or government agency, all the value it has added to the economy, has been compensated by the payments the company or the agency has made to land, labor, and capital. To be sure there are other costs, for materials and taxes and depreciation, and we shall soon turn to these. But whatever production or assembly or distribution the company or agency has carried out during the course of the year has required the use of land, labor, or capital. **Thus the total of its factor costs represents the value of the total new output that General Output by itself has given to the economy.**

Factor Costs and National Income

A second fact that strikes us is that **all factor costs are income payments. The wages, salaries, interest, rents, etc., that were costs to the company or agency were income to its recipients. So are any profits, which will accrue as income to the owners of the business.**

From here it is a simple step to add up *all* the factor costs paid out by *all* the companies and government agencies in the economy, in order to measure the total new *value added* by all productive efforts in the year. **This measure is called national income.** As we can see, it is less than gross national product, for it does not include other costs of output—namely, certain taxes and depreciation.

Thus, just as it sounds, national income means the total amount of earnings of the factors of production within the nation. If we think of these factors as constituting the households of the economy, we can see that **factor costs result directly in incomes to the household sector.** If factor costs were the only costs involved in production, the problem of buying back the gross national product would therefore be a very simple one. We should simply be paying out to households, as the cost of production, the very sum needed to buy GNP when we turned around to sell it.

But a glance at the General Output expense summary shows that this is not the case. There are other costs besides factor costs. How shall we deal with them?

Costs of Materials

The next item of the expense summary is puzzling. Called payments for "materials, supplies, etc.," it represents all the money General Output has paid not to its own factors, but to other companies for other products it has needed. We may even recognize these costs as payments for those *intermediate products* that lose their identity in a later stage of production. How do such payments become part of the income available to buy GNP on the marketplace?

Perhaps the answer is already intuitively clear. When General Output sends its checks to, let us say, U.S.X. or General Electric or to a local supplier of stationery, each of these recipient firms now uses General Output's payments to pay its own costs. And what are those costs? What must U.S.X. or all the other suppliers now do with their checks? The answer is obvious. They must reimburse their own factors and then pay any other costs that remain.

Figure 2 may make the matter plain. It shows us, looking back down the chain of intermediate payments, that what constitutes material costs to one firm are factor and other costs to another. Indeed, as we unravel the chain from company to company, it is clear that all the contribution to new output must have come from the contribution of factors somewhere down the line. **All the costs of new output —all the value added—must ultimately be resolvable into payments to the owners of land (or natural resources), labor, and capital.**

Another way of picturing the same thing is to imagine that all firms or agencies in the country were brought up by a single gigantic corporation. The various production units of the new supercorporation would then ship components and semi-finished items back and forth to one another, but there would not have to be any payment from one division to another. The only payments that would be necessary would be those required to buy the services of factors—that is, various kinds of labor or the use of property or capital—so that at the end of the year, the super-

Figure 2
HOW MATERIALS COSTS BECOME OTHER COSTS
The cost of materials to firm A consists of firm B's payments to its factors and other costs, just as firm B's materials cost is made up of firm C's factor and other costs. Eventually all costs of materials reduce to payments for the services of labor, capital and land. After all, what other ultimate costs are there?

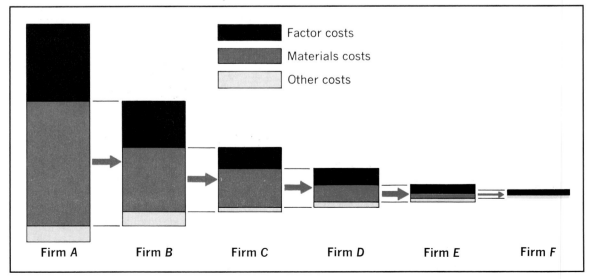

corporation would show on its expense summary only items for wages and salaries, rent, and interest (and as we shall see, taxes and depreciation), but it would have no item for materials cost.

We have come a bit further toward seeing how our gross national product can be sold. **To the extent that GNP represents new output made during the course of the year, the income to buy back this output has already been handed out as factor costs, either paid at the last stage of production or carried along in the guise of material costs.**

But a glance at the General Output expense summary shows that entrepreneurs incur two kinds of costs that we have still not taken into account: taxes and depreciation. Here are costs employers have incurred that have not been accounted for on the income side. What can we say about them?

Tax Costs

Let us begin by tracing the taxes that General Output pays, just as we have traced its material payments.* In the first instance, its taxes will go to government units — federal, state, and local. But we need not stop there. Just as we saw that General Output's checks to supplier firms paid for the suppliers' factor costs and for still further interfirm transactions, so we can see that its checks to government agencies pay for goods and services that these agencies have produced — goods such as roads, buildings, or defense equipment; or services such as teaching, police protection, and the administration of justice. General Output's tax checks are thus used to help pay for factors of production — land, labor, and capital — that are used in the *public sector.*

In many ways, General Output's payments to government units resemble its payments to other firms for raw material. Indeed, if the government *sold* its services to General Output, charging for the use of the roads, police services, or defense protection it affords the company, there would be *no* difference whatsoever. The reason we differentiate between a company's payment to the public sector and its payments for intermediate products is important, however, and worth looking into.

The first reason is clearly that with few exceptions, the government does *not* sell its output. This is partly because the community has decided that certain things the government produces (education, justice, or the use of most city parks, for instance) should not be for sale, but should be supplied to all citizens without direct charge. In part it is also because some things the government produces, such as defense or law and order, cannot be equitably charged to individual buyers since it

---

* For simplicity, we also show government agencies as taxpayers. In fact, most government units do *not* pay taxes. Yet there will be hidden tax costs in the prices of many materials they buy. No harm is done by treating government agencies like taxpaying firms in this model.

is impossible to say to what degree anyone benefits from — or even uses — these communal facilities. Hence General Output, like every other producer, is billed, justly or otherwise, for a share of the cost of government.

Indirect Taxes

Here is a second reason why we consider that the cost of taxes is a new kind of cost, distinct from factor payments: When business firms have finished paying the factors, they have not yet paid all the sums employers must lay out. Some taxes, in other words, are an addition to the cost of production. These taxes are called *indirect taxes,* and they are levied on the productive enterprise itself and on its actual physical output. Taxes on real estate, for instance, or taxes that are levied on each unit of output (such as excise taxes on cigarettes) or taxes levied on goods sold at retail (sales taxes) are all payments entrepreneurs must make as part of their costs of doing business. *They are an entirely new kind of cost of production, not previously picked up.* As an expense paid out by entrepreneurs, over and above factor costs (or material costs), these tax costs must be part of the total selling price of the goods and services in GNP.

Will there be enough incomes handed out in the process of production to cover this additional item of cost? Yes. The indirect tax costs paid out by firms will be received by government agencies who will use these tax receipts to pay income to factors working for the government. Any direct taxes (income taxes) paid by General Output or by its factors will also wind up in the hands of a government. **Thus all tax payments result in the transfer of purchasing power from the private to the public sector, and when spent by the public sector, they will again become demand in the marketplace.**

Direct Taxes

This does not mean that all taxes collected by the government are costs of production. Many taxes will be paid not by the entrepreneurs as an expense of doing business, but by the *factors* themselves. These so-called *direct taxes* (such as income taxes) are *not* part of the cost of production. When General Output adds up its total cost of production, it naturally includes the wages and salaries it has paid, but it does not include the taxes its workers or executives have paid out of their incomes. Such direct taxes transfer income from earners to government, but they are not a cost to the company itself.

In the same way, income taxes on the profits of a company do *not* constitute a cost of production. General Output does not pay income taxes as a regular charge on its operations, but waits until a year's production has taken place and then pays income taxes on the profits it makes *after* paying its costs. If it finds that it has lost money over the year, it will not pay any income taxes — although it will have paid other costs, including indirect taxes. **Thus direct taxes, such as income taxes, are not a cost paid out in the course of production that must be recouped, but a payment made by factors (including owners of the business) from the incomes they have earned through the process of production.**

Depreciation

But there is still one last item of cost. At the end of the year, when the company is totting up its expenses to see if it has made a profit for the period, its accountants do not stop with factor costs, material costs, and indirect taxes. If they did, the company would soon be in serious straits. In producing its goods, General Output has also used up a certain amount of its assets — its buildings and equipment — and a cost must now be charged for this wear and tear if the company is to be able to preserve the value of its physical plant intact. If it did not make this cost allowance, it would have failed to include all the resources that were used up in the process of production, and it would therefore be overstating its profits.

Yet this cost has something about it clearly different from other costs that General Output has paid. Unlike factor costs or taxes or material costs, depreciation is not paid for by check. When the company's accountants make an allowance for depreciation, all they do is make an entry on the company's book, stating that plant and equipment are now worth a certain amount less than in the beginning of the year.

At the same time, however, General Output *includes* the amount of depreciation in the price it intends to charge for its goods. As we have seen, one of the resources used up in production was its own capital equipment, and it is certainly entitled to consider the depreciation as a cost. Yet it has not paid anyone a sum of money equal to this cost! How then will there be enough income in the marketplace to buy back its product?

Replacement Expenditure

The answer is that in essence it has paid depreciation charges to itself. Depreciation is thus part of its gross income. Together with after-tax profits, these depreciation charges are called a business's *cash flow*.

A business does not *have* to spend its depreciation accruals, but normally it will, to maintain and replace its capital stock. To be sure, an individual firm may not replace its worn-out capital exactly on schedule. But when we consider the economy as a whole, with its vast assemblage of firms, that problem tends to disappear. Suppose we have 1,000 firms, each with machines worth $1,000 and each depreciating its machines at $100 per year. Provided that all the machines were bought in different years, this means that in any given year, about 10 percent of the capital stock will wear out and have to be replaced. It's reasonable to assume that among them, the 1,000 firms will spend $100,000 to replace their old equipment over a ten-year span.*

* What if the machines *were* all bought in one year or over a small number of years? Then replacement expenditures will *not* be evenly distributed over time, and we may indeed have problems. This takes us into the dynamics of prosperity and recession, to which we will turn in due course. For the purpose of our explanatory model, we will stick with our (not too unrealistic) assumption that machines wear out on a steady schedule and that aggregate replacement expenditures therefore also display a steady, relatively unfluctuating pattern.

This enables us to see that insofar as there is a steady stream of replacement expenditures going to firms that make capital goods, there will be payments just large enough to balance the addition to costs due to depreciation. As with all other payments to firms, these replacement expenditures will become incomes to factors, etc., and thus can reappear on the marketplace.

Profits and Demands

One last item remains. During our discussion of the circular flow, we spoke of profits as a special kind of factor cost — a payment to the factor *capital*. Now we can think of profits not merely as a factor cost (although there is always a certain element of risk-remuneration in profits), but as a return to especially efficient or forward-thinking firms who have used the investment process to introduce new products or processes ahead of the run of their industries. We also know that profits accrue to powerful firms that exact a semi-monopolistic return from their customers.

What matters in our analysis at this stage is not the precise explanation we give to the origin of profits, but a precise explanation of their role in maintaining a "closed-circuit" economy in which all costs are returned to the marketplace as demand. A commonly heard diagnosis for economic maladies is that profits are at the root of the trouble, because they cause a withdrawal of spending power or income from the community. If profits are saved or retained within the firm, this can be true. In fact, however, profits are usually distributed in three ways. They may be

1. Paid out as income to the household sector in the form of dividends or profit shares, to become part of household spending
2. Directly spent by business firms for new plant and equipment
3. Taxed by the government and spent in the public sector

All three methods of offsetting profits appear in Figure 3.

Thus, we can see that profits need not constitute a withdrawal from the income stream. Indeed, unless profits are adequate, business will very likely not invest enough to offset the savings of the household sector. They may, in fact, even fail to make normal replacement expenditures.

Thus the existence of profits, far from being deflationary — that is, far from causing a fall in income — is, in fact, essential for the maintenance of a given level of income or for an advance to a higher level. Nonetheless, there is a germ of truth in the contention of those who have maintained that profits can cause an insufficiency of purchasing power. For unless profits are returned to the flow of purchasing power as dividends that are spent by their recipients or as new capital expenditures made by business or as taxes that lead to additional public spending, there will be a gap in the community's demand. Unspent, hoarded profits are a drag on

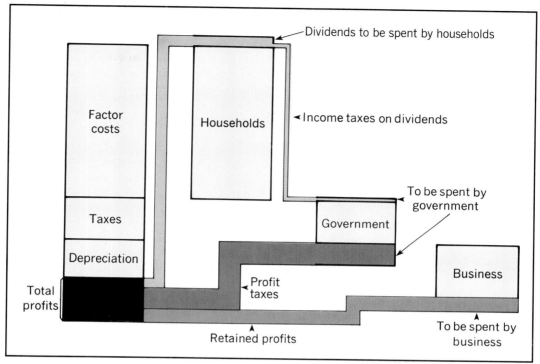

Figure 3
PROFITS IN THE CIRCULAR FLOW

There are three ways in which profits can be returned to GNP as expenditure: (1) by being distributed as dividends and spent by households, (2) by being taxed away and spent by government, and (3) by being directly spent by business for new investment.

growth, but not invested profits.* Thus we can think of profits just as we think of saving—an indispensable source of economic growth or a potential source of economic decline.

The Three Streams of Expenditure

Our analysis is now complete. Item by item, we have traced each category of cost into an income payment, so that we now know there is enough income paid out to buy back our GNP at a price that represents its full cost. Perhaps this was a conclusion we anticipated all along. After all, ours would be an impossibly difficult

---

* Here we must distinguish between the individual firm and all firms together. An individual firm that saves its profits will usually put them in a bank and thereby make them available to other firms. But if all firms collectively hold onto their profits, trouble will result.

economy to manage if somewhere along the line purchasing power dropped out of existence, so that we were always faced with a shortage of income to buy back the product we made.

But our analysis has also shown us something more unexpected. We are accustomed to thinking that all the purchasing power in the economy is received and spent through the hands of people — usually meaning households. Now we can see that this is not true. There is not only one, but *three* streams of incomes and costs, all quite distinct from one another (although linked by direct taxes).*

1. **Factor costs** → **Households** → **Consumers goods**
   ↘**Direct Taxes**
2. **Indirect taxes** → **Government agencies** → **Government goods**
   ↗**Direct Taxes**
3. **Depreciation** → **Business firms** → **Replacement investment**

The one major crossover in the three streams is the direct taxes of households and business firms that go to governments. This flow permits governments to buy more goods and services than could be purchased with indirect taxes alone.

There is a simple way of explaining this seemingly complex triple flow. Each stream indicates the existence of a *final taker* of gross national product: the consumer, government, and business itself. Since output has final claimants other than consumers, we can obviously have a flow of purchasing power that does not enter consumers' or factors' hands.†

THE COMPLETED CIRCUIT OF DEMAND

The realization that factor owners do not get paid incomes equal to the total gross value of output brings us back to the central question of this chapter: Can we be certain that we will be able to sell our GNP at its full cost? Has there surely been generated enough purchasing power to buy back our total output?

We have thus far carefully analyzed and answered half the question. **We know that all costs will become incomes to factors or receipts of government agencies or of firms making replacement items.** To sum up again, factor costs become the incomes of workers, managements, owners of natural resources and of capital; and all these incomes together can be thought of as comprising the receipts of the household sector. Tax costs are paid to government agencies and become receipts of the government sector. Depreciation costs are normally accrued within business firms, and these accruals belong to the business sector. Profits go to households, government, and business.

---

* For purposes of simplicity, we will again include profits in factor costs.

† We have not forgotten about the export sector, but we cannot integrate it into the picture until we study international trade.

Crucial Role of Expenditures

What we have not yet established, however, is that these sector receipts will become sector expenditures. That is, we have not demonstrated that all households will now *spend* all their incomes on goods and services, or that government units will necessarily *spend* all their tax receipts on public goods and services, or that all firms will assuredly *spend* their depreciation accruals for new replacement equipment.

What happens if some receipts are not spent? The answer is of key importance in understanding the operation of the economy. A failure of the sectors to spend as much money as they have received means that some of the costs that have been laid out will *not* come back to the original entrepreneurs. As a result, they will suffer losses. If, for instance, our gross national product costs $1 trillion to produce but the various sectors spend only $900 billion in all, then some entrepreneurs will find themselves failing to sell all their output. Inventories of unsold goods will begin piling up, and businesspeople will soon be worried about overproducing. The natural thing to do when you can't sell all your output is to stop making so much of it, so businesses will begin cutting back on production. As they do so, they will also cut back on the number of people they employ. As a result, business costs will go down; but so will factor incomes, for we have seen that costs and incomes are opposite sides of one coin. As incomes fall, the expenditures of the sectors might very well fall further, bringing about another twist in the spiral of recession.

This is not yet the place to go into the mechanics of such a downward spiral of business. But the point is clear. **A failure of the sectors to bring all their receipts back to the marketplace as demand can initiate profound economic problems. In the contrast between an unshakable equality of costs and incomes on the one hand, and the uncertain connection between incomes and expenditures on the other, we have come to grips with one of the most important problems in macroeconomics.**

From Recession to Inflation

We have concentrated on the problem of buying back GNP because that is the best way to understand the circular flow properties of production. But most of us these days are also worried about inflation. How does that tie into our analysis?

The answer should be clear enough. If recession arises because there is too little expenditure to cover the costs of producing GNP, inflation arises because expenditure exceeds costs. We have all heard inflation described as "too much money chasing too little goods"; as a description that is entirely correct, although it fails to explain where "too much money" comes from.

We have something of a problem in going further into an explanation of inflation at this point. We have not yet learned about money, nor have we studied the motivation of expenditure. So we will simply have to wait before we go deeply into the inflationary phenomenon. We will be back to the subject many times.

SOME IMPORTANT DEFINITIONS

We have completed the necessary economic analysis of this chapter, showing how the demand for GNP is generated. But we still need to improve and refine our economic vocabulary. Before we move on, therefore, we must learn some very useful and frequently encountered definitions.

The first of these concerns two ways of looking at GNP. One way is to think of GNP as measuring the value of a year's final output of consumption, investment, government and net export goods and services. But we also know that the value of this output is a sum of costs: factor costs, indirect tax costs, the costs of depreciation. These costs are identical with the incomes or receipts of sectors. Therefore GNP measures total incomes as well as total costs.

GNP and GNI

To express the equality with the conciseness and clarity of mathematics, we can write two equations. First, GNP as a sum of final outputs:

$$GNP \equiv C + G + I + X$$

where $C, I, G,$ and X (net exports) are designations of the four categories into which we divide our flow of production.

Next, we write an equation that describes the *same* flow not as a sum of outputs, but as a sum of costs:

$$GNP \equiv F + T + D$$

where $F, T,$ and D are familiar to us as factor, indirect tax, and depreciation costs. *But we have also learned that all costs are identical with incomes.* It follows, therefore, that we can speak of the sum of these costs as gross national income, or GNI. Hence the last set of identities:

$$\text{Gross National Product} \equiv \text{Gross National Income}$$
$$\text{or GNP} \equiv \text{GNI}$$

or

$$C + G + I + X \equiv F + T + D$$

It is important to remember that these are all accounting identities, true by definition. The National Income and Product Accounts, the official government accounts for the economy, are kept in such a manner as to make them true. As the name implies, these accounts are kept in two sets of books, one on the products produced in the economy and one on the costs of production, which we know to be identical with the incomes generated in the economy. Since both sets of accounts are measuring the same output, the two totals must be equal.

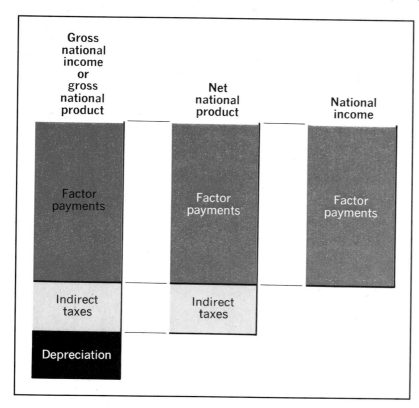

Figure 4

GNP, NNP, AND NI

GNP, NNP, and NI (or Y) fit into one another like a nest of Chinese boxes. As you can see, the basic unit of measurement of output is national income; net and gross national products are derived by adding specific costs—indirect taxes for NNP and depreciation for GNP.

NNP and National Income

It is now easy to understand the meaning of the two other measures of output. One of these is called **net national product (NNP).** As the name indicates, it is exactly equal to the gross national product minus depreciation. GNP is used much more than NNP, since the measures of depreciation are very unreliable. The other measure, **national income,** we have already met. It is *GNP minus both depreciation and indirect taxes.* This makes it equal to the sum of factor costs only. Figure 4 should make this relationship clear. The aim of this last measure is to identify the net income that actually reaches the hands of factors of production. Consequently, the measure is sometimes called the *national income at factor cost.* Its abbreviation is Y.*

---

* Why not I? Because we keep that letter for "investment."

The Circular Flow Again

The "self-reproducing" model economy we have now sketched out is obviously still very far from reality. Nevertheless, the particular kind of unreality we have deliberately constructed serves a highly useful purpose. An economy that regularly and dependably buys back everything it produces gives us a kind of benchmark from which to begin our subsequent investigations. We call such an economy, whose internal relationships we have outlined, an economy in **stationary equilibrium,** and we denote the changeless flow of costs into business receipts, and receipts back into costs, a *circular flow.*

We shall return many times to the model of a circular flow economy for insights into a more complex and dynamic system. Hence it is well that we summarize briefly two of the salient characteristics of such a system.

1. A CIRCULAR FLOW ECONOMY WILL NEVER EXPERIENCE A RECESSION. Year in and year out, its total output will remain unchanged. Indeed, the very concept of a circular flow is useful in showing us that **an economic system can maintain a given level of activity** *indefinitely,* **so long as all the sectors convert all their receipts into expenditures.**

2. A CIRCULAR FLOW ECONOMY WILL NEVER KNOW A BOOM. That is, it will not grow, and its standard of living will remain unchanged. That standard of living may be high or low, for we could have a circular flow economy of poverty or of abundance. But in either state, changelessness will be its essence. Note further that if its population rises, its per capita income will fall! This follows from the fact that its income is unchanged.

The Great Puzzle

What we have demonstrated in this chapter is an exceedingly important idea. There *can* always be enough purchasing power generated by the process of output to buy back that output.

Yet we all know, from our most casual acquaintance with economics, that in fact there is not always enough purchasing power around, or that on occasion there is too much purchasing power. With too little, we have slumps and recessions; with too much, booms and inflation.

Hence the circular flow sets the stage for the next step in our study of macroeconomics. If there *can be* the right amount of purchasing power generated, why isn't there? Or to put the question more perplexingly: If there *can be* enough purchasing power to buy *any* size output, small or large, what determines how large purchasing power will actually be, and therefore how large output will actually be?

These questions point the way for the next stage of our investigation. We must study the workings of demand much more realistically by removing some of the assumptions that were necessary to create a model of a circular flow system.

looking back

KEY CONCEPTS

The demand for GNP is generated in the act of production as firms hire factors

1 The question to be grasped is how an economy can sustain itself, how it can generate enough demand to buy back its own output. this leads at once to the origin of demand for output, or purchasing power. In turn we see that purchasing power is generated by the act of production, as firms and government employers hire factors of production. Thus we begin with the concept of a circular flow.

Factor costs are income to the factors of production

2 When factors are hired, they create costs. It is important to see that all costs are necessarily also incomes. We group all costs — including material costs — into three categories. The first category, factor costs — wages, salaries, interest payments, and the like — are obviously incomes for the factors of production who receive them.

Indirect taxes are costs that become receipts of government agencies. (Note: Income taxes are not costs of production)

3 In the second category are the costs of indirect taxation. These are not direct income taxes, which are borne by the factors out of their incomes and are not a cost of production. Indirect taxes are simply added onto factor costs as an expense of production. Such indirect taxes become part of the receipts of government agencies.

Depreciation costs accrue to firms. Profits also recirculate

4 Depreciation costs are the final category of production cost. These costs are received by business firms, which use them to finance replacement investment. Profits also can return to the income stream as dividends or investment spending or via taxation.

Thus, all costs are incomes, but all incomes may not become expenditures

5 Thus there are three separate streams in the economy: (1) Factor costs which go to the households who spend these "costs" (their incomes) for consumption; (2) indirect taxes which go to government for expenditure on public goods and services; and (3) depreciation costs that accrue to business firms for expenditure as replacement investment. It is important to see that the transition from "cost" to "income" is unbreakable — they are identities. All cost must become someone's income or receipt. This is not so for the transition from cost (or income) to expenditure. Here is a crucial area of potential malfunction.

GNP ≡ GNI

6 We can express GNP in two ways: as a sum of final outputs or as a sum of incomes (receipts). Thus there is an identity between gross national income and gross national product.

A circular flow economy has no growth

7 The model of a circular flow economy elucidates how such an economy can repurchase its own production. But a circular flow system has no vitality, no growth.

ECONOMIC VOCABULARY

QUESTIONS

1. What are factor costs? To what sector do they go? Do all factor costs become personal incomes? Do they become personal expenditures? (Careful about this last: Suppose that a household *saves* part of its income!)

2. What are direct taxes? What is "direct" about them? Why are they distinguished from "indirect" taxes? Why is an indirect tax, such as a sales tax, considered an addition to the value of GNP, whereas an income tax is not? *Think:* Does the value (or cost) of the goods or services you personally create get bigger if you pay a larger income tax? Does it get larger if the sales tax is increased?

3. To whom are material costs paid? Why do we not count them as a separate part of GNP?

4. Exactly what is depreciation? Why is it a cost? Who pays it, and how? Who receives it? Is it possible that a firm can pay depreciation to itself? How else would you describe a business that made an allowance at the end of the year for the value of the machinery that had been used up in production?

5. Why is the link between an expenditure and a receipt an identity? Why is the link between a receipt and an expenditure not an identity? Can there be any expenditure without someone receiving it? Can someone receive a payment, but not make an expenditure himself? Be sure you grasp the difference here.

CHAPTER 13
The Growth of Supply

a look ahead

We have learned some essential macroeconomic *concepts,* but we have not yet learned much macroeconomic *analysis.* We begin to do so as we move from the idea of a stationary, changeless economy to that of a dynamic, growing one.

In this chapter we take a look at growth. Here we are going to learn more about the two sources of growth that we have already singled out: changes in the quantity and quality of labor and capital inputs. Incidentally, we shall learn how difficult it is to measure those sources precisely, especially with regard to capital.

Our chapter will lead us again to the production possibility curve we first met in Chapter 7. A production possibility curve helps us understand the nature of the limits to, or constraints on, growth in terms of real output. That will pave the way for our next chapter on the dynamics of the growth in income that must accompany growth in output.

In our last chapter we became familiar with the manner in which an economy created the purchasing power needed to buy back its own output. That led to the idea of a stationary equilibrium, in which an economic system produces output and then purchases it year after year, without either increasing or decreasing the volume of its production or the incomes needed to buy that production.

The idea of a circular flow enables us to grasp the connection between costs and incomes, and the link between income and demand. Without a clear idea of how the economy generates demand from supply, and supply from demand, we cannot understand how the macro system works. But of course the picture of a changeless, level flow of economic activity is very far removed from the real world. Here activity normally grows, taking one year with another, as we have already seen. Sometimes it falls, or fails to grow fast enough.

It is these dynamic changes in the level of activity that are the main focus of macroeconomics. In this chapter we return to a historical view of growth, stressing the sources and limits of the *supply of output*. That will ready us for an analysis of the growth of demand in the chapter to follow.

A Quick Review

Macroeconomics is essentially concerned with growth. Chapter 7 opened a discussion of the long upward trend of U.S. output and the reasons for this trend. Recall that our growth trend for nearly 100 years has resulted in an average annual increase in real GNP per capita of about 1.5 percent a year — enough to double per capita income every 47 years.

Now we are going to push forward by learning much more about the underlying trends and causes of growth in the American economy. That will set the stage for the work that still lies ahead, when we will narrow our focus to the present and inquire into the reasons for the problems of our macrosystem — unemployment and inflation, booms and busts.

What determines how fast we have grown in the past, and how rapidly we may grow in the future? We already know the basic answer. **Growth comes from increases in the quantity or in the quality of the two major aspects of supply — labor and capital. Of course, it also depends mightily on the resources with which we are endowed and it is influenced by our sheer willingness to work hard. And all of these may be brought into play — or driven out of play — by the state of demand.** Therefore growth is anything but a cut-and-dried subject that can be disposed of by a simple analysis of the inputs of labor and capital. Nevertheless, by looking into these inputs, we will learn a lot.

LABOR

Output depends on work. The first source of growth is therefore the rise in the sheer number of people who work for pay — who *participate* in the national labor force. Figure 1 gives us a picture of the population and the labor force over the past

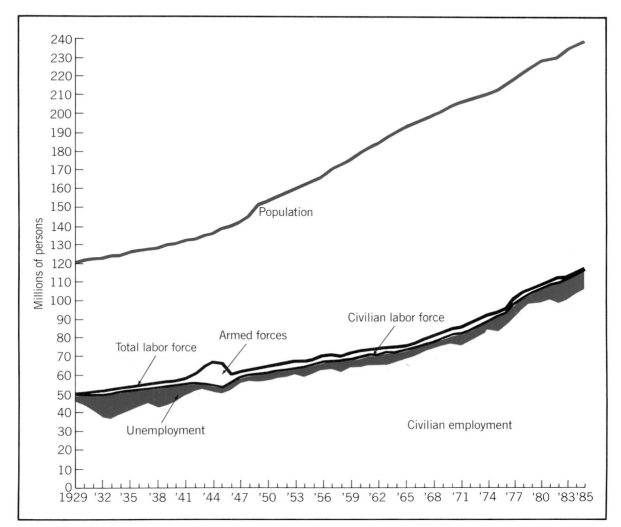

Figure 1
UNITED STATES LABOR FORCE, 1929–85
Although our eyes cannot easily make it out on the graph, the proportion of the total population seeking work has steadily risen. Today about two-thirds of the working age population is in the labor force—at work or looking for work.

half century. As we would expect, the size of the labor force has been steadily rising as our population has increased.

But there is more here than quickly meets the eye. One might expect that as our society has grown richer and more affluent, fewer people would seek employment. But that is not the case. If we go back to 1890 or 1900, we find that only 52 out of every 100 persons over age 14 sought paid work. Today about 60 out of every 100 persons of working age seek employment. Looking forward is more uncertain; but if we can extend the trend of the past several decades to the year 2000, we can expect perhaps as many as 65 persons out of 100 to be in the labor market by that date.

Participation in the Labor Force

The overall trend toward a larger **participation rate** for the entire population masks a number of significant changes:

1. MALE PARTICIPATION IN THE LABOR FORCE HAS FALLEN. In part this is because males entering the labor force are older than those who entered in the past. A larger number of young men remain in high school now or go on to college, and the ratio is steadily growing. At the same time, older males show a dramatic withdrawal from the labor force. Almost 7 out of 10 older males used to work. Now only 2 or 3 out of 10 work. The reason is the advent of social security and private pension plans. Will the proportion of older males in the labor force continue to fall? That depends: in recent years cutbacks in social security may be reducing the attractiveness of early retirement to those who can work.

2. THERE HAS BEEN A SPECTACULAR RISE IN TOTAL FEMALE PARTICIPATION. The mass entrance of women into the labor force accounts for the overall trend toward an increasing search for work. Today 55 percent of all women work outside the home, compared to 34 percent in 1950. The average American woman who marries today in her early twenties and goes on to raise a family will nevertheless spend 25 years of her life in paid employment after her children are grown.

Several changing factors in the American scene account for this surge of women into the labor market. Perhaps most important is the desire (and pressure) for the higher living standards that two incomes provide — particularly as the high-paid manufacturing jobs for men, which were once the ticket to middle-class comfort, become harder to find. Changing family structures — more single-parent households and childless couples — are another reason. The growth of the service sector has also meant more nonmanual relative to manual jobs, which are more accessible to women.

These are self-reinforcing factors: The surge of working women has helped to chip away at patterns of educational and employment discrimination, and to foster cultural acceptance of the working woman and the working wife.

Hours of Work

The total supply of labor time depends not only on how many people work, but also on how *long* they work — how many hours in a week, how many weeks in a year. Before the rise of factory production, these decisions were governed by the seasons, the crop cycle, and the calendar of religious holidays. Ever since the Industrial Revolution, working men and women have been subject to regulation by a master of their own making: the clock.

Had we asked what determined the length of the working day (or week) in the days of Adam Smith, it would have been relatively simple to answer. Wages were so close to subsistence that someone in the labor force was obliged to work extremely long hours to keep body and soul together. Paid vacations were unknown to the employees of the cotton mills. Unpaid vacations would have been tantamount to starvation.

With the passage of time, the rise of productivity, and the spread of material wealth, working men and women gradually gained higher incomes, and came to realize that a new possibility existed: that of deliberately working less than the physical maximum, using part of their increased productivity to buy leisure for themselves instead of wages.

Thus, beginning in the early nineteenth century we find that labor organizations (still very small and weak) sought to shorten the workweek. In Chapter 2 we saw that a signal victory was won in England in 1847 with the introduction of the 10-hour day as the legal maximum for women and children. In America, in the prosperity of the 1920s, the 48-hour week finally became standard; in the 1940s and 1950s, the 40-hour week; now we hear of the coming of the 3-day weekend.

Thus the total supply of labor time has not risen as fast as the labor force, because a decline in average hours has offset the rise in participation rates and in population. On balance, the total supply of labor hours has increased, but the supply of labor hours per employee, male and female, has fallen.

From Quantity to Quality

Was the change in the sheer quantity of work hours sufficient to account for the growth of total output? A very simple calculation shows us that it was not. In 1900 our labor force was approximately 30 million men and women who worked approximately 60 hours a week. As a result they expended 94 billion hours of annual labor. By 1985 the total labor force had grown to almost 117 million. The average workweek was now 36 hours. Total man-hours of labor input therefore amounted to roughly 219 billion hours of annual labor.*

Total hours of labor input over this eighty-year period therefore increased by a little more than twofold. But total economic output over the same period increased by almost tenfold. Clearly the sheer physical increase in the hours of labor was not sufficient to account for more than a small part of our growth trajectory.

Where shall we look for the remaining sources of growth? Our first move will be to examine changes in the quality of our labor hours. The 219 billion hours of labor expended in 1985 were in many cases more skillful, more knowledgeable, more

---

* This is a very rough calculation, intended for purposes of illustration. Our estimate makes no allowance for vacations, strikes, illnesses, or unemployment. But it will be legitimate enough to make the central point that soon follows: The *quantity* of labor input cannot possibly account for more than a small portion of our total growth.

Table 1
STOCK OF EDUCATION, U.S.

Here are three indicators of the huge increase in the education embodied in the labor force.

	1900	1983
Total man-years of schooling embodied in population (million)	228	2948
Percent of labor force with high-school education or more	6	72
Percent of high-school graduates entering college	17	33

Source: *Statistical Abstract of the United States,* 1985.

healthy, than the labor hours of 1900. These changes in the quality of our working abilities have come about in two ways.

1. GROWTH OF HUMAN CAPITAL. By human capital, we mean the skills and knowledge possessed by the labor force. Even though the measurement of human capital is fraught with difficulties, we cannot ignore this vital contributory element in labor productivity. Ferenc Jánossy, a Hungarian economist, has suggested a vivid imaginary experiment to highlight the importance of skills and knowledge.

Suppose, he says, that the populations of two nations of the same size could be swapped overnight. Fifty million Englishmen would awake to find themselves in, say, Nepal, and 50 million Nepalese would find themselves in England. The newly transferred Englishmen would have to contend with all the poverty and difficulties of the Nepalese economy. The newly transferred Nepalese would confront the riches of England. But the Englishmen would bring with them an immense reservoir of literacy, skills, discipline, and training, whereas the Nepalese would bring the very low levels of human capital that are characteristic of underdeveloped countries. Is there any doubt, asks Jánossy, that growth rates in Nepal, with its new, skilled population, would soon rise dramatically, and that those of England would fall catastrophically?

One way of indicating in very general terms the rising amount of human capital is to trace the additions to the stock of education that the population embodies. Table 1 shows the change in the total number of years of schooling of the U.S. population over the past three-quarters of a century, as well as the rise in formal education per capita. While these measures of human capital are far from exact or all-inclusive, they give some dimensions to the importance of skills and knowledge in increasing productivity.

2. SHIFTS IN THE OCCUPATIONS OF THE LABOR FORCE. A second source of added productivity results from shifts in employment from low productivity areas to high productivity areas. If workers move from occupations in which their productivity is low to other occupations in which output per man-hour is high, the productivity of the economy will rise even if there are no increases in productivity *within* the different sectors.

A glance at Table 2 shows that very profound and pervasive shifts in the location

Table 2
PERCENT DISTRIBUTION OF ALL
EMPLOYED WORKERS

Notice the long-term shift out of agriculture, through manufacturing and other goods-related occupations, into services.

	1900	1985
Agriculture, forests, and fisheries	38.1	2.9
Manufacturing, mining, transportation, construction, utilities	37.7	33.9
Trade, government, finance, professional and personal services	24.2	63.2

Source: Bureau of Labor Statistics, *Employment and Earnings.*

of labor have taken place. What have been the effects of this shift on our long-term ability to produce goods?

The answer is complex. In the early years of the twentieth century, the shift of labor out of agriculture into manufacturing and services probably increased the overall productivity of the economy, since manufacturing was then the most technologically advanced sector. In more recent years, however, we would have to arrive at a different conclusion. Agriculture, although highly productive, is now a very small sector in terms of employment. Moreover, the proportion of the labor force employed in manufacturing is roughly constant, up or down only a few percentage points year to year.

Today, growth in employment takes place mainly in the mixture of occupations we call the service sector: government, retail and wholesale trade, utilities and transportation, professions such as the law, accounting, and the like. The growth of output per capita is less evident in these occupations. Thus the drift of labor into the service sector means that average GNP per worker is growing more slowly today than if labor were moving into manufacturing or agriculture.

Overall Contribution of Labor

Can we sum up the overall contribution of changes in the inputs of labor to output? Clearly, changes in the *quality* of inputs — in our skills and capacities — far outweigh changes in our quantity of inputs — sheer man-hours of effort.

Knowledge and know-how, energy and initiative, enthusiasm and intelligence are powerful motors of economic growth. Indeed, economic growth expresses the gradual accumulation of these qualities of humankind much more than it expresses the increase in its sheer volume of exertion.

CAPITAL

What about capital? It must be apparent that without increases in the quantity of capital we could never achieve much growth. The rising labor force would then have to work with the same amount of machines, buildings, transportation equipment and the like, and diminishing returns would soon lower productivity severely. Therefore we have to **widen capital** — to keep the amount of capital per worker at least abreast of increases in the labor force — if we are to have any significant growth at all.

Actually, a vigorous economy does better than that. It also **deepens capital,** adding to its stock of capital wealth faster than to its labor force, so that each worker has more capital equipment than his or her predecessor, thereby experiencing the same increase in productivity that Adam Smith's workers experienced when new machinery was added to their pin factory.

The Measurement Problem

By how much has our stock of capital grown? Right away we come across a problem that we did not have to face when we considered the labor force. When we seek to measure the effects of changing labor inputs, we can at least count heads, or hours, in comparing past and present. But there is no such convenient unit of measurement when we come to capital. Is a power crane comparable to a shovel? Can we measure the amount of capital used by a bookkeeper today and in 1900 by comparing a computer (or even a desk calculator) to a pencil?

Such considerations make it plain that we cannot easily distinguish changes in the size of our capital stock from changes in its quality. Occasionally we can directly measure changes in the amount of capital; for instance, we can compare miles of railroad track over time. But even here there are changes in quality embodied in the "same" capital — modern rails are welded not riveted, roadbeds are different, tracks are electrified. In practice, we estimate the value of our capital stock by adding up the value of new investment, year after year, and subtracting an allowance for the value of capital depreciation. There are many problems in this procedure, but it remains the best we can do.

Total Capital Stock

As Table 3 shows, our total national capital in 1985 amounted to $11.3 trillion, an unimaginably vast sum, about $97,000 worth of capital for every person in the labor force.

This total capital stock is about five or six times as large as the capital stock at the beginning of the century. (Remember: To a large extent we are comparing apples and pears here. The smaller sum was not only less capital of the same kind — fewer miles of railroad track, if you will — but also very different capital: pencils instead of computers.) **One thing is indubitable from this overview. The increase in the quantity and the quality of capital is of critical importance in explaining our national growth. More and better capital are essential elements in increasing productive capacity.**

Table 3

CAPITAL WEALTH 1985 ($ BILLIONS)

Our total national capital is usually broken down as the table shows. Why do we not include the value of stocks and bonds, or money? The answer is that these are claims on our real wealth; in themselves they are not wealth.

Structures	$ 6,355	
business		$1,903
residential		2,919
public		1,533
Equipment	4,377	
priv. business and public		2,375
consumer durables		2,002
Inventories	579	
Total	11,311	

Sources: *Statistical Abstract of the United States,* 1985; *Economic Indicators.*

Investing and Inventing

How do we augment the amount of capital or improve its quality? Actually the two processes generally go hand in hand, for the very act of adding to our capital stock is usually accompanied by an improvement. But it is useful to separate the two processes in our minds.

We increase the quantity of capital by withholding resources from consumption—saving them—and by using those resources to build capital goods. This is the process of investment that we studied in the last chapter. A great deal of our macroeconomic studies in the chapters immediately ahead will be about this vital process.

We improve the quality of our capital by a process for which there is no simple name. Let us call it technology. Technology includes inventing and applying new products and processes, and achieving economies of scale—improvements that arise from sheer size.

Sources of Technology

Technology is probably the single most important factor in determining how fast we grow. Yet no one quite understands how technical change comes about. Studies have shown that inventions often follow economic demand—the late nineteenth century boom in railroad travel, for example, served to induce research and development in the expanding industry.* A famous study by Jewkes, Sawers and Stillerman, *The Sources of Invention,* has revealed that most of the major technological breakthroughs of the mid-twentieth century, from penicillin to the jet engine, were the work of individual inventors and tinkerers and not of organized laboratory work.†

* Jacob Schmookler, *Invention and Economic Growth* (Cambridge: Harvard University Press, 1966).

† John Jewkes, David Sawers, Richard Stillerman, *The Sources of Invention* (London: Macmillan, 1960).

How Technology Spreads

Diffusion of new technical knowledge is another matter entirely. The principles of nuclear physics, of aerodynamics, and of digital computing may have been discovered by individuals, but their coming into widespread use reflected a massive commitment of resources. Government has been society's technological risk-taker under the impetus of wartime needs. Sometimes, as in the case of the transistor, invented at the Bell Laboratories, the resources come from a large corporation. More recently, in the expansion of biotechnology and microcomputing, the venture capital market has supplied the resources to support large-scale commercialization of new technologies.

Thus technology has independent sources over which we have little or no control. **But there is no doubt that technical change in our economy can be nurtured by systematic investigation and research and development — R&D in industry, in universities, and under government sponsorship — and by increasing the pace of new investment.** In recent years, R&D expenditures have shown a disquieting fall in the United States — a drop of one-third, from 3 to 2 percent of GNP.

PRODUCTION POSSIBILITY CURVES

We should now have a fairly clear picture of how the growth of output originates. Let us conclude by translating the material we have covered into a production possibility curve — the graphic depiction of potential output that we have already encountered on pp. 129–30.

The Production Frontier

Increases in the quantity or quality of labor or capital move our production possibility curve to the right. Do you remember the illustration we used of an economy that produced only milk and grain? In Figure 2 we show how changes in the size of our labor force, in its skills or in its equipment, can alter the production "frontier." In panel I, we have shown the case where the production of both outputs increases; but II and III make clear that this is not always the case. Sometimes increases in education, new inventions, or other changes will affect one kind of output and not the other.

Such a two-commodity diagram may seem unreal, but remember that "milk" and "grain" can stand for consumption and investment (or any other choices available to an economy). In fact, with a little imagination we can construct a three-dimensional production possibility *surface* showing the limits imposed by scarcity on a society that divides its output among three uses such as consumption, investment, and government. Figure 3 shows what such a diagram looks like.

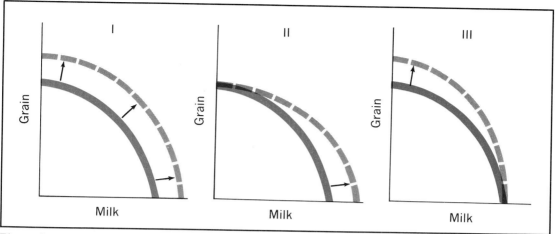

Figure 2

SHIFTS IN THE PRODUCTION FRONTIER

Changes in the quantity or quality of labor and/or capital make growth possible by pushing out our production frontier. As we can see, they may not affect all kinds of outputs equally.

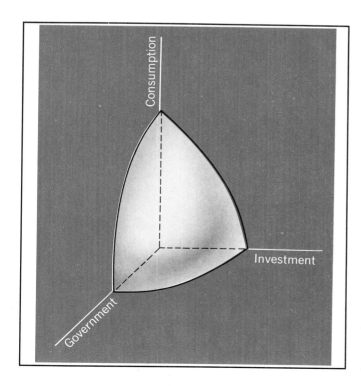

Figure 3

A PRODUCTION POSSIBILITY SURFACE

Actually, there is a frontier for every kind of output, but we have no way of depicting such a fantastic array. Here is a three-dimensional P-P surface that shows the frontier for these crucial outputs: consumption, investment, government.

Note how the production possibility surface swells out from the origin like a wind-filled sail. Any place on the sail represents some combination of consumption, investment, and government spending that is within the reach of the community. **Any place behind the efficiency frontier represents a failure of the economy to employ all its resources. It is a graphic depiction of unemployment of people or materials.**

Very few economies actually operate on their efficiency frontiers. Most have at least *some* unemployed inputs or are not using their inputs with all possible efficiency. Perhaps only in wartime do we reach the frontiers of our production possibility map. Nonetheless, we can see that a major job of economic policymakers is to move the economy as close to its frontier as possible, under normal conditions and to move the frontier out as fast as possible. Note too that the frontier does not represent a firm, immutable limit to output. It can be changed not only by the various sources of growth we have looked into, but also by *policies* that increase the quantity or quality of labor or capital.

From Supply to Demand

Everything we have discussed in this chapter relates to the ways in which our total output — our GNP — can grow. Let us emphasize *can*. The production possibility curve depicts the best we can do, given our labor force and our stock of capital goods. But it does not depict how well we will actually do. That depends on how fully we utilize our productive capacity — how far we drive the economy toward its frontiers.

What determines that? We already know the answer. It is the level of national demand, the volume of aggregate purchasing power, the size of our gross national income. How goes income grow to propel the economy to the limits established by its human and material resources? That is the vital question to which we turn next.

looking back

KEY CONCEPTS

Growth is the central trend	1 Growth is the central concern of macroeconomics and it is a central trend of the economy. In this chapter we analyze the growth of supply; in our next, the growth of demand. In Chapter 5 we saw that our real per capita growth has increased at about 1.5 percent a year, plus or minus 10 percent. This doubles real per capita living standards every 47 years.
Increases in labor inputs reflect population growth and changes in participation rates	2 Growth comes from increases in the quantity or quality of our main inputs, labor and capital. Increases in the quantity of labor have resulted from growth in population and a gradual rise in the overall participation rate, especially the entrance of women into the labor force.

Total labor hours have roughly doubled 1900–1980	3 Weekly hours have decreased since the turn of the century. Overall, it is likely that total labor hours (labor force times working hours) have slightly more than doubled, 1900–1980.
Labor hours embody more education, but the labor force works in less productive occupations	4 Changes in the quality of labor are more difficult to measure. They include increases in the amount of education embodied in the labor force and adding to the value of our human capital, and also changes in the kinds of work we do. There has been a long-term shift into service occupations which have lower than average productivity.
Total real output is up ten times since 1900. Much of this comes from capital but we cannot measure increases in quantity vs. quality	5 Total real output between 1900 and today has increased some tenfold. A major portion of this growth must come from capital inputs. However, it is almost impossible to separate changes in the quantity and quality of capital, because capital is always changing.
Investment is the process by which we add to the quantity of capital; technology adds to its quality	6 Although quantity and quality are almost impossible to separate, we speak of increases in the quantity of capital as arising through investment, and increases in its quality as arising through technology. In fact, an act of saving and investment is the means by which invention or innovation takes place.
R&D is a key activity, recently declining as a percent of GNP	7 The sources of technology are not clearly understood. Research and development activities are likely a very important source of technological improvement; recently R&D has been declining in the United States.
Changes in labor and capital inputs move out the production-possibility frontier	8 Production possibility curves can now be seen as describing provisional constraints on growth. We can move the frontiers out by the changes in labor and capital inputs we have been describing. We must now learn about the impetus that sets growth in motion.

ECONOMIC VOCABULARY

Participation rates   222   R&D   228
Human capital   224   Production possibility curves   228
Deepening vs. widening capital   226   Production frontiers   228

QUESTIONS

1. Set up a production possibilities curve for an economy producing food and steel. Show how some combinations of food and steel cannot be produced, even

though each of the goods lies within the limit of production on its own axis. Explain why the P-P curve is bowed. (If you can't, reread p. 230.)

2. Think about ways in which education can improve productivity — and ways in which it cannot. Would you think that going or not going to elementary school would have a greater or lesser effect on output per hour than going to college? In what line of work?

3. Try to think of some kinds of capital that have remained essentially unchanged over the last 50 years. How about ordinary tools, such as those that a carpenter uses? Can you picture in your mind's eye the effect of widening this kind of capital to match a growing force of carpenters, as against equipping the force with new kinds of tools such as power saws?

4. Is it possible for an economy that failed to invest to continue to grow? Suppose it worked harder? Are there limits to such kinds of growth? Are there limits to the growth that new and better capital will bring?

CHAPTER 14
The Growth of Demand

a look ahead

This key chapter explains the relationship between the growth of *potential* output and the growth of output that the economy actually enjoys. In our last chapter we learned about the elements that determine how fast we *could* grow — mainly the quantity and quality of labor and capital. We also saw that expenditure was the link in the circular flow that determined how much of our potential output we actually bought.

In this chapter we pursue that critical matter of expenditure further. Specifically, we gain an understanding of a key process by which saving becomes the necessary condition for investment, or capital formation. The savings-investment relationship is therefore at the center of this chapter. It is not the whole answer to the growth of demand — that will have to await a study of the monetary system. But the savings-investment link will give us the first deep grasp of how a macroeconomy really "works" — not in a circular flow, but in the dynamic, usually expanding fashion that is its historic hallmark.

Note: At the end of the chapter, on page 243 there are four questions. Answer them! If you can show, in words or diagrams, that you have mastered these four questions, you are well launched into the study of macroeconomics.

Our model of a circular flow economy which buys back all its output by spending all its receipts begins to explain how our economic system works —and why sometimes it does not work. Yet it leaves us in the dark with respect to the central question of growth, for an economy that merely bought back all its output by spending all its receipts would not grow. It would remain in place, reproducing itself from year to year. If we want to put growth into the picture, we have to add something that has so far been lacking from our exposition.

That missing element is a process central to all capitalist economies—indeed, to all economies whose output tends to expand. It is the process by which some of the factors of production are directed into the making of goods that will enable the economy to break out of its circular flow. As we already know, these output-creating, growth-inducing uses are called *net investment,* or *capital formation,* and the manner in which factors are put to this dynamic use is called the *savings-investment* link. That is the key process we look into in this chapter.

The Meaning of Saving

We begin by making sure that we understand a key word—*saving.* **Saving, for an economist, is not just putting money in the bank. Rather, it is refraining from spending *all or part of income for consumption goods or services.*** It should be very clear then why saving is such a key term. In our discussion of the circular flow it became apparent that expenditure was the critical link in the steady operation of the economy. If saving is not-spending, then it would seem that saving could be the cause of just that kind of downward spiral of which we caught a glimpse in that discussion.

And yet this clearly is not the whole story. The act of investing—of spending money to direct factors into the production of capital goods—requires an act of saving. To say it again, because it is very important, **we must save—that is, not use all our income for consumption—if we are to have the ability to hire factors to build capital goods. A society that did no saving would have no way of breaking out of a stationary circular flow.**

Hence, saving is necessary for the process of investment. Now, how can one and the same act be necessary for economic expansion and a threat to its stability?

The Demand Diagram

Let us use a diagram to show how saving can create both a "gap" in demand and an "opening" for investment.

In Figure 1 we trace the flow of expenditure through the economy from left to right. On the left we start with three blocks showing the factor, tax, and depreciation costs that have been incurred by businesses and government agencies as costs of production. Now we are going to follow those costs as they become incomes to different sectors, and thereafter as they are translated into new demand through the act of expenditure.

Increasing Expenditure

There are six principal methods of accomplishing this essential increase in expenditure.

1. The business sector can increase its expenditures by *borrowing* the savings of the public through the sale of new corporate bonds.
2. The government sector can increase its expenditures by *borrowing* savings of the other sectors through the sale of new government bonds.
3. Both business and government sectors can increase expenditures by *borrowing* additional funds from commercial banks.*
4. The business sector can increase its expenditures by attracting household savings into partnerships, new stock, or other *ownership (or equity)*.
5. The government sector can increase its expenditures by *taxing* the other sectors. (We will see later why total spending is likely to increase, despite higher taxes.)
6. Both business and government sectors can increase their expenditures by drawing on *accumulated past savings,* such as unexpended profits or tax receipts from previous years.

Claims

The first four of these methods have one attribute that calls them especially to our attention. **They give rise to claims that reveal from whom the funds have been obtained and to whom they have been made available, as well as on what terms.**
Bonds, corporate or government, show that savings have been borrowed from individuals, banks, or firms by business and government units. Shares of stock reveal that savings have been obtained on an equity (ownership) basis, as do new partnership agreements. Borrowing from banks gives rise to loans that also represent the claims of one part of the community against another. These claims establish the ownership of new capital assets in a growing economy.

Public and Private Borrowing

Now let us look at the upper diagram in Figure 2. This shows what happens when savings are made available to the business sector by direct borrowing from households. Note the claim (or equity) that arises. If the government were doing the borrowing rather than the business sector, the diagram would look like the lower diagram in Figure 2. Notice that the claim is now a government bond.

We have not looked at a diagram showing business or government borrowing its

* Actually they are borrowing from the public through the means of banks. We shall learn about this in Chapter 26.

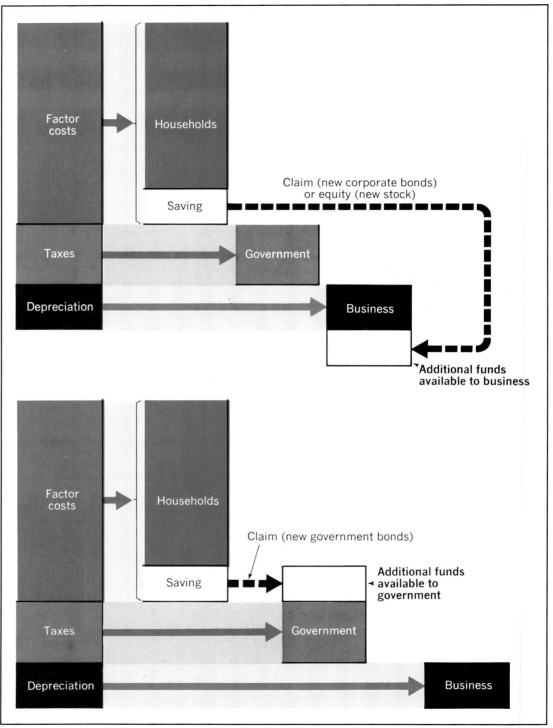

Figure 2

TWO WAYS OF TRANSFERRING SAVING BETWEEN SECTORS

Here we depict the way a demand gap can be closed by transferring the savings of one sector to another which will spend it. Our diagrams show how savings can go into business, in exchange for claims (bonds or stock) or to government, in exchange for government bonds.

funds from the banking system. (This process will be better understood when we take up the problem of money and banking, in Chapter 24.) The basic concept, however, although more complex, is much the same as above.

Completed Act of Offsetting Savings

There remains only a last step. We have seen how it is possible to offset the savings in one sector, where they were going to cause an expenditure gap, by increasing the funds available to another sector. It remains only to *spend* those additional funds in the form of additional investment or, in the case of the government, for additional public goods and services. The two completed expenditure circuits now appear in Figure 3.

While Figure 3 is drawn so that the new investment demand or new government demand is exactly equal to net saving, **it is important to understand that there is nothing in the economic system guaranteeing that these demands will exactly equal net saving — the desire for new investment or new government goods and services may be either higher or lower than new saving.**

The Key Savings–Investment Link

Here then is the essential point: An economy which is working normally, in which saving takes place, *must* generate potential demand gaps, and such an economy *must* offset those gaps if it is to function properly. But there is no guarantee that it will do so in practice.

Once this simple but fundamental point is clearly understood, much of the mystery of macroeconomics disappears, for we can then begin to see that an economy in movement, as contrasted with one in a stationary circular flow, is one in which sectors must *cooperate* to maintain the closed circuit of income and output. In a dynamic economy, we no longer enjoy the steady translation of incomes into expenditure which, as we have seen, is the key to an uninterrupted flow of output. Rather, we are faced with the presence of net saving and the possibility of a gap in final demand. This savings-investment link is the key to the volume of demand that a market economy will generate. The price of economic growth, in other words, is the risk of economic decline.

Let us take a moment to fix this key link in our mind. The problem, we recall, is to explain how growth enters the changelessness of a circular flow system. Is it by changes in the quantity and quality and labor and capital that establish the system's production possibility frontier — its potential supply? Or is it through changes in the flows of expenditure of the four great sectors that determine the level of its aggregate demand? The answer is both, and the matter is sufficiently important so that it is worth our while to review it entirely once more.

1. *The stock of our labor and capital resources are elements of supply that determine the limits of our growth.* With all the demand in the world, we cannot grow faster

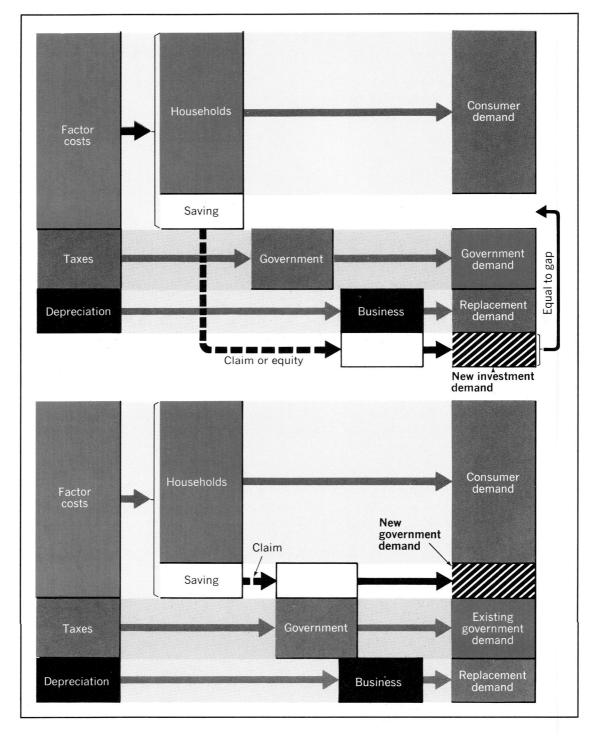

Figure 3

TWO WAYS OF CLOSING THE DEMAND GAP

There remains only to show how the savings of the household sector, now transferred to business or government, can be spent by these latter sectors to offset the gap in demand in consumption. Note: *There is no guarantee that the offsets will just balance the savings. They may be too much, bringing us growth or inflation — or too little, bringing recession.*

than these real elements allow. But we may not grow as fast as these real factors permit. The rate at which we grow depends on how much of our capacity to produce is called forth by our expenditure.

2. *Growth enters the economy when labor and capital are used to produce goods and services that increase our productivity.* Usually these are capital goods. Thus we can think of growth from the supply side as moving resources and labor into the formation of capital, which often means away from a declining industry into a booming one.

3. *Financial saving is the way in which a market economy carries out these transfers of resources.* In a command economy such as the USSR, they would be carried out by direct orders from a planning agency. When we save part of our income — for instance, when we put money into a bank — we refrain from using all our potential spending power. The saving that we perform therefore has a counterpart in the labor and capital that we "free up" by not consuming to our full abilities.

4. *These freed resources are now available for bringing about the changes in supply that will give us more (or better) output.* Thus savings are the indispensable condition for capital formation and growth. But the act of financial saving creates a problem along with this opportunity. The problem is the familiar demand gap which must be offset by additional expenditure in another sector if GNP is not to decline.

5. *Even if savings are offset by net investment, there is no guarantee that growth will be adequate.* The volume of investment spending may fall short of the amount needed wholly to compensate for the diminution of consumer spending. Or the new output may prove unsuited to the market, creating losses for investing firms instead of profits. Or government fiscal or monetary policies may interfere with the growth process.

6. *Last but not least, there may be more additional business or government spending than the flow of savings can accommodate.* The pressure of total demand, in that case, may be greater than the value of the existing, or easily available, supply, bringing inflation as well as growth.

Thus steady, adequate growth — not too slow to bring us close to the production possibility frontier, not too fast to be able to contain without inflation — is a difficult goal to achieve.

Setting the Agenda

These considerations do more than review the key saving-investment link. They also establish the agenda for the chapters to come. First, we obviously need to learn more about how savings are generated in the consumer sector, and how they are put to use in the business sector. That will occupy us in the chapters immediately ahead. Thereafter we have to look into the public sector — not only because government is itself an absorber of saving, but because government policies, including unbalanced budgets, are clearly an important part of the total growth problem and process. And that still leaves the question of money. Until we have looked at the operations of the banking system and the relation between the amount of money and the volume of spending, we cannot claim to grasp the growth mechanism.

Finally, we must confront a question that will run through all these chapters: *Can we control the growth process?* Can we avoid or mitigate recessions or slow growth? Can we avoid or curb inflationary growth? These are the large questions in macroeconomics, questions toward which much of the succeeding part will be oriented.

looking back

KEY CONCEPTS

The meaning of saving	**1** Saving is indispensable for investment. To save means to refrain from using all our income for consumption, thus freeing resources for use as capital wealth.
Saving is necessary for growth, but creates a demand gap	**2** A circular flow economy has no gaps. But if we introduce the act of saving there will be some purchasing power that is not returned to the economy. Thus the act of saving, which is necessary for growth, creates the necessity to offset the gap it leaves in spending.
Intersectoral transfers of saving against claims	**3** Demand gaps can only be offset if another sector increases its spending sufficiently to offset the gap. The second sector can do this by issuing claims or equities—such as bonds or stocks—that attract saving for its use.
Necessity of sectoral cooperation; offsets must balance gaps	**4** The essential point is that intersectoral cooperation is necessary in any modern economy that has net saving. Saving creates the conditions for growth—and for decline. There must be offsets to demand gaps if GNP is not to decline. And needless to say, if the offsets are too large, inflation will follow.
Growth requires both adequate supply and adequate demand	**5** Growth is a complicated process that requires changes in the supply of and demand for GNP. Without increases in the quantity or quality of labor and capital inputs, growth is impossible, no matter how large expenditures may be. And without adequate expenditure, growth will not take place, no matter how much labor and capital is available.
Saving releases capital and labor for the purpose of capital formation	**6** Growth takes place because financial saving releases capital and labor from consumption (or other uneconomical) tasks for the purpose of capital formation. Matching the supply of labor and capital with the right amount of demand is the central problem of macroeconomics.

ECONOMIC VOCABULARY

Saving 234
Demand gap 235
Claims 237

Linkage of savings and investment 239
Intersectoral cooperation 239

QUESTIONS

1. What do we mean by a demand gap? Show in a diagram. (And draw the diagram very, very carefully.)

2. In the same diagram show how this gap can be offset by business investment. Now show how the gap could have been filled by government spending.

3. Why is saving indispensable for investment? Can you think of any way in which a society could gather together the factors of production to undertake investment unless it had performed an act of saving? From this point of view, what does "saving" mean?

4. Can we have an act of saving without an act of investment?

CHAPTER 15
Household Demand

a look ahead

There are three chapters in this section of our macroeconomic studies. They concern the dynamics of the system, approached from the point of view of the major flows that go into GNP. Thus we first study the forces that determine the level of consumption spending; then the forces that act on investment spending; then those that are paramount in the government sector. It is hardly necessary to point out that these three chapters take us into the heart of macroeconomics by allowing us to understand the manner in which changes in the spending of households, or business firms, or government agencies affect the overall level of GNP.

We begin in Chapter 15 with the sector most familiar to us—the household sector.

1 There is one essential economic fact to be mastered in this chapter. It has to do with the basic passivity of consumption—the fact that consumption has generally followed income and has rarely been an independent economic force of its own.

2 There is a new relationship, and its associated vocabulary to learn: The propensity to consume describes how we divide our income between consumption and saving. The *average* propensity to consume describes the division of our *total* income; the *marginal* propensity to consume describes the division of any *changes* in our income.

3 Putting together the propensity to consume and the idea of consumption's passivity we will arrive at a consumption function—a simple mathematical way of depicting how the nation's consumption relates to its income.

With a basic understanding of the crucial role of expenditure and of the complex relationship of saving and investment behind us, we are in a position to look more deeply into the question of the determination of gross national product. For what we have discovered so far is only the *mechanism* by which a market economy can sustain or fail to sustain a given level of output through a circuit of expenditure and receipt. Now we must try to discover the *forces* that dynamize the system, creating or closing gaps between income and outgo. What causes a demand for the goods and services measured in the GNP? Let us begin to answer that question by examining the flow of demand most familiar to us — consumption.

THE HISTORIC PICTURE

Figure 1 shows us the flow of consumption spending since 1929. Certain things stand out.

1. Consumption Spending Is by Far the Largest Category of Spending in GNP. Total consumer expenditures — for durable goods such as automobiles or washing machines, for nondurables like food or clothing, and for services such as recreation or medical care — account for approximately two-thirds of all the final buying in the economy.

2. Consumption Is Not Only the Biggest, but the Most Stable of All the Streams of Expenditure. Consumption is *the* essential economic activity. Even if there is a total breakdown in the social system, households will consume some bare minimum. Further, it is a fact of common experience that even in adverse circumstances, households seek to maintain their accustomed living standards. Thus consumption activities constitute a kind of floor for the level of overall economic activity. Investment and government spending, as we shall see, are capable of sudden reversals; but the streams of consumer spending tend to display a measure of stability over time.

3. In Depression, Inflation, and War, the Share of Consumption in GNP Will Vary. This proportionate fluctuation must reflect changes in the relative importance of investment and government spending. And indeed this is the case. As investment spending declined in the Depression, consumption bulked relatively larger in GNP; as government spending increased during World War II, consumption bulked relatively smaller. The changing *relative* size of consumption, in other words, reflects broad changes in *other* sectors rather than sharp changes in consuming habits.

To this broad generalization, we must make a partial exception for the behavior of consumption during inflation. As we shall see, consumption can take on a life of its own in periods when consumers buy in advance of their normal needs because they hope to beat expected price rises.

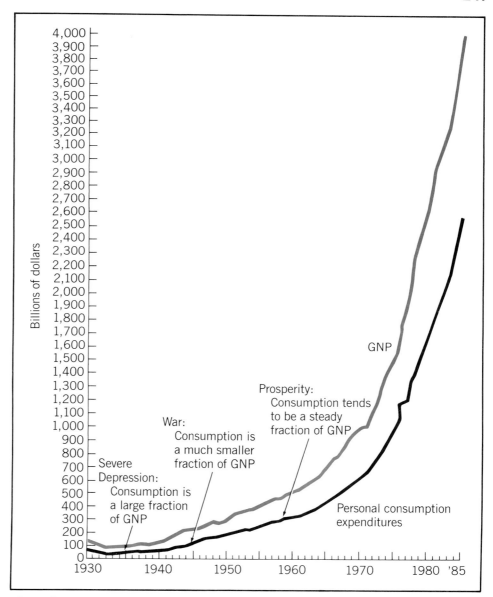

Figure 1

The statistics of consumption show that it tends to be a reliably steady share *of GNP.*
There are two big exceptions to this generalization. Wars roll back consumption to make
room for military production, so that consumption falls as a share of GNP. And severe
depressions result in a fall in business spending, so that consumption bulks larger as a
fraction of GNP.
Source: *Economic Report of the President,* February 1986.

4. Despite Its Importance, Consumption Alone Will Not "Buy Back" GNP. It is well to recall that consumption, although the largest component of GNP, is still *only* two-thirds of GNP. Government buying and business buying of investment goods are essential if the income-expenditure circuit is to be closed. During our subsequent analysis it will help to remember that consumption expenditure by itself does not provide the only impetus for demand.

Consumption, Saving, and Income

This first view of consumption activity sets the stage for our inquiry into the dynamic causes of fluctuations in GNP. We already know that the saving-investment relationship lies at the center of this problem and that much saving arises from the household sector. Hence, let us see what our knowledge of household consumption can tell us about the supply of saving.

We begin with Figure 2 showing the relationship of household saving to disposable income—that is, to household sector incomes after the payment of taxes.

What we see here are two interesting facts. First, during the bottom of the Great Depression there were *no* savings in the household sector. In fact, under the duress of unemployment, millions of households were forced to **dissave**—to borrow or to draw on their old savings (hence the negative figure for the sector as a whole). By way of contrast, we notice the immense savings of the peak war years when incomes were high, consumer goods were rationed, and prices were controlled. Clearly, then, the *amount* of saving is capable of great fluctuation, falling to zero or to negative figures in periods of great economic distress and rising to as much as a quarter of income during the managed economy of wartime.

Figure 2
SAVING AS A PERCENT OF DISPOSABLE INCOME
The ratio of savings to disposable income is remarkably steady, war and depression aside. This steadiness will become the basis of an important generalization about the macro behavior of the economy.
Source: *Economic Report of the President.*

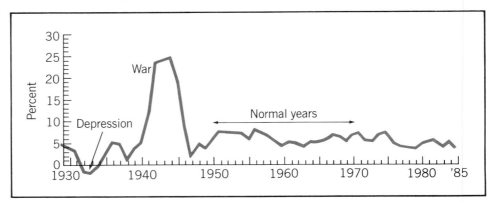

In this graph we are struck by another fact. However variable the amounts, the savings ratio shows a considerable stability in normal years. This steadiness is particularly noteworthy in the postwar period. From 1950 to the mid-1980s, consumption has ranged between roughly 92 and 95 percent of disposable personal income — which is, of course, the same as saying that savings have ranged roughly between 8 percent and 5 percent. If we take the postwar period as a whole, we can see that in an average year we have consumed a little more than 94 cents of each dollar of income and that this ratio has remained fairly constant even though our incomes have increased markedly.

Long-Run Trends

Looking at the postwar period as a whole, there seems to be a gradual declining trend to household savings, which were 50 percent higher in 1975 than they were 10 years later. Whether this represents a permanent change in behavior patterns, we do not yet know. It worries many economists, who fear that we need to encourage household savings as a source of business investment. Others believe that

Savings, Inflation, and Credit

You will note a drop in the savings rate starting in 1976 and lasting until 1980 or 1981. This seems to have been a consequence of high inflation rates and easy credit conditions. During the inflation real incomes fell and wages did not keep up with prices, mainly because imported goods like oil went up in price much more sharply than domestically produced goods. To maintain living standards, households borrowed heavily. As consumer credit soared, household savings fell.

The "tight money" policy that began in 1979 (coupled with controls put on consumer credit in 1980) broke the back of this borrowing spree. As households found that they were forced to rely more on their incomes, their spending propensities again became more cautious. All in all, the proportion of savings to disposable personal income (income after taxes) rose from 5.9 percent in 1979 to 6.7 percent by 1981. The decline in the inflationary trend after 1981 may have helped raise the savings rate by making it less tempting to buy ahead of needs, and the Reagan administration's tax proposals also aimed at augmenting savings. But these effects have not proved durable. By 1985 the personal savings rate had fallen back to 4.6 percent.

higher investment will *create* additional savings by raising our national income. This is an important macroeconomic issue to which we will return.

The long-run trends in the saving ratio interest us for another reason as well. Statistical investigations of the nation reveal that rich families tend to save a larger proportion of their incomes than poor ones. Does it not therefore stand to reason that the nation as a whole ought to save a steadily rising fraction of its total income as its wealth increases and as families move from lower to higher income brackets?

Were this so, the economy would face a very serious problem. To sustain higher levels of aggregate income, it would have to match a swelling ratio of savings with an equally fast-growing share of investment. As we shall see in the next chapter, investment is always a source of potential trouble because it is inherently a risky undertaking. If we had to keep on making proportionally larger investments, compared with GNP, to absorb our proportionally larger share of savings, we would live in an exceedingly vulnerable economic environment. Yet this is not the case. Our savings ratio, far from rising over time, has displayed a great deal of stability over the last century, and has drifted lower, not higher, in recent years. How do we square this with the fact that our real level of income is much higher than it was, and that all almost families have moved over time from lower to higher income brackets?

Relative Incomes and Saving

The explanation turns on the importance of *relative* incomes in making consumption decisions. It is well known that individuals set their living standards to conform with those of the community in which they live — this is the famous keeping-up-with-Joneses syndrome. This habit carries an important economic consequence: As income levels rise, so do consumption standards. For example, a family that earned $3,000 in 1940 probably saved a larger proportion of that income than one that earned $25,000 in 1985. The reason is that $3,000 in 1940 put one well above the median income, into the bracket of the moderately affluent. Accordingly, such a family saved a fraction of its income customary for other well-to-do households. In 1985 a family with $25,000 was just about at the median. As an average family, it felt "obliged" to maintain a standard of living that matched that of its neighbors. This resulted in a much more consumption-oriented disposition of income than the affluent family of 25 years ago, despite the huge difference in their nominal incomes.

The same relative income effect is seen in the savings rates of black families. For any given income level, the average black family saves more than the average white family. Since black family incomes are lower than white family incomes, any given income has a higher relative position among blacks than it does among whites. To keep up with their more affluent peer group, whites at that income level consequently spend more than blacks.

As a result of these and still other motivations, savings behavior in the long run differs considerably from that in the short run. Over the years, American households have shown a remarkable stability in their rate of overall savings. Its importance has already been mentioned. In a shorter period of time, however — over a few months or perhaps a year — households tend to save higher fractions of increases in their incomes than they do in the long run. The very great importance of this fact we shall subsequently note.

THE CONSUMPTION–INCOME RELATIONSHIP

What we have so far seen are some of the historical and empirical relationships of consumption and personal saving to income. We have taken the trouble to investigate these relationships in some detail, since they are among the most important causes of the gaps that have to be closed by investment. But the statistical facts in themselves are only a halfway stage in our macroeconomic investigation. Now we want to go beyond the facts to generalized understanding of the behavior that gives rise to them. Thus our next task is to extract from the facts certain behavioral *relationships* that are sufficiently regular and dependable for us to build into a new dynamic model of the economy.

If we think back over the data we have examined, one primary conclusion comes to mind. This is the indisputable fact that the *amount* of saving generated by the household sector depends in the first instance upon the income enjoyed by the household sector. Despite the long-run stability of the savings ratio, the dollar volume of saving in the economy is susceptible to great variation, from negative amounts in the Great Depression to very large amounts in boom times. Now we must see if we can find a systematic connection between the changing size of income and the changing size of saving.

Propensity to Consume

There is indeed such a relationship, lying at the heart of macroeconomic analysis. We call it the *consumption function* or, more formally, the *propensity to consume,* the name invented by John Maynard Keynes, the famous English economist who first formulated it in 1936.* What is this "propensity" to consume? **It means that the relationship between consumption behavior and income is sufficiently dependable so that we can actually *predict* how much consumption (or how much saving) will be associated with a given level of income.**

We base such predictions on a *schedule* that enables us to see the income-consumption relationship over a considerable range of variation. Table 1 is such a schedule — a purely hypothetical one for us to examine.

* See Chapter 3 for more on Keynes.

Table 1

A PROPENSITY TO CONSUME SCHEDULE

A typical propensity to consume schedule shows that savings and consumption both rise as income rises.

Income	Consumption (Billions of Dollars)	Savings
$100	$80	$20
110	87	23
120	92	28
130	95	35
140	97	43

One could imagine, of course, innumerable different consumption schedules; in one society a given income might be accompanied by a much higher propensity to consume (or a lower propensity to save) than in another. But the basic hypothesis of Keynes—a hypothesis amply confirmed by research—was that the consumption schedule in all modern industrial societies had a particular basic configuration, despite these variations. **The propensity to consume, said Keynes, reflected the fact that on the average, people tended to increase their consumption as their incomes rose,** *but not by as much as their income increased.* **In other words, as the incomes of individuals rose, so did both their consumption** *and their savings.*

Note that Keynes did not say that the *proportion* of saving necessarily rose. We have seen how involved is the dynamic determination of savings ratios. Keynes merely suggested that in the short run, the *amount* of saving would rise as income rose—or to put it conversely again, that families would not use *all* their increases in income for consumption purposes alone. It is well to remember that these conclusions hold in going down the schedule as well as up. **Keynes' basic law implies that when there is a decrease in income, there will be some decrease in the** *amount of saving,* **or that a family will not absorb a fall in its income entirely by contracting its consumption.**

What does the consumption schedule look like in the United States? We will come to that shortly. First, however, let us fill in our understanding of the terms we will need.

Average Propensity to Consume

The consumption schedule gives us two ways of measuring the fundamental economic relationship of income and saving. One way is simply to take any given level of income and to compute the percentage relation of consumption to that income. This gives us the *average propensity to consume.* In Table 2, using the same hypothetical schedule as before, we make this computation.

The average propensity to consume, in other words, tells us how a society at any given moment divides its total income between consumption and saving. It is thus a kind of measure of long-run savings behavior, for households divide their income between saving and consuming in ratios that reflect established habits and, as we have seen, do not ordinarily change rapidly.

Table 2

CALCULATION OF THE AVERAGE PROPENSITY TO CONSUME

We calculate the average propensity to consume simply by dividing consumption by income.

Income	Consumption	Consumption ÷ Income (Av. Propensity to Consume)
	(Billions of Dollars)	
$100	$80	.80
110	87	.79
120	92	.77
130	95	.73
140	97	.69

Marginal Propensity to Consume

But we can also use our schedule to measure another very important aspect of saving behavior: the way households divide *increases* (or decreases) in income between consumption and saving. This *marginal propensity to consume* is quite different from the average propensity to consume, as the figures in Table 3 (still from our original hypothetical schedule) demonstrate.

Note carefully that the last column in Table 3 is designed to show us something quite different from the last column of the previous table. Take a given income level—say $130 billion. In Table 2 the average propensity to consume for that income level is .73, meaning that we will actually spend on consumption 73 percent of our income of $130 billion. But the corresponding figure opposite $130 billion in the marginal propensity to consume table (3) is .30. This does *not* mean that out of our $130 billion income we somehow spend only 30 percent, instead of 73 percent, on consumption. It *does* mean that we spend on consumption only 30 percent *of the $10 billion increase* that lifted us from a previous income of $120 billion to the $130 billion level. The rest of that $10 billion increase we saved.

Table 3

CALCULATION OF THE MARGINAL PROPENSITY TO CONSUME

We calculate the marginal propensity to consume by dividing changes in our consumption by changes in our income.

Income	Consumption	Change in Income	Change in Consumption	Marginal Propensity to Consume = Change in Consumption ÷ Change in Income
		(Billions of Dollars)		
$100	$80	—	—	—
110	87	$10	$7	.70
120	92	10	5	.50
130	95	10	3	.30
140	97	10	2	.20

Much of economics, in micro as well as macro analysis, is concerned with studying the effects of *changes* in economic life. It is precisely here that marginal concepts take on their importance. When we speak of the average propensity to consume, we relate all consumption and all income from the bottom up, so to speak, and thus call attention to behavior covering a great variety of situations and conditions. **But when we speak of the marginal propensity to consume, we are focusing only on our behavior toward *changes* in our incomes.** Thus the marginal approach is invaluable, as we will see, in dealing with the effects of short-run fluctuations in GNP.

A Scatter Diagram

The essentially simple idea of a systematic behavioral relationship between income and consumption will play an extremely important part in the model of the economy we shall soon construct. But the relationships we have thus far defined are too vague to be of much use. We want to know if we can extract from the facts of experience not only a general dependence of consumption on income, but a *fairly precise method of determining exactly how much saving will be associated with a given amount of income.*

Here we reach a place where it will help us to use diagrams and simple equations rather than words alone. So let us begin by transferring our conception of a propensity to consume schedule to a new kind of diagram directly showing the interrelation of income and consumption.

The scatter diagram (Figure 3) shows precisely that. Along the vertical axis on the left we have marked off intervals to measure total consumer expenditure in billions of dollars; along the horizontal axis on the bottom we measure disposable personal income (income after direct taxes), also in billions of dollars. The dots tell us, for the years enumerated, how large consumption and income were. For instance, if we take the dot for 1985 and look directly below it to the horizontal axis, we can see that disposable personal income for that year was a little above $2,800 billion. The same dot measured against the vertical axis tells us that consumption for 1985 was a little less than $2,600 billion, say $2,580. If we now divide the figure for consumption by that for income, we get a value of 92.2 percent for our propensity to consume. If we subtract that from 100, our propensity to save must have been 7.8 percent.*

Returning to the diagram itself, we notice that the black line which fits the trend of the dots does not go evenly from corner to corner. If it did, it would mean that each amount of income was matched by an *equal* amount of consumption — in other words, that there was no saving. Instead, the line leans slightly downward, indicating that as income goes higher, consumption also increases, but not by quite as much.

Does the chart also show us marginal propensity to consume? Not really. As we

---

* It is difficult to read figures accurately from a graph. The actual values are: disposable income, $2,801 billion; consumption, $2,582 billion; average propensity to consume, 92.2 percent.

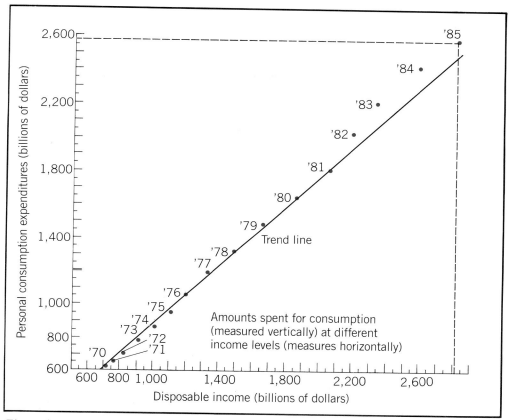

Figure 3
U.S. PROPENSITY TO CONSUME, 1970–1985

A scatter diagram shows the functional relationship between two variables—in this case between consumption and income. The trend line is fitted by a statistical technique known as "the least squares method." The trend line shows us the average propensity to consume. We get a very rough (and not very accurate) idea of the marginal propensity to consume by noting the slope of the line between two consecutive years.
Source: *Economic Indicators.*

know, our short-run savings propensities are higher than our long-run propensities. This chart shows our settled position from year to year, after the long-run, upward drift of spending has washed out our marginal (short-run) savings behavior.

Nevertheless, if we look at the movement from one dot to the next, we get some notion of the short-run forces at work. During the World War II years, for instance, as the result of high income, price controls, a shortage of some consumer goods, and a general exhortation to save, the average propensity to consume was unusually low. That is why the dots during those years form a bulge below the trend line. After the war, we can also see that the marginal propensity to consume must have been very high. As a matter of fact, for a few years consumption actually rose faster than income, as people used their wartime savings to buy things that were unavailable during the war. Between 1946 and 1947, for example, disposable income rose by some $9.8 billion, but personal outlays rose by almost $18 billion! By 1950, however, the consumption-income relationship was back to virtually the same ratio as during the 1930s.

The Consumption Function in Simple Math

There is another way of reducing to shorthand clarity the propensity to consume. Obviously, what we are looking for is a functional relationship between income (Y) the independent variable, and consumption (C), the dependent variable. In mathematical language we write

$$C = f(Y)$$

and we want to discover what f looks like.

Highly sophisticated and complex formulas have been tried to fit values of C and Y. Their economics and their mathematics are both beyond the scope of this book. But we can at least get a clearer idea of what it means to devise a **consumption function** by trying to make a very simple one ourselves. If we look at statistics, we find that during the depression years, at very low levels of income, around $50 billion, consumption was just as large as income itself. (In some years it was actually bigger; as we have seen, there was net dissaving in 1933.) Hence, we might hypothesize that a consumption function for the United States might have a fixed value representing this "bottom," plus some regular fraction designating the amount of income that would be spent for all income over that amount.

A Generalized Consumption Function

This is a very important hypothesis. **It enables us to describe the consumption function as an amount that represents rock-bottom consumption, to which we add additional consumption spending as income rises. If a is the bottom, and subsequent spending out of additional income is $b(Y)$, where b represents this marginal spending propensity, we can now write the consumption function as a whole as:**

$$C = a + b(Y)$$

We have seen that a is $50 billion, and we know that our actual spending propensity, b, is about 94 percent. Therefore, we can get a *very rough* approximation of consumption by taking $50 billion and adding to it 94 percent of our disposable income over $50 billion. In 1984, for example, disposable income was $2,577 billion. If we add $50 billion and .94 (2,577 − 50), we get $2,425. Actual consumption in 1984 was 6 percent more than this.

A 6 percent discrepancy may seem small to us, but it is much too large to be useful for econometricians who seek to project the flow of consumption. Hence the formulas that relate C and GNP are much more complex than our simple linear function. The process of translating economics into econometrics—that is, of finding ways to represent abstract theoretical relationships in terms of specific

CONSUMER CREDIT

What about consumer credit, someone will ask. Aren't many families in debt up to their ears? Doesn't the ability to buy on credit enable consumers as a group to spend more than their incomes?

Consumer credit indeed enables families to spend a larger amount than they earn as incomes or receive as transfers, for short periods of time. During the late 1970s consumers went on a credit card binge, piling up unprecedented amounts of outstanding credit. Nonetheless, consumers did not use credit to spend more than their total receipts; some consumers did, but consumers as a group did not. We know this is true because the value of all consumption spending includes purchases made on credit, such as cars or many other kinds of items bought on household loans or on installment. But this total spending was less than the total receipts of the consumer sector. Thus there continued to be net household saving, although the *rate* of saving fell.

Consumer credit was hit hard by the imposition of credit controls. The squeeze continued for several years because of extraordinarily high interest rates. As a result, consumer borrowing diminished and household saving accordingly rose.

Would there be more saving if there were no credit? In that situation, many families would put income aside until they had accumulated enough to buy cars, refrigerators, houses, and other big items. During the period that they were saving up to buy these goods, their savings rates would certainly be higher than if they had consumer credit at their disposal. But after they had bought their "lumpy" goods, their savings rates would again fall, perhaps below the level of a consumer credit economy, which tempts us to buy lumpy items and to perform our saving through installment payments.

As a result, we would expect to find high savings rates in an economy where desires for lumpy items were increasing but where consumer credit was not available. Economists cite this as one explanation of the fact that Japanese families have personal savings rates that are more than three times as high as American families, even though Japanese incomes are lower. In Japan you cannot "buy now, pay later," so you save now and buy later.

empirical relations — is a very difficult one. Nonetheless, even our simple example gives an idea of what the economist and the econometrician hope to find; a precise way of expressing functional interrelations (like those between consumption and income) so that the relations will be useful in making predictions.

Passivity of Consumption

Throughout this chapter we have talked of the dynamics of consuming and saving. **Now it is important that we recall the main conclusion of our analysis, the essential passivity of consumption as an economic process.** Consumption spending, we will recall, is a function of income. This means it is a *dependent* variable in the economic process, a factor that is acted *on,* but that does not itself generate spontaneous action.

To be sure, it is well to qualify this assertion. For one thing, consumption is so large a fraction of total spending that small changes can bring large results. In 1974 and again in 1979 consumers held back on car purchases for fear of gasoline shortages, and the effect on automobile sales had considerable impact on GNP. And we have already called attention to the push exerted by inflation-induced consumption in the late 1970s.

Yet these are exceptions to the rule. During the normal course of things, no matter how intense wants may be, consumers ordinarily lack the spendable cash to translate their desires into effective demand. Brief swings in consumption — as for automobiles — may give rise to short-run fluctuations in saving. But these swings are short-lived and therefore cannot drive the economy upward or downward for any extended period of time.

Can Consumption Drive the Economy?

This highlights an extremely important point. **Wants and appetites *alone* do not drive the economy upward; if they did, we should experience a more impelling demand in depressions, when people are hungry, than in booms, when they are well off.** Hence the futility of those who urge the cure of depressions by suggesting that consumers should buy more! There is nothing consumers would ordinarily rather do than buy more. Let us not forget, furthermore, that consumers are at all times being cajoled and exhorted to increase their expenditures by the multibillion-dollar pressures exerted by the advertising industry.

The trouble is, however, that consumers cannot steadily buy more unless they have more incomes to buy with. Of course, for short periods they can borrow or they may temporarily sharply reduce their rate of savings; but each household's borrowing capacity or accumulated savings are limited, so that once these bursts are over, the steady, habitual ways of saving and spending are apt to reassert themselves.

Thus it is clear that in considering the consumer sector we study a part of the economy that, however ultimately important, is not in itself the source of major changes in activity. Consumption mirrors and, as we shall see, can magnify disturbances elsewhere in the economy; but it does not initiate the greater part of our long-run economic fortunes or misfortunes.

looking back

KEY CONCEPTS

Consumption spending is the largest and steadiest flow in GNP. Disposable income is factor earnings after direct taxes

1 The household sector is the largest of the components of GNP. Household income is called disposable personal income —it is factor earnings minus taxes plus transfers. Household expenditures are called consumption. The main categories of consumption are nondurables, durables, and services. Altogether, consumption spending is the biggest and the steadiest of the GNP flows.

2 Despite its steadiness and size, however, consumption fluctuates and will not buy back GNP.

Long-run savings habits have been very stable at 5–8 percent a year. Inflation may be discouraging saving

3 Savings behavior is very steady over the long run. We tend to save about 5 to 8 percent of our incomes, except for exceptional periods such as war, depression, or inflation. This long-run stability is probably attributable to the sociological factor known as "keeping up with the Joneses." Inflation may be changing these spending habits.

The propensity to consume is simply a fraction: *C* to *Y*. The hypothesis is that changes in income are always used for both saving and consuming

4 The relation between saving and income is called the propensity to consume. The words themselves simply mean the ratio into which we divide income between consumption and saving. But the behavior hypothesis of the propensity to consume is that *increases* in income are never entirely spent or entirely saved, but are used for both spending and saving in regular, predictable ways.

Average and marginal propensity to consume

5 The measure of the relation between any given level of income and its associated level of consumption is called the *average* propensity to consume. The relation between a change in income and the associated change in saving or consumption is called the *marginal* propensity to consume.

$C = a + b(Y)$ where *a* is the "bottom" and *b* is the proportion of *Y* used for consumption

6 The generally accepted hypothesis about consumption behavior is that there is a "bottom"—a level of consumption that will be maintained (for a while) even if income falls below consumer spending by using up past saving to maintain a minimum standard of living. Additional income over this bottom will be divided in some regular way between consumption and saving.

Consumption is a dependent variable in the GNP flow

The bottom is designated a. The division of income (Y) between consumption and saving is designated b. Thus we write the consumption function as $C = a + b(Y)$.

7 Although changes in consumption can exert considerable effects on GNP because of the size of total consumption, consumption is usually a passive element in the flow. It is Y that is the independent variable, not C.

ECONOMIC VOCABULARY

Nondurables, services, durables 246, 262	Average propensity to consume 252
Dissaving 248	Marginal propensity to consume 253
Savings ratio 249	Scatter diagram 254
Propensity to consume 251	Consumption function 256
	Disposable personal income 261

QUESTIONS

1. Why are some components of consumption more dynamic than others? Why, for instance, does the demand for durables fluctuate more widely than that for services? (Has *durability* something to do with it?)

2. "The reason we have depressions is that consumption isn't big enough to buy the output of our farms and factories." What is wrong about this statement? Is it *all* wrong?

3. Suppose a family has an income of $30,000 and saves $1,500. What is its average propensity to consume? Can you tell from this information what its marginal propensity to consume is?

4. Suppose the same family now increases its income to $32,000 and its saving to $1,750. What is its new propensity to consume? Now can you figure out its marginal propensity to consume?

5. Draw a scatter diagram to show the following:

Family Income	Savings
$20,000	$ 0
25,000	250
30,000	750
35,000	1,500
40,000	2,500

From the figures on p. 260, calculate the average propensity to consume at each level of income. Can you calculate the marginal propensity to consume for each jump in income?

AN EXTRA WORD ABOUT

The Household Sector

Largest and in many respects most important of all the sectors in the economy is that of the nation's households — that is, its families and single-dwelling individuals (the two categories together called consumer units) considered as receivers of income and transfer payments* or as savers and spenders of money for consumption.

How big is this sector? In 1982 it comprised some 60 million families and some 22 million independent individuals who collectively gathered in $2,570 billion in income and spent $1,972 billion. As Figure 4 shows, the great bulk of receipts was from factor earnings, and transfer payments played only a relatively small role. **As we can also see, we must subtract personal tax payments from household income (or *personal income* as it is officially designated) before we get *disposable personal income* — income actually available for spending.** It is from disposable personal income that the crucial choice is made to spend or save. Notice the presence of savings in the bar on the right. This is the source of a demand gap that other sectors will have to fill.

SUBCOMPONENTS OF CONSUMPTION

Finally we see that consumer spending itself divides into three main streams. The largest of these is for an assortment of expenditures we call consumer services, comprising things such as rent, doctors' or lawyers' or barbers' ministrations, theater or movie admissions, bus or taxi or plane transportation, and other purchases that are not a physical good but work performed by someone or some equipment. Second largest is for **nondurable** goods, such as food and clothing or other items whose economic life is (or is assumed to be) short. Last is a substream of expenditure for consumer **durable** goods which, as the name suggests, include items such as cars or household appliances whose economic life is considerably greater than that of most nondurables. We can think of these goods as comprising consumers' physical capital.

There are complicated patterns and interrelations among these three major streams of consumer spending. As we would expect, consumer spending for durables is extremely volatile. In bad times, such as 1933, it has sunk to less than 8 percent of all consumer outlays; in the peak of good times in the early 1970s, it came to nearly double that. Meanwhile, outlays for services have been a steadily swelling area for consumer spending

* Remember that the word *transfer* refers to payments made unilaterally — that is, without any service being performed by the recipient. Social security (or any pension) is a transfer payment. So are unemployment insurance or business subsidies, or allowances paid to children.

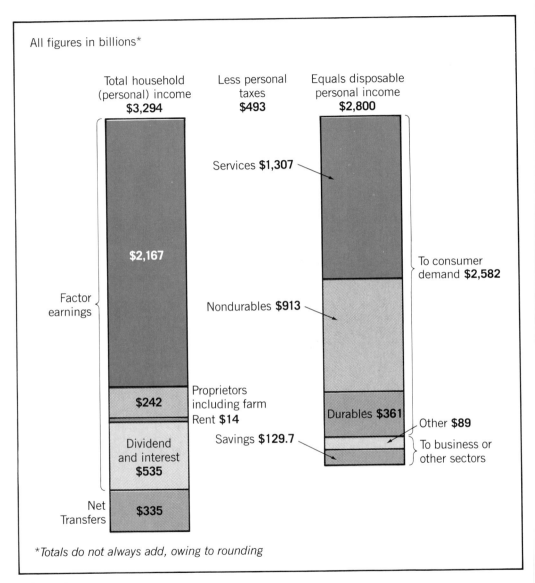

All figures in billions*

| Total household (personal) income | Less personal taxes | Equals disposable personal income |
| **$3,294** | **$493** | **$2,800** |

Services **$1,307**

$2,167

Factor earnings

Nondurables **$913**

To consumer demand **$2,582**

$242

Proprietors including farm
Rent **$14**

Dividend and interest **$535**

Durables **$361**

Other **$89**

Savings **$129.7**

To business or other sectors

Net Transfers $335

Totals do not always add, owing to rounding

Figure 4
HOUSEHOLD SECTOR, 1985
Notice that the consumption flow chart shows that the sector is a net saver. Here is the source of a demand gap that other sectors must compensate for.
Source: *Economic Indicators.*

in the postwar economy. As a consequence of the growth of consumer buying of durables and of services, the relative share of the consumer dollar going to soft goods has been slowly declining.

These internal dynamics of the household sector do not affect the basic passive behavior of that sector, but are very important for business planning.

CHAPTER 16
Business Investment

a look ahead

Warning! This is a chapter that ought to be read twice. It contains ideas that are both new and important. What is more, the vocabulary is one that most of us are not used to.

1 The vocabulary: Investment, unlike consumption, is not an activity we are familiar with at first hand; we have to learn to think of it in real terms, not financial ones.

2 There are two new ideas, both much used by economists: (a) The idea of the multiplier. You will want to learn the formula for the multiplier and to understand why it is determined by the marginal propensity to save. (b) The idea of marginal efficiency. Here you need to know about discounting future income — the key to understanding expected profit and the decision-making process behind investment.

3 Most important of all: Investment gives us the first real insight into why the macro system can be unstable. It is not only the key to growth, but the key to booms and busts. That's the idea that will unify the pages ahead.

I n studying the behavior of the consumption sector, we have begun to understand how the demand for GNP arises. Now we must turn to a second source of demand — investment demand. This requires a shift in our vantage point. As experienced consumers we know about consumption, but the activity of investing is foreign to most of us. Worse, we are apt to begin by confusing the meaning of investment, as a source of demand for GNP, with "investing" in the sense familiar to most of us when we think about buying stocks or bonds.

Investment: Real and Financial

We had best begin, then, by making certain that our vocabulary is correct. **Investing, or investment, as the economist uses the term in describing the demand for GNP, is an activity that uses the resources of the community to maintain or add to its stock of physical capital.** It is the counterpart of the real activity of saving we learned about in Chapter 14.

Investment may or may not coincide with the purchase of a security. When we buy an ordinary stock or bond, we usually buy it from someone who has previously owned it, and therefore our personal act of "investment" becomes, in the economic view of things, merely a *transfer* of claims without any direct bearing on the creation of new wealth. A pays B cash and takes his General Output stock: B takes A's cash and doubtless uses it to buy stock from C; but the transactions between A and B and C in no way alter the actual amount of real capital in the economy. Only when we buy *newly issued* shares or bonds, and then only when their proceeds are directly allocated to new equipment or plant, does our act of personal financial investment result in the addition of wealth to the community. In that case, A buys his stock directly (or through an investment banker) from General Output itself, and not from B. A's cash can now be spent by General Output for new capital goods, as presumably it will be.

Thus, much of investment, as economists see it, is a little-known form of activity for the majority of us. This is true not only because real investment is not the same as personal financial investment, but because the real investors of the nation usually act on behalf of an institution other than the familiar one of the household. **The unit of behavior in the world of investment is typically the business firm, just as in the world of consumption it is the household.** Boards of directors, chief executives, or small business proprietors are the persons who decide whether or not to devote business cash to the construction of new facilities or to the addition of inventory; and this decision, as we shall see, is very different in character and motivation from the decisions familiar to us as members of the household sector.

INVESTMENT IN HISTORIC PERSPECTIVE

Let us take a look at the flow of investment not over a single year but over many years, as we did with consumption.

In Figure 1 several things spring to our attention. Clearly, investment demand is

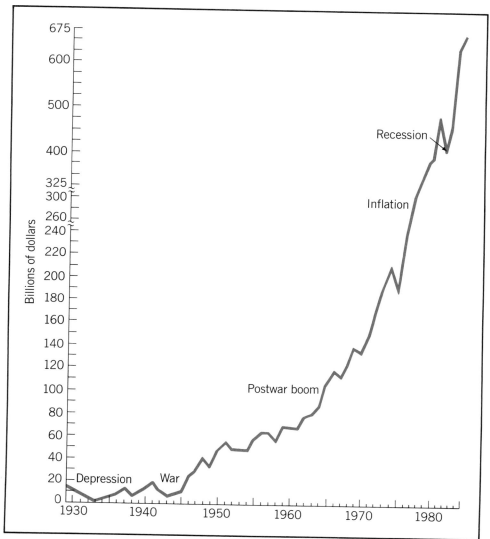

Figure 1

GROSS PRIVATE DOMESTIC INVESTMENT 1929–1985

It is evident that investment is a much more volatile item than consumption. Look at the collapse in the Great Depression. The World War II trough was different—investment was pushed aside for war spending. Then came the great postwar boom.
Sources: *Economic Report of the President; Economic Indicators.*

not nearly so smooth a flow of spending as consumption. Note that gross investment in the depths of the Depression virtually disappeared—that we almost failed to *maintain,* much less add to, our stock of wealth. (Net investment was, in fact, a negative figure for several years.) Note also investment was reduced during the war years as private capital formation was deliberately limited through government allocations.

Four important conclusions emerge from this examination of investment spending:

First, as we have many times stressed, investment is a major vehicle for growth. The upward sweep of investment is a basic explanation of our long-run rising GNP.

Second, as we have already seen, investment spending contains a component —net additions to inventory—that is capable of drastic, sudden shifts. This accounts for much of the wavelike movement of the total flow of investment expenditure.

Third, investment spending as a whole is capable of collapses of a severity and degree that are never to be found in consumption.

Fourth, unlike household spending, investment can fluctuate independently of income. It may rise when GNP is low, perhaps to usher in a boom. It can fall when GNP is high, perhaps to trigger a recession. It is an independent variable in the determination of demand.

The prime example of such a collapse was, of course, the Great Depression. From 1929 to 1933, while consumption fell by 41 percent, investment fell by *91 percent,* as we can see in Figure 1. At the bottom of the Great Depression in 1933, it was estimated that one-third of total unemployment was directly associated with the shrinkage in the capital goods industry. Conversely, whereas consumption rose by a little more than half from 1933 to 1940, investment in the same period rose by *nine times.*

THE MULTIPLIER

We shall look more closely into the reasons for the sensitivity of investment spending. But first a question must surely have occurred to the reader. For all its susceptibility to change, the investment sector is, after all, a fairly small sector. In 1982, total expenditures for gross private domestic investment came to less than one-seventh of GNP, and the normal year-to-year variation in investment spending in the 1960s and 1970s is only about 1 to 2 percent of GNP. To devote so much time to such small fluctuations seems a disproportionate emphasis. How could so small a tail as investment wag so large a dog as GNP?

Snowball Effect

The answer lies in a relationship of economic activities known as the *multiplier.* The multiplier describes the fact that additions to spending (or diminutions in spending) have an impact on income that is greater than the original increase or decrease in spending itself. In other words, even small increments in spending can *multiply* their effects (whence the name).

It is not difficult to understand the general idea of the multiplier. Suppose we have an island community whose economy is in a perfect circular flow, unchanging from year to year. Next, let us introduce the stimulus of a new investment expenditure in the form of a stranger who arrives from another island (with a supply of acceptable money) and who proceeds to build a house. This immediately increases the islanders' incomes. In our case, we will assume that the stranger spends $1,000 on wages for construction workers, and we will ignore all other expenditures he may make. (We also make the assumption that these workers were previously unemployed, so that the builder is not merely taking them from some other task.)

Now the construction workers, who have had their incomes increased by $1,000, are very unlikely to sit on this money. As we know from our study of the marginal propensity to consume, they are apt to save some of the increase (and they may have to pay some to the government as income taxes), but the rest they will spend on additional consumption goods. Let us suppose that they save 10 percent and pay taxes of 20 percent on the $1,000 they get. They will then have $700 left to spend for additional consumer goods and services.

But this is not an end to it. The sellers of these goods and services will now have received $700 over and above their former incomes, and they too will be certain to spend a considerable amount of their new income. If we assume that their family spending patterns (and their tax brackets) are the same as the construction workers', they will also spend 70 percent of their new incomes, or $490. And now the wheel takes another turn, as still *another* group receives new income and spends a fraction of it.

Continuing Impact of Respending

If the newcomer then departed as mysteriously as he came, we would have to describe the economic impact of his investment as constituting a single "bulge" of income that gradually disappeared. The bulge would consist of the original $1,000, the secondary $700, the tertiary $490, and so on. If everyone continued to spend 70 percent of his new income, after ten rounds all that would remain by way of new spending traceable to the original $1,000 would be about $28. Soon the impact of the new investment on incomes would have virtually disappeared.

But now let us suppose that after our visitor builds his house and leaves, another visitor arrives to build another house. This time, in other words, we assume that the level of investment spending *continues* at the higher level to which it was raised by the first expenditure for a new house. We can see that the second house will set into motion precisely the same repercussive effects as did the first, and that the new series of spendings will be added to the dwindling echoes of the original injection of incomes.

In Figure 2 we can trace this effect. The succession of colored bars at the bottom of the graph stands for the continuing injections of $1,000 as new houses are steadily built. (Note that this means the level of new investment is only being maintained, not that it is rising.) Each of these colored bars now generates a series of secondary, tertiary, etc., bars that represent the respending of income after

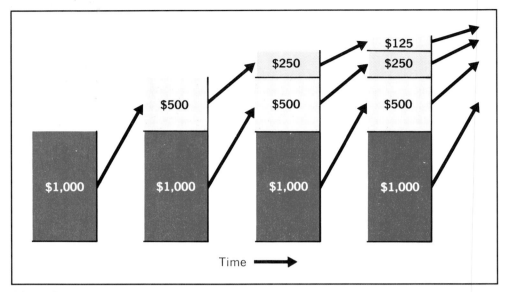

Figure 2
THE MULTIPLIER

This flow chart shows how respending creates additional income from one period to the next. This addition to income is called the multiplier. The size of the multiplier is the relation between the original new spending ($1,000) and the total new income created ($2,000). In this case, the multiplier is 2.

taxes and savings. In our example we have assumed that the respending fraction is 50 percent.

Let us now examine the effects of investment spending in a generalized fashion, without paying attention to specific dollar amounts. In Figure 3, we see the effects of a single, *once-and-for-all* investment expenditure (the stranger who came and went), contrasted with the effects of a *continuing* stream of investment.

Our diagrams show us two important things:

1. A single burst of investment creates a bulge of incomes larger than the initial expenditure, but a bulge that disappears.
2. A continuing flow of investment creates a new steady level of income, higher than the investment expenditures themselves.

Marginal Propensity to Save

We can understand now that **the multiplier is the numerical relation between the initial new investment and the total increase in income.** If the initial investment is $1,000 and the total addition to income due to the respending of that $1,000 is $3,000, we have a multiplier of 3; if the total addition is $2,000, the multiplier is 2.

What determines how large the multiplier will be? The answer depends entirely on our marginal consumption (or, if you will, our marginal saving) habits — that is,

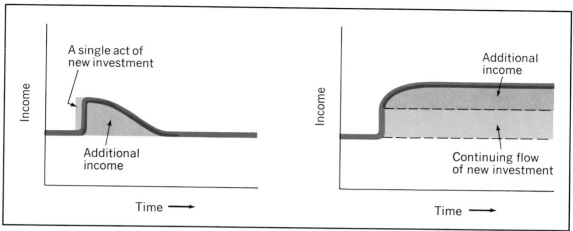

Figure 3

ONCE-OVER AND CONTINUING EFFECTS OF INVESTMENT

A single act of new spending creates a bulge in income that gradually disappears as successive receivers save part of their receipts and therefore do not respend them. A continuing flow of new spending creates a permanent addition to incomes that is larger than the new investment. Here the gradual retirement of new receipts into saving is offset by pumping out fresh additions to income.

on how much we consume (or save) out of each dollar of additional income that comes to us. Let us follow two cases in Figure 4. In the first, we will assume that each recipient spends only half of any new income that comes to him, saving the rest. In the second case, he spends three-quarters of it and saves one-quarter.

It is very clear that the amount of income that will be passed along from one receiver to the next will be much larger where the marginal propensity to consume is higher. In fact, we can see that the total amount of new incomes (total amount of boxes below) must be mathematically related to the proportion that is spent each time.

What is this relationship? The arithmetic is easier to figure if we use not the consumption fraction, but the *saving fraction* (the two are, of course, as intimately related as the first slice and the remaining cake). If we use the saving fraction, the sum of new incomes is obtained by taking the reciprocal of (i.e., inverting, or turning upside down) the fraction we save. Thus, if we save ½ our income, the total amount of new incomes generated by respending will be ½ inverted, or 2 (twice the original increase in income). If we save ¼, it will be the reciprocal of ¼, or 4 times the original change.

Basic Multiplier Formula

We call the fraction of new income that is saved the *marginal propensity to save* (often abbreviated as *mps*). As we have just seen, this fraction is the complement of an already familiar one, the marginal propensity to consume (*mpc*). If our marginal

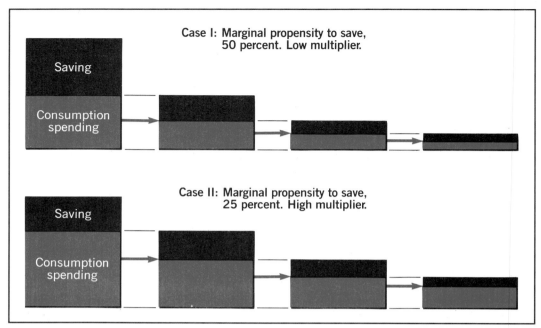

Case I: Marginal propensity to save, 50 percent. Low multiplier.

Saving

Consumption spending

Case II: Marginal propensity to save, 25 percent. High multiplier.

Saving

Consumption spending

Figure 4
COMPARISON OF TWO MULTIPLIERS

The graph makes visually apparent the obvious fact that the amount we can respend is determined by the amount we save. Therefore, the lower our savings ratio, the higher the total of our respending. Or vice versa, high marginal propensities to save result in low multipliers.

propensity to consume is 80 percent, our marginal propensity to save must be 20 percent; if our mpc is three-quarters, our mps must be one-quarter. *In brief, mps + mpc ≡ 1.*

Understanding the relationship between the marginal propensity to save and the size of the resulting respending fractions allows us to state a very simple (but very important) formula for the multiplier:

change in income = multiplier × change in investment

Since we have just learned that the multiplier is determined by the reciprocal of the marginal propensity to save, we can write:

$$\text{multiplier} = \frac{1}{\text{mps}}$$

If we now use the symbols we are familiar with, plus a Greek letter Δ, delta, that means "change in," we can write the important economic relationship above as follows:

$$\Delta Y = \left(\frac{1}{\text{mps}}\right) \times \Delta I$$

Thus, if our mps is ¼ (meaning, let us not forget, that we save a quarter of increases in income and spend the rest), then an increase in investment of $1 billion will lead to a total increase in incomes of $4 billion:

$$\$4 \text{ billion} = \left(\frac{1}{\frac{1}{4}}\right) \times \$1 \text{ billion}$$

Note that the multiplier is a complex or *double* fraction: it is $1/(\frac{1}{4})$ and *not* $1/4$. If the mps is $1/10$, $1 billion gives rise to incomes of $10 billion; if the mps is 50 percent, the billion will multiply to $2 billion. And if mps is 1? This means that the entire increase in income is unspent, that our island construction workers tuck away (or find taxed away) their entire newly earned pay. In that case, the multiplier will be 1 also, and the impact of the new investment on the island economy will be no more than the $1,000 earned by the construction workers in the first place.

LEAKAGES

The importance of the size of the marginal savings ratio in determining the effect additional investment will have on income is thus apparent. Now, however, we must pass from the simple example of our island economy to the more complex patterns of real life. The average propensity to save (the ratio of saving to disposable income) runs around 6 to 7 percent. In recent years, the *marginal* propensity to save (the ratio of additional saving to increases in income) figured over the period of a year has not departed very much from this figure. If this is the case, then, following our analysis the multiplier would be very high. If mps were even as much as 10 percent of income, a change in investment of $1 billion would bring a $10 billion change in income. If mps were nearer 6 percent—the approximate level of the average propensity to save—a change of $1 billion would bring a swing of over $16 billion. Were this the case, the economy would be subject to the most violent disturbances whenever the level of spending shifted. For example, the $70 billion swing in inventory investment in 1981 would have produced a sixteenfold fall in GNP—a fall of over $1 trillion!

Taxes. In fact, however, the impact of the multiplier is greatly reduced because the successive rounds of spending are dampened by factors other than personal saving. One of them we have already introduced in our imaginary island economy. This is the tendency of *taxation* to "mop up" a fraction of income as it passes from hand to hand. This mopping-up effect of taxation is in actuality much larger than that of saving. For every dollar of change in income, federal taxes will take about 30 cents, and state and local taxes another 6 cents.

Business Saving. Another dampener is the tendency of respending to swell *business savings* as well as personal incomes. Of each dollar of new spending, perhaps 10 cents goes into business profits, and this sum is typically saved, at least for a time, rather than immediately respent.

Imports. Still another source of dampening is the tendency of consumers and businesses to increase purchases from abroad as their incomes rise. Historically, increasing imports have diverted 4 to 5 percent of new spending to foreign nations and accordingly reduce the successive impact of each round of expenditure. In recent years this marginal propensity to import has risen sharply, and is now in the 10 to 20 percent range.

The Effect of Leakages. All these withdrawals from the respending cycle are called *leakages,* and the total effect of all leakages together (personal savings, business savings, taxes, and imports) is to reduce the overall impact of the multiplier from an impossibly large figure to a very manageable one. In dealing with the multiplier equation ($\Delta Y = 1/\text{mps} \times \Delta I$), we usually interpret mps to mean the total withdrawal from spending due to all leakages. The combined effect of all leakages brings the actual multiplier in the United States in the 1980s to a little more than 2 over a period of 2 years.

To be sure—and this is very important—all these leakages *can* return to the income stream. Household saving can be turned into capital formation; business profits can be invested; tax receipts can be disbursed in government spending programs; and purchases from foreign sellers can be returned as purchases *by* foreigners. What is at stake here is the regularity and reliability with which these circuits will be closed. In the case of ordinary income going to a household, we can count with considerable assurance on a "return expenditure" of consumption. In the case of the other recipients of funds, the assurance is much less; hence we count their receipts as money that has leaked out of the expenditure flow, for the time being.

The Downward Multiplier

The multiplier, with its important magnifying action, rests at the very center of our understanding of economic fluctuations. Not only does it explain how relatively small stimuli can exert considerable upward pushes, but it also makes much clearer than before how the failure to offset a small savings gap can snowball into a serious fall in income and employment.

For just as additional income is respent to create still further new income, a loss in income will not stop with the affected households. On the contrary, as families lose income, they cut down on their spending, although the behavior pattern of the propensity to consume schedule suggests that they will not cut their consumption by as much as their loss in income. Yet each reduction in consumption, large or small, lessens to that extent the income or receipts of some other household or firm.

We have already noted that personal savings alone do not determine the full impact of the multiplier. This is even more fortunate on the way down than on the way up. If the size of the multiplier were solely dependent on the marginal propensity to save, an original fall in spending would result in a catastrophic contraction of consumption through the economy. **But the leakages that cushion the upward pressure of the multiplier also cushion its downward effect.** As spending falls, business savings (profits) fall, tax receipts dwindle, and the flow of imports declines. We shall discuss this cushioning effect when we look into the government sector.

All of these leakages now work in the direction of mitigating the repercussions of the original fall in spending. The fall in business profits means that less will be saved by business and thus less withdrawn from respending; the decline in taxes means that more money will be left to consumers; and the drop in imports similarly releases additional spending power for the domestic market. Thus, just as the various leakages pulled money away from consumption on the way up, on the way down they lessen their siphoning effect and in this way restore purchasing power to consumers' hands. **As a result, in the downward direction as in the upward, the actual impact of the multiplier is about 2, so that a fall in investment of, say, $5 billion will lower GNP by $10 billion.**

Even with a reduced figure, we can now understand how a relatively small change in investment can magnify its impact on GNP. If the typical year-to-year change in investment is around $10 billion to $20 billion, a multiplier of 2 will produce a change in GNP of $20 billion to $40 billion — by no means a negligible figure.

The Multiplier and Inflation

Is the multiplier an inflation-breeding process? It is easy to think so, because the very word *multiplier* suggests inflation.

But that is not a correct way of looking at the question. The multiplier itself only describes the outcome of a basic pattern of economic behavior — the fact that we spend part of any additional income we receive. In itself, respending is not inflationary. But two things could make it so.

1. **If there are no more goods available — if we have reached a ceiling on production — then indeed our efforts to spend more money will only succeed in driving up prices.** Here is really "too much money chasing too few goods." But in that case the inflation-creating condition is the ceiling on production. The effort to use our income for more enjoyments is still perfectly normal.

2. **If we begin to expect inflation and therefore spend more of our incomes than we ordinarily would, or if we rush to get rid of our income as soon as possible for fear that prices will be higher tomorrow, then indeed our spending pushes us toward inflation.** This kind of panicky spending is a very important perpetuating mechanism for inflation, and we will be considering it more carefully in the chapter devoted to inflation. But even here, it is the expectations that are the cause of inflation. The respending itself is a normal part of economic behavior.

THE DEMAND FOR INVESTMENT

Consumption demand, we remember, is essentially directed at the satisfaction of the individual — at providing him with the "utilities" of the goods and services he buys. An increasingly affluent society may not be able to say that consumer expenditure is any longer solely geared to necessity, but at least it obeys the fairly constant promptings of the cultural and social environment, with the result that consumer spending, in the aggregate, fluctuates relatively little, except as income fluctuates.

Profit Expectations

A quite different set of motivations drives the investment impulse. Whether the investment is for replacement of old capital or for the installation of new capital, the ruling consideration is not apt to be the personal use or satisfaction the investment yields to the owners of the firm. **Instead, the touchstone of investment decisions is** *expected profit.*

Note the stress on *expectations.* One firm may be enjoying large profits on its existing plant and equipment at the moment; but if it anticipates no profits from the sales of goods that an *additional* investment would make possible, the firm will make no additions to capital. Another firm may be suffering current losses; but if it anticipates a large profit from the production of a new good, it may launch a considerable capital expenditure. The view is never backward, always forward.

There is a sound reason for this anticipatory quality of investment decisions. Typically, the capital goods bought by investment expenditures are expected to last for years and to pay for themselves only slowly. In addition, they are often highly specialized. If capital expenditures could be recouped in a few weeks or months, or even in a matter of a year or two, or if capital goods were easily transferred from one use to another, they would not be so risky and their dependence on expectations not so great. But it is characteristic of most capital goods that they *are* durable, with life expectancies of ten or more years, and that they tend to be limited in their alternative uses, or to have no alternative uses at all. You cannot spin cloth in a steel mill or make steel in a cotton mill.

The decision to invest is thus always forward-looking. Even when the stimulus to build is felt in the present, the calculations that determine whether or not an investment will be made necessarily concern the flow of income to the firm in the future. These expectations are inherently much more volatile than the current drives and desires that guide the consumer. Expectations, whether based on guesses or forecasts, are capable of sudden and sharp reversals of a sort rare in consumption spending. Thus in its orientation to the future we find a main cause for the volatility of investment expenditures.

The Determinants of Investment

We speak of consumption as a function of income because we know there is a behavior pattern that relates the flow of consumer spending to household incomes. Can we speak of a similar investment function relating capital spending to corporation incomes?

No such simple function exists. This is because the forward-looking nature of investment makes it inherently independent of past influences. Some investment is "induced" by past consumption—inventories, for example, may follow sales—but other investment is "autonomous"—quite independent of consumption. Much investment depends on technology, which is largely unpredictable. And other erratic or unknowable events also bring their effects to bear—the gyrations of the stock market, changes in the inflationary outlook, the ups and downs of foreign relations, and the like.

THE ACCELERATION PRINCIPLE

Nevertheless, investment expenditure is not just a random variable. There are patterns in investment, even though they may be upset by sudden, unforeseen shifts in total investment spending.

One such pattern of considerable importance is called *acceleration principle*, or sometimes just the *accelerator*. The name springs from the fact that investment often depends upon the rate of growth of the economy.

Table 1 is a model that explains this phenomenon. It shows us an industry whose sales rise for six years, then level off, and finally decline. We assume it has no unused equipment and that its equipment wears out every 10 years. Also, we will make the assumption that it requires a capital investment of $2 to produce a flow of output of $1.

Now let us see the accelerator at work.

In our first view of the industry, we find it in equilibrium with sales of, let us say, $100 million, capital equipment valued at $200 million, and regular replacement

Table 1

A MODEL OF THE ACCELERATOR

The accelerator model shows how investment spending can fall, even though sales are rising. Compare the total amount of investment in the last column with the change in sales in the second column. In the third year sales are up by $10 million. But investment spending is down by $20 million!

Year	Sales (Millions)	Existing Capital (Millions)	Needed Capital (2 × Sales) (Millions)	Replacement Investment (Millions)	Induced New Investment (2 × Addition to Sales) (Millions)	Total Investment
1	$100	$200	$200	$20	—	$20
2	120	200	240	20	$40	60
3	130	240	260	20	20	40
4	135	260	270	20	10	30
5	138	270	276	20	6	26
6	140	276	280	20	4	24
7	140	280	280	20	—	20
8	130	280	260	—	—	0
9	130	260	260	20	—	20

demand of $20 million, or 10 percent of its stock of equipment. Now we assume that its sales rise to $120 million. To produce $120 million of goods, the firm will need (according to our assumptions) $240 million of capital. This is $40 million more than it has, so it must order new equipment. Note that its demand for capital goods now shoots from $20 to $60 million: $20 million for replacement as before, and $40 million for new investment. Thus investment expenditures *triple*, even though sales have risen only 20 percent!

Now assume that in the next year sales rise further, to $130 million. How large will our firm's investment demand be? Its replacement demand will not be larger, since its new capital will not wear out for 10 years. And the amount of new capital needed to handle its new sales will be only $20 million, not $40 million as before. Its total investment demand has *fallen* from $60 million to $40.

What is the surprising fact here? It is that *we can have an actual fall in induced investment, though sales are still rising!* **In fact, as soon as the** *rate of increase* **of consumption begins to fall, the** *absolute amount* **of induced investment declines. Thus a slowdown in the rate of improvement in sales can cause an absolute decline in the orders sent to capital goods makers. This helps us to explain how weakness can appear in some branches of the economy while prosperity seems still to be reigning in the market at large. It will play a role when we come to explain the phenomenon of the business cycle.**

Now look at what happens to our model in the eighth year, when we assume that sales slip back to $130 million. Our existing capital ($280 million) will be greater by $20 million than our needed capital. That year the industry will have no new orders for capital goods and may not even make any replacements, because it can produce all it needs with its old machines. Its orders to capital goods makers will fall to zero, even though its level of sales is 30 percent higher than at the beginning. The next year, however, if sales remain steady, it will again have to replace one of its old machines. Its replacement demand again jumps to $20 million. No wonder capital goods industries traditionally experience feast or famine years!

There is, in addition, an extremely important point to bear in mind. **The accelerator's upward leverage usually takes effect only when an industry is operating at or near capacity.** When an industry is not near capacity, it is relatively simple for it to satisfy a larger demand for its goods by raising output on its underutilized equipment. Thus, unlike the multiplier, which yields its effects on output only when we have unemployed resources, the accelerator yields its effects only when we do *not* have unemployed capital.

Interest Rates and Cost of Investment

There is a second element in the economy that imposes a certain degree of orderliness on investment. This is the influence of interest rates on investment.

Interest rates affect investment in two ways. The first is to change the costs of investment. If businesses must borrow to make capital expenditures, a higher rate of interest makes it more expensive to undertake an investment. For huge firms that target a return of 15 to 20 percent on investment projects, a change in the interest rate from 10 to 11 percent may be negligible. But for certain kinds of investment—notably utilities and home construction—interest rates constitute an important component of the cost of investment funds. To these firms, the lower the cost of borrowed capital, the more stimulus for investment. The difference in *interest costs* for $1 million borrowed for 20 years at 10 percent instead of 11 percent is $200,000, by no means a negligible sum. Since construction is the largest single component of investment, the interest rate therefore becomes an important influence on the value of total capital formation.

THE STOCK MARKET AND INVESTMENT

How does the stock market affect business investment? There are three direct effects. One is that the market has traditionally served as a general barometer of the expectations of the business-minded community as a whole. We say "business-minded" rather than "business," because the demand for, and supply of, securities mainly comes from securities dealers, stockbrokers, and the investing public, rather than from nonfinancial business enterprises themselves. When the market is buoyant, it has been a signal to business that the "business climate" is favorable, and the effect on what Keynes called the "animal spirits" of executives has been to encourage them to go ahead with expansion plans. When the market is falling, on the other hand, spirits tend to be dampened, and executives may think twice before embarking on an expansion program in the face of general pessimism.

This traditional relationship is, however, greatly lessened by the growing power of government to influence the trend of economic events. Business once looked to the market as the key signal for the future. Today it looks to Washington.

A second direct effect of the stock market on investment has to do with the ease of issuing new securities. One of the ways in which investment is financed is through the issuance of new stocks or bonds whose proceeds will purchase plant and equipment. When the market is rising, it is much easier to float a new issue than when prices are falling. This is particularly true for certain businesses that depend heavily on stock issues for new capital rather than on retained earnings.

Finally, when the market is very low, companies with large retained earnings may be tempted to buy up other companies, rather than use their funds for capital expenditure. Financial investment, in other words, may take the place of real investment. This helps successful companies grow, but does not directly provide growth for the economy as a whole.

Interest Rates as a Guide to Discounting

A second guide is offered to business not directly seeking to borrow money for investment, but debating whether to invest the savings (retained earnings) of the firm. This problem of deciding on investments introduces us to an important idea: the discounting of future income.

Suppose that someone gave you an ironclad promise to pay you $100 a year hence. Would you give him $100 *now* to get back the same sum 365 days in the future? Certainly not, for in parting with the money you are suffering an *opportunity cost,* or a cost that can be measured in terms of the opportunities that your action (to pay $100 now) has foreclosed for you. Had the going rate of interest been 10 percent, for example, you could have loaned your $100 at 10 percent and had $110 at the end of the year. Hence, friendship aside, you are unlikely to lend your money unless you are paid something to compensate you for the opportunities you must give up while you are waiting for your money to return. **Another way of saying exactly the same thing is that we arrive at the** *present value* **of a specified sum in the future by discounting it by some percentage.** If the discount rate is 10 percent, the present value of $100 one year in the future is $100 ÷ 1.10, or approximately $90.90.

Discounting the Future

This brings us back to the business that is considering whether or not to make an investment. Suppose it is considering investing $100,000 in a machine that is expected to earn $25,000 a year for 5 years, over and above all expenses, after which it will be worthless. Does this mean that the expected profit on the machine is therefore $25,000—the $125,000 of expected earnings less the $100,000 of original cost? No it does not, for the expected earnings will have to be discounted by some appropriate percentage to find their present value. Thus the first $25,000 to be earned by the machine must be reduced by some discount rate; and the second $25,000 must be discounted *twice* (just as $100 to be repaid in *two* year's time will have to yield the equivalent of *two* years' worth of interest); the third $25,000, three times, etc.*

Clearly, this process of discounting will cause the present value of the expected future returns of the machine to be less than the sum of the undiscounted returns. If, for example, its returns are discounted at a rate of 10 percent, the business will find that the present value of a five-year flow of $25,000 per annum comes not to $125,000, but to only $94,700. This is *less* than the actual expenditure for the

---

* The formula for calculating the present value of a flow of future income that does not change from year to year is:

$$\text{present value} = \frac{R}{(1 + i)} + \frac{R}{(1 + i)^2} + \cdots + \frac{R}{(1 + i)^n}$$

where R is the annual flow of income, i is the interest rate, and n is the number of years over which the flow will last.

machine ($100,000). Hence, at a discount rate of 10 percent, the business would not undertake the venture.

On the other hand, if it used a discount rate of 5 percent, the present value of the same future flow would be worth (in round numbers) $109,000. In that case, the machine *would* be a worthwhile investment.

Marginal Efficiency of Investment

What rate should our business use to discount future earnings? Here is where the rate of interest enters the picture. Looking out at the economy, the business manager sees that there is a whole spectrum of interest rates, ranging from relatively low rates on bonds (usually government bonds) where the element of risk is very small, to high rates on securities of the same maturity (that is, coming due in the same number of years) where the risk is much greater, such as "low-grade" corporate bonds or mortgages. Among this spectrum of rates, there will be a rate at which he or she can borrow — high or low, depending on each one's creditworthiness in the eyes of the banking community. By applying that rate, the manager can discover whether the estimated future earning from the venture, properly discounted, is actually profitable or not.

We can see the expected effect of interest rates on investment in Figure 5. Suppose a businessman has a choice among different investment projects from which he anticipates different returns. The technical name for these discounted returns is the **marginal efficiency of investment.** Suppose he ranks those projects, as we have in Figure 5, starting with the most profitable (*A*) and proceeding to the least profitable (*G*). How far down the list should he go? The rate of interest gives the answer. Let us say that the rate (for projects of comparable risk) is shown by *OX*. Then all his investment projects whose marginal efficiency is higher than *OX* (investments *A* through *D*) will be profitable, and all those whose marginal efficiency falls below *OX* (*E* through *G*) will be discarded or at least postponed.

Note that if the interest rate falls, more investments will be worthwhile; and that if it rises, fewer will be. As the figure on the right shows in generalized form, a fall in the rate of interest (say from *OX* to *OY*) induces a rise in the quantity of investment (from *OC* to *OG*).

Interest and Investment

Thus, whether we figure interest as a cost or as a guideline against which we measure the expected returns of a capital investment, we reach the important conclusion that low interest rates should encourage investment spending — or in more formal language, that investment should be inversely related to the rate of interest.

To be sure, the fact that a given investment, such as project *B* above, has a marginal efficiency higher than the interest rate is no guarantee that a business actually will undertake it. Other considerations — perhaps political, perhaps

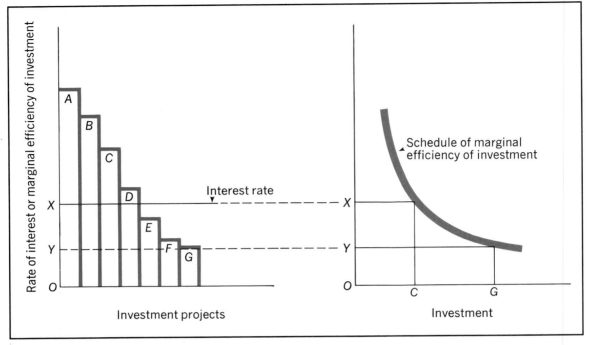

Figure 5
MARGINAL EFFICIENCY OF CAPITAL

A businessman calculates profitability by discounting the expected returns of various ventures. This gives him the marginal efficiency of those ventures. By comparing these marginal efficiencies with the rate of interest for projects of the same degree of risk, he can tell whether the opportunity cost of putting his money into the venture is worthwhile or not.

psychological — may deter management, despite its encouraging calculations. But assuredly a business will not carry out a project that yields less than the interest rate, because it can make more profit by lending the money, at the same degree of risk, than by investing it.

looking back

KEY CONCEPTS

Real vs. financial investment

1 By the term *investment,* economists usually refer to the use of resources to create new capital, not to using money to buy assets. Investment is crucial as the key to growth.

Differences of investment and consumption: expectations a key factor	**2** Investment is in large degree an independent, not a dependent, variable. It is subject to swings or even collapses of a kind unknown to consumption. Above all, investment is keyed to expectations of future profit, and not to past income.
Investment exerts an upward or downward multiplier, determined by the respending fraction mps = 1 − mpc. Respending in itself is not inflationary	**3** Investment exerts a larger effect on GNP than the direct change in investment spending. This is because income created by new investment (or income reduced by a fall in investment) is multiplied. The multiplier depends on the degree to which the original change in investment is respent. This respending fraction is the marginal propensity to consume, or its reciprocal, the marginal propensity to save. Respending is normal, not inflationary. It creates inflation only when there is too little production or when respending becomes panicky.
$$\Delta Y = \frac{1}{mps} \times \Delta I$$	**4** The effect of a change of investment on GNP therefore depends on the mpc or the mps. The simplest way to calculate the multiplier is to use the formula $Y = 1/mps$. Do not forget that mps is itself a fraction: If mps $= \frac{1}{4}$, then the multiplier is $1 \div \frac{1}{4} = 4$.
Leakages: savings imports taxes business savings	**5** The actual mps is not just determined by our personal savings. Imports, marginal taxes, and business savings also absorb increases in income and therefore lower respending. These are all leakages, which together reduce the actual effect of the multiplier to about 2 over the period of a year.
The acceleration principle links investment to increases in output; investment may fall even though output is still rising	**6** Although investment can be highly unstable, it does have some internal patterns and regularities. One of these is the accelerator or acceleration principle. This is a wavelike pattern that is induced in investment, to the extent that increases in output require ("induce") increases in investment. As output rises, induced investment at first rises faster; then investment may actually fall even though output is still growing.
Interest rates affect investment through cost	**7** Interest rates also influence investment spending. One obvious effect is that interest is a cost of investment.
Future income must be discounted to calculate the marginal efficiency of investment	**8** Interest rates are also a guide to investment profitability. Businessmen discount the expected future earnings of investment, because future income represents an opportunity cost. Interest rates show the returns available for various kinds of risk. A businessman compares the discounted earnings of any project — its marginal efficiency — with the interest rate to see if it is worth the opportunity cost.
Low interest rates encourage investment	**9** Whether as a cost or as a guide to marginal efficiencies, interest rates encourage investment when they go down and discourage it when they go up.

ECONOMIC VOCABULARY

Real vs. financial investment   266
Multiplier   268
Marginal propensity to save   270
Multiplier formula   271
Leakages   273

Acceleration principle   277
Discounting   280
Marginal efficiency of investment   281

QUESTIONS

1. If you buy a share of stock on the New York Stock Exchange, does that create an equal amount of investment?
2. Why are inventories subject to such sudden shifts?
3. Why do we face the possibility of a large-scale collapse in investment spending but not in consumption spending?
4. Draw a diagram of boxes showing the multiplier effect of $100 expenditure when the marginal propensity to spend is one-tenth. Draw a second diagram showing the effect when the mps is nine-tenths. The larger the savings ratio, the larger or smaller the multiplier?
5. Calculate the impact on income if investment rises by $10 billion and the multiplier is 2. If it is 3. If it is 1.
6. A simple problem: Income is $500 billion. Inventories decline by $5 billion. The multiplier is 2. What is the new level of income?
7. Suppose you had the following leakages: mps, 10 percent; marginal taxation, 20 percent; marginal propensity to import, 5 percent; marginal addition to business saving, 15 percent. What will be the size of the second round of spending, if the first round is $1 billion? What will be the size of the third round? What will be the final total of new spending?
8. Explain the relationship between the marginal propensity to consume and the marginal propensity to save. Why must these two fractions always add up to 1?
9. Complete the following accelerator model, assuming that you need $2 of equipment to produce $1 of output, and that replacement is at 20 percent per year. Check back on p. 277 if you need guidance.

Year	Output	Replacement Investment	New Equipment Needed	Total Investment
1	100	$40	$ 0	$—
2	120	—	40	—
3	130	—	—	—
4	135	—	—	—

10. If the rate of interest were 10 percent, what would be the present value of $100 due a year hence? Two years hence? Remember: The first year's discounted value has to be discounted a second time.

AN EXTRA WORD ABOUT

The Business Sector

Let us gain a quick acquaintance with the business sector as a whole, much as we did with the household sector.

Figure 6 gives a first general impression of the investment sector in a recent year. Note that the main source of gross private domestic investment expenditure is the retained earnings of business; that is, the expenditures come from depreciation accruals or from profits that have been kept in the business. However, as the next bar shows, gross investment *expenditures* are considerably larger than retained earnings. The difference represents funds that business obtains in the various ways — mainly borrowing or issuing new equity.

Our chart enables us to see that most gross investment is financed by business itself from its *internal* sources — retained earnings plus depreciation accruals — and that external sources play only a secondary role. In particular, this is true of new stock issues, which, during most of the 1960s and early 1970s, raised only some 3 to 8 percent of the funds spent by the business sector for new plant and equipment.

CATEGORIES OF INVESTMENT

From the total funds at its disposal, the business sector now renews its worn-out capital and adds new capital. Investment, as we know, is one of the main vehicles for growth. Let us say a word concerning some of the main categories of investment expenditure.

1. Inventories At the top of the expenditure bar in Figure 6 we note an item of minus $1 billion for *additions to inventory*. Note that this figure does not represent total inventories, but only *changes* in inventories, downward in this case. If there had been no change in inventory over the year, the item would have been zero even if existing inventories were huge. Why? Because those huge inventories would have been included in the investment expenditure flow of *previous* years when they were built up.

Inventories are often visualized as completed TV sets sitting in some warehouse. While some inventories are completed goods sitting in storage, most are in the form of goods on display in stores, half-finished goods in the process of production, or raw materials to be used in production. When a steel company adds to its stock of iron ore, it is adding to its inventories.

Investments in inventory are particularly significant for one reason. Alone among the investment categories, inventories can be *rapidly* used up as well as increased. A positive figure for one year or even one calendar quarter can quickly turn into a negative figure the next. *This means that expenditures for inventory are usually the most volatile element of*

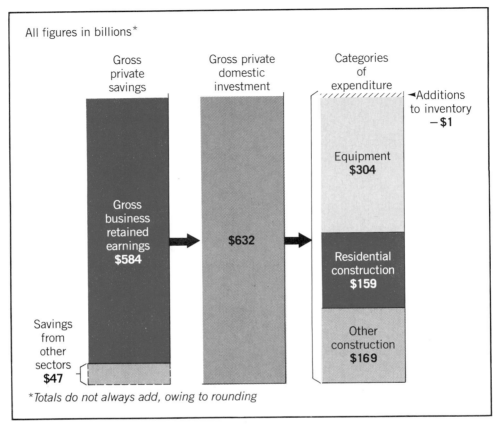

All figures in billions*

Gross private savings

Gross private domestic investment

Categories of expenditure

◄Additions to inventory −$1

Gross business retained earnings $584

$632

Equipment $304

Residential construction $159

Savings from other sectors $47

Other construction $169

*Totals do not always add, owing to rounding

Figure 6
BUSINESS SECTOR, 1985

There is one essential difference between this flow chart and that for consumption. The consumption chart shows net saving — the source of a demand gap. Investment typically shows net spending — an excess of business expenditures over the retained earnings of business.
Sources: *Economic Report of the President; Economic Indicators.*

any in gross national product. A glance at Figure 7 shows a particularly dramatic instance of how rapidly inventory spending can change. In the third quarter of 1982, we were reducing inventories at an annual rate of $61 billion a year. Five quarters later, we were building up inventories at a rate of $74 billion, on an annual basis. Thus, within a span of 18 months there was a swing of $135 billion in the rate of spending. Rapid inventory swings, although not quite of this magnitude, are by no means uncommon.

As we see more clearly later, this volatility of investment has much significance for business conditions. Note that while inventories are being built up, they serve as an offset to saving — that is, some of the resources released from consumption are used by business firms to build up stocks of inventory capital. But when inventories are being "worked off," we are actually making the demand gap bigger. As we would expect, this can give rise to serious economic troubles.

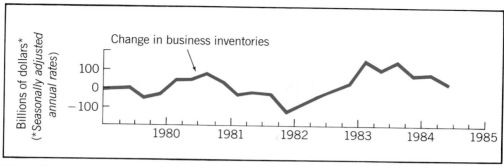

Figure 7
INVENTORY SWINGS

Inventories are a crucial portion of investment because they can change so rapidly. Compare 3Q (3rd quarter) 1981 with 1Q 1982.
Sources: *Economic Indicators; Survey of Current Business.*

2. Equipment   The next item in the expenditure bar (Figure 6) is more familiar; $206 billion for *equipment*. Here we find expenditures for goods of a varied sort — lathes, trucks, generators, computers, office typewriters.* The total includes both *new equipment* and *replacement equipment*.

New equipment is obviously a very important means of widening and deepening capital — that is, of promoting growth. But let us take a moment to consider *replacement investment*. Exactly what does it mean to "replace" a given item of equipment? Suppose we have a textile loom that cost $100,000 and is now on its last legs. Is the loom replaced by spending another $100,000, regardless of what kind of machine the money will buy? What if loom prices have gone up and $100,000 no longer buys a loom of the same capacity? Or suppose prices have remained steady but that owing to technological advance, $100,000 now buys a loom of double the old capacity?

Such problems make the definition of "replacement" an accountant's headache and an economist's nightmare. At the moment there isn't even a generally accepted estimate of replacement investment. We need not involve ourselves deeper in the question, but we should note the complexities introduced into a seemingly simple matter once we leave the changeless world of stationary flow and enter the world of invention and innovation.

3. Construction — residential   Our next section on the expenditure bar (Figure 6) is *total residential construction,* another big growth item. But why do we include this $96 billion in the investment sector when most of it is represented by new houses that householders buy for their own use?

Part of the answer is that most houses are built by business firms, such as contractors and developers, who put up the houses *before* they are sold. Thus the original expenditures involved in building houses typically come from businesses, not from households. Later, when the householder buys a house, it is an existing asset. His or her expenditure does not pump new incomes into the economy, but only repays the contractor who *did* contribute new incomes.

---

* But *not* typewriters bought by consumers. Thus the same good can be classified as a consumption item or an investment item, depending on the use to which it is put.

Actually this is a somewhat arbitrary definition, since business owns *all* output before consumers buy it. However, another reason for considering residential construction as investment is that, unlike most consumer goods, houses are typically maintained as if they were capital goods. Thus their durability also enters into their classification as investment goods.

Finally, we class housing as investment because residential purchases behave very much like other items of construction. Therefore it simplifies our understanding of the forces at work in the economy if we classify residential construction as an investment expenditure rather than as a consumer expenditure.

4. *Other construction — plant* Last on the bar, $130 billion of other construction is largely made up of the "plant" in "plant and equipment" — factories and stores and private office buildings and warehouses. (It does not, however, include public construction such as roads, dams, harbors, or public buildings, all of which are picked up under government purchases.) It is interesting to note that the building of structures, as represented by the total of residential construction plus other private construction, accounts for over half of all investment expenditures. This total would be further swelled if public construction were included. This tells us that swings in construction expenditure can be a major lever for economic change. It is one reason why high interest rates depress the economy, because the construction business depends heavily on borrowed money.

THE EXPORT SECTOR

The export sector is always added up separately in the calculation of GNP. It is *not* lumped together with investment. Nevertheless, it bears some very important resemblances to investment, so we take a quick look at it here, before we meet it again when we study international competition.

Impact of Foreign Trade We must begin by repeating that our initial overview of the economic system, with its twin streams of consumption and investment, was actually incomplete. It portrayed what we call a "closed" system, an economy with no flows of goods or services from within its borders to other nations or from other nations to itself.

First a word of explanation. Exports are the total value of all goods and services we sold to foreigners. Imports are the total value of all goods and services we bought from foreigners. The difference between the value of the goods we sold abroad and the value we bought from abroad is called *net exports,* and it constitutes the net contribution of foreign trade to the demand for GNP.

If we think of it in terms of expenditures, it is not difficult to see what the net contribution is. When exports are sold to foreigners, their expenditures add to American incomes. Imports, on the contrary, are expenditures we make to other countries (and hence that we do not make at home). If we add the foreign expenditures made here and subtract the domestic expenditures made abroad, we will have left a net figure that will show the contribution (if any) by foreigners to GNP.

The Export Multiplier What is the impact of this net expenditure on GNP? It is exactly the same as net private domestic investment. If we have a rising net export balance, we will have a net increase in spending in the economy.

Conversely, if our net foreign trade balance falls, our demand for GNP will decline, exactly as if the demand for domestic investment fell. Thus, even though we must defer for a while a study of the actual forces at work in international trade, we can quickly include the effects of foreign trade on the level of GNP by considering the net trade balance as a part of our investment demand for output.

One point in particular should be noted. If there is a rise in the net demand generated by foreigners, this will have a *multiplier effect,* exactly as an increase in investment will have. Here is, in fact, our illustrative story of an individual visiting an island come to life. Additional net foreign spending will generate new buying; and decreased net foreign spending will diminish incomes, with a similar train of secondary and tertiary effects. We will look into this problem again as we encounter the foreign trade difficulties of the United States.

CHAPTER 17

Public Spending and Deficits

a look ahead

This chapter begins our coverage of the government's role in the economy. Three basic ideas should be kept in mind as you go through the chapter.

1 The nature of the influence public spending exerts on the flow of GNP. Whether one thinks that influence is too great or too small, it is vital to know precisely how it works.

2 The meaning of a government "deficit," and the role a deficit plays in the determination of GNP.

3 The confusions that surround the deficit—as a source of growth and as a source of trouble.

We will learn in this chapter that there is no clear and simple rule about deficits. They can be useful—and they can be destructive. The most important task for an economist is to understand that deficits are a tool of fiscal policy—a tool that can be wisely or unwisely used.

THE PUBLIC SECTOR

We have become familiar with the general size and shape of the government establishment in Chapters 4 and 5. Now we are going to review and expand that familiarity by taking a careful look at the public sector.

We begin by recalling the general magnitude of government in the economy. In 1929 total government purchases of goods and services were still very small — only half as large as total private investment spending. By 1985 that had changed dramatically; government purchases had expanded to twice the size of total private investment spending. In terms of its contribution to GNP, government is now second only to consumption.

We are, of course, also interested in the composition of public spending, and Table 1 gives us a first look. Note that the columns do not add to the totals: federal grants to the states get counted again when the states spend the money. We correct for this and other forms of double-counting when we calculate the contribution of government to GNP. Two features of Table 1 you should note are: (1) most of the growth of federal spending has been of transfers, not purchases, and (2) most of the growth of state and local spending has been of purchases, not transfers.

Measuring the Public Sector

The growth of government activity within the economy has become a matter of political as well as economic importance in recent years. Opinions are sharply polarized by the question of whether or not government is "too big." That is not a question we will tackle head on — yet. And one reason why we want to defer the issue is that people can very easily argue at cross purposes if they are not very clear about what they mean when they say that "government" is too big, or possibly not big enough.

Table 1
GOVERNMENT PURCHASES AND TRANSFERS (BILLIONS OF DOLLARS)

Note that the states outspend the Federal government for purchases, but that the Federal government far outspends the states for transfers.

	1960	*1965*	*1970*	*1975*	*1980*	*1985*
Total government expenditures ($ billions)						
	$141	$193	$329	$561	$932	$1459
Federal purchases	52.9	64.6	97.1	117.9	189.3	342.2
Federal transfers	29.2	38.8	70.5	156.2	290.1	501.7
Social security	11.6	16.5	30.8	69.9	122.1	200.9
Medicare/Medicaid	0	0	6.3	16.1	31.1	70.7
Interest	6.8	8.2	13.5	21.7	50.7	128.7
Grants in aid to states	6.9	10.9	22.6	48.4	86.7	97.8
State and local purchases	46.5	71.1	124.4	217.2	340.8	460.7
State and local transfers	5.9	8.8	20.1	38.9	65.7	98.8

Sources: *Economic Report of the President; Statistical Abstract of the U.S.; U.S. Historical Statistics;* Federal Budgets.

Table 2

A COMPARISON OF GOVERNMENT SIZE AND PER CAPITA INCOMES, 1983

Table 2 shows two things: (1) the U.S. ratio of total government spending to GNP is somewhat lower than in most other major capitalist economies; and (2) there is no relation between the share of government and the level of per capita GNP.

Country	Total Government Spending as % of GNP	Per Capita Income, US $
United States	38.1%	$14,110
Japan	34.8	10,120
West Germany	48.6	11,430
France	51.5	10,500
United Kingdom	47.2	9,200
Canada	46.8	12,310

Source: *OECD Historical Statistics.*

One way to gauge the size of government is to measure its total impact on the national economy. We can do this adding up its contribution to GNP and its transfer payments, including payments of interest on all government debt. This mixed measure of purchases plus transfers can be thought of as the total contribution of government to the incomes received by its citizens.* In 1983 this contribution was equal to 38 percent of GNP.

Table 2 compares this measure of government in several major Western industrial nations. From this comparison, we see that the United States occupies a low-intermediate position among capitalist economies. We generate a larger fraction of incomes than the government of Japan, mainly because Japan relies more heavily on private pensions rather than government transfers for older citizens. We have a considerably smaller government sector than West Germany or France, where transfers to private citizens are not only larger, but the government directly owns and operates businesses such as airlines (and in the case of France, a number of other heavy industries).

Effects of the Public Sector

Table 2 also shows us a very important and interesting fact: **There is no relationship between the size of government in a country and the standard of living that country enjoys.** Some countries that we consider to have a very high standard of living have a higher share of government spending, while others that we consider to be very dynamic have a lower share. The size of government does not seem to affect the rate of economic growth.

---

* It also includes contributions to incomes of foreign citizens who own U.S. or state bonds or who receive social security payments.

Stabilizing Effects: Sheer Inertia. **From an economic standpoint, what distinguishes big government from small government countries is not the effects of the size of government per se, but the stability or instability the government sector imparts to the stream of total spending.** We have already seen that household consumption tends to be a very stable stream of spending, while business investment tends to be much more volatile. Government purchases, in peacetime, tends to be the most stable sector of all. The reason is simple: Government spending is planned by a centralized political process and administered by large bureaucratic agencies that tend to do the same things year after year, unaffected by interest rates or past profits or the state of demand or the climate of expectations.

Ceteris paribus, then, we would expect that countries with proportionately larger government sectors would enjoy a higher degree of macro stability than countries with proportionately smaller public sectors. And by and large that is what we seem to find.

Stabilizing Effects: Countercyclical Movements. **A second key fact about government spending is that its variations tend to run counter to the movements of spending in the private economy.** That is because many government programs are entitlements, whose outlays are related to need. Thus when GNP declines and the unemployment rate rises, unemployment compensation rises automatically, along with outlays for food stamps, aid to dependent children, and other relief programs. In 1982, for example, when unemployment neared 11 percent, total federal outlays were $25 billion higher than they would have been if unemployment had been only 5 percent. That $25 billion helped offset the drop in private spending caused by the recession.

We call this tendency for government spending to rise or fall countercyclically an **automatic stabilizer.** An even more powerful automatic stabilizer is the tax system. The mechanism is very obvious. Because income tax rates are higher on big incomes than on small ones, the national tax bite rises faster than national income. When income falls it works the other way around; the tax flow decreases faster than income does.

Note that government of any size can have automatic stabilization built into the way it functions; however, the larger the size of government, the smaller the proportionate change in all government spending has to be in order to achieve a given stabilizing effect.

THE DEFICIT

Now we turn to the great issue of the budget deficit, central to the macroeconomic role of the public sector in the twentieth century. Under what conditions will deficit spending help the performance of the economy? When will it hurt? How long can large-scale deficit spending be sustained? What will happen if it continues for too long?

Let us begin by understanding what the budget deficit is. **The federal budget deficit is defined as the difference between all federal spending and all federal tax revenues.** For the purposes of calculating the deficit and its economic effects, we disregard the distinctions between government purchases, transfers, grants, and interest and their differing effects on GNP, and count them all together as spending. Likewise, we aggregate all tax revenues, whether general-purpose (like the income tax) or special-purpose (like the payroll tax which finances social security outlays). We pay no heed to whether government spends money for warfare or welfare, for consumption purposes, or to build capital. We are concerned only with the difference between these two gross concepts, total outlays and total receipts.

The Deficit and the Debt

The government raises the cash to bridge the difference between outlays and receipts by selling bonds to the public, which increases the outstanding stock of the federal debt. The debt is therefore the sum of all outstanding past borrowings. Table 3 shows us the trend in both debt and deficit from 1960 to the present — and into the near future.

Is the deficit a danger? Is the debt much too large? These are obviously questions for which we are eager to have the answers. But we cannot rush into the questions unprepared. For the moment, then, let us rein our impatience until we have first mastered the mechanics of deficit spending.

Table 3

THE DEFICIT AND THE DEBT ($ BILLIONS)

The table shows the rise in both debt and deficit over the last quarter century. The estimate for 1991 comes from the President's budget for fiscal year 1987 and is based on a "current services" concept. The table shows the gross federal debt, which includes that part of the debt held by federal agencies such as the Social Security Trust Fund. In 1985 the debt held by the public was about $1,515 billion.

Year	Deficit	Gross Federal Debt	Debt Held by Public
1960	.3	$ 291	$ 225
1970	−2.8	383	263
1975	−53.2	544	397
1980	−73.8	914	596
1981	−78.9	1,004	678
1982	−127.9	1,147	895
1983	−207.8	1,382	1,044
1984	−185.3	1,577	1,256
1985	−222.2	1,841	1,515
1991 (est.)	−103.9	—	—

Source: Federal Budget documents.

The Mechanics of the Deficit

Deficits are caused in the first place because the government needs revenues, over and above taxes, to finance its expenditures. But deficits do not arise only because governments need more revenues than taxes provide. **Deficits also serve the purpose of stimulating the economy. A government can choose to incur a deficit as part of its fiscal policy, deliberately setting expenditures above taxes, or arranging matters so that expenditures will automatically rise and taxes automatically fall under certain economic conditions, such as a recession. As such, deficits are a key tool of fiscal policy.***

The basic idea behind the stimulative function of the deficit is simple enough. We have seen that economic recessions have their roots in a failure of the business sector to offset the savings of the economy through sufficient investment. If savings or leakages are larger than intended investment, there will be a gap in the circuit of incomes and expenditures. That gap can cumulate downward, at first by the effect of the multiplier, and thereafter, even more seriously, by further decreases in investment brought about by falling sales and gloomy expectations.

But if a falling GNP is caused by an inadequacy of expenditure, corresponding to a surplus of saving in one sector, our analysis suggests an answer. Could not the public sector serve as a supplementary avenue for the transfer of savings into expenditure?

Filling in the Demand Gap

As Figure 1 shows, a demand gap can indeed be closed by transferring savings to the public sector and spending them. The diagram shows savings in the household sector partly offset by business investment and partly by government *deficit spending*. It makes clear that at least so far as the "mechanics" of the economic flow are concerned, the public sector can serve to offset savings or other leakages equally as well as the private sector.

How is the transfer accomplished? It is accomplished much as business does it, by offering bonds that individuals or institutions may buy with their savings. (Unlike business, government cannot offer stock because it is not run as a profit-making enterprise). Thereafter, the proceeds of the bonds are deposited into the government's checking accounts, and enable the government to pay its bills by writing checks against those accounts.

---

* What is *fiscal* policy? As the word suggests, it is any policy affecting the overall level of operation of the economy that involves the government's *fisc*, or treasury. All spending or taxing measures are "fiscal" tools of the government. The other great branch of government economic influence is monetary policy. This uses its powers of money creation, not its powers of spending or taxation.

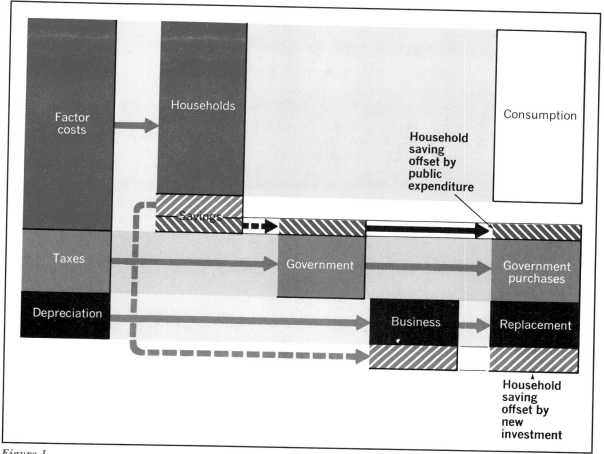

Figure 1

PUBLIC EXPENDITURE AND THE DEMAND GAP

The economics of filling a demand gap by government spending are exactly like those of investment spending. The politics are not.

UNDERSTANDING DEFICITS

Thus the sheer mechanics of government deficit spending are almost exactly like that of business investment spending. This parallel now enables us to go a little deeper into the pros and cons of deficit spending. Let us begin to inquire into the safety or dangers of a government deficit by asking whether business can also afford to incur deficits.

Deficits vs. Losses

There is one kind of deficit that a private business *cannot* afford: a deficit that comes from spending more money on current production than it will realize from sales. This kind of deficit is called a *business loss;* and if losses are severe enough, a business firm will be forced to discontinue its operations.

But there is another kind of deficit, although it is not called by that name, in the operations of a private firm. This is an excess of expenditures over receipts brought about by spending money on *capital assets.* When the American Telephone and Telegraph Company or the Exxon Corporation uses its own savings or those of the public to build a new plant and new equipment, it does not show a loss on its annual statement to stockholders, even though its total expenditures on current costs and on capital may have been greater than sales. Instead, expenditures are divided into two kinds, one relating current costs to current income, and the other relegating expenditures on capital goods to an entirely separate capital account. Instead of calling the excess of expenditures a deficit, they call it investment.*

Debts and Assets

Can AT&T or Exxon afford to run deficits of the latter kind indefinitely? The surprising answer is yes! To be sure, after a stated number of years, AT&T's or Exxon's bonds will come due and must be paid back. Perhaps the companies can do that out of their accumulated earnings. Usually, however, when a bond becomes due, a corporation issues *new* bonds equal in value to the old ones. It then sells the new bonds and uses the money it raises to pay off its old bondholders.

Many big corporations do, in fact, continuously "refund" their bond issues, paying off old bonds with new ones, and never paying back their indebtedness as a whole. AT&T, for instance, increased its total indebtedness over tenfold between 1929 and 1985. Exxon ran up its debt from $170.1 million in 1929 to over $5 billion in 1985. And the credit rating of both companies today is as good as, or better than, it was in 1929.

Government Assets

Can government, like business, borrow indefinitely? The question is important enough to warrant a careful answer. Let us begin by comparing government borrowing and business borrowing.

One difference that springs quickly to mind is that businesses borrow in order to acquire productive assets. That is, matching the new claims on the business sector is additional real wealth that will provide for larger output. From this additional wealth, business will also receive the income to pay interest on its debt or dividends on its stock. But what of the government? Where are its productive assets?

---

* Investment does not *require* a deficit, since it can be financed out of current profits. But many expanding companies do spend more money on current and capital account than they take in through sales, and thereby incur a deficit for at least a part of their investment.

We have already noted that the government budget includes dams, roads, housing projects, and many other items that might be classified as assets. During the 1960s, federal expenditures for such civil construction projects alone averaged about $5 billion a year. Thus the total addition to the public debt during the 1960s (it rose from roughly $240 billion in 1960 to $279 billion in 1969) could be construed merely as the financial counterpart of the creation of public assets.

Between 1970 and 1985, when debt held by the public rose from $285 billion to $1,515 billion, assets also kept pace. Total assets owned by government rose from $537 billion in the earlier year to over $2 trillion in 1985. Of these $2 trillion in assets, slightly more than half were tangible wealth of various kinds, such as public buildings, structures, equipment, and land. The remainder were financial assets — mortgages, loans due the government, gold, and cash in the government's own checking accounts.

Why do we not treat the government's debt the way we do a corporation's, weighing assets against liabilities? The reason is simply that the United States national income accounts lump together all public expenditures, without regard to purpose. In some European countries, public capital expenditures are sharply differentiated from public current expenditures. If we had such a system, the government deficit on capital account could then be viewed as **the public equivalent of a business deficit on capital account.** As government spends money on capital assets like dams or roads or schools, the nation's productivity rises. As a result tax revenues also rise, just like the sales of a company that has invested shrewdly.

Such a view of government spending, which stresses its potential usefulness — or wastefulness — in terms of the effects on tax revenues would greatly improve the level of discussion concerning government's finance.

Government's Power of Taxation

There is, in addition, another and much more powerful argument that applies to federal deficits. It is that national governments, unlike the biggest corporations — and unlike states or municipalities — have the ability to "capture" the spending power of their citizens through taxation.

Thus even if government does not use its expenditures to increase the productive assets of a nation — even if it squanders the money — the expenditures themselves remain within its reach in a manner not enjoyed by a spending entity that does not have the power of national taxation. **Whatever goes into the income stream is always available to government as a source of revenue, whereas whatever goes into the income stream from a corporation's expenditures is not available to it in the same way.** In normal circumstances, the federal government will recover about one-half to two-thirds of its expenditures in this way through normal taxes.*

* We can make a rough estimate of the multiplier effect of additional public expenditure as 2 and of the share of an additional dollar of GNP going to federal taxes as about ⅓ (see p. 293). Thus $1 of public spending will create $2 of GNP, of which 67¢ will go back to the federal government.

This reasoning helps us understand why federal finance is different from state and local government finance. An expenditure made by New York City or New York State is apt to be respent in many other areas of the country. Thus taxable incomes in New York will not, in all probability, rise to match local spending. As a result, state and local governments must look on their finances much as an individual business does. The power of full fiscal recapture belongs solely to the federal government.

Internal and External Debts

This difference between the limited powers of recoupment of a single firm and the relatively limitless powers of a national government lies at the heart of the basic difference between business and government deficit spending. It helps us understand why the government has a capacity for financial operation that is inherently of a far higher order of magnitude than that of business. We can sum up this fundamental difference in the contrast between the *externality of business debts* and the *internality of national government debts*.

What do we mean by the externality of business debts? We simply mean that business firms owe their debts to someone distinct from themselves — someone over whom they have no control — whether bondholders or the bank from which they borrowed. To service or to pay back its debts, business must transfer funds from its own possession into the possession of outsiders. If this transfer cannot be made, if a business does not have the funds to pay its bondholders or its banks, it will go bankrupt.

The government is in a very different position. Its bondholders, banks, and other people or institutions to whom it owes its debts belong to the same community as that whence it extracts its receipts.* In other words, the government does not have to transfer its funds to an outside group to pay its bonds. It transfers them instead from some members of the national community over which it has legal powers (taxpayers) to other members of the *same* community (bondholders).

The contrast is much the same as that between a family that owes a debt to another family, and a family in which the husband has borrowed money from his wife; or again between a firm that owes money to another, and a firm in which one branch has borrowed money from another. **Internal debts do not drain the resources of one community into another, but merely redistribute the claims among members of the same community.**

To help bring home the point, imagine that you and your roommate exchange $1,000 IOUs. Each of you now has a $1,000 asset (an IOU from the other person) *and* each of you also has a $1,000 liability (the IOU each owes the other). The total debt of the room is now $2,000. But is your room richer or poorer, or is any individual in the room richer or poorer? The answer is obviously no. No one is better or worse off than before. And what happens if you now each pay off your

---

* Except for foreigners, who these days are coming to own a higher and higher proportion of the national debt.

IOUs? Once again no one is richer or poorer than before. The same thing is true at the national level. The national debt makes us neither richer nor poorer, since we (as taxpayers) owe it to ourselves (as bondholders).

The Inflation Factor

Last but by no means least, there is a tendency to view the deficit and the debt unrealistically by failing to apply an inflation correction to their size. Do you remember the tremendous difference in the growth of GNP before and after the figures were scaled down from nominal to real magnitudes? (See pp. 195–96.) The same is true of the debt and deficit. Inflation has steadily multiplied the number of dollars of both figures, but their real growth is much less. In Table 4 we show the debt held by the public, before and after correcting for inflation. (Note that this figure, "debt held by public," is different than the total debt number.)

The Growth Factor

Thus inflation seriously distorts the real size of the debt. But even inflation-proof figures do not reflect another necessary correction—the fact that our real GNP rises, along with our real debt, so that debt as a proportion of GNP grows even more slowly than debt corrected for inflation alone.

We can best see the effects of this second correction by looking at Table 5. Here we see figures for both the national debt and annual deficits, as a percentage of GNP.

These figures may come as a surprise. They show that the national debt, as a percentage of GNP, is well *below* the level of the 1960s. This is because we greatly

Table 4
NOMINAL AND REAL DEBT

The nominal debt increased by more than sevenfold from 1960 to 1985. The real debt, measured in 1972 dollars, rose by less than twofold.

	Nominal Debt *(Billions of Current Dollars)*	*Real Debt* *(Billions of 1972 Dollars)*
1960	$ 225	$326
1970	263	281
1975	397	310
1980	596	318
1981	678	334
1982	895	423
1983	1044	476
1984	1256	552
1985	1510	635

Source: *Economic Report of the President.*

Table 5
DEFICITS, DEBTS, AND GNP

Relating debts and deficits to GNP is the best way of judging their real magnitude, for this corrects for both inflation and real growth.

	Deficits as % of GNP	Total National Debt as % of GNP
1960	−.06	57.4%
1970	.3	38.5
1975	3.4	35.1
1980	2.8	28.8
1981	2.7	33.9
1982	4.2	37.4
1983	6.3	41.8
1984	5.1	43.0
1985	5.6	46.1

Source: *Economic Report of the President.*

enlarged our debt in the 1940s to finance the war, and our growth in real GNP by 1960 had not yet reduced the debt to the proportion it would attain in the 1970s and early 1980s.

But while our debt has been decreasing in real terms, our deficits have been increasing. In 1960 we actually ran a small surplus. In the early 1970s, our deficits averaged about 1 percent of GNP. But starting in 1982, deficits began to soar, until by 1984 and 1985 they had risen to around 5 percent of GNP.

Is that increase alarming? Has deficit spending now become a source of danger for our economy? We are back to the questions that impelled us into a study of federal finance some pages back, but now we are in a position to consider the problem much more knowledgeably.

DEFICITS AND GROWTH

The overall answer is probably already clear to you. **Deficits can indeed be too big — and they can also be too small. There is no absolute magnitude that separates a useful deficit from a useless or even dangerous one.**

Two overall considerations have to be borne in mind before we can judge the positive or negative effects of any deficit, large or small:

1. The Impact of the Deficit Will Depend on the Kinds of Government Goods and Services for Which It Is Used. A deficit that is mainly incurred to create public assets — or public growth-producing services, such as education — will clearly have a different significance from one that is incurred to produce war materiel that will never (we hope) be used, or one that is the result only of transfer payments that help to sustain demand, but do not increase productivity.

The trouble is that government spending is normally a mixture of growth-producing and non-growth-producing expenditures, so it is difficult or impossible to attribute the deficit just to one set of programs. Because we do not have a national capital budget, we can only bear in mind that some portion of public spending is indeed the equivalent of capital investment. When we argue about the ways of using the public sector, we should not overlook its contribution to economic growth.

2. The Impact of the Deficit Will Also Depend on the Level of Aggregate Demand. When the sum of all private spending—households, businesses, and foreign demand—is not enough to bring the economy to a high level of employment, deficit spending can use the public sector to increase demand. As we have now seen, the mechanism of public spending is exactly the same as that of private investment. Each helps to offset a demand gap with additional expenditure. The only difference, from this point of view, is that private investment spending increases our stock of capital wealth, whereas public spending may or may not do this, depending on the purposes for which public expenditure is used.

PERSONAL DEBTS AND PUBLIC DEBTS

In view of the fact that our national debt today figures out to almost $7,000 for every man, woman, and child, it is not surprising that we frequently hear appeals to "common sense," telling us how much better we would be without this debt, and how our grandchildren will groan under its weight.

Is this true? We have already discussed the fact that internal debts are different from external debts, but let us press the point home from a different vantage point. Suppose we decided that we would pay off the debt. This would mean that our government bonds would be redeemed for cash. To get the cash, we would have to tax ourselves (unless we wanted to roll the printing presses), so that what we would really be doing would be transferring money from taxpayers to bondholders.

Would that be a net gain for the nation? Consider the typical holder of a government bond—a family, a bank, or a corporation. It now holds the world's safest and most readily sold paper asset from which a regular income is obtained. After our debt is redeemed, our families, banks, and corporations will have two choices: (1) They can hold cash and get *no* income, or (2) they can invest in other securities that are slightly *less* safe. Are these investors better off? As for our grandchildren, it is true that if we pay off the debt they will not have to carry its weight. But to offset that, neither will they be carried by the comfortable government bonds they would otherwise have inherited. They will also be relieved from paying taxes to meet the interest on the debt. Alas, they will be relieved as well of the pleasure of depositing the Treasury checks for interest payments that used to arrive twice a year.

But will not public expenditure be inflationary, if it is added to private expenditure? Indeed it may be, if we are at the borderline at which added spending affects prices as strongly as (or more strongly than) it affects employment and output. *But in that case, the same inflationary effects would also follow from more private spending!* There is no inflationary difference between an additional dollar spent by the Treasury or by General Motors. The only difference lies in the effects of each expenditure on our productivity. By and large, public spending probably adds less to productivity, dollar for dollar, than private investment spending. But this is not necessarily so. General Motors investment will not exert a strong effect on growth unless there are good roads on which to run its cars. Public expenditure for basic research will boost growth in the long run more than private expenditure for luxury hotels.

DEFICIT DANGERS

Up till now, we have mainly stressed the constructive aspects of deficit spending and sought to take away some of the fears that get in the way of an intelligent discussion of fiscal policy. Yet the last impression that we wish to leave with a reader is that deficits are always useful, or that there is nothing to worry about when expenditures exceed revenues. We have made the point that under the right conditions, deficits are useful or even necessary for economic growth. Now let us make the complementary point—under different conditions, deficits are useless and even detrimental for growth.

We have already made clear what those conditions are. **If we are at or near full employment of labor and full utilization of resources, additional government spending will add to demand—but cannot add to supply.** Additional spending will therefore push the economy out of equilibrium. Three possibilities may follow.

1. Crowding Out. The first possibility is *crowding out.* This means that the effect of excess total demand is felt primarily through an intense competition for capital in the financial markets. Business will be seeking funds to invest, and the government will be seeking funds to cover the gap between intake and outgo. As the total demand for funds rises, *interest rates rise sharply.* As a result, private business will curtail its investment plans (remember our analysis of the marginal efficiency of investment?).

Public needs will "crowd out" private ones, and business growth will suffer. This might be accepted if we were all of one mind that public needs were more important than private ones, as is usually the case during wars. But in peacetime there is no such agreement. Crowding out is therefore regarded with unease as enforcing a priority for public spending that may not be in accord with our public sentiments.

2. Inflation. The fear of crowding out has been much talked about as economists contemplate the huge budget deficits expected for at least the rest of the present decade. But notice that it rests on the assumption that competition for funds occurs exclusively in the capital markets, and does not spill over into the markets for real goods, precipitating a general rise in prices. Suppose that instead of merely competing for limited funds in the capital markets, governments, business, and households actually go out and collectively spend more dollars than the maximum value of output the economy can produce. Here is a simple case of too many dollars chasing too few goods.

Prices must rise. At the end of the inflationary process everyone, including government, will have received less real product than it had hoped for. If government tries to compensate for this by again raising its spending — and its deficit — the inflationary process will worsen. Here an unpleasant reality must be faced. We have seen that the carrying capacity of the United States for its national debt is limited only by the taxing power of the government on national income. But we must also recognize another possibility: *Inflation can be used as a substitute for taxation in "servicing" the national debt.*

Recall that the national debt is fixed in *dollars.* But the size of dollar GNP is a product of two forces: real growth and inflation. So if inflation increases tax revenues will rise, and the government will have more dollars in revenue with which to pay the interest on its debts. At the same time, the bonds that make up the debt will have lost real purchasing power over goods and services. Thus the debt will have *depreciated* by the amount of the inflation. This is another way in which governments can ensure that they always have the wherewithal to repay their debts. This mechanism is known to economists as the **inflation tax.**

Needless to say, this is a very unjust and potentially dangerous method of financing a debt. Nevertheless, as long as inflation persists, to some extent it is a means that has been used by all governments, including our own.

3. FOREIGN INDEBTEDNESS. A third possibility is to borrow the needed extra savings from foreigners. This was the course adopted by the United States in the first half of the 1980s. High interest rates made it very attractive for foreigners to seek dollar-denominated assets, like Treasury bonds. Foreigners bought $225 billion of U.S. debt (public *and* private) in 1985, 100 percent of that year's government deficit and 13 percent of the national debt.

Running up a foreign debt is a time-honored way to have your cake and eat it too — to spend in excess of production while avoiding inflation or crowding out. But can it last? That depends on how productive the investments being made with the money prove to be. In the 1870s the United States opened the West with borrowed money — U.S. railroad bonds, sold in the markets of London and Paris. This was perhaps the most lucrative investment any nation has ever made. But in the 1970s many Latin American countries tried to do the same thing and fell flat on their faces when the markets for their oil and copper and other commodities collapsed in the recession of 1979–82. Were the dollars borrowed by the American government in 1985 put to productive use in building infrastructure that would increase American productivity? We know they were not.

There is a second risk attached to foreign borrowing, over and above simply living beyond our means. It is the risk of moving from an internally held debt toward an externally held one. We cannot tax foreigners to service our own debt that way we can tax Americans. To the extent that our debt is externally held its burdens become much heavier, because we must transfer our own wealth to other nations, not merely from one group of U.S. citizens to another.

An even greater burden would fall on us should we begin to issue debts denominated in foreign currencies — say, treasury bonds payable in Swiss francs. Then we would truly begin to get into a position of owing obligations over whose ultimate value we had no control. This is the road down which Argentina, Mexico, Brazil, and Poland went, as they issued bonds payable not in their currencies, but in dollars. When the dollar became very expensive, they found they could no longer afford to buy the dollars to repay the interest they owed. Defaults, or hairbreadth escapes from defaults, followed, with painful results for the borrowers, who were now unable to receive any further credit abroad. The United States is still very far from such a grim end, but the recourse to foreign borrowing should make us aware that the risk exists.

A LEGISLATED BALANCED BUDGET?

Because of these arguments there exists a considerable body of public opinion firmly opposed to federal budget deficits under any conditions. This opinion has been mobilized behind a suggested amendment to the Constitution requiring an overwhelming majority in Congress — 60 percent — to enact a deficit budget except for emergency purposes such as war.

Would a balanced budget amendment be useful? It must be apparent from our discussion that we do not think so. Nor does the great majority of the economics profession, which has registered its opposition to such a proposed amendment in a message conveyed to President Reagan from the American Economic Association. To enact such an amendment, most economists fear (and we with them), would place a straitjacket on our ability to use the federal sector effectively not only as a means of creating and financing national capital projects, such as roads or buildings that normally require financing through borrowing, but also in mounting programs to sustain purchasing power when recessions shrink private activity.

The Gramm-Rudman Approach

As we put this book to press, the problem of the deficit is being met in yet a different way. Despairing of finding the consensus to reduce expenditures, and faced with President Reagan's adamant opposition to any tax increase, Congress has passed the Gramm-Rudman balanced-budget bill. Under this bill, budgets must be progressively reduced each year by scheduled percentages until a balanced budget is attained five years hence. If the President and Congress do not agree on spending cuts or tax increases needed to achieve the mandated reductions, the cuts are imposed by law "across the board," with certain limited exceptions. Gramm-

THE POWER TO PRINT MONEY

Ultimately the federal government has the power to incur an unlimited deficit because it has the power to print money. If a local government such as New York City incurs too much debt, investors lose confidence in the ability of the city to buy back its bonds when they come due. Therefore they will refuse to buy the city bonds and the municipality can go bankrupt.

This cannot happen to the federal government because by constitutional authority it has the power to create money. It could, therefore, simply print up the money needed to buy back its own obligations!

Needless to say, this is a cure that might well be worse than the disease. We hear about "rolling the printing presses" as the worst symptom of inflation. If the government actually began printing money wholesale to buy its own bonds, there would be a flight from the currency—maybe from the country!—and the specter of a runaway inflation might become a reality. We will discuss printing money again in Chapter 29. But we must recognize that the *unused* power of the printing press still reassures investors that they will never face default on a federal bond. It is odd, isn't it: The power to print money is the most important safeguard for government bonds—as long as it isn't used!

Rudman has been found partly unconstitutional because it abrogates the separation of powers between the President and Congress. But its very existence raises the question: should Congress try to specify a rigid track toward a balanced budget?

The Public Sector as a Balancing Force

Is it imperative to balance the budget at all costs? If there is any single lesson we should like to drive home, it is that the government sector must be considered in conjunction with the private sectors before any intelligent judgment can be passed on its size, or on whether it should show a surplus, be in balance, or run a deficit.

There may be sound arguments to diminish the size of government spending or to increase it—arguments based on national security considerations, or on feelings with respect to the proper role of the government with regard to poverty, or on convictions respecting the influence that government exerts on the private sector. These arguments may incline their holders to advocacy of a large, moderate, or small government presence.

But in our view, the decision to run a government sector deficit or not hinges entirely on the fact that it is the only part of the economy that is directly under our control. To repeat what we have said before, we cannot (and do not want to) command the households of the nation to save or spend, nor can we force businesses to invest or not. We can tempt both private sectors with tax and other incentives, but in the end a free enterprise system will do as it wishes. That leaves only the public sector to serve as a balancing mechanism. We do not preach that the mechanism be used in a particular way. But we must teach what it means when that mechanism is used to create a surplus or a deficit.

looking back

KEY CONCEPTS

Understanding the makeup of the public sector

1 It is vital to understand what we mean by the public sector. It can be usefully thought of in two ways. One of them is a flow of expenditures that contributes to GNP. In this view, state and local governments are more important than federal. The other is the source of transfer payments plus purchases. Here the federal government plays a crucial role. Neither as a provider of GNP or of incomes is the public sector large compared with other capitalist nations.

Not size but stability is important

2 There is no clear relationship between the size of the public sector and the size of GNP per capita. What counts is the stability or instability the public sector imparts to the economy as a whole.

Automatic stabilizers lend stability to the overall economy.

3 Stability is enhanced by the tendency of government to serve as an automatic stabilizer. This results from the tendency of taxes to rise or fall faster than GNP, because individuals move into higher or lower brackets. This slows down booms and cushions recessions. The "countercyclical" flows of certain transfers such as unemployment benefits and farm subsidies has the same effect.

Debt and deficit

4 Deficits refer to excesses of government expenditures over tax revenues. The amount of the deficit must be borrowed, and the sum of borrowings constitutes the national (or state or local) debt.

Public spending can be used to fill demand gaps

5 The mechanics of the public sector show that government spending can be used to offset a demand gap exactly as the business sector can. The difference is that the public sector can be deliberately used to manage the economy in a way that the private sector cannot.

Corporation deficits are safe if they create earning assets. Government deficits can also create assets	6 Are public deficits safe? A comparison with private corporations is useful. Corporations run two kinds of excesses of expenditures over receipts. One of these is a loss. No corporation can withstand prolonged losses. The other is capital investment. This is a form of "deficit spending" that can be maintained indefinitely if the assets built by the corporation are profitable. A government does not keep its books in the same way. But it too has assets—dams, roads, schools—that also create revenues for it by increasing GNP.
Real vs. nominal debts and deficits	7 Debts and deficits must be corrected for inflation and real growth. In real terms, the national debt is much reduced in size, but deficits have shown a real increase.
The difference internality makes	8 The government has one power that corporations do not. It can recapture its own expenditures through taxation. As long as its debts are internally held—held by U.S. citizens—it can always tax the revenues needed to pay interest or repay bonds. That is a power possessed only by the federal government, not by states or localities or businesses.
Deficits can be useful or dangerous	9 Deficits can be useful in generating demand. They can be dangerous in generating excess demand—more demand than can be satisfied by the supply capabilities of the economy at going prices.
Three dangers: crowding out (high interest); inflation and the inflation tax; and the need for foreign borrowing	10 Three possibilities then impend. One is crowding out, which forces up interest rates as the public sector competes for funds with the private sector. A second possibility is inflation, as public and private demands force up prices. The rise of prices serves as an inflation tax, to help service the debt. A third is the need to borrow from foreign borrowers. This can be useful—but it also makes debt an external and not an internal burden.
A balanced budget amendment has been suggested to avoid these risks and the Gramm-Rudman bill enforces balanced accounts within five years. Most economists oppose such straitjacket measures	11 Because of these dangers, there exists considerable public sentiment for a balanced budget amendment to the Constitution or for legislation, like the Gramm-Rudman bill, to enforce budgetary balance within a stated time period. Most economists, including ourselves, oppose such measures. We need the ability to run deficits *when they are useful,* which a balanced budget amendment would very probably deprive us of. The public sector, with all its problems, remains a powerful means for influencing our economy, a means that we would not wish to see disappear.

ECONOMIC VOCABULARY

Automatic stabilizers   294
Deficits and debts   295
Internal and external debts   300

Crowding out   304
Inflation tax   305

QUESTIONS

1. What is the "size" of government? Can you distinguish the economic effects of government purchases from transfers? Are the effects of regulation counted in the GNP?

2. We have seen that the "size" and the "growth" of government are not related to the size or the growth of GNP. Do you feel that the size of government affects economic well-being in other ways? Are these effects desirable, undesirable, or neutral? Explain your reasoning.

3. Show in a diagram how increased government spending can offset a demand gap. Can you show how decreased taxation can do the same?

4. Show how the automatic stabilizers might work if we have a rise in unemployment of 1 million and a corresponding fall of production of 3 percent. Assume that (a) at the outset expenditures and taxes are both $600 billion; (b) every unemployed worker receives $5,000 in (tax-free) unemployment compensation; (c) every point drop in production reduces taxes by 1.5 percent; and (d) the multiplier is 2.

5. If the government is going to go into debt, does it matter whether it spends money for roads or relief? Weapons or education? Distinguish short-run income effects from long-term wealth-generating effects.

6. If the government invests in an aircraft carrier that is deemed necessary to the national defense, is that different from a company investing in a new headquarters deemed necessary for efficient operations? How are the two actions treated in their respective governmental and corporate accounts?

7. Suppose that you were a member of the Council of Economic Advisors and that the president wanted the opinion of the Council on the effect of a deficit totaling 5 percent of GNP. What facts would you take into consideration before recommending whether or not such a deficit would be growth-producing or not?

8. How would you answer someone who claimed that deficits were always bad because: (a) "The government, just like a household, can't live beyond its means." (b) "You can't spend what you don't have." (c) "Debts are the royal road to bankruptcy."

AN EXTRA WORD ABOUT

Controlling the Domestic Deficit

As these words are being written, the deficit in the federal government budget is approximately $200 billion. The difficulty of getting rid of the deficit is revealed by Table 1.

Could we get rid of it just by cutting the military? That would require a reduction in our defense budget of two-thirds. The American people would not stand for that. Then could we get rid of it by cutting entitlement programs, such as social security and Medicare? To pick up the deficit from those items alone would require that they also be slashed by about two-thirds. No one would stand for that. Then suppose we eliminate the deficit by reducing all the other costs of government — congressional and diplomatic expenses, the array of Washington agencies, Amtrak, space, and the rest. To balance the budget at the expense of these items would virtually wipe them out altogether. There would be nothing left.

Then how about a mixture of all three? It is just the failure to produce such a mixture that has put us where we are — unable to agree on acceptable cuts, and bowing our heads to the Gramm-Rudman ax.

THE TAX SIDE

Then how can we reduce a deficit that most agree is still too large? It seems to us that the best way out of this dilemma is to raise taxes substantially. This would not only reduce the deficit, but also lower interest rates, because government's need to borrow would be cut.

Table 1
PRINCIPAL ITEMS IN THE
FY 1987 FEDERAL BUDGET

		($ Billions)
Revenues	Total	$850.4
	Income taxes	$386
	Corporate profit taxes	87
	Social security taxes	303
	All other	75
Expenditures	Total	$994
	Defense	$282
	Social security and Medicare	$283
	Health and income maintenance	153
	Interest	148
	International affairs	19
	All other	109

Lower interest rates, in turn, would spur investment and diminish the cost of interest on the debt. Not least, increased government revenues would make it possible to preserve a level of public expenditure that seems to us necessary to improve the quality of both public and private life.

But what taxes? There is the rub. To raise the needed revenues from income taxes might be the fairest way, but it is certainly not the most politically expedient way. For example, a tax boost sufficient to cut the 1985 deficit in half would require a one-quarter increase in income taxes. Most Americans would not accept that. In similar fashion, an effort to raise a large sum by a much higher payroll tax would also encounter very stiff general opposition —and would, in addition, fall much more heavily on the low-paid worker than on the more highly paid one.

Some economists have advocated moving toward a European *value added tax*—a sales tax paid by businesses on the value they add to the commodities they handle. Value added taxes are passed along from business to business and are finally paid by the consumer. A large enough VAT (value added tax) could wipe out the deficit, but the tax rate would be so high — about 15 percent at retail — as to give rise to a number of serious side effects, simultaneously giving a boost to the cost of living and dealing a severe blow to the buoyancy of consumption.

A WAY OUT?

So raising taxes is easier said than done. Nevertheless, if we are to bring the budget into manageable shape, we believe it is the best way out of our present fix.* Therefore we favor tax increases large enough to change the present budgetary picture in a dramatic way, but not so large as to pose impossible political or dangerous economic strains.

How large should such tax increases be? As we write these words, we would favor a tax increase sufficient to reduce the deficit over several years by a third to a half. The size of the tax hike cannot be specified more precisely than that, because it will vary with the state of the economy. If we are experiencing a severe recession when these words are read, we would not favor any tax increase at all. The full deficit would then be needed to sustain our level of employment and expenditure. If we should be enjoying a strong boom, we would favor a tax rise that might even exceed a 50 percent reduction in the deficit, for the advantages of reducing government borrowing would become greater the stronger the investment spending of the private sector. In such a strong economy, however, revenues would be higher, and the deficit smaller, to begin with.

THE CRITERION OF FAIRNESS

Where would the additional tax revenues come from? Many sources might have to be tapped: oil or gas taxes, or a moderate VAT with a basic exemption to avoid burdening families in the lower income levels. Best of all would be income tax reform to remove loopholes and restore a modestly progressive overall incidence. None of this will be easy, though as we write, ''revenue-neutral'' income tax reform may be nearing passage in

---

* In the long run, the very best way is to recast the national income accounts so that we have a *national capital budget,* against which long-term debt is allocated. We would then quite properly concentrate on balancing the current budget, except in recessions when we deliberately incurred an expansionary deficit. Alas, such proposals will get a proper hearing only after the electorate has learned some basic macroeconomics.

Congress — a good start, but not yet a solution to the deficit since the bill does not attempt to raise new revenue. But the real difficulty is not to devise a reasonable package of new taxes. It is to persuade the American public to accept any kind of higher taxes. We strongly believe that a tax increase will be accepted *if it is perceived as fair and necessary.* That is one of the advantages of writing a textbook! It gives us a soapbox from which to talk.*

* We get back on the soapbox in the extra word on "Fair Taxation", in Chapter 31.

CHAPTER 18
Aggregate Demand

a look ahead

We have gradually assembled the parts of the puzzle. We now have a good idea of the way that the various sectors behave and interact. It remains only to piece them together to get a picture of how GNP is determined. That is what we do in this chapter.

1 We will clarify the idea of a supply curve for GNP—a curve that will establish the costs of producing a larger or smaller output within our production possibility frontier.

2 We will add a demand curve for GNP—a curve that will show how much output the sectors will want to buy at different levels of utilization.

3 Putting the curves together will give us an equilibrium GNP. We will take a look at how this GNP can move upward or downward as the sectors alter their activity.

We have reached the destination toward which we have been traveling for several chapters. We are finally in a position to understand how the forces of supply and demand determine the actual level of GNP that confronts us in daily life — "the state of the economy" that affects our employment prospects, our immediate well-being, our satisfaction or dissatisfaction with the way things are going.

SUPPLY AND DEMAND IN MACRO

As we have begun to see, the short-run level of GNP is determined by the outcome of two opposing tendencies of supply and demand, just as the level of prices and quantities in a marketplace is set by the counterplay of these forces. **In fact, the opposition of supply and demand plays just as central a role in macroeconomics as in microeconomics. The crucial difference is that in macroeconomics we talk of supply and demand in relation to GNP, whereas in microeconomics we speak of them mainly in relation to price.**

The Utilization of Our Potential

What determines the supply of GNP? For the long run, the answer hinges on the quantity and quality of our inputs, a question we looked into in Chapter 13. These inputs determine the limits of our productive power — the production possibility frontiers that constrain our capacity to produce.

But in the short run our supply of GNP depends on how much of our production potential we actually use. Here we come up against the impossibility of going beyond the production possibility curve. **Therefore it is the degree of utilization of our production capacity — the extent to which we achieve full employment of human and material capital — that determines how close we come to the production frontier.**

What will we use as supply and demand curves to establish where that point will be? The demand curve is easy to imagine — it will be determined by the amount of expenditure the community generates at different levels of employment and utilization. Obviously, the more fully we employ our labor power, the more incomes individuals will have and the more output they will want. We shall shortly see how the demand for output can be represented in graphic form.

But what about the supply of output? Here we want to show how the value of output will change as we use more or less of our available productive power. The supply curve will show how much output costs at different levels of utilization. **The supply curve will therefore relate output and costs, and the demand curve will relate output and expenditure.**

The Supply Curve of Income

What does such a supply curve look like? **Here we make use of identities that we learned about in Chapter 12. Incomes and the costs of output are always the same. The amount of income made available to the community must rise, dollar for dollar, with the amount of production, because every dollar going into production must become income to some individual or institution.**

Our supply curve must show this identity, and Figure 1 makes clear that the resulting curve will be a 45° line. Notice that $OX = OY$, $OX' = OY'$, and so on. Notice also that this supply curve is fixed, in that the relation between incomes (GNI) and output (GNP) is always the same — identical. Again, for each dollar that we increase output, we add a dollar to income. Thus the supply of income is identical with the cost of output.

Demand Curve for GNP

Now what about the demand for GNP? **We already know that the demand curve will show us the amount of spending (demand for output) that will be generated by the community as output rises from zero to the full utilization of existing resources.**

Of course such a curve will slope upward. In Figure 2 we see why this is so. Panels I through IV sum up the demand of consumption, investment, and government. *They show that total spending, or aggregate demand, will rise as output rises: Here is our upward-sloping demand curve.*

It now remains only to put the demand and supply curves together, as in Figure 3.

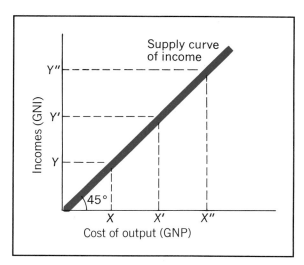

Figure 1

SUPPLY CURVE OF INCOME

The supply curve of income makes use of the identity between output costs $(C + I + G + X)$ and income $(F + T + D)$. Every unit of output generates incomes that exactly match its costs. This identity gives rise to a 45° line, which lies equidistant between the two axes at all points.

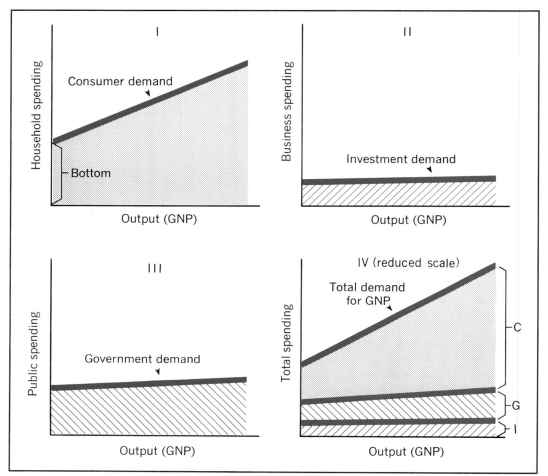

Figure 2
THE DEMAND FOR GNP

These panels show the amounts of spending that will take place in each sector (and then the three combined) as the degree of utilization increases. Spending rises in the household sector because of the propensity to consume. The accelerator and various governmental "propensities" give a slight positive slope to spending in those sectors as well.

This equilibrium shows us the money value of GNP brought about by the flow of demand against supply. It might, for example, indicate that this value of GNP was $4 trillion. It does *not* tell us whether $4 trillion is a *good* size for GNP, any more than a price of $20 for a commodity tells us whether that is a good or bad price from the viewpoint of buyers, producers, or the economy at large. We return to this critical point at the end of our chapter.

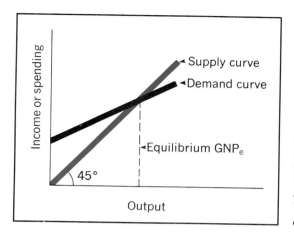

Figure 3
SUPPLY AND DEMAND FOR GNP
*Here the supply curve shows the amount
of income associated with different
amounts of output. They are identical.
The demand curve shows the amount of
spending at different levels of output.
Where spending equals income we have
an equilibrium level of GNP.*

ANOTHER VIEW OF EQUILIBRIUM

Saving and Investment

Equilibrium is always a complicated subject to master, so let us fix the matter in our minds by going over the problem once more. Suppose that by means of a questionnaire we are going to predict the level of GNP for an island community. To simplify our task, we will ignore government and exports, so that we can concentrate solely on consumption, saving, and investment.

We begin by interrogating the island's business community about their intentions for next year's investment. Now we know that some investment will be induced and that therefore investment will partly be a result of the island's level of income; but again for simplification, we assume that businesses have laid their plans for next year. They tell us they intend to spend $30 million for new housing, plant, equipment, and other capital goods.

Next, our team of pollsters approaches a carefully selected sample of the island's householders and asks them what their consumption and savings plans are for the coming year. Here the answer will be a bit disconcerting. Reflecting on their past experience, our householders will reply: "We can't say for sure. We'd *like* to spend such-and-such an amount and save the rest, but really it depends on what our incomes will be." Our poll, in other words, will have to make inquiries about different possibilities that reflect the island's propensity to consume.

Now we tabulate our results, and find that we have the schedule shown in Table 1.

Table 1

The interplay of saving and investment reveals the equilibrium output just as schedules of supply and demand show an equilibrium price.

Income	Consumption (in Millions)	Saving	Investment
$100	$75	$25	$30
110	80	30	30
120	85	35	30

Interplay of Saving and Investment

If we look at the last two columns of Table 1, those for saving and investment, we can see a powerful cross play that will characterize our model economy at different levels of income, for the forces of investment and saving will not be in balance at all levels. At some levels, the propensity to save will outrun the act of purposeful investment; at others, the motivation to save will be less than the investment expenditure made by business firms. In fact, our island model shows that at only one level of income — $110 million — will the saving and investment schedules coincide.

What does it mean when intended savings are greater than the flow of intended investment? It means that people are *trying* to save out of their given incomes a larger amount than business is willing to invest. Now if we think back to the exposition of the economy in a circular flow, it will be clear what the result must be. The economy cannot maintain a closed circuit of income and expenditure if savings are larger than investment. This will simply give rise to a demand gap, the repercussions of which we have already explored.

But a similar lack of equilibrium results if intended savings are less than intended investment expenditure (or if investment spending is greater than the propensity

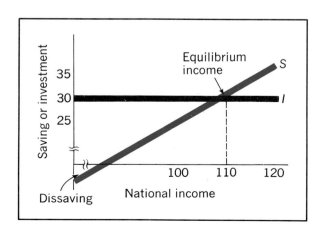

Figure 4
SAVING AND INVESTMENT

Here we simply put into graphic form the schedules of saving and investment (or leakages and injection). The equilibrium point is easy to see.

to save). Now business will be pumping out more than enough to offset the savings gap. The additional expenditures, over and above those that compensate for saving, will flow into the economy to create new incomes—and out of those new incomes, new savings.

Income and output will be stable, in other words, only when the flow of intended investment just compensates for the flow of intended saving. Investment and saving thus conduct a tug of war around this pivot point, driving the economy upward when intended investment exceeds the flow of intended saving; downward when it fails to offset saving. In Figure 4 we show this cross current in schematic form. Note that as incomes fall very low, householders will *dissave*.

Injections vs. Leakages

We can easily make our graph more realistic by adding taxes (T) and imports (M) to savings, and exports (X) and government spending to investment. The vertical axis in Figure 5 now shows all *leakages and injections*.

We recall that leakages are any acts, such as savings, increased taxes, profits, or imports, that reduce spending. Similarly, injections are any acts, such as investment or higher government spending or rising exports or even a spontaneous jump in consumption, that lead to higher spending. And just to introduce another feature of the real world, we will tilt the injection line upward, on the assumption that induced investment will be an important constituent of total investment. The leakages curve will not be exactly the same shape as the savings curve, but it will reflect the general tendency of savings and imports and taxes to rise with income.

Intended and Unintended *S* and *I*

The careful reader may have noted that we speak of *intended* savings and *intended* investment as the critical forces in establishing equilibrium. This is because there is a formal balance—an identity—between *all* saving and investment (or all leakages and all injections) at every moment in the economy. In the same way, pur-

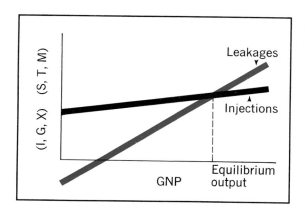

Figure 5
LEAKAGES AND INJECTIONS

chases in any market must exactly equal sales at each and every moment, but that does not mean the market is in equilibrium at all times.

Economists distinguish between the formal identity between total saving and investment (or between all leakages and all injections) and the active difference between *intended* savings and investment (or *intended* saving, *intended* imports, *intended* business saving, etc., and *intended* additional expenditures of all kinds).

What matters in the determination of GNP is the *actions* people are taking — actions that lead them to try to save or to invest or that make them struggle to get rid of unintended inventories or to build up desired inventories. These are the kinds of activities that will be moving the economy up and down in the never-ending "quest" for its equilibrium point. The fact that at each moment past savings and investment are identical from the viewpoint of the economy's balance sheet is important only insofar as we are economic accountants. As analysts of the course of future GNP, we concentrate on the inequality of future, intended actions.

The Paradox of Thrift

The fact that income must always move toward the level where the flows of intended saving and investment are equal leads to one of the most startling — and important — paradoxes of economics. **This is the so-called paradox of thrift, a paradox that tells us that the attempt to increase intended saving may, under certain circumstances, lead to a fall in actual saving.**

The paradox is not difficult for us to understand at this stage. An attempt to save, when it is not matched with an equal willingness to invest or to increase government expenditure, will cause a gap in demand. This means that business will not be getting back enough money to cover costs. Production will be curtailed or costs will be slashed, with the result that incomes will fall. As incomes fall savings will also fall, because the ability to save will be reduced. Thus, by a chain of activities working their influence on income and output, the effort to *increase* savings may end up with an actual *reduction* of savings.

This frustration of individual desires is perhaps the most striking instance of a common situation in economic life, the incompatibility between some kinds of individual behavior and some collective results. An individual farmer, for instance, may produce a larger crop in order to enjoy a bigger income; but if all farmers produce bigger crops, farm prices are apt to fall so heavily that farmers end up with less income. So too, a single family may wish to save a very large fraction of its income for reasons of financial prudence; but if all families seek to save a great deal of their incomes, the result — unless investment also rises — will be a fall in expenditure and a common failure to realize savings objectives. The paradox of thrift, in other words, teaches us that the freedom of behavior available to a few individuals cannot always be generalized to all individuals.*

* The paradox of thrift is actually only a subtle instance of a type of faulty reasoning called the *fallacy of composition.* The fallacy consists of assuming that what is true of the individual case must also be true of all cases combined. The flaw in reasoning lies in our tendency to overlook "side effects" of individual actions (such as the decrease in spending associated with an individual's attempt to save more, or the increase in supply when a farmer markets his larger crop) which may be negligible in isolation, but which are very important in the aggregate.

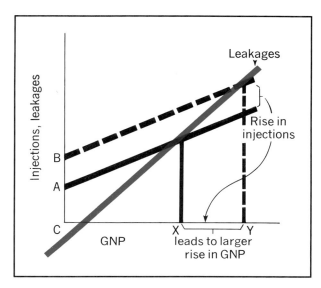

Figure 6
MULTIPLIER IN GRAPHIC FORM
An increase of injections of AB leads to a larger increase in GNP, XY. This is a graphic presentation of the multiplier. It is important to understand why AB creates XY. The reason is that the leakage curve slopes. And why does it slope? Because its slope represents the marginal propensity to save. And that is the cause of the multiplier.

THE MULTIPLIER

There remains only one part of the jigsaw puzzle to put into place. This is the integration of the *multiplier* into our analysis of the determination of GNP.

We remember that the essential point about the multiplier was that changes in investment, government spending, or exports resulted in larger changes in GNP because the additions to income were respent, creating still more new incomes. Further, we remember that the size of the multiplier effect depended on the marginal propensity to consume, the marginal propensity to tax, and the marginal propensity to buy imports as GNP rises. Now it remains only to show how this basic analytic concept enters into the determination of equilibrium GNP.

Let us begin with the diagram that shows injections and leakages, and let us now draw a new line showing an increase in injections (Figure 6). Notice that the increase in GNP is larger than the increase in injections. *This is the multiplier itself in graphic form.*

Slope of the Leakage Curve

Both diagrams also show that the relation between the original increase in injections and the resulting increase in GNP depends on the *slope* of the leakage line. Figure 7 shows us two different injection—GNP relationships that arise from differing slopes.

Notice how the *same* increase in spending (from *OA* to *OB* on the injections axis) leads to a much smaller increase in panel I GNP (from *OX* to *OY*), where the leakage slope is high, than in panel II (from *OX'* to *OY'*), where the slope is more gradual.

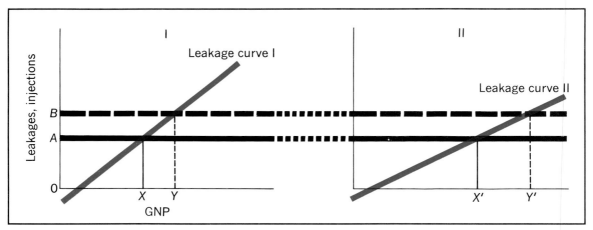

Figure 7
TWO MULTIPLIERS

Here is another chance to relate the graphics of the multiplier to the underlying behavior that causes the multiplier. The two differently sloped leakage curves generate different multipliers. This is because their different slopes picture different patterns of spending and saving.

Why is the increase greater when the slope is more gradual? The answer should be obvious. The slope represents the marginal propensity to save, to tax, to import — in short, all the marginal propensities that give rise to leakages. If these propensities are high — if there are high leakages — then the slope of the leakage curve will be high. If it is low, the leakage curve will be flat.

A Last Look at Equilibrium

Thus we finally understand how GNP reaches an equilibrium position after a change in demand. Here it is well to reiterate, however, that the word *equilibrium* does not imply a static, motionless state. Nor does it mean a desired state. We use the word only to denote the fact that *given* certain behavior patterns, there will be a determinate point to which their interaction will push the level of income; and *so long as the underlying patterns of injections and leakages remain unchanged, the forces they exert will keep income at this level.*

In fact, of course, the flows of spending and saving are continually changing so that the equilibrium level of the economy is constantly shifting, like a ping-pong ball suspended in a rising jet of water. Equilibrium can thus be regarded as a target toward which the economy is constantly propelled by the push-pull between leakages and injections. The target may be attained but momentarily before the economy is again impelled to seek a new point of rest. What our diagrams and the underlying analysis explain for us, then, is not a single determinate point at which our economy will in fact settle down, but the *direction* it will go in quest of a resting place as the dynamic forces of the system exert their pressures.

Equilibrium and Full Employment

Like the market for any single good or service, the market for all goods and services will find its equilibrium where the total quantity of goods demanded equals that supplied. But now we must note something of paramount importance. While the economy will automatically move to this equilibrium point, the point need not bring about the full employment of the factors of production, particularly labor. In Figure 8, the economy at equilibrium produces a GNP indicated by GNP_e, but as our diagram indicates, this may be well short of the volume of production needed to bring about full employment (GNP_f). Equilibrium can thus occur at any level of capacity utilization. All we can say about it — exactly as in the market for goods and services — is that it is the level toward which the system will move, and from which it will not budge unless the demand curve shifts. It is certainly not necessarily the "right" level in any sense, and it may indeed be a very poor or unsatisfactory level, as during the Great Depression.

The aim of macroeconomic policy making is therefore to raise or lower the demand curve for GNP so that it crosses the supply curve at, or near, full employment or some other desired level of output. As we have already seen, this is an objective that is exceedingly difficult to accomplish. But at least we possess, in the body of macroeconomics itself, the basic intellectual tools needed to understand the nature of the task.

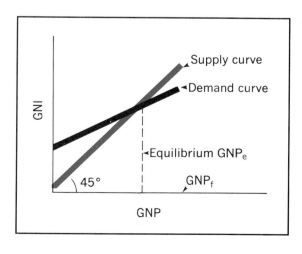

Figure 8
SUPPLY AND DEMAND FOR GNP

This last, simple-looking graph is perhaps the most important of all. It shows that equilibrium GNP_e may not be full utilization GNP — that we may be at rest far behind production possibility.

REMEDYING UNEMPLOYMENT

How can unemployment be lessened? Economists differ about specific measures, and they even disagree as to whether macro or micro policies are best suited for the task. When we come to our microeconomic studies, we will look into some of the micro policies to help the problem, such as reducing frictional or structural unemployment.

Most economists acknowledge the importance of these elements, but see unemployment essentially as a macro problem. The analysis of this chapter makes it clear that the level of employment will be determined, first and foremost, by the intersection of the aggregate demand for output with the supply curve of potential output. **As a first requirement of full employment, GNP must be high enough to generate the demand for willing and able workers to work.**

Dynamics of Aggregate Demand

This is only the first step in our analysis, however, for we must recognize that a level of demand adequate to produce full or high employment in one year will not be adequate the next. First, there is a normal growth of the labor force as a consequence of population growth. This growth may accelerate if an unusually large number of young people, products of an earlier baby boom, are leaving school. In the 1960s there was a flood of such young entrants; now, fortunately, the flood has ebbed.

Second, even if there were no increase in the labor force, we experience a normal growth in productivity as the consequence of adding capital equipment, of improving our techniques of production, and of increasing our stock of skill and knowledge. This year-to-year increase in per capita productivity varies, partly over the business cycle and partly from longer-run causes that we will devote some time to in Chapter 24. In the past, the normal rate of increase in per worker productivity was about 2½ percent per year. Add to that a normal 1 percent increase in population, and you can see that GNP must grow by at least 3½ percent each year to absorb the output of the labor force. **A constant rate of employment therefore requires a rising GNP, the rate of rise varying as population and productivity increases dictate.** This is a very important relationship to bear in mind.

Running to Stay in Place

But suppose we have too much unemployment and want to grow fast enough to absorb it? Now comes an important twist that results from the elasticity of the labor force. As employment grows, more people enter the labor force and hours lengthen. **This means that we have to increase the level of GNP enough to absorb the original unemployed, plus the addition to the labor force that results from higher participation rates and more hours worked.**

The difficulty with revving up GNP to eliminate unemployment is that we rapidly run into inflationary bottlenecks, once unemployment reaches the 5 to 6 percent level. This brings us to familiar terrain, where we must fight out the battle between unemployment and inflation, a battle we will think about many times in the chapters to come.

looking back

KEY CONCEPTS

Actual output depends on the degree of utilization of human and other resources

1 The potential output of the economy is determined by its production possibilities. But the amount actually produced depends on how close we can get to the production possibility frontier. This depends on the degree to which we utilize our human and other resources.

Demand for GNP relates spending and output; supply for GNP relates cost and output

2 The degree of utilization depends on the demand and supply for GNP. The demand for GNP is determined by the amounts the sectors will want to buy at different levels of utilization. The supply of GNP will relate the cost of GNP to its level of output.

The identity of cost and income means that the supply curve will be a 45° line

3 The supply curve of GNP uses the identity between costs and incomes to show that at all levels of utilization, output will generate incomes equal to its cost. The relation of identity between cost and income means that the supply curve of GNP will be a 45° line. Whatever the level of output, the supply of income (or spending power) will be identical with the cost of producing that output.

Equilibrium GNP is most easily shown as the level of output where $S = I$, or leakages equal injections

4 Equilibrium GNP is determined by the interplay of the supply of and demand for GNP. It is most easily depicted in terms of the interaction of the savings and investment, or leakage and injection, schedules. At equilibrium, saving must equal investment, and leakages must equal injections.

Investment or injection determine the level of income, via the multiplier. Attempts to increase S without increasing income

5 In the interplay between S and I (or leakages and injections), it is investment (or injections) that play the critical role in establishing the equilibrium level of output. Saving or leakages are dependent, passive variables in the process. Changes in intended investment will lead, via the multiplier, to changes in income that permit the economy to save the amount that matches intended investment. Attempts to save more, without boosting income first, are doomed to failure — the paradox of thrift.

Equilibrium GNP may not be full utilization GNP

6 An equilibrium GNP may not be a socially satisfactory GNP. The economy may be at rest although it is well behind its production frontiers.

The dynamics of GNP—
population, productivity,
and participation—create
a need for high growth to
reduce unemployment

7 To reduce unemployment, GNP must grow. Growth is also needed because the labor force increases as population increases, because rising productivity will displace workers unless demand increases, and because a rising GNP tempts more people into the work force. Thus we need a rapid growth in aggregate demand to create full employment in a dynamic economy. This brings us once again to the dilemma of high growth and inflation, versus slower growth and unemployment.

ECONOMIC VOCABULARY

Utilization   316
Injections vs. leakages   321

Intended and unintended S and I 321
Paradox of thrift   322

QUESTIONS

1. Suppose an economy turns out to have the following consumption and saving schedule (in billions). Fill in the missing numbers.

Income	Saving	Consumption
$400	$50	$350
450	—	395
—	60	440
550	70	—
600	85	—

Now suppose that firms intend to invest $60 billion. What will be the level of income? If investment rises to $85 billion, what will be the new level of income? What would be the multiplier?

2. Diagram the model above assuming that $I = 60$, then that $I = 85$.

3. Show in the diagram that the multiplier is determined by the slope of the leakage curve. What does this slope represent?

4. Copy Figure 3 showing the supply and demand curves that establish where equilibrium GNP will be. Now draw a new, higher demand curve, and drop a perpendicular line to the horizontal axis to show where the new equilibrium

GNP will be. Measure the distance showing the rise in the demand for GNP and the distance showing the change in equilibrium GNP. Can you see that GNP will increase by more than the rise in demand? And that this is simply another way of showing the multiplier? And that, as in Figure 7, the multiplier will depend on the slope of the leakage curve, here depicted as its twin, the marginal propensity to spend?

5. Here is a question to be thought about very carefully. Why does GNP have to increase if we are to maintain a given level of employment? Would this be true if the size of the labor force were constant and if people did not expect to improve levels of consumption? How does growing productivity figure into the picture? If the population grows at 1 percent a year, if people strive for an increase in real living standards of 2 percent a year, and if productivity grows by 2 percent, by how much will *real* aggregate demand have to grow?

CHAPTER 19
Money and Banking

a look ahead

This next section of four chapters is focused on the subject of money. No one needs to be told that it is a key section for understanding how the macrosystem works. We will tackle it in stages. First, in Chapter 19, we learn the ABCs of money—what it is, and what we call the "money supply." Next we learn how the Federal Reserve, together with the banking system, regulates the supply of money. In Chapter 21 we study money in action—the impact of changes in the money supply on the level of the macrosystem. And finally we turn to the Great Debate about money—how important is it in moving the economy?

In this chapter we begin by studying two things.

1 What is money, and how is it created by the banking system?
2 How do banks work?

This is another chapter to read twice. The basic ideas are not hard to get, but it takes some time until the practice of banking becomes clear. The questions at the back will help.

We have almost completed our analysis of the major elements of macroeconomics, and soon we can bring our analysis to bear on some major problems of the economy. But first there is a matter we must integrate into our discussion. This is the role that money plays in fixing or changing the level of GNP, along with the other forces that we have come to know.

Actually, we have been talking about money throughout our exposition. After all, one cannot discuss expenditure without assuming the existence of money. But now we must look behind this unexamined assumption and find out exactly what we mean when we speak of money. This will entail two tasks. In this chapter we investigate the question of what money *is*—for money is surely one of the most perplexing inventions of human society. In our next chapter, once we have come to understand what currency and gold and bank deposits are and how they come into being, we will look into the effect money has on our economic operations.

THE DEFINITION OF MONEY

Let us begin by asking "What is money?" Coin and currency are certainly money. But are checks money? Are the deposits from which we draw checks money? Are savings accounts money? Government bonds?

The answer is somewhat arbitrary. Basically, money is anything we can use to make purchases with. But there exists a spectrum of financial instruments that serve this purpose—a continuum that varies in liquidity, or the ease with which it can be used for purchasing. By law, coin and currency are money because they are defined by law as "legal tender": A seller *must* accept them as payment. Checks do not have to be accepted (we have all seen signs in restaurants saying, "WE DO NOT ACCEPT CHECKS"), although in fact checks are overwhelmingly the most prevalent means of payment. In 1984, 40 billion checks were written.

Thus, a variety of things can be counted as money. By far the most important general definition is the sum of all cash in the hands of the public (including travelers checks) and checkable deposits. This amount is called M1 by the Federal Reserve, which also keeps track of M2 (M1 plus dollar balances abroad, money market funds, and savings accounts), and M3 (M2 plus large savings deposits and some other special types of accounts), up to L, M3 plus all other liquid assets. The difference is very large—in 1985, for instance, M1 was $625; M2 $2,564; M3 $3,214; and L was $3,684 billion.

Which is the correct figure? That depends on many things. For our purposes, while we are learning about our monetary system, we will just settle for M1, meaning cash in the hands of the public plus checking accounts. This is the figure that most people are primarily concerned about.

Currency

In 1985, for example, M1 was $625 billion, of which $171 billion was currency held by the public and $271 billion was the total of ordinary checking accounts, or **demand deposits,** to give them their technical name.

CREDIT CARDS

Money serves as a mechanism for storing potential purchasing power and for actually purchasing goods and services. Since cash and personal checks are the principal means for making these purchases, money has come to be defined as cash outside banks plus checking accounts. But what about credit cards. Shouldn't they be considered money?

Credit cards clearly can be used to make purchases, so that they appear on the surface to have a vital attribute of money. But a moment's reflection shows that in fact they *substitute* for cash or checks in which payment is finally made. The moment you pay your credit card bill, or the moment the credit card company pays the local merchant, the credit card is replaced by standard money. Thus credit cards play the role of money only to the extent that credit bills are unpaid!

In this role credit cards are not unique. Any unpaid bill or charge account is like money, in that you are able to purchase goods and services in exchange for your personal IOU. In a sense, each person is able to "print" money to the extent that he can persuade people to accept his IOUs. For most of us, that extent is very limited.

From an economist's point of view, the value of all outstanding trade credit (unpaid bills, unpaid charge accounts, or credit cards) *should* be considered money. It is not included in the official statistics for two reasons. First, it is difficult or impossible to figure how much trade credit is outstanding at any moment. Second, fluctuations in trade credit do not have a big impact on the economy. Ordinarily, the value of trade credit does not vary much, and therefore trade credit does not give rise to substantial changes in the effective money supply.

Of the two main kinds of money, currency is the most familiar to us. Yet there is a considerable mystery even about currency. Who determines how much currency there is? How is the supply of bills or coins regulated?

We often assume that the supply of currency is set by the government that issues it. Yet when we think about it, we realize that the government does not just hand out money, and certainly not coins or bills. When the government pays people, it is nearly always by check.

Then who does fix the amount of currency in circulation? You can answer the question by asking how you yourself determine how much currency you will carry. If you think about it, the answer is that you cash a check when you need more currency than you have, and you put the currency back into your checking account when you have more than you need.

What you do, everyone does. **The amount of cash that the public holds at any time is no more and no less than the amount it *wants* to hold.** When it needs more—at Christmas, for instance—the public draws currency by cashing checks on its own checking accounts; and when Christmas is past, shopkeepers (who have received the public's currency) return it to their checking accounts.

Thus the amount of currency we have bears an obvious, important relation to the size of our bank accounts, for we can't write checks for cash if our accounts will not cover them. Does this mean, then, that the banks have as much currency in their vaults as the total of our checking accounts? No, it does not. But to understand that, let us follow the course of some currency that we deposit in our banks for credit to our accounts.

Bookkeeping Money

When you put money into a checking account, the bank does not hold that money for you as a pile of specially earmarked bills or as a bundle of checks made out to you from some payer. The bank takes notice of your deposit simply by crediting your account, a computer entry recording your present balance. After the amount of the currency or check has been credited to you, the currency is put away with the bank's general store of vault cash and the checks are sent to the banks from which they came, where they will be charged against the accounts of the people who wrote them.

There is probably no misconception in economics harder to dispel than the idea that banks are warehouses stuffed with money. In point of fact, you might search as hard as you pleased in your bank, but you would find no money that was yours other than a computer entry in your name. This seems like a very unreal form of money. And yet, the fact that you can present a check at the teller's window and convert your computer entry into cash proves that your account must nonetheless be real.

But suppose that you and all the other depositors tried to convert your accounts into cash on the same day. You would then find something shocking. There would not be nearly enough cash in the bank's till to cover the total withdrawals. In 1985 for instance, total demand deposits in the United States amounted to about $271 billion. But the total amount of coin and currency held by the banks was only $21 billion!

At first blush, this seems like a highly dangerous state of affairs. But second thoughts are more reassuring. After all, most of us put money into a bank because we do *not* need it immediately, or because making payments in cash is a nuisance compared with making them by check. Yet, there is always the chance—more than that, the certainty—that some depositors *will* want their money in currency. How much currency will the banks need then? What will be a proper reserve for them to hold?

Federal Reserve System

For many years, the banks themselves decided what reserve ratio constituted a safe proportion of currency to hold against their demand deposits. Today, however, most large banks are members of the Federal Reserve, a central banking system established in 1913 to strengthen the banking activities of the nation. Under the Federal Reserve System, the nation is divided into twelve districts, each with a **Federal Reserve Bank** owned (but not really controlled) by the member banks of its district. In turn, the twelve Reserve Banks are themselves coordinated by a seven-member Federal Reserve Board in Washington. Since the president, with the advice and consent of the Senate, appoints members of the board for fourteen-year terms, they constitute a body that has been purposely established as a formally autonomous monetary authority.*

One of the functions of the Federal Reserve Board is to establish reserve ratios for different categories of banks, within limits set by Congress. Historically these reserve ratios have ranged between 13 and 26 percent of demand deposits for city banks, with a somewhat smaller reserve ratio for country banks. Today, reserve ratios are determined by size of bank and by kind of deposit, and they vary between 18 percent for the largest banks and 7 percent for the smallest. The Federal Reserve Board also sets reserve requirements for time deposits (the technical term for savings deposits). These range from 1 to 6 percent, depending on the ease of withdrawal.

The Banks' Bank

Yet here is something odd! We noticed that in 1985 the total amount of deposits was $271 billion and that banks' holdings of coin and currency were only $21 billion. This is much less than the 16 percent reserve against deposits established by the Federal Reserve Board. How can this be?

The answer is that cash is not the only reserve a bank holds against deposits. Claims on other banks are also held as its reserve.

What are these claims? Suppose, in your account in bank A, you deposit a check from someone who has an account in bank B. Bank A credits your account and then presents the check to bank B for payment. Bank A does not expect to be paid coin and currency, however. Instead bank A and bank B settle their transaction at still *another* bank where both bank A and bank B have their own accounts. These accounts are with the twelve Federal Reserve Banks of the country, where all banks who are members of the Federal Reserve System (and this accounts for banks holding most of the deposits in our banking system) *must* open accounts. Thus at the Federal Reserve Bank, bank A's account will be credited, and bank B's account will be debited, in this way moving reserves from one bank to the other.†

---

* The independence of the Federal Reserve is a perennially controversial issue. See "An Extra Word" at the end of Chapter 20.

† When money is put into a bank account, the account is credited; when money is taken out, the account is debited.

The Federal Reserve Banks serve their member banks in exactly the same way as the member banks serve the public. Member banks automatically deposit in their Federal Reserve accounts all checks they get from other banks. As a result, banks are constantly clearing their checks with one another through the Federal Reserve System, because their depositors are constantly writing checks on their own banks payable to someone who banks elsewhere. Meanwhile, the balance that each bank maintains at the Federal Reserve — that is, the claim it has on other banks — counts, as much as any currency, as part of its reserve against deposits.

In 1985, therefore, when demand deposits were $271 billion and cash in the banks only $21 billion, we would expect the member banks to have had heavy accounts with the Federal Reserve banks. And so they did — $23 billion in all. Thus, total reserves of the banks were $44 billion ($21 billion in cash plus $23 billion in Federal Reserve accounts), enough to satisfy the legal requirements of the Fed.

Fractional Reserves

Thus we see that our banks operate on what is called a *fractional reserve system*. That is, a certain specified fraction of all demand deposits must be kept on hand at all times in cash or at the Fed. The size of the minimum fraction is determined by the Federal Reserve, for reasons of control that we shall shortly learn. It is *not* determined, as we might be tempted to think, to provide a safe backing for our bank deposits. For under *any* fractional system, if *all* depositors decided to draw out their accounts in currency and coin from all banks at the same time, the banks would be unable to meet the demand for cash and would have to close. We call this a "run" on the banking system. Needless to say, runs can be terrifying and destructive economic phenomena.*

Why, then, do we court the risk of runs, however small this risk may be? What is the benefit of a fractional banking system? To answer that, let us look at our bank again.

Loans and Investments

Suppose its customers have given our bank $1 million in deposits and that the Federal Reserve Board requirements are 20 percent, a simpler figure to work with than the actual one. Then we know that our bank must at all times keep $200,000 either in currency in its own till or in its demand deposit at the Federal Reserve Bank.

But having taken care of that requirement, what does the bank do with the remaining deposits? If it simply lets them sit, either as vault cash or as a deposit at the Federal Reserve, our bank will be very "liquid," but it will have no way of

---

* A "run" on the banking system is no longer much of a threat as in the past, because the Federal Reserve could supply its members with vast amounts of cash. We shall learn how, later in this chapter.

making an income. Unless it charges a very high fee for its checking services, it will have to go out of business.

And yet there is an obvious way for the bank to make an income while performing a valuable service. **The bank can use all the cash and check claims it does not need for its reserve to make *loans* to businesses or families or to make financial *investments* in corporate or government bonds. It will thereby not only earn an income, but assist the process of business investment and government borrowing.** Thus the mechanics of the banking system lead us back to the concerns at the very center of our previous analysis.

INSIDE THE BANKING SYSTEM

Fractional reserves allow banks to lend, or to invest in securities, part of the funds that have been deposited with them. But that is not the only usefulness of the fractional reserve system. It works as well to help enlarge or diminish the supply of investible or loanable funds, as the occasion demands. Let us follow the workings of this process. To make the mechanics of banking clear, we are going to look at the actual books of the bank — in simplified form, of course — so we can see how the process of lending and investing appears to the banker himself.

Assets and Liabilities

We begin by introducing two basic elements of business accounting: *assets* and *liabilities.* Every student at some time or another has seen the balance sheet of a firm, and many have wondered how total assets always equal total liabilities. The reason is very simple. Assets are all the things or claims a business owns. Liabilities are claims against those assets — some of them the claims of creditors, some the claims of owners (called the *net worth* of the business). Since assets show everything that a business owns, and since liabilities show how claims against these self-same things are divided between creditors and owners, it is obvious that the two sides of the balance sheet must always come to exactly the same total. **The total of assets and the total of liabilities are an identity.**

T Accounts

Businesses show their financial condition on a *balance sheet* on which all items on the left side represent assets and all those on the right side represent liabilities. By using a simple two-column balance sheet called a T account (because it looks like a T), we can follow very clearly what happens to our bank as we deposit money in it or as it makes loans or investments (see Table 1).

Table 1
ORIGINAL BANK
T accounts always balance, because liabilities show claims on assets.

Assets	Liabilities
$1,000,000 (cash and checks)	$1,000,000 (money owed to depositors)
Total $1,000,000	Total $1,000,000

We start off with the example we have just used, in which we open a brand new bank with $1 million in cash and checks on other banks. Accordingly, our first entry in the T account shows the two sides of this transaction. Notice that our bank has gained an asset of $1 million, the cash and checks it now owns, and that it has simultaneously gained $1 million in liabilities, the deposits it *owes* to its depositors (who can withdraw their money).

As we know, however, our bank will not keep all its newly gained cash and checks in the till. It may hang on to some of the cash, but it will send all the checks it has received, plus any currency that it feels it does not need, to the Fed for deposit in its account there. Table 2 shows the resulting T account.

Excess Reserves

Now we recall from our previous discussion that our bank does not want to remain in this very liquid, but very unprofitable, position. **According to the law, it must retain only a certain percentage of its deposits in cash or at the Federal Reserve — 20 percent in our hypothetical example. All the rest it is free to lend or invest.** As things now stand, however, it has $1 million in reserves — $800,000 more than it needs. Hence, let us suppose that it decides to put these *excess reserves* to work by lending that amount to a sound business risk. (Note that banks do not lend the excess reserves themselves. These reserves, cash and deposits at the Fed, remain right where they are. Their function is to tell the banks how much they may loan or invest.)

Table 2
ORIGINAL BANK
This is how the T account looks after checks have been cleared through the Federal Reserve. If you will examine some bank balance sheets, you will see these items listed as "Cash and due from banks." This means, of course, cash in their own vaults plus their balance at the Federal Reserve.

Assets		Liabilities	
Vault Cash	$100,000	Deposits	$1,000,000
Deposit at Fed	900,000		
Total	$1,000,000	Total	$1,000,000

Making a Loan

Assume now that the Smith Corporation, a well-known firm, comes in for a loan of $800,000. Our bank is happy to lend it that amount. **But making a loan does not mean that the bank now pays the company in cash out of its vaults. Rather, *it makes a loan by opening a new checking account for the firm* and by crediting that account with $800,000.** (Or if, as is likely, the Smith firm already has an account with the bank, it will simply credit the proceeds of the loan to that account.)

Now our T account shows some interesting changes (see Table 3).

There are several things to note about this transaction. First, our bank's reserves (its cash and deposit at the Fed) have not yet changed. The $1 million in reserves are still there.

Second, notice that the Smith Corporation loan counts as a new asset for the bank because the bank now has a legal claim against the company for that amount. (The interest on the loan is not shown in the balance sheet; but when it is paid, it will show up as an addition to the bank's cash.)

Third, deposits have increased by $800,000. Note, however, that this $800,000 was not paid to the Smith firm out of anyone else's account in the bank. It is a new checking account, one that did not exist before. As a result, the supply of money is also up! More about this shortly.

The Loan Is Spent

Was it safe to open this new account for the company? Well, we might see whether our reserves are now sufficient to cover the Smith Corporation's account as well as the original deposit accounts. A glance reveals that all is well. We still have $1 million in reserves against $1.8 million in deposits. Our reserve ratio is much higher than the 20 percent required by law.

It is so much higher, in fact, that we might be tempted to make another loan to the next customer who requests one, and in that way further increase our earning capacity. But an experienced banker shakes his head. "The Smith Corporation did not take out a loan and agree to pay interest on it just for the pleasure of letting that money sit with you," he explains. "Very shortly, the company will be writing

Table 3
ORIGINAL BANK

The bank has used its excess reserves to make a loan. The loan itself is a signed IOU which is a new asset for the bank. The corresponding liability is the new deposit opened in the name of the borrower.

		Liabilities	
Cash and at Fed	$1,000,000	Original deposits	$1,000,000
Loan (Smith Corp.)	800,000	New deposit (Smith Corp.)	800,000
Total	$1,800,000	Total	$1,800,000

Table 4

ORIGINAL BANK

The borrower uses the loan, and its deposits fall to zero. But the assets (and deposit liabilities) of another bank have risen.

Assets		Liabilities	
Cash and at Fed	$ 200,000	Original deposits	$1,000,000
Loan (Smith Corp.)	800,000	Smith Corp. deposits	0
Total	$1,000,000	Total	$1,000,000

SECOND BANK

Assets		Liabilities	
Cash and at Fed	$800,000	Deposit (Jones Corp.)	$800,000
Total	$800,000	Total	$800,000

checks on its balance to pay for goods or services; and when it does, you will need every penny of the reserve you now have."

That, indeed, is the case. Within a few days we find that our bank's account at the Federal Reserve Bank has been charged with a check for $800,000 written by the Smith Corporation in favor of the Jones Corporation, which carries its account at another bank. Now we find that our T account has changed dramatically. Look at Table 4.

Let us see exactly what has happened. First, the Smith Corporation's check has been charged against our account at the Fed and has reduced it from $900,000 to $100,000. Together with the $100,000 cash in our vault, this gives us $200,000 in reserves.

Second, the Smith Corporation's deposit is entirely gone, although its loan agreement remains with us as an asset.

Now if we refigure our reserves we find that they are just right. We are required to have $200,000 in vault cash or in our Federal Reserve account against our $1 million in deposits. That is exactly the amount we have left. Our bank is now fully "loaned up."

Continuing Effects

But the banking *system* is not yet fully loaned up. So far, we have traced what happened only to our bank when the Smith Corporation spent the money in its deposit account. Now we must trace the effect of this action on the deposits and reserves of other banks.

We begin with the bank in which the Jones Corporation deposits the check it has just received from the Smith Corporation. Another look at Table 4 will show you that the Jones Corporation's bank now finds itself in exactly the same position as our bank was when we opened it with $1 million in new deposits, except that the addition to this second-generation bank is smaller than the addition to the first-generation bank.

As we can see, our second-generation bank has gained $800,000 in cash and in deposits. Since it needs only 20 percent of this for required reserves, it finds itself with $640,000 excess reserves, which it is now free to use to make loans as investments. Suppose that it extends a loan to the Brown Company and that the Brown Company shortly thereafter spends the proceeds of that loan at the Black Company, which banks at yet a third bank. The two T accounts in Table 5 show how the total deposits will now be affected.

As Figure 1 makes clear, the process will not stop here but can continue from one bank to the next as long as any lending power remains. Notice, however, that this lending power gets smaller and smaller and will eventually reach zero.

Figure 1
EXPANSION OF THE MONEY SUPPLY

As the relending process continues, successive banks add to their deposits, and the money supply increases. Note the resemblance to the multiplier process.

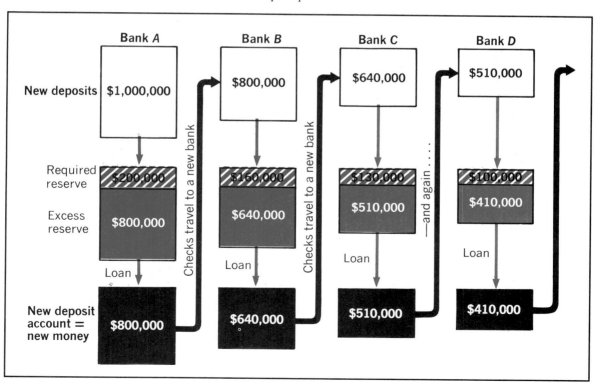

Table 5
SECOND BANK
(after Brown Co. spends the proceeds of its loan)
Here is a repetition of the same process, as the Second Bank uses its lending capacity to finance Brown Co.

Assets		Liabilities	
Cash and at Fed	$160,000	Deposits (Jones Corp.)	$800,000
Loan (to Brown Co.)	640,000	Deposits (Brown Co.)	0
Total	$800,000	Total	$800,000

THIRD BANK
(after Black Co. gets the check of Brown Co.)

Assets		Liabilities	
Cash and at Fed	$640,000	Deposit (Black Co.)	$640,000
Total	$640,000	Total	$640,000

EXPANSION OF THE MONEY SUPPLY

If we now look at the bottom of Figure 1, we will see something very important. **Every time any bank in this chain of transactions has opened an account for a new borrower,** *the supply of money has increased.* Remember that the supply of money is the sum of currency outside the banking system (i.e., in our own pockets), plus the total of demand deposits. As our chain of banks kept opening new accounts, it was simultaneously expanding the total checkwriting capacity of the economy. Thus, money has materialized, seemingly out of thin air.

Now how can this be? If we tell any banker in the chain that he has "created" money, he will protest vehemently. The loans he made, he will insist, were backed at the time he made them by excess reserves as large as the loan itself. Just as we had $800,000 in excess reserves when we made our initial loan to the Smith Corporation, so every subsequent loan was always backed 100 percent by unused reserves when it was made.

Our bankers are perfectly correct when they tell us that they never, never lend a penny more than they have. Money is not created in the lending process because a banker lends money he doesn't have. **Money is created because you and I generally pay each other by checks that give us claims against each other's bank.** If we constantly cashed the checks we exchanged, no new money would be created. But we do not. We deposit each other's checks in our own bank accounts; and in doing so, we give our banks more reserves than they need against the deposits we have just made. These new excess reserves make it possible for our banks to lend or invest, and thereby to open still more deposit accounts, which in turn lead to new reserves.

MONEY AND DEBT

All this gives us a fresh insight into the question of what money is. We said before that it is whatever we use to make payments. But what do we use? The answer is a surprising one. We use *debts*—specifically, the debts of commercial banks. Deposits are, after all, nothing but the liabilities that banks owe their customers. Furthermore, we can see that one purpose of the banking system is to buy debts from other units in the economy, such as businesses or governments, in exchange for its own debts (which are money). For when a bank opens an account for a business to which it has granted a loan or when it buys a government bond, what else is it doing but accepting a debt that is *not* usable as money, in exchange for its deposit liabilities that *are* usable as money. And why is it that banks create money when they make loans, but you or I do not when we lend money? Because we all accept bank liabilities (deposits) as money, but we do not accept personal or business IOUs to make payments with.

The Expansive Power of Money

This all sounds a little frightening. Does it mean that the money supply can go on expanding indefinitely from a single new deposit? Wouldn't that be extremely inflationary?

In our next chapter we will tackle the relation between the money supply and the level of prices directly. But we ought to say a preliminary word here. **Clearly bank reserves have an inflationary potential in a fractional reserve system, simply by virtue of the fact that they are capable of creating a multiple of themselves. That is why economists pay careful attention to the volume of reserves when they are considering the extent of the inflationary dangers facing an economy.**

But the fact that bank reserves *can* become the basis for inflation is not at all the same as saying that inflation is directly caused by bank reserves. It merely tells us that the existence of a flexible money supply poses a problem for monetary management—the theme of Chapter 21.

But monetary management quite aside, we must also understand that there are powerful forces preventing the creation of a single new deposit from expanding indefinitely throughout the system. Here are five very important counterforces that must be borne in mind.

Limits on Expansion

1. **NOT EVERY LOAN GENERATES AN INCREASE IN BANK DEPOSITS.** If our bank had opened a loan account for the Smith Corporation at the same time that another firm had paid off a similar loan, there would have been no original expansion in

bank deposits. In that case, the addition of $800,000 to the Smith account would have been exactly balanced by a decline of $800,000 in someone else's account. Even if that decline had taken place in a different bank, it would still mean that the nation's total of bank deposits would not have risen, and therefore no new money would have been credited. **Thus, only net additions to loans have an expansionary effect.** We will shortly see how such net additions arise in the first place.

2. There Is a Limit to the Rise in Money Supply from a Single Increase in Deposits. As Figure 1 shows, in the chain of deposit expansion each successive bank has a smaller increase in deposits, because each bank has to keep some of its newly gained cash or checks as reserve. Hence the amount of *excess* reserves, against which loans can be made, steadily falls.

Further, we can see that the amount of the total monetary expansion from an original net increase in deposits is governed by the size of the fraction that has to be kept aside each time as reserve. **In fact, we can see that just as with the multiplier, the cumulative effect of an increase in deposits will be determined by the reciprocal of the reserve fraction.** If each bank must keep one-fifth of its increased deposits as reserves, then the cumulative effect of an original increase in deposits, when it has expanded through the system, is five times the original increase. If reserves are one-fourth, the expansion is limited to four times the original increase, and so on.*

3. The Monetary Expansion Process Can Work in Reverse. Suppose the banking system as a whole suffers a net loss of deposits. Instead of putting $1 million into a bank, the public takes it out in cash. The bank will now have too few reserves, and it will have to cut down its loans or sell its investments to gain the reserves it needs. In turn, as borrowers pay off their loans, or as bond buyers pay for their securities, cash will drain from other banks that will now find *their* reserves too small in relation to their deposits. In turn, they will have to sell more investments or curtail still other loans, and this again will squeeze still other banks and reduce their reserves, with the same consequences.

Thus, just as an original expansion in deposits can lead to a multiple expansion, so an original contraction in deposits can lead to a multiple contraction. The size of this contraction is also limited by the reciprocal of the reserve fraction. If banks have to hold a 25 percent reserve, then an original fall of $100,000 in deposits will lead to a total fall of $400,000, assuming that the system was fully loaned up to begin with. If they had to hold a 20 percent reserve, a fall of $100,000 could pyramid to $500,000.

4. The Expansion Process May Not Be Fully Carried Through. We have assumed that each bank in the chain always lends out an amount equal to its excess reserve, but this may not be the case. The third or fifth bank along the way may have trouble finding a creditworthy customer and may decide — for the moment,

---

* If M is the money supply, D is net new deposits and r is the reserve ratio, then $\Delta M = 1/r \times \Delta D$. Notice that this formula is exactly the same as that for the multiplier.

anyway—to sit on its excess reserves. Or borrowers along the chain may take out cash from some of their new deposits and thereby reduce the banks' reserves and their lending powers. Thus the potential expansion may be only partially realized.

5. THE EXPANSION PROCESS TAKES TIME. Like the multiplier process, the expansion of the money supply encounters many "frictions" in real life. Banks do not instantly expand loans when their reserves rise; bank customers do not instantly spend the proceeds of bank loans. The time lags in banking are too variable to enable us to make an estimate of how long it takes for an initial increase in new deposits to work its way through the system, but the time period is surely a matter of months for two or three rounds.

Why Banks Must Work Together

There is an interesting problem concealed behind this crisscrossing of deposits that leads to a slowly rising level of the money supply. Suppose that an imaginary island economy was served by a single bank (and let us forget about all complications of international trade, etc.), and this bank, which worked on a 20 percent reserve ratio, was suddenly presented with an extra 1 million dollars worth of reserves— let us say newly mined pure gold. Our bank could, of course, increase its loans to customers. By how much? By *5 million dollars!*

In other words, our island bank, all by itself, could use an increase in its reserves to create a much larger increase in the money supply. It is not difficult to understand why. Any borrower of the new 5 million, no matter where he spent his money on the island, would only be giving his checks to someone who also banked at the single, solitary bank. The whole 5 million, in other words, would stay *within* the bank as its deposits, although the identity of those depositors would, of course, shift. Indeed, there is no reason why such a bank should limit its expansion of the money supply to 5 million. As long as the soundness of the currency was unquestioned, such a bank could create as much money as it wanted through new deposits, since all those deposits would remain in its own keeping.

The imaginary bank makes it plain why ordinary commercial banks *cannot* expand deposits beyond their excess reserves. Unlike the monopoly bank, they must expect to *lose* their deposits to other banks when their borrowers write checks on their new accounts. As a result they will also lose their reserves, and this can lead to trouble.

Overlending

This situation is important enough to warrant taking a moment to examine. Suppose that in our previous example we had decided to lend the Smith Corporation not $800,000 but $900,000, and suppose as before that the Smith Corporation used the proceeds of that loan to pay the Jones Corporation. Now look at the condition of our bank after the Smith payment has cleared (Table 6).

Table 6

ORIGINAL BANK

A bank that lends an amount larger than its excess reserve will be in trouble. Its reserves will fall below the level required by law.

Assets		Liabilities	
Cash and at Fed	$ 100,000	Original deposits	$1,000,000
Loan (Smith Corp.)	900,000	Smith Corp. deposit	0
Total	$1,000,000	Total	$1,000,000

Our reserves would now have dropped to 10 percent! Indeed, if we had loaned the company $1,000,000, we would be in danger of insolvency.

Banks are, in fact, very careful not to overlend. If they find that they have inadvertently exceeded their legal reserve requirements, they quickly take remedial action. One way a bank may repair the situation is by borrowing reserves for a short period (paying interest on them, of course) from another bank that may have a temporary surplus at the Fed; this is called borrowing *federal funds*. Or a bank may quickly sell some of its government bonds and add the proceeds to its reserve account at the Fed. Or again, it may add to its reserves the proceeds of any loans that have come due and deliberately fail to replace these expired loans with new loans. Finally, a bank may borrow reserves directly from its Federal Reserve Bank and pay interest for the loan. We shall shortly look into this method when we talk about the role of the Federal Reserve in regulating the quantity of money.

The main point is clear. A bank is safe in lending only an amount that it can afford to lose to another bank. But of course one bank's loss is another's gain. That is why, by the exchange of checks, the banking system can accomplish the same result as the island monopoly bank, whereas no individual bank can hope to do so.

Investments and Reserve

If a bank uses its excess reserves to buy securities, does that lead to the same multiplication effect as a bank loan?

It can. When a bank buys government securities, it usually does so from a

Table 7

ORIGINAL BANK

Excess reserves can be used to buy bonds as well as to finance loans.

Assets		Liabilities	
Cash and at Fed	$ 200,000	Deposits	$1,000,000
Government bonds	800,000		
Total	$1,000,000	Total	$1,000,000

Table 8
SECOND BANK
When the seller of the bond deposits his check, the same money-expanding process will be set into motion.

Assets		Liabilities	
Cash	$800,000	New deposit of bond seller	$800,000
Total	$800,000	Total	$800,000

securities dealer, a professional trader in bonds.* Its check (for $800,000 in our example) drawn on its account at the Federal Reserve will be made out to a dealer, who will deposit it in his bank. As a result, the dealer's bank suddenly finds itself with an $800,000 new deposit. It must keep 20 percent of this as required reserve, but the remainder is excess reserve against which it can make loans or investments as it wishes.

Is there a new deposit, corresponding to that of the borrower? There is: the new deposit of the securities dealer. Note that in his case, as in the case of the borrower, the new deposit on the books of the bank has not been put there by the transfer of money from some other commercial bank. The $800,000 deposit has come into being through the deposit of a check of the Federal Reserve Bank, which is not a commercial bank. Thus it represents a new addition to the deposits of the private banking system.

Let us see this in the T accounts. Table 7 shows what our first bank's T account looks like after it has bought its $800,000 in bonds (paying for them with its Federal Reserve checking account).

As we can see, there are no excess reserves here. But look at the bank in which the seller of the government bond has deposited the check he has just received from our bank (Table 8). Here there are excess reserves of $640,000 with which additional investments can be made. It is possible for such new deposits, albeit diminishing each time, to remain in the financial circuit for some time, moving from bank to bank as an active business is done in buying government bonds.

Yields

Meanwhile, however, the very activity in bidding for government bonds is likely to raise their price and thereby lower their rate of interest.

This is a situation you will probably be faced with in your personal life, so you should understand it. A bond has a *fixed* rate of return and a stated face value. If it is a 9 percent, $1,000 bond, this means it will pay $90 interest yearly. If the bond now sells on the market for $1,200, the $90 yearly interest will be less than a 9 percent return ($90 is only 7.5 percent of $1,200). If the price should fall to $900, the $90

---

* The dealer may be only a middleman who will in turn buy from, or sell to, corporations or individuals. This doesn't change our analysis, however.

return will be more than 9 percent ($90 is 10 percent of $900). **Thus the** *yield* **of a bond varies inversely — in the other direction — from its market price.**

When the price of government bonds changes, all bond prices tend to change in the same direction. This is because all bonds are competing for investors' funds. If the yield on "governments" falls, investors will switch from governments to other, higher-yielding bonds. But as they bid for these other bonds, the prices of these bonds will rise — and their yields will fall, too!

In this way, a change in yields spreads from one group of bonds to another. A lower rate of interest or a lower yield on government securities is quickly reflected in lower rates or yields for other kinds of bonds. In turn, a lower rate of interest on bonds makes loans to business look more attractive. Thus, sooner or later excess reserves are apt to be channeled to new loans as well as new investments. Thereafter the deposit-building process follows its familiar course.

looking back

KEY CONCEPTS

The supply of money is usually defined as cash in the public's hands, plus demand deposits

1 The supply of money is generally defined as the cash in the possession of the public (not the cash in bank vaults) plus checking deposits, technically known as demand deposits. The total is called M1. Other measures of money include savings accounts and other liquid assets.

Banks must keep stated fractions of reserves against their deposits: these reserves are cash or accounts at a Federal Reserve Bank. Banks can lend or invest sums equal to excess reserves

2 Banks are required by the Federal Reserve Act to maintain stated proportions of actual cash (in their own vaults) or claims on other banks as reserves against their deposits. These reserves are largely maintained as accounts with one of the twelve Federal Reserve banks of the country. This is called the fractional reserve system. It permits banks to make loans or investments equal in amount to their excess reserves.

Banks make loans by opening deposits for the borrower. These deposits, when spent, become new deposits for other banks, enabling them in turn to expand their loans or investment

3 When a bank makes a loan against its excess reserve, it opens a deposit in the name of the borrower. That deposit is normally used for business purposes, and thereby becomes a new deposit in some other bank. In turn that bank must keep a legal reserve to cover part of its new deposit, but is free to lend or invest an amount equal to its excess reserve.

The process of successive relending expands the money supply.
The banking system can increase M, although no bank by itself could long do so

4 The successive spending of loans creates additional deposits through the system, acting like a multiplier. These new deposits are additions to the money supply. No single bank on its own would dare to expand the total of deposits, but working together as a system, the member banks can increase this supply to the extent that fractional reserve requirements permit.

The expansion process has limits, set by the reserve fraction. It applies only to net loans, and it may work in reverse	**5** The money expansion has several limits: Only net loans create new money, not loans that are offset by repayments; expansion is controlled by the reserve fraction, just like the multiplier process; monetary expansion can work in reverse if repayments exceed new loans; the expansion process may not be carried all the way through; and the process takes time.
Using excess reserves to buy bonds also increases the money supply	**6** A bank that uses its excess reserve to buy bonds also creates new deposits when the seller of the bond deposits his check. This too can expand the money supply.
As bond prices change, bond yields also change. The higher the price, the lower the yield	**7** As bonds are bought and sold, their price changes. Because bonds have fixed interest obligations, a higher or lower price for a bond changes its yield. As bond prices rise, yields fall, and vice versa.

ECONOMIC VOCABULARY

Money supply   332
Demand deposits   332
Federal Reserve System   335
Fractional reserves   336
Assets and liabilities   337

T accounts   337
Excess reserves   338
Overlending   345
Yields   347

QUESTIONS

1. Why do we not count cash in the tills of commercial banks in the money supply? When you deposit currency in a commercial bank, what happens to it? Can you ask for your particular bills again? If you demanded to see "your" account, what would it be?

2. What determines how much vault cash a bank must hold against its deposits? Would you expect this proportion to change in some seasons, such as Christmas? Do you think it would be the same in worried times as in placid times? In new countries as in old ones?

3. What are excess reserves? Suppose a bank has $500,000 in deposits and a reserve ratio of 30 percent is imposed by law. What is its required reserve? Suppose it happens to hold $200,000 in vault cash or at its account at the Fed. What, if any, is its excess reserve?

4. If the bank above wanted to make loans or investments, how much would it be entitled to lend or invest? Suppose its deposits increased by another $50,000. Could it lend or invest this entire amount? Any of it? How much?

5. If a bank lends money, it opens an account in the name of the borrower. Now suppose the borrower draws down his new account. What happens to the reserves of the lending bank? Show this in a T account.

6. Suppose the borrower sends his check for $1,000 to someone who banks at another bank. Describe what happens to the deposits of the second bank. If the reserve ratio is 20 percent, how much new lending or investing can it do?

7. If the reserve ratio is 20 percent and the original addition to reserves is $1,000, what will be the total potential amount of new money that can be created by the banking system? If the ratio is 25 percent?

8. Suppose you own a $1000, 10% bond from the U.S. government which you bought for $1000. Now suppose that the rate of interest for comparable securities rises from 10% to 20%. Would you be able to sell your bond for $1000? Suppose the rate of interest sank to 5%. Would you be able to get more than $1000 for your bond? Think about this question very carefully. If you find it puzzling, never fear. We will take it up again in detail in Chapter 21.

CHAPTER 20
The Federal Reserve

a look ahead

In the last chapter we learned what money was and how the money supply could be increased. But we have not yet investigated the methods by which the national government exercises control over the money supply; this we shall do here.

1 First we look into the workings of the Federal Reserve System, particularly with respect to the three ways in which it can loosen or tighten the monetary strings. This brings us to the question of how the Fed is involved in the international exchange market.

2 Second, we look into the question of gold and paper money. Where do those famous "printing presses" get into the money question?

3 Third, we look again at the involvement of the United States in the world economy and ask to what extent we can still speak of "our own" money supply.

W e have now seen how a banking system can create money through the creation of excess reserves. But the key to the process is the creation of the *original* excess reserves, for without them the cumulative process will not be set in motion. We remember, for example, that a loan will not result in an increase in the money supply if it is offset by a decline in lending somewhere else in the banking system; neither will the purchase of a bond by one commercial bank if it is only buying a security sold by another. **To get a net addition to loans or investments, however, a banking system — assuming that it is fully loaned up — needs an increase in its reserves.** Where do these extra reserves come from? That is the question we must turn to next.

ROLE OF THE FEDERAL RESERVE

In our example we have already met one source of changes in reserves. When the public needs less currency and deposits its extra holdings in the banks, reserves rise, as we have seen. When the public wants more currency, it depletes the banks' holdings and thereby lowers their reserves. In the latter case, the banks may find that they have insufficient reserves behind their deposits. To get more currency or claims on other banks, they will have to sell securities or reduce their loans. This might put a very severe crimp in the economy. Hence, to allow bank reserves to be regulated by the public's fluctuating demand for cash would be an impossible way to run our monetary system.

But we remember that bank reserves are not mainly currency; in fact, currency is a relatively minor item. Most reserves are the accounts that member banks hold at the Federal Reserve. If these accounts could somehow be increased or decreased, we could regulate the amount of reserves—and thus the permissible total of deposits—without regard to the public's changing need for cash.

This is precisely what the Federal Reserve System is designed to do. Essentially, the system is set up to regulate the supply of money by raising or lowering the reserves of its member banks. When these reserves are raised, member banks find themselves with excess reserves and are thus in a position to make loans and investments by which the supply of money will increase further. Conversely, when the Federal Reserve lowers the reserves of its member banks, they will no longer be able to make loans and investments, or they may even have to reduce loans or get rid of investments, thereby extinguishing deposit accounts and contracting the supply of money.

Monetary Control Mechanisms

How does the Federal Reserve operate? There are three ways.

1. CHANGING RESERVE REQUIREMENTS. It was the Federal Reserve itself, we will remember, that originally determined how much in reserves its member banks should hold against their deposits. By changing that reserve requirement for a given level of deposits, it can give its member banks excess reserves or create a shortage of reserves.

This has two effects. First, it immediately changes the lending or investing capacity of all banks. In our imaginary bank we have assumed that reserves were set at 20 percent of deposits. Suppose now that the Federal Reserve determined to lower reserve requirements to 15 percent. It would thereby automatically create extra lending or investing power for our *existing* reserves. Our bank with $1 million in deposits and $200,000 in reserves could now lend or invest an additional $50,000 without any new funds coming in from depositors. On the other hand, if requirements were raised to, say, 30 percent, we would find that our original $200,000 reserve was $100,000 short of requirements, and we would have to curtail lending or investing until we were again in line with requirements.

Second, the new reserve requirements raise or lower the reserve multiplier — expanding or contracting the limits of the flexible money system. Because these new reserve requirements affect *all* banks, changing reserve ratios is a very effective way of freeing or contracting bank credit on a large scale. But it is an instrument that sweeps across the entire banking system in an undiscriminating fashion. It is therefore used only rarely, when the Federal Reserve Board feels that the supply of money is seriously short or dangerously excessive and needs remedy on a countrywide basis.

2. CHANGING DISCOUNT RATES. A second means of control uses interest rates as the money-controlling device. Recall that member banks short on reserves have a special privilege, if they wish to exercise it. They can *borrow* reserve balances from the Federal Reserve Bank itself and add them to their regular reserve account at the bank.

The Federal Reserve Bank, of course, charges interest for lending reserves, and this interest is called the discount rate. By raising or lowering this rate, the Federal Reserve can make it attractive or unattractive for member banks to borrow to augment reserves. In contrast with changing the reserve ratio itself, changing the discount rate is a mild device that allows each bank to decide for itself whether it wishes to increase its reserves.

Although changes in the discount rate can be used as a major means of controlling the money supply and are used to control it in some countries, they are not used for this purpose in the United States. The Federal Reserve Board does not allow banks to borrow whatever they would like at the current discount rate. The discount "window" is a place where a bank can borrow small amounts of money to cover a small deficiency in its reserves, but it is not a place where banks can borrow major amounts of money except in an emergency. **As a result, the discount rate serves more as a signal of what the Federal Reserve would like to see happen than as an active force in determining the total borrowings of banks.**

3. OPEN-MARKET OPERATIONS. Most frequently used is a third technique called open-market operations. This technique permits the Federal Reserve Banks to

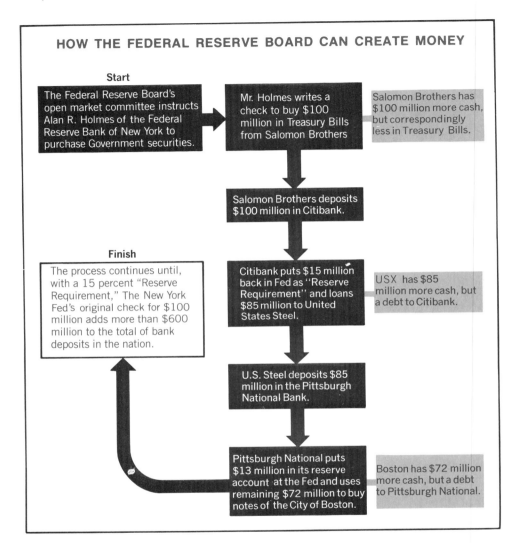

HOW THE FEDERAL RESERVE BOARD CAN CREATE MONEY

Start

The Federal Reserve Board's open market committee instructs Alan R. Holmes of the Federal Reserve Bank of New York to purchase Government securities.

Mr. Holmes writes a check to buy $100 million in Treasury Bills from Salomon Brothers

Salomon Brothers has $100 million more cash, but correspondingly less in Treasury Bills.

Salomon Brothers deposits $100 million in Citibank.

Finish

The process continues until, with a 15 percent "Reserve Requirement," The New York Fed's original check for $100 million adds more than $600 million to the total of bank deposits in the nation.

Citibank puts $15 million back in Fed as "Reserve Requirement" and loans $85 million to United States Steel.

USX has $85 million more cash, but a debt to Citibank.

U.S. Steel deposits $85 million in the Pittsburgh National Bank.

Pittsburgh National puts $13 million in its reserve account at the Fed and uses remaining $72 million to buy notes of the City of Boston.

Boston has $72 million more cash, but a debt to Pittsburgh National.

change the supply of reserves by buying or selling U.S. government bonds on the open market.

How does this work? Suppose the Federal Reserve authorities wish to increase the reserves of member banks. They will begin to buy government securities from dealers in the bond market, and they will pay these dealers with Federal Reserve checks.

Notice something about these checks: *They are not drawn on any commercial bank!* They are drawn on the Federal Reserve Bank itself. The security dealer who sells the bond will, of course, deposit the Federal Reserve's check, as if it were any other check, in his own commercial bank; and his bank will send the Federal Reserve's check through for credit to its own account, as if it were any other check. *As a result, the dealer's bank will have gained reserves, although no other commercial bank has lost reserves.* On balance, then, the system has more lending and investing capacity than it had before. In fact, it now has *excess* reserves and these, as we have seen, will spread out through the system. **Thus by buying bonds the Federal Reserve has, in fact, deposited money in the accounts of its members, thereby giving them the extra reserves that it set out to create (see box p. 354).**

Conversely, if the authorities decide that member banks' reserves are too large, they will sell securities. Now the process works in reverse. Security dealers or other buyers of bonds will send their own checks on their own regular commercial banks to the Federal Reserve in payment for these bonds. This time the Fed will take the checks of its member banks and charge their accounts, thereby reducing their reserves. **Since these checks will not find their way to another commercial bank, the system as a whole will have suffered a diminution of its reserves.** By selling securities, in other words, the Federal Reserve authorities lower the Federal Reserve accounts of member banks, thereby diminishing their reserves.

Isn't this, you might ask, really the same thing as raising or lowering the reserve ratio? If the Fed is really just putting money into member bank accounts when it buys bonds and taking money out when it sells them, why does it bother to go through the open market? Why not just tell the member banks that their reserves are larger or smaller?

Analytically, you are entirely right. But there are cogent reasons for working through the bond market. The open-market technique allows banks to *compete* for their share of the excess reserves that are being made available or taken away. Banks that are good at attracting depositors will thereby get extra benefit from an increase in the money supply. Thus, rather than assigning excess reserves by executive fiat, the Fed uses the open market as an allocation device.

A FLEXIBLE MONEY SUPPLY

There are many important questions to be examined with regard to the problem of controlling the money supply. We shall examine them in some detail in our next chapter. But at this point, where we are still learning about how the Fed works, we must examine a question we have heretofore passed over in silence. We have taken for granted that we need a larger supply of money in order to expand output. But why should we? Why could we not grow just as well as if the supply of money were fixed?

Theoretically we could. If we cut prices as we increased output, a given amount of money (or a given amount of expenditure) could cover an indefinitely large real output. Furthermore, as prices fell, workers would be content not to ask for higher wages (or would even accept lower wages), since in real terms they would be just as well or better off.

It is not difficult to spot the flaw in this argument. In the real world, prices of many goods cannot be cut easily. If the price of steel rose and fell as quickly and easily as prices on the stock exchange or if wages went down without a murmur of resistance or if rents and other contractual items could be quickly adjusted, then prices would be flexible and we would not require any enlargement of the money supply to cover a growing real output.

In fact, as we know, prices are extremely "sticky" in the downward direction. Union leaders do not look with approval on wage cuts, even when living costs fall. Contractual prices cannot be quickly adjusted. Many big firms administer their prices and carefully avoid price competition: Note, for example, that the price of many customer items is printed on the package months before the item will be sold.

An Economic Straitjacket

Thus we can see that a fixed, unchanging, supply of money would put the economy into a straitjacket. As output tended to increase, business would need more money to finance production, and consumers would need more money to make their larger expenditures. If business could get more money from the banks, all would be well. But suppose it could not. Then the only way it could get a larger supply of cash would be to persuade someone to lend the money, and persuasion would be in the form of a higher rate of interest. But this rising interest rate would discourage other businesses from going ahead with their plans. Hence the would-be-boom would be stopped dead in its tracks.

A flexible money supply avoids this economic suffocation. The fact that banks can create money (provided they have excess reserves) enables them to take care of businesses that wish to make additional expenditures. The expenditures themselves put additional money into the hands of consumers. And the spending of consumers in turn sends the enlarged volume of purchasing power back to business firms to complete the great flow of expenditure and receipt.

THE FEDERAL RESERVE AND FOREIGN EXCHANGE

There is one further function of the Federal Reserve that we must understand. It concerns the role of the Federal Reserve in the foreign exchange market.

Perhaps you recall from our early discussion of America in the world economy (Chapter 6) that exporting and importing required the participation of banks as well as producers or merchants or transportation companies. If an American automobile importer wants to bring Hondas into this country, someone has to find the yen with which to pay the Japanese exporter, and if a Japanese importer wants to bring American wheat into Japan, someone has to find the dollars to pay the American grain merchant. Banks provide the needed foreign exchange in both cases. But where do banks acquire their supplies of other countries' currencies?

In part the answer is that banks participate in foreign trade to help both importers and exporters, and thereby acquire claims on foreign currencies as a result. But the answer also involves the Federal Reserve — or more correctly, all central banks. **For central banks are agencies of their governments in the international currency markets.** When the Federal Reserve buys yen or francs, it pays out dollars and builds up deposits of foreign money. When it sells foreign exchange, it exchanges these foreign reserves for dollars. Central banks are therefore potential sources and absorbers of foreign exchange for their own banks.

For example, if the Chase Manhattan Bank finds it has deposits of ten million more yen in its Tokyo branch than it can use there, it can exchange those extra yen (at the going exchange rate) for a credit in dollars to its dollar account at the Federal Reserve. The Federal Reserve then holds the yen as part of its Japanese reserve account. In the same way, a Japanese bank with more dollars in its New York branch than it knows what to do with can do the same thing with its central bank, the Bank of Japan. The Bank of Japan will transfer the unwanted dollars to its own dollar reserve account, giving the Japanese bank a credit in yen.

What the Federal Reserve Can Do

As a result the Federal Reserve, like all central banks, becomes a repository for **international reserves** — the supplies of foreign exchange that establish the international creditworthiness of a nation. As a central bank it therefore plays a very important role in the market in which the exchange rate for dollars is established. By selling its reserves, it would tend to lower the price of the currencies it sold and to raise the price of the dollar. And by selling dollars, it tends to lower their price and to raise the exchange rate for foreign currencies.

As we know, the United States is staggering today under a tremendous deficit in its balance of trade. One reason for this, we recall from Chapter 6, is that the exchange rate for the dollar has been very high, making imports cheap and exports dear. Then why doesn't the Federal Reserve sell dollars and bring down the exchange rate?

How would it sell dollars? Exactly the same way as it "sells dollars" when it buys bonds on the open market. The Federal Reserve would simply buy yen or francs or marks, instead of bonds, paying for them with checks written on itself — just as it does at home. Because the credit of the United States is still the strongest in the world, no one would dream of refusing a Federal Reserve check. Then why doesn't the Federal Reserve get us out of our foreign trade problem?

Risks of a Falling Dollar

The answer is that international capital markets are extremely volatile, and the Federal Reserve fears — not without reason — the consequences of even a small move to change exchange rate values. The fears are twofold: fears that the fall may get out of hand, and fears that a return to a low dollar may rekindle inflation.

Seeing the Federal Reserve embark on an operation of dumping dollars—buying other currencies right and left by writing checks on itself—private investors, domestic and foreign, would understandably become nervous about the dollar's value. To some extent, they would worry about the direct effects of the Federal Reserve's actions—but *mostly they would worry about each other.* If the dollar is going to fall, who wants to be the last person holding dollars? With such a psychology, even a small commitment to exchange rate intervention could, at any moment, turn into a stampede. In that case, the dollar might fall by much more than desired or planned.

What would happen if the dollar did fall precipitously? As foreign depositors removed their dollars *en masse,* many United States banks might find themselves in a precarious position, exactly as they would if many domestic depositors closed their accounts. However, in the international case, the withdrawn dollars might not be redeposited in another American bank, but might instead end up in a foreign country. The Federal Reseve could therefore be forced to lend reserves to member banks—possibly in massive amounts—to prevent a domestic credit crunch.

No doubt we could weather such a crisis. But over a year or so, we would confront a different problem. United States exports, suddenly more competitive, would rise—that would be a good thing; United States imports, suddenly more expensive, would fall. Thus the trade deficit would shrink. But if domestic markets were tight, the rising prices of imports might well lead to rising prices of domestically produced goods, and thereafter to rising wages as workers tried to offset the fall in their standard of living. Inflation could return via rising costs and expenditures.

The Internationalization of Finance

Scenarios such as these make it clear that the power of the Federal Reserve, vast though it is, is limited. Together with its sister institutions in other countries, the Federal Reserve remains a major force in international finance. But its power of action is constrained by the immensely greater forces of the international financial network of exchange. At best, the Federal Reserve can mobilize a few billions of foreign exchange to put on the market. But the average value of a day's trading in foreign currencies around the world is estimated to come to $150 billion!* Thus the impact of the Federal Reserve is primarily psychological, not economic.

Indeed, the power of the Federal Reserve is not only limited in the international financial markets, but at home as well. As we have seen, that is because the actions of international investors, choosing where to place their assets and on what terms, can have a dramatic effect on conditions in the U.S. economy itself. To a very large extent, there is now only one international financial market in the world, established by the collective and uncoordinated operations of the world's financial institutions—including its central banks, its commercial banks, and its markets in stocks, bonds, and other securities.

* *The New York Times,* September 27, 1985, p. D7.

International Banking

This internationalization of finance is the consequence of many developments. One of them is the greatly expanded activities of multinational corporations, which maintain very large bank balances in many nations, switching them around to earn the highest possible rate of return on their funds. This creates a constant flow of "hot money" across national frontiers, as money rushes in to take advantage of an interest rate edge or an expected rise in the exchange rate, and then rushes out if the interest edge becomes negative or the currency threatens to devalue.

Equally significant is the rise of international banking. In 1965 the twenty biggest U.S. banks had a total of only 211 branches around the world. By 1972 the number had grown to 627, and the number of branches today is well over a thousand. This same multiplication of banking facilities has taken place in other major nations: In New York City alone there are branches of at least a hundred foreign banks listed in the telephone directory.

These banks create an international money mechanism that also ties together capitalist economies. Using electronic techniques, banks lend money literally around the world for a few hours at a stretch, so that deposits that are not "working" in Citibank after banking hours can be loaned overnight to a bank in Hong Kong or New York, where they will serve as deposit reserves until Hong Kong shuts down and New York opens up, and the deposits are "returned."

These international deposits add to the vast pool of domestic money deposited in other countries that we call Eurodollars (or Euromarks, Euroyen, and the like). The total volume of all these internationally located funds has been estimated at close to $3 trillion. Their consequence is that there is now a single (unofficial) money supply in the world. Unlike the supply of dollars or francs or marks, however, it is not controlled by any single central bank or by any international agency. Instead, it rises and falls, with all the effects of changes in the domestic money supply, as a result of the expansion or contraction of the bigger units in the world economy, of which the United States is the biggest of all. Thus **the international money network serves as a transmission mechanism by which booms or busts in powerful economies exert upward or downward effects on other economies.**

PAPER MONEY AND GOLD

Finally, let us clear up one last mystery of the monetary system—the mystery of where currency (coin and bills) actually comes from and where it goes. If we examine most of our paper currency, we will find that it has "Federal Reserve Note" on it: That is, it is paper money issued by the Federal Reserve System. We understand, by now, how the public gets these notes: It simply draws them from its checking accounts. When it does so, the commercial banks, finding their supplies of vault cash low, ask their Federal Reserve district banks to ship them as much new cash as they need.

And what does the Federal Reserve Bank do? It takes packets of bills ($1 and $5 and $10) out of its vaults, where these stacks of printed paper have *no monetary significance at all,* charges the requisite amount against its member banks' balances, and ships the cash out by armored truck. So long as these new stacks of bills remain in the member banks' possession, they are still not money! But soon they will pass out to the public, where they will be money. Do not forget, of course, that as a result the public will have that much *less* money left in its checking accounts.

Could this currency-issuing process go on forever? Could the Federal Reserve print as much money as it wanted to? Suppose the authorities at the Federal Reserve decided to order a trillion dollars worth of bills from the Treasury mints. What would happen when those bills arrived at the Federal Reserve banks? The answer is that they would simply gather dust in their vaults. There would be no way for the Federal Reserve to "issue" its money unless the public wanted cash. And the amount of cash the public could want is always limited by the amount of money in its checking accounts.

Thus the specter of "rolling the printing presses" has to be looked at skeptically. In a nation such as pre-Hitler Germany, where most individuals were paid by cash, not by check, it was easier to get the actual bills into circulation than it would be in a highly developed check money system such as ours. The roads to inflation are many, but the actual printing of money is not likely to be one of them.*

The Gold Cover

Are there no limitations on this note-issuing or reserve-creating process? Until 1967 there *were* limitations imposed by Congress, requiring the Federal Reserve to hold gold certificates equal in value to at least 25 percent of all outstanding notes. (Gold certificates were a special kind of paper money issued by the U.S. Treasury and backed 100 percent by gold bullion in Fort Knox). Prior to 1964 there was a further requirement that the amount of gold certificates also be sufficient to give a 25 percent backing as well to the total amount of member bank deposits held by the Fed. Thus the legal obligation not to go beyond this 25 percent gold cover provided a strict ceiling on the amount of member bank reserves the Federal Reserve System could create or on the amount of notes it could ship at the request of its member banks.

All this presented no problem in, say, 1940, when the total of member bank reserves plus Federal Reserve notes came to only $20 billion, against which we held gold certificates worth almost $22 billion. Trouble began to develop, however, in

---

* We have all seen pictures of German workers being paid their wages in wheelbarrow loads of marks. The question is this: Why didn't the German authorities simply print paper money with bigger denominations, so that someone who was paid a billion marks a week could get ten 100 million mark notes, not ten thousand 1 million mark notes? The answer is that it takes time to go through the bureaucratic process of ordering a new print run of higher denomination notes. Imagine a young economist at the finance ministry suggesting to his chief that they ought to stock up on billion mark notes to be put into circulation six months hence. His superior would certainly be horrified. "You can't do that," he would protest. "Why, an order for billion mark notes would be — inflationary!"

the 1960s when a soaring GNP was accompanied by a steadily rising volume of both member bank reserves and Federal Reserve notes. By 1964, for example, member bank reserves had grown to $22 billion, and outstanding Reserve notes to nearly $35 billion. At the same time, our gold stock had declined to just over $15 billion. With $57 billion in liabilities ($22 billion in member bank reserves plus $35 billion in notes) and only $15 billion in gold certificates, the 25 percent cover requirement was clearly imperiled.

Congress thereupon removed the cover requirement from member bank reserves, leaving all our gold certificates available as backing for our Federal Reserve notes. But even that did not solve the problem. Currency in circulation continued to rise with a record GNP until it exceeded $40 billion in 1967. Our gold stock meanwhile continued to decline to $12 billion in that year and threatened to fall further. The handwriting on the wall indicated that the 25 percent cover could not long be maintained.

There were basically two ways out. One would have been to change the gold cover requirements from 25 percent to, say, 10 percent. That would have made our gold stock more than adequate to back our paper money (and our member bank deposits, too). The second way was much simpler: *eliminate the gold cover entirely.* With very little fuss, this is what Congress did in 1967.

Gold and Money

Does the presence or absence of a gold cover make any difference? From the economist's point of view it does not. Gold is a metal with a long and rich history of hypnotic influence, so there is undeniably a psychological usefulness in having gold behind a currency. But unless that currency is 100 percent convertible into gold, *any* money demands an act of faith on the part of its users. If that faith is destroyed, the money becomes valueless; so long as it is unquestioned, the money *is* "as good as gold."

Thus the presence or absence of a gold backing for currency is purely a psychological problem, so far as the value of a domestic currency is concerned. But the point is worth pursuing a little further. Suppose our currency *were* 100 percent convertible into gold — suppose, in fact, that we used only gold coins as currency. Would that improve the operation of our economy?

A moment's reflection should reveal that it would not. We would still have to cope with a very difficult problem that our bank deposit money handles rather easily. This is the problem of how we could increase the supply of money or diminish it, as the needs of the economy changed. With gold coins as money, we would either have a frozen stock of money (with consequences we shall trace in the next chapter), or our supply of money would be at the mercy of our luck in goldmining or the currents of international trade that funneled gold into our hands or took it away. And incidentally, a gold currency would not avoid inflation, as many countries have discovered when the vagaries of international trade or a fortuitous discovery of gold mines increased their holdings of gold faster than their actual output.

GOLDFINGER AT WORK

Some years ago a patriotic women's organization, alarmed lest the Communists had tunneled under the Atlantic, forced an inspection of the gold stock buried at Fort Knox. It proved to be all there. An interesting question arises as to the repercussions, had they found the great vault to be bare. Perhaps we might have followed the famous anthropological example of the island of Yap in the South Seas, where heavy stone cartwheels are the symbol of wealth for the leading families. One such family was particularly remarkable insofar as its cartwheel lay at the bottom of a lagoon, where it had fallen from a canoe. Although it was absolutely irretrievable and even invisible, the family's wealth was considered unimpaired, since everyone knew the stone was there. If the Kentucky depository had been empty, a patriotic declaration by the ladies that the gold really was in Fort Knox might have saved the day for the United States.

Money and Belief

How, then, do we explain the worldwide fascination with gold? Once again, the economist offers no rational explanation for such a phenomenon. There is nothing in gold itself that possesses more value than silver, uranium, land, or labor. Indeed, judged strictly as a source of usable values, gold is rather low on the spectrum of human requirements. **The sole reason why people want gold — rich people and poor people, sophisticated people and ignorant ones — is that gold has been for centuries a metal capable of catching and holding our fancy, and in troubled times it is natural enough that we turn to this enduring symbol of wealth as the best bet for preserving our purchasing power in the future.**

Will gold in fact remain valuable forever? And if so, how valuable? There is absolutely no way to answer such a question. As we cautioned at the outset, money is a highly sophisticated and curious invention. At one time or another nearly everything imaginable has served as the magic symbol of money: whales' teeth, shells, feathers, bark, furs, blankets, butter, tobacco, leather, copper, silver, gold, and (in the most advanced nations) pieces of paper with pictures on them, or simply numbers on a computer printout. In fact, anything is usable as money, provided that there is a natural or enforceable scarcity of it, so that people can usually come into its possession only through carefully designated ways. Behind all the symbols, however, rests the central requirement of faith: **Money serves its indispensable purposes as long as we believe in it. It ceases to function the moment we do not. Money has well been called "the promises men live by."**

looking back

KEY CONCEPTS

The Federal Reserve is the source of most of the net increases (or decreases) in deposits

1 The volume of demand deposits can increase only if there is an increase in deposits that is not matched by a decrease elsewhere. This net increase in deposits and reserves mainly comes from the Federal Reserve system. In the same way the money supply will contract only if a fall in deposits at one bank is not balanced by a rise elsewhere. Again, the Federal Reserve is the source of such net decreases.

Three methods of changing the money supply:
1. Raising or lowering reserve requirements (this is a powerful but undiscriminating weapon)

2 The Fed has three methods by which it can change the net total of deposits. The first is by changing the reserve requirement. This directly freezes or frees a portion of the reserves of each bank and also changes the deposit multiplier. This is a potent means of bringing about large changes in money supply, but it exerts its effect across the board in an undiscriminating fashion.

2. Changing discount rates signals a policy of tighter or easier money

3 The Federal Reserve can also change discount rates—the rate at which member banks can borrow. This action not only directly encourages or discourages member bank borrowing, but is widely regarded as a signal to the financial world that the Fed is eager to make money tight or easier.

3. Open-market operations are an important week-to-week means of control. When the Fed buys government bonds it creates net deposits; selling bonds reduces total deposits

4 Most important in week-to-week activities are open-market operations. These operations are the buying and selling of government bonds conducted by the New York Federal Reserve Bank in the bond market. When the Fed buys bonds, it pays for them by its own check. This check, when deposited in a bank, creates a new deposit that is not gained from another bank. It is a net increase in money supply. Selling a bond withdraws deposits in the same way. Open market operations enable banks to compete for their share of the new deposits that will be created.

A flexible money system is necessary for an economy with sticky prices

5 A flexible monetary system is necessary because prices are sticky. This is the consequence of long-term contracts, wage agreements, and similar institutional rigidities that make it impossible for prices to fall so that a fixed money supply could finance a growing volume of real output.

The Federal Reserve acquires foreign exchange; its power of intervention is, however, limited

6 The Federal Reserve, like all central banks, buys and sells foreign exchange. All national banks can "unload" unwanted exchange on their central bank where they become part of the central bank reserves of foreign exchange. Thus the Fed can affect the exchange value of dollars by buying or selling its reserves. It cannot greatly lower the price of dollars, however,

	without the danger of an international flight from American banks.
The internationalization of money	7 This limited power of the Fed is one aspect of the degree to which an internationalized money supply has constrained the power of all banks. National money supplies are now international — especially around the fringes.
Paper money has no gold backing. It only passes into use when the public converts its demand deposits into cash	8 Printed money is not actually money until it passes into the hands of the public. The amount depends on the demand for cash and the size of checking accounts. There is no longer a gold cover behind printed money.
Gold is valuable because of its long symbolic importance	9 Gold has long held a special place in the human imagination, and this accounts for its value. There is no way of knowing whether gold will continue to hold that special place.

ECONOMIC VOCABULARY

Changing reserve requirements   352   International reserves   357
Discount rates   353   Gold cover   360
Open-market operations   353

QUESTIONS

1. Suppose that a bank has $1 million in deposits, $150,000 in reserves, and is fully loaned up. Now suppose the Federal Reserve System lowers reserve requirements from 15 to 10 percent. What happens to the lending capacity of the bank? What happens to the deposit multiplier?

2. The Federal Reserve banks buy $100 million in U.S. Treasury notes on the open market. How do they pay for these notes? What happens to the checks? Do they affect the reserves of member banks? Will buying bonds increase or decrease the money supply?

3. Now explain what happens when the Fed sells Treasury notes. Who buys them? How do they pay for them? Where do the checks go? How does payment affect the accounts of member banks at their Federal Reserve bank?

4. Suppose you had $1,000 in the bank. Would you be more willing to invest it if you could earn 5 percent or 8 percent? What factors could make you change

your mind about investing all or any part at, say, 8 percent? Could you imagine conditions that would make you unwilling to invest even at 10 percent? Other conditions that would lead you to invest your whole cash balance at, say, 3 percent?

5. Suppose the going rate of interest is 7 percent and the monetary authorities want to curb expenditures and act to reduce the quantity of money. What will the effect be in terms of the public's access to cash? What will the public do if it feels short of cash? Will it buy or sell securities? What would this do to their price? What would thereupon happen to the rate of interest? To investment expenditures?

6. Suppose the monetary authorities want to encourage economic expansion. What are the general measures it will take? What problems might arise because of the international character of money?

7. Why do you think gold was a monetary standard for so long?

AN EXTRA WORD ABOUT

Independence of the Fed

The Federal Reserve Board is run by seven governors, each appointed to a 14-year term by the president with the approval of Congress. The governors of the Federal Reserve System cannot be removed during their terms of office except for wrongdoing. Thus, although fiscal policy is located in the executive and legislative branches of the government, monetary policy is vested in an independent board.

There were two initial justifications for this institutional arrangement. The first was that monetary policies were necessarily subject to quick changes. Second, it was felt that monetary policies ought to be insulated from the political process.

Are these reasons still valid? Some economists think so; others, including ourselves, think not. To take the first argument: It is true that Congress cannot be expected to operate an efficient open-market system on a daily basis. But this is not an argument for divorcing the responsibility for such operations from the *executive* branch. In most of the world's governments, central banks (the equivalent of the Fed) are located within the executive establishment, usually as a part of the Treasury or Finance ministries or departments. These banks have no trouble making quick decisions. Moreover, even if Congress could not be expected to approve of every jiggle in monetary measures, there is no reason why it could not endorse or direct the major thrust of monetary strategy toward an expansionary or a contractionary general objective.

The argument about "insulation" depends on one's view of democracy, where values once again reign supreme. There is a curious inconsistency, however, in trying to insulate only monetary policies, not fiscal policies. Why should we trust the democratic mechanism to establish expenditures and taxes, but not the supply of money?

As in most institutional debates, dramatic changes are unlikely, although we seem to be moving in a more democratic direction in our monetary management. Congress now expects to be briefed every six months on the Fed's monetary objectives for the following year. There are also bills pending in Congress to integrate the Fed more fully by altering the tenure of the chairman to be concomitant with that of the president; or to require the Fed to issue an economic report directly after the president's economic report, stating what differences, if any, lie between them, and justifying the Fed's course of action if it differs from that of the administration.

Meanwhile, a high degree of integration exists in fact, although not in law. More and more, the Fed bows to public pressure or to pressure from the administration. This is hardly surprising. As we shall see in the next chapter, we live at a time when the importance of money in the economy is more highly regarded than it used to be. The idea of an independent Fed does not sit so well when we think of the Fed as bearing prime responsibility for our economic well-being. Having created the Federal Reserve Board in the first place, Congress can alter it, as it wishes; and it undoubtedly would alter it, were the Fed to risk a direct confrontation with congressional or presidential economic objectives. Constitutionally, the power to create money is vested in Congress, which could, if it wished, legislate rules for the Fed. The more important money management becomes, the more powerful are the pressures to place it within, not outside, the main political mechanisms of the nation.

CHAPTER 21
Money and the Macro System

a look ahead

In our last chapters we learned what money was and how the money supply could be increased. Now we must turn to the much more complicated question of how money affects the macro system. Here we encounter two distinct and opposing views. The first is probably the most famous theory in economics — the quantity theory of money, which holds that the key relationship is between *money* and *prices.* The opposing view, associated with John Maynard Keynes, holds that the key relationships are between *money* and *interest rates,* and between *interest rates* and *demand.*

In this chapter we will

1 Learn the old fashioned quantity theory of money.
2 Find out what was missing from that theory.
3 Learn the alternative Keynesian theory.

We will take up some newer approaches to money, especially the "monetarist" view, in the next chapter.

THE QUANTITY THEORY OF MONEY

O ne relation between money and economic activity must have occurred to you by now. It is that the quantity of money must have something to do with *prices.* Does it not stand to reason that if we increase the supply of money, prices will go up, and that if we decrease the amount of money, prices will fall?

Quantity Equation

Something very much like this belief lies behind one of the most famous equations (really identities) in economics. The equation looks like this:

$$MV \equiv PT$$

where

$M =$ *quantity of money* (currency outside banks plus demand deposits);

$V =$ *velocity of circulation,* or the number of times per period or per year that an average dollar changes hands;

$P =$ *the general level of prices,* or a price index;

$T =$ *the number of transactions made in the economy* in a year, or a measure of physical output.

If we think about this equation, its meaning is not hard to grasp. What the quantity equation says is that the amount of *expenditure* (M times V, or the quantity of money times the frequency of its use) equals the amount of *receipts* (P times T, or the price of an average sale times the number of sales). Naturally, this is an identity. In fact, it is our old familiar circular flow. What all factors of production receive *(PT)* must equal what all factors of production spend *(MV)*.

Just as our GNP identities are true at every moment, so are the quantity theory of money identities true at every instant. They merely look at the circular flow from a different vantage point. And just as our GNP identities yielded useful economic insights when we began to inquire into the functional relationships within those identities, so the quantity theory can also shed light on economic activity if we can find functional relationships concealed within its self-evident "truth."

Assumptions of the Quantity Theory

To move from identities to functional relationships, we need to make assumptions that lend themselves to investigation and evidence. In the case of the GNP = C + G + I + X identity, for instance, we made a critical assumption about the propensity to consume which led to the multiplier and to predictive statements about the influence of injections on GNP. In the case of $MV = PT$, we need another assumption. What will it be?

The crucial assumptions made by the economists who first formulated the quantity theory were two: (1) The velocity of money—the number of times an average dollar was used per year—*was constant;* and (2) transactions (sales) *were always at a full employment level.* If these assumptions were true, it followed that the price level was a simple function of the supply of money:

$$P = \frac{V}{T} \cdot M$$

$$P = kM$$

where k was a constant defined by V/T.

If the money supply went up, prices went up; if the quantity of money went down, prices went down. Since the government controlled the money supply, it could easily regulate the price level.

Testing the Quantity Theory

Is this relation true? Can we directly manipulate the price level by changing the size of our stock of money?

The original inventors of the quantity equation, over half a century ago, thought this was indeed the case. And of course it *would* be the case if everything else in the equation held steady while we moved the quantity of money up or down. In other words, if the **velocity of circulation,** V, and the number of transactions, T, were fixed, changes in M would have to operate directly on P.

Can we test the validity of this assumption? There is an easy way to do so. Figure 1 shows us changes in the supply of money compared with changes in the level of prices. A glance at Figure 1 answers our question. Between 1929 and 1982 the supply of money in the United States increased over elevenfold, while prices rose only a little more than fourfold. Clearly, something *must* have happened to V or to T to prevent the elevenfold increase in M from bringing about a similar increase in P. Let us see what those changes were.

Changes in V

Figure 2 gives us a first clue as to what is wrong with a purely mechanical interpretation of the quantity theory. In it we show how many times an average dollar was used to help pay for each year's output.* We derive this number by dividing the total expenditure for each year's output (which is, of course, the familiar figure for GNP) by the actual supply of money—currency plus checking accounts—for

---

* Note that final output is not quite the same as T, which embraces *all* transactions, including those for intermediate goods. But if we define T so that it includes only *transactions that enter into final output,* PT becomes a measure of gross national product. In the same way, we can count only those expenditures that enter into GNP when we calculate MV. It does no violence to the idea of the quantity theory to apply it only to final output, and it makes statistical computation far simpler.

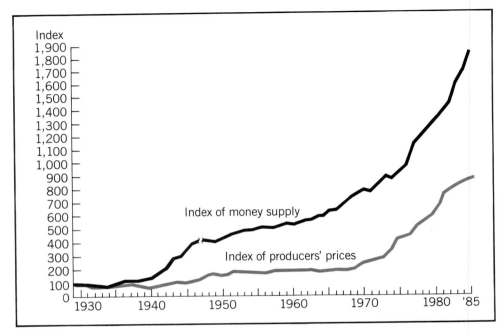

Figure 1

MONEY SUPPLY AND PRICES

Money supply has risen faster than price levels, proof that there is no iron link between M and P. V and T must be taken into account.

Sources: *Statistical Abstracts of the United States.*

each year. As the chart shows, the velocity of circulation of money fell by 50 percent between 1929 and 1946, only to rise above the 1929 level over the post-war years.

We shall return later to an inquiry into why people spend money less or more quickly, but it is clear that they do. This has two important implications for our study of money. First, it gives a very cogent reason why we cannot apply the quantity theory in a mechanical way, asserting that an increase in the supply of money will *always* raise prices. For if people choose to spend the increased quantity of money more slowly, its impact on the quantity of goods may not change at all. If they spend the same quantity of money more rapidly, prices can rise without any change in *M*.

Second, and more clearly than we have seen, the variability of *V* reveals that money itself can be a destabilizing force — destabilizing because it enables us to do two things that would be impossible in a pure barter economy. We can:

1. Delay between receiving and expending our rewards for economic effort.
2. Spend more or less than our receipts by drawing on, or adding to, our cash balances.

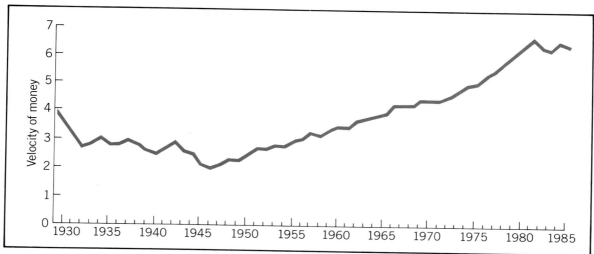

Figure 2
VELOCITY OF MONEY

Velocity is an important source of change. The quicker we spend money, the more dollars we send chasing after goods.
Sources: *Statistical Abstracts of the United States.*

Classical economists used to speak of money as a "veil," implying that it did not itself play an active role in influencing the behavior of the economic players. But we can see that the ability of those players to vary the rate of their expenditure — to hang onto their money longer or to get rid of it more rapidly than usual — makes money much more than a veil. Money (or rather, people's wish to hold or to spend money) becomes an independent source of change in a complex economic society. **To put it differently, the use of money introduces an independent element of uncertainty into the circular flow.***

Changes in *T*

Now we must turn to a last and perhaps most important reason why we cannot relate the supply of money to the price level in a mechanical fashion. This reason lies in the role played by *T*; that is, by the volume of output.

Just as the early quantity theorists thought of *V* as essentially unvarying, so they thought of *T* as a relatively fixed term in the quantity equation. In the minds of nearly all economic theorists before the Depression, output was always assumed to be as large as the available resources and the willingness of the factors of produc-

---

* Technically, the standard economic definition of money is that it is both a means of exchange and a store of value. It is the latter characteristic that makes money a potentially disturbing influence.

tion would permit. While everyone was aware that there might be minor variations from this state of full output, virtually no one thought they would be of sufficient importance to matter. **Hence the quantity theory implicitly assumed full employment or full output as the normal condition of the economy.** With such an assumption, it was easy to picture T as an unimportant term in the equation and to focus the full effect of changes in money on P.

The trauma of the Great Depression effectively removed the comfortable assumption that the economy naturally tended to full employment and output. At the bottom of the Depression, real output had fallen by 30 percent. Aside from what the Depression taught us in other ways, it made unmistakably clear that changes in the volume of output (and employment) were of crucial importance in the overall economic picture, and that the economy does *not* naturally gravitate to full employment levels.

Output and Prices

It is clear, then, that the old-fashioned quantity theorists were mistaken. (For an explanation of *why* they erred, see box on this page).

What should we put in the place of the original $MV = PT$ theory? That is a very important question, but we shall postpone it for a moment. For there are still things

WHY THE OLD QUANTITY THEORISTS ERRED

Modern economists can easily show that the velocity of money is not constant and that the volume of transactions (GNP) is not always at full employment. But it should not be thought that the originators of the quantity theory were stupid or too lazy to look up the basic data. Most of the numbers on which economists now rely were simply not in existence then. The national income, for example, was not calculated until the early 1930s, and the GNP was not "invented" until the early 1940s. You cannot calculate the velocity of money unless you know the national income or the gross national product.

Neither did the original quantity theorists have accurate measures of unemployment or capacity utilization. They used the only method available to them: direct observation of the world, a method that is notoriously inaccurate when one's view is much smaller than "the world." The idea of mass involuntary unemployment required the idea of an equilibrium output that would be less than a full employment output, an idea completely foreign to pre-Keynesian thought.

to be learned about how money works, and we cannot tackle monetary theory until we have done so.

The first thing to understand is how our modern emphasis on the variability of T — that is, of output and employment — fits into the overall question of money and prices. The answer is very simple, but very important. **We have come to see that the effect of more money on prices cannot be determined unless we also take into account the effect of spending on the volume of transactions or output.**

It is not difficult to grasp the point. Let us picture an increase in spending, perhaps initiated by a business launching a new investment program or the government a new public works project. These new expenditures will be received by many other entrepreneurs as the multiplier mechanism spreads the new spending through the economy. But now we come to the key question. What will entrepreneurs do as their receipts increase?

It is at this point that the question of output enters. For if factories or stores are operating *at less than full capacity,* and if there is an *employable supply of labor available,* the result of their new receipts is almost certain to be an increase in output. That is, employers will take advantage of the rise in demand to produce and sell more goods and services. They may also try to raise prices and increase their profits further. But *if their industries are reasonably competitive, it is doubtful that prices can be raised very much.* Other firms with idle plants will simply undercut them and take their business away. An example is provided by the period 1934 through 1940, when output increased by 50 percent while prices rose by less than 5 percent. The reason, of course, lay in the great amount of unemployed resources, making it easy to expand output without price increases.

Full Employment vs. Underemployment

This is a very important finding for macroeconomics, for it helps us see that policies that make sense in one economic situation make no sense in another. This is particularly the case with policies that promote spending of any kind — public spending or private spending, spending out of earned income or deficit spending. If an economy is suffering from large numbers of unemployed workers and from large amounts of underutilized capacity, it *must* spend more if it is to move back to its production frontiers. As we have learned in Chapter 12, expenditure is the necessary precondition for output. Unless we spend more, we are doomed to remain permanently underemployed.

But spending more will not bring us more output if we are at, or close to, the production frontier. Then more spending — for consumption or investment, for private use or public use — can only send prices higher, with little or no effect on the volume of output.

Until recently, this distinction between the beneficial effects of expenditure when unemployment was high, and the bad effects of expenditure when unemployment was low, was a central premise of modern macroeconomics. Today, the distinction is not so sharp as it once was, for we seem to have moved into a condition in which spending sends prices up even though we are certainly not in a state of full employment or utilization. This is a problem that greatly complicates the management of the nation's money supply. **We live, more and more, in an environment that certainly cannot be called "fully employed" or "fully utilized" by conventional standards, but that is nonetheless very inflation-prone.** We will look more fully into this question in Chapter 23.

THE KEYNESIAN THEORY

The quantity theory of money reigned supreme until the 1930s, when it first became apparent that the assumption of full employment was not a satisfactory basis for a theory of the price level. John Maynard Keynes set about trying to construct an alternative view of the role of money which could fit into an economic system in which unemployment and underemployment might be the normal or equilibrium conditions.

Keynes's solution was published as his *General Theory of Employment Interest and Money* in 1936. The title gives away the heart of his argument. Keynes simply threw away the quantity theory, and with it the notion that the principal effects of a change in money are necessarily to be found on *prices*. Not so, said Keynes: **Changes in the money supply affect not prices, but the rate of interest.** Changes in the rate of interest in turn affect the demand for investment spending — as we have seen in our chapter on the investment sector — and hence the *level of aggregate demand*. Any effects on prices depend on the level of employment and unemployment, as we have just noted.

The Demand for Money

The bold innovation of Keynes's theory was the idea that there was a demand schedule for money — that actors did not merely accept the volume of money supplied by the authorities, but actively sought to acquire more money, or to get rid of money they did not want or need. Once the idea was entertained that individuals could have changing needs for money, it was a short step to the idea that individuals would pay a price to satisfy their needs. The price was the rate of interest.

But what sorts of needs and wants could give rise to a demand curve for money? Keynes distinguished two separate kinds of demands: transactions and financial.

1. TRANSACTIONS DEMAND. The first and most evident reason for individuals to want more or less money, said Keynes, was that they required different amounts to finance their regular purchases and sales. When business was brisk and consumption demand ran high, individuals would ordinarily require larger deposits in their bank accounts. As a result, they would be willing to turn other kinds of assets, such as stocks or bonds, into money by selling them. In doing so, they would have to give up the income that those other investments offered. Cash is very useful for meeting payrolls or for paying other bills, but cash on hand (or in a bank) will not pay you the return you can get from bonds or many other forms of wealth.

2. FINANCIAL DEMAND. A second, quite different, motive for holding money, said Keynes, arose from financial rather than transactional considerations. Keynes saw that the demand schedule for cash for financial purposes related the quantity of

INTEREST RATES AND BOND PRICES

Most bonds are a promise to pay a certain stated amount of interest and to repay the principal at some fixed date. To simplify things, forget the repayment for a moment and focus on the interest. Suppose that you paid $1,000 for a perpetual bond that had a "coupon" — an interest return — of $100 per year with no date of repayment. And suppose that you wanted to sell that bond. What would it be worth?

The answer depends wholly on the current market rate of interest for bonds of equal risk. Suppose this rate of interest were 10 percent. Your bond would then still be worth $1,000, because the coupon would yield the buyer of the bond 10 percent on his money. But suppose interest rates had risen to 20 percent. You would now find that your bond was worth only $500. A buyer can go into the market and purchase other bonds that will give him a 20 percent yield on his money. Therefore he will pay you only $500 for your bond, because your $100 coupon is 20 percent of $500. If you want to sell your bond, that is the price you will have to accept.

On the other hand, if interest rates have fallen to 5 percent, you can get $2,000 for your bond, for you can show the buyer that your $100 coupon will give him the going market return of 5 percent at a price of $2,000. (If you were to buy a *new* $1,000 bond at the going 5 percent interest rates, it would carry a coupon of only $50.)

These calculations also show that it can be very profitable at times to hold money. When interest rates are rising, bond prices are falling. Therefore, the longer you wait before you buy, the bigger your chances for a capital gain if interest rates turn around and go the other way. This means that we tend to get "liquid" whenever we think that interest rates are below normal levels and bonds are too high; and that we tend to get out of money and into bonds whenever we think that interest rates are above normal levels, and therefore bonds are cheap. The trick, of course, is being right about the course of interest rates before everyone else.

cash wanted to the opportunity cost of acquiring that amount of cash. The cost was the income that had to be sacrificed by giving up earning types of assets for ready cash.* It followed that the higher the rate of interest — that is, the larger the income available from bonds — the greater the cost of holding cash. As interest rates rose, therefore, Keynes reasoned that individuals or firms would seek to minimize their cash holdings. We have seen dramatic confirmation of this relationship in the years of sky-high interest rates in the early 1980s, when companies and households put every available cent into money market funds and interest-bearing CDs (certificates of deposit) rather than allowing funds to sit idle in checking accounts.

All these financial considerations, led individuals or firms to seek to hold more cash when interest rates were low than when they were high, and more when business was brisk than when it was slack. In all cases, however, the common consideration was how **liquid** or **illiquid** the economic actor wanted to be — that is, how he wished to divide his assets between cash or bonds and other kinds of holdings.

The Supply and Demand for Money

From these motives, we can construct a demand schedule for money. Like other normal demand curves, the demand for money is a downward-sloping curve: in general, at a given interest level, the lower the rate of interest, the greater the demand for money. And what is the supply curve of money? It is very simple: It consists of the actual quantities of money made available at any moment by the monetary authorities. It will be drawn, therefore, as a vertical line, like the supply curve for fish on page 150.

If we now put together the supply and demand curves for money, we have a result that looks like Figure 3. Our diagram shows that at interest rate *OA*, there will be *OX* amount of money demanded for transactions purposes and *OY* amount for various liquidity purposes. The total demand for money will be *OM* (=*OX* + *OY*), which is just equal to the total supply at interest rate *OA*.

Changing the Supply of Money

Let us suppose the monetary authorities reduce the supply of money. We show this in Figure 4. Now we have a curious situation. The supply of money has declined from *OM* to *OM'*. But notice that the demand curve for money shows that firms and individuals want to hold *OM* at the given rate of interest *OA*. *Yet they cannot hold amount OM, because the monetary authorities have cut the supply to OM'.* What will happen?

---

* In Keynes's day, commercial banks did not pay interest on checking accounts. Today a checking account may earn interest, but it is usually much less than the interest available from bonds or other nonliquid assets.

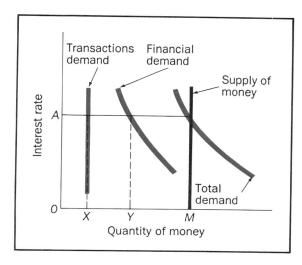

Figure 3

TRANSACTIONS AND FINANCIAL
DEMANDS FOR MONEY

*The demand for money has a
negative slope, whether we want
money to spend or to hold as a liquid
investment. The lower interest rates
fall, the more money we will seek.
The supply of money, as we can see,
is a fixed quantity in the short run.*

The answer is very neat. As bank reserves fall, banks will tighten money — raise lending rates and screen loan applications more carefully. Individuals and firms will be competing for a reduced supply of loans and will bid more for them. At the same time, individuals and firms will feel the pinch of reduced supplies of cash and will try to get more money to fulfill their liquidity desires. The easiest way to get more money is to sell securities, to get out of bonds and into cash. **Note, however, that selling securities does not create a single additional dollar of money. It simply transfers money from one holder to another. But it does change the rate**

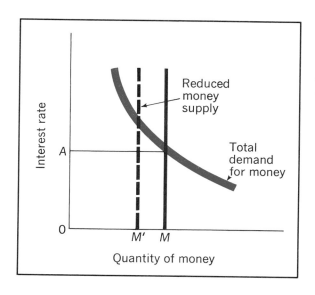

Figure 4

REDUCING THE SUPPLY OF MONEY

*The Fed reduces the money supply
from OM to OM′. OA is no longer a
price for money that will clear the
market. Now see Figure 5.*

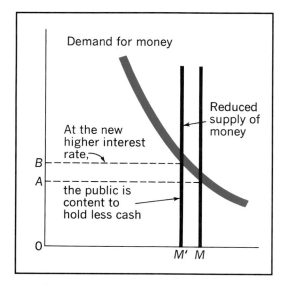

Demand for money

Reduced
supply of
money

At the new
higher interest
rate,

B

A

the public is
content to
hold less cash

0

M' M

Figure 5
DETERMINATION OF NEW EQUILIBRIUM
*When the quantity of money shrinks, the
public will try to acquire money by selling
bonds. As they do so, bond yields rise. As
yields rise, the demand for money falls.
The market now finds a new clearing
price (OB) for its smaller quantity of OM'.*

of interest. **As bonds are sold, their price falls; and as the price of bonds falls, the
interest yield on bonds rises (see p. 375).**

Our next diagram (Figure 5) shows what happens. Because interest rates have
risen, the public is content to hold a smaller quantity of money. Hence a new
interest rate, *OB*, will emerge, at which the public is *willing* to hold the money that
there *is to hold.* The attempt to become more liquid ceases, and a new equilibrium
interest rate prevails.

Suppose the authorities had increased the supply of money. In that case, individuals and firms would be holding more money than they wanted at the going rate of
interest. They would try to get out of money into bonds, sending bond prices up
and yields down. Simultaneously, banks would find themselves with extra reserves
and would compete for loans, also driving interest rates down. As interest rates fell,
firms and individuals would be content to hold more money until a new equilibrium was again established. Figure 6 shows the process at work.

Determination of Interest Rates

This gives us the final link in our argument. We have seen that interest rates
determine whether we wish to hold larger or smaller balances. But what determines the interest rate itself?

The Federal Reserve can, of course, raise or lower the discount rate, and big
banks from time to time can announce a new *prime rate*—the rate at which they will
lend to their best customers. But neither the Fed nor the biggest bank could make a
rate stick if there were no bidders for money at that level, or conversely, if everyone
converged on the bank for a loan. Although rates are announced by the monetary
authorities or by big banks, they must match the forces of the marketplace if they

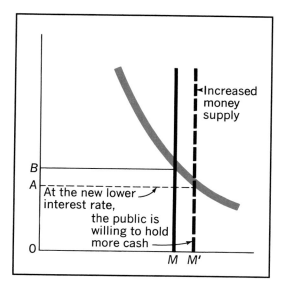

Figure 6

INCREASING THE SUPPLY OF MONEY

Here is the opposite story. The Fed increases M to OM'. Individuals do not want more money at the old price (OB). They use the new supply of money to buy bonds. Bond prices rise, yields fall. At a lower interest rate (OA) the public will be willing to hold OM'.

are to hold steady. And we can now see that the forces of the marketplace are summed up in the interplay of supply and demand we have been discussing.

Our demand for money is made up of our transactions demand curve and our financial demand curve. The supply of money is mainly controlled by the monetary authorities. The price of money — interest — is therefore determined by the demand for, and supply of, money, exactly as the price of any commodity is determined by demand and supply.

Money and Its Effects: A Review

What our analysis enables us to see is that once the interest rate is determined, it will affect the use to which we put a given supply of money. Now we begin to understand the full answer to the question of how changes in the supply of money affect GNP. Let us review the argument, and supply the last link.

1. Suppose the monetary authorities want to increase the supply of money. They will lower reserve ratios or (more likely these days) buy government bonds on the open market.

2. Banks will find that they have larger reserves. They will compete with one another and lower lending rates.

3. Some of the money will come to rest in rising financial balances as interest rates fall, and will have no further financial or real effects. But this typically will not be a large part of the total increase in the supply of money.

4. Here is the last link: Lower lending rates will cause investors to reevaluate the investment projects they have before them. (Recall the schedule of the marginal efficiency of investment we learned about in Chapter 16). They will discover newly profitable projects, will place new orders with companies that

supply equipment and materials, and will take on new workers. The total level of demand will rise, and with it the transactions demand for money.

5. A new equilibrium will be reached at which the total demand for money will just come to equal the supply.

KEYNES VS. THE QUANTITY THEORY

Finally, back to the quantity theory. What is the essential difference between the old *MV-PT* view of the relation between money and prices and the Keynesian view?

There are two ways of describing the difference. The first is that Keynes recognized *two kinds* of needs for money—one for carrying on business, the other for being more or less liquid so that wealth was protected. The older economists made no such distinction; all money to them was considered as a transaction requirement, and the level of transactions, as we have noted, was always considered to be at a level corresponding to full employment. *Thus there was no demand curve for money.* Individuals or firms simply used all the money available to carry on their affairs. They did not consider whether or not they wanted to economize on money because the interest rate was high, and the cost of being "in" money also high. So one way of describing Keynes's contribution is that he introduced a financial calculation into the money equation—making it more complicated, but much more realistic.

The other way of describing the difference between Keynes and the classical economists is that Keynes's demand for money hinges on *expectations*. It is future interest rates, more than present interest rates, that establish liquidity preferences. If we expect rates to go higher, we will want to be more liquid than we are today. If we expect them to fall, we will want to be less liquid. Thus expectations—our imperfectly formed, uncertain, almost surely incorrect views about the future—become a central force in the economic mechanism. This explanation of the working of the world becomes correspondingly less tidy, but also correspondingly closer to the way things really happen.

looking back

KEY CONCEPTS

Originally the quantity theory was formulated as *MV* ≡ *PT*, where *P* and *T* were taken as fixed. We know that they are not

1 The quantity theory, in its original formulation, directly related increases in *M*, the stock of money, to increases in *P*, the price level. The formula for the theory was $MV \equiv PT$, where *V*, velocity, and *T*, transactions (output) were assumed to be unchanging.

2 Empirical evidence, not available at the time of the original formulation, has made it clear that *V* and *T* are both variables,

not constants. This is particularly the case with T, which can no longer always be assumed to tend to full utilization levels.

More spending should not send up prices when unemployment is high

3 As a general rule, increases in spending will generate additional output, with or without price increases, as long as there is large unused capacity in the labor and capital markets. But additional spending, private or public, will generate only price rises and no more output as we reach full employment.

Bond prices rise and fall to make their yields equal to the going interest rate

4 Bonds are promises to pay fixed amounts at stated periods until the bond matures. Basically, the price at which you can sell a bond on the market depends on the going rate of interest. If your bond will pay $10 per year, and the going rate of interest is 5 percent, the value of the bond—regardless of what you paid for it—will be the price that gives its buyer a 5 percent return. That will be $200, because the $10 interest payment is a 5 percent return on $200. If the market rate of interest rises, say to 10 percent, the value of the bond on the market will fall to whatever price again makes $10 a year equal to the interest rate. At 10 percent, this new price will be $100. Thus, as interest rates rise, bond prices fall, and vice versa.

The rate of interest is set by S and D for money

5 By changing the stock of money, the authorities create more or less money than the public wants to hold at existing interest rates. The public will buy bonds to get out of money or sell them to get into cash. Buying and selling will not change the amount of money, but it will change bond yields. Thus interest rates are determined by the supply of and demand for money.

Transactions and financial demands for money

6 Keynes's contributions were two: First, he differentiated the financial uses of money from their transactional uses. This was a considerable advance from the older views, where no such differentiation was made. Second, he introduced the notion of expectations, with all its uncertainties, into the very heart of macroeconomics. Looking forward is the most difficult of all economic tasks, but it is the one on which the trend of things depends.

The importance of expectations

ECONOMIC VOCABULARY

QUESTIONS

1. Why is the quantity equation a truism? Why is the interpretation of the quantity equation that M affects P not a truism?

2. If employment is full, what will be the effects of an increase in private investment on prices and output, supposing that everything else stays the same?

3. Suppose you had $1,000 in the bank. Would you be more willing to invest it if you could earn 5 percent or 8 percent? What factors could make you change your mind about investing all or any part at, say, 8 percent? Could you imagine conditions that would make you unwilling to invest even at 10 percent? Other conditions that would lead you to invest your whole cash balance at, say, 3 percent?

4. Suppose the going rate of interest is 7 percent and that the monetary authorities want to curb expenditures and act to reduce the quantity of money. What will the effect be in terms of the public's access to cash? What will the public do if it feels short of cash? Will it buy or sell securities? What would this do to their price? What would thereupon happen to the rate of interest? To investment expenditures?

5. You hold a bond that pays $80 a year, for which you paid $1000. What is its percentage return or "yield"? If the market rate of interest is 8 percent, at what price could you sell the bond to someone else? Suppose the market rate rose to 15 percent. Will people still give you $1000 for your bond? What would they give you — what price would make its $80 coupon worth 15 percent? Suppose the market rate fell to 7 percent? How much will the bond then bring on the market?

6. Suppose that the monetary authorities want to encourage economic expansion. What are the general measures they will take? What problems might changing liquidity preference interpose?

7. Do you unconsciously keep a "liquidity balance" among your assets? Suppose your cash balance rose. Would you be tempted to spend more?

8. Show in a diagram how a decrease in the supply of money will be reflected in lower transactions balances and in lower financial balances. What is the mechanism that changes these balances?

9. Do you understand (a) how the rate of interest is determined; (b) how it affects willingness to hold cash? Is this in any way different from the mechanism by which the price of shoes is determined or the way in which the price of shoes affects our willingness to buy them?

CHAPTER 22

The Debate about Monetary Policy

a look ahead

In our last chapter we looked into the difference between the old quantity theory and Keynes's views as to the role of money in determining output, employment, and the price level. In this chapter we explore the modern debate on this issue, perhaps the most important policy question in macroeconomics today.

1 First we take a look at monetarism, the view of monetary policy largely inspired by Professor Milton Friedman. This is a powerful attempt to resurrect the quantity theory on the basis of a new explanation of economic behavior called rational expectations.

2 Second, we explore the objections to the monetarist thesis.

3 We try to discover what the fuss is ultimately about: Can we control the direction of economic affairs?

W here do we stand today with respect to the theory of money? We know that the old mechanical quantity theory is inadequate because it assumes that V is a constant, which is not the case, and because it assumes that T — output — is also fixed. Do we have something to put in its place?

There is probably no area of macroeconomics where there is less consensus. Some economists firmly believe that money is the key variable in the determination of prices (and hence of the dollar value of GNP); others believe that it is only one of many variables, and not necessarily the most important. We cannot resolve that often technical debate here. But we would like to present the arguments on both sides of the case, as we see them.

MONETARISM

In the 1960s and 1970s, much controversy was generated by an approach to monetary management called *monetarism,* originally advanced by Nobel Laureate Milton Friedman. Monetarism, at its base, is part of a larger view of the self-correcting, self-propelling nature of our economic system which has long characterized one major strand of economic thinking. But monetarism has three specific, and highly interesting, propositions about monetary management that we should study now.

1. Monetarists Claim That Changes in the Supply of Money Affect Spending Directly, Not through Indirect Effects on the Rate of Interest and the Demand for Investment. Monetarists claim that an increase in the lending capabilities of banks — for that is what an increase in the supply of money comes down to — must result in an increase in bank loans. As these loans are spent MV will rise, even though there has been no previous drop in interest rates.

The original monetarist formulation did not explain why there would be a *demand* for additional loans without a fall in interest. It simply asserted that a larger supply of money would give rise to more spending: "Money matters" became a kind of monetarist slogan. Only recently has a new theory of "rational expectations" put a causal foundation under the slogan. We shall shortly see what it is.

2. Monetarists Hold That Monetary Policy Exerts No Lasting Effect on Output. Behind this claim is a belief, much like that of the classical economists, that money is only a "veil" thrown over the real forces in the economy. These real forces are expressed in what Friedman has called the economy's **natural rate of unemployment.** This is the rate that reflects the willingness of individuals to work, given the prevailing wage. An injection of money, by raising prices, may tempt people to seek work in the belief that real wages have risen. But they will soon discover their error and withdraw from the labor market.

Thus the economy will gravitate toward a rate of growth that reflects its natural desire to work (at a given wage). Changes in the money supply may cause short-lived flurries, but cannot change this real growth-setting pacemaker. Booms and busts will therefore be transient—more often than not the result of futile interventions into the economy. In the long run the economy will express the energy and drive of its working force and its managerial talent, and these guiding forces will not be substantially or permanently affected by changes in the supply of money.

3. THE LASTING EFFECT OF MONETARY POLICY IS ON THE PRICE LEVEL. Although monetarism has scant belief in the power of the monetary authorities to change the pace of the economy, it has a profound belief in the importance of money management in determining the nominal prices at which output will be sold. Here the reasoning is very much like that of the old quantity theory. A belief in a natural rate of unemployment is much like a belief in an unvarying level of T in the $MV = PT$ formulation. Increases in spending (MV) will therefore drive up prices, but not production. It follows that if the government spends more money by borrowing, it may succeed in capturing a larger share of the total flow of spending, but only at the expense of private spending.

As a consequence, monetarists see no merit in Federal Reserve policies that aim to reduce interest rates or stimulate demand. Any efforts in this direction, they argue, will only create more money than needed at the existing level of prices. No effort to bring unemployment below the level to which it naturally gravitates can have any lasting effect, except to flood the economy with money—and to raise prices.

Monetarist Policy

This seems like a prescription for inaction. But that is not quite the monetarist proposal. Rather, Friedman advocates that **the supply of money should be expanded by an unvarying percentage that corresponds with the growth of the real productive capacity of the economy.** That way, he asserts, the supply of money will accommodate the need for growing payrolls and inventories and loans, but with no risk of inflation.

Moreover, the very steadiness of monetary growth will serve to keep the economy on the track. If we find ourselves headed into a recession, let us say because of a downturn of confidence and investment, the steady increase in the money supply will add to banks' reserves, encouraging them to lower interest rates, expand their loans, and thereby move us out of recession. On the other hand, if we experience a surge of inflation, the same steady and unchanging rate of growth of bank lending capability will act as an automatic curb, holding down the banks' ability to finance the inflation-swollen demands of their customers, thereby mitigating the inflationary pressure.

Rational Expectations

One of the questions monetarism originally left unanswered was how an increase in the money supply became an increase in incomes and spending. To put it concretely, if the Federal Reserve decided to buy bonds, why should this result in individuals spending more? For if individuals did not spend more, monetarism would be without the crucial link between an increase in M and an increase in P.

Keynes, of course, did supply such a link. As we have seen, he believed that an increase in M would lead to a fall in the rate of interest, and that this in turn would stimulate investment spending. But in Keynes's answer to the question, money is no longer "neutral" — merely a veil. A change in the supply of money is not like an incoming tide that lifts all boats; it is like the opening of a sluiceway, forcing some boats along and leaving others alone.

The missing link in monetarism was provided in the early 1960s by economist John Muth. Muth argued that individuals continually form "rational expectations" about the future and guide their behavior accordingly. The theory of rational expectations does not mean *correct* expectations. Rather, it means that people are always thinking about the future and that they apply their best available economic knowledge to predict how things will go. This process would lead individuals "rationally" to foresee the likely consequences of government policies and to act accordingly.

Essentially the theory lays the basis for a belief that government policy cannot affect the economy because people anticipate its effects and thereby annul them.

Suppose, for instance, that people read about efforts of the Federal Reserve to increase the money supply in order to stimulate demand. Will not a rational person anticipate that more spending will send prices up, and will not he or she go shopping right away so that he or she buys before prices actually rise? In that case, when the Fed actually does increase the money supply, there will be no increase in demand because ordinary citizens will have beaten it to the punch!

Many economists, including ourselves, take a skeptical view of the theory of rational expectations, which rests on far-reaching claims as to the knowledge individuals possess and on the competitive nature of markets. It seems very clear, for instance, that the market for stenographers or steelworkers does not react with the quick omniscience of the market for stocks or bonds. Unquestionably, however, rational expectations has been useful in reminding economists that they are not the only predictors in a market system. The theory may overstate the case seriously when it goes on to claim that because everyone is in the forecasting business to some degree, government can never change the way individuals perceive the economy — and therefore the way they act.

ANTIMONETARISM

Can the propositions of monetarism be proved? Here is where the economics profession is still deeply divided. Let us consider the rejoinders antimonetarists offer to the three points we have enumerated above.

1. DO CHANGES IN THE MONEY SUPPLY DIRECTLY AFFECT EXPENDITURE? Antimonetarists believe they do not. They do not believe the Federal Reserve "controls" the money supply the way the monetarists claim it does. The monetarists assert that when the Federal Reserve increases M, P goes up. This means that the direction of causality runs from MV to PT, thus $MV \rightarrow PT$. But that is not the way the world works, say the antimonetarists. In real life, the causal influence runs the other way, $MV \leftarrow PT$!

How could this be? The answer, according to the antimonetarists, is that the monetarists fail to understand the overriding aim of the Federal Reserve (or any central bank). That purpose, they say, is not to control inflation or interest rates, or to stimulate or hold back the economy. It is to be sure that the banks have enough reserves to be able to cover their deposits as required by law.

The critics charge that monetarists speak as if the monetary authorities first decided how large the lending capacity of the banking system should be, after which the banks went around looking for customers. But the realities are quite the other way around. Half of all new business loans are made to big corporations under credit lines the companies have negotiated with their bankers, legally entitling them to borrow agreed-upon amounts. As Alan Holmes of the New York Federal Reserve has put it, "In the real world, banks extend credit . . . and look for reserves later. In one way or another, the Federal Reserve will accommodate them." Thus tight money may bring very high interest rates, but it will not prevent large companies from having access to credit.

2. Antimonetarists Doubt That the Economy Tends to Full Employment or Even to a Steady "Natural" Rate of Unemployment. Far from regarding the business cycle as transient and unimportant, antimonetarists think of fluctuations in the rate of growth as an intrinsic part of the capitalist mechanism. Many of these cycles, they willingly admit, are short and limited in scope, but others are deep and protracted. In 1873, for example, the United States experienced a depression that lasted six long years. In 1893, a depression brought an unemployment rate of 14 percent that lasted for four years. And of course in 1930 the economy went into a veritable tailspin in which GNP dropped by 30 percentage points and unemployment almost touched 25 percent. That depression was still with us, although in milder form, in 1940.

Were these depressions only transient phenomena, or the product of ill-advised monetary policy? Four years, six years, or ten years is too long to be called transient, say the critics of monetarism. Moreover, the earlier depressions, at least, cannot be blamed on the actions of the Federal Reserve, because there *was* no Federal Reserve in 1873 or 1893.

In 1932, the Federal Reserve did indeed pursue a wrong policy of keeping money tight (it was afraid that the gold flowing into the United States would create an inflation!). But later, when it came to its senses and turned its policy around, it could not raise prices and turn the economy around. "You can't push with a string" was the way antimonetarist economists describe the failure of the Federal Reserve to get banks to offer loans, or businesses to seek them, in the climate of terrible pessimism to which the Depression gave rise.

Thus to antimonetarists the record of the past gives ample proof that money does not matter to the exclusion of everything else: The Federal Reserve cannot be blamed for starting depressions that occurred before it existed, and it cannot be credited with curing a depression that proved indifferent to its expansionary monetary policy.

3. Antimonetarists Argue That the Price Level Can Be Influenced by Many Nonmonetary Factors. Antimonetarists hold that prices are above all determined by *costs.* Thus any number of influences can affect the price level: a shock to the price of oil, an inertial spiral of wages and prices, a massive Soviet wheat purchase, the disappearance of anchovies off the coast of Peru (once an essential component of animal feedstocks), or a change in the value of the dollar on foreign exchange markets. Perhaps a too-easy monetary policy will have inflationary effects.* But antimonetarists argue that to assign to every change in price level a monetary cause stretches the concept of causality — and the responsibility of the central bank to maintain a stable price level — past a reasonable limit. Hence antimonetarists argue (as we will in Chapter 23), for a wide range of alternative anti-inflation policies.

For a Discretionary Money Policy

Antimonetarists therefore reject the goal of a stable increase in the money supply. It would perhaps be nice to live in a world that was free of supply shocks, wage explosions, commodity cycles, and technological revolutions — a world in which a steady increase in money might accompany a steady increase in output. However, we do not live in such a world, antimonetarists say, and so it is pointless, and perhaps counterproductive, to conduct policy as though we did.

Antimonetarists point to two situations in particular in which the rule of a steady growth in the money supply leads to an undesirable result. The first is a change in the demand for money. Suppose, for example, that as a result of a drop in the inflation rate, the public decides it would like to hold more cash and demand deposits (M) in relation to the given volume of transactions (T). What happens? Under a monetarist growth rule, no accommodation would be made. But if V does not rise, P or T must fall. **Antimonetarists argue that shifting demands for money balances can cause wholly unnecessary fluctuations in output under a money growth rule.**

Second, suppose the economy is hit with an external shock, such as the OPEC oil price increases of the 1970s, which suddenly raises the value of P relative to M and V. Under a monetarist rule, again, there can be no accommodation, and so T — output — must fall. Antimonetarists argue that this is unnecessary: **M should be increased in such a situation so as to stabilize output at the new level of prices.**

---

* Recently, there has been growing skepticism even about this point. During 1985 the money supply grew very rapidly, and monetarists warned that the inflation rate would turn up as a consequence. Instead, the inflation rate fell! There were, of course, many reasons why inflation did not worsen — cheaper imports, falling oil prices, easier wage bargains. But don't forget — monetarism has always claimed that *only* an increase in money would give rise to inflation, and also that an increase in money would *always* give rise to inflation. The increase took place, but not the expected result.

FROM ECONOMICS TO POLITICS?

Is it possible to say which side is right in this dispute? It must be evident that our own judgments incline us to the antimonetarist position. But we would be the first to stress the importance of the contribution the monetarists have made in insisting that money matters. Money does indeed matter. Our position is that money does not always matter in precisely the way the monetarists believe; and that not *only* money matters.

Beyond that is a more serious issue. Monetarist policies seem to us to be most effective in ordinary times, when the actions of the Fed can indeed urge on a mildly lagging system or curb a slightly overheated one. **In our view, however, monetary policies act least well when we most need effective measures, namely in deep depressions and dangerous inflations. In depressions, easy money may not create the desire to spend and invest; and in bad inflations, tight money operates unevenly and in a very costly manner.**

That last matter seems crucial. A tight money policy, applied in the United States from 1979 to 1982 and in England for an even longer period, did indeed succeed in its main objective, which was to bring down the rate of inflation. Inflation rates fell because tight money policy slowed down borrowing, greatly intensified competitive pressures, forced unions to accept lower wage raises, and businesses to accept lower profits.

Costs vs. Benefits

Is that not a very convincing proof that monetary policies work, even if some parts of the system escape the noose? The problem is that it is very hard to compare costs and benefits. For while inflation rates were cut in half, unemployment rates were almost doubled. Bankruptcies soared to levels that had not been experienced since the Great Depression. Indeed, the high cost of money, combined with other problems of the system, brought about the most serious depression since the 1930s. Was monetary policy a success then, or a failure?

The trouble is that the answer will not be gained by a simple calculus of dollars and cents. Inflation and unemployment involve considerations of equity as well as performance — that is, considerations of what we consider to be fair and just, as well as what we deem to be economically effective. The balance between good and bad policies is determined more often than not by considerations of political and moral preference, rather than by economic judgments alone.

The Core of the Issue

Is monetarism simply a technical disagreement over the working of the monetary system? That is certainly part of the issue, but not the crux of it. At the core of monetarism is a profound belief in the natural tendency of a capitalist economy to grow in an orderly manner *if it is not interfered with by government.* At the core of the antimonetarist stance is an equally profound conviction that a capitalist economy, left to its own devices, will encounter serious difficulties which require government intervention to cure. That fundamental disagreement—a disagreement that harks back to the views of Adam Smith and of Marx or Keynes—is at the crux of the controversy.

What can we say about this philosophical disagreement? Perhaps we can venture two conclusions that award something to both sides and yet present the issue as we see it.

1. UNQUESTIONABLY WE ARE GOING TO PURSUE INTERVENTIONIST ECONOMIC POLICIES BOTH IN THE SHORT AND THE LONG RUN. The interventionists argue that we no longer have the social or political option of not intervening. In the great depressions of the past the public accepted a passive government response because it was generally believed that government had no right (as well as no capacity) to deal with economic misfortunes. That point of view is now as dead as the dodo, interventionists insist. When growth slows down or inflation speeds up, the public cry is that government should "do something." To be told that doing nothing is the best response to economic trouble is an idea that no Western electorate would accept, and that no Western government would propose. Therefore an interventionist response is forced on us, the activists say, and the attitude of those who advocate noninterventionism is simply irresponsible.

This argument seems correct. The noninterventionist position is a *long-run* point of view. It requires a degree of patience that we do not think modern democracies will (or should) display. There is no doubt in our minds that some form of active policy will be followed.

2. OUR POLICY DETERMINATIONS WILL BE SERIOUSLY HAMPERED BY THE KINDS OF PROBLEMS RAISED BY THE NONINTERVENTIONISTS. Thus we are going to try to improve our short-run economic performance. But how well will we succeed in doing so? The objections raised by the noninterventionists suggest that efforts to accelerate or decelerate, redirect or guide the economy will be much more difficult than we have thought in the past. It was not so very long ago that economists spoke of "fine tuning" the economy as if it were a vast stereo set that could be regulated with precision by turning the knobs labeled "fiscal policy" and "monetary policy." We now know that this cannot be done. Some knobs are stuck; others turn without much affecting the quantity or quality of sound; still others seem to set up feedback that distorts the results we seek.

But this is not to say that we cannot regulate the economy at all. Our own belief is that we can intervene to our collective benefit, provided that we have realistic expectations of what it lies within our power to do. Modern industrial economies are very complex systems, and we should not expect that we can fiddle with them like radios. But some success is better than none—and some success seems possible.

looking back

KEY CONCEPTS

Monetarism has three tenets

1 The most important new development in the controversy over the relation between money and output (and prices) is known as monetarism. It is the product of Professor Milton Friedman and has attracted wide attention and generated much controversy.

Changes in M directly affect spending

2 Monetarism has three basic tenets. The first is that changes in the supply of money do not affect the economy via their effect on interest rates and investment. Changes in the money supply—in the banks' ability to make loans—result directly in changes in expenditure.

There is a natural rate of unemployment that controls the rate of growth

3 The second tenet concerns the effect of M (or MV) on output. One of the basic beliefs in monetarism is that the economy naturally gravitates to a rate of growth that reflects the natural rate of unemployment—the willingness of individuals to work, given the prevailing wage. Changes in expenditure (MV) may result in bursts of activity, but will not budge that fundamental controlling force. Hence attempts to accelerate growth through increasing the supply of money or government spending will only "crowd out" private activity. The system will return to its natural path. So too, booms and busts will be transient—indeed they are more often caused than cured by government intervention.

Changes in M affect P

4 Where money matters most is in its effect on the price level. An increase in M leads to an increase in MV; but because the level of output is "fixed" by the natural rate of unemployment, its effects will be felt in changes in P. It is these changes that are the only source of rising or falling prices.

Monetarist policy calls for a steady increase in M

5 The monetary policy urged by Friedman and other monetarists is a steady increase in M, geared to the natural rate of productivity growth of the economy. This rate would not vary. If circumstances pushed the economy ahead faster than the fixed rate of growth of M, the steady rate would tend to hold it back. If the economy lagged for any reason, the steady increase in M would stimulate it to grow up to its natural rate.

Rational expectations link M and MV

6 Rational expectations round out monetarism by providing a causal link between M and MV. Rational expectations theory asserts that all individuals are guided by commonsense predic-

tions about the future. When they read that the authorities are increasing M, they expect P to rise. Therefore they spend their incomes more quickly to "beat" the coming price rise. As intuitive monetarists, they make monetarist theory come true.

Antimonetarists contend that $MV \leftarrow PT$

7 The antimonetarists contest all these tenets. First, they deny that the Fed controls the money supply as the monetarists state. Rather, they suggest that the demand for money (for transactions needs) forces the Fed to change the money base. The linkage runs $MV \leftarrow PT$, not $MV \rightarrow PT$.

They deny a natural rate of unemployment or the uselessness of intervention, and assert that costs, not M, determine P

8 They doubt that there is a natural rate of unemployment or that depressions are caused by government intervention. They point to very deep depressions that occurred before there was a Federal Reserve, and to the inability of the Federal Reserve to raise prices during the depression of the 1930s. And they argue that cost, not the quantity of money, is the fundamental element in establishing the price level. The bases for inflation, they state, are such changes as supply shocks or changes in wages.

A discretionary monetary policy

9 Therefore antimonetarists favor a discretionary monetary policy that will try to fit the supply of money to changing needs.

Interventionism vs. noninterventionism

10 Beneath the dispute over monetarism lies a deeper disagreement over the possibilities for intervention in the economy. Essentially monetarism is based on a belief that the economy manifests behavior that cannot easily be turned around by government policy, at least in a free market system. Interventionists argue that policy can indeed make a difference, although often it falls short of the policy maker's hopes, for the very reasons suggested by the noninterventionists.

ECONOMIC VOCABULARY

Monetarism   384

Natural rate of unemployment   384

Rational expectations   385

QUESTIONS

1. Why would a monetarist object to Keynes's view that increases in M affect the economy via the interest rate? *Hint:* Think of the natural rate of unemployment. Doesn't this require that money be "neutral"?

2. Do you think there is a natural rate of unemployment? If an unemployed engineer refuses even to inquire about a "Help Wanted" sign in a supermarket, does this show that he prefers not to work at the prevailing wage? How could you test the idea that there was, or was not, a "natural rate" of unemployment? (For one answer, see the box on involuntary unemployment in Chapter 35.)

3. What is "tight" about a tight money policy? How does it bring down inflation? Can you describe how such a policy works in terms of the $MV = PT$ formulation?

4. What would be an antimonetarist policy to lower inflation? Would direct price controls be such a policy? What might a monetarist assert about the efficacy of such controls?

5. If wages rise, will that necessarily push up prices? Does the answer depend on productivity? Suppose that wages rise faster than productivity. Then must they push up costs? What would a monetarist argue about the effect of rising costs on P? Might he assert that the good which now cost more would simply "crowd out" other goods because PT was fixed? Fixed by what?

AN EXTRA WORD ABOUT

What Caused the Great Recession?

The recession of 1979–82 was the most severe and painful setback suffered by the American economy since the Great Depression of the 1930s. Do we know what caused it? Yes and no. It's the same way with the Great Depression. With one as with the other, we have a number of plausible candidates for the role of villain. The problem is to decide the degree of responsibility we would assign to different causes (see Chapter 9).

Inflation is assigned a role in many persons' minds in explaining the Great Recession (not the Great Depression, when inflation had not yet appeared on the scene.) But inflation, in and by itself, does not cause GNP to fall, as we shall see in our next chapter. So when economists assign some portion of the blame to inflation, they look for a causative link. They find it in the increased uncertainty inflation brings with respect to future earnings. How important was this factor in bringing on the recession? The statistical evidence implies that it was not a major factor because business investment as a share of GNP did not fall.

But there is no lack of other places to look in explaining the recession. One of them is the *second oil shock,* which doubled oil prices in 1979. In addition to giving inflation another boost, the higher price of oil acted exactly like a tax increase on the purchasing power of the U.S. economy—except that the U.S. government could not offset the tax easily because it did not receive the "tax" proceeds. Most economists agree that the oil shock was a contributory factor in the 1979 decline. How contributory? Probably not a major cause, simply because the tax was not *that* punitive.

Another frequently cited cause for the recession is the *productivity lag* we have already noted in Chapter 6. As we have seen, this remains a poorly understood phenomenon, but certainly not one to be dismissed on that account. Probably the productivity lag *weakened* the economy, making it susceptible to shocks of all kinds.

Thus a number of elements must bear some part of the responsibility for the Great Recession. Which was the most important? Probably none of the above, but a factor we have not yet mentioned: *government policy.* That policy was a high-interest, tight-money position adopted by the Federal Reserve in October 1979 in a determined effort to bring the inflationary spiral to a halt. After the Reagan administration took office, tight money was made even tighter and prime interest rates rose to over 20 percent for six months in the spring and summer of 1981.

Tight money had one bad effect and one good one. The bad effect was to bring on a wave of bankruptcies in industries that depended heavily on easy credit — housing, automobile dealerships, farmers, small business generally. Failing businesses laid off help, cut back on inventory orders, and tightened belts. The tight-money recession thereupon became the nucleus of a falling-demand recession.

The good effect? The tight-money-induced recession did bring the inflationary momentum to a near-halt. What economists disagree about, of course, is whether the gain was worth the cost — whether inflation could not have been stopped in some other way.

What caused the recession to come to an end? The main reason follows from what we have just seen. Government policy changed. As inflation fell from over 12 percent a year in 1980 to under 4 percent in 1982, it became possible to relax tight money to some degree. At the same time, the huge tax cuts enacted by the Reagan administration began to take effect, along with the boost in military spending, so that the demand-induced recession was offset by an demand-induced recovery. Then oil prices stopped rising and actually fell — in effect giving the U.S. economy a ''tax cut.''

The moral of all this? Growth and decline are complicated processes, when examined up close. Theories of cycles and waves take their place in the bankground, casting an indispensable illumination over the events of history, but the day-to-day, cycle-by-cycle sequences of events is multicausal, political, and never — even after it is all over — entirely clear.

CHAPTER 23
Inflation

a look ahead

In this last section of our macro studies, we take up the challenges that macro-economists face. They are two: the stubborn problem of inflation—not so much as an immediate danger as a long-term chronic tendency; and, in Chapter 24, the challenge of growth itself, the fundamental necessity and uncertainty of the macro process.

In this chapter we take up inflation in a long-term historical perspective. This leads us to ask the question that underlies the whole chapter: Why has capitalism, in the late twentieth century, shown an inflationary tendency that it never manifested before?

At the same time we examine a number of more technical issues.

1 We learn about the famous Phillips curve, a way of relating the level of unemployment and the rate of inflation.

2 We stop to think about the actual costs and risks of inflation—whom it threatens and why people fear it.

3 We look into the possibility that the inflationary wave has spent its force and that we may possibly be moving into a more stable price environment.

And in the extra word at the conclusion of the chapter we examine ways and means of bringing inflation under control, if the tendency becomes once again acute.

INFLATION IN RETROSPECT

L et us begin our investigation into inflation by setting it in historical perspective. Inflation is both a very old problem and a very new one. If we look back in history, we discover many inflationary periods. Diocletian tried in vain to curb a Roman inflation in the fourth century A.D. Between 1150 and 1325, the cost of living in medieval Europe rose fourfold. Between 1520 and 1650, prices doubled and quadrupled, largely as a result of gold pouring into Europe from the mines of the New World. After the Civil War, the American South experienced a ferocious inflation. And during World War I, prices in the United States rose 100 percent.

Now we focus on the American experience up to 1960, as Figure 1 shows. Two things should be noted about this chart. **First, major wars are regularly accompanied by inflation.** The reasons are obvious enough: War greatly increases the volume of public expenditure, but governments do not often curb private spending by an equal amount through taxation. Invariably, wars are financed largely by borrowing; the total amount of spending, public and private, rises rapidly. Meanwhile, the total amount of goods available to households is cut back to make room for war production. The result fits the classic description of inflation: Too much money chasing too few goods. Only in two instances, World War II and the Korean war, has this patten been largely avoided, by a combination of price controls and

Figure 1
INFLATION IN PERSPECTIVE
Looking back in history, inflation is a chronic consequence of war. But in the past it was always short-lived.
Source: *Historical Statistics of the United States.*

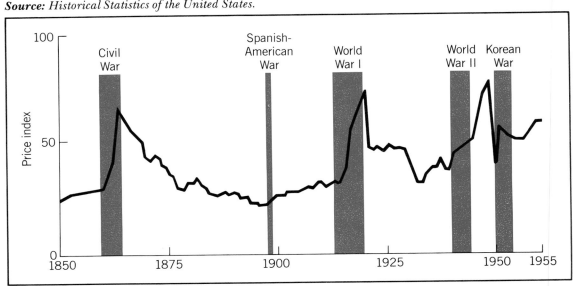

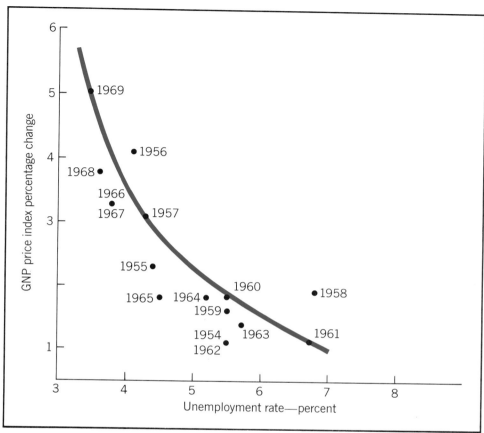

Figure 3
UNEMPLOYMENT-INFLATION RELATION 1954 TO 1969

Until 1969, the Phillips curve looked very clear.
Source: *Historical Statistics of the United States.*

problems. What follows, therefore, we loudly and clearly state, is *our* diagnosis of the nature of the inflationary phenomenon. It is to be thought about, and perhaps argued with. We hope that it will shed light; we cannot promise total illumination.

Basic Market Instability

Our argument begins with a simple but essential fact: It is that market systems are easily disturbed. Wars, changes in political regimes, resource changes, new technologies, shifts in demand—all disturb the equilibrium of the market system as stones cast ripples in a pond.

These unsettling events have caused different kinds of disturbances at different periods in capitalism's political and economic development. For economists, the

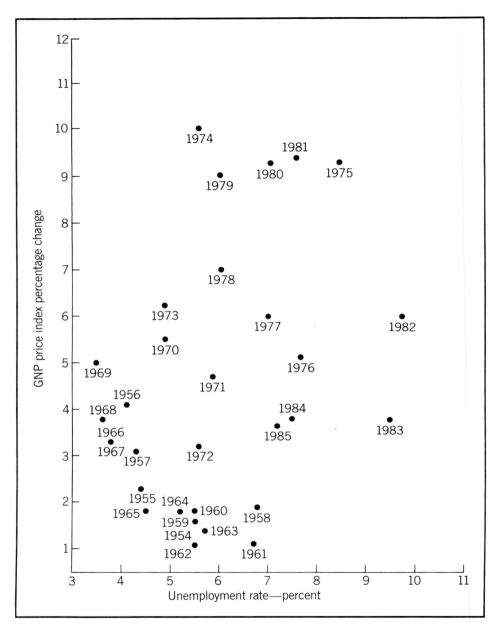

Figure 4

UNEMPLOYMENT-INFLATION RELATION REEXAMINED

Recent experience makes it clear that there is no reliable unemployment-inflation relation within the "normal" range of unemployment.

Sources: *Historical Statistics of the United States; Economic Report of the President, 1986.*

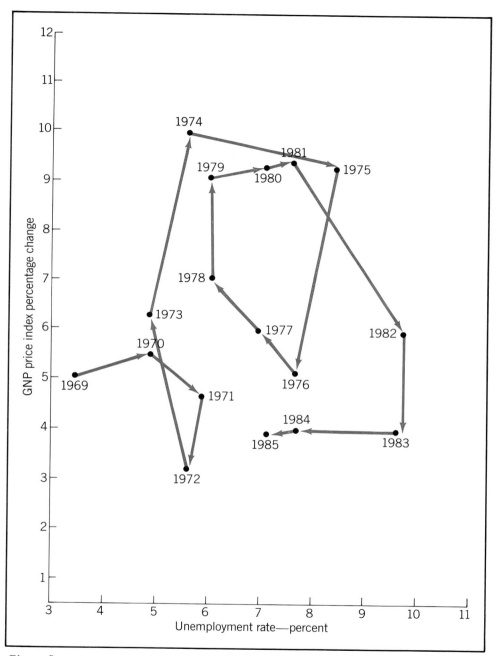

Figure 5

THE "EXPLODING" INFLATION UNEMPLOYMENT RELATION

As we can see, the unemployment-inflation combination seemed to worsen until 1983. But will the end of the 1980s see the curve "implode"?

Sources: *Historical Statistics of the United States; Economic Report of the President, 1986.*

most important of these disturbances has been the tendency of the market system to develop instabilities in production and prices and employment. We have already encountered these instabilities in the form of business cycles, or tendencies to recession, or in the inflationary propensities of recent years.

It may not seem important to begin from a stress on this deep-seated vulnerability characteristic of capitalist systems. But once we place the fact stage center, a striking question immediately faces us: How does it happen that nowadays the vulnerability so often results in inflation, and not depression or some other malfunction? For when we think of it, it was not inflation but other kinds of dysfunctions that troubled capitalism in previous periods — think of the collapse of the 1930s.

From this perspective, inflation appears as the way in which the capitalist system responds to shocks and disruptions in the institutional setting of the late twentieth century. Take, for example, the impetus given to inflation by the oil price rises of 1973 or 1979. Suppose an exactly comparable shock had been administered a century earlier, say by the Pennsylvania coal companies banding together as a coal cartel and suddenly announcing a fourfold increase in coal prices. Would such a coal cartel have produced inflation? The question is ludicrous. It would have brought on a massive depression. Coal mines would have closed, steel mills shut down, car loadings fallen. That imaginary but unchallengeable scenario then puts the right question: **What happened between 1873 and 1973 so that the same shock — an abrupt rise in energy prices — would have produced depression in one era and did produce inflation in another?**

Public Barriers against Depression

We know the answer. Far-reaching changes have taken place within the social structure of accumulation all over the world. Of these, by far the most visible and important has been the emergence of large and powerful public sectors. In 1890 government expenditures were less than 7 percent of GNP in the United States, the same in Germany, and less than 5 percent in Great Britain. In 1983 the ratio had risen to 38.1 percent in the United States, 48.6 percent in West Germany, and 47.2 percent in Britain.* In Sweden it was an astonishing 62.2 percent.†

Whatever else their significance, these public expenditures provide a floor for economic activity that did not exist before. In itself that is enough to shift a depression-prone world toward an inflation-prone one.

The floors of public expenditure do not prevent the arrival of all recessions, as we know from recent experience. The difference is that a market system with a core of public spending does not easily move from recession into ever-deeper depression. The downward tendency of production and employment is limited by the support of government spending such as social security, unemployment insurance, and the like. **Cumulative, bottomless depressions are changed into limited, although persisting, stagnations.**

---

* *OECD Historical Statistics*, 1985. Table 6.5.

† 1982 data for Sweden.

Increased Private Power

A second aspect of the sea change that has come over capitalism in the last century is the rise in private power. We see it in the vast organizations — the icebergs — that dominate the waters of business and labor.

The emergence of massive institutions of private power makes an important contribution to our inflationary propensity. A striking difference between today and yesterday is that in the past, inflationary peaks were regularly followed by long deflationary periods. Prices trended irregularly *downward* over most of the last half of the nineteenth century. Why? One reason is that the economy was much more heavily agricultural in those days, and farm prices have always been more volatile, particularly downward, than the prices of manufactured goods. Hence an industrial economy, just by virtue of being dominated by manufactures, is much less likely to have price declines than a farming economy.

A second reason is that the character of the manufacturing sector has also changed. In the early decades of the twentieth century, it was not unusual for big companies to announce across-the-board wage cuts when times were bad. In addition, prices declined as a result of technological advances, and as a consequence of the price wars that continually broke out among industrial competitors.

That is all part of a chapter of economic history largely ended. Agriculture is now only a small part of GNP. Technology continues to lower costs, sometimes dramatically — look what has happened to the computer during the last decade! — but these lower industrial costs have been offset by a "ratchet tendency" shown by wages and prices since World War II. **A ratchet tendency means that prices and wages go up, but rarely or never come down** — always excepting technological revolutions or market debacles such as the chaos of the American automobile industry. In normal times and normal business, we see the ratchet at work. Concentrated business and union power, coupled with a general abhorrence for the tactics of cutthroat competition, mean that wages and prices generally move in one direction only — up. These tendencies also add to our inflationary drift.

Demand-Pull and Cost-Push

These changes help us understand why we live in a world which, in distinction to that of our fathers, has become inflation-prone. We "catch" inflation the way capitalism of the late nineteenth and early twentieth centuries caught deflation.

But inflation susceptibility is one thing, its actual advent is another. Our inflationary experience has its origin in specific events that started the process off, just like the depressions of bygone eras. In our case, inflation probably received its initial impetus from the boost to spending that resulted from the Vietnam war. A powerful stimulus to inflation in *other* countries then resulted from the manner in which the United States used its global power to force other nations to accept our dollars in lieu of gold, building up inflationary expansions of credit abroad that eventually fed back on our own price levels. And then came the famous oil shocks of 1973 and 1979.

Directly or indirectly, the average American consumer spends 10 cents out of every consumption dollar on energy. When energy prices doubled, this increase, all by itself, generated a 10 percent rise in the cost of living. In contrast to the inflation-inducing effects of spending, called *demand-pull,* these boosts to inflation are called *cost-push.*

Transmitting Inflation by Indexing

We have already reflected on the difference between the inflation-creating effects of that oil shock and the depression-creating effects that would have accompanied an imaginary "coal shock" in 1873. Now we must pay heed to a very important institution that made the higher prices of the oil shock so contagious. This is the presence of indexing arangements in social security and many wage contracts. Higher prices no longer serve as a deterrent to buying, as they would have in 1873. **Under indexing, the additional income needed to cover the higher-cost items is automatically provided by COLAS (cost-of-living adjustments) or by social security and other indexed payments.**

When prices rise suddenly, as a consequence of oil shock or wage shock or any other cost increase, the economy momentarily shudders as sales lag and employment declines. But then the higher oil or wage or other costs show up in a higher cost-of-living index number, and as the index rises so do the checks that go to social security recipients, or the wage adjustments paid out on indexed contracts. All this serves the excellent purpose of short-circuiting recession. But it also greases the skids for further inflation.

Expectations

With this inflation-transmitting change in institutions comes an even more dangerous inflation-transmitting change in the way people think. In the old days the prevailing point of view about economic life was summed up in the adage, "What goes up must come down," so that booms and price rises typically (although not always) generated a salutary degree of caution. Today, attitudes have changed. When we learn that a commodity is going up, our first reaction is that it will probably continue to go up, maybe faster, so that we had better get in there while the getting is good. **Thus the very expectation of higher prices becomes an inflation-sustaining mechanism, much like during the Depression, when bad times were stretched out because businesses *expected* them to go on and on.** Expectations are self-fulfilling, self-generating.

In the inflationary process, the widespread and unchallenged belief that "Next year will be 10 percent higher" leads to the very kind of buy now, pay later behavior which guarantees that next year will, in fact, be 10 percent higher.

An Inflation-Prone Economy

All this allows us to see that many of the conventional explanations given for inflation play some role in sustaining the chronic malfunction of our economy.

Government is indeed responsible for inflation, insofar as it has introduced floors under the economy, indexed important payments, and bolstered security to the point at which our expectations and attitudes are much more aggressive than formerly. The massing of union and business power also contributes to inflation through the ratcheting of wages and prices. And most of the other villains can be seen at work in the background or the foreground.

The difference in our perceptions is that these various explanations can now be seen as taking their various places within an overall coherent framework of understanding. Inflation — our kind of chronic inflation accompanied by a sagging undertow of recession — comes about because capitalism exerts its nervous, thrusting, expansive energy in a changed social environment. Capitalism is now government-supported capitalism, power-bloc capitalism, a capitalism of high public expectations. This is its mid-twentieth century social structure of accumulations, the milieu within which growth takes place.

THE DANGERS OF INFLATION

Why is inflation widely regarded as such a threat? As we shall shortly see, it cannot be for the reason that inflation makes us poorer — even though we may *feel* poorer. Indeed, one of the perplexing things about inflation is that it is not an economic process that brings a clearly identifiable loss to the nation's wealth.

Recession vs. Inflation

This fact is important enough to warrant very careful attention. In recessionary times incomes fall; unemployed individuals especially suffer real losses in purchasing power. Moreover, there is no gain to set against the loss. The purchasing power given up by an unemployed person does not appear in someone else's pocket. Not so during inflation. Here the decline in the buying power of one unlucky person is *always* offset by a rise in the buying power of another. *This is because a rise in prices always creates a rise in someone's income.* Perhaps the gainer is a strategically placed group of workers enjoying higher wages. Perhaps it is a group of businesspeople for whom higher prices mean higher profits. Perhaps it is a cartel of domestic enterprises and foreign governments that collectively monopolize the supply of a strategic commodity. Whoever may gain, higher prices for one person always mean a higher income for another.

Thus inflation is a zero-sum game — a game of redistribution in which you win what I lose, or vice versa. Recessions, on the other hand, are not zero sum, but negative sum: Losses incurred by some individuals will not be transferred to others as income.

Winners and Losers

In analyzing the economic costs of inflation therefore, we always have to look for winners and losers. And here we encounter the first of many puzzles in this area. It

Table 1
SHARES OF INCOME BY FAMILY, 1970 AND 1981
Despite inflation, income shares are almost unchanged.

	1970	*1981*
The poor (bottom 20 percent)	5.4%	5.0%
Working class (next 40 percent)	29.8	28.7
Middle class (next 35 percent)	49.2	50.9
Upper class (top 5 percent)	15.6	15.4

is very hard to identify economic winners and losers from inflation in any systematic way. From 1970 to 1984, our real GNP grew by $553 billion in 1972 dollars during a period of substantial, though highly variable, inflation. Someone had to be receiving that larger real income, and the inflation — we suspect — had a lot to do with just precisely who. So who was it? Just the very rich? The oil companies? Municipal workers? The elderly? The answer is: all of us. While some groups may have gained somewhat more than others, major shifts in the distribution of income overall did not occur. Table 1 shows that even at the peak of inflation, the shares of income going to the poor, the working class, the middle class, and the rich, remained very little changed.

THE REAL COSTS OF INFLATION

The difficulty of isolating inflation's winners and losers forces us to ask whether there are economic costs of inflation to the system *in general,* costs that are shared in common by all who experience inflation, even though the measurable effects on any one household's or company's real income may be small. Economists have sought to define a number of such systemic economic costs.

Information Costs

One real cost stems from the fact that inflation tends to upset the normal relationships among prices. Real estate typically soars; commodities often go through the roof (and then sometimes through the floor); speculative fevers are endemic. The sober consequence is that rational forward planning becomes more difficult. Economists speak of this as *raising the cost of information* about prices. The practical effect is that businesses are less able to count on established price relationships in projecting costs and incomes. It becomes increasingly necessary to allow for inflationary distortions. All this raises the degree of business uncertainty and depresses business confidence. As a consequence, investment and productivity are both likely to decline.

MORE ON WINNERS AND LOSERS

It is always surprising to discover that inflation's winners and losers are much harder to find than we imagine. Here are a few additional facts:

Pensioners: The conventional wisdom has always held that pensioners on fixed incomes would suffer most in inflation. No doubt that is true. But today pensioners largely have indexed incomes. Between 1972 and 1985, the average social security recipient found his or her real income improved, not worsened.

Stockholders: We were all brought up to believe that stocks were a "hedge" against inflation because the value of company assets would rise as prices rose. In fact, between 1970 and 1982, prices doubled, but stocks remained unchanged. The real purchasing power of portfolios was halved during that period. Not until 1982 did the market finally begin to make up lost time.

Workers: Have working families suffered from inflation? Many workers were badly hurt during the inflationary years, as the steel and auto industries declined, as imports came flooding in, and as food and energy prices soared. But steel, auto, and foreign trade problems cannot be blamed squarely on inflation; and the rise in food prices and in oil came about in large part because of foreign economic developments.

All of Us: Then why do we all feel hurt by inflation? One reason is that we are aware of prices rising all through the year as we go shopping. We are unaware — except perhaps once a year — that our incomes are also rising! When we get a pay raise, we feel we have earned it — *forgetting that part of the raise is simply a cost of living allowance given to us to keep up with inflation.* As our total raise is nibbled away at by constantly rising prices, we feel cheated. No one keeps books to show us that at the end of the year we are still ahead in real terms. By that time we feel battered and bruised. We complain that inflation robs us. We have forgotten about that *inflated* pay raise.

This is assuredly a real cost of inflation, but it is a cost that is very difficult to measure. This is because we can never know what investment or productivity growth would have been if business confidence had been greater.

Misallocation and Disincentive Effects

A second real cost concerns the effect of inflation in bringing about *uneconomic behavior.* Firms and households both typically become hoarders — rationally trying to build up stores of supplies before prices go higher. It is never possible to build up enough supplies to ride out the inflation for good, and the effort to protect oneself against the immediate future simply sends out wrong signals to the economy and ties up purchasing power in unused materials.

More serious than the effects on inventories are the consequences of inflation on work. If inflation begins to show serious cumulative tendencies, workers may find that they can do better for themselves wheeling and dealing than working at steady jobs, and businessmen may decide they can make more by putting out money in short-term loans at very high rates of interest than in carrying on their normal affairs. During the terrible German inflation of the 1920s, many workers left the factories to roam the countryside, seeking to exchange their work for food rather than for nearly worthless currency. Such misallocations and disincentives can have uncountably high costs: They can bring an economy to ruin.

Cumulative Tendencies

There is one further aspect of inflation that figures large in everyone's assessment of its consequences. This is the fear that inflation may run away.

There is a reason behind this fear. Inflation has a built-in tendency to worsen because it is a process in which individuals try to get ahead of inflation — and in so doing, worsen it. Union leaders, for example, will normally try to win a pay increase for their constituencies higher than the going rate of inflation. Suppose the going rate is 5 percent. Union leaders may try to win a real increase of 3 percent, which means that they will bargain for 8 percent — 5 percent to stay even with inflation, 3 percent to get ahead of it. But if all union leaders do this, the inflation rate is very likely to rise from 5 to 7 or 8 percent. The next year, union leaders will have to ask for 10 or 11 percent — just to stay even and get their 3 percent real raise.

There is no question that one of the most disturbing aspects of inflation has been its tendency to accelerate. As we have seen, a pattern of irregularly accelerating inflation can be discovered in most parts of the world. In the 10 leading industrial nations the price level rose by about 2.5 percent a year during the 1950s; by not quite 3.5 percent a year in the 1960s; by over 9 percent in the 1970s. We can see this irregularly upward-tending pattern in Figure 6. (The sharp spike in 1974 is the result of the OPEC price boost. If you cover the spike with your finger, you can see the upward trend more clearly, together with the general subsidence after 1981.)

The Political Cost of Inflation

We cannot call the endemic cumulative tendency of inflation a "cost." It is better understood as a *threat*—a threat that the economic process of inflation will exact its last and most terrible true cost—political chaos.* For most Europeans, for

---

* We put a very important point into a footnote. True runaway inflations—called *hyperinflations*—are very rare. They are almost always the consequence of previous military or social collapse, such as the demoralization of the German economy following World War I or of the American South after the Civil War. They remain, quite properly, vivid examples of inflation's ravages, but they should be seen for what they are—political breakdowns with hideous economic consequences.

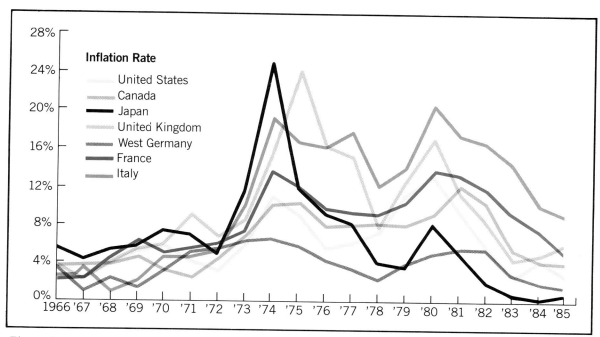

Figure 6
GLOBAL PATTERNS OF INFLATION 1966–1985
All around the world inflation is diminishing, mainly owing to tight money and economic slowdown.
Source: *Economic and Energy Indicators.*

whom the political experience of the twentieth century is living history, the evil of inflation is axiomatic: Inflation destroys constitutional regimes. It does so, as Keynes wrote in 1919, by a process of pernicious and arbitrary redistribution, by turning the ordinary business of economic life into a lottery that deprives the individual of control over his economic fate, and hence undermines faith in the justice of the system.

Keynes's argument likened the effects of inflation to those of a political revolution. In *The Economic Consequences of the Peace*—a polemic against the Versailles Treaty that ended World War I on harsh terms for Germany—Keynes wrote:

> *The sight of this arbitrary rearrangement of riches strikes not only at the security, but at the confidence in the equity of the existing distribution of wealth. Those to whom the system brings windfalls, beyond their deserts and even beyond their expectations or desires, become "profiteers," who are the object of the hatred of the bourgeoisie, whom the inflationism has impoverished, not less than of the proletariat. As the inflation proceeds . . . all permanent relations between debtors and creditors, which form the ultimate foundation of capitalism, become so utterly disordered as to be almost meaningless, and the process of wealth-getting degenerates into a gamble and a lottery.*

Then comes the famous passage:

Lenin was certainly right. There is no subtler, no surer means of overturning the existing basis of society than to debauch the currency. The process engages all the hidden forces of economic law on the side of destruction, and does it in a manner which not one man in a million is able to diagnose.

CONTROLLING INFLATION

Can we put an end to the threats and costs of the inflationary process? The question is certainly not an easy one, for we *have* got rid of a great deal of our inflation — but perhaps not of our inflationary tendency. Let us look into the matter carefully.

Disinflation

As we write these pages, the United States economy, and to a lesser extent the economies of Europe, are in the midst of a very deep and rapid process of disinflation — a slowing down of the inflationary process. In March 1980, inflation in the United States was running at a 14 to 15 percent rate. By the end of 1985, the index of producers' prices had ceased to rise, and the consumer price index was increasing at a rate of under 4 percent. Thus we have seen a massive decline in the inflation rate, all the more dramatic because it was unexpected.

What has accounted for this remarkable turnabout? Economist Allen Sinai identifies five main reasons. First, there were *the back-to-back recessions of 1980 and 1981–82*—recessions brought about by tight money. These created heavy unemployment and large underutilization, and greatly weakened the self-reinforcing tendencies of the wage-price spiral. Second was a *change in the oil situation*. Oil prices began to fall in 1983 and collapsed in late 1985, giving us a downward oil shock in place of an upward one. Third, the long, hard recessionary period *changed the pattern of wage negotiations*. Many unions agreed to "givebacks." In important industries, union agreements broke old forms in a search for wage scales that would improve U.S. foreign competitive abilities. Not least, the very fact of declining inflation allowed union leaders to lower their bargaining demands because they did not have to anticipate as much inflation as before. Fourth, the *deregulation of a number of strategic industries,* such as transportation, increased competition and lowered the costs of doing business. And not least, *the flood of imports* served as a powerful force for disinflation by bringing in cheaper foreign goods.*

* Allen Sinai, "The Soaring Dollar Did It," *Challenge*, September–October 1985.

Can Disinflation Continue?

If these disinflationary forces continue, we have every right to expect that the momentum of inflation will remain weak, and that we may enter a period of relative price stability.

But will they continue? That question makes many economists uneasy. **For our disinflationary pressures all stem from two elements in our general state of affairs that we do not want — or expect — to continue.** One of these is the continuing effects of a prolonged recession. The other is the heavy pressure of a seriously unbalanced trade relationship. If these two general elements were to disappear — if our recession would give way to full and sustained growth, and if our trade imbalance were to disappear — would inflation again rear its head?

That is the prospect that has economists worried. It implies that the price of a return to a healthy economy, rid of its recessionary and trade deficitary ills, will be a resumption of the very ailment that troubled us before these difficulties began.

A Permanent Inflationary Propensity?

It is a question to which we may not know the answer for some time. As we write these pages, the United States is enjoying a strong recovery that has *not* brought a resumption of inflation. On the other hand, the recovery has not brought unemployment down to the levels of the inflationary 1960s, and our lopsided foreign trade balance continues to exert its strong anti-inflationary pressure. So we do not know whether we have "wrung" inflation out of our system once and for all — or whether it is merely a matter of time before the price level begins to resume its unsettling upward-trending pattern.

In this period of uncertainty, our own analysis brings us to a prognosis that may or may not be shown to be correct. We expect that an inflationary tendency will manifest itself as soon as we succeed in throwing off the effects of our recession and ridding ourselves of our unhealthy import exposure. This is because, as we have explained in this chapter, we see inflation as a deep-rooted tendency of modern capitalism, comparable to the equally deep-rooted depressionary tendency of earlier twentieth-century capitalism.

Moreover, in each case we see that the tendency wreaks its social havoc because the socioeconomic system has not yet developed the institutions it needs to buffer and contain its own destabilizing forces. In the case of earlier capitalism, what was lacking were the institutions necessary to put a floor under economic activity — institutions largely based in a strong, permanent public sector. In the case of present-day capitalism, what seems to be lacking are the institutions required to put restraints on the destabilizing tendencies that otherwise lead to self-feeding price rises. As to what those restraints might be, see the extra word at the end of this chapter.

looking back

1 Inflation, in our belief, stems from the instability of capitalist economic systems. This instability no longer creates cumulative depressions, due to the intervention of the government sector. Increased institutional rigidity also limits downward price adjustments. In this new situation shocks to the economy create only mild recessions; and upward tendencies in costs, transmitted by indexing, result in inflationary expectations. The new social structure of accumulation makes the system inflation-prone, much as the old social structure, without a large public sector, was depression-prone.

2 Unlike inflations in the past, contemporary inflation has persisted beyond the end of war and despite the presence of unemployment. Hence it is called stagflation—stagnation combined with inflation.

3 Stagflation is reflected in the "exploding" Phillips curve. It used to be thought that inflation and unemployment were tradeoffs— that an increase in unemployment was accompanied by a decrease in inflation rates. During the 1970s, that relation largely disappeared.

4 Inflation is a redistributive process, a zero-sum game. Actually, it has not significantly redistributed money incomes among the main classes of income receivers.

5 Inflation poses real but not easily measurable economic costs to the system. One of these is the loss of reliable guides to price relationships. This adds risk to business investment. A second real cost is the tendency to hoard, and at worst, to speculate or scrounge, instead of working.

6 Inflation has an endemic cumulative tendency. An important source of this is the effort of union leaders to win wage increases greater than existing inflation. When generalized throughout the system, this simply pushes up prices. Western experience since World War II shows a marked cumulative pattern, but it has not ended in a runaway hyperinflation. Nor does this seem likely to happen. The runaway tendency raises a real fear, but is not itself a true cost of inflation.

7 The most damaging of all the costs of inflation is political: It is the loss of political faith in a system that has replaced the norms of economic conduct with mere chance.

| Disinflation has resulted from recession and imports | 8 We have had a sharp disinflation since 1981. The main contributory elements have been two back-to-back recessions; cheaper oil; reduced wage demands; deregulation; and the pressure of imports. Perhaps the most important question is whether these disinflationary pressures would continue if we resumed strong growth and ended our trade imbalance. |
| We believe that modern capitalism is inflation-prone and will require restraints of some kind | 9 We do not know the answer to this question, but our analysis leads us to perceive modern capitalism as having a built-in inflationary propensity analogous to the depressionary tendencies of early twentieth-century capitalism. These tendencies require institutional restraints. |

ECONOMIC VOCABULARY

Stagflation   398
Phillips curve   398
Demand-pull   403
Cost-push   403

Indexing   404
Zero-sum game   405
Information costs   406
Disinflation   410

QUESTIONS

1. Is war spending *inherently* inflationary? Would this be true if it were fully financed by taxes?
2. What is the difference between inflation, stagnation, and stagflation?
3. How does the Phillips curve "work"—in theory? How would you explain its curious tendency to show such a clear-cut relationship for the 1960s—and such a confusing one for the 1970s?
4. Capitalism in the 1880s was certainly not plagued by constant inflationary tendencies. Yet that seems to be the case in the 1980s. How do you explain the difference?
5. Do you think the day will come when you will buy a 4 percent U.S. bond, payable in 20 years, and be perfectly content that you will not be a loser because of inflation? What sorts of changes in institutions do you think might be needed to instill that frame of mind?

6. How does indexing transmit inflation? Spell out carefully the difference in the scenario of a "coalpec" in the 1870s and an OPEC in the 1970s.

7. What is meant by a zero-sum game? Is chess such a game? The stock market? Is being successful in economic life such a game? Why is inflation considered to be zero sum and recession to be negative sum?

AN EXTRA WORD ABOUT

Restraining Inflation

Can we restrain inflation? Of course we can. The question is: Can we restrain it without plunging into a recession? We think we can do that too. Here are five broad policy proposals that suggest the kinds of steps we could take.

1. DEINDEXING

Indexing has been spreading through the economy for over a decade now, and in each instance a case can be made for it. Workers who sign three-year contracts argue that it is only fair that they be protected against unforeseeable price increases during the life of their contract. Social security recipients argue that old people living on retirement incomes ought not to be penalized because of inflation. Middle and upper classes who benefit from the indexation of income taxes believe they should not be hit with higher tax rates due to "bracket creep" — higher money (not real) incomes that raise them into stiffer tax brackets.

All these arguments have merit, but they ignore one big problem. It is that indexing, which is supposed to protect us against inflation, in fact tends to increase the likelihood of inflation. Do you recall how the OPEC oil shock of 1973 gave us an inflationary impetus, whereas imaginary "coal shock" of 1873 did not? That is an instance of the way that indexing greases the inflationary skids — *by matching increased costs with increased incomes.*

For these reasons, *a systematic deindexing of many parts of the economic system —* wage contracts, the income taxes, and federal entitlement and retirement programs — *could contribute to the reestablishment of a more price-stable system.* Need we add that this is a suggestion that would be difficult to put into practice? Everyone is for deindexing those parts of the economy that do not affect him or her, but not so quick to accept it for those that concern his or her income. A young wage earner wouldn't object too strenuously to deindexing social security, but would fight like a steer against taking out the COLA (cost of living adjustment) clause in his own wage contract. His elderly relatives would likely feel just the other way. The lesson, of course, is that the economic aspects of inflation control are a lot easier to design than their political aspects.

2. INCOMES POLICY

Another way of improving the inflation picture is to institute a voluntary *incomes policy —* an agreement freely entered into by unions and corporations to limit wages or dividend payments in accord with some standard such as a productivity index. Then, if national productivity showed an increase of, say, 3 percent, wages or dividend payments would rise by no more than that amount. In addition, corporations would have to agree not to raise prices unless they could demonstrate that costs had increased for reasons beyond their control. If everyone would agree to such a guideline, the inflation-producing momentum would immediately drop *and no one would be any worse off.* Such a collective decision would halt the escalator, but would not change our respective positions on it.

The idea of such a voluntary incomes policy is very attractive, but the difficulty is obvious. It is to make the policy stick. For if everyone does not cooperate, the scheme will not work. Just as it helps everyone see the game on the football field if all remain seated (and just as no one sees better if everyone stands), so an incomes policy will only work if everyone "sits," by abiding by the productivity standard. But again, just as at a football game, where the few who stand *will* see better (thereby tempting others to rise), anyone who disregards the voluntary limitations on income will gain, so that soon everyone will be leaving his or her seat.

3. TIP PLANS

Because of this weakness in voluntary schemes, a number of clever plans have been suggested that would retain the voluntary element of a freely accepted incomes policy, but would add inducements and incentives that would increase the likelihood of its effectiveness. Among these are *tax incentive plans (TIPs)* which would levy tax penalties against companies that gave wage settlements in excess of guideline rates. TIPs have generated considerable interest, but like all incomes policy ideas, they encounter formidable obstacles. They would put the government at the collective bargaining table in a way that would seem, to workers, to favor the employer. And they would require the establishment of a monitoring bureaucracy that would surely seem, to employers, to be an unwarranted intrusion of the tax system into business decisions. For these and other reasons, TIPs have not yet caught on.

4. PROFIT SHARING

A related idea, which has been advanced in various forms by Professor Martin Weitzman at MIT* and by Professor Daniel J. B. Mitchell of UCLA, would urge corporations to change the way in which they pay wages to synchronize rises in workers' incomes with rises in productivity. To do this would entail scrapping the system of fixed hourly wages in favor of a system of *wages plus profit sharing* or *revenue sharing,* in which workers would be paid a fixed proportion of what the company earns.

In good years earnings would automatically rise, and in bad years they would fall. Weitzman argues that such a system would help bring price stability with full employment because it would make variations in earnings, not variations in employment, the balance wheel that would bring supply and demand for labor into equilibrium.

Like TIP schemes, profit-sharing plans seem worth exploring — they are one of the ways that Japan manages to combine low inflation and high employment rates. In the United States, profit-sharing plans have not, as a rule, been greeted with much enthusiasm by labor or management. That may now change. Still, it seems unlikely that so large a change in labor-management relations will rapidly become generalized across the business world.

* *The Share Economy* (Cambridge: Harvard University Press, 1984).

5. MANDATORY CONTROLS

What about controls, such as legal ceilings on prices and wages? These are drastic measures, although they have a long history in the United States. In the present century they have been imposed four times: in World War I, World War II, the Korean war, and during the period August 1971 through January 1973.

Do controls work? They do — for a time. They were certainly applied successfully during World War II and Korea, and helped bring inflation down quite sharply while they were in effect in 1971 to 1973, despite a lack of wartime spirit or enforcement resources.

Controls do not work well, however, over extended periods. We are not prepared to place wage and price authority in the hands of government on a permanent basis, with all the bureaucratization and loss of efficiency such a step would entail. Especially during peacetime, controls — when kept in place too long — foster evasion: black markets, shortweighting, quality deterioration, product differentiation to get around legal categories, and still other control-evading stratagems become more prevalent as time goes on.

On the other hand, controls have one major benefit. More effectively than any other measure, they halt the inflationary spiral. The halt may be only temporary, but it does provide a breathing space in which more durable anti-inflation reform can be put into effect, such as deindexing or changes in wage-setting institutions. If inflation returns, therefore, and if other measures fail to contain it, we may yet again turn to this last remedy.

BACK TO POLITICS

Can policies such as these control our inflationary propensity? Perhaps. Each of the suggested measures makes economic sense. The question is whether it makes political sense. For there is no magic *economic* cure for inflation. The objective in all anti-inflationary policies is to find measures that will change people's attitudes and actions. This is difficult because all effective anti-inflation measures require individuals to accept some kind of restraint over their *own* incomes, not just over others' incomes. It is easy to agree that wages should be restrained — if you are not a worker yourself.

Successful anti-inflation policy therefore requires the ability to convince individuals to put the general interest ahead of their own in the short run, as the only way to advance their own interest in the long run. To win such forward-looking agreement is the very essence of effective economic policy in a democracy. Economists can suggest ways and means toward such an agreement, but that is child's play compared with the business of winning the active trust of the community itself.

CHAPTER 24
Prospects for Long-Term Growth

a look ahead

Perhaps we remember the great problem with which our study of macroeconomics began. It was the problem of growth—how it originates, how it is sustained, how it can be influenced by government. It is not surprising that this is the problem to which we return at the end of our macroeconomic study, for growth remains the central problem for all capitalist economies.

In this "challenge" chapter, we first look at two growth problems that we have heretofore ignored. One of these is the tendency of a market system to develop business cycles—cyclical fluctuations—as it follows its growth path. The other is the possibility that capitalist economies may develop tendencies toward stagnation—not cycles, but long-lasting decelerations in rate of growth. That will prepare the way for a consideration of our long-term growth prospects.

L et us begin by taking a moment to reexamine the patterns of our national economic growth as shown in the first three figures of Chapter 5. These long-run charts impress us with their sense of an uninterrupted momentum, save only for the severe dips associated with great depressions or the superbooms that accompany wars.

But if we look at these charts under a magnifying glass, so to speak, we find that the smooth-seeming historic trend is in fact marked by many sharp rises and falls. Take the years 1895 to 1905. As Table 1 below reveals, these years were anything but the steady climb they appear to be in the charts.

Or examine a more recent period, not year by year, but in groups of years. As we can see in Figure 1 the rate of growth has varied greatly over the last fifty years. At times, such as the severe recessions of 1974–75 and 1981–82, the economy has even shown negative rates of growth. These episodes may show up only as small dips in the graph of our long-term advance, but they have meant suffering and deprivation for millions of persons who were robbed of work or income as a consequence.

BUSINESS CYCLES

This sequence of ups and downs, periods of growth followed by doldrums, introduces us to the question of business cycles. For if we inspect the profile of the long ascent carefully, we can see that its entire length is marked with irregular tremors or peaks and valleys. Indeed, the more closely we examine year-to-year figures, the more of these tremors and deviations we discover, until the problem becomes one of selection: Which vibrations shall we consider significant, and which shall we discard as uninteresting?

The problem of sorting out the important fluctuations in output (or in statistics of prices or employment) is a difficult one. Economists have actually detected dozens of cycles of different lengths and amplitudes. Cycles vary from the very short rhythms of expansion and contraction that can be found, for example, in patterns of inventory accumulation and decumulation, to large background pulsations of 17 or 18 years in the housing industry. In addition, there may be swings of 40 to 50 years in the path of capitalist development as a whole, called *Kondratief cycles* after their Russian discoverer.

Generally, however, when we speak of the business cycle, we refer to a wavelike movement that normally lasts (in peacetime years) from 2.5 to 5 years, averaging

Table 1
U.S. RATES OF GROWTH 1895–1905

1895–1896	−2.5%	1900–1901	+11.5%
1896–1897	+9.4	1901–1902	+ 1.0
1897–1898	+2.3	1902–1903	+ 4.9
1898–1899	+9.1	1903–1904	− 1.2
1899–1900	+2.7	1904–1905	+ 7.4

Source: Long-Term Economic Growth (U.S. Dept. of Commerce, 1966), p. 107.

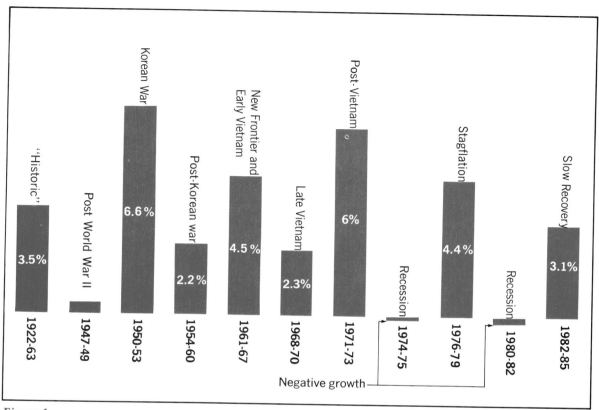

Figure 1

SHORT-TERM VARIATIONS IN THE RATE OF GROWTH

Except in periods of real recession, such as 1974–75 or the 1980s, the economy always shows growth. But the rate of growth varies considerably, as we can see.

46 months. We have had 25 such peacetime cycles between 1854 and 1982.* This major oscillation of the American economy stands forth very clearly in Figure 2, for the chartist has eliminated the underlying tilt of growth so that the profile of economic performance looks like a cross-section at sea level rather than a cut through a long incline.

Stylized Cycles

In a general way we are all familiar with the meaning of business cycles, for the alternation of ''boom and bust'' or prosperity and recession is part of everyday speech. It will help us study cycles, however, if we learn to speak of them with a

* Victor Zarnowitz, ''Recent Work on Business Cycles,'' *Journal of Economic Literature,* June 1985, Table 1.

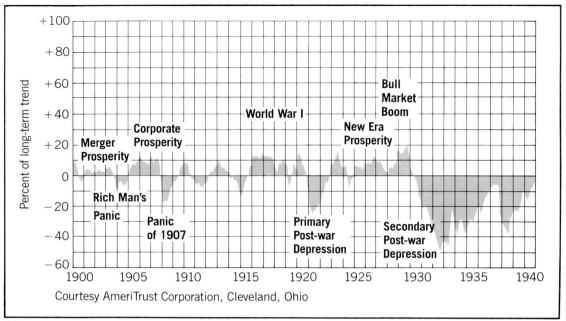

Figure 2

THE BUSINESS CYCLE

This chart, prepared by the AmeriTrust Corporation, vividly shows our swings. Note that the swings lie around a base line called "long-term trend." That is actually an upward-tilting line reflecting our long-term growth rate of 1.5 percent per capita.

standard terminology — **peak, contraction, trough, recovery.** We can do this by taking the cycles from actual history, superimposing them, and drawing the general profile of the stylized cycle that emerges. It looks like Figure 3. This model of a typical cycle enables us to speak of the length of a business cycle as the period from one peak to the next or from trough to trough. If we fail to measure from *similar* points on two or more cycles, we can easily get a distorted picture of short-term growth — for instance, one that begins at the upper turning point of one cycle and measures to the trough of the next. Much of the political charge and countercharge about growth rates can be clarified if we examine the starting and terminating dates used by each side.

Causes of Cycles

What lies behind this more or less regular alternation of good and bad times?

Many theories, none of them entirely satisfactory, have been advanced to explain the business cycle. A common business explanation is that waves of optimism in the world of affairs alternate with waves of pessimism — a statement that is true enough, but that describes the sequence of events rather than their cause. Hence economists have tried to find the underlying cyclical mechanism in firmer stuff than an alternation of moods. One famous late nineteenth-century economist,

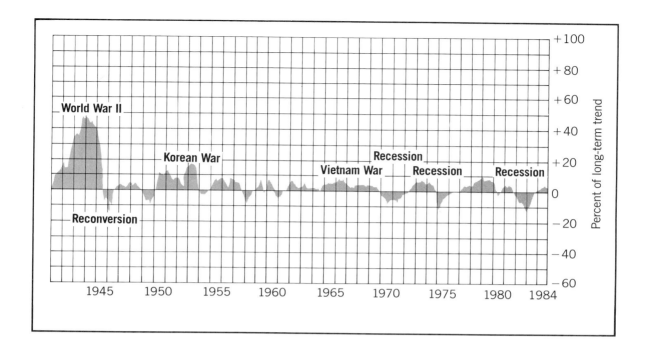

W. S. Jevons, explained business cycles as the consequence of sunspots — perhaps not as occult a theory as it might seem, since Jevons hypothesized that the sunspots caused weather cycles that caused crop cycles that caused business cycles! The trouble was that subsequent investigation showed that the periodicity of sunspots was sufficiently different from that of rainfall cycles to make the connection impossible.

Figure 3
THE STYLIZED CYCLE

An idealized cycle serves to give us standard nomenclature, so that we can compare two or more cycles.

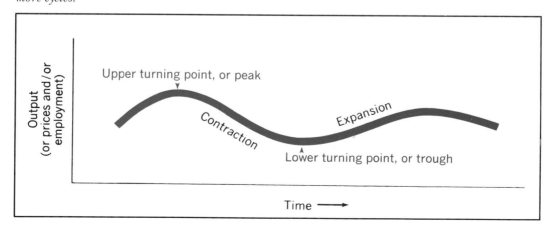

Other economists have turned to causes closer to home: to variations in the rate of gold mining (with its effects on the money supply); to fluctuations in the rate of invention; to the regular recurrence of war; and to yet other factors. There is no doubt that many of these events can induce a business expansion or contraction. The persistent problem, however, is that not one of the so-called underlying causes itself displays an inherent cyclicality — much less one with a periodicity of 2.5 to 5 years.

The Multiplier–Accelerator Cycle

Then how do we explain cycles? **Economists no longer seek a single explanation of the phenomenon in an exogenous (external) cyclical force. Rather, they tend to see cycles as our own eye first saw them on the growth curve — as variations in the rate of growth induced by the dynamics of growth itself.**

We can gain considerable insight into this uneven pace of growth if we combine our knowledge of the multiplier and the accelerator — the latter, we recall, showing us the investment induced by the growth of output.

Boom and Bust. Let us assume that some stimulus such as an important industry-building invention has begun to increase investment expenditures. We can easily see how such an initial impetus can generate a cumulative and self-feeding boom. As the multiplier and accelerator interact, the first burst of investment stimulates additional consumption, the additional consumption induces more investment, and this in turn reinvigorates consumption. Meanwhile, this process of mutual stimulation serves to lift business expectations and to encourage still further expansionary spending. Inventories are built up in anticipation of larger sales. Prices firm up, and the stock market rises. Optimism reigns. A boom is on.

What happens to end such a boom? There are many possible reasons why it may peter out or come to an abrupt halt. It may simply be that the new industry will get built and thereafter an important stimulus to investment will be lacking. Or even before it is completed, wages and prices may have begun to rise as full employment is neared, and the climate of expectations may become wary. ("What goes up must come down," is an old adage in business too.) Meanwhile, perhaps tight money will choke off spending plans or make new projects appear unprofitable.

Or investment may begin to decline because consumption, although still rising, is no longer rising at the earlier *rate* (the acceleration principle in action). We have already noticed that the action of the accelerator, all by itself, could give rise to wavelike movements in total expenditure (see p. 277). The accelerator, of course, never works all by itself, but can exert its upward and downward pressures within the flux of economic forces and in this way give rise to an underlying cyclical impetus.

Contraction and Recovery. It is impossible to know in advance what particular cause will retard spending — a credit shortage, a very tight labor market, a saturation of demand for a key industry's products (such as automobiles). But it is all too easy to see how a hesitation in spending can turn into a general contraction.

Perhaps warned by a falling stock market, perhaps by a slowdown in sales or an end to rising profits, business begins to cut back. Whatever the initial motivation, what follows thereafter is much like the preceding expansion, only in reverse.

The multiplier mechanism now breeds smaller rather than larger incomes. Downward revisions of expectations reduce rather than enhance the attractiveness of investment projects. As consumption decreases, unemployment begins to rise. Inventories are worked off. Bankruptcies become more common. We experience all the economic and social problems of a recession.

But just as there is a natural ceiling to a boom, so there is a more or less natural floor to recessions. The fall in inventories, for example, will eventually come to an end, for even in the severest recessions, merchants and manufacturers must have *some* goods on their shelves and so must eventually begin stocking up. The decline in expenditures will lead to easy money, and the slack in output will tend to a lower level of costs; and both factors will encourage new investment projects. Meanwhile, the countercyclical effects of government fiscal policy will slowly make their effects known. Sooner or later, in other words, expenditures will cease falling, and the economy will tend to bottom out.

Government-Caused Cycles

We have spoken about business cycles as if they were initially triggered by a spontaneous rise in investment or by a natural cessation of investment. But our acquaintance with the relative sizes of the components of GNP should make us wary of placing the blame for recessions solely on industry. More and more, as government has become a major source of spending, cycles have resulted from variations in the rate of government spending, not business spending. Cycles these days, more often than not, are made in Washington.

Take the six recessions (periods of decline in real GNP lasting at least six months) since World War II. Every one of them can be traced to changes in government budget policies. The first four recessions — in 1949, 1954, 1957–58, and 1960–61 — resulted from changes in the military budget. In each case, the federal government curtailed its rate of military expenditure without taking compensatory action by increasing expenditure elsewhere or by cutting taxes. The result in each instance was a slackening in the rate of growth.

The 1969–70, 1974–75 and the 1980–82 recessions are even more interesting. They represent cases in which the federal government deliberately created a recession through fiscal and monetary policies aimed at slowing down the economy. The purpose, as we know, was to dampen inflation. The result was to reverse the trend of growth. Thus it is no longer possible, as it once was, to discuss business cycles as if they were purely the outcome of the market process.

There is no doubt that the market mechanism has produced cycles in the past, and would continue to produce them if the government were miraculously removed from the economy. But given the size of the public sector these days, we often need to look first to changes in government spending as the initiating source of a cycle.

FROM CYCLES TO STAGNATION

Cycles, as we have described them, resemble the oscillations of a pendulum — years of boom alternating with years of bust. But the pendulum does not suggest another aspect of the challenge of growth. This is the possibility that our growth trend fails to give us a large enough GNP over the long pull. Economists call this deeper problem *stagnation*. Stagnation does not mean that the economy stands still; it refers to a chronic tendency to underachieve — to grow too slowly to reach reasonably high levels of employment and robust prosperity.

Loss of Potential Output

Do we face a condition of stagnation in the United States today? The evidence is not clear. Figure 4 shows us one possible measure of stagnation — the amount by which our potential output ran behind our actual output. We derive **potential growth** by multiplying the rising labor force (adjusted for normal unemployment) by an index of its growing productivity. As the figure shows, this potential output far outpaced actual output during the recession year of 1974 and then narrowed during the recovery that followed.

But the stunning loss came during the two recessions that followed. Here actual GNP fell far below the level of potential GNP. The gap over the years 1980–83

Figure 4
ACTUAL AND POTENTIAL OUTPUT
The graph shows the difference between what we could have produced at "full" employment and what we did produce.
Sources: *Economic Reports the President.*

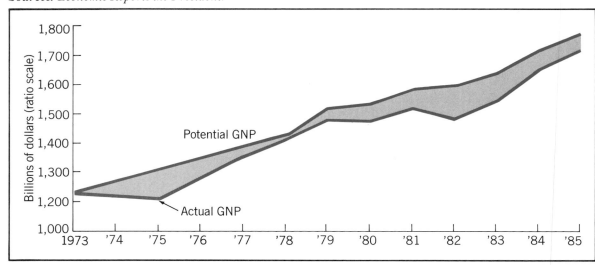

can be estimated at $268 billion — some $4,300 per family. Even in the recovery of 1985 we could have added $60 billion to GNP if we had brought unemployment down from its level of just over 7 percent to the 5.1 percent that is used to calculate potential output.

The Trend in Unemployment

Next, let us look at the data for unemployment. Table 2 gives the record of recent years, as well as some benchmark years for further comparison.

The terrible percentages of the Great Depression years speak for themselves. At the very depth of the Depression, a quarter of the work force was jobless at a time when unemployment insurance and welfare were largely nonexistent. Note too that massive unemployment persisted until 1940. Only the advent of World War II finally brought unemployment below 1929 levels.

The record of the 1960s and 1970s is mixed. During the early 1960s, unemployment was at a level considered to be uncomfortably high — roughly between 5 and 6 percent of the labor force. This percentage dropped in the second half of the decade, partly as a consequence of higher spending on armaments.

It is the record of the 1970s and 1980s that is disturbing. First we watched the unemployment rate rise from 5 percent in 1970 to almost 8 percent in 1980 — an increase of 60 percent. Then, as the recessions began to take their toll, we saw unemployment rates reach an alarming figure close to 10 percent in 1982–83. Finally, we witnessed a decline in unemployment as the recovery of 1983 began to

Table 2
UNEMPLOYMENT IN THE UNITED STATES

Unemployment reached its worst level in 1933. But it was still severe up to World War II. The record throughout the 1970s was poor, and in the 1980s, terrible.

Year	Unemployed (Thousands)	Percent of Civilian Labor Force
1929	1,550	3.2%
1933	12,830	24.9
1940	8,120	14.6
1944	670	1.2
1960–65 av.	4,100	5.5
1965–70 av.	3,117	3.9
1970	4,993	5.9
1980	7,637	7.1
1981	8,273	7.6
1982	10,678	9.7
1983	10,717	9.6
1984	8,539	7.5
1985	8,312	7.2

Source: *Economic Report of the President.*

Table 3
TOTAL NUMBER OF WEEKS OF UNEMPLOYMENT

A measure of unemployment that multiplies the number of those without work times the length of time they have been jobless presents a much graver picture of the impact of the depression of the 1980s.

Period	Unemployment Rate	Number Unemployed (Thousands)	Average Duration (Weeks)	Total Weeks of Unemployment (Millions)
1979	5.8%	6,137	10.8	66.3
1980	7.1	7,637	11.9	90.9
1981	7.6	8,273	13.7	113.3
		. . .		
1982	9.7	10,678	15.6	166.6
1983	9.6	10,717	20.0	214.3
1984	7.5	8,539	18.2	155.4
1985	7.2	8,312	15.6	129.7

Sources: *Economic Report of the President; Employment and Earnings.*

gather momentum, but the rate of joblessness hardly fell below 7 percent. **A level of unemployment that would have been considered unacceptable only a few years earlier had become the best the economy could do despite vigorous growth.**

Even these figures may understate the severity of the problem. Paul Manchester, staff economist for the Joint Economic Committee of Congress, has proposed as a truer measure of labor market distress the number of the unemployed multiplied by the average length of unemployment. This yields a figure of the *total number of weeks of unemployment.* As Table 3 shows, that number increased alarmingly as the depression was prolonged through 1982.

PROSPECTS FOR THE FUTURE

The figures on unused output and nagging unemployment are troubling and worrisome, but they do not present an ironclad case for the existence of stagnating tendencies in the American economy. It is certainly a possibility that the American economy may not be able to work up a full head of economic steam, but it is not a certainty. We will not know, one way or the other, for a number of years.

As we write, the shape of things to come is also uncertain for Europe. In 1985 there were 20 million unemployed in the European Economic Community. The unemployment rate in Great Britain was 14 percent, double that of the United States. In Europe there remain fears that the deep recessions of the early 1980s might be only precursors of a still deeper depression to come. Here too there are worries about stagnation—worries that cannot be clearly substantiated by the available data, but that are deep enough to cloud thinking about the future.

Is it possible, however unclearly, to peer into the future? Alas, it is not. History has produced too many surprises, too many unexpected reversals and turnabouts, to enable us to pronounce the likelihood that prosperity or recession will dominate the scene as these pages are read. We can, however, venture a few remarks that can clarify the future by suggesting the preconditions for successful economic growth. Let us look into three of them: technological stimulus, wages and profits, and the social structure of accumulation.

1. Technological Stimulus

All economists agree that the motor of capitalist growth is capital accumulation, to use Adam Smith's term for the saving and investing process by which the system works. But what determines the volume of accumulation? What makes capitalists eager to risk vast sums in one period, and unwilling to do so in another? **One explanation lays the basic cause for vitality and stagnation at the doorstep of technology. Economists such as Joseph Schumpeter (1883–1950) attribute the momentum of long booms to technological breakthroughs that create entire new horizons for profitable expansion.** The era of railroad building in the mid-nineteenth century was one such achievement that literally required the building up of an entirely new underpinning for the economies of the West. Railroads were thus, in Schumpeter's view, the basic cause of the buoyancy of the 1850–70 period, and the saturation of the railroad network was the fundamental cause for the absence of momentum that lengthened the downturns of 1873 and 1893 into full-scale depressions.

That same argument provides a cogent explanation of the upswing that followed in the early twentieth century. Now the technological stimulus came from two sources: The introduction of electricity into the home, with the consequent building of huge utility systems; and the perfection of the gasoline-driven internal combustion engine that gave us the automobile, perhaps the most capital-generating invention ever made. And as before, the "completion" of the first huge wave of utility and automotive investment helps account for the stagnant tendencies that dragged out the depression of the 1930s.

So technology—or rather, the absence of a strong enough technological stimulus—helps explain why growth lags from time to time. It is at least plausible that the recurrent periods of history when booms were short and slumps dragged on—the troughs of the Kondratief "long waves" we mentioned earlier—can be attributed to lack of an adequate technological stimulus.

Technological Prospects. Is it possible to hazard a guess as to technological prospects today? One aspect of that question is clearer than is usually the case in history. By general assent, the achievements and promise of modern science are dazzling. The taming of the nuclear force, the adventure into space, the beginning of genetic engineering, and the ubiquitous computer have opened an era of scientific and technical advance that bids fair to change life as deeply and widely as did the first Industrial Revolution. *Ceteris paribus,* that should supply the preconditions for a long investment boom.

But *ceteris* are not quite *paribus* with respect to the impact of modern technology. Also by common consent, the new technology brings unprecedented threats as well as promises. It is hugely destructive (nuclear explosives), risky (genetic engineering), of dubious profitability (space), and possibly disruptive — the arrival of the automated office and the robotized assembly line, for example, may swell the ranks of the unemployed with displaced white-collar as well as blue-collar workers.*

So the verdict on the *economic* impact of the new technology must remain guarded. That we will witness remarkable scientific progress seems beyond question. That this process will become translated into strong economic growth of output and employment is less certain. It is very likely that the new technology will require brand-new safeguards and safety nets. Perhaps the conclusion to which we are led is that the new technology may provide the basis for a long boom — *if we succeed in controlling it.* More on this later.

2. Wages and Profits

A second area in which to look for clues as to our long-term prospects directs our attention to an aspect of the economic process we have not considered since we looked into Adam Smith's and Karl Marx's theories in Chapter 3. This is the crucial relation between wages and profits. If wages are too high, Smith pointed out, profits will be squeezed and accumulation will be choked off. If wages are too low, Marx stressed, the system will suffer from the consequences of **underconsumption** because workers will not be able to match the supply of output with enough working-class demand.

Thus, like a number of other economic variables, such as the flow of savings or the supply of money, wages can interfere with economic growth by being too high — or too low! It is probable, for example, that the Great Depression was brought on, in part, because wages lagged behind productivity during the 1920s; and it is equally likely that the end of the post-World War II boom was hastened by the pressure of wage costs against business.†

Business profitability, then, clearly depends to a considerable degree on the *wage bargain.* How is this crucial bargain determined? In the past, the level of wages has been largely left to the play of market forces, the supply of and demand for labor. Yet as both Smith and Marx made clear, the wage bargain was never left to these forces operating in an economic vacuum. On the contrary, we saw in Smith's theory that population pressure played a critical background role in preventing wages from encroaching too deeply on profits, and in Marx's theory we found a similar disciplining force in the continuous displacement of labor by labor-saving machinery.

---

* See the extra word following this chapter.

† These wage costs include the transfer payments that comprise a considerable portion of total workers' remuneration — not only fringe benefits, but the unemployment compensation, health payments, and retirement benefits payable to labor. So-called *social wages* are 5 to 15 percent higher than direct wages, and in a number of European countries are a considerable burden on business.

Negotiating the Wage Bargain. And in the modern world? Population growth no longer plays a significant role in setting wage levels, at least in the advanced industrial nations. The displacement of labor by machinery still exerts its pressure on wages, but this pressure is greatly tempered by the existence of unemployment insurance and welfare benefits that act as wage-supporting, not wage-depressing, forces. Nonetheless the level of wages is not left to the free play of supply and demand, like the price of wheat. In every capitalist nation, the critical variable of wage levels is arrived at by a process of *negotiation,* quite a different matter from pure competition.

In many capitalist nations, the wage negotiation has become a main item on the national agenda. In Japan, for instance, an annual meeting of labor leaders, employers' representatives, and government officials, works out the wage bargain for the coming year. In Sweden, a national labor union and a unified employers' federation do the same thing, but without direct government intervention. In West Germany, cost of living increases are outlawed and the main labor unions and big businesses conduct their negotiations under the watchful eye of the government. In the United States, the process of negotiation is much less unified or supervised, but even here both labor's and capital's objectives are considerably influenced by public policy.

All these differing institutional forms of arriving at the wage bargain ultimately have the same objective — to find a middle course between a level of wages so low as to create an undertow of inadequate demand, and a level so high as to choke off investment. What institutional arrangement will best attain this goal? The question leads us to the next element in the prospects for growth.

3. The Social Structure of Accumulation

That last element in our macroeconomic prospects brings us to what labor economist David Gordon has called *the social structure of accumulation.* By this term Gordon means, first, the manner in which employers deploy and supervise their work forces — a relationship that is an immediate determinant of the productivity and profitability of labor. But Gordon extends the concept outward from the factory floor to include the relationship of business to government, equally important in establishing the milieu in which profits are made; and from the government into the general relationship between business and the public; and then into the world economy itself.

All these levels and layers of institutions, Gordon suggests, shape the capital-accumulating process, opening up profitable horizons for business or closing them down. Furthermore, Gordon puts forward the idea that a social structure of accumulation that works very successfully in one period may be unsuccessful in another. Like a river that becomes silted up, a given combination of labor, government, public, and world relationships will eventually lose its capacity to serve as a conduit for the accumulation process. When that happens, accumulation slows, and we enter a period of malfunction during which business and government leaders seek new ways of making the system work.

THE MAKING OF THE MIXED ECONOMY

We have already noted two periods in history when the social structure of accumulation played a decisive role in establishing the general tenor of economic growth. The first of these was the period preceding the Great Depression. The immediate cause of that depression was a stock market crash that triggered a wave of bankruptcies and a general collapse of confidence. This was worsened by a Federal Reserve policy that tightened credit, rather than loosening it, and by a general belief that the remedy for a slump was "budget balancing."

Underneath these immediate causes, however, were deeper weaknesses—a lagging wage and farm sector (that gives support to an underconsumptionist view), and a cresting of the great automotive boom that we have already noted. But the inability of the economy to regain its former momentum was testimony to a still deeper problem: This was the vulnerability of an economic system that had embarked on a long accumulation boom of private growth, *without laying in any support system in the event that growth failed.*

In the nineteenth century, America was still a small-town, small-business, heavily rural economy where economic setback had self-limitations by virtue of the remaining high degree of independence of so many of its citizens. By the end of the great upswing that ended in 1929 small-business America had become big-business America, small-town America was dwarfed by big-city America, and farming America was decisively displaced by factory and office America.

When the Great Crash came, therefore, it toppled a vast interlocked structure of business and finance in a social setting that was no longer even modestly self-sufficient. With no underpinning under the banks, no dependable stream of expenditures for business, no floors under household income, the economy simply went into free fall.

From the wreckage, business and government leaders gradually assembled a structure of institutions that significantly altered the way in which capitalism worked. **Beginning with the New Deal and ending with its endorsement in the mid-1950s by Republican president Dwight D. Eisenhower, a new form of capitalism came into being, distinguished from its previous form by the much larger role played by government as a provider of demand.** This is a development we are familiar with. But we can now see the evolution of the "mixed economy" and the "welfare state" as a process of transformation whose purpose was to create a milieu in which the accumulation drive would once again take place.

The Long Boom

Did the new social structure of accumulation create a setting in which investment would again flourish? There can be no doubt that it did. The period of economic growth from 1950 to 1973—the year in which the OPEC oil shock dealt the first destabilizing blow to the long boom—was the most buoyant, least interrupted, and most widely shared period of economic expansion capitalism had ever known.

Throughout the world, capitalist nations were consciously aware that they had left behind a long history of financial insecurity and meager comforts for the majority of their populations, and entered upon an era in which something like a modest affluence was attained by perhaps three-fifths of their citizens. A degree of well-being and social assurance unimaginable in the 1920s (not to mention the nineteenth century) became generalized throughout the west. During the 1950 to 1973 boom, modern capitalism virtually eliminated dire poverty and provided a previously unknown level of material comfort to its older people, its citizens, and most important of all, to its working classes.

The rise in the general standard of well-being was both the cause and the effect of the rising social wage we previously discussed. The increase in real output made possible higher real wages and a larger volume of welfare transfers, and these in turn helped to sustain the buying power that supported the boom.

The End of the Boom

What happened then? The question brings us back to the macroeconomic issues and challenges of our text. The new social structure, as often before, began to produce unforeseen and negative consequences. It changed the momentum of growth into an inflationary spiral. In ways that we do not fully understand, the new milieu seems to have sapped the sources of productivity all over the world, not just in the United States. The new social structure brought government more deeply than ever before into the direction of economic affairs, but it did not match the increased involvement of government with a clear agreement as to how public power should be used. It promoted an internationalization of economic life, but no intergovernmental means capable of dealing with the problems. It brought unprecedented advances in government and private scientific exploration, but no clear idea of how to control its own laboratory products.

When we look into the prospects for the future, the organization of our social structure of accumulation seems to take center stage. The way in which we will encourage, winnow, and monitor our technological thrust, the manner in which the all-important wage bargain will be worked out, the success we will have in coping with inflation, productivity, and the national and the international deficits —all these seem finally to hinge not so much on this or that specific policy, as on the overall framework within which policies will be made.

What should that framework look like? Will it be characterized by an increasing reliance on the extraordinary mechanism of the self-adjusting market, or on the development of new instruments of control over the market? Will it be distinguished from the present social structure by the emergence of vast international business enterprises that provide the global regulation we require, or will new international government agencies be set into place to stabilize trade and currency flows? Will government play a larger or a smaller role in determining the level of investment, the supply of money, and the degree of protection given to threatened industries?

We cannot answer these questions, although our general predilections and expectations have been spelled out more than once in this text and will be made explicit again at the very end of the book. But it is useful to end our overview of the prospects ahead by returning to the central issue of the political framework within which economic life unfolds. Macroeconomics thereby takes on its proper importance—not just as a "subject" to be dutifully learned, but as an effort to understand how our society copes with the problem of pushing its way through history, like a great ship opening a channel in ice-filled seas.

looking back

KEY CONCEPTS

The business cycle exhibits the fluctuating rhythm of economic growth

1 Growth is not an even process, but is marked by fluctuations that we designate as a business cycle. There are many kinds of cycle, of varying periodicities (durations). We speak of their phases as four: upper turning point or peak, contraction, lower turning point or trough, and expansion.

The 2.5- to 5-year cycle is analyzed in terms of a multiplier-accelerator inter-action, often triggered by government

2 No entirely satisfactory explanation has been found for 2.5- to 5-year periodicity of the principal business cycle. Economists analyze the alternation of boom and bust mainly in terms of the interaction of the multiplier and accelerator. The cause of the cyclical pattern lies as much in government actions as in the spontaneous behavior of the business economy.

Potential growth focuses on the output that full employment would yield

3 The attention of economists today is focused less on cycles than on the difference between potential and actual growth. Potential growth is the trend of output that would result from the continuous full employment of the labor force. Actual growth is the value of GNP in fact produced. In recent years there has been a serious growth gap.

Stagnation, or inadequate growth, may be a problem of our time

4 There is some evidence, not yet clear, that our economy has been displaying signs of stagnation, or growth too slow to reach healthy levels of output.

Three preconditions for sustained growth

5 The future remains unpredictable. But we can identify three important preconditions for sustained and vigorous growth: (1) technological stimulus, (2) a wage bargain that avoids underconsumption or profit squeeze, and (3) a favorable social structure of accumulation.

Technology is strong but presents many problems

6 The technological outlook is strong with respect to the opening of new frontiers of scientific advance. It is not so clear that the new technology will not also bring many problems—dangers to

<table>
<tr><td>The wage bargain today is conducted by private or public negotiation</td><td>7 The wage bargain was earlier set in a milieu in which population increase or technological displacement provided strong pressures against a profit squeeze. Today's extra-market regulatory force takes the form of wage negotiations—business-union, labor-capital, and labor-capital-government.</td></tr>
</table>

ecology and survival, and unemployment from automation and robotization. Technology seems to require new social controls.

7 The wage bargain was earlier set in a milieu in which population increase or technological displacement provided strong pressures against a profit squeeze. Today's extra-market regulatory force takes the form of wage negotiations—business-union, labor-capital, and labor-capital-government.

A social structure of accumulation forms the framework in which accumulation occurs. We are likely to build new frameworks for the future

8 The social structure of accumulation refers to the framework of labor-capital and capital-government relationships. The success of accumulation reflects a favorable social structure, but typically the institutions favorable for one period gradually lose their effectiveness. In setting the prospects for the future, a new institutional framework may be the first requirement.

ECONOMIC VOCABULARY

Business cycles   418
Peak, contraction, trough, recovery   421
Multiplier-accelerator   422

Potential growth   424
Stagnation   424
Underconsumption   428
Social structure of accumulation   429

QUESTIONS

1. Explain how the interaction of the multiplier and the accelerator can give rise to cycles. Why does not such a multiplier-accelerator interaction shed light on the question of periodicity? Suppose that capital goods tended to wear out in about three years. Would this give rise to a cycle if their replacement were bunched in time?

2. What facts would you have to know to calculate potential growth? In addition to the size of the labor force, would you need information on productivity? How would you calculate this?

3. How would you design a research program to decide whether capitalism was essentially a stagnation-prone system marked by bursts of prosperity, or a prosperity-prone system marked by interruptions of depression? Can you think of some ways of deciding which of the two tendencies was more "fundamental"?

(Remember this is a question about which economists sharply disagree. All the more reason to think about it.)

4. Can you make a scenario in which the technical breakthroughs of our day create an industrial boom comparable to that of the railroads or autos? What sorts of economic effects would they have to exert? Why do some inventions, like helicopters, have virtually no impact on economic growth, while others, like the airplane, obviously have a great effect?

5. Consider the problem of "underconsumption." Do you think it likely that there would be high investment if workers were paid starvation wages? Would there be high investment if workers were paid astronomical wages? What do you think the *optimal* wages would be, from the viewpoint of encouraging investment? Would you have to know something about wages as a component of total spending and wages as a component of costs?

AN EXTRA WORD ABOUT

Technological Unemployment

Unemployment caused by the introduction of machines is a problem that vexes and worries us, partly because it is real, partly because we do not understand it very well. Technology can be a source of job creation, especially when it brings whole new industries into being. But machines can also displace people from established jobs — and may not create new industries to absorb them.

Looking back over the history of the United States, it seems that machines have steadily pushed people out of the agricultural sector, through the factory, and into the office. Fifty years ago it took almost 40 percent of the work force to feed us; today it takes only 3 percent. The proportion of the labor force that works in manufacturing has been falling very slowly over the last 50 years. It is the service employments that have burgeoned, employing 70 percent of our labor force today, compared with 25 percent in 1900.

ROBOTIZATION AND OFFICE AUTOMATION

One of the more disquieting technological trends of the last few years has been the development of "robotization," the fancy term for machines that display humanlike capacities for "recognizing" objects, handling and orienting their tools in complex ways, and obeying long and often complex series of built-in commands. As is often the case with new levels of technology, ominous projections have accompanied the appearance of the new robots: In March 1982, *Business Week* took seriously one estimate that the computer revolution would, over 30 years, do away with more than 80 percent of all manufacturing jobs.

Office automation can have the same effect on white-collar workers as robots on blue-collar workers. In the automated office there will be much less need for people.

Machines will do much of the typing, filing, accounting, and other paper-shuffling jobs that occupy so many of us now.

Robotization and office automation bring into play a new level of technological sophistication, but the economic problem they raise is not new. Technology affects production in two ways. It may introduce a new *product,* in which case its effect on employment is to increase the number of jobs in the new areas it opens, and to decrease employment in other fields from which purchasing power is withdrawn. Alternatively, technology may affect the *process* by which goods or services are brought into being. In such cases, the technology will not be introduced unless it cheapens the cost of making the item. If — as in the case of the technology of robotization — the new machines perform tasks formerly undertaken by men and women, it is called labor-saving. If it undertakes more effectively tasks formerly performed by other kinds of machinery or equipment, we call it capital-saving.

Does labor-saving technology reduce employment? Initially the effect is precisely the same as in the case when the new techniques create a brand new good or a new way of making an old good. The new ''robotized'' product will be cheaper, because it would not otherwise pay to use the new technology. Because it is cheaper, more of it will be demanded; and if demand is price-elastic, this will tend to reemploy some of the labor that has been pushed aside by machinery. **But as before, the additional demand that is directed to the cheaper product must be taken from some other good or service. The effect of labor-saving technology, in the first instance then, is to rearrange consumer spending — not to increase or decrease it.** Its effect on employment will depend on such matters as the wage levels in the newly robotized process compared with those in the product from which demand has been withdrawn.

THE ROLE OF INVESTMENT

That is not, however, an end to the matter. The crucial effect of technology on employment comes through its impact on investment spending. When technology creates a new product that displaces an older one, the new product will require investment in factories for its production. This will be employment-generating because more labor is needed to build a new factory (or a whole new industry) from scratch than was required merely to maintain the older factory or industry whose knell has been sounded. The same is true with a process-cheapening technology, like robotization or word processing. If the new robot-produced items are much cheaper than the old ones, investment may boom in the robotized industry. This may well create more employment than any labor that is laid off in other industries whose products have been crowded out by competition.

Can we then predict what will happen, if robotization arrives on a major scale? We cannot, unless we can foretell whether the new technologies will bring into being new kinds of products, or much cheaper products that will give rise to large investment expenditure. It is entirely possible that robots will create new ''needs,'' or new possibilities for expenditure, that will easily provide a high level of employment.

And if not? Several alternatives are open. One is to use incentives of various sorts to expand private demand. This is a remedy we have often discussed. Its availability depends first and foremost on our ability to control the inflation that a program of stimulation might cause. A second, quite different tack, has been suggested by Nobelist Wassily Leontief. He suggests that we may adapt to a high level of technological unemployment by reducing the workday or the work week. This has been a historic mode of adjustment

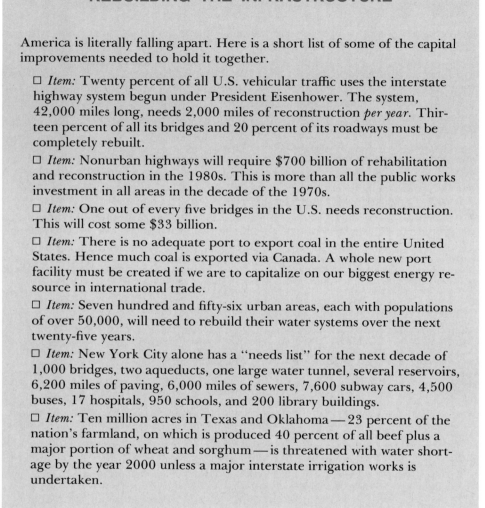

REBUILDING THE INFRASTRUCTURE

America is literally falling apart. Here is a short list of some of the capital improvements needed to hold it together.

☐ *Item:* Twenty percent of all U.S. vehicular traffic uses the interstate highway system begun under President Eisenhower. The system, 42,000 miles long, needs 2,000 miles of reconstruction *per year.* Thirteen percent of all its bridges and 20 percent of its roadways must be completely rebuilt.

☐ *Item:* Nonurban highways will require $700 billion of rehabilitation and reconstruction in the 1980s. This is more than all the public works investment in all areas in the decade of the 1970s.

☐ *Item:* One out of every five bridges in the U.S. needs reconstruction. This will cost some $33 billion.

☐ *Item:* There is no adequate port to export coal in the entire United States. Hence much coal is exported via Canada. A whole new port facility must be created if we are to capitalize on our biggest energy resource in international trade.

☐ *Item:* Seven hundred and fifty-six urban areas, each with populations of over 50,000, will need to rebuild their water systems over the next twenty-five years.

☐ *Item:* New York City alone has a "needs list" for the next decade of 1,000 bridges, two aqueducts, one large water tunnel, several reservoirs, 6,200 miles of paving, 6,000 miles of sewers, 7,600 subway cars, 4,500 buses, 17 hospitals, 950 schools, and 200 library buildings.

☐ *Item:* Ten million acres in Texas and Oklahoma — 23 percent of the nation's farmland, on which is produced 40 percent of all beef plus a major portion of wheat and sorghum — is threatened with water shortage by the year 2000 unless a major interstate irrigation works is undertaken.

that for some reason has become "stuck" in modern times. Last, we can launch a program of public employment designed to offer work to those who cannot find it in the private sector (see the box). The critical factor, once again, is our ability to control the inflationary tendency it would be likely to create.

In the long run, robotization and office automation are the very ingredients that lead to higher levels of productivity and higher standards of living. They are no different in terms of their impact than the railroad or electricity. Railroads could deliver the same freight with many fewer workers than were needed in the age of horses and carts. Electricity let us do things that could not previously be done. In both the past and the present, if each of us can produce more because we are working with better machinery, then each of us can achieve a higher material level of consumption. That is, in fact, the only way we can enjoy a higher standard of living. There is no other way.

The difficulty, now as before, is to balance the gains over the long run with the costs in the short run. How to move from an existing structure of social and material life into a new one, with a minimum of wrenching dislocation and a maximum of lasting benefits, is a problem capitalism has never handled very well. Neither has any other social system. Before the life-rearranging powers of technology, our capacity for reasonable and orderly social adaptation was, as it still is, terribly lacking.

PART FOUR

microeconomics

CHAPTER 25
Prices and Allocation

a look ahead

With Chapter 25, we enter the world of microeconomics — or rather, we reenter it, because we have already learned some basic microeconomics when we studied supply and demand in Chapters 7 and 8. In this three-part section, we extend that basic knowledge considerably. In Chapter 25 we investigate the market mechanism as a vast coordinating device, a rationing and allocating mechanism for society. In Chapter 26 we add the necessary concept of elasticity, which will enable us to speak of the market's functions with much greater precision. Chapter 27 will then turn the coin over and show us the inherent limitations of the market as a goods allocator.

In our present chapter we learn simple but central things.

1 The market mechanism is a device for organizing the production and distribution activities of society. It does so through two vast market networks. The factor market, in which businesses, households, and government agencies are brought together to produce and distribute wealth; and the goods market, in which products and services are allocated.

2 The market is a rationing device. This is one of the most important ideas in microeconomics. The price mechanism is a way of determining who will participate in economic activity as buyer or seller, and who will not.

Bear in mind as you read the chapter, that all societies must find some means of solving this rationing, or allocation, problem. The things to look for here are the strong points and the weak points of price rationing.

THE WEB OF TRANSACTIONS

W̱e began our study of macroeconomics by learning how the economy looked from a macro perspective. Now that we are about to start a study of microeconomics, there is no more effective way to illustrate the difference between the two approaches than to look over the economic panorama from our new vantage point.

Once again our eye is caught by the enormous activity taking place in the offices, factories, and fields of the nation. But now our micro perspective brings a hitherto unnoticed aspect of the process to the fore. We are no longer much interested in the river of total output or its component parts. Instead, we direct our attention to the activity taking place in a thousand corners of the economy where individuals and firms are conducting their daily business. We look at the economic flow as a *vast web of transactions* into which virtually everyone enters as either a buyer or a seller.

Production

We are all familiar with this *market system* in which we participate as buyers of goods and services. We are not as used to thinking about it as a mechanism for organizing production. Yet that is actually one of the two vital services the market performs.

Figure 1 shows us how the market takes charge of production. Let us first look at the black arrows that go clockwise from households to business, and then from business to households. These arrows represent the movement of *actual services or products* from one place to another. Starting from households, these services consist of the skills and energies of labor (and the physical services of capital goods or land) that householders produce and make available to business. Thereafter, as the black arrows show, the products that business has made from these services of labor and resources move back to the households, where they will be consumed.

Thus we can see that the market mechanism organizes the indispensable economic activity of production as a great circular motion of economic activity. Labor, land, and capital — the factors of production — are combined into commodities that will return to the owners of these resources as goods and services needed for the renewal or growth of society.

Distribution

The other vital service the market performs is *allocation,* for the goods and services which have been produced must be shared in the community. This leads us to take notice of a second loop in Figure 1 which goes in the opposite direction from the production loop. This is the flow of money payments. With every individual market transaction, goods or services move in one direction and money moves in the other.

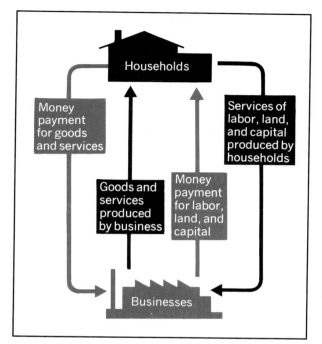

Figure 1

THE BASIC MARKET MECHANISM

This diagram shows us two loops. The black loop represents production. Real labor and other services move from households to firms, and return as real goods and services. The blue loop represents distribution. Money payments leave businesses for households and return to firms as payments for business output.

Our blue arrows show us this second circular flow of payments going in the opposite direction to the flow of real activity. With every household purchase of a business product, money moves from the hands of householders to the hands of business. And with every purchase of the services of the factors of production, money moves from business into the owners of these factors—wages and salaries going to labor, rent to landowners, profit or interest to owners of capital resources. **Thus we can see that in addition to organizing production, the market mechanism organizes the distribution or sharing of incomes.**

Of course, Figure 1 does not depict the entire market mechanism. It has omitted a vital flow of goods and services from one business to another, matched by a return flow of payments from business to business. No less vital, government has been left out, both as a buyer of goods and services and as a producer of outputs of its own, thereby linking the government with households and business. Figure 2 shows these complicated interlocks.

Two Kinds of Markets

Another way of revealing how the market mechanism works is to divide its activities into two kinds of market: a factor market and a goods market, as in Figure 3.

The factor market is another name for the loop where production takes place. Here the services of labor, land, and capital are bought and sold, hired and fired,

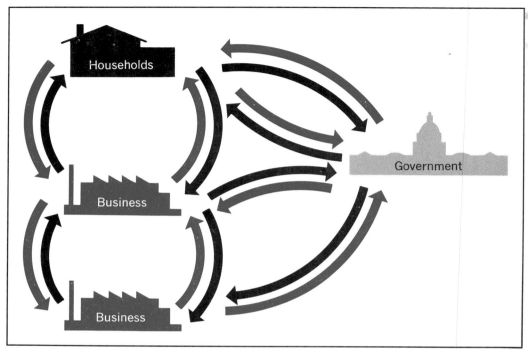

Figure 2

THE COMPLETE BUSINESS MECHANISM

Here we begin to get some idea of how complex the flow of the market mechanism actually is. But notice that the blue and black flows are essentially the same as in Figure 1.

offered and withheld in a vast number of transactions whose outcome is the production of goods and services.

The market for goods and services is the loop where allocation is organized. Here shoes and ships and sealing wax are sold to, and thereby distributed among, the buyers of society.

Breaking the market system down into two kinds of markets further clarifies the working of the overall mechanism. For we can see that households and firms (including government units) both participate in each of the two basic markets, *but on different sides of each market.* In the market for goods, the household is a buyer. In the market for factors, the household is a seller as its members offer their services for hire. In the market for goods, the firm is a seller. In the market for factors, the firm buys. Thus we can redraw our model of the circular flow as in Figure 4, with supply and demand curves that show the twofold participation of each of the basic participants in the two markets.

Here we can see that the household is the source of the demand curve in the market for goods. We also see it is the source of the supply curve in the market for factors. On the other hand, the firm shapes the supply curve in the goods market, and the demand curve in the factor market.

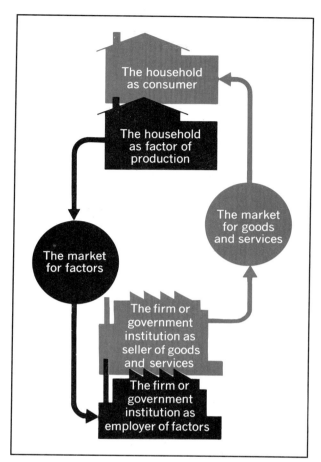

Figure 3
CIRCULAR FLOW IN TWO MARKETS
Here we see how households, businesses, and government agencies participate in two markets, acting as buyer in one and as seller in the other.

Thus, far from being a chaos of buying and selling, the market system is a **network of transactions with demand on one market reflected in supply in another, and supply in one market reflected in demand on another.** This circular flow — this link of demand and supply — will be one of the main keys to understanding how the economy works as a whole.

Looking at the System as a Whole

Now for a last important insight. The two markets — for factors and for goods — are also connected. This is because the household income that will be spent in the goods market is earned in the factor market. For businesses, the income that will be spent on hiring factors has to be earned in the goods market. **Production and distribution are therefore mutually dependent, not wholly independent, activities.** The outcome of the production circuit determines how the distribution cir-

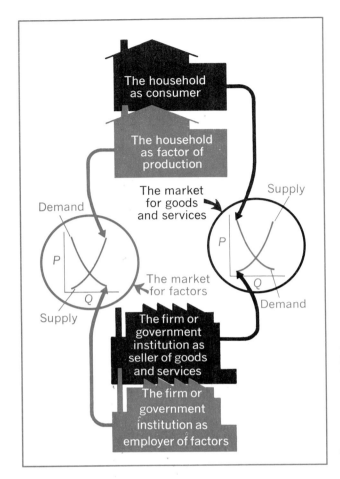

Figure 4

DEMAND AND SUPPLY CURVE IN THE CIRCULAR FLOW

Our final diagram shows how supply and demand curves represent the activities of the participants in the market mechanism. Notice especially that the household is the source of the demand curve in the goods market and of the supply curve in the factor market. What is the role of business?

cuit will operate; and the outcome of the distribution circuit determines the ability of business firms to enter the factor market.

Thus once again we see the market mechanism as a complex system, a network of actions that impose order and pattern on the economic life of society.

Like many models, ours operates at a very high level of abstraction. It lumps together the richest investor and the poorest laborer in the market for factors. It jumbles the sale of caviar and hospital care into one undifferentiated market for goods and services. Nevertheless, this abstract conception begins to untangle the flux of market activities in the world around us. It even clarifies our task in the chapters ahead. We must study the two different markets and the two different institutions, one at a time, to find out the actions and motivations characteristic of each. We begin in our next chapter by taking a searching look at households and their demand for goods and services.

THE ALLOCATION PROBLEM

From Chapter 8, "Supply and Demand," we know how prices are formed in the marketplace. We understand in general that prices for goods reflect the interplay of the demand schedules of consumers and the supply schedules of producers. In the next chapter, changes in demand will affect prices, and various characteristics of demand will exert different influences on the price structure.

Individual and Collective Supply and Demand

We must add one word before we investigate the market at work. Thus far we have considered only the factors that make an *individual* more willing and able to buy or less willing and able to sell as prices fall. Generally when we speak of supply and demand, we refer to markets composed of *many* suppliers and demanders. That gives us an additional reason for relating price and behavior. If we assume that most individuals have somewhat different willingnesses and abilities to buy, because their incomes and their tastes are different, or they have unequal willingnesses or abilities to sell, then we can see that a change in price will bring into the market new buyers or sellers: **As price falls, it will tempt or permit one person after another to buy, thereby adding to the quantity of the good that will be purchased at that price. Conversely, as prices rise, the number of sellers drawn into the market will increase, and the quantity of goods they offer will rise accordingly.**

We can see this graphically in Figure 5. Here we show three individuals' demand curve. At the going market price of $2, A is either not willing or not able to buy any of the commodity. B is both willing and able to buy 1 unit. C buys 3 units. If we add up their demands, we get a *collective or market demand curve.* At the indicated market price of $2, the quantity demanded is 4 units. What would it be (approximately) for each buyer, and for the group, at a price of $1?

The same, of course, applies to supply. In Figure 6 we show individual supply curves and a collective or market supply curve that is 7 units at $2 market supply. What would total supply be at a price of $1? What would seller A's supply be at $1?

Rationing

In one form or another, *rationing*—or the allocation of goods among claimants—is a disagreeable but inescapable task every economic system must carry out; for in all societies, the prevailing reality of life has been the inadequacy of output to fill the wants and needs of the people. In traditional economies, rationing is performed by a general adherence to rigidly established rules. Whether by caste or class or family position or whatever, these rules determine the rights of various

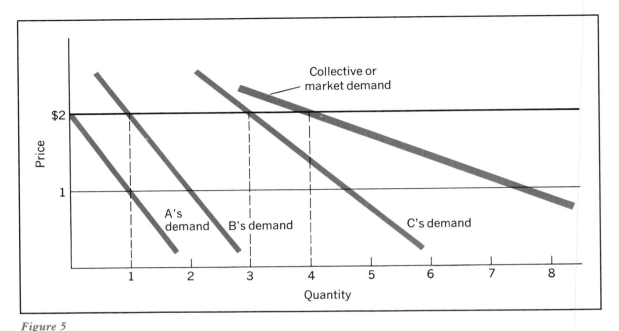

Figure 5
INDIVIDUAL AND MARKET DEMAND CURVES
The demand curve for a product on a market is the sum of the individual demand curves for it.

individuals to share in the economic product. In command societies, the division of the social product is carried out in a more explicitly directed fashion, as the governing authorities determine the rights of various groups or persons to share in the fruits of society.

A market society, as we know, minimizes the heavy hand of tradition and the authoritative one of command. It cannot escape some system of rationing, though, to prevent what would otherwise be an impossibly destructive struggle among its citizens. This critical allocative task is also accomplished by the price mechanism. One of the prime functions of a market is to determine who shall be allowed to acquire goods and who shall not.

How the Market Rations

Imagine a market with ten buyers, each willing and able to buy one unit of a commodity, but each having a different maximum price. Imagine ten suppliers, each also willing and able to put one unit of supply on the market, again each at a different price. Such a market might look like Table 1.

Remember that the maximum prices may differ because different people have different desires for the commodity or because they have different incomes. Those willing to pay the highest prices may not desire the commodity the most. They may simply have the most income and be willing and able to pay more for everything.

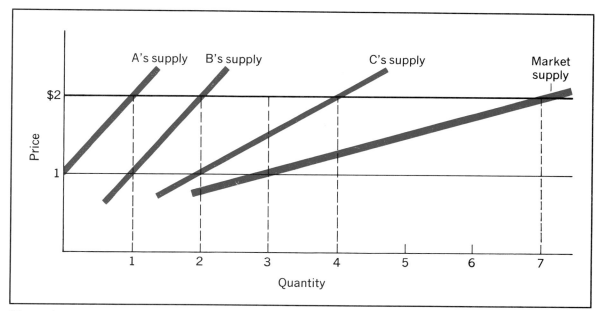

Figure 6

INDIVIDUAL AND MARKET SUPPLY CURVES

Like market demand curves, market supply curves sum up the willingness and ability of individuals into a market total.

As we can see, the equilibrium price will lie at $6, for at this price there will be five suppliers of one unit each and five purchasers of one each. Now let us make a graph and let each bar stand for one person. The height of the bar tells us the maximum each person will be willing to pay for the unit of the commodity or the minimum he or she would sell it for. If we line up our marketers in order of their demand and supply capabilities, our market will look like Figure 7.

What we have drawn is in fact nothing but a standard supply and demand diagram. But look what it shows us. All the buyers who can afford and are willing to pay the equilibrium price (or more) will get the goods they want. All those who cannot will not. So too, all the sellers who are willing and able to supply the

Table 1

The table shows a line-up of buyers and sellers, each one with a different maximum or minimum price (also called a "reservation price"). Can you see why $6 is an equilibrium price?

Price	$11	$10	$9	$8	$7	$6	$5	$4	$3	$2	$1
Number willing and able, at above price, to											
buy one unit	0	1	2	3	4	5	6	7	8	9	10
sell one unit	10	9	8	7	6	5	4	3	2	1	0

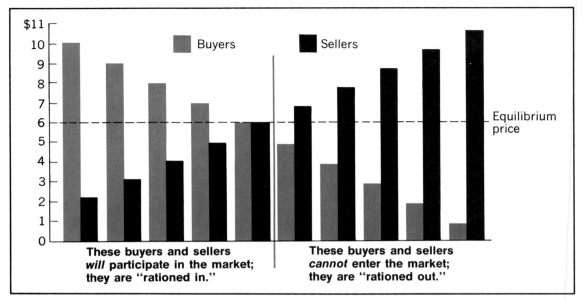

Figure 7
HOW THE MARKET RATIONS

commodity at its equilibrium price or less will be able to consummate sales. All those who cannot will not.

Thus the market, in establishing an equilibrium price, has in effect allocated goods among some buyers and withheld goods from others. It has permitted some sellers to do business and denied that privilege to others. In our case in Chapter 7 anyone who could pay $25 or more got a pair of shoes. Those who could not pay that much were unable to get shoes. All producers who could turn out shoes for $25 or less were able to do business, and those who could not meet that price were unable to make any sales at all.

Note that the market is in this way a means of *excluding* certain people from economic activity; namely, customers with too little money or with too weak desires or suppliers unwilling or unable to operate at a certain price.

Later we will see that the market mechanism allocates incomes in much the same way as it allocates goods. Those who successfully enter the market as factors of production get paid wages, rents, or interest. Those who do not, don't.

PRICE VS. NONPRICE RATIONING

The rationing system of the market is both its triumph and its trouble.

Let us look first at the triumphs. Nonmarket systems typically suffer from two difficulties. If they are run mainly by tradition, they tend to be inert, passive, changeless. It's very hard to get things done in a traditional economy, if anything has to be done in a new way.

A command system has a different inherent problem. It is good at getting things done, but it acquires its problem-solving capacity at a price. The price is the presence of political power in the economic mechanism, either as a large bureaucracy or as an authority capable of sticking its nose into daily life.

Against these two difficulties, the price system has two great advantages: (1) *It is highly dynamic,* **and (2)** *it is self-enforcing.* **That is, on the one hand it provides an easy avenue for change to enter the system; on the other, it permits economic activity to take place without anyone overseeing the system.**

The second (self-enforcing) attribute of the market is especially useful with regard to the rationing function. In place of ration tickets with their almost inevitable black markets or cumbersome inspectorates or queues of customers trying to be first in line, the price system operates without any kind of visible administration apparatus or side effect. The energies that must go into planning or the frictions that come out of it are alike rendered unnecessary by the self-policing market mechanism.

Market Problems

On the other hand, the system has the defects of its virtues. It is efficient and dynamic, but it is also devoid of values. It recognizes no valid claim to the goods and services of society except those of wealth and income. Those with income and wealth are entitled to the goods and services the economy produces; those without income and wealth receive nothing.

This blindness of the market to any claim on society's output except wealth or income creates very serious problems. It means that those who inherit large incomes are entitled to large shares of output, even though they may have produced nothing themselves. More important, it means that individuals who have no wealth and who cannot produce—perhaps because they are ill, or simply because they cannot find work—have no way of gaining an income. To abide just by the market system of distribution we would have to be willing to tolerate individuals starving on the street.

Therefore every market society interferes to some extent with the outcome of the price rationing system. In times of emergency it issues special permits that take precedence over money and thereby prevent the richer members of society from buying up all the supplies of scarce and costly items. In depressed areas, it may distribute basic food or clothing to those who have no money to buy them. To an ever increasing extent it uses taxes and transfer payments to redistribute the ration tickets of money in accordance with the prevailing sense of justice, or the overriding needs of political pressures.

Shortages

Our view of the price system as a rationing mechanism helps to clarify the meaning of two words we often hear as a result of intervention into the rationing process: *shortage* and *surplus.*

What do we mean when we say there is a *shortage* of housing for low-income groups? The everyday meaning is that people with low incomes cannot find enough housing. Yet in every market there are always some buyers who are unsatisfied. We have previously noted, for instance, that in our shoe market, all buyers who could not or would not pay $25 had to go without shoes. Does this mean there was a shoe shortage?

Certainly no one uses that word to describe the outcome of a normal market, even though there are always buyers and sellers who are excluded because they cannot meet the going price. Then what does a "shortage" mean? **We can see now that shortage usually refers to a situation in which some nonmarket agency such as the government, fixes the price below the equilibrium price.**

An Example in Gasoline. Figure 8 shows us such a situation in gasoline—for instance after the OPEC shock of 1973. Note that the price established by the oil companies and the government was *below* the price that would have cleared the

Figure 8
THE SHORTAGE: GAS

Here is a graphic portrait of a shortage of a critical commodity such as gasoline. The supply of gas in the short run is fixed, as the vertical supply curve SS shows. That is, there is only so much gas on hand, no matter wht the price. (We'll discuss such vertical curves in our next chapter.) The demand for gas (DD) indicates that quantity OS' is sought at the going price OA. There isn't that much gas. A shortage of SS' exists, creating lines of cars at the gas pumps. Suppose the government puts on a gas tax AA", raising gas prices from OA to OA'. At the new higher price the quantity demanded is OS, just equal to supply. There is no more shortage. But there is a lot of complaint about high prices!

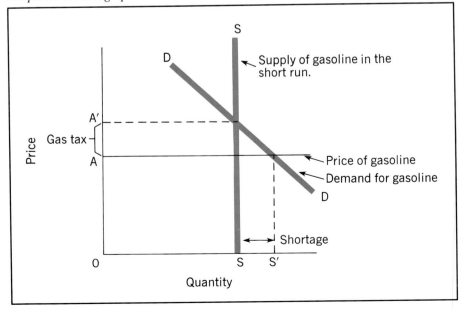

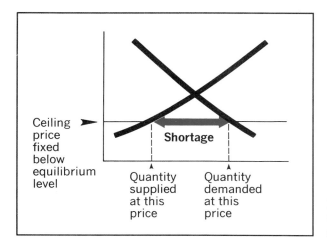

Ceiling price fixed below equilibrium level

Shortage

Quantity supplied at this price

Quantity demanded at this price

Figure 9
SHORTAGES

The graph makes clear that a "shortage" means that prices are not able to rise to equilibrium levels, so that quantity demanded exceeds quantity supplied.

market.* As a result, the quantity of gas demanded (OS') was greater than the quantity supplied (OS). The result was that people waited in long lines at the pumps and that those who failed to get to the pumps on time had to do without gas.

How could the shortage have been "cured"? Obviously by raising the price to an equilibrium level. But we did not want the oil companies to make much larger profits, nor were we willing greatly to increase the taxes on gas. At a price of, say, $3 including taxes, the lines would probably have disappeared.

Why did we not do that? Because the public would have objected violently to paying such high prices. People preferred to wait in line and take their chance of going without gas to paying the amount needed to remove the shortage. They preferred rationing by luck or by the clock to rationing by price.

Price Controls

This bears directly on the problem of price controls. The problem with such controls is that they tend to fix prices below the level that would be established in a free market. As a result, some buyers who would ordinarily have been priced out of the market remain *in* the market, although there are not enough goods offered to satisfy their demands. The result tends to be queues in stores to buy things before they are gone, under-the-counter deals to get on a preferred list, or black or gray markets selling goods illegally at higher prices than are officially sanctioned. We show this in Figure 9.

* Why did the companies not set the price at OA'? Simply because they feared the public outcry that would have accompanied this price. It would have been an economic equilibrium price, but not a political one.

Surpluses

The opposite takes place with a surplus. In this situation, the quantity supplied is greater than that demanded (note we should *not* say that "supply is greater than demand"). In a free market, the price would fall until the two quantities were equal. If the government continues to support the commodity, then the quantity bought by private industries will not be as large as the quantity offered by farmers. Unsold amounts will be a surplus, bought by government.

Thus the words *shortage* and *surplus* mean situations in which there are sellers and buyers who are willing and able to enter the market at the going price but who remain active and unsatisfied because the price mechanism has not

RATIONING BABIES

Because the market is such an efficient distributive mechanism, it has been proposed as a means to achieve zero population growth, assuming that this were the declared national policy. Since a sizable minority (probably about 15 percent) of all families voluntarily choose to have no children or only one, a country can achieve ZPG even if some families have more than two children. The question is how to decide which families should be allowed to have the extra children. Professor Kenneth Boulding has ventured an answer that leans heavily on the market mechanism. He proposes that each girl and boy at adolescence be given 110 green stamps, of which 100 are required if a woman is to have a legal child. (The penalty for having an illegal child would be very severe.) Unwanted or surplus stamps would then be sold in a market organized for that purpose. It can be seen that the total number of stamps would permit the population as a whole to have 2.2 children per family—the ZPG rate. The market would therefore serve to ration the extra stamps, making them available to those with higher incomes or a greater desire for children. "As an incidental benefit," writes Boulding, tongue in cheek, "the rich will have loads of children and become poor, and the poor have few children and become rich."*

When this scheme was first published, it provoked a storm of criticism. Commenting on its reception, Boulding observes: "This modest and humane proposal, so much more humane than that of Swift, who proposed that we eat the surplus babies, has been received with so many cries of anguish and horror that it illustrates the extraordinary difficulty of applying rational principles to processes involving human generation."

* Kenneth E. Boulding, *Economics as a Science* (New York: McGraw-Hill, 1970), p. 39.

eliminated them. This is very different from a free market where there are unsatisfied buyers and sellers *who cannot meet the going price* and who are therefore not taken into account. Poor people, who have no demand for fresh caviar at $60 per pound, do not complain of a caviar shortage. If the price of fresh caviar were set by government decree at $1 a pound, there would soon be a colossal "shortage."

When Price Rationing Fails

What about the situation with low-cost housing? Essentially what we mean when we talk of a shortage of inexpensive housing is that we view the outcome of this particular market situation with noneconomic eyes and pronounce the result distasteful. By the standards of the market, the poor who cannot afford to buy housing are simply buyers at the extreme lower right end of the demand curve. Their elimination from the market for housing is only one more example of the rationing process that takes place in *every* market. **When we single out certain goods or services (such as dialysis or private nursing care) as being in "short supply," we imply that we do not approve of the price mechanism as the appropriate means of allocating scarce resources in these particular instances.** An economic problem becomes a social problem. This does not imply that the market is not as efficient a distributor as ever. What we do not like is the social outcome of the market rationing process. The underlying distribution (or maldistribution) of income clashes with other standards of the public interest that we value more highly than efficiency.

looking back

KEY CONCEPTS

Market mechanism: Two loops or circuits

One central idea of this chapter has been to show that the vast array of buying and selling activity we call "the market" is actually a *system*—that is, a social institution that displays regular, orderly patterns of operation. We follow the operations of this mechanism by observing that it can contain two loops or circuits, one having to do with production, one with distribution.

The production loop: Business buys factor services and makes goods that are used by the factors

1 First, production. The market network is the means by which a market society organizes its factors of production so as to bring about production. This shows up as a flow of services (labor power, or the services of capital or land) from households that own them to businesses that put them to productive use. The loop is completed when the goods that business produces return to the household to be consumed or put to further use.

The distribution loop: Payments to factors who buy business's output	**2** The distribution loop is a circuit of money payments, not of real services or goods. It goes in the opposite direction to the production loop as businesses pay households for their services as factors of production, and as households pay businesses for the products they buy.
Two kinds of markets: factors and goods	**3** Another way of revealing the connectedness of the market mechanism is to divide the complex totality of market activity into two kinds of markets: the market for factors and the market for goods (and services). The factor market regulates production; the goods market organizes allocation.
Households enter the factor market as sellers; business as a buyer. In the goods market, households shape demand and business determines supply	**4** In the factor market, households offer their services to business as labor or as owners of land and capital. Their activities therefore shape the supply curves in that market. It is just the reverse in the market for goods and services. Here it is business that shapes the supply curve because businesses are the sellers in this market, whereas demand is formed by the factors of production (behaving as households).
The market as rationing or allocation mechanism	**5** A second central idea of this chapter is one of the most important in this entire section. It is the idea of the market as a rationing system—a means of allocating output (or, as we will later see, income)—is fundamental to understanding our form of economic society.
Price as rationer	**6** The rationing device used by the market is simplicity itself. Price determines who will and who will not enter the market, whether as buyer or seller. Those who cannot or do not wish to sell or buy at existing prices are rationed out of the marketplace.
Strengths of the market system: flexibility and self-governance	**7** The price system of allocation has two great advantages. It avoids the stodginess and unresponsiveness of tradition-bound systems, and it makes unnecessary the bureaucracy or political intervention of command-run systems. Markets govern themselves. Those who are rationed in and those who are rationed out usually—although not always—acquiesce in the market's determinations.
Weaknesses: no social conscience or political awareness	**8** Price rationing has one great disadvantage: It recognizes no claim on output except the ability to enter the market. Therefore it has no "heart," no political awareness. As a result all market systems make allowances for those it considers are unfairly or unwisely kept out of the market.
Shortages: when prices are below equilibrium, $Q_d > Q_s$	**9** The function of price as an allocator throws light on shortages and surpluses. What we mean by a shortage is that price is held below an equilibrium or clearing level by government or other means. As a result the quantity demanded is greater than that supplied. The result of this is queues or black markets or a scramble to get to the front of the line.

Surpluses are just the opposite: $Q_d < Q_s$	**10** A surplus comes about just the other way. When prices are held up above clearing levels by price supports or some other means, more is supplied to the market than is demanded. The supply for which there are no buyers at the support price is called a surplus.

ECONOMIC VOCABULARY

QUESTIONS

1. What is the difference between the market for goods and for factors? Can a household be a buyer in the market for factors? Suppose it hires a maid? Are a maid's activities a factor of production or a kind of service? Can a household be a seller in the goods market? Suppose it sells homegrown vegetables? In that case, is it acting as a household or a firm?

2. Can you describe other ways in which the factor and the goods markets interact? Will a firm's behavior on the goods market (its supply curve) be affected by a household's behavior on the factor market (the household supply curve or the price that a household asks for its services)? How about a firm's behavior as a buyer of factors being determined by a household's behavior as a buyer of goods?

3. What is meant by describing the market as a "system"? What exactly do we mean by a system? Does it imply that there is something mechanical — machinelike — about the way a social organism works? Can you see that all these words, such as *system, mechanism,* even *works,* imply a regular, orderly, predictable process?

4. Why is rationing an inescapable problem in our kind of society? Is it inescapable even in traditional societies, like the Eskimo? How is it solved there?

5. Explain how the market rations automobiles. What other means of allocating cars could you imagine in a capitalist society? In a socialist one?

6. Under what circumstances is the market not regarded as a good rationer? Take a newly perfected vaccine as an example. Why would people object to selling it to the highest bidder? Why don't the same arguments apply to aspirin?

7. Is there a shortage of low-cost housing? High-cost housing? What do we mean by the term?

8. Would you be in favor of a gas tax that would remove any shortages or do you prefer rationing on a nonprice basis? Which basis strikes you as best?

9. Diagram a situation in which a government subsidy holds up farm prices and creates a surplus. (You might check your diagram with Fig. 7 on page 450.)

AN EXTRA WORD ABOUT

Optimal Allocation of Individual Income

There is another way in which a market allows us to allocate income efficiently. Let us see how the market mechanism maximizes the total utilities of a person who shops in many markets for many goods.

An intuitive example may help us begin. Suppose you had to spend your weekly income each Monday, but you had to make up your shopping list, once and for all, before leaving your house. If you had enough price catalogs that would not be impossible to do, although you might debate the merits of this item versus that one. *Suppose you had to make up the list without knowing what prices were!*

Two problems would present themselves. First, you would not know how many goods you could buy, *in toto,* because you would not know whether your income would suffice to buy a few goods or many. Second, you would have no way of ranking the priority of your purchases. Knowing the prices of bread and cake, you can decide how much you want to spend on each. Not knowing these prices, how could you make a rational decision whether to buy many units of bread and no cake, or fifty-fifty or some other combination?

You might think, perhaps, that a rational man would buy bread first, then cake. But suppose after he had made his irrevocable decision he found that bread was very expensive and cake very cheap. He might then regret having decided to buy so much bread and wish he had chosen cake instead.

This seemingly trivial example contains more than may at first meet the eye, for it shows us how the existence of prices enables us to behave as rational maximizers in disposing of our incomes. Therefore let us pursue this line of reasoning a little further.

In Figure 10 we show our reservation prices for three commodities. *Reservation price* is a term meaning the highest price that we are willing to offer as buyers, or the lowest price we'd take as sellers. In each case, our reservation price for another unit of the same good diminishes because the good gives us less marginal utility. At the same time, as the diagram makes clear, the schedule of reservation prices is very different for each good. Good A is very important to us, so our initial reservation price is very high; good B less so; good C still less. (We have drawn our reservation prices in steplike fashion and overlaid a

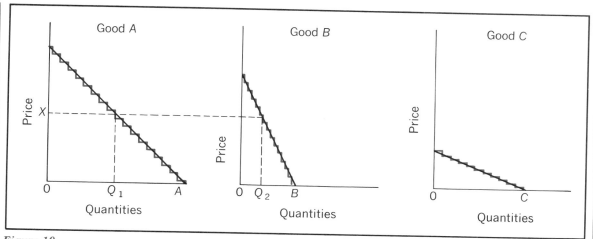

Figure 10
ALLOCATING INCOME

The graph shows us different schedules of reservation prices (the most we would pay) for successive units of three commodities. At price OX we will just be tempted to buy an amount OQ_1 of good A, OQ_2 of good B, but none of good C. At zero price, how much do we want of each?

generalized schedule of reservation prices, which is, of course, our familiar demand curve.)*

MARGINS VS. TOTALS

The question we want to elucidate is this: *How much of each good will we buy to get the largest possible satisfaction from our income?*

Suppose we had an unlimited income. This is the same thing as supposing that the goods were free, that their prices were zero. How much of A, B, and C would we then acquire? An unlimited amount? Certainly not. As our diagram shows, we don't want unlimited quantities of A, B, and C. Beyond a certain point, their marginal utilities are negative. They are nuisances. We could even have negative reservation prices: We would pay someone to take the stuff away. Thus, with no budget constraint, we consume quantities $OA + OB + OC$.

Now notice something interesting about this unlimited consumption. The three demand curves reflect differing marginal utilities of the three goods. Looking at these curves, we see that the *total* utility we get from A will be greater than that we get from B or C, and that the *total* utility of B will be greater than that of C. Why then don't we take more of A and B, since their total utility is so large? The answer, also apparent from the graph, is that after we have acquired quantity *OA* of good A, *we don't get any further utility from it.* The same is true of B after we have *OB* of it, and of course of C, after *OC*.

This begins to clarify a very important point. To get the maximum amount of enjoyment from our income — even from an *unlimited* income — we need pay no attention to the total

* Remember that each of these schedules of reservation prices depends on our income as well as our tastes. With different incomes we might have a different set of desires for the three goods.

utilities we get from various commodities. Their marginal utilities are all we need to know. We will reach a maximum of satisfaction from our total expenditure when we get as much utility from the marginal unit of one good as from another. *Indeed, the rule for maximizing our total satisfaction is to acquire goods until their marginal utilities per dollar of expenditure are equal.*

THE EQUIMARGINAL RULE

This equimarginal rule has many applications in economics, for it has an astonishing property. It means that we don't have to stop to compare totals when we maximize values. *We need compare only margins.* Later we will see that this applies to entrepreneurs trying to maximize total revenues and to minimize total costs. They too will need to look at only marginal costs and incomes. For ourselves as consumers, it means that we do not have to try to compare whether we get more "total" satisfaction out of bread or out of cake. All we have to do is worry about whether we want one more loaf of bread or one more piece of cake. If we buy whichever we want more of at the moment, we will automatically be maximizing our total well-being. When we equally desire another unit of each, we have spent our income as efficiently as possible.

BUDGET CONSTRAINTS

So far, we have imagined that we had no budget constraint. Of course we do have such constraints. Our incomes are limited, and prices are not zero. Then how does the equimarginal principle apply?

If you will turn back to Figure 10 you will see an *X* on the price axis of good A. We can imagine that this is the price of goods A, B, and C. We picture them having the same price: e.g., $5 for a basket of fruit (good A), a necktie (good B), a movie ticket (good C). (We could draw different prices for each good, but that would only complicate the diagram without changing the principle.)

Now how much of A, B, and C do we buy? You can see that we buy (approximately) OQ_1 of good A, and OQ_2 of good B. We buy none of good C. Why? Because the price is higher than our top reservation price. We don't want to go to the movies at $5, given our budget constraint.

Now look at goods A and B. You obviously have much more total utility from A than from B. Why then don't you buy more of A and less of B? The answer is that you are getting as much satisfaction *at the margin* for good A as for good B. If you bought another unit of good A and one less unit of good B, you would be giving up more utility than you would be getting. *Thus budget constraints limit the amount of goods we can buy, but we still maximize our well-being by seeking equal marginal utilities from those we buy.*

EQUALIZING MARGINAL UTILITIES

Now let us take one last step. We have just seen that we maximize our personal well-being by equalizing the marginal utilities of goods, not their total utilities. *We can then see that we will spend our income optimally when we get the same satisfaction from the last dollar spent on each good.* If the marginal utility of a dollar's worth of bread is equal to that of a dollar's worth of cake, we have obviously achieved our aim.

When we speak of "a dollar's worth" of bread, we are speaking of its price. Therefore we can set up a formula that will describe the way we allocate our incomes to maximize our satisfactions.

$$\frac{\text{marginal utility of good A}}{\text{price of good A}} = \frac{\text{marginal utility of good B}}{\text{price of good B}}$$

or in more abstract terms:

$$\frac{MU_1}{P_1} = \frac{MU_2}{P_2} = \frac{MU_n}{P_n}$$

where *MU* stands for the marginal utilities of goods 1, 2 . . . *n*, and P_1, P_2 . . . P_n stand for their respective prices.

Here is the equimarginal principle at work. We are maximizing our well-being by equating the *marginal* utilities of different goods in proportion to their prices, so that each dollar expenditure for each good gives us the same enjoyment. We may still get a much larger amount of enjoyment from one kind of good than from another, but we will only decrease our total welfare if we lose sight of the equimarginal principle.

CHAPTER 26
Market Dynamics

a look ahead

We have already learned how the interaction of supply and demand schedules establishes price, and about how movements in these schedules (and in the curves that represent them) help us explain changes in price. But we still need to explore the concept of price formation a little more deeply.

In this short but important chapter, we concentrate on two problems.

1 The idea of elasticity, one of the most useful notions in the economist's kit of tools. Elasticity will provide a much more complete understanding of how supply and demand work.

2 The idea of substitution. It has been said that substitution is one of the central organizing concepts of economics. We will use it here to shed light on the much misunderstood words *necessity* and *luxury*.

We have seen how shifts in demand or supply affect price, but *how much* do they affect price? Suppose, for example, that demand schedules have increased by 10 percent. Do we know how large an effect this change will have on price?

These questions lead us to a still deeper scrutiny of the nature of supply and demand, by way of a new concept called elasticity or, more properly, **price elasticity**. Elasticities describe the shapes of supply and demand curves and thereby tell us a good deal about whether a given change in demand or supply will have a small or large effect on price. Figure 1 illustrates the case with two supply curves. Our diagrams show two commodities selling at the same equilibrium prices and facing identical demand schedules. Note, however, that the two commodities have very different supply curves. In both cases, demand increases by the same amount. Notice how much greater is the price increase for the good with the inelastic (steep) supply curve.

Similarly, the price change that would be associated with a change in supply will be greater for a commodity with an inelastic demand curve than for one with an elastic (gently sloping) demand curve. Figure 2 shows two identical supply curves matched against very different demand curves. Notice how the commodity with inelastic demand suffers a much greater fall in price.

Elasticities are powerful factors in explaining price movements, because the word *elasticity* refers to sensitivity of response to price changes. An elastic demand (or supply) means that changes in price strongly affect buyers' or sellers' willingness or ability to buy or sell. When schedules are inelastic, the effect of price is small. **In**

Figure 1
ELASTICITY OF SUPPLY

Elasticity describes the shapes of supply or demand curves. These shapes in turn represent the sensitivity of buyers or sellers to price changes. On the left we have an inelastic supply curve. The increase in demand from DD to D'D' brings about a big jump in prices (much like the effect on the short-run market for fish, Figure 3, top). On the right, the same increase in demand coaxes forth a lot of additional supply. Therefore price rises much less than in the first case.

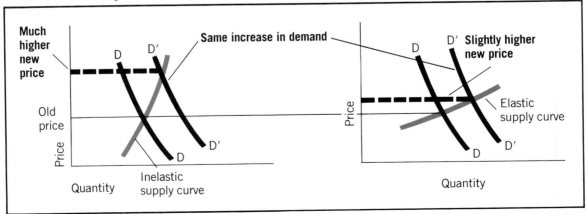

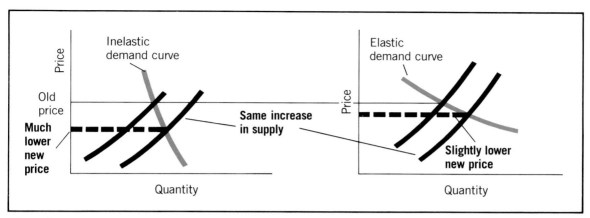

Figure 2
ELASTICITY OF DEMAND

Elasticity obviously affects demand curves as well as supply curves. Rule: *The* more *elastic demand is, the less will a given shift in supply change prices.*

more precise terms, an elastic demand (or supply) is one in which a given percentage change in prices brings about a larger percentage change in the quantity demanded (or supplied). An inelastic schedule or curve is one in which the response in the quantities we are willing and able to buy or sell is proportionally less than the change in price.

The Elasticity Formula

It is helpful to have a precise idea of how we measure elasticity. The method is simple enough. We measure the percentage change in the quantity demanded over the percentage change in price. If the percentage change in quantity demanded is greater than that of price, our measure of elasticity will be greater than unity, and we have an elastic curve. If it is less than unity, we have an inelastic curve. If the two variables are equal, we have unit elasticity.

In algebra:*

$$\frac{\Delta Q/Q}{\Delta P/P} = \text{measure of elasticity}$$

* A footnote to the mathematically inclined student. You have probably noticed that the change in quantity is likely to be a positive number when the change in price is a negative number — we buy more when the price goes down. Therefore the measure of elasticity will also be a negative number. For convenience sake, economists disregard this and speak as if the measure were positive. You should also note that there are a number of refinements in measuring elasticity which we do not go into here. The main one concerns the difference between measuring elasticity at a single point and measuring it along a section of the curve.

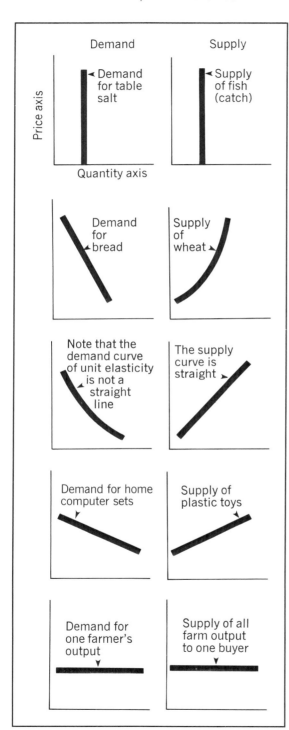

Demand Supply

Price axis

Demand for table salt

Supply of fish (catch)

Quantity axis

Demand for bread

Supply of wheat

Note that the demand curve of unit elasticity is not a straight line

The supply curve is straight

Demand for home computer sets

Supply of plastic toys

Demand for one farmer's output

Supply of all farm output to one buyer

Figure 3
A FAMILY OF SUPPLY AND DEMAND CURVES

Totally inelastic demand or supply. The quantity offered or sought is unchanged despite a change in price. Examples: Within normal price ranges there is probably no change at all in the quantity of table salt bought. Similarly, a fisherman bringing a catch of fish to a market will have to sell it all at any price within reason.

Inelastic demand or supply. Quantity offered or sought changes proportionately less than price. Examples: We probably do not buy twice as much bread if the price of bread drops to half. Neither are we likely to halve our bread purchases if bread prices double. On the supply side, the price of wheat may double, but farmers are unable (at least for a long time) to offer twice as much wheat for sale.

Unit elasticity. This is a special case in which quantities demanded or supplied respond in exact proportion to price changes. (Note the shape of the demand curve, a rectangular hyperbola.) Many goods may fit this description, but it is impossible flatly to state that any one good does so.

Elastic demand or supply. Price changes induce proportionally larger changes in quantity. Examples: Many luxury goods increase dramatically in sales volume when their price is lowered. On the other side, elastic supply usually affects items that are easy to produce, so that a small price rise induces a rush for expanded output.

Totally elastic demand or supply. The quantity supplied or demanded at the going price is "infinite." Examples: This seemingly odd case turns out to be of great importance in describing the market outlook of the typical small competitive firm. Merely as a hint: For an individual farmer, the demand curve for his output at the going price looks horizontal because he can sell all the grain he can possibly grow at that price. A grain dealer can also buy all he wants at that price.

where:

ΔQ is the *change* in quantity demanded

Q is the *original* quantity demanded

ΔP is the *change* in price

P is the original price.

It helps if we see what elasticities of different kinds look like. Figure 3 is a family of supply and demand curves that illustrates the range of buying and selling responses associated with a change in prices.

Elasticities and Business Fortune

In Chapter 32 we will discover a very important effect of elasticities in determining the incidence of taxation — that is, who pays a given tax. But while we are still studying the marketplace, we should note that elasticities have a great effect on the fortunes of buyers and sellers. It makes a big difference to a buyer whether the supply curve of a commodity he wants is elastic or not, for that will drastically affect the amount he will have to spend on that particular commodity if its price changes. It makes an equal amount of difference to a seller whether the demand curve for his output is elastic or not, for that will determine what happens to total revenues as prices change.

Here is an instance in point. Table 1 shows three demand schedules: elastic, inelastic, and of unit elasticity. Let us see how these three differently constituted schedules would affect the fortunes of a seller who had to cater to the demand represented by each.

A very interesting result follows from these different schedules. The amounts spent (price times quantity) are in Table 2. **The total amount spent for each commodity (and thus the total amount received by a firm) will be very different over the indicated range of prices.**

Table 1

DEMAND SCHEDULES FOR THREE GOODS

The three demand schedules are different in elasticity because each reveals a different ability or willingness to buy as prices change.

| | Quantities Demanded | | |
Price	Inelastic Demand	Unit Elasticity	Elastic Demand
$10	100	100	100
9	101	111⅑	120
8	102	125	150
7	103	142⁴⁄₇	200
6	104	166⅔	300
5	105	200	450
4	106	250	650
3	107	333⅓	900
2	108	500	1,400
1	109	1,000	3,000

Table 2

TOTAL EXPENDITURES (OR RECEIPTS)

Compare what happens to receipts of the three goods when price drops from $10 to $9.

Price	Inelastic	Unit Elastic	Elastic
		Goods with Demand Schedules That Are	
$10	$1,000	$1,000	$1,000
9	909	1,000	1,080
8	816	1,000	1,200
7	721	1,000	1,400
6	624	1,000	1,800
5	525	1,000	2,250
4	424	1,000	2,600
3	321	1,000	2,700
2	216	1,000	2,800
1	109	1,000	3,000

To a seller of goods, it makes a lot of difference whether or not the demand he faces is elastic. If demand is elastic and he cuts his price, he will take in more revenue. If his demand is inelastic and he cuts his price, he will take in *less* revenue.

Conversely, a business that raises its price will be lucky if the demand for its product is inelastic, for then receipts will actually increase. Compare the fortunes of the two businesses depicted in Figure 4. Note that by blocking in the change in price times the change in quantity, we can show the change in receipts. (Because we have ignored changes in costs, we cannot show changes in profits.)

Our figure shows something else. If we reverse the direction of the price change, our businesses' fortunes suffer a sharp change. A demand curve that is elastic spells bad news for a business that seeks to raise prices, but the same demand

Figure 4

ELASTICITIES AND RECEIPTS

Notice the striking difference in the receipts of two businesses facing demand curves of different elasticities if each firm raises price by the same amount.

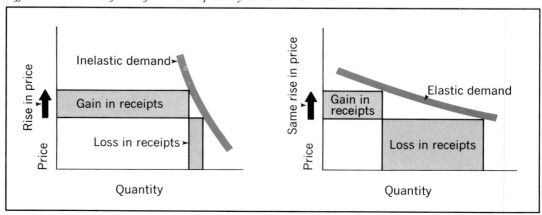

curve brings good fortune to one that intends to cut prices. Just the opposite is the case with an inelastic demand curve: Now the condition of demand is favorable for a price rise, since the seller will hold most customers even at the higher price; but inelastic demand is bad for one who cuts prices, since it will gain few additional customers (or the old ones will increase their purchases only slightly) when prices fall.

INCOME ELASTICITIES

We should notice that we can use another term—*income elasticity*—to describe how our willingness or ability to buy or sell responds to a change in *income,* rather than price. With many commodities, income elasticities of both demand and supply are more significant than price elasticities in actual economic life.

The idea of income elasticity is exactly the same as price elasticity. Sales of an income-elastic good or service rise proportionately *faster* than income. Sales of an income-inelastic commodity rise *less than proportionately* with income. These relationships are graphed in the accompanying figure.

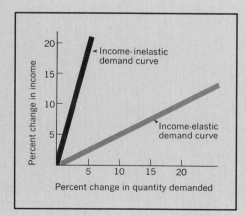

Figure 5
INCOME ELASTICITIES

Do not be fooled into thinking that these are supply curves because they slope upward. "Income" demand curves show a functional relation different from that of "price" demand curves. In the curves shown, we assume that prices are unchanged, otherwise we would not have *ceteris paribus.*

As an exercise, try drawing an income-elastic and an income-inelastic supply curve.

Obviously, what all businesspeople would like to have is a demand for their product that was inelastic in an upward direction and elastic at lower than existing prices, so that they stood to gain whether they raised or lowered prices. As we shall see when we study pricing under oligopoly, just the opposite is apt to be the case!

BEHIND ELASTICITIES OF DEMAND: SUBSTITUTION

Because elasticities are so important in accounting for the behavior of prices, we must press our investigation further. We must leave the supply side of elasticity to be studied when we look into the behavior of factors and firms. Here we will ask why demand curves are shaped the way they are. Why is our price (or income) sensitivity for some commodities so great and for others so slight?

If we think of a good service for which our demand might be very inelastic — say eyeglasses (assuming we need them) — and compare it with another for which our demand is apt to be highly elastic — say a trip to Europe — the difference is not difficult to grasp. One thing is a necessity; the other is a luxury. But what do we mean by *necessity* and *luxury*?

One attribute of a necessity is that it is not easily replaced by a substitute. If we need eyeglasses, we will spend a great deal of money, if we must, to acquire a pair. Hence such a necessity has a very inelastic demand curve.

Marginal Utility Again

Necessities are never absolute in the sense that nothing can be substituted for the commodity in question. High enough prices will drive buyers to some substitute, however imperfect.* Just when will the buyer be driven to the "next best thing"? As we know, economists say that the decision will be made by a comparison of the marginal utility derived from a dollar's worth of the high-priced item with that derived from the lower-priced substitute. As the price of champagne goes up and up, there comes a point at which we would rather spend our next dollar for a substantial amount of beer than a sip of champagne.

---

* What *would* be the substitute for eyeglasses? For a very nearsighted person, the demand for one pair of glasses would be absolutely inelastic over a considerable price range. But when glasses got to be, say, $500 a pair, substitutes would begin to appear. At those prices, one could hire someone to guide him around or to read aloud. Admittedly this is less satisfactory than having glasses; but if the choice is between spending a very large amount on glasses and on personal help, the latter might seem preferable. Of course, there are some goods without any substitutes — air, for example. Such goods are "free goods," because no one owns them. If a good such as air could be owned, it would have to be subject to stringent public control to prevent its owners from exacting a horrendous price for it.

Necessities and Elasticity

We have seen that necessities have inelastic demand curves, so that we stick to them as prices rise. What about when they fall? Won't we rush to buy necessities, just because they *are* necessities? Won't that make their demand curves elastic?

Surprisingly, we do not rush to buy necessities when their prices fall. Why? The answer is that necessities are the things we buy *first,* **just because they are necessities.** Having bought what we needed before the fall in price, we are not tempted to buy much more, if any more, after the fall. Bread, as we commented before, is a great deal more valuable for life than diamonds are. But we ordinarily have enough bread, so the marginal utility of another loaf is no greater than that of an equivalent expenditure on any other good. Thus, as the price of bread drops, the quantity we seek expands only slightly. So too with eyeglasses.

Compare the case with a luxury, such as a trip to Europe. There are many substitutes for such a trip: trips out West, trips East, or some other kind of vacation. As a result, if the price of a European trip goes up, we are easily persuaded to switch to some alternative plan. Conversely, when the price of a European trip gets cheaper, we are quick to substitute *it* for other possible vacation alternatives, and our demand accordingly displays its elastic properties.

Do not make the mistake, however, of thinking that elasticity is purely a function of whether items are expensive or not. Studies have shown that the demand for subway transportation in New York City is price-elastic, which hardly means that riding in the subways is the prerogative of millionaires. The point, rather, is that the demand for subway rides is closely affected by the comparative prices of substitutes — bus fares and taxis. **Thus it is the ease or difficulty of substitution that always lies behind the various elasticities of demand schedules.**

The Importance of Substitutes

Time also plays an important role in shaping our demand curves. Suppose, for example, that the price of orange juice suddenly soared owing to a crop failure. Would the demand for orange juice be elastic or inelastic?

In the short run, it would generally be more inelastic than in the longer run. Lovers of orange juice would likely be willing to pay a higher price for their favorite juice because (they would believe) there was really no other juice quite as good. As weeks went by, they might be tempted to try other breakfast juices, and no doubt some of these experiments would take. Substitutes would be found, after all.

The point is that it takes time and information for patterns of demand to change. Thus demand curves generally become more elastic as time goes on and the range of discovered substitutes becomes larger.

Because substitutes form a vast chain of alternatives for buyers, changes in the price of substitutes change the position of demand curves. Here is a new idea to be thought about carefully. Our existing demand curve for bread or diamonds has the shape (elasticity) it does because substitutes exist at various prices. When the prices of those substitutes *change,* the original commodity suddenly looks "cheaper" or "more expensive." If the price of subway rides rises from 75 cents to $1 while the price of taxi rides remains the same, we will be tempted to switch part of our transportation from subways to taxis. If subway rides went to $1.50, there would be a mass exodus to taxis.

Thus we should add changes in taste and in income when we consider the possible causes of a shift in demand. If the price of a substitute commodity rises, the demand for the original commodity will rise. As the price of substitutes falls, demand for the original commodity will fall. This may, of course, bring changes in the price of the original commodity.

Complements

In addition to substitution, there is another connection between commodities. This is the relationship of *complementarity.* **Complementarity means that some commodities are technically linked, so that you cannot very well use one without using the other, even though they are sold separately.** Automobiles and gasoline are examples of such complementary goods, as are cameras and film.

Here is another instance of change in the price of one good actually affecting the position of the demand curve for the other. If the price of film goes up, it becomes

THE SEARCH FOR SUBSTITUTES

The search for substitutes is a complicated process that can lead to equally complicated supply and demand reactions. Just after a taxi strike in New York City, when fares went up 50 percent, people switched to substitutes (they rode buses, subways, or walked) and the taxi business suffered severely. Then after the shock of the increase wore off, business revived. People got used to higher fares; that is, they discovered that the marginal utility of a high-priced taxi ride was still greater than the marginal utility of the money they saved by using other transportation, plus the marginal utility of the time they wasted or the business they lost because they weren't taking taxis. In other words, the substitutes weren't satisfactory. Gradually, people began taking more cab rides, and taxi receipts were higher than before the fare hike. The quantity of taxi service consumed was down somewhat, but not by as much as the original drop. In this case, demand proved to be more *inelastic* over time than it was in the very short run.

more expensive to operate cameras. Hence the demand for cameras is apt to drop. Note that the price of cameras has not changed in the first instance. Rather, when the price of the complementary good, the film, goes up, the whole demand curve for cameras shifts to the left. Thereafter the price of cameras is apt to fall too.

Behavior and Nature, Again

There is a last point we should make before we leave the subject of elasticity. We have seen that the substitutability of one product for another is the underlying cause of elasticity. Indeed, more and more we are led to see products themselves as bundles of utilities surrounded with competing bundles that offer a whole range of alternatives for a buyer's satisfaction.

What is it that ultimately determines how close the substitutes come to the commodity in question? As with all questions in economics that are pursued to the end, the answer lies in two aspects of reality before which economic inquiry comes to a halt. One of these is human behavior, with its tastes, drives, and wants. One person's substitute will not be another's.

The other ultimate basing point is the technical and physical nature of the world that forces certain constraints upon us. Cotton may be a substitute for wool because they both have the properties of fibers, but diamonds are not a substitute for the same end use, because they lack the requisite physical properties. Diamonds, as finery, may be a substitute for clothes made out of cotton; but until we learn how to spin diamonds, they will not be a substitute for the cloth itself.

looking back

KEY CONCEPTS

Elasticity measures our quantity response to price changes:

$$\frac{\Delta Q/Q}{\Delta P/P}$$

Elasticities affect receipts and expenditures

1 The use of curves gives us a quick, graphic sense of the market at work. In particular, it highlights our responsiveness as buyers or sellers to changes in price (or income). We call this responsiveness the elasticity of our supply or demand curves. You should learn the formula for this elasticity and the definition of elastic and inelastic curves.

2 Elasticities greatly affect the way markets work. One important effect is the relation between elasticities and business receipts. A firm facing an inelastic demand curve will be glad to raise prices, sad to lower them. Why? A buyer with an elastic demand for a commodity will be sad when prices go up, glad when they go down. Again why? (If you don't know, review pages 463–469.

Substitution lies behind elasticity	**3** Finally, we go behind elasticity to find the all-important element of substitution. It is the ease of finding substitutes that shapes our behavior as buyers and sellers. If we can't find substitutes, we change our buying habits relatively little even if prices go up. This is another way of describing a necessity. If substitutes abound, even a small price rise will bring a larger reduction in the quantity we consume—we have given up a luxury.
Necessities and luxuries are created by ease of substitution	It has been said that substitution is the law of economic life, the key to everything. Think about the kinds of substitutes we have for even the most necessary items. What are the substitutes for water? Bread? There are surprisingly many. Indeed, it is hard to find items like eyeglasses, for which substitutes are very few.
	4 *Last, be sure you do the questions to this chapter.* They will help you discover what you know—and don't yet know.

ECONOMIC VOCABULARY

QUESTIONS

1. Draw the following: an elastic demand curve and an inelastic supply curve; an inelastic demand curve and an elastic supply curve; a demand curve of infinite elasticity and a totally inelastic supply curve. Now give examples of commodities each one of these curves might represent.

2. Show on a diagram why elasticity has so much effect in determining price changes. (Refer back to the diagrams on pp. 464–465 to be sure that you are right.)

3. Draw a diagram that shows what we mean by an increase in the quantity supplied; another diagram to show what is meant by an increase in supply. Now do the same for a decrease in quantity supplied and in supply. (*Warning:* It is very easy to get these wrong. Check yourself by seeing if the decreased supply curve

shows the seller offering less goods at the same prices.) Now do the same exercise for demand. Refer back to Chapter 7 if you have forgotten.

4. Show on a diagram (or with figures) why you would rather be the seller of a good for which demand was elastic, if you were in a market with falling prices. Suppose prices were rising — would you still be glad about the elasticity of demand?

5. How does substitution affect elasticity? If there are many substitutes for a product, is demand for it elastic or inelastic? Why?

6. If you were a legislator choosing a product on which to levy an excise tax, would you choose a necessity or a luxury? Which would yield the larger revenue? Show how your answer hinges on the different elasticities of luxuries and necessities.

7. By and large, are luxuries apt to enjoy elastic or inelastic demands? Has this anything to do with their price? Can high-priced goods have inelastic demands?

8. Why is demand more apt to become elastic over time?

9. The price of pipe tobacco rises. What is apt to be the effect on the demand for pipes? On the demand for cigars?

CHAPTER 27
Where the Market Fails

a look ahead

We have been learning about how the market works as an efficient allocator of goods. Now we must learn about how the market fails to work in certain instances. Two general categories of cases will interest us in this chapter.

1 The first has to do with situations in which the market operates badly or inefficiently.

2 The second concerns a class of transactions that entirely escape the market's organizing powers. In the second class we come across the very important problem of pollution, and we will consider ways of coping with it.

U p to this point we have been concerned with learning about the ways in which the market operates as a self-enforcing mechanism for allocating goods. We have noted that the results of its allocation may not necessarily please us because the market has a very mercenary attitude toward allocation, but we have made a point of stressing how efficiently and effectively it operates compared with other rationing systems.

In this chapter we must round out our understanding of the market by probing two areas of economic activity where the market works very inefficiently or not at all. One of these has to do with instances where marketers have no way of making intelligent decisions and where therefore the results of the market will reflect ignorance, luck, or accident, rather than informed maximizing behavior. The second case involves a large category of production that we call public goods — goods that escape the ministrations of the market entirely.

INFORMATION PROBLEMS

The whole market system is built on the assumption that individuals are **rational maximizers.** But buried in that assumption is the implicit expectation that marketers will have at least roughly accurate information about the market. A good example to the contrary is the situation faced by the tourist in a bazaar of a country where he or she doesn't know a word of the language. Such a buyer has no way of knowing what the price of an article "ought" to be. That's why tourists so often return triumphantly with their bazaar trophies — only to discover that they were for sale in their hotel at half the price.

The Prevalence of Ignorance

Without correct or adequate information, marketers obviously cannot make correct decisions. But often marketers do not have adequate information. Consumers guide themselves by hearsay, by casual information picked up by random sampling, or by their susceptibility to advertising. Who has time to investigate which brand of toothpaste is really best or even tastes best? Even professional buyers, such as industrial purchasing agents, cannot know every price of every product, including all substitutes.

The lack of information can be remedied, at least up to a point; but the remedy costs money or its equivalent — time. Few of us have the resources or patience to do a complete research job on every item we buy. Would it even be rational to do so? **Thus a certain amount of ignorance always remains in all markets, causing prices and quantities to differ from what they would be if we had complete information.** These differences can be very great, as anyone knows who has ever discovered, with sinking heart, that he or she paid "much too much" for a given article or sold it for "much too little."

MARKET INSTABILITY

One important class of market failure that stems from inadequate information is market instability. We have concentrated thus far on the tendency of markets to gravitate toward an equilibrium price. But markets may not equilibrate if the information marketers have is faulty; instead, they may gyrate or race back and forth, as the stock market does when investors are particularly "nervous" about the future.

Cobwebs

One interesting kind of market instability is called a *cobweb*, for reasons that become clear when we look at Figure 1. In this graph we show the supply and demand curves for some commodity that is produced a long time before it is sold, so that producers can't quickly change their outputs to correspond with the state of the market. They have to gear production to the demand they *expect* six months or even longer into the future. If these expectations are unfounded, trouble can ensue.

In Figure 1 we begin by supposing that Christmas tree growers initially put the quantity *OA* on the market. We can see that quantity *OA* will sell at price *OB*. Figuring that this will be *next year's* price, tree growers now plant the amount they are willing and able to offer at price *OB*—quantity *OC*. Alas, when the harvest comes, it is found that quantity *OC* will fetch only price *OD*. Now the process goes into reverse. Growers will figure that next year's price will be *OD*, and they plant amount *OA*, since at price *OD* the quantity they wish to supply is no more than that. Thereupon, next harvest time the price goes back to *OB* and around we go. If the

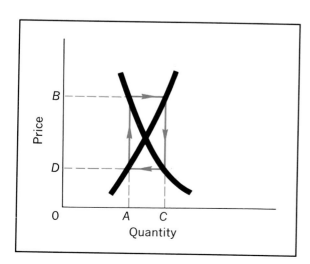

Figure 1
THE COBWEB
See text for the explanation of this cobweb. If expectations and information remain unchanged, producers will go on chasing their tails forever.

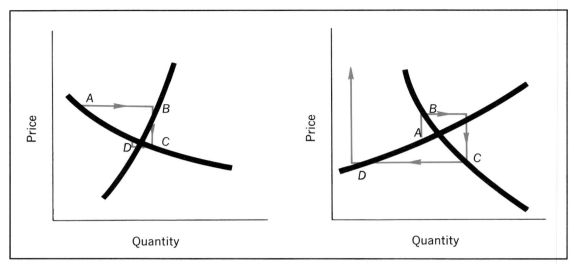

Figure 2
STABILIZING AND EXPLOSIVE COBWEBS

The cobweb on the left spirals into an equilibrium and the one on the right "explodes." The reason in both cases lies in the position and shape of the supply and demand curves. In other words, if supply and demand are favorable, a cobweb can lead to stability. If they are wrong, terrible instability can result.

supply and demand schedules were differently sloped, we could have a cobweb that converged toward equilibrium, as we show on the left of Figure 2; and we could have one that "exploded," as we see in the diagram on the right.

EXPECTATIONS AND SPECULATION

Expectations are so important in making markets work smoothly that we must spend a little more time with them.

Let us quickly learn how expectations work. Suppose buyers of a commodity discover that its price is rising. If they expect that this rise in price will be short-lived or even if they think that the new higher price will persist for a fairly long time, they will behave the way textbooks say they should. In the face of higher prices, quantities demanded will decline, a new equilibrium price will be established, and that will be that. The market will have performed its task.

Perverse Reactions

Now suppose that the rise in prices sets off expectations that prices will rise still more. This is a common experience in inflationary times, when the mounting prices of goods leads us to believe that prices will be still higher tomorrow, not that they will be lower or remain at their new levels. **In this case of inflationary expectations, we do not behave as normal demanders. Instead of curtailing our willingness to buy, the rise in prices spurs it on. Better to buy more today than wait till tomorrow when prices will be higher still. Thus, expectations can induce perverse reactions in the marketplace.** Of course, the same kinds of perverse reactions can affect the supply curves of sellers. Ordinarily, a rise in prices brings about an increase in the quantities offered. Not, however, if expectations point in the direction of still higher prices. Then sellers will hold back, causing the supply curve to shift leftward.

The result, as we can see in Figure 3, is that prices can move violently upward and that the movement of prices can continue to feed upon itself, because demand and supply curves (D_1, D_2, D_3 and S_1, S_2, S_3) are themselves being shifted by the very fact that prices have changed. In deflationary times, the same process can work in reverse.

Such perverse price movements can lead to very dangerous consequences. They play a major role in the cumulative, self-sustaining processes of speculation or collapse. They can cause commodity prices to shoot to dizzying heights or plummet to the depths. At their worst, perverse behavior threatens to make an

Figure 3
A SELF-FEEDING PRICE RISE

Suppose we have a market in which D_1 is the demand curve and S_1 the supply curve, with price at P_1. Now suppose that supply shifts to S_2, as when the OPEC countries in 1973 raised their prices. If D_1 did not change we would simply have a new stable market with price at P_2. But if the change in supply serves as a trigger to move demand upward to D_2, price will rise to P_3. And if OPEC sellers, seeing that the market is buoyant, contract offerings further—the S_3 supply curve—prices will continue to go up, if demand also shifts to D_3. This kind of market instability, based on expectations, can also work in reverse. Can you see its relevance to a "collapse" in stock prices?

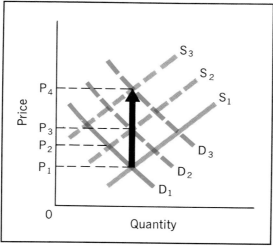

entire economy go out of control, as in the case of hyperinflations or panics. At best, they disrupt smooth, orderly markets and bring shocks and dislocations to the economy.

Remedying Information Lacks

Can these market failures be remedied? Some can; some cannot. Ignorance can certainly be reduced by better economic reporting or by truth-in-advertising laws. Cobwebs can be mitigated by accurate economic forecasting or just by learning. Perverse behavior can be lessened by persuasive pronouncements from important public figures.

But we must recognize that there is a residue of arbitrariness even in the best-intentioned remedies. Take the matter of consumer information. We "inform" the consumer, through labels on cigarette packages, that smoking is dangerous; but we do not prohibit the advertising of cigarettes. We spread "market information" by having the incomprehensible contents of medications printed on their containers, but we allow the consumer to be misinformed through advertising that claims superiority of one kind of aspirin over another.

Why? There is no clear rationale in these cases. Essentially we are trying to repair omissions in the market system — injecting information, so that consumers can make better choices — without becoming paternalistic. Maybe we think it is better to allow the consumer to make some mistakes than to allow the government to make them for him.

That is perhaps as it should be. But the consequence is that the market will continue to produce less than wholly satisfactory or efficient results because a residue of ignorance or misinformation is allowed to remain — or remains despite our best efforts.

PUBLIC GOODS

Now we must turn to the range of problems that derive from the fact that certain kinds of output in our system do not have the characteristics of ordinary goods or services because they are not sold. That is, they never enter the market system in the first place, so it is not surprising that the market cannot allocate them. We call such outputs *public goods*. Since public goods are not easy to define, let us start by illustrating the properties of goods such as defense, the national weather service, or lighthouses. Such goods have these peculiar characteristics:

1. **The consumption of a public good by one individual does not interfere with its consumption by another.** A lighthouse is as effective for ten boats as for one. A weather service is as useful for 100 million TV viewers as for 100. By way of contrast, private goods cannot be consumed in the same way. Food, clothing, or doctors' services that I use cannot also be consumed by you.

2. **Private individuals have no control over the use of a public good.** I can deny you the use of my car. There is no way of denying you the use of "my" national defense system, or of "my" road system.

3. **Most important of all, public goods can be provided only by collective decisions.** My private consumption depends on my individual decision to spend or not spend my income. But there is no way that I can, by myself, buy defense, weather services, or a lighthouse service.* We must not only agree to buy the public good or services, but agree *how much* to buy!

Not all public goods are entirely "pure." Highways, education, the law courts, or sanitation services are not so universally available as lighthouses or defense. The amount of education, road space, court time, or garbage service that I consume does affect the amount left over for you. It is possible to exclude some citizens from schools or roads. But even these less perfect examples share in the third basic attribute of public goods: They must all be produced by collective decisions, usually by the voting system of the community.

Free Riding

Because of their characteristics, all public goods share a common difficulty. *Their provision canot be entrusted to the decision-making mechanism of the market.*
In the use of ordinary goods, each person can consume only as much as that person buys. Here the market works very well. The marginal utility of the goods he or she consumes determines how much the buyer will spend. By way of contrast, in the use of public goods, the utility calculus doesn't work. Each person will not buy an amount that he or she really wants, because each can enjoy the goods *someone else* buys. Do not forget that there is no way of excluding others from the use of a pure public good (or from most not-so-pure ones). Therefore each of us would try to get a free ride if we attempted to use the market to determine the level of output.
An example may help. Lighthouse service is a pure public good. Why couldn't we make it a private good? The answer is that no boat owner would be willing to pay what the lighthouse is actually worth to him. Why should he? So long as someone else builds a lighthouse, the boat owner can enjoy its services free!

Voting Instead of Buying

How do we then determine the level of provision of such goods? By eschewing the useless market mechanism and availing ourselves of another means of decision-making voting. **We vote for the amount of public goods we want; and because voting is a curious mechanism, sometimes we oversupply ourselves with these**

---

* Not even if I were immensely rich or an absolute monarch? In that case we would not have a market system, but a command economy catering to one person. Then indeed there would be no distinction between public and private goods.

goods, and sometimes we undersupply ourselves. We swim in defense and starve in prison reform because defense has "friends in Congress" and prisons do not.

Is there a remedy for the problem? Some economists have suggested that we should try to bring as many public goods as possible into the market system by getting rid of their "public" characteristics. We could charge admission to the city's parks, so that we could produce only as much park service as people were willing to buy. We could charge tolls on all roads, even streets, and limit the building or repair of highways to the amount of private demand for road services. We might limit the use of law courts to those who would hire the judge and jury, or ask the police to interfere on behalf of only those citizens who wore a badge attesting to their contribution to the police fund.

Privatizing Public Goods?

Such a **privatization** of public goods might indeed bring the level of their production up, or down, to the amount that we would consume if they were strictly private goods, like cars or movie tickets. The problems are twofold. First, there are innumerable technical difficulties in making many public goods into private ones. Imagine the problems in charging a toll for each city street!

Second, and more arresting, the idea offends our sense of justice. Suppose we could convert defense into a private good. The defense system would then defend only those who bought its services. Presumably the more you bought, the better you would be defended. Few believers in democracy would like to see our national defense converted into a bastion for the rich. Nor would we remove from public use the law courts, the schools, the police, and so on. Unlike private goods, which we have the *privilege* of buying from our incomes, public goods are thought of as our *rights*.

There are valid arguments and clever techniques for returning *some* public goods into the market's fold. **The main point to keep in mind is that it is impossible to make all goods private; and for the ones that should remain public, the market cannot be used to establish a desirable level of output. Here the market mechanism must give way to a political method of making economic decisions.**

EXTERNALITIES

Our next instance of market failure is closely connected with the attributes of public goods. It is the problem of allowing for the "externalities" of production; that is, for the effects of the output of private goods and services on persons other than those who are directly buying or selling or using the goods in question.

Pollution

Externalities bring us to one of the most vexing and sometimes dangerous problems in our economic system — controlling pollution.

What is pollution, from an economic point of view? It is the production of wastes, dirt, noise, congestion, and other things that we do not want. Although we don't think of smoke, smog, traffic din, and traffic jams as part of society's "production," these facts of economic life are certainly the consequence of producing things we do want. Smoke is part of the output process that also gives us steel or cement. Smog arises from the production of industrial energy and heat, among other things. Traffic is a by-product of transportation. In current jargon, economists call these unwanted by-products "bads" to stress their relation to things we call "goods."

"Bads" Escape the Market

Why do externalities exist? The basic answer is technological: We do not know how to produce goods "cleanly"; i.e., without wastes and by-products such as smoke— at least within acceptable cost limitations. But the economic answer calls our attention to another aspect of the problem. **Externalities refer to the fact that the output of bads does not pass through the market system.** A factory may produce smoke, etc., without having to pay anyone for producing these harmful goods. Certain inputs used by firms—air, water, even space in an esthetic rather than economic sense—are available without charge, so that there is no constraint to urge a firm to use air or water sparingly or to build a handsome rather than an ugly factory or building.

In other words, pollution exists because it is the cheapest way to do many things, some having to do with producing goods, some with consuming them. It is cheaper to litter than to buy waste cans (and less trouble, too); cheaper to pour wastes into a river than to clean them up. That is, it is cheaper for the individual or the firm. But it may not be cheaper for the community. A firm may dump its wastes "for free" into a river, but people living downstream will suffer the costs of having to cope with polluted water.

Marginal Private and Social Costs

The point is so fundamental it is worth elaborating. In back of the conception of the marketplace as an *efficient* allocator of goods and incomes is a silent assumption. It is that all the inputs going into the process are owned by some individual and that all the outputs are bought by some person or firm or agency. Presumably, then, the price at which commodities are offered will include all the costs that are incurred in the process. Presumably also, the price that will be offered will reflect all the prospective benefits accruing to the buyer. **In other words, prices established in the marketplace are supposed to take into account *all* the disutilities involved in the process of production, such as fatigue or unpleasantness of work, and *all* the utilities ultimately gained by the final consumer of those goods.**

What the problem of pollution has brought home is that the market is not a means for effectively registering a great many of these costs and benefits. The examples of the damage wrought by smoke that is not charged against the factory or of a neighborhood nuisance such as a loud bar or a hideous advertising sign are instances of economic activities in which *private costs are less than social costs.* These social costs are, of course, private costs incurred by other people. Contrariwise, when a person spends money to educate himself, he benefits not only himself but also the community, partly because he becomes a more productive citizen and partly because he presumably becomes a more responsible one. Thus the *social benefits* of some expenditures may be greater than their *private benefits.*

Some externalities are not "bads," but "goods." A new office building may increase the property value of a neighborhood. Here is a positive externality. The benefit gained by others results from the new building but is not paid to the owners of that building. Such externalities give some private goods the partial attributes of public goods.

CONTROLLING EXTERNALITIES

How can we bring the process of pollution under social control? Basically, we can attack the problem in three ways. We can

1. Regulate the activity that creates it
2. Tax the activity that creates it
3. Subsidize the polluter to stop (or lessen) the activity

1. Regulation

Faced with the ugly view of smoke belching from a factory chimney, sludge pouring from a mill into a lake, automobiles choking a city, or people being injured by contaminants, most ecologically concerned persons cry for regulation: "Pass a law to forbid smoky chimneys or sulfurous coal. Pass a law to make mills dispose of their wastes elsewhere or purify them. Pass a law against automobiles in the central city."

What are the economic effects of regulation? **Essentially the idea behind passing laws is to internalize a previous externality. That is, a regulation seeks to impose a cost on an activity that was previously free for the individual or firm, although not free, as we have seen, for society.** This means that individuals or firms must stop the polluting activity entirely or bear the cost of whatever penalty is imposed by law, or else find ways of carrying out their activities without giving rise to pollution.

Costs of Regulation. Let us take the case of a firm that pollutes the environment as a joint product of producing goods or services. Suppose a regulation is passed, enjoining that firm to install antipollution devices—smoke scrubbers or waste treatment facilities. Who bears this cost?

The answer seems obvious at first look: The firm must bear it. But if the firm passes its higher costs along in higher selling prices, we arrive at a different answer.

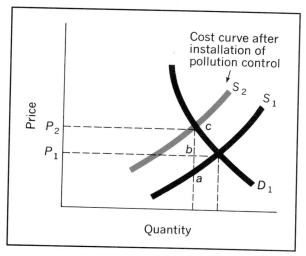

Figure 4

EFFECTS OF REGULATION

Regulation imposes costs on buyers, sellers, and employees. See text if you don't understand why.

Examine Figure 4. Our firm's original marginal cost (or supply) curve is S_1. The need to install new antipollution equipment raises it by an amount ac to S_2. Now a little economic analysis will show us that the cost is in fact borne by three groups, not just by the firm. First, the firm will bear some of the cost because at the higher price, it will sell less output, OY instead of OX. How much less depends on the elasticity of demand for its product. But unless demand is totally inelastic (a vertical line), its sales and income must contract.

Two other groups also bear part of the cost. One group is the factors of production. Fewer factors will be employed because output has fallen. Their loss of income is therefore also a part of the economic cost of antipollution regulation. Last, of course, is the consumer. Prices will rise from P_1 to P_2. Note that consumers lose satisfaction in two ways: They must pay a higher price, bc, for the units that they do buy, and certain consumers are discouraged by the higher price from buying at all. (The satisfaction they lose is measured by the area under the demand curve, abc.)

Gains from Regulations. Offsetting all these costs is the fact that each of these three groups and the general public now have a better environment. There is no reason, however, why each of these three groups, singly or collectively, should think that *its* benefit outweighs *its* costs. Most of the benefit is likely to go to the general public, rather than to the individuals actually involved in the production or consumption of the polluting good or service.

Thus a regulation forcing car manufacturers to make cleaner engines will cost the manufacturers some lost sales, will cost the consumer added expense for a car, and will cost lost income for whatever land, labor, and capital is no longer employed at higher production costs. As part of the public, all three groups will benefit from cleaner air, but each is likely to feel its specific loss more keenly than its general gain.

Is Regulation Useful? Regulations are good or bad, partly depending on their ease of enforcement. Compare the effectiveness of speed limits, which attempt to lessen the externality of accidents, and of regulations against littering. It is difficult enough to enforce speed laws, but it is almost impossible to enforce antilittering laws.

This in turn is largely a matter of cost. If we were prepared to have traffic police posted on every mile of highway or every city block, regulation could be fully effective for speed violations or for littering. Obviously the cost would be horrendous, and so would people's reaction to being overpoliced.

2. Taxation

A second way to cope with pollution is to tax it. When a government decides to tax pollution (often called effluent charges), it is essentially creating a price system for disposal processes. If an individual company found that it could clean up its own pollutants more cheaply than paying the tax, it would do so. If the company could not clean up its own pollutants more cheaply than the tax cost (which is often the case because of economies of scale in pollution control), it would pay the necessary tax and look to the state to clean up the environment.

The effluent charge looks like, but is not, a license to pollute. It is a license that allows you to give some of your pollutants to the state *for a price.*

As a result of effluent charges, an activity that was formerly costless is no longer so. Thus, in terms of their economic impacts, these charges are just like government regulations. In fact, they are a type of government regulation. They raise the supply curve for the good in question, with all the corresponding ramifications. The difference is that each producer can decide whether it pays to install clean-up equipment and not pay the tax, or to pollute and pay whatever tax costs are imposed.

Antipollution Taxes vs. Regulations. Which is better, regulation or taxation? As we have seen, regulation affects all polluters alike, and this is both its strength and its weakness. Taxation enables each polluter to determine what course of action is best. Some polluters will achieve low pollution targets more cheaply by installing antipollution equipment, thereby avoiding taxes on their effluents, while other polluters will find it more profitable to pay the tax.

Here practical considerations are likely to be decisive. For example, taxation on effluents discharged into streams is likely to be more practical than taxation on smoke coming from chimneys. The state can install a sewage treatment plant, but it cannot clean up air that is contaminated by producers who find it cheaper to pay a pollution tax than to install smoke-suppressing equipment. Moreover, to be effective, a pollution tax should vary with the amount of pollution—a paper mill or a utility plant paying more taxes if it increases its output of waste or smoke. One of the problems with taxation is installing monitoring equipment. It is difficult to make accurate measurements of pollution or to allow for differences in environmental harm caused by the same amount of smoke coming from two factories located in different areas.

3. Subsidies

The third way of dealing with pollution is to subsidize polluters to stop polluting. In this case the government actually pays the offending parties to clean up the damage they have caused or to stop causing it. For example, a township might lower the taxes on a firm that agreed to install filters on its stacks. This is, of course, paying the firm to stop polluting.

Economists typically object to subsidies because they camouflage the true economic costs of producing goods and services cleanly. When regulations or taxes increase the price of paper or steel, the individual or firm becomes aware that the environment is not free and that there may be heavy costs in producing goods in a way that will not damage the environment. The increased price will lead them to demand less of these goods. But when they get clean environment through the allocation of a portion of taxes, there is no price signal to show them the cost of pollution associated with particular commodities.

Nevertheless, there are cases when subsidies may be the easiest way to avoid pollution. For example, it might be more effective to pay homeowners to turn in old cans and bottles than to try to regulate their garbage disposal habits or to tax them for each bottle or can thrown away. Subsidies may therefore sometimes be expedient means of achieving a desired end, even if they may not be the most desirable means from other points of view.

Externalities in Review

In one way, the problem of externalities differs markedly from the problem of public goods. The difference is that it is possible to allow the market system itself to handle the otherwise hidden costs of pollution by using the various techniques we have examined.

Therefore, in offsetting externalities in the production of private goods, we avoid some of the arbitrariness that troubles us in the provision of public goods. We can internalize the costs of pollution in a way that we cannot privatize the costs or benefits of pure public goods.

Nonetheless, we must keep in mind one theme of this chapter. It is that a market system has weak spots or ineffective areas peculiar to its institutional nature. Its inability to put a price on external effects or to give a producer the rewards of producing external benefits means that the system, left to itself, may work poorly or even dangerously. The remedy requires political intervention of one kind or another—regulation, taxation, or subsidy. As we have seen, practical considerations determine which method is likely to be the best.

Market Strengths and Weaknesses

This is not a conclusion that should be interpreted as a kind of general plea for more government. Many economists who severely criticize the market want less government—certainly less bureaucratic, nonparticipatory, nondemocratic government. The point, however, is to recognize that the existence and causes of market malfunction make some government intervention inescapable. We can then seek to use government power to repair individual market failures in order to strengthen the operation of the system as a whole.

After so much criticism of the market system, perhaps it is well to conclude by recalling its strengths. Basically they are two. **First, the market encourages individuals to exert energies, skills, ambition, and risk-taking in the economic pursuits of life. This gives to market systems a high degree of flexibility, vitality, inventiveness, and change.** For all their failures, market economies have displayed astonishing growth, and the source of that growth lies ultimately in the activities of their marketers.

Second, the system minimizes the need for government supervision, although for reasons we now understand it cannot dispense with it. It would be a mistake to suppose that every instance of government intervention is an abridgment of freedom, or that every area of market activity is an exemplar of liberty. The truth is that government and market are equally capable of promoting liberty or giving rise to oppression. Nonetheless, in a world in which the concentration of government power has been one of the greatest scourges of humankind, there is clearly something to be said for a mechanism capable of handling the basic economic tasks of society without exaggerated dependence on political authority.

looking back

KEY CONCEPTS	This chapter is a very important complement to our previous chapters. There we stressed the advantages of the market as a rationing device. Here we point out its shortcomings or inadequacies.
Inadequate information yields poor market results	1 The first class of serious market failure arises from inadequate or erroneous information. Without correct information, marketers cannot make correct decisions and market results may be seriously deficient.
Cobwebs result from erroneous expectations	2 One consequence of inadequate information is a tendency to generate instability under certain conditions. The most interesting of these is the cobweb, where prices may rise and fall and may never zero in on equilibrium.
Expectations can also lead to inflationary markets	3 Cobwebs in turn reveal the importance of expectations in making markets work smoothly. When expectations are inflationary we get perverse behavior, where rising prices make the entire demand curve shift outward. This can be an important element in perpetuating inflation.

Public goods escape the market and cause free riding. Privatization is sometimes possible but may offend our sense of justice

4 A second large category of market failure arises when the market cannot allocate at all because outputs have no price. One of these cases concerns public goods—goods collectively bought. Public goods result in free riding. In some cases this can be corrected by privatizing public outputs. Often, however, we do not wish to sell public goods because they are deemed to be a citizen's right, and therefore felt to be properly available without specific charge.

Externalities are "bads" that exist because there is no charge based on polluting behavior

5 Externalities have certain of the attributes of public goods. The production of "bads" is a kind of free ride for polluters. Pollution arises because there is no way of charging for the "bads" that production or consumption create—the litter a consumer throws on the road, the smoke a factory generates, the congestion to which each automobile adds.

Regulation, taxation, and subsidy are three ways of coping with externalities

6 There are three basic ways of coping with externalities. The first is to regulate; the second is to tax; the third is to subsidize. No one of these is always superior to the others, but each has its strengths and weaknesses. Each situation must be judged separately to discover which method is most likely to be effective.

ECONOMIC VOCABULARY

Rational maximizing   478
Cobwebs   479
Perverse reactions   480
Public goods   482
Free riding   483
Privatization   484

Externalities   484
Bads   485
Regulation   486
Taxation   488
Subsidies   489

QUESTIONS

1. As a seller who seeks to maximize, would you increase or decrease your offerings if prices rose and you expected them to rise further? Suppose you expected them to fall—then what is your rational maximizing response?

2. Can you imagine an industrial process that might result in a cobweb? How about a process in which you had to make heavy commitments in plant and equipment

long before production actually took place? Suppose hydroponic farming takes over, so that agriculture becomes more industrialized and less dependent on seasons. Would you expect the cobweb type of reaction to become less common? Why?

3. Explain the mechanism of a free ride. Are there free rides in private goods? How about window displays? Skywriting?

4. Explain carefully why the market system will not work in supplying the appropriate level of goods that have "public" characteristics.

5. What kinds of public goods do you think should be made private? The national parks? Public schools? Public beaches? Public hospitals? (By "private," we mean charging a user fee sufficient to cover costs). Explain your preference in each case.

6. Can you think of an externality imposed by a producer on a consumer? (That's easy.) One imposed by one producer on another? One consumer on another?

7. What do you think would be the best way to handle the following externalities: (1) a smoky factory, (2) roadside littering, (3) overfishing a pond, (4) noise from an airport, (5) radiation hazards in a hospital, (6) billboards, (7) pornography, (8) overcutting forests, (9) noise from motorcycles, (10) disruption to traffic caused by parades. In each case, discuss the relative advantages of regulation, taxation, and subsidy.

CHAPTER 28
Operating a Competitive Firm: I

a look ahead

With Chapter 28 we begin a new section in our microeconomic studies. We leave behind the market mechanism as a whole (though we return to it in the Challenge section ahead) to consider an area of microeconomics heretofore unexamined. This is the manner in which the basic unit of production, the competitive business firm, is run. In this and the next chapter we take a look at this kind of firm and go over the ground at two levels of abstraction. Then in Chapter 30 we move to a tour of big business, and of smaller but less than perfectly competitive firms. And last, in Chapter 31, we apply our microeconomic scrutiny to taxing and government spending. There we shall find that the vocabulary and techniques we have mastered will apply to the public as well as the private sector.

In this chapter we meet for the first time a decisive economic personage. This is the entrepreneur, the person who makes the decisions that affect the business enterprise. Our task in this chapter is to analyze the three main tasks the entrepreneur must carry out.

1 Deciding on the scale of operations.
2 Combining the factors of production as profitably as possible.
3 Determining the volume of output.

In this visit we do no more than familiarize ourselves with the entrepreneur's task in general terms. In Chapter 29 we return, pad and pencil in hand, to calculate the firm's course.

M ost of us have firsthand knowledge of the household, whose role is crucial in determining the demand for goods. We know a lot less about the firm, whose function is to supply us with goods. In this chapter we enter the gates of a competitive firm for a quick look around. We will come back in our next chapter to study the operation in greater detail.

ECONOMICS OF THE FIRM

The first person we encounter inside the factory gates is an economic personage we have not previously studied. It is the boss of the works, the organizer of the firm, the *entrepreneur*.

Entrepreneurship

An entrepreneur is not necessarily a capitalist; that is, the person who has supplied capital to the business. The entrepreneur may act as the risker of capital, but so may a bank. The capitalist may be a group of people who have lent money to the business but never visited the premises. **An entrepreneur provides a service that is essentially different from that of putting up capital. His or her contribution is** *organizational.* Indeed, some economists have suggested that it is proper to think of four factors of production: labor, land, capital, and entrepreneurship, instead of the traditional first three alone.

Economic Profit

As a fourth factor of production, the entrepreneur is paid a wage, *the wage of management.* It can, of course, be very high, since entrepreneurship is a valuable skill, the skill of maximizing a firm's *economic profit.*

This is not the profit of everyday usage. In ordinary usage we call "profit" any sum left over after a firm has paid its wages and salaries, rents, cost of materials, taxes, etc. Included in that ordinary profit is an amount an economist excludes from the definition of a true economic profit. This is the interest owed to the capitalist for the use of his or her capital. In other words, if a firm has a plant and equipment worth $1 million and makes a profit of $50,000, an economist, before declaring the $50,000 to be a true economic profit, would first ask whether the firm had taken into account the interest owing to it on this capital. If interest rates were 5 percent, and no such allowance had been made (and it usually is not the ordinary accounting practice when the firm owns its own capital), an economist would say that no economic profits were earned. **Economic profit is what is left after paying all explicit costs and after allowing for implicit interest. It is the final residual.**

Our analysis shows us how an entrepreneur tries to create economic profits after appropriately remunerating all the factors, including capitalists, and how the operation of the market constantly tends to make this economic profit disappear, despite the best entrepreneurial efforts. (That will become clear in our next chapter, rather than in this one.)

One last point. Who gets the residual? It goes to the owner of the business, who is legally entitled to any profits it enjoys. That owner, as we have said, may or may not be the entrepreneur. In a cooperatively owned factory it might be the work force. Usually it is a proprietor, a group of partners, or shareholders including, of course, the management, to the extent that it owns shares. In all cases this residual economic profit is over and above any recompense for the services these factors supply, including the service of making capital available.

THE TASKS OF THE ENTREPRENEUR

What does our entrepreneur do for his or her wages of management?* In actual practice, he will do many things: bargaining with labor unions, establishing credit lines with a bank, arranging complex real estate deals, hiring production and design experts, gauging "what the market will bear" when it comes to pricing and selling output. Some of these tasks we shall investigate in Chapter 30, when we look into the operation of firms that are not perfectly competitive.

But we must begin with a simpler model. We are going to start by analyzing the basic tasks of an entrepreneur in an environment of *pure competition.* As we see later, this is more the exception than the rule. Nevertheless, studying the operation of a firm in pure competition reveals more clearly than any other model the essential tasks of entrepreneurship.

Pure Competition

Exactly what do we mean by pure competition? In general, economists mean three things:

1. LARGE NUMBERS OF SELLERS OR FIRMS. A *monopoly,* as we shall see in Chapter 30, means there is only one firm in an industry. An *oligopoly* means there are a few firms. **But a competitive market means that there are many firms. By "many" we mean enough so that no single firm by itself can affect the prices it pays for the factors of production or the prices it receives for its output, regardless of how much or how little it produces.**

---

* *His or her* is an important point to make, but tedious to repeat. We mainly use the male pronoun for convenience sake. We ought to note, however, that there are plenty of women entrepreneurs, especially in retail trade, and their numbers are increasing.

Are there such markets? Of course. Farms operate in a market situation very close to that of pure competition. So do many small businesses, where the field is so numerous each entrepreneur knows that he or she has no power to influence the market for the firm's outputs.

2. EASY ENTRY AND EXIT. A competitive industry is not only characterized by large numbers of firms. **It is also an industry into which new firms can move with ease and out of which unsuccessful firms can easily exit.**

This has very important consequences for the conduct of business. We can readily see why: In a competitive industry, if profits are high there will soon be an invasion of entrepreneurs from other fields seeking to reap some of that profit. If business is bad, there will be a general exodus toward greener pastures.

3. THE OUTPUTS OF COMPETITIVE FIRMS ARE UNDIFFERENTIATED. A differentiated output is one that is recognizable as belonging to its producer. A cereal with a brand name, an automobile with a distinctive look, and fashion garments with their labels are all differentiated goods. The ability of a producer to differentiate his output gives him the ability to gain a loyal clientele and to charge prices that may differ from those of competitors.

No such advantage of differentiation exists in a market characterized by pure competition. One output is exactly like another. Thus, wheat is wheat and bears no identification of the farm it comes from; paper clips are paper clips (although they may have differentiated boxes); coal is coal; one taxi ride is like another.

The absence of product differentiation carries a consequence of great importance. It means that competition among firms must be carried out entirely by trying to beat the prices offered by rivals. There is no way of attracting buyers to a particular output except by price.

Pure Competition and the Entrepreneur

As we can see, the conditions for pure competition are stringent indeed. In effect, they rob the entrepreneur, as the chief executive of the business, of much of the power he would like to have (and that he *does* have in industries which are not so competitive, as we shall see). In fact, in a market of pure competition — farming, much wholesale trading, or small retail business for example — the operating powers of an entrepreneur are reduced to three:

1. **The entrepreneur can decide on the scale of the enterprise.**
2. **He can determine how best to combine the factors of production.**
3. **He can choose the level of output that will maximize profits.**

And that is all he can do! There is no chance of striking a special arrangement with the factors of production, such as signing a sweetheart contract with a labor union.

There is no point in hiring a design expert or an advertising firm because it is impossible to differentiate his firm's corn, or paper notebooks, or wire coat hangers from his competitors'. There is no strategy in pricing because if he is as much as a penny over his competitors, he will not sell any of his production.

HOW AN ENTREPRENEUR OPERATES

What does an entrepreneur actually do under such demanding conditions?

Task No. 1: The Decision on Scale

The first task lies in the determination of the scale of output — how big the firm is to be. In each industry a certain minimum size, mainly dictated by technology, is needed to operate in the existing market. Suppose we were considering opening a bookstore. A bookstore may be very small, but it must occupy *some* space. It must stock a reasonable number of books and someone must sell them. If we were in agriculture, we would need a farm of at least a certain area, depending on the crop, and a basic amount of capital in the form of buildings, equipment, fertilizer, seed. If we were in manufacturing, there would be a minimum size of plant or machinery essential for our operation. If we were in a mass production business, such as steel, the smallest efficient plant might run into an investment of millions of dollars and a work force of thousands; but that would take us well out of the world of atomistic competition to which we are still devoting our attention.

In other words, the first decision of an entrepreneur involves the physical (or engineering) fact that there is a certain amount of each factor that we must hire for technical reasons. This is what we mean by minimum scale. If problems of scale did not exist, we could produce television sets as efficiently in a garage as in a vast plant or raise cattle as cheaply in our backyard as on a range.

Economies of Scale. The choice of a scale of operation has important consequences for the costs the entrepreneur's firm will incur. Every plant has a cost curve that describes how much it costs to produce one unit of output at various levels of production. In Figure 1 we see such a curve. Notice that when we are producing only small quantities (such as OX), the cost for each unit of output is high (OY); and that costs per unit typically fall as production increases, after which they eventually rise again. This produces a dish-shaped curve.

We will learn a lot more about curves as we move along. Here we should note that a cost curve applies to a given scale of output. A bigger plant may well lower unit costs because it can utilize technologies in large-scale production that are unavailable to small producers. If a small firm is successful, it may be able to

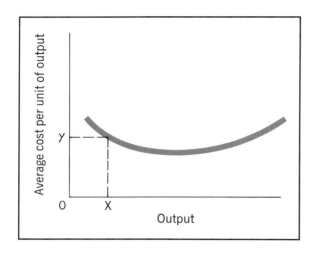

Figure 1
TYPICAL AVERAGE COST CURVE

A curve of average costs usually falls at first and then rises. We call such curves "dish-shaped" or "U-shaped." Remember that they show how average costs change as we vary output. Total cost is shown by multiplying average cost by the number of units produced. At output OX, total cost is OY × OX.

gain these *economies* of scale by building a larger plant. In Figure 2 we show how successively bigger plants can reduce costs, at least up to a point where the limits of efficiency are reached and mounting costs per unit of output are encountered, creating *diseconomies of scale.*

The actual choice of an appropriate scale of plant is more important for big, oligopolistic firms than for small, competitive ones. But even in atomistic competition there are decisions to be made with regard to scale. A farmer has to decide whether to build another barn. A stationery store owner has to decide whether to buy additional space. The decision on scale, with its economies and its diseconomies, is a very important first task of entrepreneurship.

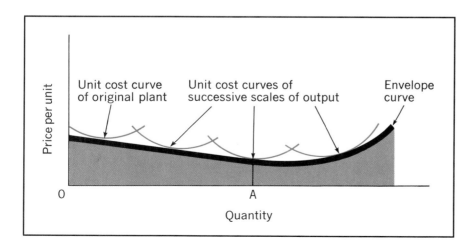

Figure 2
LONG-RUN COST CURVE OR ENVELOPE CURVE

Cost curves change as the scale of output changes. This long-run cost curve, or "envelope" curve, shows how a larger scale first lowers unit costs, then increases them. These curves refer to individual plants, not to firms, which may have many plants.

Task No. 2: Combining the Factors

Having chosen the appropriate scale, our entrepreneur now has to make two decisions on how to combine labor, land, and capital; or in more ordinary business language, how much to pay in wages, rent, and interest.

The Profitability Rule: MR > MC. The first decision is whether it is profitable to hire a given factor, say an additional salesperson or an additional amount of inventory. This decision is very simple to make. Our entrepreneur merely compares two figures: (1) the cost of adding the additional factor; and (2) the income he expects to gain from the additional factor. In economic language, he compares the marginal cost of a factor with the marginal revenue he expects from the factor.

By "marginal" we mean the additional cost or the additional revenue in question. If he is thinking of taking on a salesperson and the wage for salesclerks is $10,000, then the marginal cost of such a unit of labor is $10,000. Obviously the person will not be hired unless the entrepreneur expects that the clerk will bring into the firm at least $10,000 of marginal revenue—that is, of additional income.

Hence the cardinal rule for hiring is: Compare marginal cost and marginal revenue. If marginal revenue is greater than marginal cost, hire the factor. If not, get rid of the factor because it is costing more than its keep.

Comparing Factor Returns. And now for the second decision. Assuming that marginal revenue is greater than marginal cost for all factors, the entrepreneur has to decide whether to spend the firm's money on one factor or another. Suppose an additional salesperson costs $10,000 and is expected to bring in $12,000 of additional income; 100 square feet of space would cost $1,000 and would yield $1,300 of new income; and a new piece of equipment would cost $10,000 but would increase revenues by $15,000.

Here all the factors are profitable buys. But which is the *most* profitable? The answer is not difficult. Our entrepreneur simply compares the return per dollar for each factor or the percentage return on each factor. A dollar of additional labor cost brings in $1.20 ($12,000 of revenue divided by $10,000 of cost); a dollar of space brings in $1.30 ($1,300 divided by $1,000); and a dollar of capital expense yields $1.50. Clearly the most profitable use of the firm's money will be to use it all on equipment as long as the ratios of marginal cost and marginal revenue stay the same.

Maximizing Profits. Will they stay the same? No. For reasons we will investigate more closely in the next chapter, they will not. As the entrepreneur hires more and more equipment (or more and more of any one factor), its marginal revenue will eventually decline because it will be used beyond the point of greatest efficiency. Our entrepreneur will then switch to some other factor that has become more profitable at the margin. In the end he will maximize his profits by mixing factors so that their marginal returns are all equal, with no special advantage accruing to any one.

Here is a rule to remember. The entrepreneur maximizes profits first by seeking equal marginal revenues.* If returns at the margin are not equal, there must exist opportunities for greater profit by adding more of the factor whose marginal return is highest. This is true whether the entrepreneur is running a competitive business or a monopoly. It is how the entrepreneur ensures that the firm will be as efficient as possible, getting as much return as possible from every dollar it spends.

Task No. 3: Determining the Level of Output

Now we come to the last and most complicated part of the entrepreneur's task. We have seen how he or she determines the initial scale of the enterprise, and how he or she decides whether to hire factors, and if so, which factors to hire. Now we must see how the entrepreneur determines how much output to produce.

The basic rule for determining output is very simple, and resembles the basic rule for hiring factors. An entrepreneur is constantly comparing marginal costs and marginal revenues for his output, just as he is comparing them for the factors he hires. The price at which he sells his last unit of output is his marginal revenue. The amount it costs him to produce that last unit of output is his marginal cost.

It's not difficult to see that he will decide on his volume of production by comparing the two. **If marginal revenue *(MR)* is greater than marginal cost *(MC)*, he will be making money on that unit of output and he will want to increase his production to make more money. If *MR* is less than *MC*, he will be losing money on his marginal output and he will want to contract production.**

The Marginal Revenue Curve.   It is possible to describe this task of the entrepreneur in a very revealing and helpful graph. Let us start by showing what marginal revenue looks like to a farmer, small businessman, or other competitive entrepreneur.

Remember, the conditions of pure competition rule out any possibility that the small firm, by itself, could affect the level of prices. The prices of wheat or corn, paper clips or coal are just *there,* and the entrepreneur has no choice but to take them as the market offers them. Therefore, the demand curve for his product looks to him like Figure 3. It is a horizontal line showing that the market will absorb all the corn or paper clips he can produce at a given price. The price may not be a profitable one, but that is another matter we will look into in the next chapter.

The point is that the competitive firm's selling price does not change, whatever its levels of output. Each unit therefore brings in exactly as much revenue as the one before or after. That is why its marginal revenue curve is a horizontal line. When we study monopolies and oligopolies we will see that this is not the case for them.

---

* This is just like a consumer seeking to maximize total utilities by equating the marginal enjoyments of different goods. See "An Extra Word" to Chapter 25.

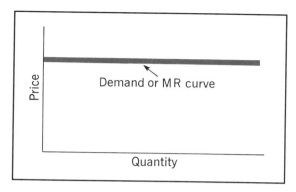

Figure 3

DEMAND CURVE FOR A COMPETITIVE FIRM

Because a competitive firm by definition cannot affect the market whether it sells all or nothing at all, each unit of item will fetch the same price. Therefore the marginal revenue of each unit will be the same. This means that the demand curve and the marginal revenue curve are one and the same — perfectly elastic, horizontal lines.

The Marginal Cost Curve. Perhaps we can anticipate what comes next. We are going to discover what the marginal cost curve looks like, and by putting that curve against the marginal revenue curve, we will find out how the entrepreneur solves his third task, determining the level of output.

We already know that *average* costs of output give us a dish- or U-shaped curve (refer back to Figure 1 if you've forgotten). Not until the next chapter will we analyze the reasons for the similar shape of the marginal cost curve. But in this first look around a competitive plant, it will suffice if we intuitively understand that it's likely to cost an entrepreneur a lot to start up production, so that marginal costs per unit — the cost of each additional unit — are apt to start out high. We can further see that it is plausible for marginal costs to fall as output gets up to the levels for which the scale of the plant is designed; and that marginal costs are likely to rise beyond that point. Thus we get the idea that a marginal cost curve will look like Figure 4.

Marginal Revenue and Marginal Cost. Finally we have all the information we need to understand how an entrepreneur performs the last of this three basic tasks.

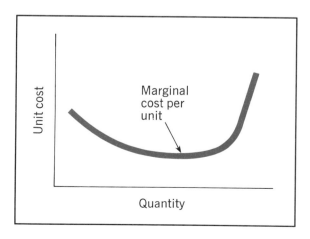

Figure 4

A TYPICAL MARGINAL COST CURVE

A marginal cost curve shows the additional costs of each unit as we increase output. Usually the marginal cost of the first units is high; then it falls; and finally rises, often sharply. Our next chapter will analyze this curve more carefully.

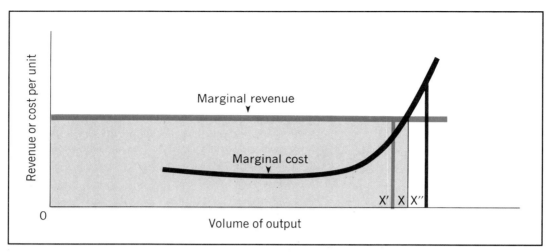

Figure 5
POINT OF OPTIMUM OUTPUT
Marginal cost and marginal revenue provide the guide to the level of output where profit is maximized. Think about costs and revenues for units marked X' and X''. Can you see why X' makes money and X'' does not? What should the entrepreneur do in each case?

We have a marginal cost profile that tells us what happens to unit costs as we hire or fire factors. We have a marginal revenue profile that tells us what happens to the firm's income as we do the same. It remains only to put the two together to discover just how much output a firm should make to maximize its profits.

We can do this very simply by superimposing the revenue diagram on the cost diagram. **The point where marginal revenue and marginal cost meet indicates exactly where the most profitable volume of output lies.** If our entrepreneur was producing to the left of this point, he would be missing the chance of making more money by expanding output. We can see that this is the case because up to point *OX* in Figure 5 each additional (marginal) unit of production will bring in more than it costs. If production goes beyond *OX*, on the other hand, the entrepreneur will have miscalculated, because each unit of output beyond *OX* will cost more than it yields.

End of the Tour

There is a great deal that remains to be explained. Is our firm making money? Why do the curves have the shapes they do? Is there an equilibrium level of operation for the firm?

These questions will necessitate a second trip with pad and pencil in hand, ready to do some calculations. Our first visit has prepared the way by showing us in bold terms what the entrepreneur has to do; now we should be ready to put ourselves more directly into his or her shoes.

looking back

KEY CONCEPTS

The entrepreneur seeks an economic profit

1 The key person within the firm is the entrepreneur, the organizer of production. The entrepreneur (who may or may not be a capitalist) seeks to make an economic profit. An economic profit is a residual—what is left after paying all costs, including the implicit costs of interest on the firm's capital.

Three conditions of pure competition: large numbers; easy entry and exit; no product differentiation.

Competition by price alone

2 We are first going to study the entrepreneur's task under pure competition. Pure competition refers to a market in which three conditions prevail: a large number of firms; easy entry or exit of firms; and no differentiated products. The only competitive weapon available to the firm is therefore price.

Three entrepreneurial tasks: Choosing the right scale

3 The entrepreneur in such a competitive milieu has only three variables under his command. The first is scale. A plant must be the right size to enter the market in the first place.

Hiring factors if their $MR > MC$. The factor whose profitability is highest is always hired

4 Second, the entrepreneur must combine factors as profitably as possible to get costs as low as possible. He does so by applying two simple rules. (a) He hires a factor only if its marginal revenue is greater than its marginal cost (if $MR > MC$). (b) He always hires the factor whose profitability is greatest, giving the largest return per dollar of cost.

Expanding output until $MC = MR$

5 Third, the entrepreneur determines the level of output. He does this by comparing the marginal cost of each unit of additional output with the marginal revenue obtained from that unit. The marginal cost of most firms has a dish or U shape. We shall investigate the reasons for this more carefully in the next chapter. By expanding output until marginal revenue equals marginal cost, the entrepreneur maximizes the firm's profit.

ECONOMIC VOCABULARY

Entrepreneur 494
Economic profit 494
Pure competition 495
Entry and exit 496
Undifferentiated output 496
Scale 497

Economies of scale 497
Marginal cost 499
Marginal revenue 499
Profitability rule: $MR > MC$ 499
MR curve 500
MC curve 500

QUESTIONS

1. Suppose you were about to open a small business—say a drugstore. What do you think would be the factors critical in determining the scale of your operation? Suppose it were a farm? A factory?

2. Why does pure competition require a large number of sellers? Does this mean that a drugstore is not competitive if it is the only such store in town? What does this suggest about the difficulties of defining a market?

3. Which of the three conditions for pure competition do you think is missing from the following industries: (a) aircraft construction; (b) fashion design; (c) gold mining?

4. Suppose a manufacturer had the following alternatives. It would be possible to (a) spend $1,000 on a machine that would add 115 units to sales (each unit selling at $10); (b) spend $5,000 to hire a new worker who would increase output by 510 units; (c) rent new space for $10,000 that would make possible an increase in output of 1,100 units. How would one know which was the best factor to hire? Show that the manufacturer would begin by asking what the dollar return would be per dollar of cost for each factor. What is this in the case of the machine? The new worker? The land?

5. Why is the demand curve the same as the marginal revenue curve for a manufacturer of wire coat hangers? Draw the demand curve for such a firm. Draw a separate diagram for its marginal revenue curve. Are they exactly the same? (They should be.)

6. Superimpose a firm's MR curve on its MC curve and explain carefully why the point of highest profit is where the curves intersect.

AN EXTRA WORD ABOUT

Helping the Farmer

The farmer is the very prototype of the entrepreneur of a competitive firm. But farming is an industry with very special problems. Traditionally, it has been a trouble-ridden occupation. All through the 1920s, the farmer was the "sick man" of the American economy. Each year saw more farmers going into tenantry, until by 1929 four out of ten farmers in the nation were no longer independent operators. Each year the farmer seemed to fall further behind the city dweller in terms of relative well-being. In 1910 the income per worker on the farm had been not quite 40 percent of the nonfarm worker. By 1930, it was just under 30 percent.

Part of this trouble on the farm, without question, stemmed from the difficult heritage of the past. Beset now by drought, now by the exploitation of powerful railroad and storage combines, now by his own penchant for land speculation, the farmer was proverbially an ailing member of the economy. In addition, American farmers had traditionally been careless of the earth, indifferent to the technology of agriculture. They were not model entrepreneurs. Between 1910 and 1920, for instance, while nonfarm output per worker rose by nearly 20 percent, output per farm worker actually fell. Between 1920 and 1930, farm productivity improved somewhat, but not nearly so fast as productivity off the farm. For the great majority of the nation's agricultural producers, the trouble appeared to be that they could not grow or raise enough to make a decent living.

INELASTIC DEMAND

If we had looked at farming as a whole, however, a very different answer would have suggested itself. Suppose farm productivity *had* kept pace with that of the nation. Would farm income as a whole have risen? The answer is disconcerting. The *demand* for farm products was quite unlike that for manufactured products generally. In the manufacturing sector, when productivity rose and costs accordingly fell, the cheaper prices of manufactured goods attracted vast new markets, as with the Ford car. Not so with farm products, however. When food prices fell, people did not tend to increase their actual consumption very greatly. Increases in overall farm output resulted in much lower prices but not in larger cash receipts for the farmer. Faced with an *inelastic demand,* a flood of output only leaves sellers *worse* off than before.

That is very much what happened during the 1920s. From 1915 to 1920, the farmer prospered because World War I greatly increased the demand for his product. Prices for farm output rose, and his cash receipts rose as well; in fact, they more than doubled. Following the war, when European farms resumed production, American farm crops simply glutted the market. Although prices fell precipitously (40 percent in the single year 1920–21), the purchases of farm products did not respond in anything like equal measure. As a result, the cash receipts of the farmer toppled almost as fast as prices. In turn, an ailing farm sector contributed to a general economic weakness that would culminate in the Great Depression.

THE NEW DEAL

At its core, the trouble with the farm sector was that the market mechanism did not yield a satisfactory result for farmers. Two causes were evident. One was the inelastic demand for food. The second was the inability of a vast, highly competitive industry like agriculture to limit its own output, so that it would not constantly "break the market" every time a bumper crop was harvested.

This chronic condition of agriculture was one of the first problems attended to by Franklin Roosevelt's New Deal administration. The New Deal could not alter the first cause, the inelasticity of demand, for that arose from the nature of the consumer's desire for food. It could change the condition of supply, which hurled itself, self-destructively, against an unyielding demand. One of the earliest pieces of New Deal legislation — the Agricultural Adjustment Act — sought to establish machinery to be used by farmers, as a group, to accomplish what they could not do as competitive individuals: curtail output.

The curtailment was sought by offering payments to farmers who agreed to cut back their acreage or in other ways hold down their output. In the first year of the act there was no time to cut back acreage, so that every fourth row of growing cotton had to be plowed under, and 6 million pigs were slaughtered. In a nation hungry and ill-clad, such a spectacle of waste aroused sardonic and bitter comment. Yet if the program reflected an appalling inability of a society to handle its distribution problem, its attack on overproduction was not without results. In both 1934 and 1935 more than 30 million acres were taken out of production in return for government payments of $1.1 billion. Farm prices rose as a result. Wheat, having slumped to 38¢ a bushel in 1932, rose to $1.02 in 1936. Cotton doubled in price, hog prices tripled, and the net income of the American farmer climbed from the fearful low of $2.5 billion in 1932 to $5 billion in 1936.

SUPPORT PRICES

Later the New Deal sought to raise farm incomes by establishing *support prices* at which the government would, if necessary, buy farm output. Because the New Deal sought to raise incomes, not to stabilize production, these prices were set at a level *higher* than equilibrium market prices. Given these support prices, farmers could confidently plan their future production, since they knew their output would be bought. But because prices were above equilibrium levels, they chose to grow more than the consumer was willing to consume at the support price. In other words, surpluses emerged, as in Figure 6.

To avoid these surpluses, the government limited the acreage that farmers could plant if they wanted to qualify for support payments, as Figure 7 shows. The strategy might have worked were it not for the extraordinary increase in agricultural productivity resulting from new technologies. Between 1940 and the late 1960s, harvested acreage declined by 15 percent, but the yield per acre increased by over *70 percent.* The result was a flood of output. Huge quantities had to be purchased and stored by the government. Only the massive distribution of these supplies to the underdeveloped lands during the early 1960s prevented the surplus problem from becoming a permanent national embarrassment.

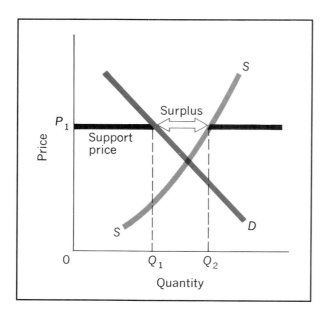

Figure 6
PRICE SUPPORT SURPLUS

At support price P_1 consumers want to buy quantity Q_1. Farmers, however, produce quantity QQ_2. The difference, Q_1Q_2, has to be bought and stored by the government. In 1960, government warehouses bulged with unsold crops worth $6 billion.

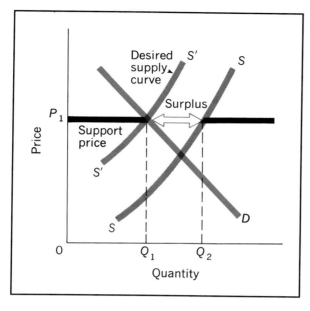

Figure 7
THE EFFORT TO LIMIT SUPPLY
The government tried to eliminate the surplus by restricting acreage. It sought to move SS to S'S' to bring about equilibrium output OQ_1.

PRICE CONTROLS ON FOOD?

Whenever food prices rise, we hear the cry for price controls on food. Would such a "freeze" help?

If food prices were at or above their equilibrium levels when controls were imposed and if these equilibrium levels were not changing, price freezes would have no immediate impact, since they would be the same prices that the market would have sooner or later set. Let us assume that this is not the case and that the controls are going to hold some prices below their equilibrium level, as in Figure 8.

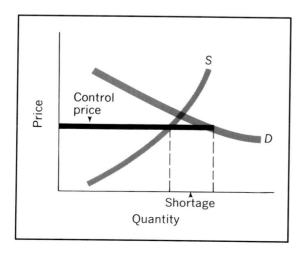

Figure 8
PRICE CONTROLS
Price ceilings below equilibrium create shortages.

As we have seen, whenever prices are held below their equilibrium level, shortages will occur; that is, people will want to buy more of the commodity than suppliers are willing to supply. Since price is not being used to ration the existing supplies, some other technique must be found. The only alternatives are to distribute goods and services on a first-come, first-served basis or to establish formal rationing. Note that if government control procedures break down and black markets are established, *we are right back to rationing by prices.* The only difference is that in the black market, prices are illegal. Purchasers or sellers at these illegal prices can be thrown in jail.

If formal rationing is used, governments seek to reduce the demand curve for the commodity by insisting you must have both money *and* ration coupons to buy a pound of beefsteak. By limiting the amount of beef covered by ration coupons to the known supply of beef, it becomes possible to push the demand curve back to the point where it just crosses the supply curve at the desired price. The problem with this procedure is that the farmer now has no incentive to expand production. The only way he will produce more is if he is able to get a higher price. Thus the controls that reduce the price of food retard the expansion of the food supply.

Suppose, instead, that we ration on a first-come, first-served basis. Now the problem is the opportunity cost of shopping time. The price of purchasing a good is now the money you must pay, plus the time you must wait in line to get what you want. For most people, beefsteak that sells for 50¢ per pound but requires a 2-hour wait in line is not cheap beefsteak.

Now let's assume that the farmer has the option of selling his production to foreigners as well as to Americans. A freeze on retail prices is not a freeze on prices on the farm. Foreign buyers can therefore offer farmers more than American retailers can. Accordingly, farmers sell their crops to foreign buyers. This not only leads to greater U.S. shortages, but can also create other problems. After the freeze is established, suppose soybean prices rise because of foreign demand. With higher soybean prices, U.S. chicken growers may find that chickens sell below the cost of feeding them. If this occurs, they will stop raising chickens and further aggravate the shortage of meat. Another possibility is that producers may simply hang onto their production, waiting for the freeze to be lifted. If cattle are withheld from the market, for example, shortages are once again exacerbated.

As a result, there are a host of adverse consequences stemming from the effort to control the increase in retail food prices. If retail controls are to be effective in holding prices below their equilibrium levels, they require formal rationing as a complement to price ceilings, plus some nonprice effort to increase the supply of foodstuffs. Eliminating acreage controls would be one nonprice action to increase production in the face of a price freeze.

THE FARM PICTURE IN PERSPECTIVE

As any agricultural economist can tell you, the farmer leads anything but a serene life. He must make difficult guesses about the course of prices years into the future. Prices take large swings, seldom settle into stable patterns, and may not be a very good guide to the future.

Yet, in all this it is important to gain a sense of long-term perspective. We have seen that the farmer, unable to control economic swings, has traditionally been their victim. What we have tried to do in the last four decades is to intervene in the market process to make it yield results more in accord with our conceptions of social justice. Despite all the difficulties we have discussed, the results are substantial. In 1940 only a third of all farm families had electricity and only a quarter had telephones. Today these are virtually ubiquitous. The standard of living of the independent farm operator is today close to that of urban middle-class families.

The important lesson is that it is possible to intervene in the market process to bring about desired social ends, although as our discussion should have made clear, the process of intervention is far from simple and full of unexpected pitfalls.

It would be misleading, however, to leave this brief discussion of farming with the impression that all is now well. Small-scale farming (say under 200 acres), once the mainstay of the American economy, is in a precarious state, and the majority of the million-odd small farmers now depend as much or more on income from nonfarm jobs — perhaps tending a gas pump — as they do on selling their small crops. Middle-scale farming (200 to 500 acres), as we have mentioned, is sorely pressed by rising costs and heavy debts. Meanwhile the importance of food exports has steadily increased as a portion of total American foreign sales. The farm sector is today severely hurt by the high dollar, which costs us much of our traditional export market. How much of this will return with the dollar's eventual decline, we do not know. The average American farmer has by no means achieved a degree of financial security commensurate with the contribution he makes to the national economy; and he will not achieve this security until the United States has again established a competitive place in the world economy.

CHAPTER 29
Operating a Competitive Firm: II

In this chapter we will go over some material we have already covered, but much more carefully. There are a lot of numbers and a lot of graphs, but you should already be generally familiar with the situation that they analyze.

Three big questions tie the chapter together.

1 Why do unit costs rise, after their initial fall? This will bring us the very important role of the law of diminishing returns.

2 What are the conditions for equilibrium of the competitive firm? This will again bring home the need to equate MC and MR and will introduce a new criterion for equilibrium in the industry: Average cost must equal average revenue (or price).

3 How can profit be earned by a firm in a competitive setting? Here we will learn about intramarginal earnings, or quasi rents.

Keeping these three main ideas in mind will help you move steadily through the analysis.

THE COST PROBLEM

Once again, let us become imaginary entrepreneurs. Since we are familiar with the firm's calculations in regard to buying factor services, let us extend our knowledge to a full appreciation of what the cost problem looks like to us.

Fixed and Variable Costs

We know that a firm's *total* costs must rise as it hires additional factors. Yet as businesspeople, we can see that our total costs will not rise proportionally as fast as our additional factor costs, because some costs of production will not be affected by an increase in factor input. Real estate taxes, for example, will remain unchanged if we hire one person or 100 — so long as we do not acquire additional land. We can assume that the depreciation cost of machinery will not be affected by additions to land or labor. Rent will be unchanged unless the premises are expanded. The cost of electric light will not vary appreciably despite additions to labor or machinery. Neither will the salary of the president. **Thus some costs, determined by legal contract or by usage or by the unchanging use of one factor, do not vary with output. We call these fixed costs.**

In sharp contrast with fixed costs is another kind of cost that does vary directly with output. Here are many factor costs, for generally we vary inputs of labor and capital (and sometimes land) every time we seek a new level of production. To increase output almost always requires the payment of more wages and the employment of more capital (if only in the form of inventories or goods in process) and sometimes the rental of more space. **All costs that vary with output are called variable costs.**

Average Costs

Now we must move from considering *total* costs — fixed or variable — to considering **costs *per unit* of output.** These are called *average costs.* Instead of thinking about the costs of bringing in a crop or producing a batch of output, we fasten on the costs per bushel, or per item of manufacture. Both variable and fixed costs can be translated from their total amounts to their average basis by dividing the total by the number of bushels or items the firm makes. We shift from total to average costs because they allow us to focus on, and to compare, *marginal* revenues and expenses in a way that total costs do not.

There is certainly no difficulty in picturing what happens to *fixed costs* per unit of output as output rises. By definition, they must fall. Suppose a manufacturer has fixed costs (rent, certain indirect taxes, depreciation, and overhead) of $10,000 a

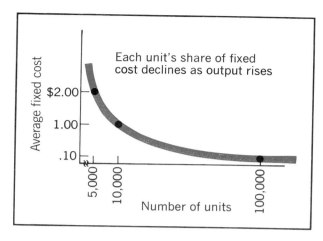

Each unit's share of fixed
cost declines as output rises

Figure 1
PROFILE OF FIXED COSTS PER UNIT

As output increases, fixed costs are spread over a larger number of units, and therefore fixed costs per unit steadily decline.

year. If 5,000 units of the product are produced per year, each unit will have to bear $2 of fixed cost as its share. If output rises to 10,000 units, the unit share of fixed costs will shrink to $1. At 100,000 units it would be a dime. Thus a curve of average fixed costs would look like Figure 1.

We notice that the curve of fixed costs per unit falls steadily. This stands to reason, because the costs *are* fixed, and they are spread over an ever larger output. But this does not explain why the cost curve eventually turns up—why it has a dish or U shape. That question brings us to the question of variable costs.

Variable Costs and Diminishing Returns

Variable costs must be the reason that cost curves per unit eventually turn up. This means that variable costs per unit—wages, for example—must rise after a time. Why should that be the case?

The answer takes us away from the firm, for a moment, to think again about a constraint of nature we have encountered in Chapter 6—the law of diminishing returns.

Let us begin with a case that is very simple to imagine. Suppose we have a farmer who has a farm of 100 acres, a certain amount of equipment, and no labor at all. Now let us observe what happens as he hires one man, then a second man of the same abilities, then a third, and so on. Obviously, the output of the farm will grow. What we want to find out, however, is whether it will grow in some clearly defined pattern that we can attribute to the changing amount of the factor which is being added.

What would such a curve of productivity look like? Assume that one man, working the 100 acres alone as best he can, produces 1,000 bushels of grain. A second man, helping the first, should be enormously valuable, because the two men can begin to specialize and divide the work, each doing the jobs he is better at and saving the time formerly wasted by moving from one job to the next. As a consequence of this division of labor, output may jump to 3,000 bushels.*

Marginal Productivity

Since the *difference* in output is 2,000 bushels, we speak of the *marginal productivity of labor,* when two men are working, as 2,000 bushels. Note that we should not (although in carelessness we sometimes do) speak of the marginal productivity of the *second* man. Alone, his efforts are not more productive than those of the first man; if we fired the first man, worker number 2 would produce only 1,000 bushels. What makes the difference is the jump in the combined productivity of the *two* men, once specialization can be introduced. Hence we should speak of the changing marginal productivity of *labor,* not of the individual.

It is not difficult to imagine an increasing specialization taking place with the third, fourth, and fifth man, so that the addition of another unit of labor input in each case brings about an output larger than was realized by the average of all the previous men. Remember that this does not mean the successive factor units themselves are more productive. **It means that as we add units of one factor, the total mix of these units plus the fixed amounts of other factors forms an increasingly efficient technical combination.** Remember Adam Smith's pin factory!

We call the range of factor inputs, over which average productivity rises, a range of *increasing average returns.* It is, of course, a stage of production that is highly favorable for the producer. Every time he adds a factor, efficiency rises. (As a result, as we shall shortly see, costs per unit of output fall.) The rate of increase will not be the same, for the initial large marginal leaps in productivity will give way to smaller ones. But the overall trend of productivity, whether we measure it by looking at *total* output or at *average* output per man, will still be up. All this keeps on happening, of course, because the factor we are adding has not yet reached its point of maximum technical efficiency with the given amount of other factors.

Diminishing Returns

At a certain point, the farmer notices a disconcerting phenomenon. Marginal output no longer rises when he adds another man. Total output will still be rising, but a quick calculation reveals that the last man on the team has added less to output than his predecessor.

---

* With each additional man, the proportions of land, labor, and capital are altered, so that the change in the level of output should rightfully be ascribed to new levels of efficiency resulting from the interaction of *all three factors.* But since labor is the factor whose input we are varying, it has become customary to call the change in output the result of a change in "labor productivity." If we were altering land or capital alone, we would call the change the result of changes in their productivities, even though, as with labor, the real cause is the changing efficiency of *all* factors in different mixes.

What has happened is that we have overshot the point of maximum technical efficiency for the factor we are adding. Labor is now beginning to crowd land or equipment. Opportunities for further specialization have diminished. **We call this condition of falling marginal performance a condition of decreasing or diminishing returns.** As the words suggest, we are getting back less and less as we add the critical factor — not only from the "marginal" man, but from the combined labor of all men.

If we now go on adding labor, we will soon reach a point at which the contribution of the marginal man will be so small that average output per man will also fall. Now, of course, costs will be rising per unit. If we went on foolishly adding more and more men, eventually the addition of another worker would add nothing to total output. In fact, the next worker might so disrupt the factor mix that *total* output would actually fall, and we would be in a condition of negative returns.

Total, Average, and Marginal Product

This changing profile of physical productivity is one of the most important generalizations economics makes about the real world. It will help us to think it through if we now study the relationships of marginal and average productivity and of total output in Table 1. All three columns are integrally related, and it is important to understand the exact nature of those relationships.

1. **The column for total output is related to the column for marginal productivity, because the rise in total output results from the successive marginal increments. For instance, the reason total output goes from 7,800 bushels with 4 men to 9,800 with 5 men is that the marginal output associated with the fifth man is 2,000 bushels. Thus, if we know the schedule of total outputs, we can always figure the schedule of marginal productivity simply by observing how much total output rises with each additional unit of factor input.**

Table 1

It is important to understand the relation among the three columns. If you knew only the successive totals, how would you calculate the marginal products? If you knew the marginal column, how do you figure the total? From there, how do you get the average?

Number of Men	Total Output	Marginal Productivity (Change in Output)		Average Productivity (Total Output ÷ No. of Men)	
1	1,000	1,000	Increasing marginal productivity	1,000	Increasing average productivity
2	3,000	2,000		1,500	
3	5,500	2,500		1,833	
4	7,800	2,300		1,950	
5	9,800	2,000	Decreasing marginal productivity	1,960	
6	11,600	1,800		1,930	Decreasing average productivity
7	13,100	1,500		1,871	
8	14,300	1,200		1,790	

2. It stands to reason, therefore, that if we know the schedule of marginal productivity, it is simple to figure total output: We just add up the marginal increments.

3. Finally, the meaning of average productivity is also apparent. It is simply total output divided by the number of men (or of any factor unit in which we are interested).

One thing must be carefully studied in this example. Note that marginal productivity begins to diminish with the fourth man, who adds only 2,300 bushels to output, and not 2,500 as did his predecessor. Average productivity, however, rises until we hire the sixth man, because the fifth man, although producing less than the fourth, is still more productive than the average output of all four men. Thus marginal productivity can be falling while average productivity is still rising. That is a sentence worth reading twice — or even three times — until it sinks in.

The three curves in Figure 2 all show the same phenomenon, only in a graphic way. The top curve shows us that as we add men to our farm, output at first rises

Figure 2
THE LAW OF VARIABLE PROPORTIONS
The graph simply enables us to visualize the relationships of Table 1. Note that marginal productivity falls before average productivity.

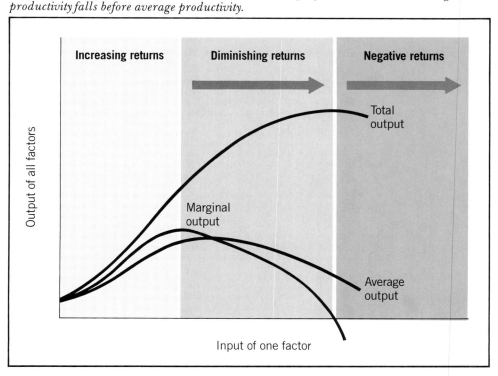

very rapidly, then slowly, then actually declines. The marginal productivity curve shows us *why* this is happening to total output. As we add men, the contribution they can make to output changes markedly. At first each man adds so much that average output grows rapidly. Thereafter marginal output falls, although average output still rises. Finally, each man adds so little that he actually pulls down the average obtained before his hiring. The average curve, as we have just indicated, merely sums up the overall output in an arithmetical way by showing us what the average person contributes to it.

The Law of Variable Proportions

To sum up: If we add successive units of one factor to fixed amounts of others, marginal productivity will at first increase and then decrease. We call this the law of diminishing returns, or the law of variable proportions (both terms are used).

Bear in mind two things about the law. (1) It applies to all factors, land and capital as well as labor; and (2) we can't speak of the law in operation if we don't hold all factors fixed except one. Otherwise, we do not know the cause of any change in output.

Average Variable Costs

Now we return to our firm. Perhaps we can already anticipate that the law of variable proportions will explain why average costs turn up, despite falling average fixed costs. Let us work our way through the actual figures.

We will begin by setting up an imaginary but plausible schedule of output for our manufacturer in Table 2. Once again we see the law of variable proportions at work. The total number of units produced will rise at first rapidly, then more slowly, with the addition of labor input to the plant.

Table 2

Can you see the law of diminishing returns at work in these figures?

Number of Men	Total Output (Units)	Marginal Product
0	0	
1	5,000	5,000
2	13,000	8,000
3	23,000	10,000
4	32,000	9,000
5	39,000	7,000
6	44,000	5,000
7	47,000	3,000
8	49,000	2,000

Table 3

Total variable costs rise steadily at $5,000 per worker. Average costs first fall, then rise. Why? Because changing marginal productivity first makes output rise rapidly, then more slowly. Therefore the $5,000 increments of variable cost at first get spread more thinly, lowering cost per unit from $1 to $.63. Then (starting with the fifth man, the share of variable costs begins to rise, from $.63 to over $.80.

Number of Men	Total Variable Cost @ $5,000 per Man	Total Output (Units)	Average Variable Cost (Cost ÷ Output)
1	$ 5,000	5,000	$1.00
2	10,000	13,000	.77
3	15,000	23,000	.65
4	20,000	32,000	.63
5	25,000	39,000	.64
6	30,000	44,000	.68
7	35,000	47,000	.74
8	40,000	49,000	.82

To convert this schedule of physical productivity into a curve of average costs, we must do two things:

1. Calculate the total cost for the variable factors used for each level of output. This is total variable cost.

2. Then divide the total variable cost by the number of units, to get average variable cost.

Figure 3

PROFILE OF CHANGING VARIABLE COSTS PER UNIT (AVERAGE VARIABLE COST)

This is simply a graph of the last column in Table 3. We now see that the upward slope of the dish-shaped curve is the result of the law of diminishing returns.

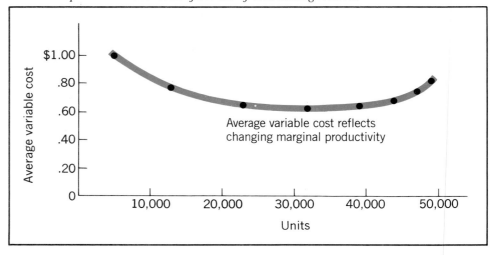

Let us assume that the going wage is $5,000. Table 3 then shows the total, marginal, and average costs for different levels of output. Notice that average variable costs decline at first and thereafter rise. The reason is by now clear enough. Variable cost increases by a set amount: $5,000 per man, as factors are added. Output, however, obeys the law of variable proportions, increasing rapidly at first and then displaying diminishing returns. **It stands to reason, then, that the variable cost *per unit* of output will be falling as long as output is growing faster than costs, and that it will begin to rise as soon as additions to output start to get smaller.**

If we graph the typical variable cost curve per unit of output (or average variable cost), it will be the familiar dish-shaped or U-shaped profile Figure 3 shows.

Total Cost per Unit

We can now set up a complete cost schedule for our enterprise by combining fixed and variable costs, as in Table 4. Notice how marginal costs begin to turn up *before* average costs.

If we graph the last two columns of figures—average and marginal cost per unit—we get the very important diagram in Figure 4.

Table 4

Here we show total cost—fixed plus variable—and total output. It's simple thereafter to figure average and marginal costs. Technical note: *Ideally, we should like to show how marginal cost changes with* each *additional unit of output. Here our data show the change in costs associated with considerable jumps in output as we add each man. Hence we estimate the marginal cost by taking the change in total costs and dividing this by the change in total output. The result is really an "average" marginal cost, since each individual item costs actually a tiny fraction less, or more, than its predecessor. We have shown the data this way since it is much closer to the way businessmen figure.*

			Total Cost per Unit of Output	
Number of Men	Total Cost ($10,000 Fixed Cost + $5,000 per Man)	Output (Units)	Average (Total Cost ÷ Output)	Marginal (Change in Total Cost ÷ Change in Output)
1	$15,000	5,000	$3.00 ⎤	$ ⎤ Falling
2	20,000	13,000	1.54 ⎪ Falling	.63 ⎬ marginal
3	25,000	23,000	1.09 ⎬ avg.	.50 ⎦ cost
4	30,000	32,000	.94 ⎪ cost	.55 ⎤
5	35,000	39,000	.90 ⎦	.71 ⎪ Rising
6	40,000	44,000	.91 ⎤ Rising	1.00 ⎬ marginal
7	45,000	47,000	.96 ⎬ avg.	1.67 ⎪ cost
8	50,000	49,000	1.02 ⎦ cost	2.50 ⎦

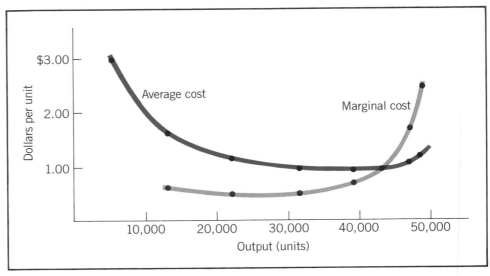

Figure 4
AVERAGE AND MARGINAL COST

When we graph average and marginal costs, we really see what a difference the phenomenon of diminishing returns makes.

The Cost Profile

We have reached the end of our cost calculations, and it will help to take stock of what we have done. Actually, despite all the figures and diagrams, the procedure has been quite simple.

1. We began by seeing what would happen to our *fixed costs* per unit as we expanded output. Since fixed costs, by their nature, do not increase as production increases, the amount of fixed cost that had to be charged to each unit of output fell as output rose.

2. Next we calculated the *variable costs* that would have to be borne by each unit as output increased. Here the critical process at work was the law of variable proportions. As the marginal productivity of factors increased, variable cost per unit fell. When the inevitable stage of diminishing returns set in, variable costs per unit had to rise.

3. Adding together average fixed and variable costs, we obtained the average *total cost* of output. Like the variable cost curve, average total costs are dish-shaped, reflecting the changing marginal productivity of factors as output grows.

4. Finally, we show the changing *marginal cost*—the increase in total costs divided by the increase in output. As before, it is the changing marginal costs

that the entrepreneur actually experiences in altering output. It is the increase at the margin that alters total cost and therefore determines average cost.

The Common Sense of Changing Average Cost

Actually, the cost profile we have worked out would be known by any businessperson who had never studied microeconomics. Whenever a firm starts producing, its cost per unit of output is very high. A General Motors plant turning out only a few hundred cars a year would have astronomical costs per automobile.

As output increases, unit costs come down steadily, partly because overhead (fixed cost) is now spread over more units, partly because the factors are used at much greater efficiency. Finally, after some point of maximum factor efficiency, average costs begin to mount. Even though overhead continues to decline, it is now so small a fraction of cost per unit that its further decline does not count for much, while the rising inefficiency of factors steadily pushes up variable cost per unit. If General Motors tries to jam through more cars than a plant is designed to produce, the cost per auto will again begin to soar.

So much for the *average* cost. By directing our attention to the changes that occur in total cost and total output every time we alter the number of factors we engage, the *marginal* cost curve simply tells us why all this is happening. In other words, as our plant first moves into high gear, the cars we add to the line (the marginal output) will cost considerably less than the average of all cars processed previously. Later, when diminishing returns begin to work against us, we would expect the added (marginal) cars to be high-cost cars, higher in cost than the average of all cars built so far.

Average and Marginal Costs

Since the cost of marginal output always "leads" the cost of average output in this way, we can understand an important relationship that all marginal and average cost curves bear to each other. **The marginal cost curve always cuts the average cost curve at the lowest point of average cost.**

Why? Because as long as the additional cars are cheaper than the average of all cars, their production must be *reducing* average cost; that is, as long as the marginal cost curve is lower than the average cost curve, the average cost curve must be falling. Conversely, as soon as additional output is more expensive than the average for all previous output, that additional production must *raise* average costs. Again (look at the previous diagram), as soon as marginal cost is above average cost, average cost must begin to rise. Hence it follows that the *MC* (marginal cost) curve

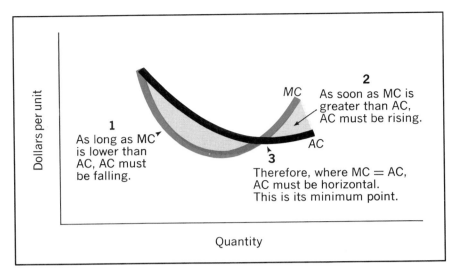

Figure 5
RELATION OF MARGINAL
AND AVERAGE COST
The marginal cost curve cuts the average cost curve at its lowest point. For reasons, read the information on the graph.

must cross the *AC* (average cost) curve at the minimum point of average cost. This relationship has nothing to do with economics as such, but with simple logic, as Figure 5 may elucidate.*

FROM COST TO REVENUE

The cost profile gives us a clear picture of what happens to unit costs as our firm hires additional factors. But that is only half the information we need for understanding how a firm operates with one foot in the factor market and the other in the market for goods. Now we need a comparable profile of what happens to revenues as the firm sells the output its factors have made for it.

Average and Marginal Revenue

We already know what the demand curve looks like for a competitive firm. It is a horizontal line, reflecting the fact that the firm's output is too small to affect the market price of the good. Let's now assume that our firm makes such a competitive product — say a metal stamping, whose price is $1.50.

---

* It follows that the marginal productivity curve always crosses the average productivity curve at its peak. Look at Figure 2. As long as marginal productivity is *higher* than average productivity, the average curve must be *rising*. As soon as additional (marginal) output is *less than* the preceding average output, the lower marginal output must *diminish* the average. The relation is exactly that of Figure 5, only upside down.

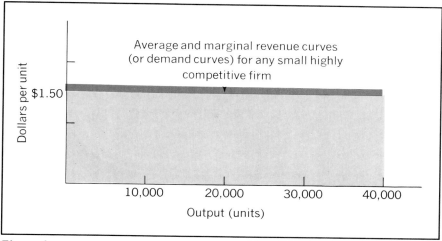

Figure 6

AVERAGE AND MARGINAL REVENUES UNDER COMPETITION

This is the same flat curve we saw in the previous chapter. We reproduce it here because its flatness holds the key to analyzing the competitive firm's situation. (Can you anticipate why the marginal and average revenue curves will not be flat, and will not be the same, when we get to monopolistic markets?)

The entrepreneur can easily calculate his revenue curves, knowing there is a limitless demand for his product.* Each unit will sell at the same price as the one before or the one after. The revenue brought in by each unit—the marginal revenue—will therefore be unchanged. So will the average revenue, which is the same thing as the selling price. As the schedule of Table 5 and the graph of Figure 6 show, marginal and average revenues are the same. (They won't be when we get to less than competitive markets in the next chapter.)

Marginal Cost and Supply

Now we have all the information we want. We have a cost profile that tells us what happens to unit costs as we hire or fire factors. We have a revenue profile that tells us what happens to unit revenues as we do the same. It remains only to put the two

Table 5

Output (Units)	Price	Marginal Revenue	Total Revenue	Average Revenue
5,000	$1.50	$1.50	$ 7,500	$1.50
10,000	1.50	1.50	15,000	1.50
20,000	1.50	1.50	30,000	1.50
40,000	1.50	1.50	60,000	1.50

* So why doesn't an ambitious firm produce a limitless amount and become limitlessly rich? Because rising unit costs will soon bring it limitless losses.

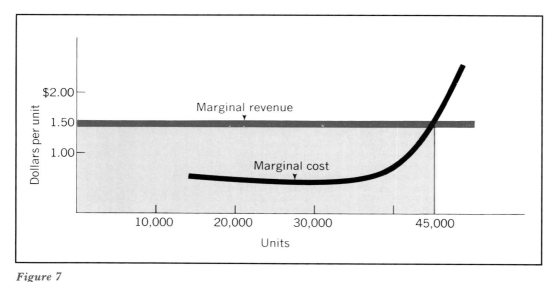

Figure 7
THE POINT OF OPTIMUM OUTPUT
Here is the same MC = MR diagram we used in the previous chapter, this time calibrated to show the actual number of units at optimal output.

together to discover just how much output the firm should make to maximize its profits. As we can see in Figure 7, it is just about at 45,000 units.

We already know why this is the most profitable level of output. But we can now see a new meaning for the marginal cost curve. **The rising portion of the marginal cost curve is the firm's supply curve.**

Suppose price rises from P_1 to P_2 in Figure 8. As far as the firm is concerned, it does not matter where its average cost is. What counts is whether additional

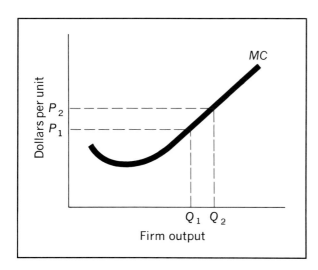

Figure 8
THE FIRM'S SUPPLY CURVE
We have often talked about a firm's supply curve. Now we can see that the rising portion is its marginal cost curve.

production will be profitable. Further, it will be profitable only if the marginal cost of that additional production does not exceed marginal revenue. Therefore, when price rises, the firm's output increases from Q_1 to Q_2, a point determined by the intersection of the *MC* curve and the new price.

The point we must bear in mind is more than just a geometrical demonstration. **It is that marginal costs, not average costs, determine most production decisions.** When prices rise or fall, the change in quantity will reflect the ease or difficulty of adding to or diminishing production, as that ease or difficulty is reflected in the shape of its *MC* schedule.

Profits

Now let us return to the firm producing the quantity of stampings that just equates marginal cost and marginal revenue. What is the total amount of economic profit at the firm's best level of output? This is very difficult to tell from diagrams that show only marginal costs and marginal revenues. As we have just seen, these curves tell us how large *output* will be. But we must add another curve to enable us quickly to see what the *profit* will be at each level of output.

This is our familiar average cost curve. Average costs, we know, are nothing but total costs reduced to a per-unit basis. Average revenues are also on a per-unit basis. **Hence, if we compare the average revenue and cost curves at any point, they will tell us at a glance what total revenues and costs look like at that point.**

Figure 9 reveals what our situation is at the point of optimum output. (This time we generalize the diagram rather than putting it into the specific terms of our illustrative firm.) The diagram shows several things. First, as before, it indicates our most profitable output as the amount *OA* — the output indicated by point *X*, where the marginal revenue and marginal cost curves meet. Remember: We use marginal costs and marginal revenues to determine the point of optimum output. Second, it shows us that at output *OA*, our *average cost* is *OC* ($=AB$) and our *average*

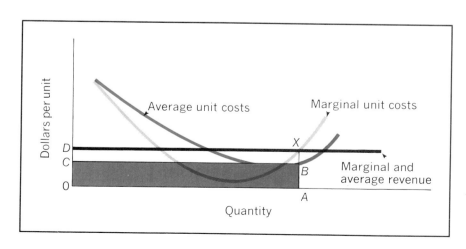

Figure 9

THE FIRM IN EQUILIBRIUM WITH PROFITS

How well is our firm doing? Total costs = OABC: output times average costs. Total revenues = OAXD: output times average revenue. Profits equal the difference, or CBXD — a profit of BX per unit times the number of units.

Labels within figure: Dollars per unit / Average unit costs / Marginal unit costs / X / D / C / 0 / B / A / Marginal and average revenue / Quantity *revenue* is *OD* (=*AX*), the same as our marginal revenue, since the demand curve for the firm is horizontal. Our profit on the *average* unit of output must therefore be *CD* (=*BX*), the difference between average costs and average revenues at this point. The *total* profit is therefore the rectangle *CDXB*, which is the average profit per unit (*CD*) times the number of units. Remember again: We use average costs and average revenues to calculate profits.

Working Out an Example

We can translate this in terms of our firm. At the point where $MC = MR$, it is making about 45,000 stampings, as Figure 7 shows. Table 4 does not show us the exact cost at 45,000 units, but we will assume it is 1¢ more than the 91¢ cost of making 44,000 units. We will therefore estimate average cost for 45,000 stampings to be 92¢ per unit. Since the selling price is $1.50, we are now taking in a total of $1.50 × 45,000 units, or $67,500, while our total cost is 92¢ × 45,000 units or $41,400. Our profit is the difference between total revenues and total costs, or $26,100.

Entry and Exit

However satisfactory from the point of view of the firm, this is not yet a satisfactory stopping point from the point of view of the system as a whole. If our firm is typical of the metal stamping industry, small firms throughout this line of business are making profits comparable to ours. In other lines of endeavor, though, numerous businesses do not make $26,100 in economic profit. Hence entrepreneurs in these lines will now begin to move into our profitable industry.

Figure 10
INDUSTRY IN ADJUSTMENT TO PROFITS
On the left we see that supply and demand lower the price as new firms move in. On the right we see how this affects each individual firm.

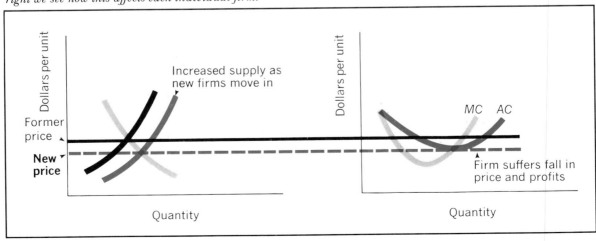

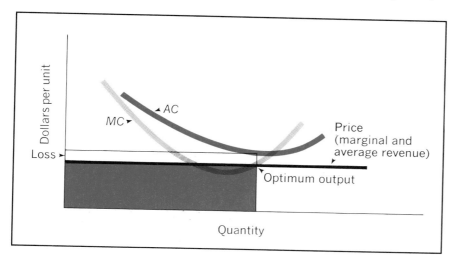

Figure 11
THE FIRM SUFFERING A
LOSS

*If price sinks too low, the
firm will seek optimum
output (MR = MC), but
its price will fail to cover
average costs. It will make
a loss.*

Perhaps we can anticipate what will happen now. **As other firms move into our
line of business, output will increase. The supply curve of the industry will
move to the right. The price of our product will therefore fall, as Figure 10
shows.**

How long will this influx of firms continue? Suppose it continues until price falls
below the average cost curve of our representative firm. Now its position looks like
Figure 11. Output will still be set where $MC = MR$ (it always is), but now the
average cost curve is above the average revenue curve at this point. The unavoid-
able result is a loss for the firm, as the diagram shows.

What will happen? Clearly, we need a reverse adjustment process — an exodus of
firms into greener pastures, so that the supply curve for our industry can move to
the left, bringing higher prices for all producers. This may not be a rapid process.
Eventually, the withdrawal of producers should bring about the necessary adjustment shown in Figure 12.

Minimizing Losses

The process of minimizing losses (which is as close as an unfortunate entrepreneur
can get to maximizing profits) is worth a careful look. Figure 13 shows two curves:
AC is our familiar curve of average costs. *AVC* is the curve of average variable costs
(Figure 3). It is not *total* cost because it does not include the items like rent that go
into fixed cost.

Suppose that price falls to P_1. Should the firm quit? No, because it covers its
out-of-pocket expenses (*AVC*) and even makes a little over to cover some, although
not all, fixed cost. **As long as price is high enough to cover variable costs, a firm
will continue to produce. Only when price fails to cover out-of-pocket AVC costs
will it be rational to shut down.**

How long can a firm go on incurring losses? The answer depends on how rapidly
it can terminate its fixed costs, such as getting rid of its buildings, machinery, etc.,

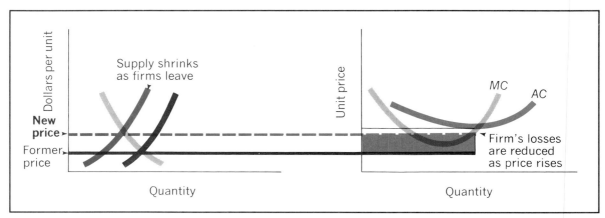

Figure 12
INDUSTRY ADJUSTMENT TO LOSSES

As firms gradually leave an industry, the supply curve moves to the left, prices rise, and firms' losses are reduced.

or how long it can incur losses without going bankrupt. The firm may limp along for an extended period, continuing to add production to the market and thereby delaying the leftward shift of the industry's supply curve.

Long-Run Equilibrium

Sooner or later, whether through the entry of new firms or the gradual withdrawal or disappearance of old ones, we reach a point of equilibrium for both the firm and the industry. It looks like Figure 14. Note that this position of equilibrium has two characteristics for the firm:

1. **Marginal cost equals marginal revenue, so there is no incentive for the individual entrepreneur to alter output.**
2. **Average cost equals average revenue (or price), so there is no incentive for firms to enter or leave the industry.**

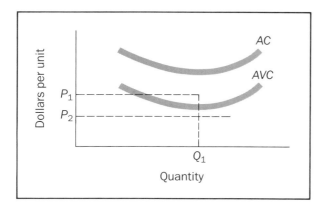

Figure 13
ADJUSTING TO LOSSES

If price is at P_1 the firm is covering variable costs although not total costs. Perhaps it makes enough to cover its wages and some of its rent. It stays in business despite its economic loss. At price P_2 it can't even cover out-of-pocket costs. It has to shut down.

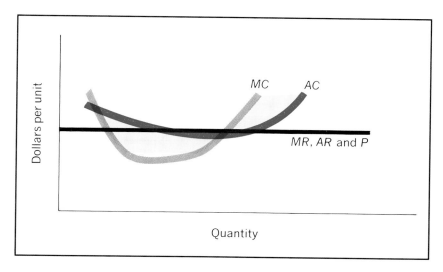

Figure 14
MARGINAL FIRM IN EQUILIB-
RIUM WITH NO PROFITS
*Here is a diagram to be fully
grasped. It shows the
conditions for equilibrium of
the competitive firm: (1) No
incentive to change output
(MR = MC). (2) No
incentive for entry or exit
(AC = P).*

Thus we can state the condition for the equilibrium resting point of our firm and
industry as being a four-way equality:

$$MC \quad = \quad MR \quad = \quad AC \quad = \quad P$$

$$\underset{\text{cost}}{\text{marginal}} = \underset{\text{revenue}}{\text{marginal}} = \underset{\text{cost}}{\text{average}} = \underset{\substack{\text{(average} \\ \text{revenue)}}}{\text{price}}$$

We have reached an equilibrium for the firm and for the industry. It is certainly
an uncomfortable one for us as typical manufacturers; for in the final resting point
of the firm, it is clear that *profits have been totally eliminated.* We are driven to the
conclusion that in a "perfect" competitive market, the forces of competition would
indeed press toward zero the returns of the *marginal* firms in all industries, so that
the cost and revenue profile of the last firms able to remain alive in each industry
would look like our diagram.

Quasi Rents

Note, however, that these are marginal firms. Here is a clue to how profits can exist
even in a highly competitive situation. In Figure 15 we show the supply curve of an
industry broken into the individual supply curves of its constituent firms. Some of
these firms, for reasons we will discuss below, will be lower-cost producers than
others. When the industry equilibrium price is finally established, they will be the
beneficiaries of the difference between the going price, which reduces the profits
of the *marginal* firm to zero, and the lower unit costs attributable to their superior

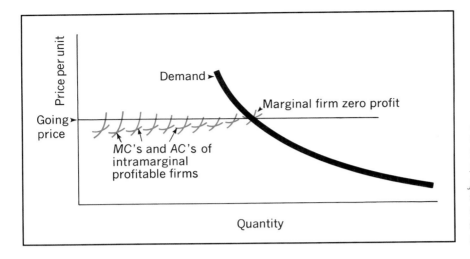

Figure 15
QUASI OR ECONOMIC
RENTS
Even though the marginal firm makes no profit, intramarginal firms may realize quasi rents. Entry into the industry will tend to eliminate them.

efficiency. Industry equilibrium leaves them in the enviable position of the firm shown in Figure 9.

These intramarginal profits are called quasi rents.* They are the only true economic profits we find in competitive industries.

Sources of Quasi Rents

Where do these quasi rents arise? From several sources. One source may be personnel. Workers hired at the same wage are not always equally productive. A superior manager will recruit or organize a superior work force and gain rents as a result. Another source can be location. A retail store may enjoy a movement of population into its area. The value of its location increases, but its actual rental payments may not rise until a new lease is signed. Third, just plain luck or the uncertainties of the business world constantly create positive or negative quasi rents. Not all prices adjust quickly to changed conditions. An entrepreneur goes into a business having calculated costs and revenues, then finds that costs have fallen or revenues risen, for reasons that could not be anticipated. Positive or negative quasi rents — profits or losses — will ensue. Uncertainty is, in fact as well as in proverb, fundamental to life and a major source of the good or bad fortune that besets the best-laid plans of entrepreneurs.

Thus, economic profits enter the competitive world from changes in the economic setting, from random runs of good and bad luck, from unequal distributions of talent or resources. As a general rule, these sources of quasi rent are ephemeral, and the normal, profit-seeking movement of the industry will erode and eventually erase them. Badly run firms will go out of business or hire a better manager. Badly located firms will pick up and move. Contracts will come to an end and be renegoti-

* Sometimes they are called "economic rents" or even plain "rents."

ated to remove quasi rents. Movements of the marketplace that create positive rents one year will create negative ones the next. Luck evens out. **Thus in the long run we can expect a tendency in a competitive market to eliminate existing quasi rents, although new ones may be created as conditions change.**

looking back

| KEY CONCEPTS | There are a great many graphs and tables in this chapter, but they all dovetail into an overall concept. The concept is the idea of the competitive firm seeking to maximize its profit. Keeping that in mind will help organize your understanding |

Fixed and variable cost

1 All firms have two kinds of costs, fixed and variable. Fixed costs, which do not vary with output, decline when figured on a per unit basis as output grows. Variable costs display the familiar U shape.

Law of diminishing returns gives first increasing, then diminishing returns

2 Variable costs rise because of the law of diminishing returns — also called the law of variable proportions. This law tells us that as we add more and more of any one factor to a fixed amount of other factors, output will first rise — increasing returns — and then fall — diminishing returns.

This gives falling, then rising average variable costs

3 This change in productivity means that costs per unit — average costs — first fall, then rise, as we add variable costs — usually labor — to a fixed amount of plant and equipment.

Eventually average and marginal cost both rise. *MC* curve always cuts *AC* curve at lowest point

4 If we add variable to fixed costs, we get the familiar dish-shaped curve. As output increases, eventually both average and marginal cost will rise, marginal cost more sharply. The marginal cost curve always cuts the average cost curve at its lowest point.

***AR* and *MR* curves are identical**

5 Average and marginal revenues for a competitive firm are identical and horizontal. This is because the firm's output is too small to affect price, whether it expands or contracts output.

***MC* = *MR* is always optimal output**

6 The firm maximizes its own profit by setting output where $MC = MR$. The marginal cost curve always determines the point of optimal output. It is the firm's supply curve.

Entry and exit will change the supply curve for the industry. A firm will produce as long as *AR* > *AVC*

7 $MC = MR$ is the "solution" for the firm, but it may not be the equilibrium for the industry. If the firm is making profits, there will be entry from other firms. Supply will increase. Price will drop. Profits will tend to disappear. If there are losses, some firms will leave the industry. Supply will diminish, prices will rise, losses will be cut. A firm will continue to produce as long as price (average revenue) is greater than average variable cost (out-of-pocket expenses).

| Long-run equilibrium: $MC = MR = AC = P$ | **8** Long-run equilibrium requires that the firm be at the $MC = MR$ point and that it also have $AC = AR$ (or price). The firm must have no incentive to change output, and there must be no incentive to enter or leave the industry. |
| Quasi rents are intramarginal profits | **9** Profits at the margin thus tend toward zero. But intramarginal profits, called quasi rents, may persist. |

ECONOMIC VOCABULARY

Fixed costs   512
Variable costs   512
Unit costs   512
Diminishing returns   513
Marginal productivity   514
Marginal product   515

Law of variable proportions   517
Average and marginal costs   521
Average and marginal revenue   522
Entry and exit   526
Quasi rents   529

QUESTIONS

1. If you were a retail grocer, what kind of costs would be fixed for you? If you were a manufacturer who owned a large computer, would its maintenance be a fixed cost? If you *rented* the computer, would maintenance be a fixed cost?

2. Assume your fixed costs are $500 a week and your output can vary from 100 to 1,000 units, given the scale of your enterprise. Graph what happens to fixed costs per unit. Is this diminishing returns?

3. Assume your plant hires 6 workers successively and that output changes as follows:

Number of workers	1	2	3	4	5	6
Total units of output per week	100	300	550	700	750	800

   What is the marginal product of each worker? The average product? If each worker costs $100 per week, what is the variable cost per unit as you add personnel? Explain the relation between the shape of the curve and the law of variable proportions.

4. If you add fixed costs of $500 per week to the variable cost you have just ascertained, what is the average cost? What is the marginal cost? (Remember, this is figured by dividing the *change in total cost by the change in total output*.)

5. Graph the curve of average total costs and marginal costs. Why does the marginal cost curve cross the average cost curve at its lowest point?

6. What does average revenue mean, and what is its relation to price? What is meant by marginal revenue? Why is marginal revenue the same as average revenue for a competitive firm?

7. Suppose (in the example above) you sell the output of your firm at $1.35 per unit. Draw in such a marginal revenue curve. Now very carefully indicate where the *MR* and *MC* curves meet. Show on the diagram the output corresponding to this point. What is the approximate average cost at this output? Is there a profit here? Indicate by letters the rectangle that shows the profit per unit of output and the number of units. Is it a quasi rent?

8. What will be the result, in a competitive industry, of such a profit? Draw a diagram showing how an influx of firms can change the ruling market price. Will it be higher or lower?

9. Draw a diagram showing how price could drop below the lowest point on the average total cost curve and indicate the low the firm would suffer. Explain, by means of a diagram, why a manufacturer may remain in business even though the firm cannot sell its output for the full cost of producing it. What will determine whether or not it is worth the firm's while to quit entirely?

10. Carefully draw a diagram showing the equilibrium position for the firm. Explain how *MR* and *MC* are all the firm is concerned with. How do *AR* and *AC* enter the picture? Why do *MR* and *MC*, by themselves, fail to give an equilibrium price in a competitive industry?

11. Suppose you are a druggist and you know that the least efficient druggist in town makes virtually no profit at all. Assuming that you both sell in the same market at the same prices, and that you hire factors at the same prices, what could bring a profit to your enterprise? What would you expect to be the trend of these profits?

CHAPTER 30
Operating a Big Business

a look ahead

In this chapter we move from the world of perfect competition to that of imperfect competition—monopolies, oligopolies, and monopolistically competitive businesses. We will study the operation of these business firms and compare it with the operation of the perfectly competitive firm we have already studied.

The crucial difference, as we will soon see, is that firms operating in conditions of imperfect competition have falling marginal revenue curves rather than horizontal ones. This means that at optimum output, where $MR = MC$, average cost will not equal average revenue or price. The main objective of this chapter is to see what difference this makes.

In Chapter 32 we make a social assessment of big business and consider various ways to deal with the problems it presents.

MOTIVES AND MARKETS

Monopoly and, nowadays, oligopoly, are bad words to most people, just as competition is a good word, although not everyone can specify exactly what is good or bad about them. Often we get the impression that the aims of the monopolist are evil and grasping, while those of the competitor are wholesome and altruistic. Therefore the essential difference between a world of pure competition and one of very impure competition seems to be one of motives and drives—of well-meaning competitors and ill-intentioned monopolists.

The truth is that exactly the same motives drive the monopoly and the competitive firm. Both seek to maximize profits. Indeed, the competitive firm, faced with the necessity of watching costs and revenues in order to survive, is apt to be, if anything, more pennypinching and more intensely profit-oriented than the monopolist, who (as we shall see) can afford to take a less hungry attitude toward profits. The lesson to be learned—and to remember—is that motives have nothing to do with the problem of less-than-pure competition. **The difference between a monopoly, an oligopoly, and a situation of pure competition is entirely one of market structure; that is, of the number of firms, ease of entry or exit, and the degree of differentiation among their goods.**

Price Takers vs. Price Makers

We have noted a very precise distinction between the competitive situation (numerous firms, undifferentiated goods) and markets with few sellers or highly differentiated goods. In the competitive case, as we have seen, each firm caters to so small a section of the market that the demand curve for its product is, for all intents and purposes, horizontal. By way of contrast, in a monopolistic or oligopolistic market structure there are so few firms that each one faces a downward-sloping demand curve. Each monopoly firm, in fact, faces the demand curve of its own *industry*. That means each firm, by varying its output, can affect the price of its product.

Another way of describing this difference is to call purely competitive firms, who have no control over price, *price takers* and to label monopolies or oligopolies or any firm that can affect the price of its product *price makers*.

"Pure" Monopolies

Before examining the economic problems of a "pure" monopoly, let us see how such a price maker operates. Why do we place the word "pure" in quotes? Because monopoly is not as easy to define as one might think. Essentially, the word means that there is only *one* seller of a particular good or service. The trouble comes in defining the "particular" good or service. In a sense, any seller of a differentiated good is a monopolist, for no one else dispenses *quite* the same utilities. Each shoeshine boy has his "own" customers, some of whom would probably continue to patronize his stand even if he charged slightly more than the competition.

Thus, at one end of the difficulty is the fact that there is an element of monopoly in many seemingly competitive goods, a complication we come back to later. At the other end of the problem there are so-called natural monopolies, where economies of scale lead to one seller supplying the whole market, such as a local utility company. Yet even here there are substitutes. If power rates become exorbitant, we *could* switch from electric light to candlelight. Hence, before we can draw conclusions from the mere fact that a company provides the "only" service of its kind, we need to know how easy or difficult it would be to find substitutes, however imperfect, for its output.

Limits of Monopoly

Evidently the problem of defining a "pure" monopoly is not easily resolved. Let us, however, agree to call the local power company a monopoly, because no one else sells gas and electricity to the community. In Figure 1 we show what the demand curve of such a monopoly looks like.

One point is immediately clear. **The monopolistic *firm* faces the same kind of demand curve the competitive *industry* faces.** That is so because both cater to *all* the demand for that particular product. A corollary follows. The demand curve itself imposes a fundamental limitation of the monopolist's power to control the market. Suppose a monopoly is selling quantity *OX* at price *OA*. The firm would prefer to sell quantity *OY* at price *OA,* but there is no way of forcing the market to take a larger quantity of its product — unless it lowers the price to *OB*.

The situation is very similar (on the seller's side) to a *union.* A union can raise the price of labor since it controls the supply of labor, but it cannot force employers to hire more labor than they want. Hence the question "Can unions raise wages?"

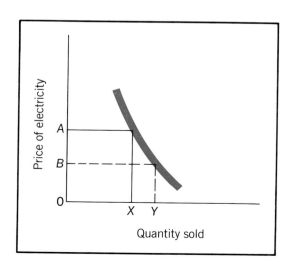

Figure 1

DEMAND CURVE FOR A MONOPOLY

A monopolist's demand curve is never horizontal. It slopes like the demand curve of a competitive industry. A demand curve constrains the monopolistic firm as decisively as it constrains the competitive industry.

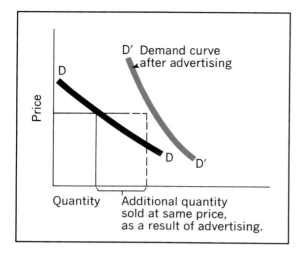

D' Demand curve
after advertising

D

Price

Quantity

D

D'

Additional quantity
sold at same price,
as a result of advertising.

Figure 2
ADVERTISING AND DEMAND

Any firm that advertises tries to do two things: (1) move DD to the right, and (2) make D'D' more inelastic than DD was.

must be answered "Yes," insofar as those who continue to be hired are concerned. But until we know the elasticity of the demand for labor, we cannot say if unions can raise the total amount of labor's revenues.

Advertising

There is one thing a monopoly can do, however, that neither a union nor a purely competitive firm can do. **A monopoly can advertise and thereby seek to move the demand curve for its product to the right, or to change its slope.** Advertising does not "pay" for a purely competitive firm selling undifferentiated goods, because such a firm has no way of being sure that *its* goods — and not a competitor's — will benefit. But advertising *can* be profitable for a monopoly that will get all the demand it can conjure up. We can think of advertising as an attempt to sell larger quantities of a good or service without reducing prices, by shifting the demand curve itself. Figure 2 shows us this important effect, and we will talk about it further in a moment.

Cost Curves for the Monopolist

We have seen in what way the shapes of the demand curves faced by monopolists differ from those faced by competitive firms. Are cost curves similarly different?

In general, they are not. We can take the cost profile of a monopoly as being essentially like that of a competitive firm.* The monopoly, like the competitive firm, buys factors and exerts no control over their prices. The local utility does not

* One difference is that monopolies (and oligopolies, to be discussed next) have *selling costs.* Some of their costs are variable, like advertising; others are fixed, such as long-term merchandising contracts.

HOW MONOPOLISTIC IS A MONOPOLY?

How do we recognize a monopoly? Because of the problem of substitutes, there is no very clear sign, except in a few cases such as the "natural" monopolies. Usually when we speak of monopolies we mean (*a*) very large businesses with (*b*) much higher than competitive profits and (*c*) relatively little direct product competition. Not many firms satisfy all three conditions. Exxon is a monopoly by criteria *a* and *b*, but not by *c*; Polaroid (until recently) by *b* but not *a*, and perhaps not by *c* (Kodak is its direct product competitor). Note, furthermore, that even small businesses can be monopolies, like "the only gambling house in town" famed in all Westerns.

affect the level of wages or the price of land or capital by its decision to expand or not to expand production. The monopolist, like the competitive entrepreneur, experiences the effects of changing productivity as he hires additional factors and, again like the competitive firm, shops for the best buys in the factor markets. Thus the same U-shaped average cost curve and the same more steeply sloped marginal cost curve will describe the cost changes experienced by a monopolist quite as well as those of a competitive firm.

FROM COST TO REVENUE

Monopoly Revenues

It is when we come to the revenue side of the picture that we meet the critical distinction of monopoly. **Unlike a competitive firm, a monopoly has a marginal revenue curve that is different from its average revenue curve.** The difference arises because each time a monopoly sells more output, it must reduce the price not on just the last unit sold, but on *all* units, whereas a competitive firm sells its larger output at an unchanged price. Therefore, as the monopoly's sales increase, its *marginal* revenues will fall.

A table may make this clear. Suppose we have a monopoly that is faced with an average revenue or price schedule as in Table 1. The graph of such a marginal revenue curve looks like Figure 3. Note that at an output of 6 units, AR (price) = \$15; MR = \$10.

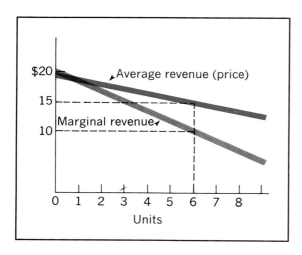

Figure 3

AVERAGE AND MARGINAL REVENUE FOR A MONOPOLIST

When we graph the monopolist's situation we can see how a sloping demand curve creates an MR curve different from the AR curve.

What determines the shape of the marginal revenue curve? Obviously, the change in quantity demanded that will be brought about by a drop in price. In turn, this reflects — as we remember from our discussion in Chapter 29 — the elasticity of demand which, in turn, hinges on our tastes and the availability of substitutes. The more inelastic the demand, the faster the marginal revenue curve will fall. Note especially that the *MR* curve lies below the *AR* curve because the monopolist must lower prices on *all* units sold, not on just the marginal unit. Thus each additional item drags down the revenue of all output.

Equilibrium for the Monopoly

The next step is obvious. We must superimpose the cost and the revenue profiles to determine the equilibrium position for the monopolist. We can see it in Figure 4.

What will be the equilibrium position? **The monopoly seeking to maximize profit is guided by exactly the same rule as the competitive firm: It adds factors so long as the marginal revenue they bring in is greater than their marginal cost.**

Table 1

As price, AR, falls, MR falls even more rapidly

Quantity Sold	Price	Total Revenue	Marginal Revenue
1	$20	$20	$20
2	19	38	18
3	18	54	16
4	17	68	14
5	16	80	12
6	15	90	10

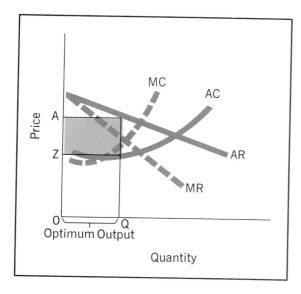

Figure 4
MONOPOLY EQUILIBRIUM
The intersection of MR and MC here tells us three things: (1) best output, OQ; (2) price at OQ = OA; and (3) average cost at OQ = OZ. Profit is the spread between price and cost (AZ) times the number of units sold (OQ).

Hence we look for the intersection of the *MC* and *MR* curves on Figure 4 to discover its optimum output.

We can see that optimum output is *OQ*. What about price? To discover this, we go up from the intersection of *MC* and *MR* to the *AR* (price) curve, and then over to the price axis. Optimum price obtainable for output *OQ* is *OA*.

As always, profit reflects the spread between average cost and average revenue. As we can see, this spread is *AZ*, the difference between average cost at output *OQ* and average revenue at that output. Total profit is therefore *AZ* times *OQ*, the rectangle we have shaded in.

Monopoly vs. Competitive Prices

What is the difference between this price and that of a purely competitive market? We remember the formula for the equilibrium price of such a market: $MC = MR = AC = $ price. In the monopoly situation, *MC* still equals *MR* (this is always the profit-maximizing guide), but price certainly does not equal *AC*. Whereas the competitive firm is forced to price its goods at the lowest point on its cost curve, the monopolist will sell at a price above cost. If this were the case in a competitive market, we know what the remedy would be. An influx of firms would move the supply curve to the right. As a result, prices would fall until excess profits had been wiped out. **But in a monopoly situation, by the very definition of a monopoly, there is no entry into the market. Hence the monopoly is able to restrict its output to the amount that will bring in the high profit it enjoys.**

OLIGOPOLY

Monopoly in its pure form is a rarity. Most big corporations operate in a market structure of oligopoly rather than monopoly. **In an oligopolistic market situation, a few sellers divide the bulk of the market.** Sometimes there is a long tail of smaller competitors who share the leftovers.

The aircraft industry is a typical oligopoly. In 1982 there were 166 manufacturers of planes or airframes in the United States, but the top five accounted for two-thirds of all sales. There were over 723 makers of soaps and detergents, but the top four in that industry accounted for over half of the market. In tires and tubes, 164 companies made up the industry, but the top four cornered two-thirds of all sales. In automobiles, the top four manufacturers out of 284 had 71 percent of the market.

Oligopoly Cost and Demand

What does a typical oligopoly look like under the lens of price theory? On the cost side, it is much the same as a monopoly, with a dish-shaped cost curve that includes selling expense. There is, however, an essential difference between the demand curve of a monopolist and that of an oligopolist. The demand curve for a monopolist, since it comprises the entire demand for the commodity, has the familiar downward-sloping shape. The demand curve for the oligopolist, although also downward-sloping, does not have the clear-cut position of the monopolist's curve.

On the contrary, the essence of the oligopoly's demand curve is that it is uncertain; and moreover, that its position depends on what the oligopoly and its competitors do. Like the monopoly, the oligopoly is free to raise or lower its price. Unlike the monopoly, the oligopoly does not do so against a fixed demand curve. If one firm raises its price, the competitors may meet competition by raising theirs. Or they may keep their prices unchanged. Or an oligopoly may ignore price raises or cuts and lure business away by altering the product or simply by changing its image in advertising. Each of these responses will have a different impact on the demand curves of all its competitors.

The Fight for Market Shares

This extreme indeterminacy brings its effects to bear on the character of oligopolistic competition. It makes price competition the least favored rather than the standard mode of competition. Instead of price wars, a fight for shares of the market becomes the normal mode of competition. This is, of course, totally unlike the other market structures we have examined. **No competitive firm fights for a share of the market, because its output is insignificant. A monopoly does not worry about its share, because it has the whole market for itself. But a fight for**

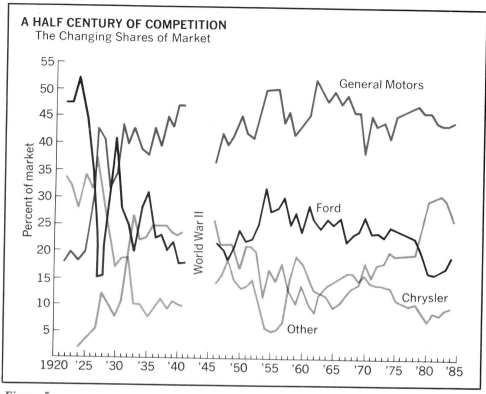

A HALF CENTURY OF COMPETITION
The Changing Shares of Market

Figure 5

Fortune magazine writes: During the last half century, the auto industry has reached a few crucial turning points that affected the fortunes of competitors for many years. In the 1920s, Alfred Sloan of General Motors wrested the lead from Henry Ford. Then, when car production resumed after World War II, Henry Ford II restored his company to a strong No. 2 position. The "other category" now consists mainly of imports. The chart is based on R. L. Polk & Company's compilation of new-car registration figures.

shares is the very heart of the oligopolistic struggle. Figure 5 shows how intense this struggle has been in the automobile industry.

Moreover, because each producer tries to be better than its main competitors in one way or another, the fight usually takes the form of winning customers to a carefully *differentiated* product. A Ford is made to be distinguishable from a Chevy; a Chevy from a Chrysler.

In the fight for market shares, price cutting becomes a much feared means of competing resorted to only when the going gets very tough. Each oligopolist thinks he is better than the competition at designing or advertising or at serving customers. No one thinks he is better at price cutting. Moreover, each oligopolist fears that a price cut will be met by retaliatory price cuts, leaving market shares more or less unchanged and everyone worse off.

CONCENTRATION RATIOS: WHAT IS AN INDUSTRY?

Economists generally measure the degree of concentration by comparing the ratio of total sales or assets of the top 4 or the top 8 companies to the total sales or assets of their industry. But immediately we encounter the difficult problem of defining *industry*. For example, the top 4 companies make 81 percent of a commodity for which there is really no adequate substitute: salt. Yet if we put salt into an industrial classification called "chemical preparations not elsewhere specified," the share of the top 4 companies falls to a paltry 23 percent of the output of that larger group of products.

Take another example. A housewife shopping for salad dressing is a consumer in an "industry" in which the top 4 producers sell 57 percent of the product. If she thinks of herself as a consumer browsing in an industry called "pickles and sauces," the top 4 salad dressing makers' share of output is only 29 percent. A farmer looking for a tractor is buying in a "market" in which the top 4 companies make 72 percent of the total output: but if we think of a tractor as belonging to a larger industry called "farm machinery and equipment," the share of the top 4 is only 44 percent.

How *should* we draw lines around industries or products? One way is by measuring how much sales of product A increase if the price of product B rises. Here is the idea of substitution applied to an important problem of economic policy. We call the measure of interproduct influence the *cross-elasticity of substitution*. If a rise in the price of A leads *many* customers to switch to B, there is at least a prima facie case for drawing the line of the industry to include both. Of course, the argument then arises as to how many consumers it takes to make "many" of them.

The Kinked Demand Curve

Thus we can see that it is not possible to arrive at neat models of oligopolistic behavior that predict how big companies will respond. But one among many models of behavior has been worked out and is worth familiarizing ourselves with, because it allows us to show graphically why oligopolists do not like to resort to price competition.

Suppose you were the president of a large company that, along with three other very similar companies, sold roughly 80 percent of a certain commodity. Suppose also that a price had been established for your commodity. It yielded you and your competitors a reasonable profit, but you and your fellow officers were trying to increase that profit.

One possibility that would certainly be discussed would be to raise the price of your product and hope your customers would continue to be loyal to you. Your company economists, however, might point out that their analyses showed a very elastic demand for your product *if you raised your price, but your competitors did not.* That is, at the higher price, many of your "loyal" customers would switch to a competitive brand, so your revenues would fall sharply and your profits decline.

Suppose, then, you took the other tack and gambled on that very elasticity of demand by cutting your prices. Would not other firms' customers switch to you and thereby raise your revenues and profits? This time your advisors might point out that if you cut your price, your competitors would almost certainly do the same, to *prevent* you from taking a portion of their market. As a result, with prices cut all around, you would probably find your market share unchanged, and your demand curve inelastic.

As Figure 6 shows, you are facing a "kinked" demand curve. In this situation, you might be tempted to sit tight and do nothing, for a very interesting thing happens to the marginal revenue curve that is derived from a kinked demand curve.

In Figure 7 we now get two marginal revenue curves: one applicable to the upper, elastic section of the demand curve; the other applicable to the lower, inelastic section. At the point of the kink, the marginal revenue curve is discontinuous, dropping vertically from the end of one slope to the beginning of the next. **As a result, there is no single point of intersection of the marginal revenue and marginal cost curves.** This means that an oligopoly's costs can change considerably before it is forced to alter its optimum volume of output or selling price.

The kinked demand curve helps explain why oligopoly prices are often so unvarying even without collusion among firms. It does not really explain how the existing price is arrived at; for once cost or demand conditions have changed

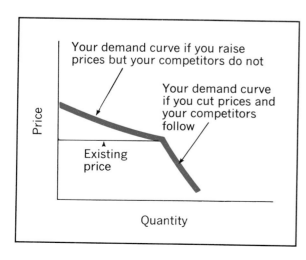

Figure 6

KINKED DEMAND CURVE

The kinked demand curve is a graphic way of showing why oligopolies tend to shy away from price cutting. Their demand curve is elastic going up, inelastic going down — exactly the opposite of what they would like it to be.

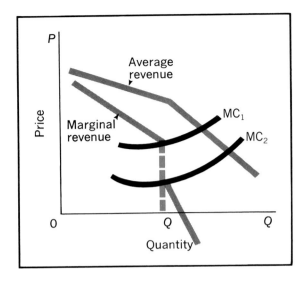

Figure 7
DISCONTINUOUS *MR* CURVE

The kinked AR curve gives rise to a strangely shaped MR curve with a vertical discontinuity. Hence costs can change considerably (from MC_1 to MC_2) without altering optimum output, OQ.

enough to overcome oligopolistic inertia, a new kink will again appear around the changed price. The kinked curve thus shows what forces affect *changes* in the oligopolistic situation, rather than how supply and demand originally determine the going price.

Collusion and Price Leadership

Another way of avoiding price competition has probably already occurred to the reader. It is for the dominant firms to agree not to undersell one another.

Such agreements have existed, undoubtedly do exist, and certainly minimize price cutting. They are, however, illegal under the antitrust laws. When unearthed, they lead to prosecution, fines, and even jail sentences. Therefore, outright collusion is probably used as a last resort. Moreover, outright collusion is often not necessary because a kind of tacit collusion called *price leadership* can do just as well.

Price leadership exists when one company sets prices for the entire industry. For years, CPC International set the price of corn starch. From time to time, when the market situation seemed to warrant it, CPC would announce a change in price. Immediately thereafter its two or three big competitors and its host of small fry competition would change their prices.

Did CPC confer with its major competitors over lunch before changing its price? Probably not. Its competitors were glad to follow the leader, because all recognized that this was the best way to maximize profits for the industry as a whole.*

---

* How are price leaders chosen? The situation varies from one industry to another. Sometimes it is the biggest firm; sometimes the most aggressive. Sometimes leadership shifts around. There is no fixed pattern.

GAME THEORY

A competitive firm has no strategy, because it has no options. It is forced to maximize its short-run profits, or it will soon be forced out of business. But the introduction of market imperfections opens the way for numerous strategies.

The problems of strategy have led to the development of game theory, a new approach to economic analysis. Suppose we have two arch-rival firms who dominate an industry. The board of directors of firm A meets one day to decide on price policy. The president opens with, "Trustworthy sources I am unable to reveal inform me that if we raise our prices, firm B, our main competitor, will raise its prices. I calculate that firm B and ourselves will each boost profits by $10 million as a consequence. Therefore, I recommend that we raise prices immediately.

At this point, the president is interrupted by the company treasurer, who is a graduate of the Harvard Business School. "I must recommend against this proposal on two counts. First, firm B may well be baiting a trap for us. If we raise our prices, they will *not* raise theirs. We will thereupon lose a vast amount of business to B. I estimate that this will cause us a loss of $10 million, and that firm B will make a profit of $20 million.

"Second, suppose firm B *does* raise prices. Then, as profit-maximizing directors, we should certainly not raise ours; for in that case, by keeping our prices low, we will steal away a great deal of business from B, and we will make a profit of $20 million, while they lose $10 million."

"Well reasoned," says the chairman of the board. "It is not only clear that we should not raise prices, but I suggest that we inform company B—discreetly, of course—that we *will* raise prices, as they suggest, in order to tempt them to do so. That will make our strategy foolproof."

In due course, this information is transmitted to firm B, where a similar discussion takes place. Firm B resolves to "accept" firm A's offer, but in fact not to raise prices at all. Result: Neither firm raises prices, because neither trusts the other. Instead of each gaining $10 million, which would have been the result of a price rise by both firms, the two firms stand pat and accept the much smaller profits that accrue from *minimizing risk.*

Excess Capacity and Price Wars

Price leadership may lead to comfortable price relations within an industry, and it is a very common mode of pricing in oligopolistic markets. From time to time, however, the system breaks down. As long as business is good, firms gladly abide by

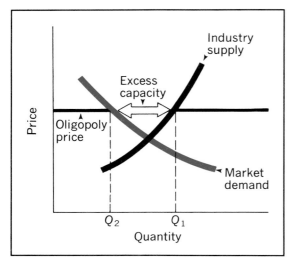

Figure 8
EXCESS CAPACITY

The ability of oligopolies to establish prices above equilibrium or clearing prices results in excess capacity. This is just like the "surplus" in earlier diagrams.

a live and let live philosophy that permits competition to focus on the relatively safe means of product differentiation.

When business is poor, price leadership is not always accepted. This difference is generated by the fact that prices above the equilibrium for a competitive market lead to a condition known as *excess capacity.* Each seller within the industry is tempted to enlarge his production capacity to the size that the "administered" price indicates. The result, as Figure 8 shows, is excess capacity; that is, the ability to supply more output (Q_1) than the market will take at that price (Q_2). In desperation, the rivals turn to price cutting, and price wars are apt to break out until stability is once more achieved.

The Drive for Growth

We have concentrated on the tactics of competition among oligopolies, but we must not leave this form of industrial market structure without paying heed to a central aspect of oligopolistic life. This aspect is the drive for growth that characterizes virually all oligopolistic firms.

To be sure, all firms in a market system seek to grow. But small competitive firms are hampered in their efforts because their rising marginal cost curves do not permit a single plant or business to expand very far. Monopolies, as we have seen, are few; and their growth, by definition, is limited to expansion of their industries. The growth situation is very different for an oligopoly. **To begin with, because an oligopoly is a large firm, it normally has many plants and therefore tends to enjoy economies of scale or long-run unit cost curves that are horizontal rather** than upward-climbing. Thus there is no cost impediment to growth, at least not for a long time.*

Second, the typical oligopolist is not as highly concentrated as the auto or tire manufacturers. The share of the industry served by the top 4 companies is frequently less than 50 percent, and the biggest single company often serves only about a quarter or less of the business. **Thus the field for expansion is very great, and the drive to widen one's share correspondingly powerful.** Growth may be the dream of the small business in a competitive industry, but it is the stuff of daily life for the oligopolist.

Growth within Markets

How is growth achieved? Usually by plowing back profits into more capital equipment or by buying up the ready-made plant and equipment of smaller companies in the field. It is virtually impossible to expand sales without an increase in capital assets, and therefore we find all successful oligopolies steadily building up the value of their capital.

For a considerable period a successful oligopoly can increase its share of the market in this way. But at a certain point, further growth within the market becomes difficult. The cost of gaining additional business rises, as indifferent customers are wooed and other customers remain loyal to competitive brands. Or the specter of an antitrust suit may loom because a company threatens, by virtue of its growth, to monopolize a market.

MNCs and Conglomerates

Two responses are open to the successful oligopoly. **First, it may transfer its fight for market shares from a national to an international basis.** The big corporation today considers the world to be its potential market—not merely as a market to which it may ship its home-produced goods, but as a market within which it may actually manufacture its product. We shall be investigating this extremely important aspect of modern competition in the extra word about multinational corporations following this chapter.

Or the oligopolist may decide to become a conglomerate; that is, to acquire capital in other industries. By diversifying its sales, it not only escapes the eye of

---

* We recall from page 520 that long-run cost curves turned up at high levels of output. This is because they referred to economies and eventually diseconomies of scale for a *given plant.* It is indeed likely that unit costs increase in a given plant, because eventually it becomes so large that it is no longer convenient to administer. An oligopoly or a monopoly may, however, decide to build a new plant rather than to push an existing one beyond its economical size. Do big oligopolistic firms that spread production among several plants also experience rising unit costs? We really do not know. It may be that the new technology of information retrieval has so increased the efficiency of management that multiplant firms *never* experience rising unit costs. For all practical purposes, their long-run cost curves are horizontal or perhaps even falling.

the Justice Department antitrust lawyers, but also avoids putting all its eggs in one basket.

The rise of the conglomerate helps explain a curious and seemingly contradictory state of affairs that we noticed in Chapter 5. There we saw that the share of total assets coming under the control of giant companies—virtually all of them oligopolists—had risen dramatically, so that the top 100 industrial companies in 1970 owned about 50 percent of all the assets of all manufacturing companies, about the same share as the top 200 companies had owned in 1948. We also noted that the concentration of sales did not parallel that of assets. Actually, a study of the nation's markets shows no overall drift toward a more highly concentrated pattern *within* markets.

Now we can understand the dynamics of this phenomenon. The concentration of assets is partly explained by the continued growth of some companies within their industries, and by the very rapid rise of conglomerates, often through mergers. From 1974 to 1984 there were some 23,000 mergers and aquisitions, and 82 of the largest 500 corporations disappeared. In 1985–86 alone, 17 of the Fortune 500 lost their corporate independence in the merger game.

MONOPOLISTIC COMPETITION

We will return to the world of oligopolies, but we must first continue our survey of competition in the real world. For oligopoly, although perhaps the most significant departure from the ideal of pure competition, is not the most common departure. Once we pass from the manufacturing to the retail or service sectors where competition is still intense and characterized by numerous small units, we encounter a new kind of market situation, equally strange to the pages of a text on pure competition. **This is a situation in which there are many firms, with relatively easy entrance and exit, but where each firm sells a product slightly differentiated from that of every other.** Here is the world of the average store or the small competitive manufacturer of a brand-name product—indeed, of all sellers who can identify their products for the public and who must face the competition of many other makers of similar but not exactly identical products.

Economists call this market situation tinged by monopoly *imperfect competition or monopolistic competition.* How does it differ from pure competition? Once again, there is no difference on the cost side. That is the same for both a perfectly competitive and an imperfectly competitive firm, except for the presence of selling costs in imperfect competition. The difference, again, comes in the nature of the demand curve.

We recall that the special attribute of the demand curve facing a firm in a purely competitive situation is its horizontal character. By way of contrast, **in a market of imperfect competition, the demand curve facing each seller slopes gently downward** because one seller's good or service is not exactly like that of competitors, and because the seller therefore has some ability to raise price without losing all his business.

Equilibrium in Monopolistic Competition

What is the equilibrium position of such an imperfectly competitive firm — say a dress manufacturer? In Figure 9 on the left, an imperfect competitor is obviously making substantial profits. Note that the firm's best position where $MR = MC$ is *exactly* like that of any firm, monopolies included. But our firm is not a monopolist and its profits are therefore not immune to erasure by entry into its field. In Figure 9 we show the same firm after *other entrepreneurs have moved into the industry* (with additional similar, although not identical, products) and taken away some of our firm's market and *moved its demand curve to the left.*

Note that our final position for the marginal dress firm has no more profit than that of a purely competitive seller because $AC = AR$. On the other hand, because its demand curve slopes, the equilibrium point cannot be at the lowest point on the average cost curve, nor will output have reached optimum size.

This outcome clearly dissipates economic well-being. The fact that firms are forced to operate to the left of the optimums on their cost curves means that they have not been able to combine factors to yield their greatest efficiency. This failure penalizes factors, once when they are paid too little because their potential marginal productivity has not been reached, and again as consumers when they are

Figure 9
MONOPOLISTIC COMPETITION

Here we can see that initial equilibrium for a small dress manufacturer looks exactly the same as equilibrium for a monopoly. In both cases MC and MR determine output. But unlike the case for monopolies, the dress manufacturer experiences the competition of entry. His demand curve AR_1 moves to the left to AR_2. Again, he seeks $MC = MR$, but now there is no spread between AC and AR. He has no profit and no advantage from his monopolistic MR curve.

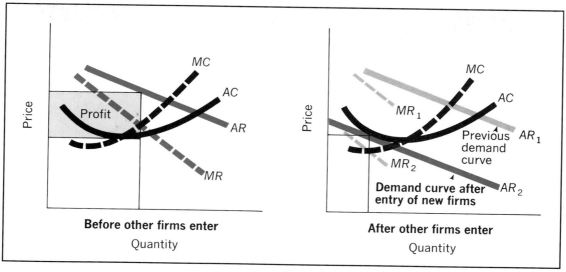

Before other firms enter

After other firms enter

forced to pay too much for products that have not been produced at lowest possible cost. In addition, waste is incurred because the attempt to differentiate products leads in many instances to too many small units; for example, four gas stations at one intersection.

Inefficient though it may be, monopolistic competition yields no profit for the marginal firm in an industry. The entrepreneur therefore feels fully as hard-pressed as would the producer of an undifferentiated commodity. The difference is that a monopolistic competitive businessperson has the possibility of *further differentiating* a product, hoping thereby to tilt the demand curve in a more inelastic position. In turn, this might permit a slight price rise to squeeze out a tiny "pure monopoly" profit. The result is that monopolistic competition fosters a tremendous variety of goods—the ladies garment industry being a prime example.

THE WORLD OF REAL COMPETITION IN COMPUTERS

Once we leave the world of homogenous products such as wheat, the problems of pricing and product design become much more complicated than any economics text can indicate. Let us take the case of the personal computer industry. At the moment there are over 200 firms making computers. They range in price from a few hundred to several thousand dollars. They offer a wide range of options, "compatibilities," gadgets, service facilities, and the like.

Ten years from now, if past experience is a reliable guide, it is likely that only a few dozen or so firms will have survived. What will determine which of the 200 firms will be among the survivors? Will it be price alone? That is very unlikely. Design alone? Equally unlikely. The winners will be those companies that have found a niche for themselves, where a combination of price and product design suits the needs of enough consumers to allow production to be carried on profitably.

What will that combination be? The managers of the present-day 200 companies do not know—if they did, they would all be producing the "correct" product, instead of searching around to discover what the correct product will be. In the end we will probably have a spectrum of computers, just as we have a spectrum of cars or appliances or TV sets. The process of actual competition is one of "sorting out" and structuring the market itself, as well as finally locating oneself in it.

Social Consequences

Are monopolies as evil as their reputations? Are oligopolies a bad thing? Are monopolistically competitive industries simply wasteful?

These are questions of major importance, but they take us outside the firm to a public point of view. We take up these issues shortly.

looking back

KEY CONCEPTS

Markets vs. motivation Price makers vs. price takers

1 Imperfect competition—monopoly, oligopoly, and monopolistic competition—refers to different kinds of market structure than pure competition; it does *not* refer to different motivations. Competitive firms have no option but to take existing prices. Firms in imperfect competition can make prices—although not entirely as they would like.

Monopoly demand curves are like those of a competitive industry

2 Monopolies are firms that cater to all the demand of a given market. They face the same demand curve as a competitive industry. By advertising, a monopolist hopes to move his demand curve out and to make it more inelastic.

$MR < AR$ for a monopolist

3 Because a monopoly faces a sloping demand curve, its marginal revenue curve is not horizontal, but falling. This is because it must cut price to increase sales. For a competitive firm $MR = AR$; for a monopoly, $MR < AR$.

Monopoly equilibrium: $MR = MC$, $AR > AC$ = profit

4 Monopoly equilibrium is determined by the intersection of MR and MC. This gives optimum output. Optimum output indicates selling price. Profit is determined by the spread between selling price and average cost at point of optimum output. This profit is not subject to erosion by entry because by definition our firm is the only one—a monopoly.

An oligopoly may have a kinked demand curve reflecting competitors' reactions

5 Oligopoly is much more frequent than monopoly. It is a market structure in which a few firms dominate the market. An oligopolist's demand curve is likely to be kinked. The kink simply tells us that each firm's price policy invites a response, so that if it raises prices, competitors won't, whereas if it cuts them, they will.

The fight for market shares, diversification and multinationals

6 Oligopolies often use price leadership to avoid price competition. The fight for market shares is the most conspicuous feature of their strategies. To avoid undue concentration, oligopolies may diversify or go multinational.

Monopolistic competition: entry removes monopoly profits	**7** Monopolistic competition refers to market situations in which each firm has a monopoly (a sloping demand curve), but where entry is easy. The result is that demand is pushed to the left and equilibrium is reached without any monopoly profit.

ECONOMIC VOCABULARY

QUESTIONS

1. How would you define a monopoly? Are monopolies necessarily large? What constraints does a demand curve put on the behavior of a monopoly?

2. Suppose that you were the only seller of a certain kind of machinery in the nation. Suppose further that you discovered that your demand curve looked like this:

Price	$100	$90	$80	$70
Quantity of machines sold	1	2	3	4

What is the average revenue at each price? What is the marginal revenue at each price? Draw a diagram showing the marginal and average revenues.

3. Now superimpose on this diagram a hypothetical cost profile for your business. Where is the point of equilibrium for the monopolist? Is this the same, in terms of MC and MR, as the point for the competitive firm? Now show the equilibrium output and price.

4. Does the equilibrium output of the monopolist yield a profit? What are the relevant costs for figuring profit, average cost per unit, or marginal cost? Show on your diagram the difference between average cost and selling price.

5. Why will a monopolist's selling price not be pushed to the lowest point on the cost curve?

6. What is the difference between monopoly and oligopoly? Between oligopoly and pure competition? Between pure competition and monopolistic (or imper-

fect) competition? Between the latter and oligopoly? Can these differences be expressed in demand curves?

7. What is a differentiated commodity? Give examples. Draw the demand curve for a farmer selling wheat and that for a toy manufacturer selling a special kind of doll. What will happen if the doll manufacturer makes a large profit? What will the doll maker's final point of equilibrium look like if there are many competitors?

8. Is excess capacity possible in a truly competitive industry? A monopoly? Why in an oligopoly?

AN EXTRA WORD ABOUT

The Multinational Corporation

The problem of big business is one of old standing, dating back to the period just after the Civil War. But recently that problem has been given a new twist by the appearance of enormous corporations whose business empires literally straddle the globe — the multinational corporations. Take PepsiCo, for example. PepsiCo does not ship its famous product around the world from bottling plants in the United States. It *produces* Pepsi Cola in more than 600 plants in 148 countries. When you buy a Pepsi in Mexico or the Philippines, Israel or Denmark, you are buying an American product that was manufactured in that country.

PepsiCo is a far-flung, but not a particularly large multinational corporation: In 1982 it was the 156th largest company. More impressive by far is the Ford Motor Company, a multinational that consists of a network of 26 major subsidiary corporations, 19 of them foreign-based. Of the corporation's total assets of $23 billion, nearly one-half is invested in 19 foreign nations; and of its 383,700 employees (as of 1984) more than 210,000 were employed outside the U.S. And if we studied the corporate structures of GM or IBM or the great oil companies, we would find that they, too, are multinational companies with substantial portions of their total wealth invested in productive facilities outside the United States.

If we broaden our view to include the top 100 American firms, we find that two-thirds have such production facilities in at least six nations. Moreover, the value of output that is produced overseas by the largest corporations by far exceeds the value of the goods they still export from the United States. In 1984, assets of foreign affiliates of U.S. multinational firms (which means their wholly or partially owned overseas branches) came to over $233 billion.

INTERNATIONAL DIRECT INVESTMENT

Another way of establishing the spectacular rise of international production is to trace the increase in the value of U.S. foreign direct investment; that is, the value of foreign-located, U.S.-owned plant and equipment (not U.S.-owned foreign bonds and stocks). In 1950 the value of U.S. foreign direct investment was $11 billion. In 1984 it was over $226 billion. Moreover, this figure, too, needs two upward adjustments.

The value of foreign direct investment is calculated by adding up the actual money spent each year in acquiring assets. But no adjustment is made for increases in the current value of those assets because of inflation. That is, the replacement value of American (or European) foreign assets would be much higher than its "book" value if assets were revalued according to current prices. In 1984, for example, the earnings of America's overseas direct investment came to $28 billion. If we assume the ratio between assets and earnings was roughly the same abroad as at home, the value of America's overseas assets would have been $350 billion, not $226 billion.

A second correction to the value of foreign investment arises because the stated value of overseas assets includes only the dollars actually invested, not the value of the total enterprise the investment may control. It is frequently the case that a direct investment will control a larger amount of capital than the investment itself — it only takes 51 percent of the voting stock to wield decision-making power in a corporation, and frequently control is gained with a much smaller holding than that.

The actual value of American foreign direct investment (or its counterpart, European or Japanese foreign investment) is therefore difficult or impossible to calculate with exactitude. In all likelihood something between a quarter and a half of the real assets of our biggest corporations are located abroad, and probably the same ratio applies to other advanced capitalist economies.

THE INTERNATIONAL CHALLENGE

The movement toward the internationalization of production is not a strictly American phenomenon. If the American multinationals are today the most imposing (of the world's biggest 50 corporations, over 23 are American), they are closely challenged by non-American multinationals (see Table 1). Notably, these non-American companies are either petroleum-related or huge Japanese trading conglomerates. Philips Lamp Works is a huge Dutch multinational company with operations in 68 countries. Of its 343,000 employees, 260,000 work in nations other than the Netherlands, Royal Dutch/Shell is another vast multinational, whose home is somewhere between the Netherlands and the United Kingdom (it is jointly owned by nationals of both countries): Shell *in the United States* ranks among "our" top 20 biggest companies. Another is Nestle Chocolate, a Swiss firm, 97 percent of whose $2 billion revenues originate outside Switzerland.

MOTIVES FOR OVERSEAS PRODUCTION

What drives a firm to produce overseas rather than just sell overseas? One possible answer is straightforward. A firm is successful at home. Its technology and organizational skills give it an edge on foreign competition. It begins to export its product. The foreign market grows. At some point, the firm begins to calculate whether it would be more profitable to organize an overseas production operation. By doing so, it would save transportation costs. It may be able to evade a tariff by producing goods behind a tariff wall. It may be able to take advantage of lower wage rates. Finally it ceases shipping goods abroad and instead exports capital, technology, and management — and becomes a multinational.

Calculations may be more complex. By degrees a successful company may change its point of view. First it thinks of itself as a domestic company, perhaps with a small export

Table 1
THE TOP 15 MULTINATIONALS, 1982

Company	Total Sales ($billions)	Foreign Sales as % of Total Sales	Number of Countries in which Subsidiaries are Located
1. Exxon Corp.	$102.1	70%	>80
2. Shell/Royal Dutch Petroleum	83.8	60*	87
3. AT&T	65.1	3	15
4. Mobil Oil	63.1	60	22
5. Mitsubishi Corp.	61.5	N/A	>80
6. General Motors	60.0	16	20
7. Mitsui & Co.	55.4	25	>80
8. British Petroleum	52.9	81	70
9. C. Itoh & Co.	51.6	N/A	>80
10. Marubeni	48.3	N/A	>70
11. Texaco	47.0	66	32
12. Sumitomo Corp.	45.9	N/A	81
13. Ford Motor	37.2	45	19
14. Standard Oil Co. of California	35.2	53	39
15. IBM	34.4	37	15

* Outside Europe.
Sources: *The Times 1000, 1983–84,* annual reports.

market. Then it builds up its exports and thinks of itself as an international company with a substantial interest in exports. Finally its perspective changes to that of a multinational, considering the world (or substantial portions of it) to be its market. In that case, it may locate plants abroad *before* the market is fully developed, in order to be firmly established abroad ahead of its competition.*

ECONOMICS OF MULTINATIONAL PRODUCTION

Whether or not the multinational boom continues at its past rate, the startling rise of multinationals has already changed the face of international economic relationships. **One major effect has been a dramatic shift in the *geographic location* and the *technological* character of international economic activity.**

The shift away from exports to international production has introduced two changes into the international economic scene. One change is a movement of foreign investment away from its original concentration in the underdeveloped areas of the world toward the richer markets of the developed areas. Fifty years ago, in the era of high imperialism, most of the capital leaving one country for another flowed from rich to poor lands. Thus foreign investment in the late nineteenth and early twentieth centuries was largely associated with

---

* The internal dynamics that send some firms overseas, but not others, are by no means wholly understood. The internationalization of *production* is much more widely spread in some industries, such as glass, than in others, such as steel. Drugs are widely produced on an international basis; machine tools are not.

the creation of vast plantations, the building of railways through jungles, and the development of mineral resources.

But the growth of the multinational enterprise has coincided with a decisive shift away from investment in the underdeveloped world to investment in the industrial world. In 1897, 59 percent of American foreign direct investment was in agriculture, mining, or railways, mainly in the underdeveloped world. By the end of the 1970s, our investment in agriculture, mining, and railways, as a proportion of our total overseas assets, had fallen to about 20 percent; and its geographical location in the Third World came to only 36 percent of all our overseas direct investments. More striking, almost three-quarters of our huge rise in direct investment during the decades of the 1960s and 1970s were in the developed world; and the vast bulk of it was in manufacturing (and oil) rather than in plantations, railroads, or ores. **Thus the multinational companies were investing in each others' territories rather than invading the territories of the underdeveloped world.** This is not to say that they do not wield great power in the less developed regions, as we shall see, but that their thrust of expansion has been in other industrial lands.

The second economic change is really implicit in the first. **It is a shift away from heavy- to high-technology industries — away from enterprises in which vast sums of capital were associated with large, unskilled labor forces as in the building of railways or plantations — toward industries in which capital is perhaps less strategic than research and development, skilled technical manpower, and sophisticated management techniques typical of the computer, petrochemical, and other new industries.** Table 2 sums up the overall shift.

Note the dramatic shift away from Latin America and away from transport, mining, and agriculture into Europe and manufacturing, a shift that would be even more accentuated if we were not still dependent on oil as a major source of the world's energy. If nuclear power or the fuel cell displace oil within the next two decades, we can expect a still more rapid decline in investment in the less developed areas (especially in the Middle East), and a proportionately still larger concentration of foreign direct investment in manufacturing.

Table 2
AMERICAN FOREIGN DIRECT INVESTMENT

Total (Millions)	1929 $7,528	1950 $11,788	1984 $233,412
		Distribution by market (%)	
Canada	$27	30%	22%
Europe	18	14	44
Latin America	47	41	12
Asia, Africa, other	8	15	22
		Distribution by industrial sector (%)	
Manufacturing	24	31%	40%
Petroleum	15	29	27
Transport and utilities	21	12	N/A
Mining	15	9	3
Trade	5	7	13
Agriculture	12	5	N/A
Other	8	6	N/A*

* The other 17% now is in banking (6%), finance (6%), other (5%).
Source: *Survey of Current Business,* June 1985, p. 30.

In recent years a still more dramatic trend has come to the fore. This is the capacity of big companies to combine high technology and low-wage labor by setting up modern production facilities in such areas as Mexico, South Korea, Singapore, and the like. This is by no means a movement confined to the multinationals. High-tech, low-wage operations have often been organized by companies of relatively small size. But the new capability of combining the two has often aided the big MNCs in consolidating their global positions.

PROBLEMS FOR POLICY MAKERS

Multinationals have not only changed the face of international economic activity, but also have added considerably to the problem of controlling domestic economies. Assume that a country wants to slow down its economy through monetary policies designed to reduce plant and equipment spending. A restrictive monetary policy at home may be vitiated by the ability of a multinational to borrow *abroad* in order to finance investment at home. Conversely, a monetary policy designed to stimulate the home economy may end up in loans that increase production in someone else's economy. Thus the effectiveness of national economic policy making is weakened. Moreover, it is not easy to suggest that monetary policies should be coordinated among countries, since the economic needs of different countries may not be the same: What is right for one country at a given time may be wrong for another.

HOST AND HOSTAGE

The jealous claims of nation-states who seek to retain national control over productive activity within their own borders and the powerful thrust of pan-national corporations for new markets in foreign territories introduces profound tensions into the political economics of multinational production. **On the one hand, the multinational is in a position to win hard bargains from the host country into which it seeks to enter because the corporation is the main bearer of new technologies and management techniques that every nation seeks.** Therefore, if one country — say France — refuses to give a would-be entrant the right to come in (and possibly to cause financial losses to its established firms), the multinational may well place its plants, with their precious economic cargo of productivity, in another country, leaving the recalcitrant nation the loser in the race for international growth.

On the other hand, the power is by no means entirely one-sided; for once a multinational *has* entered a foreign nation, it becomes a *hostage* of the host country. It is now bound by the laws of that country and may find itself forced to undertake activities that are "foreign." In Japan, for example, it is an unwritten law that workers engaged by giant corporations are *never* fired, but become permanent employees. Japan has been extremely reluctant to allow foreign capital to establish manufacturing operations on Japanese soil, to the great annoyance of foreign companies. But if, as now seems likely, Japan is opened to American and European capital, we can be sure that American or European corporations will be expected to behave in the Japanese way with their employees. This will not be an easy course to follow, since these corporations are not likely to receive the special support the Japanese government gives to its own big firms.

Or take the problem of a multinational that is forced by a fall in demand to cut back the volume of its output. A decision made along strictly economic lines would lead it to close its least profitable plant. But this may bring very serious economic repercussions in the particular nation in which that plant is located — so serious that the government will threaten to take action if the plant is closed. What dictates shall the multinational then follow: those of standard business accounting or those of political accounting?

Or consider the multinational seeking to expand or to alter its operations in an underdeveloped country. This, too, may lead to friction, for as former Under Secretary of State George Ball has candidly asked: "How can a national government make an economic plan with any confidence if a board of directors meeting 5,000 miles away can, by altering its pattern of purchasing and production, affect in a major way the country's economic life?"

AN UNWRITTEN ENDING

There are no answers to these questions as yet. In all likelihood the tension between the pull of economic and of political life will go on, unsatisfactorily resolved, for a long time. The big corporations are certain to continue their multinational thrust. As global producers, they will be the main international carriers of efficiency and development, especially in the high technology areas for which they seem to be the most effective form of organization. But if the power of the nation-state will be challenged by these international production units, it is not likely to be humbled by them. There are many things a nation can do that a corporation cannot, including, above all, the creation of the spirit of sacrifice necessary both for good purposes such as development and for evil ones such as war.

Perhaps all we can say at this stage of human development is that both nation-states and huge corporations are necessary, in that they seem to be the only ways in which we can organize mankind to perform the arduous and sustained labor without which humanity itself would rapidly perish. Perhaps after the long age of capital accumulation has finally come to an end and sufficient capital is available to all peoples, we may be able to think seriously about dismantling the giant enterprise *and* the nation-state, both of which overpower the individual with their massive organized strength. However desirable that ultimate goal may be, in our time both state and corporation promise to be with us, and the tension between them will be part of the evolutionary drama of our period of history.

CHAPTER 31
The Microeconomics of Taxing and Spending

a look ahead

Taxing and government spending are usually thought to be macroeconomic problems — and of course they are macroeconomic problems when we consider the levels of taxing and spending in relation to the flows of gross national product. But there are also important microeconomic aspects to both of the great fiscal functions of government. Specifically in this chapter we look into

1 The basic structure of the U.S. tax system.
2 The complicated question of tax incidence — who pays taxes.
3 The criteria for rational government expenditure.

All this should pave the way for some hard questions in the coming chapters.

THE STRUCTURE OF TAXATION

Taxation in the United States is complex. It occurs on three basic levels of government—federal, state, and local—and through a myriad of entities and forms. There are a total of some 38,000 units of government in our country with taxing power. They tax sales, they tax property, and they tax income. There is no rhyme, reason, or logic to this system: It is simply the way our country grew up, and the way it is. That is why, in part, our system of taxation is so hard to justify or even to understand.

All in all, in 1984 federal, state, and local government raised $1.33 trillion in taxes, or 30.9 percent of our gross national product. How does this figure compare with other industrial nations? Table 1 provides the answer: It is relatively low. Japan, with its heavier reliance on private pensions, manages to tax a smaller share of total income. Major European countries and Canada, with nationalized health care, take on a higher tax share than ourselves. For smaller, wealthy, social democratic states like Norway and Sweden, the tax share is highest of all.

One big difference, though, is the federal character of our tax system. Only 62 percent of all taxes raised in the United States in 1984 ($703 billion) went to the federal government. The remainder, $430 billion, was raised by states and localities. No other major industrial country has anything like this degree of federalism and diversity in tax raising.

Sources of Revenue

Moreover, the sources of taxation are diverse. The principal tax source of the federal government is the *personal income tax,* in existence since 1913. The personal income tax contributed $345 billion to the federal coffers in 1985, or nearly half of the total. Personal taxes (including personal property taxes) also contrib-

Table 1
TAXES AS PERCENT OF GDP, 1983

Country	Current Receipts
Japan	30.4%
United States	31.7
Canada	39.0
United Kingdom	42.5
Germany	45.2
Italy	45.3
Austria	46.6
France	47.0
Norway	52.6
Denmark	53.1
Sweden (1982)	59.3

Source: *OECD Historical Statistics,* p. 64.

uted about one quarter of their tax revenues to state and local governments in 1985.

The second largest source of tax revenue for the federal government — and the most rapidly growing in recent years — is *contributions for social insurance,* primarily social security, unemployment insurance, and Medicare. These are levied on payrolls — half on the employer, half on the employee. In theory — and by and large in fact — they go only toward the payment of retirement, health care, and unemployment insurance benefits. These sources contributed $289 billion to federal revenues in 1985, over a third of the total. State and local governments, in contrast, got only about a tenth of their taxes from this source.

So far, we have accounted for over four-fifths of federal government revenues, but only for a third of state and local tax income. Where does the rest come from? We know the answer: from taxes on corporate income and on business sales, officially designated as *corporate profits taxes* and *indirect business taxes.*

Corporate profits taxes have been a tax source of declining relative importance in recent years. In 1960, for example, they contributed nearly a quarter of all federal revenues; by 1984 they were down to less than a tenth. Corporate profits taxes are also a minor component — less than 4 percent — of state and local tax revenue. Figure 1 shows these trends.

That leaves "indirect business taxes" — primarily the city and state sales taxes that you pay on virtually everything you buy, unless you happen to live in one of the very few states that has managed to avoid adopting one. Federal excise taxes, such as the telephone tax, and taxes on cigarettes and alcohol account for the remaining tenth of federal revenues. But this source is vastly more important to the state and local sector, accounting for $249 billion in revenue in 1984, or over half of the grand total.

TAX INCIDENCE

Regressive, Progressive, and Proportional

What is a fair tax? As with so many questions that affect policy, there is no economic criterion for fair or unfair. But there are some objective measures that enable us to talk about the question more intelligently.

We start by recognizing that all taxes can be classified into three different kinds by their incidence — that is, by analyzing who pays them. Regressive taxes bear more heavily, in percentage terms, on low incomes than high ones: a highway toll, for example, is regressive because 25¢ is a bigger part of a poor driver's income than of a rich driver's. Proportional taxes bear equally on all income groups. Any tax that takes a fixed percent of all incomes — say 25

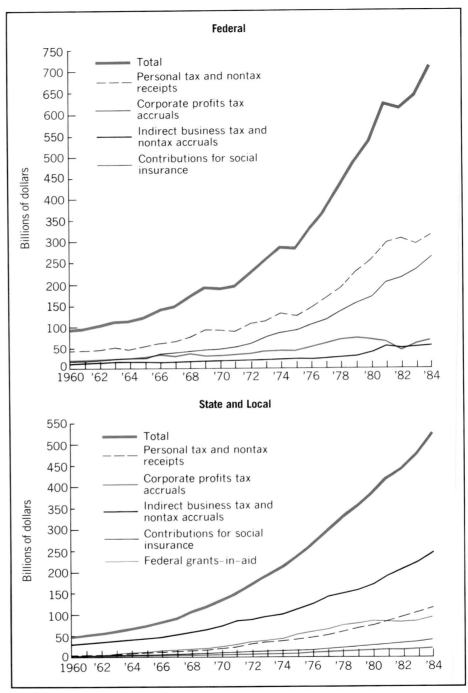

Figure 1

TAX TRENDS

This figure provides the basic data on federal and state and local tax trends over the past twenty-five years. Note the rise in social insurance and the fall in corporate income taxes at the federal level.

percent — would be a proportional tax. And a progressive tax is a tax that takes a larger bite — a larger percentage as well as a larger amount — as income rises.

There are no economic or even moral rules that enable us to say that one category of taxes is fairer than another. Yet there is no doubt that most economists, politicians, and members of the public do not openly admire regressive taxes. Sometimes we favor regressive revenue measures, such as lotteries, which tend to bear more heavily on the poor than the rich, but then we find ways of rationalizing our decision, such as the popularity of such measures, or their convenience. On the whole, everyone favors proportional taxes or mildly progressive ones. But when progressivity goes "too far" — when very successful entrepreneurs are penalized by taxes that virtually wipe out all their incomes — we tend to call that unfair.

By these criteria, are our taxes fair or unfair? The answer depends, of course, on their incidence; and as we shall see, it is surprisingly difficult to determine what that incidence is. To take the most simple-looking case, suppose that the state levies a 5 percent sales tax on all commodities sold at retail. Who pays such a tax? The question seems nonsensical. Doesn't the consumer pay the tax? Not all of it. When the state levies a sales tax, the cost of commodities rises. This is the same thing as an upward shift to the supply curve, as we see in Figure 2. As a result, price rises from P_1 to P_2.

Now, who has paid the tax? The consumer has paid some, but not all. He pays the rise in price $P_2 - P_1$, and he also loses the utilities of the goods he can no longer buy, $Q_1 - Q_2$. But the producer has also paid some of the tax — the amount $P_1 - P_3$, and he has also suffered a loss in revenues because his sales have dropped.

And even this is not an end to the matter. Because the producer's income has fallen, his demand for factors has dropped from D_1 to D_2 (See Figure 3). Hence the

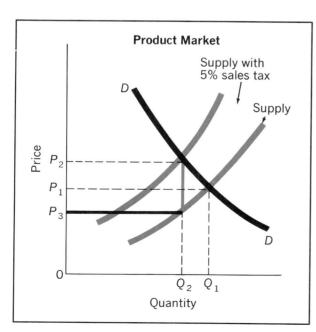

Figure 2
INCIDENCE OF SALES TAXES

Sales tax per unit is $P_2 - P_3$. The consumer pays part, $P_2 - P_1$, and the producer part, $P_1 - P_3$. The consumer also suffers a fall in consumption from Q_1 to Q_2, and the producer a fall in sales of like amount. Both consumer and producer bear some of the tax.

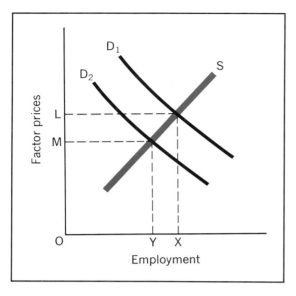

Figure 3
IMPACT OF SALES TAX ON FACTORS
Factors also bear some of the tax because a fall in producer's revenues shifts his demand curve leftward. Factor income falls from OX times OL to OY times OM.

prices of the factors and the quantities employed will fall. So *factors, too, bear part of the tax.* In Figure 3 factors of production suffer a cutback in price from *L* to *M* and a reduction in quantities employed from *X* to *Y*. Hence their incomes will fall from *OL* $\times$ *OX* to *OM* $\times$ *OY*.

As a result, the sales tax will actually be shared by consumers, producers, and factors of production. The point is that the retail storekeeper, who actually makes out the check to the government, or the consumer who pays his pennies of sales tax is very likely not the sole bearer of the tax.

Effects of Elasticity

How much of the tax will the consumer bear? That depends on the elasticity of demand for the product. If demand is very inelastic the storekeeper will mark up items by the amount of the sales tax and will sell as many items as before. In that case, the consumer will pay it all, and the retailer or seller will simply act as the collection agency for the government, as Figure 4 shows.

More likely, when a sales tax is imposed, sellers will shave profit margins to avoid a serious loss of volume. They will make up price by less than the tax and make up the difference out of profits. Sellers and consumers both will then bear the tax.

Complexity of Incidence

Are sales taxes fair or unfair? Perhaps we can now see how difficult it is to answer the question. Even in what seems to be a clear case we have to know two things:

1. How much of the tax is shifted "forward" to the consumer, how much is absorbed by the seller or producer, and how much is shifted backward to the

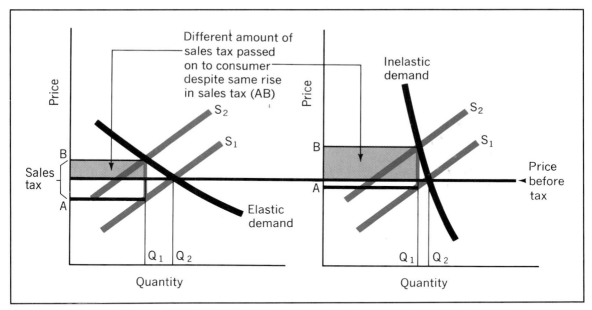

Figure 4
EFFECT OF ELASTICITY ON TAX INCIDENCE FOR CONSUMERS

Elasticity again makes all the difference. Compare the amount of tax that can be passed along to the consumer in the two cases above. Both goods bear the same sales tax. In the case of the left, demand is elastic, and therefore consumers find substitutes. Quantity sold falls markedly, and the actual rise in price—the amount of the sales tax passed on to the consumer—is only about half the sales tax. Observe how the inelastic demand curve on the right allows a much larger proportion of the tax to be shifted forward.

factors of production? That requires a knowledge of elasticities of demand and supply we often do not possess.

2. To determine how much of a sales tax is paid by any one person, we also have to know the extent to which that individual is a consumer, a producer, or a factor. Think about the impact of a 5¢ tax per pack of cigarettes on a tobacconist who does not smoke but who owns 10 shares of American Tobacco. Such are the difficulties of coming to clear-cut pronouncements about tax incidence.

Regressivity of Sales Taxes

Nonetheless, we can venture one generalization. **A sales tax on necessities is sure to be passed on to the consumer to a much greater extent than one on luxuries.** This is because the demand curve for necessities is, by definition, less elastic than the demand curve for luxuries. Most necessities, such as food, bulk larger in the budgets of low-income families than of high-income families. On the average, food costs absorb about 30 percent of an $8,000 family budget, in contrast with just over 20 percent of an $18,000 budget. Therefore sales taxes on necessities are regressive.

Does this mean that a sales tax on luxuries is progressive? Not necessarily. Because the demand for luxuries is likely to be elastic, the sales tax on luxuries may not be shifted forward, but will fall instead on the yacht-builders, the furrier, the Cadillac maker, and their employees—who may not be wealthy at all!

PERSONAL INCOME TAXES

Progressivity of Income Taxes

Income taxes, levied by federal, state, or local (usually municipal) authorities are generally progressive in their structure. That is, the rate of taxes rises as income rises. The federal income tax, as we write these words, begins at 11 percent and increases to 50 percent at a taxable income level of $85,000 for a married couple filing separate returns or for a single taxpayer. Tax reductions to a top level of around 30 percent are likely in 1986 and after.

However, there is a great deal of difference between rates on paper and actual income taxes paid by families. This is because we do not pay taxes on our total or gross income, but on our taxable incomes. Taxable incomes are our gross incomes less various exemptions and deductions permitted by law. For example, we are allowed to deduct $1,040 for each dependent (including ourselves) in figuring our income tax. We can deduct interest that we pay, which is usually interest on mortgages on our houses. We can deduct all state and local taxes from our federal income tax. We can take off charitable contributions, legitimate business expenses, and a long list of other items.

Effect of Deductions

Deductions affect the incidence of the income tax structure in two ways. In the first place, they often create "horizontal" inequities. Two families or individuals with identical incomes may pay very different taxes because one can use a deduction and another cannot. For years, owners of oil properties enjoyed a deduction known as a depletion allowance. It enabled them to reduce their taxable income from oil by as much as a third below the actual oil income. Owners of state and local bonds have for years enjoyed the privilege of not paying any federal tax on the interest from these bonds.

Thus, two households, side by side in identical houses, enjoying identical incomes, may pay hugely different taxes. Because of deduction loopholes, a few—actually a very few—wealthy people escape taxation entirely.

Loss of Progressivity

In the second place, deductions greatly lessen the progressivity of taxes. Deductions have this antiprogressive effect because a deduction is worth much more to a high-income family than to a low-income one. Example: charitable donations. A rich family, whose marginal tax bracket is 50 percent, gives away $100. As a result, its pretax income is reduced by $100, but its tax is reduced by $50. The net cost of the $100 gift is therefore $50 in reduced after-tax spendable income. A poorer family, whose marginal tax bracket is 25 percent, also gives away $100. It thereby saves a tax of $25. Its spendable, after-tax income is reduced by $75. Not only is this loss of spendable income larger in *absolute* terms than for the richer family, but it is certainly larger as a percentage of its total income. We see these effects in Table 2, calculated on the basis of tax rates in the early 1980s.

Yet another study conducted by the Treasury Department showed that 4.4 percent of all taxpayers who earned $50,000 a year and up enjoyed a third of the benefits from thirty-three specific tax loopholes. Highest on the list of such tax benefits was the exclusion from taxation of all interest on state and municipal bonds: 93 percent of all such interest goes to those earning $50,000 or more.

Do Taxes Impinge on Effort?

Personal income taxes—particularly at high marginal rates on high incomes—have come under intense attack in recent years. Does this reflect good economics, or merely special interest greed? We look into the details of this attack again in Chapter 35. Here, we simply need to set out the outlines of the critics' case.

The essence of the argument has been that high tax rates on *income* are the equivalent of high tax rates on *effort*. Progressive income taxes, it is claimed, lessen the marginal utility of additional work because they take away an increasing proportion of the after-tax income that can be derived from it. Therefore they move those subject to high taxes up the classical supply curve of labor, encouraging the wealthy, in effect, to spend their time by the pool and on the golf course rather than in productive effort.

Studies—both before and after the tax reductions of 1981—have failed to support this "supply-side" case. Neither hours worked nor intensity of effort seems to respond to changes in marginal tax rates. And the reasons are easy to understand. First, a change in taxes affects more than the relative value of labor as against leisure: It also affects *income*. After a tax cut, a wealthy person has more after-tax income than before, and this increase in wealth may induce him or her to work less, even though the after-tax return *from working* has risen. Second, for many of the truly wealthy, there never was a strong connection between hours worked and income. Top-bracket income comes more from nonwork—capital gains, interest and dividends, and other property income—than from active economic effort. Property income is not at all affected by the number of hours put in at the office, so that lowering taxes on *income* (not just on salaries) offers no spur to work.

Table 2

REAL AND NOMINAL TAX RATES, 1985

Actual taxes paid in different income brackets have been less progressive than marginal tax rates would suggest.

Adjusted Family Income (Married Taxpayers)	Scheduled Marginal Federal Income Tax Rates	Actual Average Federal Income Tax Rates
$0–3,540	0%	0%
3,540–5,720	11	4
5,720–7,910	12	4
7,910–12,390	14	6
12,390–16,650	16	9
16,650–21,020	18	11
21,020–25,600	22	12
25,600–31,120	25	14
31,120–36,630	28	16
36,630–47,670	33	18
47,670–62,450	38	21
62,450–89,090	42	25
89,090–113,860	45	30
113,860–169,020	49	33
169,020– . . .	50	39

Single Taxpayers

$0–2,390	0%	0%
2,390–3,540	11	4
3,540–4,580	12	4
4,580–6,760	14	5
6,760–8,850	15	8
8,850–11,240	16	10
11,240–13,430	18	11
13,430–15,610	20	12
15,610–18,940	23	13
18,940–24,460	26	15
24,460–29,970	30	18
29,970–35,490	34	20
35,490–43,190	38	22
43,190–57,550	42	25
57,550–85,130	48	29
85,130– . . .	50	35

Source: Form 1040 IRS

Turning the coin over, we find that lowering marginal tax rates has little effect on factory or office or service workers generally because they do not control the number of hours they work. Work schedules are largely set by managers, not by the work force. In addition, whatever incentive might result from higher take-home pay owing to an income tax reduction is offset, under the 1981 tax changes, by increases in social security taxes on payrolls.

Income taxes may, however, change income tax payment habits. Unlike most other forms of taxation, the income tax demands a huge degree of voluntary taxpayer cooperation. High tax rates, accompanied by widespread distrust of the uses to which tax revenue is put, may foster tax evasion, or resort to methods of exchange that evade the tax collector's notice. A lawyer will offer free advice to a carpenter in exchange for a weekend's work on the lawyer's garage. A house-painter will submit two estimates: a high one if the transaction is to be reported, a low one if it is to be cash. At the top of the income ladder, a commodity speculator will work overtime on such devices as butterfly straddles to show paper losses each year and avoid the capital gains tax. At the bottom end, a housekeeper will take the weekly payment in cash, and not insist that the employer make the mandatory contribution to the social security system.

SOCIAL SECURITY TAXES

Social security taxes pose another problem. There is no question who pays them. They reduce the income of the wage earner and the employer, who may or may not be able to pass forward his share of the tax. The more interesting question is whether this tax is regressive.

At first glance there is no doubt in the matter. Social security taxes today take 14.3 percent of all wages, half paid by a reduction in the salary check, the other half by the employer. This percentage is the same on all taxed wages, so that the tax seems quite proportional. But there is no tax levied above an established level ($42,000 in 1986), so that high wage earners pay smaller proportions of their earnings. In addition, although social security taxes are taken from even the lowest earned income, property income of any kind—interest, rent, dividends, or royalties—is exempt from social security. Thus, measured against total income, the social security levy is regressive.

Yet in the end, matters are not quite that simple. The payout formula for social security is set to give low-income earners more dollars of benefit, per dollar paid in, than high earners. **Therefore, if we offset the regressive tax with the progressive payment schedule, the net impact of social security becomes progressive.**

The difficulty is that social security taxes are paid at one stage in an individual's life cycle, and the benefits are received at another, later stage. It is not easy to compare the costs and benefits of such *intergenerational transfers* when they are separated by long periods of time. This problem is worsened because the ratio between the number of persons working (and paying tax) and those not working (and receiving benefits) is changing in favor of the retired population. An ever larger proportion of our population is living on social security, at much higher benefit levels than formerly; and these trends will certainly continue.

CORPORATE INCOME TAXES

Let us next take a look at the corporate income tax, no longer a prime source of funds for the federal government.

Who pays a corporation's income tax? Few questions are more uncertain.

Some economists think the corporate income tax is essentially a sales tax, borne partly by consumers, partly by the business (in the form of reduced income), partly by the factors of production who suffer a loss in earnings. Others think it is a tax on capital, serving to reduce the flow of capital into the corporate sector. Still others believe that its impact cannot be clearly depicted because most corporate income taxes are paid by big oligopolistic companies, who may use tax increases as an excuse to raise prices in their industry, laying the blame for this on "the government." Some economists even go so far as to say that one of the virtues of the corporate tax is that no one can state with certainty who pays it; therefore, it serves as an excellent way for the government to raise money without clearly imposing a tax on anyone!

Double Taxation

Many critics claim that corporate taxes are unfair because they tax the owners of corporations twice on the income their companies have earned. They are taxed once when the corporation pays half of its income to the government — income

MAKING MONEY OUT OF TAXES

Whether or not corporation income taxes are a useful means of raising revenues, they are certainly an effective way of *making* money for those corporations able to take advantage of the Byzantine provisions of the tax code that allow for various kinds of writeoffs, shelters, and other perfectly legal avenues of tax avoidance.

In 1984, for example, the 275 biggest corporate money-makers paid about 15 percent of their net income to the federal government — not the 46 percent that the tax code presumably levied. Of these companies, 129 paid no taxes or received tax rebates, although their profits amounted to $66.5 billion. Of this group, 9 companies have paid no taxes at all for the years 1981–84. For example, the Boeing Corporation received rebates during this period of $285 million, although its reported income came to over $2 billion. General Electric received tax rebates of $98 million over the period, although its income came to $9,577 million. In all, the 9 companies with the biggest rebates earned $25.1 billion *before* federal income tax — and an additional $1.4 billion *after* taxes!

Source: Data from *Corporate Taxpayers and Corporate Freeloaders* (Washington, DC: Citizens for Tax Justice, August 1985).

that would otherwise belong to the shareowner. And they are taxed again when dividends are paid and the owners receive their income.

Many who favor progressive taxes would protest that abolition of the corporate income tax would aid the rich. Actually, if corporate income taxes were abolished and all corporate earnings were distributed to shareowners, the bite on wealthy stockholders might well be greater, not smaller, than today!

PROPERTY TAXES

Property taxes are also very important sources of revenue for states and localities —and hot political items since Proposition 13 put a ceiling on them in California in 1976, followed by Proposition 2½ in Massachusetts in 1980. One difficulty with property taxes is that inflation can raise the assessed value of real estate much more rapidly than it increases the income of homeowners. What happened in California was that owners found themselves unable to meet taxes that were mounting steadily higher. To be sure, homeowners could sell their houses at a profit. But to buy a new house cost just as much, and did not get around the problem of rising real estate taxes.

Are property taxes always paid by homeowners? Not when they are levied on an owner who rents his property. Then the taxes are usually passed along as higher rents. Because rent payments are a more important budget item for low-income families than for high-income families, these tax-induced rent raises are regressive in their impact. For slum dwellers who cannot afford to move, they may be terribly high.

Even in the case of a landlord, however, sometimes property taxes are progressive, not regressive. Suppose property taxes are $250,000 per year on a building whose rentals yield $1 million a year. Net earnings are therefore $750,000. As we know, the building is worth a capital sum that will yield $750,000 at the going rate of return for similar properties. At 10 percent, it will be worth $7,500,000. If property taxes are now raised and cannot be passed along, the capitalized value of the building will fall. Even though the taxes may be passed forward to renters, the heaviest cost will fall on the owner of the building whose capital has been diminished.

So it is not altogether clear that property taxes are as regressive as they are thought to be. They are regressive only if we estimate their incidence on incomes. If we include their impact on wealth, they can be a very progressive form of taxation!

TOTAL INCIDENCE

Can we sum up total tax incidence in our tax system? It must be clear that it is difficult to do so for two reasons. First, the horizontal variances are so great that average figures are often very little guide to reality. Second, incidence depends on elasticities of supply and demand that are often unknown to us.

In Table 3 we see a sophisticated effort to discover total tax incidence, carried out by Joseph Pechman and Benjamin Okner, both of the Brookings Institution. Although the study refers to 1966, there is no reason to believe that the conclusion would differ for more recent years.

Notice the tremendous difference between variant 1 and variant 2. In variant 1, millionaires pay 49 percent of their incomes in taxes. In variant 2, they pay less than 30 percent. In variant 1, a very poor family pays less than 20 percent of its income in taxes. In variant 2, it pays 28 percent.

The difference between the variants lies in the assumptions that are made about the elasticity of supply and demand curves. In variant 1, where total taxation seems quite progressive, it is assumed that property taxes are borne mainly by landlords and that corporate income taxes ultimately descend on shareholders. In variant 2, which is roughly proportional and regressive at the lowest and upper-most ends, it is assumed that property taxes are passed forward to the renter, and that corporate income taxes lower consumers' incomes through higher prices, not stockholders' incomes through lower dividends.

A Proportional System

Which of these variants is more likely to be true? **The actual incidence of taxation remains a matter for conjecture. We should note, however, that the uncertainties relate to the very lowest and highest incomes. Under both sets of assump-**

Table 3

EFFECTIVE RATES OF FEDERAL, STATE, AND LOCAL TAXES UNDER TWO INCIDENCE ASSUMPTIONS, 1966

Pechman's study reveals two different tax bites, depending on various assumptions. We do not know which is true.

Adjusted Family Income ($000)	*Federal*	*Variant 1 State and Local*	*Total*	*Federal*	*Variant 2 State and Local*	*Total*
$0-3	8.8%	9.8%	18.7%	14.1%	14.0%	28.1%
3-5	11.9	8.5	20.4	14.6	10.6	25.3
5-10	15.4	7.2	22.6	17.0	8.9	25.9
10-15	16.3	6.5	22.8	17.5	8.0	25.5
15-20	16.7	6.5	23.2	17.7	7.6	25.3
20-25	17.1	6.9	24.0	17.8	7.4	25.1
25-30	17.4	7.7	25.1	17.2	7.1	24.3
30-50	18.2	8.2	26.4	17.7	6.7	24.4
50-100	21.8	9.7	31.5	20.1	6.3	26.4
100-500	30.0	11.9	41.8	24.4	6.0	30.3
500-1,000	34.6	13.3	48.0	25.2	5.1	30.3
1,000 and over	35.5	13.8	49.3	24.8	4.2	29.0
Total	17.6	7.6	25.2	17.9	8.0	25.9

tions, the tax burden for the groups that we have called the working class, the middle class, and the top 5 percent (although not the top 2 percent) are the same. Under both sets of assumptions, state and local taxes are regressive, and federal taxes are progressive — the two balancing each other out to produce an overall system that is roughly proportional.

Is this overall system fair? If by fairness we mean that our tax incidence should be mildly progressive, the answer is mixed. Some elements of the system, such as social security, are not fair. Other elements, such as the federal income tax, are fair. Still others, such as the property tax, are sometimes fair and sometimes not.

To make things even more complicated, we must remember that the taxes a person pays depend very much on where he or she lives. There are, as we mentioned above, some 38,000 taxing authorities in the United States. States, municipalities, water districts, school districts, transportation authorities, and a host of other agencies can impose public charges, fees, and taxes. The fairness of our personal tax situation is very much determined by our geographic situation.

Horizontal Equity

It's very difficult, in other words, to pass any kind of overall judgment about the United States tax system(s). On one issue, however, everyone feels alike. Whatever the values that incline us toward progressive or proportional taxation, few people would go on record as favoring preferential or discriminatory taxation. Yet that is, in fact, the kind of tax system that we have.

Tax reform, in fact, is no longer basically focused on the question of progressivity or regressivity in general. The battle rages over the hundreds or thousands of loopholes that benefit small numbers of persons. Because the closing of any particular loophole would bring a tax saving of only a few dollars for most taxpayers, they cannot work up much enthusiasm in mounting an attack on any one provision. The beneficiaries of that provision, on the other hand, stand to gain enormously by it, and they mount an all-out campaign in its favor. Thus lobbying for individual tax breaks is intense. Lobbying against any one loophole is weak.

There have been sporadic efforts to simplify and make more equitable the tax system of our 38,000 tax-levying governments. Until 1986 they have been failures. Only wars, with their overriding imperatives, have proved capable of moving the vested interests and inertias that defend our complex system. Perhaps, though, the tax reform act of 1986 signals the dawn of a new day, at least on the federal level.

PUBLIC SPENDING

Taxing is, of course, only half the government's activity. The other half is spending. Is government spending wasteful? Many people think so. But how can we answer such a question analytically? One way is to reflect on how we would decide if *private* expenditure were wasteful. But notice: **We do not judge whether a firm's**

output is wasteful! If there is a demand for the product, that is presumed to be sufficient justification for its existence. Outputs may be illegal if they are forbidden by government, but economists do not speak of "wasteful" outputs as long as there is a market for them.

The public sector is intrinsically different from the private sector. With minor exceptions it does not sell its output and therefore cannot justify it by pointing to market demand. Moreover, as we have seen, much public output consists of public goods such as defense, from which no individual can be excluded, even if he or she did not contribute to its cost. For such goods, there is no conceivable market test to determine whether the "right" level of output has been attained. In the absence of such a test, we tend to call "wasteful" all government spending we do not approve of.

Voting vs. Spending

How do we determine, in the absence of a market, whether a program should be undertaken in the first place? The answer, as we know, is through the representative political process, through voting. We vote for or against the general economic programs of candidates or parties. Within Congress or the state legislatures, our representatives vote again. The voting process is the subject of intense efforts to influence its outcome: leadership (or lack of it) provided by the President and his administration, lobbying, pressure from constituents, log-rolling deals of many sorts. From this pulling and hauling emerges the national economic budget with its appropriations for different public purposes, a process duplicated again at state and local levels.

Some economists argue that this process leads to an inherent bias in favor of increasing expenditures. The reason is that each proposed expenditure is touted in terms of the specific benefits it will create. This rallies a group of intense supporters. Meanwhile the increased expenditure means only a small average increase in taxes. Therefore it will not result in an equally vociferous lobby of opponents. The presence of staunch supporters and the absence of strong objectors for specific expenditures thus tips the scales in favor of raising, not lowering, total expenditures, according to the argument of the "public choice" school.

But if this were so, why wouldn't total expenditures rise without limit? Why have federal purchases in relation to GNP remained so stable over the years? The answer is that there are *many competing interests, each seeking a larger share of federal spending at any given time.* In a political process, albeit with much fuss and rhetoric, these interests strive for and eventually reach a workable bargain with each other over the relative shares each will receive. While such an implicit bargain lasts, no single interest can achieve a disproportionate increase in spending for its pet purpose without exciting the intense opposition of all the others. Only something like a war, or a major reform movement, is likely to disrupt this bargain. Thus total spending tends to rise, but at a fairly slow rate, restrained by the competition of many different interests for what all perceive to be a limited total spending pie.

Is Spending "Rational"?

There is nothing inherently "rational" about the public allocation of resources so achieved. But it is not "irrational" either. Perhaps the most that can be said is that our public expenditure decision-making process is legitimated by the support most of us give to our political system. We recognize that without some orderly, open mechanism—however imperfect—to settle the many nonmarket resource-allocation decisions and conflicts that we face, we would be much worse off—less democratic, and less free—than we are. **Economic analysis alone can give us no ultimately correct division between public and private expenditure.**

COST-BENEFIT ANALYSIS

Still, at the level of the individual public project, we are not helpless. We do have certain analytical tools at our disposal. The most important of these is known as **cost-benefit analysis.**

Calculating Costs and Benefits

Because a public expenditure is rarely planned to make money, a legislator must try to estimate the public benefits that will flow from the expenditure as an offset against its cost. These benefits may be fairly easy to calculate, as when a government agency plans to build a hospital, and estimates what a comparable private hospital might earn. Even if the public hospital provides its services free, these services are presumably worth approximately that much to the public, since it has been relieved of expenditures it would otherwise have made at a private facility.

But often the benefits of a project are exceedingly difficult to calculate. How can we estimate the benefits of a new road? By the tolls that might be collected? What about the indirect benefits gained by townspeople who are now served more rapidly and efficiently? What about improvements in the landscape if billboards are banned?

There is no perfectly objective way of adding up all the benefits of a public project. We can make more or less sophisticated guesses and estimates, but these estimates always contain a large element of uncertainty. We can easily overestimate—or underestimate—the benefit of a project.

Cost Effectiveness

Once a project is decided on—a road, a school, a training program—considerations of cost-effectiveness are exactly the same as they are in a factory, a private house, or any other private venture.

The principle is the use of the most economic combination of inputs to achieve a given output. Here "wastefulness" has the same definition in the public and private sector. It is certainly not easy to translate principles of efficiency, as an economist describes them, into the complex specifications of a construction job. But the aim is in no way different between the public and private sectors.

Sunk Costs

Many public projects are large, uncertain, one-of-a-kind ventures whose costs and benefits cannot be accurately forecasted. Often, as work goes forward, new difficulties and new costs come to light. The concept of benefit-cost analysis often has to be applied at several stages in such a public project. This raises the question of how one should treat sunk costs — expenditures that have been made in the past and that cannot be undone.

Here, too, is a parallel between public and private efficiencies. Suppose that you have a dam or a factory half built. A decision must be made whether to continue with the project or abandon it. At this point neither the public legislator nor the private entrepreneur should go back and review whether the project should have been started in the first place. The money that has been spent on it is irretrievably lost, both to the public and to the private enterprise. The only relevant question is whether the *remaining cost* will be justified by the benefits or revenues that are expected ultimately to accrue.

Although a private firm may regret having decided to start up a new branch, an intelligent decision on going through with the project will measure only the remaining costs against the expected revenues. A legislator may rue having voted for a public project, but he will intelligently vote to complete it if the remaining costs will be justified by the total ensuing benefits.

"Throwing Good Money after Bad"

In other words **all sunk costs are irrelevant in making decisions about future actions.** Rather, they *should be* irrelevant. In fact, it is very difficult for decision makers, public or private, to understand that costs incurred in the past are now beyond recall and can be recouped, in part if not in full, only by continuing with a project even though the total undertaking is now deemed to be a losing proposition. The impulse is to stop a project once it has been decided that the initial decision was in error. The common phrases "don't throw good money after bad" and "cut your losses" are heard, even though, *at the margin,* the investment would be highly profitable (relative to the investment as a whole).

It only makes sense to cancel a project if the *remaining* costs are greater than the *total* benefits. Of course, such a situation will arise only when the original cost-benefit analysis was badly in error, or if circumstances have changed dramatically since the project was begun. In real life, where specialists often dispute each other's estimates of costs and valuation of benefits, such cancellation decisions are often highly controversial.

THE MARKET IN A FINAL RETROSPECT

This seems a good place to make a final assessment of the wastefulness with which resources are allocated through votes and through spending. Many people look askance at how the public sector allocates its resources. No one needs to be reminded of innumerable scandals having to do with influence peddling or abuse of the public trust by members of federal or state legislatures.

What we should remember, however, is that the voting process is a substitute rationing mechanism. Where one-dollar-one-vote does not work, or is deemed an improper rationing mechanism, a democratic society must choose one-person-one-vote.

The abuses of the voting mechanism may be many and its problems are assuredly difficult. Nonetheless, voting is the way a democracy rations its public output, just as spending is the way a market system rations its private output. Before we wax too indignant about the shortcomings of the voting process, pointing to the waste that accompanies government programs, etc., etc., we should remind ourselves of the inequities that accompany private rationing decisions.

The market mechanism has enormous strengths, but it is certainly not perfect. In fact, we know that it must be imperfect. There are problems the market cannot cope with at all. Moreover, those it does handle reveal the pervasive bias of a voting system in which individuals are measured by their incomes, not by any other gauge of their human value.

Thus all market systems must have public counterparts and complements. It is impossible to have an economic system in which government would play no role whatsoever. The exercise of the political will that is so much (and so properly) distrusted is also essential for social survival. In this struggle between the authority of politics and that of the market lies a central issue, not merely of microeconomics but of modern economic society itself.

looking back

KEY CONCEPTS

The U.S. tax system is complex	**1** The United States has an immensely diverse federalized tax structure. Personal income taxes and payroll taxes for social insurance are the most important federal tax sources. Sales

taxes are the most important state and local tax sources, with personal taxes on incomes and property a distant second. Corporate profits taxes contribute a declining share of federal revenue.

Incidence of taxation is important for equity. Incidence depends heavily on elasticity but is hard to determine

2 The key question, from the point of view of fairness or equity, concerns the incidence of taxation—who actually pays a given tax. Most Americans favor proportional or mildly progressive taxes. But most taxes are shifted forward or backward—to the consumer or to the factors of production. The amount of shifting depends very considerably on the elasticity of the demand curve or supply curves in the product or factor markets. Actual incidence is often very difficult to determine.

Regressive taxes hit low incomes hardest. Sales taxes are such a tax. Graduated income taxes are progressive, hitting upper-income groups proportionately harder than lower, but loopholes greatly lessen this effect

3 Sales taxes tend to be regressive—to bear more heavily on lower incomes than higher ones. Individual income taxes tend to be progressive, although deductions and loopholes greatly lower the actual (as opposed to the scheduled) degree of progressivity. Corporate income taxes are so complex in their incidence that we do not know whether they are passed forward or backward, or are progressive or regressive. Social security taxes are very regressive, because they reach a ceiling on high incomes, but the payout formula makes up for this regressivity. Property taxes can be regressive when they are passed along as higher rentals, but they can also be progressive when they result in lower capitalized values.

The total tax system has large horizontal inequities

4 The overall incidence of the total tax system is unclear. This is especially true because there is such a multiplicity of tax systems in the United States. There is no doubt that substantial horizontal inequities exist and that it is very hard to get rid of them.

Waste as an economic concept involves efficiency, not the justification of output

5 Waste is an important economic idea. In microeconomics it describes the criteria for efficiency, but it does not refer to the justification for output. In the public sphere it often describes our judgment about the worthwhileness of public efforts, as well as their efficiency.

Allocation problems of voting: asymmetry of spending and taxing

6 We allocate public funds among various purposes by voting, not by market decisions. Voting has many problems as an allocation mechanism. One is that we tend to vote for programs that increase our incomes, but not for programs that increase others' incomes. This leads to an asymmetry between spending and taxing. It is easier to raise budgets by stressing particular advantages which rally strong supporters, than to cut them which spreads benefits diffusely and wins no strong support.

Cost-benefit considerations should ignore sunk costs

7 Expenditures should be justified by weighing benefits against costs. This is often difficult to do, because sunk costs, although irrelevant to a rational decision, are hard to ignore.

Public and private sectors both necessary	8 It is impossible to have an economy without a public sector— that is, without taxation and government expenditure. The public sector has many problems—but it must not be forgotten that the private sector also has its allocational difficulties. This is an inescapable problem of modern society.

ECONOMIC VOCABULARY

Tax incidence   563
Regressive, proportional, and
  progressive taxes   563
Deductions   568

Double taxation   572
Horizontal equity   575
Cost-benefit   577
Sunk costs   578

QUESTIONS

1. Can you think of arguments that would incline you in favor of a regressive tax system? How about encouraging the rate of saving? Or the idea that those who are richer deserve to be given preference because they have made a larger contribution to society?

2. Assume a payroll tax is levied in all firms. Using supply and demand curves, show who might bear such a tax if the demand for factors was very price-elastic.

3. Suppose family A has $1 million in stocks and bonds and an income of $35,000. Family B has no property but an earned income of the same amount. How would you decide which tax system would yield horizontal equity for the two families? For example, would corporate income taxes affect each alike? Straight income taxes? Capital gains taxes? Is horizontal equity possible when the source of income differs, even though the amount is the same?

4. Suppose there were a flat tax of 20 percent on all income. How would you go about determining whether a business's expenses were a legitimate deduction from its gross income? Assume that no entertainment expenses were allowed for any business. Would this result in horizontal inequities in different businesses? Would this be sufficient argument not to press for this tax change?

5. A congressional committee is considering the construction of a moving sidewalk in Washington, D.C. It is estimated to cost $1 billion, and will give benefits of an estimated $1.5 billion. After six months of work, $1 billion has been spent and the remaining costs are still $600 million. Should you throw "good money after bad" or discontinue the project? What are the project's opportunity costs and sunk costs?

AN EXTRA WORD ABOUT

Fair Taxation

Two thousand years ago, in Book One of *The Republic,* Plato wrote "When there is an income tax, the just man will pay more and the unjust less on the same amount of income." Americans today widely agree with Plato's maxim. The income tax, that annual headache, has long since lost most of the moral authority it once derived from the perception that it was a fair tax, levied on the public in reasonable relation to the ability to pay. To the contrary, most Americans today regard the income tax as riddled with unjustified and obsolete exemptions, deductions, loopholes, and special provisions that shift the tax burden from the wealthy and well-lawyered to the average household.

For this reason, tax reform — an effort to achieve a comprehensive restructuring of the system of income taxation — has been high on the political agenda. Indeed, President Reagan declared such reform to be the highest domestic priority of his second administration, and as we write, a major tax reform act is on the verge of enactment.

But what would constitute a good system of taxation? Are there broad principles of tax reform around which reasonable people can rally? In a recent study for the Joint Economic Committee, economist William Buechner set forth seven such criteria, with which we are broadly sympathetic.*

1. **REVENUES.** First, and perhaps foremost, a tax system should have the potential to raise revenue adequate to cover most of the expenditures of government in normal times. Since 1981, our tax system has failed to meet this objective by a wide margin; hence a good tax reform must include measures that increase revenue, or at least make it politically easier to raise revenues after the reforms are in place.

2. **STABILIZATION.** A good tax system should help to stabilize demand in the economy, allowing tax burdens to fall sharply in recessions but causing them to rise sharply when inflation is the threat. Progressivity improves the stabilizing properties of the tax system; as the income tax has become less progressive in recent years, it has also become less stabilizing. Indexation of tax rates to inflation, enacted in 1981, also has destabilizing effects since it reduces tax rates by increasing amounts as inflation rises — putting fuel rather than water on the inflationary fires.

3. **FAIRNESS.** There are two basic criteria of fairness or equity in taxation: *horizontal equity,* meaning that those with nearly equal incomes pay a nearly equal tax, and *vertical equity,* or progressivity, meaning that those with higher incomes pay a higher proportionate tax.

Despite its many faults, the income tax that we have been paying during the last decade has been a broadly progressive tax, as we may recall from Table 2. It is when we come to the problem of horizontal equity that problems emerge. Buechner writes:

The main source of tax inequity is the long list of preferences that are not available to all taxpayers on even terms. The Joint Committee on Taxation lists 108 deductions, credits,

---

* *Tax Reform,* A Staff Study Prepared for the Use of the Subcommittee on Economic Goals and Intergovernmental Policy of the Joint Economic Committee, Congress of the United States, Washington, DC: GPO, November 29, 1984.

exemptions, and other preferences in the tax code, including those affecting corporations, that can be used to shelter income from taxes. This is double the number listed in 1970. Many tax preferences, particularly those which reduce the rate of tax on capital income, primarily benefit those at the top of the income scale. In addition, according to the Joint Committee on Taxation, the benefits of even the most widely used itemized deductions are concentrated among those earning $30,000 or more.

Hence, any effective tax reform must restore the perception of fairness and broaden the tax base by eliminating all but the most indispensable exemptions, credits, deductions, and preferences.

4. EFFICIENCY. Any tax system will influence economic activity and the allocation of resources. Still, our present tax system clearly attempts far too much in this area, spreading too many incentives too thinly over too vast a ground. It drains the government of needed resources, providing help only wastefully and inefficiently to activities ranging from business capital investment through solar energy development to charitable contributions. A good tax reform would strip away inefficient or wasteful incentives, replacing them where necessary with direct subsidies, and otherwise returning the functions they serve to the discretion of the free market.

5. SIMPLICITY and **6. COMPLIANCE.** Elimination of many special preferences would also serve the basic goal of making the tax system comprehensible again to the individual taxpayer. This would help reduce the nearly 2 billion hours spent each year on tax preparation in the United States, and the $3 billion spent on professional assistance. More important, it would help restore voluntary compliance with the code, since taxpayers would have less reason to feel that they were falling behind in a rat race to save every possible tax dollar. As Table 4 shows, compliance—voluntary reporting of taxable

Table 4

VOLUNTARY REPORTING PERCENTAGES FOR INDIVIDUAL FILERS AND NONFILERS, BY SOURCE OF INCOME, 1973 AND 1981

Category	Percent of Income Reported	
	1973	1981
Wages and salaries	95.4%	93.9%
Dividends	90.7	83.7
Interest	87.6	86.3
Capital gains	75.7	59.4
Nonfarm proprietor income and partnership and small business corporation income	84.0	78.7
Farm proprietor income	88.6	88.3
Informal supplier income	20.7	20.7
Pensions and annuities	81.5	85.2
Rents	94.7	95.6
Royalties	74.3	61.2
Estate and trust income	82.0	76.2
State income tax refunds, alimony, and other income	66.0	62.0
Total income	91.2	89.3

Source: Internal Revenue Service, *Income Tax Compliance Research: Estimates for 1973–1981.* Washington, DC: Internal Revenue Service, July 1983, p. 10.

income — has been declining in recent years, with the worst offenders being taxpayers with income from personal services (informal supplies income) and capital gains.

7. FEDERALISM. Unlike most other countries, the United States raises more tax revenue at the level of state and local government than at the federal level. Our system of federalism must therefore also be considered in a discussion of tax reform.

The autonomy of our state and local governments is an established — though by no means unlimited — national principle. We foster it through the tax system in two ways: (1) by reserving to the state and locality certain types of taxation, such as property taxation, and (2) by permitting taxpayers to deduct taxes paid to other levels of government from their income for federal tax purposes. To change the federal tax system in either respect could have serious repercussions on the ability of states and localities to raise their own needed revenues.

As this book goes to press, tax reform goes to Washington. Very likely, top brackets will be reduced from the 50 percent level to under 30 percent. Many of the exceptions and special provisions of the tax code will be repealed. At the end of the process we can expect some greater degree of horizontal equity, and perhaps a vertical incidence that American taxpayers will regard as more equitable. Whether the tax burden as a whole can be lightened is a doubtful question, given the size of the federal deficit. So the issue remains in the air. It will be interesting to see how many of economist Buechner's recommendations find their way into the bill that will determine the taxes we pay for the next several years of our lives.

CHAPTER 32
The Control of Market Power

a look ahead

We end our study of microeconomics with a section of four chapters devoted to the central unsolved issues of the market mechanism. One of these, discussed here, concerns the control of market power—the perennial issue of "big business." The next two chapters focus on the patterns of income that the market distributes in fact, compared with those that would be distributed if the criterion of marginal productivity were the sole determining factor. Finally, in Chapter 35 we look at unemployment and poverty, in many ways the most important measures we possess of the success or failure of any market system.

No single analytical problem comes to the fore in the present chapter. Instead, the central theme is power—economic power in the marketplace. As we shall see, the problem of power is neither so easy to define, nor to offset, as we sometimes tend to believe. The purpose of the chapter is to make you aware of the complexity of a public policy issue of great importance.

Chapter 30 was devoted to the problem of market power from the firm's point of view: How should a monopoly price its products to maximize profits? What is an oligopolist's best strategy? What can a monopolistically competitive firm do to hang on to its minuscule market advantage? Now we address ourselves to the issue of market power from the public's point of view. And here the place to begin is with a simple question: Why oppose monopoly or any other form of market imperfection? What difference does it make?

IS THE CONSUMER KING?

In theory, the answer is clear: The consumer is king. Each individual comes to the marketplace fully equipped with definite views, or *preferences,* about the goods and services he or she would like to consume and the range of prices he or she is willing to pay. *Consumer sovereignty* is the term we use to assert that the consumer's given preferences are the ultimate source and determinant of market behavior.

Consumer Sovereignty

Under pure competition, the business of competition consists of efforts to satisfy those preferences. The consumer enjoys goods that are sold as cheaply and produced as abundantly as possible. Each firm produces the goods consumers want, in the largest quantity at the lowest possible cost—given the levels of wages, and materials costs, and the limits of technology. As we have seen, in a purely competitive market there exist no profits (except transitory rents). Business, in short, has no economic power in this world.

In an imperfectly competitive market, the situation changes. Firms have leverage over total supply. Hence they develop *strategies,* including the strategy of restricting output and raising prices. Profits are not competed away to the benefit of consumers. **Output is reduced, prices rise above the competitive level, and some consumer satisfaction is transferred to producers.** Business power enters the scene, countering the power of the consumer. In this situation, it is important to realize that the consumer is still "sovereign," as we have defined the term. His or her preferences are not as well satisfied as they would be under pure competition, but they have not actually been *altered* by the absence of it. The consumer has become, as it were, a constitutional monarch. The control of business power in this situation is then straightforward in principle, if difficult to achieve in practice. It consists of finding ways to make monopolies and oligopolies behave "as if" they were competitive firms—through regulation, the pressure of public opinion, antitrust action, or other means.

For the most part in this chapter, we will stick with the concept of the sovereign consumer, and explore the responses that are available when this sovereignty comes under challenge because business wields market power. But first, we need to explore a serious dissent from the entire conceptual framework. This dissent holds that the power of modern corporations goes well beyond the ability merely to *obstruct* consumer preferences. Rather, power reaches the point of helping to determine how preferences are formed.

Producer Sovereignty: A Dissenting View

John Kenneth Galbraith, in a famous argument,* asserts that it is quite wrong to take preferences as "given" by forces outside the economic system. Galbraith argues that consumer preferences are determined, at least in part, *within* the economic system — by product design and differentiation, and by the advertising strategies of large corporations. Insofar as business *creates* the tastes of the public, we have *producer sovereignty* instead of consumer sovereignty. Not only must consumers pay the higher than competitive prices and accept the particular kinds of product design that business offers on the market, but consumers are actually conditioned through advertising and social pressures to like the world that corporations have created. If widely accepted, Galbraith's view would overturn much of traditional economic analysis. Let us look into it more carefully by examining two means by which producer sovereignty may be exercised: advertising and product differentiation.

Advertising as Information

Galbraith's dissent can be seen in part as an argument over the social role of advertising. In 1867 we spent an estimated $50 million to persuade consumers to buy products. In 1900 advertising expenditures were $500 million. In 1985 they were $95 *billion,* roughly one-third as much as we spend on primary and secondary education. Advertising is not omnipotent — highly advertised products from the Ford Edsel to the IBM PCjr have been known to fail. But even if we are not slaves of advertising, few would deny that advertising is a powerful and pervasive force in our economic lives.

The question is: to what effect? Does advertising infringe on consumer sovereignty? The question is perplexing. If one regards the consumer as coming to the marketplace in search of specific goods to satisfy already well-formed needs and values, then one can think of advertising as merely providing *information* to that consumer. For example, I may know I need furniture for my house. I may even know that I prefer traditional natural woods over modern stainless-steel and glass designs, without knowing *exactly* what model or which manufacturer is producing what I want. Advertising then tells me where to find what I want, at the best price. This kind of advertising does not change tastes; it merely informs them.

* John Kenneth Galbraith, *The Affluent Society* (Boston: Houghton Mifflin, first published 1957).

Advertising as Manipulation

Yet it is obvious that all advertising is not merely informational and that consumer tastes can be shaped by appeals to their instincts, their insecurities — or to their children: Is a two-year old screaming for Cap'n Crunch cereal at the Safeway expressing a "natural" preference for this item?

Adults, too, can be manipulated. We are mainly creatures of brand preference not because we have sampled all the choices and made up our minds, but as a result of advertising exposure. It is difficult to contemplate the battles of aspirin, toothpaste, soup, soap (up to 10 percent of the price of soap is selling expense), cars, cigarettes, and whisky without recognizing that there is an element of what might fairly be termed consumer exploitation. Brand-name aspirin, for example, sells for as much as three times the price of nonbrand versions of the identical product.

Product Differentiation

Product differentiation is another such case. Corporations proliferate models and styles prodigiously, whether we are talking about cars or stereos or furniture or clothing. Are they doing so strictly to meet a comparable diversity of tastes? Or do they find that product differentiation, combined with advertising, *creates* a diversification of tastes, along with a little range of monopoly power — enabling companies to raise prices and make a little more profit on each item?

As with advertising, the question is where to draw the line. Should an affluent society aim to produce the largest possible quantity of a standardized product at the least possible cost, or to offer an array of differing products that please our palates, admittedly at somewhat higher prices? Most of us would say that American consumers do not want to dress in some kind of "uniform," however inexpensive, or to drive a standardized cheap car. Yet sometimes a company succeeds just because it does produce a commodity that is cheap and standardized — the Volkswagen Beetle and Levi Strauss jeans are cases in point. Does that not suggest there is nothing "natural" about the desire for a wide range of products?

Thus product differentiation, like advertising, poses a conundrum for theory. Do we take the diversity of consumer preferences as given, or as created? Sociologists and anthropologists tend to see tastes as formed by the cultural influences that surround us — including advertising and product differentiation. Economists tend to regard advertising as primarily informational, and product differentiation as a response to a preexisting diversity of tastes. Even economists, however, recognize the force of Galbraith's dissent, which is that the whole *theoretical* structure of consumer sovereignty depends on the assumption that consumer preferences are *given*, not made.

BUSINESS AND POWER

For the moment let us go along with the profession and accept consumer sovereignty as a point of departure. What happens when the monopolistic corporation comes into conflict with this "sovereign" consumer? To what extent does monopoly or oligopoly introduce inefficiency or restrictions on output, preventing the consumer from buying goods as cheaply as possible in the quantity he or she desires? What, in other words, are the consequences of business power?

Do Profits Bring Progress?

Once again the evidence is murky. For one thing, we tend to leap to the conclusion that the competitive firm, which has managed to combine its factors of production as profitably as possible, has also reached the frontiers of technological efficiency. Is this really so? Suppose the frontiers of technology are themselves variable — capable of being advanced by determined efforts in research, development, and product design? Will a small competitive firm, on the margin of existence with low, competitive profits, ever actually advance the state of technological knowledge? Or do such efforts require a cushion, resources to spare, a "monopoly" profit?

These are not idle questions. There is ample evidence that the diffusion of new technologies often — but not always — occurs in large corporations, capable of employing battalions of scientists and engineers. Thus the transistor came from Bell Labs and the research on the semi-conductor occurred at IBM. The economist Joseph A. Schumpeter thought that this process of big business advance represented the core mechanism of capitalist development — the "gales of creative destruction" in which today's monopoly profits are the price we pay for tomorrow's technological advance.

Coping with Power

This brings us again to the question of power — the ability to impose one's will on others. Power has long been an issue of central concern for political scientists and philosophers. It has not been so much an object of examination for economists because, as we have seen, they picture the world as tending to a competitive situation in which power disappears.

But obviously power in the marketplace is not going to disappear — neither Galbraith's power to influence tastes and wants nor power in the conventional economic view as less than perfect competition. The question is what to do about it.

A Conservative View

The first suggestion is most prominently associated with the name of Milton Friedman. Professor Friedman is a philosophic conservative whose response to the question of what a corporation should do to discharge its social responsibility is very simple: Make money.

The function of a business organization in society, argues Friedman, is to serve as an efficient agent of production, not as a locus of social improvement. It

serves that productive function best by striving after profit—conforming, while doing so, to the basic rules and legal norms of society. It is not up to business to "do good"; and it is up to government to prevent it from doing bad.

Moreover, says Friedman, as soon as a businessman tries to apply any rules other than moneymaking, he takes into his own hands powers that rightfully belong to others, such as political authorities. Friedman would even forbid corporations to give money to charities or universities. Their business, their responsibility to society, he insists, is *production*. Let the dividend receivers give away the money the corporations pay them, but do not let corporations become the active social welfare agencies of society.

The Corporation as Social Arbiter

It is interesting to note that few corporate heads espouse Friedman's position. They take the view that the corporation, by virtue of its immense size and strength, has power thrust upon it, whether it wishes to have it or not. The solution to this problem, as executives see it, is for corporations to act "responsibly" in using their power, doing their best to judge fairly among the claims of the many groups to whom they are responsible: labor, stockholders, customers, government, and the public at large.

Thus many top corporate executives think of themselves as referees among contending groups, and no doubt many of them use caution and forethought in exercising the power of decision. But the weaknesses of this argument are also not difficult to see. There are no recognized criteria for qualifying as a "responsible" corporate executive.* Nor is there any clear guideline, even for the most scrupulous executive, for defining the correct manner in which to exercise responsibility. Should an executive's concern for the prevention of pollution take precedence over a good year-end profit statement? Over labor's request for wage increases? Over reducing the price of the product? Is the company's contribution to charity supposed to represent the executives' preferences, or those of the owners or consumers or workers? On what grounds should a company decide to do business, or not to do business, in South Africa? Has Mobil a right to help the cause of public broadcasting? The makers of firearms to support the National Rifle Association?

The questions begin to indicate the complexity of the issue of social responsibility and the problems implicit in allowing important *social* decisions to be made by private individuals who are not publicly accountable for their actions.

---

* The plea of professionalism is further placed in doubt by considerable evidence of white-collar crime in high corporate places. In 1985 a rash of scandals, including a plan by E. F. Hutton to defraud banks in which it placed its deposits, led to an unprecedented admission of guilt by the company, accompanied by a heavy fine. Half the bank failures in the nation, according to the FDIC, arose at least in part from criminal conduct. A former cabinet official and board chairman of a major steel company was sent to jail for passing inside information. Quipped *Time* magazine: "The ways things are going, *Fortune* may soon have to publish a 500 Most Wanted list." (June 10, 1985).

Antitrust

Only a few decades ago, there was virtually unanimous agreement among economists that a strict application of antitrust laws was one of the most effective remedies for the problems of oligopoly. Today this zeal is on the wane, although, as we shall see, it is probably too early to write *finis* to antitrust prosecutions designed to break big companies into little ones.

Why has the zeal for antitrust declined? There are a number of reasons. One is that economists have come to recognize that an industry with one or two giant firms and a tail of small firms does not operate very differently—if at all—from an industry with five or six leading members. Whether concentration ratios give the top four firms 30 percent or 60 percent of an industry does not seem to affect their oligopolistic decision-making. Product differentiation continues. The struggle for market shares goes on. Price leadership persists. Even the breakup of the aluminum industry from a near-monopoly under the domination of Alcoa to an industry in which four firms have big shares of the market does not appear to have changed aluminum prices or aluminum pricing policies.

Economists have also begun to pay more attention to a matter we have stressed several times in our text. This is the fact that industries dominated by big firms have the ability to create technical advances. Competitive firms, as we have seen, may be more efficient at any moment, selling their output at lower prices, but over time many competitive industries have remained technologically static, whereas the oligopolistic industries—with some exceptions—have been innovators.

A third consideration is the tremendous time lag and cost involved in major antitrust cases. A big antitrust case may go on for twenty or thirty years before it is finally resolved. One may ask whether the eventual savings are worth the huge legal costs. Moreover, many antitrust actions seem to make little economic sense. For example, antitrust laws prohibit the merger of two firms whose combined assets would be less than those of the industry leader, but the courts do nothing to break up the leader itself. This situation exists because antitrust is against "combination" on principle, but not against bigness, as such. Yet the price policies of one big business often restrain trade as much as if two former competitors were combined.

Moreover, the increasing importance of international trade—a theme that bulks larger and larger as we penetrate into the workings of the economy—makes obsolete the narrowly national focus within which antitrust legislation was conceived. General Motors, for example, can no longer be considered as just competing against Ford and Chrysler. Toyota is number 2 in the American car market.

Defenders of antitrust legislation do not question these views. It is not really imaginable that General Motors, for example, will ever be broken into a thousand firms each with a capitalization of $50 million, even though GM is big enough to yield that many pieces. In all likelihood, trustbusting GM would result in the formation of 3 or 4 giant firms, each worth $20 billion or so and each still possessing enormous market power.

But the defenders of antitrust do not want to give up the implicit threat that antitrust prosecution carries. The ghost of Senator Sherman, the sponsor of the

THE BREAKUP OF MA BELL

In 1984, history's biggest antitrust case came to an end with the breakup of the American Telephone and Telegraph Corporation. AT&T was a classic monopoly, dominating telephone service in the nation. But interestingly the antitrust case did not allege that AT&T had used its monopoly power to exploit the consumer. To the contrary: Before the breakup, nearly every U.S. household had relatively cheap, efficient access to the phone network. AT&T was, moreover, the world's top-quality telephone system, providing phones that never broke, and clear and instantaneous connections across the country, and via satellites, around the world.

AT&T had been accused instead of abusing its *technological* stranglehold on the U.S. telephone system. It had used its control of local telephone service in order to prevent the establishment of alternative long distance services, and to prevent alternative manufacturers of telephone equipment from attaching their products to AT&T lines. Thus households could not take full advantage of new microwave transmission technologies, nor of the full range of telephone equipment manufacturers were capable of providing. With its monopoly profits from equipment and long distance services, AT&T kept local telephone rates low and engaged in funding a wide range of research activities through Bell Labs.

The court decree split AT&T away from its equipment manufacturer (Western Electric) and split off eleven companies to provide local service in different parts of the country. The results? MCI, Sprint, Allnet soon began an aggressive campaign to expand their share of the long distance market. As a result, long distance costs fell. At the same time, telephone equipment costs also fell, though often so did the quality of the equipment. But local telephone rates rose, since local companies no longer had AT&T's deep pockets behind them. Phone bills suddenly got more complex, as did the business of getting phone equipment repaired. Perhaps the biggest loser was the AT&T research effort, which was cut back sharply in the new competitive environment.

So antitrust actions create winners and losers. Perhaps the poet Ogden Nash had the last word on the Ma Bell breakup when he wrote, years ago:

If there is one principle to Americans unknown;
It is, "leave well enough, alone."

original antitrust legislation, sits on the board of directors of all large firms, according to George Stigler, an eminent economist. There the ghost exercises a cautionary influence against actions that might be taken if there were no threat of antitrust action. The ghost serves to prevent the rise of supergiant firms whose political and social power might be considered inimical to our democracy, if not injurious to our economy.

Regulation

Regulation has been a traditional American response to the problem of business power. Regulation has sought to influence or prohibit business actions in many fields: pricing, advertising, product design, dealing with unions and minority groups, pollution, workplace and product safety, and still other areas. Given the variety of ways in which corporations are regulated, it is hardly surprising that the effectiveness of the regulatory process is very uneven.

It is useful to distinguish *economic regulation,* which is concerned with pricing and market access, from *social regulation,* which is concerned with a host of other issues, such as pollution and safety and civil rights. (Of course the distinction is somewhat artificial, since social regulation may have strong economic effects.)

Economic Regulation

Historically, the United States government has been most concerned with economic regulation of industries providing transportation and communications services, and with "natural monopolies" — utilities such as electric power companies — that have declining cost curves through their whole range of output.

The first great regulatory agency was the Interstate Commerce Commission, established in 1887 to regulate the railroads, which were at that time a natural monopoly in much of the country. The ICC's role was dual: to prevent abuses of market power by the railroads, and also to ensure that the country was adequately served by rail transportation. Later, buses and trucks and pipelines came under ICC jurisdiction, but the dual function remained: The ICC both restricted and protected these transportation sectors.

The Civil Aviation Board (CAB) was designed in the same mold to promote the airline industry and also to protect it from "cutthroat competition"; still later, the Federal Communications Commission (FCC) came to play a similar role for television, as did the original Atomic Energy Commission for nuclear power. As time went by, many observers came to feel that the regulators were not doing both sides of their job. Having lived with their industries, the regulating agencies had come to adopt the industry viewpoint, protecting the industry against competition more than protecting the broader interests of the public.

Social Regulation

In contrast to economic regulation, social regulation is not industry-specific. Rather, it represents the efforts of government to lay down guidelines for conduct for whole classes of industries to promote one or another social purpose. The first social regulations were laid down in 1906 during the Progressive era, with the federal Food and Drug Administration (FDA). Others followed, until the list today includes the Federal Trade Commission (FTC) concerned with advertising, truth-in-lending and other trade practices; The Securities and Exchange Commission (SEC); the National Labor Relations Board (NLRB); the Equal Employment Opportunity Commission (EEOC) and Office of Federal Contract Compliance (OFCC), concerned with civil rights; the Occupational Safety and Health Administration (OSHA); the Environmental Protection Agency (EPA); and the Consumer Product Safety Commission (CPSC). Quite a list!

Social regulations have often proved effective — as when FDA testing prevented the pregnancy antinausea drug thalidomide, which resulted in seriously deformed babies, from being released on the U.S. market. Sometimes they have not been effective, as in the case of the FTC's campaigns against TV advertising aimed at children in the late 1970s, or the failure of the EPA under the Reagan administration to do something about the problem of toxic waste dumps. Sometimes a regulatory failure occurs because the regulation itself was ill-conceived; at other times, simply for lack of money.

Right or wrong, social regulation is usually controversial. It imposes an economic burden on business, and what is sometimes worse, it steps on businessmen's toes, offending their sense of independence. Often, social regulations lead to court fights, as over affirmative action rulings, or to battles in Congress, as over proposed FTC rules governing used car dealers and funeral parlors. In many cases, an uneasy stalemate comes to exist, in which the regulatory agency remains in existence, but without the funding it would require to pursue its legal mandates to the full extent stipulated in the law.

Deregulation

Recently there have been great strides to curtail economic regulation, started in the late 1970s and continued under the Reagan administration. The Atomic Energy Commission was broken up and its safety functions delegated to the Nuclear Regulatory Commission (NRC), which is not intended to promote nuclear power. The CAB has actually been abolished, together with federal control over airline routes and fares. The ICC has relinquished much of its power over the trucking industry, and some of its power over railroads. The breakup of AT&T diminished regulation of telecommunications. With the rise of cable TV, the FCC has been granting much more leeway than heretofore to commercial television stations on their programming decisions. Banking services have become progressively deregulated and competitive.

To date, the best-documented example of economic deregulation has been in the airline industry — where, despite some difficulties, the verdict seems quite favorable. An immediate and dramatic effect has been a sharp fall in airline prices on those routes where the demand for service was high, permitting the use of the largest and most efficient aircraft at the lowest per passenger costs. As a result, coast-to-coast travelers have found themselves able to fly for bargain rates, especially during off-hours. Another result has been a dramatic reorganization of route structures, as big airlines have moved to systems of "hubs" — American Airlines at Dallas, United at Chicago, TWA at St. Louis, Delta at Atlanta, People Express at Newark — that maximize within-airline transfers and permit the most efficient use of equipment. Finally, many new airlines have sprung up, servicing smaller airports with a wide range of smaller equipment and competing on major commuter and shuttle routes with the established giants.

This is not to say that everyone has come out ahead. Some airlines have not been able to take the strain. One large company, Braniff, went out of business; others have hovered on the bankruptcy edge. Yet others — Continental and United — have used a bankruptcy proceeding or a strike to force pilots and other staff to take major pay cuts. Union membership in the industry has declined. And everyone has heard the complaints about how much more expensive it is to fly (on a per-mile basis) between lightly traveled destinations (say New York to Nashville or Richmond, or Indianapolis to St. Paul or Sioux City) than on the great routes. Such complaints, and allegations that small city travelers "subsidize" the intercontinental routes, overlook the economies inherent in high load factors, big aircraft, and efficient airports on those routes, and the fact that airport overheads — maintenance, baggage crews, catering and ticket services — do not depend on the distance you fly. On the whole, it seems that airline deregulation has reinvigorated the industry, providing better, cheaper, and more efficient service at a price that more closely reflects airline costs than before — pretty much what a competitive model would predict.

The Reagan administration has also aggressively moved against most forms of social regulation, although it has encountered stiff battles over the EPA, civil rights, health and safety, and many other areas. Here, as one might expect, the verdict depends on whose side of the underlying social struggle one is on. Those who feel that the government had gone too far in combatting pollution and racial inequality and in setting standards for workplace and consumer safety have supported the administration's positions; those with the contrary opinions have been opposed. It is part of the nature of social regulation that no purely *economic* criterion can adequately appraise the question.

Other Possibilities

Thus, the problem of social responsibility will not be easy to resolve, no matter what steps we choose, from Professor Friedman's laissez faire to an aggressive program of renewed social regulation. Here we merely wish to suggest some other lines of action that have been proposed in the past, and are likely to be heard from again.

Nationalization of large industries is not a characteristically American response to this issue, but effective nationalization sometimes occurs. To all intents and purposes, the Reagan administration took over the Continental Illinois Bank when the bank came near folding in 1983. A massive wave of scandals has plagued the defense industries, from reports that the government was charged with country club fees to allegations of procurement fraud in submarine contracts totaling, in just two cases, over a billion and a half dollars. As a result, the Pentagon has forced the resignation of the chairman of the board of the General Dynamics Corporation, the nation's largest military contractor. Even more decisive action in the future — nationalization *de facto* if not *de jure* — cannot be ruled out.

Expanded access to the courts for aggrieved citizens is another option. It was a private civil suit under the antitrust laws that brought about the dissolution of AT&T. And corporate liability to lawsuits is by no means limited to antitrust. The Ford Motor Company was tried for murder (though acquitted) in a case stemming from the vulnerability of the Pinto to rear-end collisions. Another murder case was brought in Chicago against a photochemical firm, one of whose workers had died of cyanide gas poisoning. That case resulted in a conviction. Less spectacular but still effective have been a rash of liability suits in product safety cases, tending to establish that a manufacturer remains responsible for its products long after they leave its factory or warehouse.

Economic democracy is another course of action that has its advocates, urging the appointment of public members to boards of directors of large companies. These public members would be charged with protecting consumer interests and with reporting behavior contrary to the public interest. A variant is to put union representatives on the board. For instance, UAW President Doug Fraser joined the Chrysler board a few years ago. And in the past few years, some corporations have actually been bought out, in whole or part, by their workers — Eastern Airlines and Weirton Steel, as two examples. Worker buy-outs have often brought a surge of productivity, but this has not usually been enough to reverse an unfavorable market position.

Power: The Unresolved Problem

It would be a mistake to conclude this recital with the implication that corporate (or union or government) power can be easily brought under control through a few legal remedies or by the power of public opinion. Certainly many abuses can be curbed, and much better levels of social performance achieved.

Yet mass organizations seem an inescapable concomitant of our age of high technology and increasing social interdependence. Here we should note that, depending on our interests, we stress different aspects of this universal phenomenon. To some, who fear the continued growth of very large-scale business, the most significant aspect is that we have not managed to control business power. To others, concerned over the emergence of large labor unions, it is labor power that most dangerously eludes effective control. And to still others who are most worried by the growth of big government, it is the growth of public power that is the main problem.

Thus the question of economic power remains, at best, only partially resolved. As A. A. Berle has written: "Some of these corporations can be thought of only in somewhat the same way we have heretofore thought of nations." Unlike nations, however, their power has not been rationalized in law, fully tested in practice, or well defined in philosophy. Unquestionably, the political and social influence and the economic power of the great centers of production pose problems with which capitalism — indeed, all industrialized societies — will have to cope for many years to come.

looking back

KEY CONCEPTS

In theory, the consumer is king

1 Consumer sovereignty is the ultimate rationale for the market system. With perfect competition, consumer sovereignty implies that (a) the consumer, not the producer, determines the allocation of resources, and (b) the consumer is offered goods produced as cheaply and as abundantly as resources and technology permit.

Market imperfections reduce consumer sovereignty

2 If monopoly or oligopoly are present, the consumer becomes a qualified sovereign. His or her preferences may be the same as before, but the market may not cater to these preferences at the lowest price.

Do advertising and product differentiation disprove consumer sovereignty?

3 Advertising is generally thought by economists to provide information consumers need, while product differentiation is generally held to reflect the diversity of preferences. Galbraith's dissenting view holds that advertising and product differentiation actually mold and create preferences. If so, consumer sovereignty would give way to producer sovereignty, and the whole basis of economic theory would have to change.

Business power has met many suggestions: Friedman suggests that profit-seeking is the only legitimate social function of business, but many businessmen prefer to think of themselves as being socially responsible

4 There are many views as to how business power should be dealt with. The view of conservatives who follow Milton Friedman is that big business is best left alone — that its main social function is to strive after profit, not to "do good." (In fact businesses should not be allowed to use their profits for philanthropy.) Many corporate executives find this view too uncomfortable and seek to define their roles as "professional" managers who deliberately follow socially responsible policies.

Dissolution of monopoly and antitrust policies have not proven very successful, mainly because big business is more technologically advanced than small business

5 The dissolution of monopoly is another approach to business power. So are antitrust measures, designed to break "combinations in restraint of trade," which have long been established policy. Yet both approaches have their limitations. Bigness is often the other side of the coin of technical efficiency and may also bring enlightened employee or social practices. And antitrust activity runs up against problems of cost and time, the

Economic and social regulation are both on the decline	6 Economic regulation of industries began to give way in the 1970s to restored competition in airlines, trucking, telecommunications, and other industries. There is a wide agreement that the results have been generally good. Social regulation—over environment, safety, civil rights, and other policies of corporations—has been cut back sharply beginning with the Reagan administration. Here the verdict remains controversial.

efficiency of big companies, and the dubious rationale of anti-trust policy itself.

Other options: power an unresolved problem	7 Various other policy options include expanded use of liability laws to enforce corporate responsibility, and economic democracy and even worker ownership; in some extreme cases, the government may itself in the future find itself in control of large corporations.

ECONOMIC VOCABULARY

Consumer sovereignty   586
Producer sovereignty   587
Product differentiation   588

Economic regulation   593
Social regulation   593
Deregulation   594

QUESTIONS

1. Make a list of the main institutional changes you can think of that would be needed if we were to institute a system of perfect competition.

2. Go through a magazine and analyze a dozen ads to see (a) how much genuine information they convey, such as price, technical features, availability, etc., and (b) how much they try to influence taste by suggesting the social or other benefits of using the product, without any economic information. Do the same for a newspaper. Why do you think that "informational" ads are more common in newspapers than magazines?

3. How do you feel about Friedman's ideas on business responsibility? Do you think that Mobil has a right to support "Masterpiece Theatre" and other such public TV shows? How about Mobil's right to publish editorials in support of its views on oil? And how about the contributions of small arms manufacturers to the National Rifle Association?

4. Do you think a businessman has any right to decide what the most socially responsible policy for his company should be? Take the case of moving a plant from one region to another. Should business management alone decide this? If not, who?

5. Would you support the nationalization of a big company such as USX (United States Steel) if it were threatened with bankruptcy that would impose terrible economic hardship on its workers and communities?

6. By and large, which do you consider to be the most dangerous *economic* problem: big business, big labor, big government? Which is the most dangerous *political* problem? The most dangerous *social* problem? Whatever your own list, can you imagine a rational argument for a different one? For a list in which the three groups were differently rank-ordered according to areas of danger? Do you think there is a "right" way of looking at this problem?

CHAPTER 33
The Distribution of Income — in Theory

a look ahead

With this chapter we enter a new area of microeconomics — income distribution. This chapter presents a discussion of how wages, rents, and interest are determined in the marketplace — in theory. In Chapter 34 we will look at the real world and discuss why and where the theory doesn't work as well as we should expect.

One by one we will consider each factor of production, deriving the forces of supply and demand that establish its level of remuneration. Actually, however, there is a central theme you will soon catch sight of: the marginal productivity theory of income distribution. This theory claims that each factor in a competitive market earns as much as the net revenue it brings into the firm. Marginal productivity theory thereby becomes the main idea for you to bear in mind — and note especially the surprising conclusion to which it points: There is no such thing, in a truly competitive world, as exploitation.

Although we have explored in some detail the demand for goods, we have left unexamined a crucial area of the market system. This is the market for factors, where wages, rent, and interest are determined.

This area is crucial for two reasons. First, it allows us to complete the analysis of the circular flow that has provided the basic pattern of our analysis. When we have understood the factor market, we will have knit together the household and the firm in their second major interaction—this time with the household acting as supplier rather than demander, and with the firm providing demand rather than supply.

Second, our analysis is crucial because it leads us to the consideration of a problem of major political and social importance: the *distribution of income,* the main theme in this and Chapter 34. In this chapter we look into the matter in theory—that is, as incomes would be determined in a perfectly competitive world. In Chapter 34, we look at the matter in fact—that is, as incomes are set in the imperfectly competitive world of our economy.

Factors and Factor Services

We must begin with a simple but distinguishing fact that separates the market for factors from that for goods. When we buy or sell goods, we take possession of, or deliver, an actual commodity. **But when we speak of buying or selling factors, we mean only that we are buying or selling a stream of services a factor produces.** When we buy or sell "labor," we do not buy or sell the human being who produces that labor—only the value of the work efforts. When we buy or sell "capital," we are not purchasing or selling a sum of money or a capital asset. We are hiring or offering the use of that money or equipment. Land too enters the market for factors as an agency of production whose services we rent but need not actually purchase.

Obviously we can buy land as real estate, and we can buy capital goods and various forms of capital, such as stocks and bonds. (We cannot buy human labor as an entity because slavery is illegal. In former times though, one *could* buy labor outright.) It stands to reason, then, that there should be a relationship between the price of factors, considered as assets (actual capital goods or real estate) and the price of the stream of services that factors produce: the *interest* earned on capital, the *rent* of land. There is such a relationship, which we will study later under the heading of "capitalization." Here we must recognize that the market for factors is not a market in which the assets are sold, but in which the productive services—the earnings—of these assets are priced.

As in every market, these prices will be determined by the interplay of supply and demand. Therefore to study the factor market, we must first look into the forces that determine the demand for factors, and then into the forces that determine their supply.

Direct Demand for Factors

Who buys factor services? Part of the answer is very simple. **A portion of the services of labor, land, and capital is demanded directly by consumers for their own personal enjoyment, exactly as with any good or service.** This kind of demand for factors of production takes the guise of the demand for lawyers and barbers and servants or the demand for plots of land for personal dwellings or the demand for cars and washing machines or other personal capital goods or the demand for loans for consumption purposes. To the extent that factors are demanded directly for these purposes, there is nothing in analyzing the demand for them that differs from the demand curves we have previously studied.

Derived Demand

Most factors of production do not earn their incomes by selling their services directly to final consumers. They sell them instead to firms. In turn, firms want the services of these factors not for personal enjoyment, but to put them to profitable use.

Thus we speak of the firm's demand for factors as derived demand. Its demand is derived from consumers' demand for the output the firm makes. Each firm will hire labor (or any other factor) until the marginal revenue from that factor just equals the marginal costs of hiring that factor.

The marginal output a factor produces multiplied by the selling price of the product is called its **marginal revenue product.** If a factor produces three extra units of output that are sold for $10 per unit, its marginal revenue product is $30. If the number of units of output falls as more and more of a factor is added to the production process, these diminishing returns cause the marginal revenue product curve or the derived demand curve to slope downward.

We see this in Figure 1, where the derived demand for a factor leads firm 1 to employ quantity *OA*. Derived demand of firm 2 results in the hire of *OB*, and the summed demand of both firms gives us a market demand of *OC*.

This, however, leaves us with the question of factor price only half explained. We understand the elements that enter into the demand curve for the factor. But we

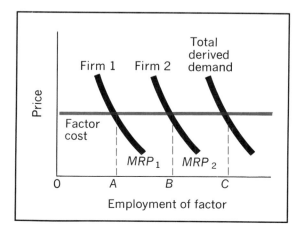

Figure 1

DERIVED DEMAND FOR FACTORS

The derived demand curve (or the marginal revenue product curve) slopes downward because each factor adds less and less to output as we add that factor. Multiply the falling marginal contribution of the factor times the selling price and you get the curves shown here.

cannot understand how the price of the factor is established until we know something about the supply curves in the factor market. That is the missing element we need to complete the circular flow.

THE SUPPLY CURVE OF FACTORS

What do we know about the willingness and ability of the owners of labor, capital, and land to offer their services in the marketplace at varying prices for these services?

Labor

By far the most important supply curve in the factor market is that of labor — meaning, let us remember, labor of all grades, from the least skilled workman to the most highly trained scientist or the most effective entrepreneur.

As Figure 2 shows, the supply curve for the labor of most individuals has a curious shape. Up to wage level *OA,* we have no trouble explaining things. Economists assume that labor involves *disutility.* Moreover, just as we assume that increasing amounts of a utility-yielding good give us diminishing marginal utility, so we assume that increasing amounts of labor involve *increasing marginal disutility.* Therefore the curve rises up to level *OA* because we will not be willing to work longer hours (to offer a larger quantity of labor services within a given time period), unless we are paid more per hour.

The Backward-Bending Supply Curve. How then do we explain the backward-bending portion of the rising curve above wage level *OA?* The answer lies in adding to the rising marginal disutility of labor the falling marginal utility of *income* itself,

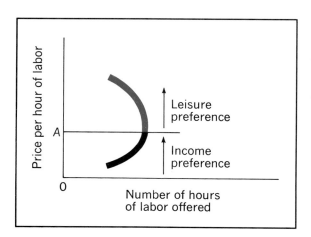

Figure 2
BACKWARD-BENDING SUPPLY CURVE OF LABOR
A typical labor supply curve bends backward because the balance between the utility of additional income and the disutility of earning it changes from "pro-work" to "pro-leisure."

on the assumption that an extra dollar of income to a person who is making $10,000 is worth less than the utility of an additional dollar when that person is making only $5,000. **Above a certain income level, leisure is preferable to more income.**

Together, these two forces explain very clearly why the supply curve of labor bends backward above a certain level. Take a designer who has been tempted to work 70 hours a week by wage raises that have finally reached $50 an hour. Now suppose that wages go up another 10 percent. It is possible, of course, that the marginal utility of the additional income may outweigh the marginal disutility of these long hours, so that the designer stays on the job or works even longer hours. If, however, his or her marginal utility of income has reached a low enough point and his or her marginal disutility of work a high enough point, the raise may bring a new possibility: The designer may work *fewer* hours and enjoy the same (or a somewhat higher) income as well as additional leisure. For example, as pay goes up 10 percent, the designer may reduce his or her workweek by 5 percent.

Backward-bending supply curves help explain the long trend toward reducing the workweek. Over the last century, weekly hours have decreased by about 40 percent. Although many factors have converged to bring about this result, one of them is certainly the desire of individual men and women to give up the marginal utility of potential income for that of increased leisure.

Individual vs. Collective Supply. A cautionary note is useful here. We can speak with some degree of confidence about the backward-bending supply curve of individual labor, especially when labor is paid by the hour or by the piece. But we must distinguish the supply curve of the individual from that of the labor force as a whole. As the price of labor rises, some persons will be tempted to enter the labor market because the opportunity cost of remaining "leisured" is now too great. This accounts for the entrance of many housewives into the market as the price for part-time office work goes up.

This is the problem of the "participation rates" of the population that enters into the macroeconomic problem of employment. **Here it is useful to understand that the collective supply curve of labor is probably upward-sloping rather than backward-bending.** (It would be backward-bending if wages rose so high that married women, for example, dropped out of the labor force as their husbands' earnings rose, but that does not seem to be the case.)

Psychic Income. The supply curve of labor is further complicated because work brings not only disutilities, but positive enjoyments. Jobs bring friendships, relieve boredom, may lead to power or prestige. Many people derive deep satisfactions from their work and would not change jobs even if they could improve their incomes by doing so. Indeed, it is very likely that most individuals seek to maximize their "psychic incomes" rather than their money incomes, combining the utilities derived from their earnings and the quite separate utilities from their work, and balancing these gains against the disutilities work also involves.

The difficulty in speaking about psychic income is that it involves us in an unmeasurable concept — a tautology. Therefore when we speak about the supply curve of labor, we generally make the assumption that individuals behave roughly as money maximizers, an assumption that has prima facie evidence in the long-run exodus from low-paying to higher-paying occupations and from low-wage to high-wage regions.

Mobility of Labor. More than a million American families change addresses in a typical year, so that over a decade the normal mobility of the labor force may transport 30 million to 40 million people (including wives and children) from one part of the country to another. Without this potential influx of labor, we would expect wages to shoot up steeply whenever an industry in a particular locality expanded, with the result that further profitable expansion might then become impossible.

We also speak of mobility of labor in a vertical sense, referring to the movement from occupation to occupation. Here the barriers to mobility are not usually geographical but institutional (for instance, trade union restrictions on membership) or social (discrimination against the upward mobility of blacks) or economic (lack of sufficient income to gain a needed amount of education). Despite these obstacles, occupational mobility is also very impressive from generation to generation, as the astounding changes in the structure of the U.S. labor force have demonstrated (see box p. 610).

This is a force tending to reduce the differences between income extremes, since the mobility of labor will not only shift the supply curve to the right in the favored occupations (thereby exerting a downward pressure on incomes), but move the supply curve to the left in those industries it leaves, bringing an upward impetus to incomes. Figure 3 shows how this process works.

Figure 3
EFFECT OF LABOR MOBILITY ON RELATIVE WAGES
The diagram shows a low-wage employment paying OA wages, and a high one O'A'. The movement of labor out of the disfavored occupation or industry and into the favored one raises OA to OB, and reduces O'A' to O'B'. Note: The labor that goes into the high-wage employment is not necessarily the same labor that leaves the low-wage area. But as long as supply curves shift, the wage differential will change as shown.

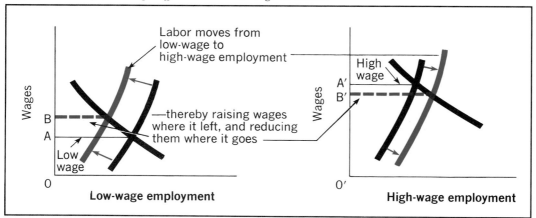

Capital

What does the supply curve of capital look like? When we say "capital," we are not much interested in the supply of actual machines or equipment. Machines will be produced, just like any other commodity, up to the point where the marginal cost of making them equals the marginal revenue from their sale.

When we speak of the supply of capital, therefore, we concern ourselves with the supply of new savings into the market, the source of the machines of the future. **How about the supply curve of savings? Economists have learned that savers change their habits of thrift much less in response to changes in the price of savings (interest) than in response to changes in the level of income.** We can see this in Figure 4.

Allocating Savings. Even though the price of savings may not greatly affect our thriftiness, it has a very important effect on what we do with our savings. As savers, we often reallocate the way we dispose of our savings, shifting our "portfolios" among checking accounts, savings accounts, insurance, or stocks and bonds, as the various returns offered by these assets change (or as our assessment of their risk changes). For example, high interest rates in the late 1970s resulted in a tremendous movement from non-interest-bearing checking accounts into interest-bearing savings accounts and then into money market mutual funds. Financial institutions also shift real investment funds in response to different rates of return.

Thus, when we picture the supply curve for saving, we should also bear in mind what this curve looks like to any particular demander. From the point of view of an

Figure 4
THE SUPPLY CURVE OF SAVINGS
We do not greatly change our saving habits if interest changes, but we do greatly change our savings as income changes. This last is a macroeconomic relationship of great importance.

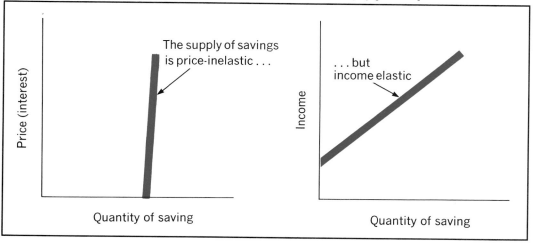

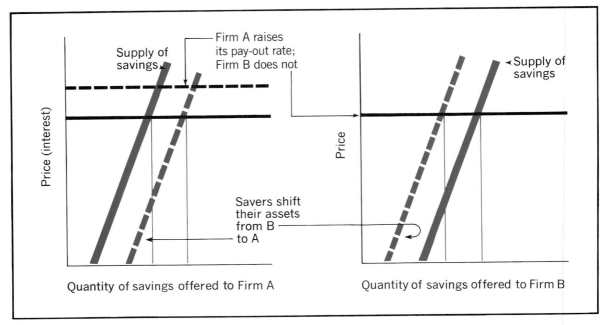

Figure 5
REALLOCATION OF SAVINGS

The diagram shows us that capital moves, just as labor does, leaving low-remuneration employment for high-remuneration employment.

enterprise in the market for capital, savings are highly price-elastic; that is, a firm can attract savings by offering a higher return than a competitive enterprise offers. As a result, savers will shift their capital from one enterprise to the other, as in Figure 5. This bears an obvious relation to the mobility of labor, and we can indeed speak of it as the *mobility of capital.*

Land

Finally, let us consider the supply curve of land. At any moment, the total supply of land, like capital, is fixed. To a limited extent, there is a counterpart to saving which adds to capital. By applying capital and labor we can slowly add to land by dredging, clearing forests, reclaiming swamps and deserts. Therefore the long-run supply curve for land is slightly price-elastic, as Figure 6 shows.

As with capital, however, it is possible to speak of the *mobility of land.* This seems strange, since land is obviously not movable. Land can, however, be used for very different purposes, depending on the returns to be had from them. If we picture the supply curve of land for, say, shopping centers or orange groves or industrial sites, we can picture an upward-sloping curve, just like the supply curve of capital

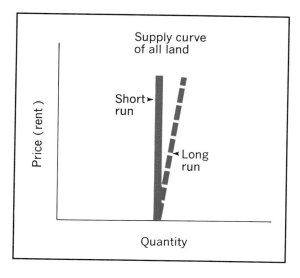

Figure 6
SUPPLY CURVE FOR LAND

We can add only small amounts to usable land as its price rises. But as Figure 7 makes plain, we can add large amounts to usable space. What do you suppose the ratio of space to land is in New York City compared to a Great Plains town? Why is it worth building skyscrapers in New York but not in the rural Midwest?

for any one use. Land can be—and constantly is—moved from use to use, as various enterprises bid for it. Thus the supply curve may be very elastic to any one user, even though the overall supply curve to society is very inelastic.

Land vs. Space. In addition, we must differentiate land from space. We can create space much more easily than we can create land. Space is essentially a function of the availability of capital and labor, not of land. Every time we put up a high-rise building where there was previously a low one, we have created more space on the same amount of land. As a result, the supply curve for space will be very price-elastic—a higher price for space (rent) bringing more onto the market, as Figure 7 shows. In the long run, space is available in indefinite amounts.

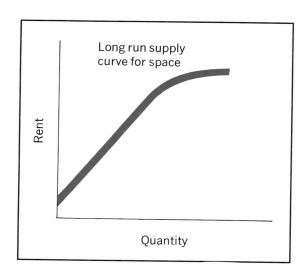

Figure 7
SUPPLY CURVE FOR SPACE

UNITED STATES' WORK PROFILE

What kinds of work do people do in the United States? The table below gives us a picture of the shifting occupational profile of the nation's work force over the last eighty odd years.

Note particularly the striking growth in professional and managerial work, together with the drift from blue- to white-collar jobs. This lies behind most discussion of "postindustrial" society as the direction in which we may be headed.

	Percent of Labor Force			Percent of Labor Force	
	1900	1985		1900	1985
Managerial and professional			**Blue-collar**		
Professional and technical workers	4.1%	16.0%	Skilled workers and foremen	10.3%	12.2%
			Semiskilled workers	12.8	11.4
Managers, officials, and proprietors (nonfarm)	5.9	11.4	Unskilled workers	12.4	4.2
			Household and other service workers	8.9	13.7
White-collar			**Farm**		
Clerical workers	3.1	16.3	Farmers and farm managers	20.0	2.7
Sales workers	4.8	12.1	Farm laborers	17.6	

Source: Bureau of Labor Statistics *Employment and Earnings.*

RENTS AND INCOMES

We are almost ready to tie together all our different supply curves, and to describe the overall working of the factor market. But the importance of time in bringing about increases in land or space alerts us to a very important reason for the existence of very large incomes (and very large disparities of incomes) in the short run. This is the phenomenon of **quasi rent** (also called *economic* rent).

Land Rent

First let us get rid of some confusing terminology, by distinguishing quasi rents from the earnings of land as a factor of production, which is also rent. The distinction is clear in thought. It is muddied only because usage has chosen similar words for dissimilar things.

The rent earned by land as a factor of production is the payment we make to its owner for its services to the market. If we cease to pay land rent or pay less rent, the amount of land offered on the market will fall. If we pay more, it will rise. This rent is both a payment made to a factor of production to compensate its owner for its services and an element of cost that must enter into the calculation of selling prices. If a farmer must pay $100 rent to get an additional field, that $100 will clearly be part of the cost of producing a new crop.

Quasi or Economic Rent

Quasi rents differ in important ways from true land rent.

1. **Quasi rent is not a return earned by the factor, in that the payment has nothing to do with inducing the factor to enter the market.**
2. **Quasi rents are not a cost that helps to determine selling price. They are earnings determined by selling price.**
3. **Quasi rents apply to all factors, not just to land.**

An illustration may clarify the problem. Figure 8 shows the supply curve for "first class" office space in New York City. Notice that over a considerable range there is an unchanging price for space. Up to amount OX, you can get all the space you want at rent OA (per square foot). This is real land rent, in the sense of being a necessary payment for a factor service. If there were no rent paid, no space would be forthcoming.

Next, look at the situation after we have used up OX amount of space. We can rent additional space up to OY, but only at rising prices (rents). Perhaps expenditures are needed to induce landlords to upgrade "second-class" space. Each new

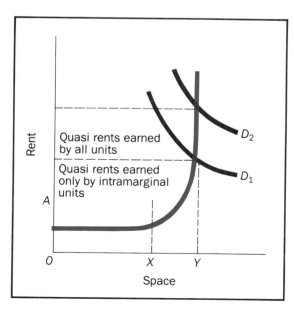

Figure 8
RENTS AND QUASI RENTS

Are quasi rents scarcity returns? The diagram makes it clear they are. Are they monopoly returns? No, because they can be enjoyed by large numbers of intramarginal firms or individuals.

area that is tempted onto the market at a higher price earns real rent, in that it would not appear unless a higher price were paid. But notice that all the offices previously offered at lower prices are now in a position to ask higher rentals because the price of the marginal unit has increased. Thus we have here a mixture of real rents and economic or quasi rents. **The marginal landlord is receiving real rent. All the other (intramarginal) landlords who can now get higher rentals are the beneficiaries of a scarcity price that gives them a bonus over the real rent they originally received. This bonus is economic or quasi rent.**

Finally we reach the point OY, at which there is no more space to be had at any price. Suppose the demand for space continues to rise from D_1 to D_2. The price of office space will rise as well, and *all* landlords will be receiving quasi rents on top of their real rents.

Rents and Prices

Here is where we make a clear distinction. True rent is a cost that must be paid to bring land into production. Quasi rent is not such a cost. It is wholly the result of scarcity and plays no role in determining the real cost to society of producing goods or services. If demand fell from D_2 to D_1, a great deal of quasi rent would disappear, although not a foot of office space would be withdrawn.

Thus true rent helps determine price, whereas economic or quasi rent is determined by price. We can see that rent must be paid if office space OX is to appear, but that quasi rent is not a necessary cost of production for space thereafter.

This conclusion, however, applies only to our analysis of costs from a social point of view. From the point of view of the individual producer, the distinction disappears. A renter must pay the landlord whatever it costs to rent space, be it rent or quasi rent. Thus quasi rents enter into the renter's costs and help determine the price that must be asked for his or her goods.

Economic Rents and Allocation

From the social point of view, quasi rent (or, by its other name, economic rent) is a waste. If we could eliminate it, say by taxing it away, it would not diminish production at all, only the incomes of the owners of scarce resources.

Quasi rents are therefore wholly "unearned" incomes. Nonetheless, they serve a useful function for society. They allocate a scarce commodity, in this case office space, among various claimants for that commodity.

The fact that quasi rents are a monopoly return is neither here nor there, so far as their rationing function is concerned. If there were no quasi rents, office space would be leased at prices that failed to equate quantities demanded and supplied. There would be a "shortage" of space and rationing would take place on some other basis — first come, first served or political influence or having an "in" with the landlord, instead of through the price mechanism.

Economic Rents and Incomes

Finally, we must make careful note of the fact that quasi rents are not returns limited to land. Take car rentals. Suppose we can rent all the car transportation we need at the going price. Suddenly there is a jump in demand, and the rentable fleet is too small. Rentals will rise. Until additional cars come onto the market, the fleet owners will simply enjoy economic rents (quasi rents) on their cars.

In the same way, the earnings of actors or authors or of anyone possessing scarce talent or skills are likely to be partly economic rents. An actress might be perfectly happy to offer her services for a good movie role at $50,000, but she may be able to get $100,000 because of her name. The first $50,000, without which she would not work, is her wage. The rest is a quasi or economic rent. A plumber who would be willing to work for standard wages, but who gets double because he is the only plumber in town, earns economic rents. And as we have already seen, these rents explain a part of business profits, as returns going to inframarginal firms.

Capitalization

Economic rents lead us to the process called *capitalization*. As we have mentioned, buyers of land and capital often have the option of buying the actual real estate or machinery they use, instead of just paying for its services. Capitalization is the means by which we place a value on a factor as an asset.

Suppose an office building makes $100,000 a year in rentals and we decide to buy the building. How much would it be worth? The answer depends, of course, on the riskiness of the investment. Some buildings, like some machines or bonds or businesses, are safer buys than others. For each class of risk there is a rate of return established by other buyers and sellers of similar assets. Suppose the rate of return applicable to our building is 10 percent. Then we will capitalize it at $1 million. This is because $1 million at 10 percent gives us a return of $100,000.

We can capitalize any factor (or any business) by dividing its current earnings by the appropriate interest rate. The appropriate interest rate tells us the opportunity cost of our money: how much we could get for it if we bought some other factor or asset of similar risk. Notice that as the interest rate falls, so does the opportunity cost. We have to be content with a smaller return on our money. Thus if we are buying land that rents for $2,000, and the appropriate interest rate is 10 percent, the land will sell for $20,000 ($20,000 × .10 = $2,000). If the interest rate *falls* to 5 percent, the value of the land will *rise* to $40,000.

Capitalization and Economic Rents

Capitalization is important in determining the asset prices of factors. It is also important because it gets rid of economic rents! Suppose the $100,000 rental income were virtually all quasi rent and that the building were sold for $1 million.

The new owners of the building will still be making $100,000 a year, *but it will no longer be an economic rent.* It will be a normal market return on the capital they expended. They will have paid for their quasi rents in the opportunity cost of their capital.

The gainer in the transaction will be the original owner of the building. Perhaps the building cost him very little and the $1 million sale price came as a great capital gain. He will have capitalized his quasi rents into a large sum of capital; but on the sum, in the future, he can expect to make no more than the normal rate of interest.

Market Price for Factors*

We are finally in a position to assemble the pieces of the puzzle. We have traced the forces that give rise to the supply curves of the different factors, and we understand the explanation for the demand curves as well. Hence we understand how factors are priced in the market, which is to say we understand the mechanism for determining *factor incomes.*

Can we generalize about the result? One would think, in light of the variety of supply curves we have discussed, that this would be impossible. If we think about the nature of the demand curve for factors, however, we see this is not so. The shape and position of the supply curve for any factor will determine how much of it appears on the market at any given price. **But whatever the amount of the factor, it will be paid a return equal to the marginal revenue product of that factor.** Remember the entrepreneur will go on hiring all factors as long as their marginal revenue products are greater than their marginal costs. Thus, whatever the shape or position of the supply curve, the earnings of the factor will always be equal to the marginal revenue it brings to the buyer, as Figure 9 shows.

We could draw other curves showing the collective supply of labor, the supply of savings to a given user, or the total quantity of land, but the conclusion would be the same. In each case, the market rate of wages, interest, and rent would be equal to the marginal revenue product of that factor.

---

* In the sixties there was a spirited controversy about the nature of capital, led by the late English economist Joan Robinson. Robinson challenged the concept of capital as a factor of production. Of course there were *capital goods* of all kinds, but what of capital itself? Labor could be measured in hours, but in what units should capital be measured? What, indeed, *is* a "unit" of capital? How could one add up all the various capital goods—shovels and machine tools and inventories—to arrive at a factor of production called *capital?*

Robinson argued on this point that conventional theory was inherently circular. Capital, unlike labor, is measured not in physical units, but by its *value.* But its value depends on its rate of return, which theory describes as the "marginal product" of capital. Now here is the problem. To know the value of capital you have to *know* its marginal product. In that case, how can one use the value of capital to *derive* its marginal product? Such considerations have shaken the foundations of the theory of capital, but they have not led to much change in the ordinary treatment of capital by businesspeople and economists. Both continue to speak of it as if no conceptual difficulties obscured its meaning—as if you could add up the stream of past investments, less depreciation—and arrive at a meaningful "value of capital" to put into a "production function." We will not probe more deeply into this complex question here, but the student ought to be aware that there are unresolved problems surrounding these basic ideas.

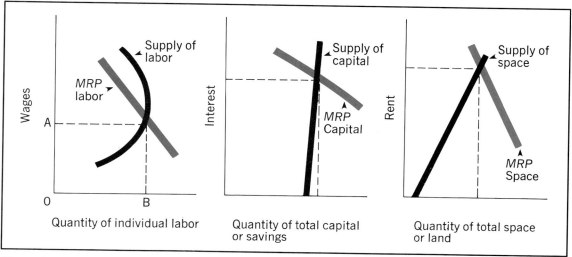

Figure 9

MARGINAL REVENUE PRODUCTS AND EARNINGS

Despite their different shapes and locations, the various supply curves of the factors always help determine the quantity of the factor that will be hired and the remuneration it will receive. In each case, the demand curve is the marginal revenue product curve — the amount of income the entrepreneur will gain from hiring the factor in question. As our graph shows, these derived demand curves may also have differing shapes or locations, but in all cases the intersection of the two curves gives us the information we want. Notice the important fact that the earnings of each factor will be equal to the marginal revenue it earns for its employer. At quantity OB of labor, labor's MRP is OA. This is its wage. The equality of earnings and MRPs is the basis for the claim that in a market of perfect competition there can be no exploitation.

The Marginal Productivity Theory of Distribution

We call this generalization about factor prices the *marginal productivity theory of distribution.* **What it tells us is very simple. The income of any factor will be determined by the contribution each factor makes to the revenue of the enterprise. Its income will be higher or lower, depending on the willingness and ability of suppliers of factor services to enter the market at different prices; but at all prices, factors will earn amounts equal to the marginal revenue they produce.**

Two conclusions follow from this theory. **The first is that in a perfect market there can be no exploitation of any factor.** That is, each factor will receive an amount exactly equal to the revenue it produces for the firm.* There can be no

---

* When a factor is bought directly by a consumer, the factor will receive the money value of the marginal utility it produces for the consumer.

unpaid labor or unrewarded land or capital. A worker or capitalist or landlord may not be willing to offer his services at going rates of pay, but none can claim that his earnings are less than the revenues he brings into the firm. For as we have seen, every profit-maximizing entrepreneur must keep on hiring factors until their marginal revenue products equal their marginal cost.

Moreover, no factor can claim that some other factor is paid too much. To be sure, some factors will earn quasi rents, a waste from society's point of view, as we have seen. But we have seen that quasi rents are a temporary phenomenon, slowly eliminated by mobility of the factor in question into an area of scarcity. **In the long run, the return to land, capital, and labor will reflect the actual dollar contribution each makes to output.**

Price and Productivity

The second conclusion follows from the first: It is that all factors will be paid in proportion to their productivity.

Suppose an entrepreneur can hire a unit of factor A, say an acre of land which will produce a marginal revenue product of $20, or an extra worker whose marginal revenue product will be $40. We know that the entrepreneur will have to pay $20 to hire the acre of land and cannot pay more than that, and that he or she will have to pay $40 for the worker and cannot pay less than that.

What accounts for the difference between the earnings of a unit of land and a unit of labor? Their marginal revenue products. But these marginal revenue products, we recall, are only the *physical* marginal products of the factors multiplied by the market value of the output to which they contribute. The value of the output must be the same, since land and labor will both be adding to the output of the same commodity. The difference in their marginal *revenue* products is therefore solely the result of the fact that (in this example) a unit of land creates fewer units of output than a unit of labor.

It follows, therefore, that factor prices must be proportional to their physical productivities, or that:

$$\frac{\text{price of factor A}}{\substack{\text{marginal productivity} \\ \text{of factor A}}} = \frac{\text{price of factor B}}{\substack{\text{marginal productivity} \\ \text{of factor B}}}$$

Marginal Productivity and "Justice"

This is a very remarkable solution to the problem of distribution. It says that in truly competitive systems, all factors will be rewarded in proportion to their contribution to output. If an acre of land is only half as productive as a unit of labor, it will be paid only half as much. If it is twice as productive, it will be paid double. If skilled labor produces three times as much as unskilled, its wage rate will be three times that of unskilled, and so on. **The resulting pattern of income distribution** thus seems both just and efficient. It seems just because everyone is getting all the income he or she produces, and because no one is getting any income he or she has not produced. It seems efficient because entrepreneurs will use factors in a way that maximizes their contribution to output, thereby not only giving the factors their largest possible reward, but giving society the greatest overall output to be had from them.

Is this conclusion valid? Do the earnings of land, labor, and capital reflect their contributions to output? The question takes us from a consideration of how the factor market works in theory — that is, under conditions of perfect competition — to a consideration of how it works in fact. It brings us also to look carefully into the question of whether or not marginal productivity establishes a pattern of rewards that can rest its case on some definition of justice. We look into these extremely important questions in our next chapter.

looking back

KEY CONCEPTS

Factor services

1 The income of the factors of production is derived from the sale of their services — the energy and intelligence of labor, the use of land and capital.

Direct and derived demand; derived demand is the marginal revenue product of the factor

2 The demand for these services sometimes arises directly from their purchaser, as in the case of land bought for a home, but generally it is derived demand — the demand of a firm for the revenues the services will bring. These revenues are called the marginal revenue products of the factor. They are the marginal physical increments to production the factor will create, times the selling price of that output.

Supply curve of individual labor is backward-bending

3 The supply side of the factor market varies with each factor. Typically, the willingness of individuals to offer their labor increases as earnings rise and then decreases, giving us a backward-bending supply curve of labor. This is because above a certain income level, individuals prefer to sacrifice some potential money income for leisure.

Supply curve of savings is price-inelastic, except for allocation

4 The supply curve of capital that most interests us is the supply of savings. The flow of savings is very responsive to income changes, much less so to price changes. But the allocation of savings among users is highly price-elastic.

Supply curve of land vs. space

5 The supply curve of land is highly price-inelastic; but the supply curve for space is very price-elastic.

Quasi rents, or economic rents, are scarcity returns. They are price-determined, not price-determining

6 Quasi rent, or economic rent, is the name for scarcity returns that accrue to factors (land, labor, or capital) by virtue of their scarcity. Unlike true rent, a quasi rent does not tempt additional factors onto the market. A quasi rent is therefore price-determined, not price-determining; it results from a high price for the factor at the margin, and does not constitute an explanation of why the marginal factor is high priced. (From the viewpoint of the person who pays a quasi rent, it is, of course, a cost and enters into his costs.)

Quasi rents are socially wasteful, but useful in allocation

7 Quasi rents are a social waste because they do not induce additional production. But they play a useful role in the allocation of scarce resources.

Capitalization determines factor values by dividing their earnings by the appropriate interest rate.

8 Capitalization is the process by which we use factor earnings (including their quasi rents) to determine the value of the factors themselves. We capitalize a factor by dividing its earnings by the appropriate interest rate for its class of risk. Thus as interest rates decline, capitalized values rise. After a capitalized factor is sold, it no longer earns a quasi rent for its purchaser, but simply a normal return for its degree of risk.

Ideally, all factors earn their MRPs

9 We can generalize about factor incomes as ideally determined by the interplay of their supply curves with their respective demand curves. The demand curves are their marginal revenue product curves or the curve of the marginal revenues they will earn for their buyer. This is called the marginal productivity theory of distribution. Under marginal productivity theory, each factor receives its full contribution to revenues as its reward. There is no possible exploitation.

This marginal productivity theory of distribution implies no exploitation

10 All factors will also be paid proportionally to their contributions to revenues. Therefore we can write:

$$\frac{P_x}{MP_x} = \frac{P_y}{MP_y}$$

$$\frac{\text{price of factor X}}{\text{marginal product of factor X}} = \frac{\text{price of factor Y}}{\text{marginal product of factor Y}}$$

ECONOMIC VOCABULARY

QUESTIONS

1. When suburban homeowners buy real estate, what services are they actually buying? When they hire domestic help, what services are they buying? When they borrow money from a bank?

2. What is meant by the *derived* demand for labor? What is its relationship to the marginal revenue product of labor? To clarify your understanding, do the following: (a) Run over in your mind the law of diminishing returns; (b) Be sure you understand how this law affects marginal *physical* productivity; (c) explain how we go from marginal physical product to marginal *revenue* product; and (d) explain how marginal revenue product influences the willingness of the employer to hire a factor.

3. If the rent of a piece of land is $500 and the rate of interest is 5 percent, what is the value of the land? Suppose the rate rises to 10 percent; does the value of the land rise or fall? If the rental increases to $1,000 and interest is unchanged, what happens to the value of the land?

4. What do you think the supply curve of executive labor looks like? Is it backward-bending? Would you expect it to be more or less backward-bending than the supply curve of common labor? Why?

5. Exactly what is rent? How does it differ from quasi rent? Is there any similarity between rent and interest, or rent and wages? What is the role of ownership in rent, profits, *and wages*?

6. What is meant by saying that rent is price-determining? What does it mean to say that economic rent is price-determined? Show this on a diagram.

7. Explain carefully how factor returns are proportional to their marginal productivities. What conditions would be necessary to make this theoretical conclusion true in the real world?

AN EXTRA WORD ABOUT

The Problem of Equity

Most people in the modern world would admit to an underlying bias in favor of equality in their social values. We hear of policies in every nation that seek to diminish the differences between rich and poor. We hear of very few policies that openly advocate greater inequality. Even policies that support greater inequality — for example tax loopholes for millionaires — are justified in terms of their ultimate effect in raising the incomes of *all,* presumably lessening poverty.

Starting with this bias in favor of equality, we need some understanding of the kind of exceptions we may make to the general rule. That is, we need to know and to look carefully into the arguments in favor of inequality. There are four of them.

1. We agree that inequality is justified if everyone has a fair chance to get ahead. Most of us do not object to inequality of outcome — in fact, we generally favor it — if we are convinced that the race was run under fair conditions with no one handicapped at the start.

What are fair conditions? That is where the argument becomes complex. Are large inheritances fair? Most Americans agree that *some* inheritance is fair but that taxes should prevent the full passage of wealth from generation to generation. What about inheritances of talent? No one is much concerned about this. Inheritances of culture? For some time we have been getting exercised over the handicaps that are inherited by persons born in the slum or to nonwhite parents.

2. We agree to inequality when it is the outcome of individual preferences. If the outcome of the economic game results in unequal incomes, we justify these inequalities when they accord with different personal desires. One man works harder than another, so he deserves a larger income. One chooses to enter the law and makes a fortune; the other chooses to enter the ministry and make do with a small income. We acquiesce in these inequalities to the degree that they appear to mirror individual preferences.

3. We abide by inequality when it reflects merit. Merit is not quite the same as fairness or personal preference. It has to do with our belief in the propriety of higher rewards when they are justified by a larger contribution to output. Here is the belief which underpins the idea that factors should be paid their marginal revenue product. We do not object to factors receiving different remunerations in the market, because we can show that each factor contributes a different amount to total output.

That is, of course, only a value judgment. Suppose there are two workers, side by side, on the assembly line. One is young, strong, unmarried, and very productive. The other is older, married, has a large family and many expenses — and is less productive. Should the first be compensated more highly than the second? We find ourselves in a conflict of values here. Our bias toward equality tells us no. Our exception for merit tells us yes. There is no correct solution for this or any other problem involving value judgments. Once again, social values prevail, sometimes paying the younger person more than the older, sometimes both the same, sometimes the older more.

4. Finally, we agree in violating the spirit of equality when we are convinced that inequality is for the common good. The common good is often translated into practical terms of gross national product. Thus we may agree to allow unequal rewards because we are convinced (or persuaded) that this inequality will ultimately benefit us all by raising all incomes as well as the incomes of those who are favored.

The difficult question here is to define the common good. There are many conceptions of what such an objective should be. All incorporate value judgments. Even the common good of survival, which might justify giving a larger reward to those who must be entrusted with survival, is a value judgment.

EQUITY AND ECONOMICS

These general principles do not describe the way we *should* think about inequality. They are an attempt to describe the way we *do* think about it — the arguments we commonly hear, or raise ourselves, to defend an unequal distribution of goods and services or of wealth.

Each of these arguments, as we can see, poses its own tangled problems. And there is every reason that they should be tangled, for the distribution of incomes poses the most perplexing of all economic problems to any society. At one extreme, it criticizes all the privileges and inequalities every society displays, forcing us to explain to ourselves why one person should enjoy an income larger than he or she can spend, while another suffers from an income too small to permit him a decent livelihood. At the other extreme, it forces us to examine the complications and contradictions of a society of absolutely equal incomes, where each individual (or family?) received the same amount as every other, regardless of differences in physical capacity, life situation, potential contribution to society.

Usually we have to compromise, to find reasons to support income distributions that are neither completely equal nor completely unequal. Here is where we lean partly on our actual knowledge of the effects of income distribution on work and output, and partly on value systems that define allowable exceptions to our basic rule that societies should seek equality as their goal. As our values change — and we are now living in a period when values seem to be changing rapidly — we accord different weights to the various arguments by which we traditionally justify unequal incomes.

THE UNAVOIDABLE PROBLEM

Economic equality is complex, confusing, and often disconcerting. It makes us uneasy not only because it confronts us with the often shaky presumptions we make about equity, but because we recognize that no solution will ever be found that can be demonstrated to be superior to all others.

Yet there is no escape from trying to specify what is meant by equity. If we fail to make such an effort, we only end up with a hodgepodge of feelings about equity, many of them contradictory or unsatisfying. This does not mean we can work out a scheme of economic equity free of contradictions or uncertainties. But at least we will have understood why certain contradictions are inherent in the problem of equity, and will be in a position to act with both intelligence and purpose when forced — as are we all — to decide which economic policies are better and which are worse.

CHAPTER 34
How Incomes Are Distributed —
in Fact

a look ahead

Here is a chapter in which we examine two matters of great importance:

1 The way in which income is actually distributed among individuals or families.
2 The various ways in which we have tried to achieve a fairer income distribution than the existing one.

Once again, it is important not to get bogged down in facts, although the basic realities are important to know. The question to think about is *why* income distribution does not seem to bear much relation to marginal productivity theory, and *why* various efforts to change income distribution have had very different impacts. Thus we are still interested in theory, even though we zero in on the distribution of income in fact.

In our last chapter we reached the conclusion that factor prices could be explained by their marginal productivities. Does this mean that we now have the key to understanding the actual distribution of income in our society? Can we explain riches and poverty, high-paid professions and low-paid ones, in terms of marginal productivity?

The quick answer to that question is no. Marginal productivity does not explain the basic facts of income distribution as we find it in the United States. Nonetheless, there is a valuable use for the theory. At the end of the chapter we will come back to the question of how we can use marginal productivity. First, however, let us discuss why it fails to explain income distribution as we find it in reality.

RICH AND POOR

Chapter 4 made us familiar with the contours of income distribution. Perhaps you recall our discussion of classes or of the income parade in the box on p. 64. How much of this panorama can marginal productivity help us understand? By and large we can eliminate two ends of the income parade. Marginal productivity theory does not explain the existence or persistence of most poverty, and it does not adequately account for the presence of most very high incomes. Let us begin by seeing why this is the case.

Poverty

Quickly let us review a few major characteristics of American families who were in poverty in 1985:

☐ About a third of them are black.
☐ About a half are families headed by a female.
☐ One-tenth of them are over 65 years of age.
☐ Forty percent are juveniles.
☐ Thirty-five percent of the family heads are unemployed.

These are not, of course, the only "reasons" for being poor, but they are causative factors that figure to some extent in many cases of poverty. **Note, however, these characteristics of poverty have very little to do with productivity.** There is no reason to believe that the potential productivity of blacks or women condemns so many of them to low-income status. (We discuss that question later.) Persons over 65 need not have low marginal productivity. Some of our most prominent artists, statesmen, lawyers, and executives are older than 65. And of course, the marginal productivity of an unemployed person is zero—not because he or she is not productive, but because he or she has no job.

Low Wages

Marginal productivity theory therefore gives us very little insight into the reasons for the low income of the bottom fifth of the nation. It sheds light on this bottom bracket only to the extent that its members are employed in very low-wage (presumably low-productivity) jobs. A considerable number of those in poverty do hold low-wage jobs: two-thirds of poor adults work. But we shall see that their low pay is better explained by market imperfections than by attributing a kind of innate low productivity to the person who holds the job.

Thus poverty is a question that we must examine from perspectives other than that of marginal productivity. Why does the economy not produce full employment? Why does it have regional differences in productivity? Why does discrimination exist? Why is there a culture of poverty in the slums, from which it is difficult to break away?

Some of these questions are dealt with in this text. Others go beyond the scope or knowledge of economists. Clearly, when we want to explain most poverty, marginal productivity theory will serve us poorly.

Riches

What about the upper end of the income scale, the top 5 percent of families enjoying incomes over $73,000 or the topmost echelon of millionaires? Can marginal productivity help us explain high incomes?

To some extent perhaps it can. The marginal revenue product—that is, the salable output—of many skilled professions helps to explain why airplane pilots, surgeons, lawyers, skilled artisans, and TV newscasters have high incomes; but even here there is a problem. Some of these high incomes are quasi rents. Pay is high partly because there are many hurdles placed in the way of learning some highly paid skills. Thus, just as in the case of low wage earners, market imperfections must be taken into account in explaining these extremes of income.

In addition, different ranges of income appear to be accepted in different nations. In the United States, for example, the range between the lowest prevailing wage in a large establishment and the income of its top management is often greater than fifty to one: $10,000 to $15,000 being an entry wage for an unskilled office or factory worker and $500,000 to $1 million the remuneration of topmost management. In Japan or Norway, much smaller differentials are the rule. Japanese managers typically make less than ten times the salaries or wages of lower-income employees. In Norway the differential is smaller yet—perhaps as low as four to one. In addition, the tax bite on upper-income salaries, at least in Norway, is proportionally much more severe than it is in the United States. The moral seems to be that the "rules of the game," as J. M. Keynes called them, are capable of considerable variation without dulling the incentive that presumably justifies the differentials in the first place.

PERPETUATION OF INCOME DIFFERENCES

Possession of wealth has the added advantage of making it easier for the wealthy, or their children, to go to college or professional school. Recall our anecdote on how poverty causes poverty in the box on page 85. Conversely, high incomes cause high incomes.

The accompanying table shows the advantage accruing to children of upper-income families in acquiring the college education that is a steppingstone toward higher incomes for themselves.

Family Income (1983)	% 1983 High-School Graduates Enrolled in College
Under $10,000	25.7%
10,000–14,999	32.3
15,000–19,999	35.9
20,000–24,999	37.2
25,000–34,999	42.7
Over 35,000	58.2

Source: *Statistical Abstract of the U.S.*, 1985, p. 152.

Another example of the tendency of different income and social levels to reproduce their respective economic levels can be seen in the second table, which compares the occupations of sons with those of their fathers, for 1973. The figures are not up to date because more recent data do not exist; but there is no reason to believe the relationships have changed much, if at all.

Father's Occupation When Son Was 16	Son's Occupation in March 1973		
	White-Collar	Blue-Collar	Farm
White-collar	60.8%	37.4%	1.8%
Blue-collar	31.6	65.1	3.3
Farm	16.5	44.1	39.4

Source: *Opportunity and Changes,* David Featherman and Robert M. Hauser (New York: Academic Press, 1978), p. 66.

Although the table shows considerable movement out of one's parent's group into other groups, it also shows that the great majority of white-collar families produce white-collar sons. The preponderance of blue-collar families produce blue-collar sons, and most young farmers come from farming families.

Property

More important, the topmost echelons of income reflect the unequal ownership of property. As we have seen, wealth is very unevenly distributed. Almost half of all property income is channeled into the hands of the top 2 percent of households. In 1985, interests, dividends, and rent amounted to $565 billion, or 17 percent of all income.

Can marginal productivity explain this concentration of property incomes? Not very well. Conventional economic theory explains the accumulation of wealth by saving. Undoubtedly some persons do accumulate modest sums by refraining from consumption, but they do not accumulate fortunes. If you start with $100,000 — a sum possessed only by a very small fraction of all families — and if you invest the sum at 10 percent, paying a 35 percent tax on your interest, it would take a long, long time (actually 37 years) to pile up $1 million.

Very few millions are put together this way. The goal of riches seems to have two approaches. One is via the road of inheritance, the source of approximately half of today's fortunes. The other is via the road of instant riches, the main source of new fortunes and in most cases the original source of the old fortunes as well.

Instant Wealth

How does someone become rich overnight? Luck is helpful — once, anyway. People who make a fortune in one endeavor rarely go on to make as great a gain in another. Financial institutions, who employ the best expertise available, actually do not fare any better with their investments than the average performance of the stock market.

If luck seems to play a crucial role in selecting the winner, another element establishes the size of the winnings. Suppose an inventor figures it will cost $1 million to build and equip a plant to make a newly patented product. The product should sell at a price that will bring a profit of $300,000. A bank puts up the money.

The plant is built and the expected $300,000 profit is realized. Now comes the instant fortune. To the nation's capital markets, the actual cost of the plant is of no consequence. *What counts is its return and the going rate of return on similar kinds of investments.* If that rate is 10 percent, the inventor's plant is suddenly worth $3 million, for this is the sum that will yield $300,000 at a 10 percent return. The inventor is now worth $2 million, over and above what he owes to the bank. He will have risen to the status of an instant millionaire because the financial markets will have capitalized his earnings into capital gains, and not because his marginal productivity — or his saving — has made him rich.

THE MIDDLE STRATA

Thus we do not look to marginal productivity theory — although we may use other elements of economic analysis — when we seek to explain the presence of very high incomes. Then what about the middle strata, the 85 percent of families who are above the status of low income and below that of the top 5 percent? Can marginal productivity help us here?

Table 1
MEDIAN EARNINGS OF MALES, 1984*

Is marginal productivity the reason for these differences? See text below.

Professionals	$32,510
Sales workers	24,053
Managers	23,218
Clerical workers	22,140
Manufacturing operatives	19,217
Service workers	15,537
Laborers, nonfarm	15,023

* Full-time, year-round

Source: Census Bureau, *Current Population Reports,* p. 60, No. 149, p. 13.

Some Basic Problems

Consider Table 1. Can we say, on the basis of marginal productivity theory, that a salaried draftsman who earns $20,000 is twice as productive as a laborer who earns $10,000? Or should we say that the draftsman is *only* twice as productive as a laborer because the former makes only twice as much? It is hard to make sense of the question, because it is very difficult to figure the marginal revenue products of engineers or laborers. Even if we knew their productivities, it would be difficult to state that earnings in different occupations reflected productivities because of the many barriers to mobility. We will soon discuss this further.

Meanwhile consider a second problem. If we examine the earnings of supposedly homogeneous groups such as female secretaries or male laborers or doctors or professors, we find that some members of the occupation may earn four or five times as much as other members. Few people would claim that a highly paid secretary is as productive as *five* low-paid secretaries or that similar productivity differences could be found in other occupations. Results such as these would be far-fetched in the world of pure competition that marginal productivity theory describes.

MARKET IMPERFECTIONS

This last sentence gives us a clue, for it brings us to problems that prevent the market from bringing about the results that theory predicts. **Marginal productivity theory only applies under conditions of pure competition. Market imperfections play the same role in the factor market that noncompetitive market structures play in the market for goods and services. They result in prices higher or lower than the long-run equilibrium prices that a competitive supply and demand setting would produce.** Let us look into some of these imperfections.

Ignorance and Luck

Markets often fail to bring about a level of earnings corresponding to relative marginal productivities, because marketers do not have all the relevant information. A skilled mason in Connecticut may not know that there is a brisk demand for masons in Arizona — or even Rhode Island. A high school graduate looking for her first job may not know that the possibilities for high wages are much greater in printing than in retailing. This is one reason why earnings depart from levels that can be explained by a theory based on rational, informed behavior. Luck and chance play roles in determining the spread of ordinary earnings, just as in the attainment of wealth.

Monopolies

Ignorance and luck are involuntary market imperfections. More striking are market imperfections introduced by institutions that deliberately seek to set factor prices above or below equilibrium prices. This is the case whenever there is an element of monopolization in the factor market; for instance, in a small town where one landowner controls virtually all the real estate or where a single bank controls the availability of local capital. In these cases we would expect the level of rents or interest to be higher than the equilibrium level. In the same way, if one company dominates the labor market, we may find that wages are *below* their equilibrium levels — that labor is paid less than its marginal revenue product because it has nowhere else to look for work.

One of the most important institutions creating factor monopolies is the labor union. Essentially, a union tries to establish a floor for wages above the equilibrium rate that the market would establish. In this way, the economic effect of a union is exactly like that of a minimum wage law.

In dealing with monopolies of all kinds in the factor market, we have to distinguish between two questions. The first has to do with the earnings of the factors. No one doubts that factor earnings can be depressed below their competitive equilibrium levels in a one-company town or can be raised above their competitive levels by a powerful union. The more interesting question is the effect of such changes on the total earnings of the factor. Can a union, by raising wages, increase total payrolls? Or will the effect of higher wages be to shrink payrolls?

Rents and High Incomes

Anything that inhibits the mobility of factors — anything that impedes their movement from lower paid to higher paid occupations — creates or perpetuates economic or quasi rents and enters into the explanation of income differences. Barriers of race and wealth, of patents and initiation fees, of geography and social custom — all give rise to shelters behind which such rents flourish. If blacks, for instance, are systematically excluded from managerial positions, the supply of managers will be smaller than otherwise. Existing (white) managers will therefore enjoy economic rents.

Discrimination

The other side of this story is that barriers can constitute sources of discrimination that lower the earnings of those who are discriminated against.

To what extent does discrimination enter into income distribution in the United States? The most obvious instance has to do with blacks. Black families in all

Table 2
MEDIAN ANNUAL INCOME BY FAMILY TYPE, 1984*

Family Type	Black	White	Black/White Ratio
Married couple families	$31,090 (64%)	$36,418 (88%)	.85
Wife in labor force	34,172 (49%)	39,026 (55%)	.88
Wife not in labor force	20,346 (15%)	31,915 (33%)	.64
Families maintained by men alone	22,476 (4%)	31,124 (3%)	.72
Families maintained by women alone	15,619 (32%)	21,390 (9%)	.73
All Families	24,814 (100%)	34,831 (100%)	.71

Black incomes fall below white incomes for every type of household.
Source: Census Bureau, *Current Population Reports,* Series P-60, No. 149.
* The distribution of families by type is shown in parentheses.

categories have incomes well below the corresponding type of white family, as Table 2 shows. The table does not show 1986 Census Bureau findings that the median white household has ten times the assets of the median black household.

In itself these facts do not establish that wage discrimination exists. An apologist for differentials in wages could claim that there is a real difference in the marginal productivity of whites and blacks. In that case the question is whether there has been discrimination at a more basic level; for instance, in the access to human capital.

Only a few years ago, it would have been simple to demonstrate that blacks were systematically prevented from acquiring equal skills or gaining access to jobs on equal terms. Their marginal productivity was lower because they were forced into the bottom jobs of society, unable to gain admission into many colleges, kept out of high-wage trades, and simply condemned by their own past poverty from accumulating the money needed to buy an education that would allow them to compete.

This picture is now changing in some important respects, as Table 3 shows. Mean earnings of blacks are closer to those of whites than in the past, especially among younger workers. Among black women aged 35 to 44 they are even higher. This change is the result of a substantial lowering of barriers against blacks entering many professions and occupations.

Table 3
MEAN EARNINGS OF BLACKS AS A %
OF MEAN EARNINGS OF WHITES, 1983

This table does not show an even more dramatic fact: Recent census studies reveal that whites have almost twelve times as much wealth (assets) as blacks.

Age	Black Workers
15–24	57%
25–34	66
35–44	64
45–54	57
55–64	43
65 and over	57
Total	62

Source: Census Bureau, P-60, No. 149.

Table 4
MALE AND FEMALE EARNING DIFFERENTIALS,
1984. FULL-TIME, FULL-YEAR WORKERS.

There is a striking male-female pay differential. Do you think this reflects differences in marginal productivity?

Occupation	Women	Men	Women's Earnings as a % of Men's
Professional	$20,899	$31,534	.66
Technical	17,566	26,336	.67
Sales workers	11,997	24,053	.50
Craft	13,777	22,580	.61
Clerical	14,417	22,140	.65
Operatives	11,817	19,217	.61
Service workers	9,506	15,537	.61
Nonfarm laborers	11,970	15,023	.80
Laborers, farm	5,089	9,564	.53

Source: Census Bureau, P-60, No. 149, p. 13.

Discrimination against Women

A second major area of discrimination militates against women. Table 4 compares women's pay (on a full-time, year-round basis) to that of men. As the table shows, women typically earn substantially less than men in all occupations. A portion of this differential may stem from women withdrawing from the labor force to have

ECONOMIC RENT IN HIGH PLACES

Much of the very high incomes of corporate managers is also probably economic rent. In 1962, according to Robert Averitt (*The Dual Economy,* Norton, p. 178) the salaries and bonuses paid to the 56 officers and directors of General Motors exceeded the combined remuneration received by the president of the United States, the vice-president, 100 senators and 435 representatives, 9 Supreme Court justices, 10 cabinet members, and the governors of 50 states.

How could we ascertain whether the incomes of the General Motors executives (or for that matter, of the officials of government) contained economic rent? The answer is simple: We would have to reduce their incomes and observe whether they reduced their output of work. Presumably that is what the income tax tries to do. Despite the rhetoric of "incentive," studies indicate that the payment of a portion of income to the government does not seem to affect the supply curve of labor for executive skill. The presumption, then, is that a good part of their income is an economic rent, which the income tax siphons off in part.

children and to nurture them in their early years, but there is no doubt that these "economic" reasons for pay differentials do not begin to account for the full differences we observe.

In recent years we have seen a good deal of stirring for equal rights for women, and we get the impression that discrimination against women is disappearing. The statistics do not support this. The proportional gap between male and female earnings of full-time workers has not changed since the 1930s!

Will it change? The women's movement has won court battles to establish the right of equal pay for equal work, as well as equal rights to jobs, regardless of sex. Perhaps this will begin to alter our prevailing sexist patterns.

The United States has been very slow to admit women to a full range of professional and occupational opportunities. Only about 15 percent of our doctors are women, for example, whereas in West Germany 20 percent, and in the USSR 70 percent, are women. These surprising percentages leave little doubt that women *could* earn a great deal more than they do, if the barriers of discrimination were removed.

PUERTO RICANS, CHICANOS, INDIANS, OTHERS

Blacks are by no means the only racial group that suffers from discrimination. The table below shows the family income of Hispanics relative to white families:

	Income as % of White Family Income	
	1969	1984
Hispanic	54%	71%

There is a shocking absence of data on the poorest and smallest group of all, the American Indians. Based on reports from about half of U.S. reservations, the median income of American Indians is on the order of *one-third* that of white families.

Now, a more cheerful word. If we look at income data of all ethnic groups, we find only three major groups with incomes below the national average: blacks, those of Spanish heritage, and Indians. Of 100 million Americans who claim ethnic backgrounds, 80 million have incomes *higher* than those of Americans who consider themselves to be ethnically native. In 1972 the ethnic groups with the highest average family income were Russians, then Poles, then Italians.

Reference Groups

Another distributional problem arises because people have strong feelings about how much they are entitled to. In our competitive model, each person is a rational income maximizer, out for himself. At no time does any supplier of labor look at the wages of *other* laborers, except to determine whether or not he is being paid the competitive rate of return.

Yet real people do not focus narrowly on their own wages, but look around them at the entire wage structure. A police officer looks at firefighters' wages, at truckers', perhaps even at schoolteachers' incomes. This interest in other incomes has different labels. Sociologists would call it an interest in *reference groups*.

Reference groups seem to be both stable and restricted — people look at groups that are economically close to themselves. This helps explain why very large inequalities in the distribution of economic rewards seem to cause relatively little dissatisfaction, whereas small inequalities can raise a great commotion. A police officer does not expect to make as much as a movie actor — Hollywood is not the reference point. He or she does expect to make as much as, or more than, a sanitation worker, perhaps as much as a teacher. Changes in the pay of his or her reference groups therefore bring immediate changes in estimation of the fairness of his or her own pay.

As a result of these comparisons, groups strongly resist changes in relative wage rates. Even the person benefiting from a change in relative wages may feel that it is unfair that he or she receive more than someone else. Consequently, labor economists have discovered that wage rates among many groups move together, almost independently of movements in the supply and demand curves in each occupation.

Uses of Marginal Productivity Theory

All these and still other difficulties explain why the distribution of income, even in the middle range, cannot be fully explained by marginal productivity theory, and why we must be very careful in assuming that the theory adequately accounts for variations in earnings — riches and poverty aside.

Should we then forget about the theory? Not quite. For just as the pure theory of competition helped to explain movements and tendencies in the real market, even if not real market prices, so marginal productivity can enlighten us with respect to economic reality. **It tells us how entrepreneurs behave in hiring factors. It explains the simple but crucial fact that entrepreneurs will not knowingly hire a factor (or a team of factors) that does not "pay its way." Thus the theory of marginal productivity serves as a first approximation to a theory of employment for the firm, even if it does not explain very much about factor incomes.** However incomes are determined — by law, power, custom, or the marketplace — entrepreneurs will be guided in hiring factors by their relative profitability, which is to say, by comparing their cost with the marginal revenue product he can hope to obtain from them. As its marginal productivities rise, more of a factor will be hired. As they fall, less of it will be used.

Thus the theory helps elucidate one aspect of economic life. We simply must be careful not to claim that it explains income distribution or that different levels of earnings are justified by marginal productivity.

CHANGING INCOME DISTRIBUTION

Can we change the distribution of income? Of course we can. Should we? That is a more difficult question. When we speak of deliberately trying to change the distribution of income, our purpose is usually to make it fairer. By *fairer,* we generally mean more equal, although not always. Sometimes we say it is not fair that certain groups, such as schoolteachers, do not get higher incomes, even though they are already receiving incomes that are above the median for the society. In the discussion that follows, we will largely be concerned with ways of making income distribution fairer by making it more equal.*

If you want to change income distribution, you must choose among four basic ways of going about your task.

1. You may try to change the marginal productivities of individuals and then let them fend for themselves on the market.
2. You may try to limit the workings of the market, so that certain people will receive larger or smaller incomes even if their marginal productivities remain the same.
3. You may let marginal productivities and markets alone and intervene by the mechanism of taxes and transfers, rearranging the rewards of society according to some principle of equity.
4. Finally, you can introduce some system of rewards wholly different from market-determined rewards.

This last is the boldest and most far-reaching method, but it is one about which economists have very little to say. Accordingly, we will confine ourselves to the first three methods.

Changing Productivities

Assuming that low marginal productivity is a basic reason — if not the only reason — for low incomes, someone who wants to change income distribution would do well to begin by boosting the marginal productivity of the least skilled and trained.

---

* See "An Extra Word" on equity at the end of Chapter 33.

Table 5

MALE EDUCATION AND AVERAGE LIFETIME EARNINGS

Education and incomes are obviously correlated. This does not mean that education causes the whole difference. The payoff on educational investment is about 7 to 10 percent.

	Lifetime Earnings (1979)
Elementary school	
0 – 12 years	$ 845,000
High school	
4 years	1,041,000
College	
1 – 3 years	1,155,000
4 years	1,392,000

How can **human capital** be improved? By and large, by giving *education,* a generalized skill, or *training,* a specialized skill, to those who lack them.

Education and Income. A glance at Table 5 makes it clear that there is a strong functional relationship between education and lifetime earnings. We must be careful not to jump to the conclusion that education is the direct cause of these earnings, however. For example, 30 percent of white high school graduates will end up making more money than the average college graduate, and 20 percent of college graduates will make less than the average high school graduate. Clearly there is no guarantee that education will pay off for everyone.

There is also a problem of scale. The table shows us that college graduates as a group have higher incomes. This may be because there are fewer of them and they earn scarcity rents. If everyone went to college, the supply and demand situation would be radically different, and the extra earnings of the college group much smaller.

Last there is the problem of circular causation that we encountered earlier in this chapter (see the box, "Perpetuation of Income Differences). Education may indeed be a factor in increasing lifetime earnings. It is also true that someone coming from a high-income family will receive more education and will probably earn a high income *because of his or her social station in life.* When we correct for the starting point on the income scale education still yields a return, but a much smaller one than the figures in Table 5 indicate. **Probably the cost of a college education gives its recipient a lifetime return of about 7 to 10 percent on that investment, hardly a bonanza.**

Investment in Human Capital. Even if the advantages of education are frequently exaggerated in terms of their strictly economic results, there is no doubt that education is a help toward higher income. For one thing, it teaches general skills such as reading, writing, and math, as well as special skills. These are the attributes we speak of as *human capital.*

Equally valuable is its teaching of behavior expected in high-level occupations: how to speak politely, how to be punctual, how to relate to authority, and other often overlooked attributes of classroom discipline that prepares us for jobs, especially managerial jobs.

Intervening on the Demand
Side of the Market: Minimum Wages

A quite different way of going about the task of changing the income distribution is to intervene on the demand side of the market. The most widespread current intervention is that of minimum wages — whether imposed by law or unions. Can unions raise wages? Can the government raise the wages of the poor by imposed minimum wages? Few questions in economics generate such heat. We'll try to throw a little economic light on them, too.

Minimum wages enforced by law and minimum wages enforced by union contract have very similar attributes. Both are equivalent to price supports for agricultural products, in that they establish a price higher than that which the market would establish by itself. If they did not, they would not serve any purpose. Thus in Figure 1 we can view the wage line *AB* as established by union or government, for in both cases its effect is to establish a wage floor above that set by the intersection of supply and demand.

Three effects follow. Some workers will lose their jobs because the new higher minimum wage is above their marginal revenue product (or above what the employer estimates their *MRP* to be). In the diagram, this amount of lost employment is represented by $Q_1 - Q_3$. Here are the delivery boys who are let go when the minimum wage is raised and small grocery stores decide to cut down their help. Here are the elevator operators who are replaced by automatic elevators when a union wage contract finally tips the balance in favor of automation.

Second, some workers — those between O and Q_3 — will find their incomes raised. Here are the grocery boys who are kept on at higher pay; the elevator operators who are not fired but have fatter pay envelopes.

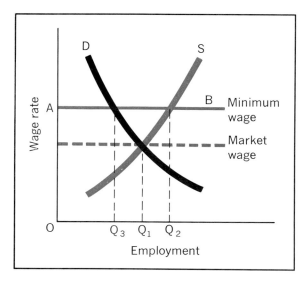

Figure 1

EFFECT OF MINIMUM WAGE LAWS

The volume of employment would be Q_1 if there were no union or minimum wage. This is also the amount of labor that workers would offer at that wage. At the new higher wage level OA employers want to hire only Q_3 worth of labor, while workers are interested in supplying Q_2 worth. As we can see, there must be a labor surplus, just as there is an agricultural surplus when farm prices are set above the market equilibrium.

Third, there will be a larger number of workers than formerly—those between Q_1 and Q_2—looking for work. Their condition will be neither better nor worse than before the union floor or the minimum wage, for at the previous wage rate these people were not seeking work, nor did they have any income. Nonetheless, their presence in the labor market will be noted in the statistics of unemployment, and it may have social and political consequences.

Net Gain or Loss?

Is there a net gain or loss in the situation? As you can see, the increase in earnings of the group that is retained can be compared with the loss in income of the group that is fired. There are, however, problems in such a comparison. It is much easier to calculate gains and losses on a diagram than to compute them in real life. This is because everything hinges on the slopes of the two curves. Suppose, for example, we think that the demand for labor is extremely inelastic. Then even though unemployment rises, no one will lose his or her job. All will remain employed with higher earnings. To make the point clear, we show this case in Figure 2, with a totally inelastic demand curve.

On the other hand, suppose the demand for labor is highly price-elastic. Then many workers could lose their jobs, as you can easily see if you draw a diagram with an elastic curve.

The Demand for Labor. What is the shape of the actual demand curve for labor? Studies indicate that it is probably quite inelastic, so that minimum wage laws do not have a severe adverse effect on total employment. Rather, their effect is likely to be heavily concentrated on certain groups, such as teenagers. The illustration of delivery boys is not an idle one. A high minimum wage may well result in substan-

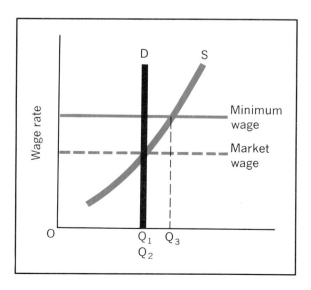

Figure 2
ELASTICITY AND INCOME
The gain to those employed at a higher wage will reflect the elasticity of the demand curve.

AFFIRMATIVE ACTION PROGRAMS

No government program to alter the distribution of earnings has been more controversial than the affirmative action requirements, for affirmative action offends people in a way that antidiscrimination laws do not. People may object violently to the results of anti-discrimination laws or to techniques of compliance, such as busing; but almost no one is willing to argue that an unequal start is a good thing. People may call training programs for the poor inefficient, but no one calls them un-American.

Affirmative action laws make people angry because they seem to be unfair. In order to find qualified members of minority groups, firms or agencies or universities have to pass over fully qualified members of majority groups. Is it fair not to hire a qualified white electrician because affirmative action gives a preference to a black one, or not to hire a young male graduate student as a teacher, because a college is short of women instructors?

The fairness issue really comes down to the obligations of one generation to redress the grievances of another. Suppose that discrimination disappeared magically tomorrow. Blacks would still be holding the jobs that were open to them in the discrimination-filled past. If nothing further were done, it would take about 45 years — the time it takes for a generation to pass through the labor market — for the effects of past discrimination to be eliminated. Affirmative action can thus be viewed as an attempt to offset the impact of past injustice.

Does it also create present injustice? Is the white electrician, passed over because of affirmative action, fairly treated? Many people say no. At the same time, we must try to see the problem from the viewpoint of the whole society as well as from that of the offended person. Is it not possible that a society is becoming more fair, even though some individuals are being treated less fairly? Those persons who suffer from affirmative action today are the victims of our efforts to overcome the unfairness of the past. The problem is therefore whether we can remedy the failures of the past generations without inflicting injuries on some members of the present generation.

Ideally there is no reason why not. To raise up a previously disprivileged person does not require that someone else be put down. But the ideal solution requires an expansive economy where the demand for talent outstrips the supply. In a sluggish environment, the fight for advancement becomes a zero-sum game, and my gain becomes possible only at the expense of your loss. This has been the situation during the past ten years of inadequate growth. In such a situation there are bound to be losers. The question is: Who will they be?

tial teenage unemployment in menial jobs. This has led to suggestions that there should be lower minimum wages for adolescents than for adults, a scheme that has been used in Europe but that has so far been opposed by labor unions in this country.

Union wage settlements also have their gains and losses exactly as do minimum wage laws. Once again the critical factor is the elasticity of the demand for labor. But there is a difference with respect to the impact of union settlements. Minimum wage laws affect only the fringe of workers whose pay is *below* the minimum. Union settlements typically affect *all* workers in the industry. The incentive to substitute machines for people or simply to economize on labor is therefore much greater. The economic consequences of a union wage settlement are, accordingly, likely to be more substantial than those of a boost in minimum wages.

Taxes and Transfers

A third means of altering income distribution is to tax high incomes and to subsidize low ones. Taxes and subsidies, or *transfers* as they are called, are used by all governments to redistribute incomes. **By and large, there seems little doubt that the overall effect of this system leaves income shares much as they were before taxes for most income receivers above the poverty line.** In all brackets, income receivers pay about 20 to 25 percent of their incomes to the government, taking federal, state, and local taxes into account.

There is one exception, however. In recent years, revolutionary changes have swept our tax system. Income tax rates, inheritance taxes, and capital gains taxes have been slashed, and income tax brackets indexed to the rate of inflation. At the same time, taxes to finance the social security system have been repeatedly raised. The net effect of these changes has been to shift the total burden of taxation away from the very wealthy. Whereas before the 1980s those with very high incomes tended to pay a somewhat higher share to the government than income receivers in the middle echelons, now that element of progressivity has been sharply reduced, if not eliminated.

Transfer payments, targeted to the poor, the elderly, and the infirm, make a much greater impact on the distribution of income than the tax system does. Without transfer payments, the share of the lowest 20 percent of families in the total income pie would be less than half of what it actually is. Lately, some critics have questioned whether transfer payments are truly an effective remedy for a maldistributed national income. They claim that such payments substitute for income that would otherwise be earned through labor, and that therefore the apparent gains from transfers are a statistical illusion. We examine these contentions in detail in the next chapter.

In Review

Can we change income distribution? Yes, of course. But not all ways of doing so are equally effective. Efforts to change marginal productivities have not shown marked results, although this does not detract from their worthwhileness on other grounds.

TOWARD AN OPERATIONAL DEFINITION OF FAIRNESS

Can we specify with certainty what a fair income distribution would look like? Of course not. Can we specify a distribution of income that would accord with what most people think is fair? Here we put the question in such a way that we could test the results, for example by an opinion poll.

If we took such a poll, most persons in the United States would probably agree that existing income is not fairly distributed. They consider it unfair that some people are as poor as they are and others are as rich as they are.

Suppose we ask whether the public would approve of an income distribution that had the same shape as that for one group in which the more obvious advantages and disadvantages of the real world were minimized. *That group consists of the white adult males who work full-time and full-year.* It ranges from surgeons to street sweepers. In general, these workers suffer minimally or not at all from the handicaps of race, sex, age, personal deficiencies, or bad economic policies. By examining their earnings rather than their incomes, we can eliminate the effects of inherited wealth. Might not such a standard appeal to many people as constituting an operational definition of a just income distribution?

Since the poll has never been taken, we cannot answer the question. But we can examine what income distribution would look like under such a dispensation. The results are shown in the table. It is interesting to note that this standard of fairness, if applied, would reduce the dispersion of income by 40 percent.

Annual Earnings, 1970 ($ Thousands)	Distribution of Income in Accordance with "Fairness" Standard	Actual Distribution of Income
$ 0–1	1.7%	10.4%
1–2	1.3	8.3
2–3	1.5	6.9
3–4	3.0	6.8
4–5	4.4	6.2
5–6	6.8	6.7
6–7	8.6	7.0
7–8	10.5	7.8
8–10	19.7	13.2
10–15	27.9	17.7
15–20	11.2	6.8
25 & over	3.3	2.3

Interventions through minimum wages, unions, and government requirements have assuredly redistributed incomes among persons, but they cannot be shown to have altered the national pattern of the distribution of income. **Only income transfers — social security, unemployment insurance, and welfare — have made a substantial and dramatic difference.** We will examine these programs in detail shortly. But first we must acquire some further understanding of the great social problem to which they are addressed.

looking back

KEY CONCEPTS

Poverty and riches are not explained by marginal productivity theory	**1** Marginal productivity theory does not explain the two ends of the spectrum of income distribution. Most poverty arises from reasons other than low productivity or from reasons that lie behind low productivity. Very high incomes stem from property, rents, capitalization, and luck rather than from measurable high *MRP*s.
Middle strata display large intra-occupational variations	**2** The middle strata of income are those most nearly explicable by marginal productivity. But here too there are inexplicable differences such as the very large variations we find in a given occupation.
Market imperfections lessen the applicability of marginal productivity theory	**3** The disturbing elements of the real world are many. One is the presence of monopoly elements in income determination. A second is the influence of discrimination. A third is the role of reference groups. All these and other elements lessen the applicability of marginal productivity theory, which assumes a world of pure competition.
The theory is a useful way of explaining how factor employment is determined	**4** Nonetheless, marginal productivity theory is useful as a means of explaining how employment is determined. Given the income of factors, however determined, employers will be guided by *MRP*s when they consider how much of a factor to hire.
Three strategies for income redistribution	**5** There are three basic strategies for changing income distribution: changing the productivity of factors, changing the demand for factors, and directly changing incomes by taxes or transfers.
It is difficult to assess the effect of education on income and productivity	**6** Efforts to change factor productivity by education — building up human capital — are difficult to measure with precision. Undoubtedly education helps individuals toward higher incomes, but the effect is not clear-cut and may not obtain if everyone is equally educated.

Intervening to offset discrimination has only limited effectiveness	**7** Intervening on the demand side by affirmative action and other programs to remedy discrimination has helped professional blacks and women, but not much affected general earnings of disadvantaged groups.
Taxes do not redistribute incomes in the main strata of recipients. Transfers are very important for low-income receivers	**8** Taxes and transfers have different impacts. The effect of taxes is small in changing the shares of income enjoyed by most groups, with the possible exception of the bottom and very top. The most effective method of transferring income seems to be transfer payments, which amount to 60 percent of the income of the lowest fifth of income receivers.

ECONOMIC VOCABULARY

Rents and discrimination 629

Human capital 635

Reference groups 633

QUESTIONS

1. How much of the differences in occupational earnings shown in Table 1 do you think can be ascribed to marginal productivity? Can you devise a research program that would enable you to study this with allowance for all market imperfections?

2. Which of the following do you consider to be market imperfections that result in earnings higher than those that would be produced by a free market: (1) certification by state boards before anyone can practice medicine; (2) limiting admission to medical school by aptitude examinations; (3) the costs of education, if these can be covered by a long-term loan.

3. Suppose it could be shown that the marginal productivity of blacks in a given occupation was less than that of whites. Would that explain their lower rates of pay? Justify them?

4. A woman patents a gadget that brings her an annual net income of $100,000. The market return for her category of risky products is 20 percent. What is her patent worth? Can you show that the higher the degree of risk, the *less* will be her capitalized gain?

5. Do you think the present educational system works to reduce or to maintain the structure of inequality in rewards? How would you suggest changing it if you wanted less inequality? If you wanted more?

CHAPTER 35

Unemployment and Poverty

a look ahead

This chapter confronts some of the theory we have previously learned with some unpleasant facts. It asks

1 What are the different types of unemployment? How serious are they? And what are the causes of each?

2 What are the causes of poverty, and what has been the record of past antipoverty efforts by government?

Finally, we will ask whether the facts of unemployment and poverty correspond well or poorly to the theories articulated by recent critics of social welfare policy.

Unemployment and poverty remain today the most serious social problems of our times. They are not so serious as *economic* problems as they were, say, fifty years ago, because unemployment insurance and the welfare system and social security all help to remove some of the privation associated with a low income. Even without these programs, the general standard of living of the whole nation is higher, and wealth is more widely distributed through the population, so that more of the unemployed have family assets to fall back on than would have been the case back then. But as *social* problems unemployment and poverty are perhaps even more serious than they were. Since the 1930s, the rural country life into which the urban poor and the unemployed could (and did) retreat has for the most part disappeared. For most people today, being without work means having no purpose in life; to be without income is to feel without worth.

UNEMPLOYMENT

All unemployment is not the same. There is a world of difference, for example, between the millworker whose plant has closed down for good and the journeyman carpenter temporarily laid over between jobs. Equally, though for less obvious reasons, we must distinguish between the secretary minding her children at home while seeking employment in a downtown office building, and the housewife who may be doing exactly the same sort of housework each day, but who is not actively seeking some other employment.

Kinds of Unemployment

Economists distinguish among several types of unemployment. The journeyman carpenter mentioned above, along with agricultural laborers migrating from one harvest to another, this year's pool of college graduates undergoing interviews for their first jobs, and many others, are described as **frictionally unemployed.** That is, their movement between jobs is part of their normal life style or a normal feature of the particular stage of their careers. It may not be pleasant, but it is temporary; it helps the economy to function efficiently; and it is not a major source of policy concern.

The secretary and the housewife are both "unemployed," if you like, and may spend their days in exactly the same way, but economists treat them as quite different cases. The secretary is counted as officially unemployed, the housewife as not. That is because the housewife is not *actively seeking work outside the home.* Her labor is not part of the market economy, and in technical terms she is said to be a nonparticipant in the labor force. (If she would like to work outside the home but is not actively looking because she has heard that no jobs are available, we would have still another term for her: *discouraged worker*). The secretary, on the other hand, is actively seeking paid employment, and therefore she is counted as unemployed. Is her unemployment frictional? That depends on how long it lasts and how often it recurs. If our secretary is a temp who regularly works only one- or two-week stints before seeking a new employer, then we would class her unemployment experiences as frictional.

Our concern for the unemployed must focus on the nonfrictional cases, on the millworker whose mill closes because of technological change or international competition, on the auto worker who receives a "pink slip" because of recession, on the teacher "riffed" in a budget cutback, or the teenager who has never held a job because she could never find one. These are the people on whom the burden of unemployment falls. We will refer to them as the *involuntarily unemployed*.

Involuntary Unemployment

Microeconomic theory, as we learned in Chapters 29 and 30, tells us that employers will hire labor as long as the revenue produced by each successive person exceeds his or her cost. The same theory also tells us that workers will seek employment as long as the (marginal) utility of their income is greater than the (marginal) disutility of their work.

This makes perfect sense from the microeconomic point of view, in which we trace the reasons for, and the consequences of, the actions of individuals or firms. But this analysis of unemployment has a curious implication. According to this theory, no one can be involuntarily unemployed! A worker may dislike a job more than he or she likes its pay and may therefore decline the job—but that can hardly be called *involuntary* unemployment. And a worker who likes or wants a job has only to offer his or her services for slightly less than the going wage to find an employer who will be glad to employ someone whose marginal revenue product will be greater than that of the existing work force. .

Keynes's Objection

That was the view of almost all economists in the 1930s, despite the fact that unemployment rates were climbing toward a quarter of the work force. It was Keynes who pointed to the flaw in the reasoning. He observed that there were circumstances which would induce employers to hire more workers even if they did not cut their wage demands. This occurred when prices rose, but money wages did not—for instance if there was a flurry of speculative buying in the midst of a depression. Then business picked up, even if momentarily, and employers took on more workers.

Now here is the point. Because there was a great deal of unemployment, these workers were easy to find. Yet the fact that they were accepting the going wage even *though prices were rising* meant that actually they were taking a cut in real wages. If they were willing to work at these reduced real wages, they certainly would have been even *more* willing to work at the wage levels that prevailed before the price rise. Yet employers did not seek to hire them at those previous real wages, nor, absent the price rise, did real wages fall to induce employers to do so. It followed, then, that unemployment in these circumstances had nothing to do with voluntary decisions. Unemployment was forced on workers because employers were not concerned with microeconomic decisions about marginal revenue and marginal product, but about *expected longer-term results* of enlarging their output. They feared that these longer-term results would simply be larger losses.

Micro vs. Macro

Involuntary unemployment therefore takes us to a different plane of analysis from voluntary employment. It involves such elements as expectations about the movements of large aggregates, like gross national product, over which employers have no control whatsoever. That is one of the fundamental differences between micro and macro economics. As microeconomists we cannot say a great deal about the unemployment that comes about because of *sectoral* movements. To understand the roots of mass unemployment, we must be macroeconomists. But to understand the nature of—and the remedies for—other kinds of unemployment, we need the kind of cost-revenue analysis for which microeconomics provides the necessary tools.

Unemployment and Social Insurance

One such microeconomic approach to unemployment is to be found in a problem raised by Professor Martin Feldstein, former chairman of the Council of Economic Advisors under President Reagan. This is the possibility that unemployment insurance—the safeguard we have erected to cushion the costs of unemployment—is itself a cause of unemployment.

Feldstein points out that unemployment insurance is not taxed, whereas earnings from employment are. Therefore, he reasons, the opportunity cost of unemployment is not the comparison of a worker's earnings and his or her unemployment compensation check; it is a comparison of the *after-tax* earnings with that check. The difference may be small. Feldstein believes that our present system encourages unemployment by making it profitable to get fired—at least for young or part-time employees. He suggests that we can alleviate the situation by making unemployment benefits taxable.

Feldstein is undoubtedly correct that the difference between the income of an employed person and an unemployed one is narrowed because of these factors. The impact of this differential on employment is, however, an empirical rather than a purely theoretical matter: What is at stake is *how much* unemployment is increased because of the post-tax considerations. Most evidence seems to point strongly to the conclusion that the effect is minute. For most workers, the intangible and fringe benefits of employment—security, seniority, pension rights, and so on—tie them tightly to their jobs. Quit rates and firing rates are not the major sources of variations in unemployment or utilization of unemployment insurance—layoff rates are.

Moreover, while the unemployment insurance system is a social safety net for some, it misses a surprisingly large fraction of the unemployed. In 1982 only 40

THE DIFFERENTIAL
IMPACT OF UNEMPLOYMENT

We need to pay heed to the extraordinarily wide variation of unemployment rates among different segments of the population. Just as an instance, unemployment rates for black teenagers, corrected for those who have dropped out of the labor force—not at school, not at work, not trying to get work—reach levels of up to 90 percent in central city slums!

The table below shows us the tremendous spread in the incidence of unemployment, disregarding the pathology of the slum. Notice that black males bear twice the impact of unemployment that white males do, black females double the impact of white females. The table bears study and thought.

STRUCTURE OF UNEMPLOYMENT

In 1985, the national unemployment rate was 7 percent. This table shows how that average figure conceals very much higher rates among certain groups.

October 1985		*October 1985*	
Males	6.5%	Females	7.2%
White males	5.5	White females	6.2
16–19	18.8	16–19	15.2
20–24	8.5	20–24	8.2
25–54	4.1	25–54	5.3
55–64	3.7	55–64	3.6
65 & up	2.9	65 & up	2.9
Black males	15.1%	Black females	14.3%
16–19	41.8	16–19	40.4
20–24	23.1	20–24	29.4
25–54	11.8	25–54	10.3
55–64	5.9	55–64	5.1
65 & up	11.5	65 & up	4.8

Source: Bureau of Labor Statistics, *Employment and Earnings*, November 1985, p. 7.

percent of those unemployed were receiving any unemployment insurance checks at all. The rest had to rely on whatever savings they had, on their family, or private charity—or simply went on relief. These large holes exist in the safety net because individuals lose their unemployment checks after they have been unemployed for more than 52 weeks, and because many have not worked long enough to be eligible for unemployment checks when they become unemployed. Even those lucky enough to get unemployment checks find that they replace less than half of their previous earnings. By contrast, the replacement rate is much higher in Europe and a much larger fraction of the unemployed are eligible for benefit. In Britain the unemployed are eligible for benefits even if they have never worked before!

POVERTY

We discuss poverty together with unemployment for a very good reason: **Changes in unemployment are the single largest cause of changes in poverty.** In recessions, when previously middle- or working-class citizens lose their jobs, the poverty

Figure 1
PEOPLE LIVING IN POVERTY
Percentage of the total population and selected groups living below the poverty line for each year. The 1984 poverty line for a family of four was an income of $10,609.
Source: Census Bureau, P-60, No. 149.

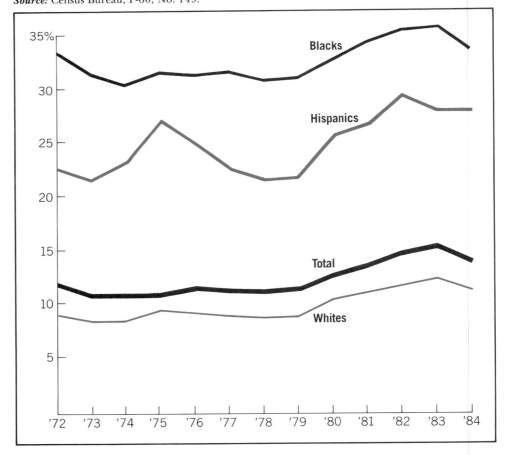

rate rises. In recoveries, new opportunities open up and poverty declines as economic conditions improve. Thus the poverty rate rose steadily from 13 percent in 1980 to 15.3 percent in 1983, before declining by nine-tenths of a percentage point—nearly 1.8 million people—in the strong growth year of 1984. Moreover, where you find a particular demographic grouping that is prone to suffer high rates of unemployment—whether it be blacks or Hispanics or teenagers—you are likely to find a high incidence of poverty in that population.

Nevertheless, the problem of poverty goes well beyond the problem of unemployment: to single and separated women with small children, to the elderly whose working years are behind them, to the disabled, the handicapped, and the educationally disadvantaged, and to those who live in parts of the country that have not enjoyed a full measure of growth and economic development.

WELFARE PROFILE

What racial characteristics do welfare recipients have? The answer depends very much on whether we are examining short-term welfare recipients, who are on welfare for one or two years out of ten, or long-term recipients, who are on welfare for eight or more years out of ten.

	Percent of Entire Population	*Percent of Short-Term Recipients*	*Percent of Long-Term Recipients*
All individuals	100.0%	12.3%	4.4%
White	88.3	84.5	44.7
Black	11.7	15.5	55.5

Source: Richard D. Coe, "Welfare Dependency: Fact or Myth?" *Challenge*, Sept.–Oct. 1982, p. 49. Reprinted with permission of publisher, M. E. Sharpe Inc., 80 Business Park Drive, Armonk, New York.

The table shows that from 1969 to 1978 short-term recipients closely mirrored the racial proportions of the entire population, whereas long-term recipients were disproportionately black. The lesson seems to be that bad luck, which forces most individuals onto welfare, is color-blind, whereas the escape from bad luck is heavily weighted against blacks. This is largely the case because forty percent of long-term black individuals on welfare were women with young children, who have a particularly hard time in finding or holding jobs. Even in this most disadvantaged group, however, approximately 60 percent were on welfare for five years or less out of ten.

Measuring Poverty

How do we know that a family is poor? This is not so simple a question as it seems. Moreover, much in our attitude toward poverty and toward the poor themselves can be shown to rest on the way in which we define it.

For the purpose of counting the poor, the government establishes a *poverty line*—an income level below which a family is considered to be poor. The poverty line is based on calculations of the cost of a minimal standard of living in different regions of the country for families of differing sizes. As part of this process, the Agriculture Department computes the cost of maintaining a basic family diet (the "Thrifty Food Plan"). In 1984, the official poverty line was $10,609 for a family of four.

Naturally, the poverty line changes from year to year with inflation, changes in the relative prices of foods and other commodities, and to some extent with changes in the standards of the community. Thus, while fifty years ago a rural family without electricity or plumbing might not be considered poor, today the costs of such necessities are incorporated in the poverty line. Still, the poverty line concept is known as an *absolute standard* for poverty, since it attempts to measure poverty by measuring purchasing power over a specific basket of consumer goods. *Such absolute measures tend to show that the incidence of poverty has declined over the past several decades,* although by all measures poverty rose in the late 1970s and early 1980s.

Absolute vs. Relative Poverty

A quite different conception holds that poverty should be thought of in *relative* terms, by comparing the income levels of the poor with those of society as a whole. The idea here is that poverty is *subjective* and *comparative,* rather than absolute: People feel poor because they cannot have what others take for granted, rather than because they cannot afford to purchase a specific item or items. Thus, a family might be considered poor if its income were less than (say) half the median income for families of the same size—a result which for a family of four would have given a poverty line of $13,215 dollars in 1984. **Measures of relative poverty, which are really measures of income distribution, show that there has been little change in such poverty over the years.** While living standards for the whole population have improved, the poor remain as far behind the average household as they ever were.

CURING POVERTY

What can be done about poverty? One large answer brings us back to the issues of macroeconomics. Anything that will raise the rate of growth of GNP will, *ceteris paribus,* reduce the level of poverty. But there is also a second category of response, closer to the analytic viewpoint of microeconomics. Let us look into the problem from this vantage point.

Welfare

Few issues are more controversial these days than such transfer programs, known as *welfare*. Defenders of welfare programs declare them to be an essential part of the "safety net" of a fair-minded society. Opponents declare that welfare may be well-intentioned, but that it spreads the deadly virus of welfare dependency — a loss of incentive that eventually condemns the poor to a lifetime of passivity and helplessness.

Recently, the critics' case has been laid out at length by Charles Murray, who argues* for the abolition of most welfare programs on the ground that, while spending for those programs has risen dramatically since 1950, poverty has not declined at all. Murray asserts that there is cause and effect here: Rising expenditures on social welfare have produced rising welfare dependency, destroying the structure of individual and family responsibility on which the work ethic itself is based.

Murray's arguments have generated much attention, but like the supply-side theories of a few years earlier, have also come under heavy criticism. Close students of the relationship between welfare programs and poverty come to just the opposite conclusion from Murray: that variations in poverty have stemmed primarily from changes in economic conditions, and not at all from a perverse effect of changes in welfare spending. They point out that welfare payments grew by the same amount from 1965 through 1969 as from 1969 through 1974, yet poverty declined in the former period and increased in the latter. The reason: declining economic performance, not a change in welfare policy.†

The Extent of Welfare

Other studies have approached this question on a case-by-case basis, to see what kind of families go on welfare and what happens to them when they do. These studies have tended to show some surprising results. One, for example, dealing with welfare recipients for the period 1969–78, came up with the following conclusions:

1. In any single year, about 10 percent of the entire population received some welfare.

2. Over the entire ten years, about one-quarter of all individuals received some welfare.

3. About one-half of all families who received welfare were recipients for only one or two years in ten.

4. Less than one family in ten who received welfare continued to receive it for eight or more years out of ten.

---

* Charles Murray, *Losing Ground* (New York: Basic Books, 1984).

† Sheldon Danziger and Peter Gottschalk, "The Poverty of Losing Ground," *Challenge,* May–June 1985, p. 490. Reprinted with permission of publisher, M. E. Sharpe, Inc., 80 Business Park Drive, Armonk, New York.

Table 1
FEMALE-HEADED HOUSEHOLDS AND AFDC AID

Despite a rising percentage of female-headed households, the real value of aid for families with dependent children has fallen.

Year	Percentage of Nonaged Families with Children Headed by Women (Percent)	Real AFDC Plus Food Stamp Guarantee (Dollars)
1960	n.a.	$6,715
1964	n.a.	6,604
1968	10.7%	7,129
1972	13.8	8,894
1976	16.7	8,743
1980	19.8	7,486
1984	20.8	6,955

Summing up an extended study into the characteristics of welfare studies, Richard D. Coe writes:

> It is difficult to conclude . . . that there is something inherently pernicious about the welfare system—that it poisons those who touch it with a debilitating dose of dependency. Quite the contrary. The welfare system would seem to be more accurately portrayed as a temporary fallback position for those individuals who suffer unexpected shocks to their more normal style of life. For nonelderly men, these shocks would most likely be an involuntary job loss; for married women, a divorce or separation; for an unmarried woman, the birth of a child. For the vast majority of these people, the welfare system serves as a stepping stone back to a more normal standard of living.*

Finally we should note that the real value of payments under the Aid for Families with Dependent Children (AFDC) and Food Stamps programs—the main welfare programs for poor families—has been declining consistently since 1972. Table 1 shows that the purchasing power of such assistance is now over 20 percent less than a decade and a half ago, despite the fact that the eligible population, measured by such indicators as the proportion of female-headed households has been rising. In other words, smaller per person benefits are being spread out to meet an increasingly needy population.

Helping Poor Families

Can poverty be helped? Or should we accept whatever levels exist as the best results of the market system? This is a difficult question on which to arrive at a balanced view.

* Coe, "Welfare Dependency," *Challenge,* p. 49.

Table 2

INCIDENCE OF POSTTRANSFER POVERTY (EXPRESSED AS A PERCENTAGE OF THE GROUP)

Social programs have affected different groups very differently.

	All Persons	Aged		Nonaged (With Children)			
		Whites	Nonwhites	White Men	Nonwhite Men	White Women	Nonwhite Women
1967	14.3%	27.0%	52.0%	7.5%	28.4%	38.2%	68.5%
1980	13.0	13.2	35.7	7.8	16.9	39.1	58.3
Change	−9.1	−51.1	−31.3	+4.0	−40.5	+2.4	−14.9

Source: Danziger and Gottschalk, "Poverty," *Challenge*, p. 490.

In the 1960s, under the leadership of President Johnson, the United States declared a War on Poverty. Everyone "knows" that it failed. But did it? If one looks at the incidence of poverty *after taking account of transfer payments* in various groups in 1967 and again in 1980, one comes to some surprising conclusions. As Table 2 shows, the incidence for nonwhite men fell sharply — by 40.5 percent! — while that for nonwhite women fell by nearly 15 percent. But the greatest progress of all came among the aged, whose poverty rates were cut in half for whites and by a third for nonwhites.

So it is clear that transfers can reduce poverty. But we must recognize that this was not entirely the result of the War on Poverty itself. James Patterson's study* identifies two different factors that were operating at the same time. The first and most important was the increase in the real value of social security payments beginning in 1972. Social security is not a welfare program — its payments flow to the poor and the nonpoor alike — but it is nevertheless America's most effective bulwark against poverty among the aged.

The second factor was a "welfare explosion" that occurred in the early 1970s. This consisted primarily of poor people taking advantage, as they had not previously, of all of the benefits Congress had made available to them in theory under the law. As a result of these two forces, poverty declined substantially, until recession and budget cuts pushed rates back up in the 1980s.

Can poverty be *eliminated*? Probably not, especially if one views poverty in relative rather than absolute terms. Still, there is no reason to think that the *level* of poverty is beyond influence or control. Indeed, the most careful studies confirm what common sense suggests: Within the modest limits of our existing assistance programs, people are better off with more money — as well as food, housing, and other essentials — than with less.

* James T. Patterson, *America's Struggle against Poverty 1900–1980* (Cambridge: Harvard University Press, 1981).

looking back

Frictional unemployment is a normal feature of an efficient economy

1 Some workers will always be in transition from one job to another, and some types of work necessarily involve periods of unemployment. These are not matters of immediate policy concern.

Involuntary unemployment

2 Involuntary unemployment occurs when workers cannot find work at any reasonable wage. The level of involuntary unemployment rises and falls with the level of aggregate demand.

Unemployment has a highly differential impact

3 Certain categories of workers, especially minorities and the young, experience more frequent and longer spells of unemployment than prime-aged white males.

Does unemployment insurance cause unemployment?

4 It has recently been suggested that the existence of unemployment insurance and other safety net provisions serves to increase unemployment, because unemployment insurance benefits are not taxable. Undoubtedly there is some effect here, but the benefits of seniority, security, fringe benefits, and psychic satisfaction would seem greatly to outweigh the purely monetary differential.

Absolute vs. relative poverty

5 Official measures of unemployment are based on calculations of the cost of a minimally decent standard of living. These tend to show progress over time. Some scholars argue that poverty is inherently relative and subjective; measures of poverty based on the income distribution tend to show little change over time.

Unemployment causes poverty

6 The most important determinant of changes in the rate of poverty is changes in the rate of unemployment. The rise in poverty in the 1980s is almost entirely due to the poor economic performance in the early part of the decade.

Transfer payments relieve poverty

7 The growth in transfer payments in the 1970s has reduced the burden of poverty, especially on the elderly. Some critics suggest that they have also removed the incentive for poor people to work, but the evidence indicates that it is changes in unemployment, not changes in transfer programs, that are responsible for the rise in pretransfer poverty rates.

ECONOMIC VOCABULARY

Frictional unemployment 644	Absolute poverty 650
Involuntary unemployment 645	Relative poverty 650

QUESTIONS

1. The Bible tells us that the poor shall always be with us. Is this true if we define poverty in absolute terms? In relative terms? Suppose we had an egalitarian society, such as the early *kibbutzim* in Israel? Was there poverty on the *kibbutz?* Were they "affluent"?

2. How are we to interpret the idea of involuntary unemployment? When 10 million people cannot find work, does that suggest forces beyond the control of individuals? And yet, would not work be available for many of these individuals if they offered their services at sufficiently low rates of pay? Is there an implicit social standard of wages that plays a role in the distinction between voluntary and involuntary unemployment?

3. Do you remember the story about poverty and its causes in Chapter 5? How would you interpret that story in terms of what you now know about poverty?

4. Do you think there is something to the idea of "welfare dependency"? If so, what changes in social institutions might reduce it? Sink-or-swim policies? Retraining? Relocation? How would you argue as an economist for these policies — or against them? How would you decide how much it would make sense to spend on policies such as job retraining?

PART FIVE

the rest of the world

CHAPTER 36
The Gains and Strains of Trade

a look ahead

In these last chapters we look again at America in the world economy, first in terms of our economic relationships; at the end, in a broader, historic perspective.

Chapter 36 takes another look at the economics of international exchange. This will introduce us to one of the most useful ideas in all of economics—that exchange can yield gains in productivity. In order to understand this, we will have to master the principle of comparative advantage—the way in which trade can benefit two nations (or regions or individuals), even though one of the two is more productive than the other in everything it does! The answer to this seeming paradox, we shall see, lies in the opportunity cost of not specializing productive effort. After we have learned about the gains from trade, we review the pros and cons of free trade.

By now we are certainly aware of the importance of the world economy for American economic prospects. Nevertheless, we have not yet analyzed the central problem of international economic relations. That central problem is the gains from trade—and the strains of trade. Until we have understood these crucial issues, we cannot grasp the underlying issue of international economics—the bias of nationalism.

The Bias of Nationalism

The bias of nationalism is the curious fact that relationships and propositions that are perfectly self-evident in the context of "ordinary" economics suddenly appear suspect, not to say downright wrong, in the context of international economics.

Suppose that the governor of an eastern state—let us say New Jersey—wanted to raise the incomes of his constituents and decided that the best way to do so was to encourage some new industry to move there. Suppose furthermore that his son was very fond of grapefruit and suggested to him one morning that grapefruit would be an excellent addition to New Jersey's products. The governor might object that grapefruit needed a milder climate than New Jersey had to offer. "That's no problem," his son might answer. "We could protect our grapefruit by growing them in hothouses. That way, in addition to the income from the crop, we would benefit the state from the incomes earned by the glaziers and electricians who would be needed."

The governor might murmur something about hothouse grapefruit costing more than ordinary grapefruit, so that New Jersey could not sell its crop on the competitive market. "Nonsense," his son would reply. "We can subsidize the grapefruit growers out of the proceeds of a general sales tax. Or we could pass a law requiring restaurants in this state to serve state grapefruit only. Or you could bar out-of-state grapefruit from New Jersey entirely."

"Now, my boy," the governor would return, "in the first place, that's unconstitutional. Second, even if it weren't, we would be making people in his state give up part of their incomes through the sales tax to benefit farmers, and that would never be politically acceptable. And third, the whole scheme is so inefficient it's just downright ridiculous."

But if we now shift our attention to a similar scene played between the prime minister of Nova Jersia and his son, we find some interesting differences. Like his counterpart in New Jersey, the son of the prime minister recommends the growing of hothouse grapefruit in Nova Jersia's chilly climate. Admittedly, that would make the crop considerably dearer than that for sale on the international markets. "But that's all right," he tells his father. "We can put a tariff on foreign grapefruit, so none of the cheap fruit from abroad will undersell ours."

"My boy," says the prime minister after carefully considering the matter, "I think you are right. It is true that grapefruit in Nova Jersia will be more expensive as a result of the tariff, but there is no doubt that a tariff looks like a tax on them and not on us, and therefore no one will object to it. It is also true that our hothouse grapefruit may not taste as good as theirs, but we will have the immense satisfaction of eating our *own* grapefruit, which will make it taste better. Finally, there may be a few economists who will tell us that this is not the most efficient use of our resources, but I can tell them that the money we pay for hothouse grapefruit — even if it is a little more than it would be otherwise — stays in our own pockets and doesn't go to enrich foreigners. In addition to which, I would point out in my television appearances that the reason foreign grapefruit are so cheap is that foreign labor is so badly paid. We certainly don't want to drag down the price of our labor by making it compete with the cheap labor of other nations. All in all, hothouse grapefruit seems to me an eminently sensible proposal, and one that is certain to be politically popular.''

Source of the Difficulty

Is it a sensible proposal? Of course not, although it will take some careful thinking to expose all its fallacies. Will it be politically popular? It may very well be, for economic policies that would be laughed out of court at home get a serious hearing when they crop up in the international arena. Here are some of the things that many of us tend to believe.

Trade between two nations usually harms one side or the other.

Rich countries can't compete with poor countries.

There is always the danger that a country may sell but refuse to buy.

Are these fears true? One way of testing their validity is to see how they ring in our ears when we rid them of our unconscious national bias by recasting them as propositions in ordinary economics.

Is it true that trade between businesses or persons usually harms one side or the other?

Is it true that rich companies can't compete with poor ones?

Is it true that one company might only sell but never buy — not even materials or the services of factors of production?

What is the source of this curious prejudice against international trade? It is not, as we might think, an excess of patriotism that leads us to recommend courses of action that will help our own country, regardless of the effect on others. For, curiously, the policies of the economic superpatriot, if put into practice, would demonstrably injure the economic interests of his own land. The trouble, then, springs from a root deeper than mere national interest. It lies in the peculiarly deceptive problems posed by international trade. What is deceptive about them, however, is not that they involve principles that apply only to relations between nations. All the economic arguments that elucidate international trade apply equally well to domestic trade. The deception arises, rather, for two other reasons.

1. **International trade requires an understanding of how two countries, each dealing in its own currency, manage to buy and sell from each other in a world where there is no such thing as international money.**

2. **International trade requires a very thorough understanding of the advantages of and arguments for, trade itself.**

Table 1	Production	Wooltown	Cottontown
UNSPECIALIZED PRODUCTION: CASE 1 *Wooltown and Cottontown each put half their populations to work at wool and cotton, with these results.*	Wool (lbs)	5,000	2,000
	Cotton (lbs)	10,000	20,000

Gains from Trade

In a general way, of course, we are all aware of the importance of trade. *It is trade that makes possible the division and specialization of labor on which our productivity is so largely based.* If we could not exchange the products of our specialized labor, each of us would have to be wholly self-supporting, and our standard of living would thereupon fall to that of subsistence farmers. Thus trade (international or domestic) is actually a means of *increasing productivity*, quite as much as investment or technological progress.

The importance of trade in making possible specialization is so great that we should take a moment to make it crystal clear. Let us consider two towns. Each produces two goods: wool and cotton; but Wooltown has good grazing lands and poor growing lands, while Cottontown's grazing is poor, but growing is good. Suppose, moreover, that the two towns had equal populations and that each town employed half its people in cotton and half in wool. The results might look like Table 1.

As we can see, the same number of grazers in Wooltown turn out two and one-half times as much wool as they do in Cottontown, whereas the same number of cotton farmers in Cottontown produce double the amount of cotton that they do in Wooltown. One does not have to be an economist to see that both towns are losing by this arrangement. If Cottontown would shift its woolworkers into cotton, and Wooltown would shift its cotton farmers into wool, the output of the two towns would look like Table 2 (assuming constant returns to scale).

Now, if we compare total production of the two towns (see Table 3), we can see the gains from specialization.

In other words, specialization followed by trade makes it possible for both towns to have more of both commodities than they had before. No matter how the gains from trade are distributed — and this will depend on many factors, such as the relative elasticities of demand for the two products — both towns can gain, even if one gains more than the other.

Table 2	Output	Wooltown	Cottontown
SPECIALIZED PRODUCTION *They move all their labor force to the more productive task, with these results.*	Wool	10,000	0
	Cotton	0	40,000

Table 3

THE GAIN FROM SPECIALIZATION

Comparing the output of the two towns together, before and after, shows the gains from specialization.

| Output | Combined Towns | | Gain from Specialization |
	Mixed	Specialized	
Wool	7,000	10,000	3,000
Cotton	30,000	40,000	10,000

Unequal Advantages

If all the world were divided into nations, like Wooltown and Cottontown, each producing for trade only a single item in which it has a clear advantage over all others, international trade would be a simple matter to understand. It would still present problems of international payment, and it might still inspire its prime ministers of Nova Jersia to forego the gains from trade for political reasons that we will examine at the end of this chapter. But the essential rationale of trade would be simple to understand.

It is unfortunate for the economics student as well as for the world that this is not the way international resources are distributed. Instead of giving each nation at least one commodity in which it has a clear advantage, many nations do not have such an advantage in a single product. How can trade possibly take place under such inauspicious circumstances?

To unravel the mystery, let us turn again to Cottontown and Wooltown, but this time call them Supraville and Infraville, to designate an important change in their respective abilities. Although both towns still enjoy equal populations, which are again divided equally between cotton and wool production, in this example Supraville is a more efficient producer than Infraville in *both* cotton and wool, as Table 4 shows.

Is it possible for trade to benefit these two towns when one of them is so manifestly superior to the other in every product? It seems out of the question. But let us nonetheless test the case by supposing that each town began to specialize.

Tradeoff Relationships

But how to decide which trade each town should follow? A look at Figure 1 may give us a clue. Production-possibility diagrams are familiar to us. Here we put them to use to let us see the results of trade.

Table 4

UNSPECIALIZED PRODUCTION: CASE II

In this case, one country is better than the other not just in one activity, but in both.

	Supraville	Infraville
Wool output	5,000	3,000
Cotton production	20,000	10,000

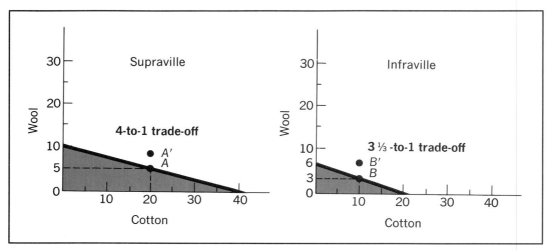

Figure 1

PRODUCTION POSSIBILITIES IN TWO TOWNS BEFORE TRADE

Production possibility curves are graphic depictions of tradeoffs, or (same thing) of opportunity costs. Supraville enjoys a wool/cotton income at point A, Infraville at point B. Note that points A' and B' are out of reach for the two towns.

What do the diagrams show? First, they establish maximums that each town could produce if it devoted all its efforts to one product. Since we have assumed that the labor force is divided, this means that each town could double the amount of cotton or wool it enjoys when it divides its workers fifty-fifty. Next, a line between these points shows the production frontier that both towns face.* We see that Supraville is located at point *A* where it has 5,000 lbs of wool and 20,000 lbs of cotton, and that Infraville is at *B*, where it has 3,000 lbs of wool and 10,000 lbs of cotton.

But the diagrams (and the figures in the preceding table, on which they are based) also show us something else. It is that each town has a different "tradeoff" relationship between its two branches of production. When either town specializes in one branch, it must, of course, give up the output of the other. **But each town swaps one kind of output for the other in different proportions, as the differing slopes of the two p–p curves show.** Supraville, for example, can make only an extra pound of wool by giving up 4 pounds of cotton. That is, it gets its maximum potential output of 10,000 lbs of wool by surrendering 40,000 lbs of cotton. Infraville can reach its production maximum of 6,000 lbs of wool at a loss of 20,000 lbs of cotton. Thus, rather than having to give up 4 lbs of cotton to get one of wool, it gives up only 3.3 lbs. Therefore, in terms of opportunity cost—how much

---

* Why are these lines drawn straight, not bowed as in Chapter 7? As we know, the bowing reflects the law of increasing cost, which makes the gains from a shift in resource allocation less and less favorable as we move from one extreme of allocation to another. Here we ignore this complication for simplicity of exposition. We have also ignored the problem of variable returns when we assumed that each town could double its output of cotton or wool by doubling its labor force.

cotton has to be given up to get a pound of wool—wool actually costs less in Infraville than in Supraville!

Not so the other way round, of course. As we would expect, cotton costs Supraville less in terms of wool than it costs Infraville. In Supraville, we get 40,000 lbs of cotton by relinquishing only 10,000 lbs of wool—a loss of a quarter of a pound of wool for a pound of cotton. In Infraville, we can get the maximum output of 20,000 lbs of cotton only by a surrender of 6,000 lbs of wool—a loss of approximately ⅓ lb of wool rather than ¼ lb of wool for each unit of cotton.*

Comparative Advantage

Perhaps the light is beginning to dawn. Despite the fact that Supraville is more productive than Infraville in terms of output per man in both cotton and wool, it is *relatively* more productive in cotton than in wool. And despite the fact that Infraville is absolutely less productive than Supraville, man for man, in both cotton and wool, it is *relatively* more productive in wool. To repeat, it requires a bigger sacrifice of wool to get another pound of cotton in Infraville than in Supraville.

We call this kind of relative superiority *comparative advantage*. It is a concept that is often difficult to grasp at first, but that is central to the reason for trade itself. When we speak of *comparative* advantage, we mean, as in the case of Supraville, that among *various* advantages of one producer or locale over another, there is one that is better than any other. *Comparatively* speaking, this is where its optimal returns lie. But just because it must abandon some lesser opportunity, its trading partner can now advantageously devote itself in the direction where *it* has a comparative advantage.

This is a relationship of logic, not economics. Take the example of the banker who is also the best carpenter in town. Will it pay him to build his own house? Clearly it will not, for he will make more money by devoting all his hours to banking, even though he then has to employ and pay for a carpenter less skillful than himself. True, he could save that expense by building his own house. But he would then have to give up the much more lucrative hours he could be spending at the bank!

Now let us return to the matter of trade. We have seen that wool is *relatively* cheaper in Infraville, where each additional pound costs only 3.3 lbs of cotton, rather than 4 lbs as in Supraville; and that cotton is *relatively* cheaper in Supraville, where an additional pound costs but ¼ lb of wool, instead of ⅓ lb across the way in Infraville. Now let us suppose that each side begins to specialize in the trade in which it has the comparative advantage. Suppose that Supraville took half its labor force now in wool and put it into cotton. Its output would change as in Table 5.

Supraville has lost 2,500 lbs of wool but gained 10,000 lbs of cotton. Now let us see if it can trade its cotton for Infraville's wool. In Infraville, where productivity is so much less, the entire labor force has shifted to wool output, where its greatly

---

* It takes long practice to master the arithmetic of gains from trade. It is important, first, to get the idea; then to master the calculations.

Table 5

Supraville uses specialization to boost cotton production at the expense of wool.

	Before the Shift	After the Shift
Wool production	5,000	2,500
Cotton production	20,000	30,000

inferior productivity can be put to best use. Hence its production pattern now looks like Table 6.

Infraville finds itself lacking 10,000 lbs of cotton, but it has 3,000 *additional* lbs of wool. Clearly, it can acquire the 10,000 lbs of cotton it needs from Supraville by giving Supraville *more* than the 2,500 lbs of wool it seeks. As a result, both Infraville and Supraville will have the same cotton consumption as before, but there will be a surplus of 500 lbs of wool to be shared between them. As Figure 2 shows, both towns will have gained by the exchange, for both will have moved beyond their former production frontiers (from A to A' and from B to B').

This last point is the crucial one. The nature of production possibility curves is such that any point lying outside the production frontier is simply unattainable by that society. In Figure 2, points A' and B' lie beyond the pretrade *PP* curves of the two towns, but trade has made it possible for both communities to enjoy what was formerly impossible.

Opportunity Cost

Comparative advantage gives us an important insight into all exchange relationships, for it reveals again a fundamental economic truth we have mentioned more than once before. It is that *cost, in economics, means opportunities that must be foregone.* **The real cost of wool in Supraville is the cotton that cannot be grown, because workers are engaged in wool production, just as the real cost of cotton is the wool that must be gone without. In fact, we can see that the basic reason for comparative advantage lies in the fact that opportunity costs vary, so that it "pays" (it costs less) for different parties to engage in different activities.

If opportunity costs for two producers are the same, then it follows that there cannot be any comparative advantage for either; and if there is no comparative advantage, there is nothing to be gained by specializing or trading. Suppose Supraville has a two-to-one edge over Infraville in *both* cotton and wool. Then, if either town specializes, neither will gain. Supraville may still gain 10,000 lbs of cotton for 2,500 lbs of wool, as before, but Infraville will gain only 2,500 lbs of wool (not

Table 6

Specialization is concentrated in wool in Infraville's case.

	Before the Shift	After the Shift
Wool	3,000	6,000
Cotton	10,000	—

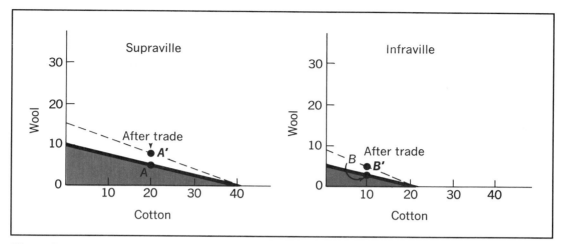

Figure 2
PRODUCTION POSSIBILITIES IN TWO TOWNS AFTER TRADE
Specialization has made more wool available. This is like moving the PP curve outward along the wool axis. Points A' and B', formerly out of reach, are now accessible to the two towns. (For clarity's sake, the graph shows a gain much larger than the 500 lbs described in the text.)

3,000) from its shift away from cotton. Thus, the key to trade lies in the existence of *different* opportunity costs.

Are opportunity costs usually different from country to country or from region to region? For most commodities they are. As we move from one part of the world to another — sometimes even short distances — climate, resources, skills, transportation costs, capital scarcity, or abundance all change; and as they change, so do opportunity costs. There is every possibility for rich countries to trade with poor ones, precisely because their opportunity costs are certain to differ.

Exchange Ratios

But we have not yet fully understood one last important aspect of trade — the *prices* at which goods will exchange. Suppose that Supraville and Infraville do specialize, each in the product in which it enjoys a comparative advantage. Does that mean they can swap their goods at any price?

A quick series of calculations reveals otherwise. We remember that Supraville needed at least 2,500 lbs of wool for which it was going to offer some of its extra production of cotton in exchange. But how much? What price should it offer for its needed wool, in terms of cotton?

Suppose it offered 7,500 lbs of cotton. Would Infraville sell the wool? No, it would not. At home it can grow its own 7,500 lbs of cotton at a ''cost'' of only 2,273 lbs of wool, for we recall that Infraville traded off one pound of wool for 3.3 lbs of cotton (7,500 ÷ 3.3 = 2,273).

Suppose, then, that Infraville counteroffered to sell Supraville 2,500 lbs of wool for a price of 12,000 lbs of cotton. Would Supraville accept? Of course not. This would mean the equivalent of 4.8 lbs of cotton for a pound of wool. Supraville can do better than that by growing its own wool at its own tradeoff ratio of only 4 lbs to 1.

We begin to see, in other words, that the price of wool must lie between the trade-off ratios of Infraville and Supraville. Infraville wants to import cotton. If it did not trade with Supraville, it could grow its own cotton at the cost of one pound of wool for every 3.3 lbs of cotton. Hence, for trade to be advantageous, Infraville seeks to get *more* cotton than that, per pound of wool.

Supraville is in the opposite situation. It seeks to export cotton and to import wool. It could make its own wool at the sacrifice of 4 lbs of cotton per pound of wool. Thus it seeks to gain wool for a *lower* price than that, in terms of cotton. Clearly, any ratio between 3.3 and 4 lbs of cotton per pound of wool will profit both sides.

The Role of Prices

Let us put this into ordinary price terms. Suppose that cotton sells for 30¢ per pound. Then wool would have to sell between 99¢ and $1.20 (30¢ × 3.3 and ×4) to make trade worthwhile.* Let us say that supply and demand established a price of $1.10 for wool. Supraville can then sell its 10,000 lbs of extra cotton production at 30¢, which will net it $3,000. How much wool can it buy for this sum? At the going price of $1.10 per lb, 2,727 lbs. Therefore Supraville will end up with the same amount of cotton (20,000 lbs) as it had before specialization and trade, and with 227 *more* lbs of wool than before (2,500 lbs produced at home plus 2,727 lbs imported from Infraville — a total of 5,227 lbs). It has gained by trade an amount equal to the price of this extra wool, or $249.70.

How has Infraville fared? It has 3,273 lbs of wool left after exporting 2,727 lbs to Supraville from its production of 6,000 lbs, and it also has 10,000 lbs of cotton imported from Supraville in exchange for its wool exports. Thus it, too, has a gain from trade — the 273 lbs of wool (worth $300.30) over the amount of 3,000 lbs that it would have produced without specialization and trade. In brief, *both* sides have profited from the exchange. To be sure, gains need not be distributed so evenly between the trading partners. If the price of wool had been $1, trade still would have been worthwhile, but Supraville would have gained almost all of it. Had the price of wool been $1.19, both sides again would have come out ahead, but now Infraville would have been the larger beneficiary by far. The actual price at which wool would sell would be determined by the supply and demand schedules for it in both communities.

---

* Obviously, these prices are used for illustrative purposes only. And once again, let us reassure you: These calculations are easy to follow, but not easy to do by yourself. Familiarity will come only with practice.

THE CASE FOR FREE TRADE

Would the prime minister of Nova Jersia be convinced by these arguments? Would his son? They might be weakened in their support for hothouse grapefruit, but some arguments would still linger in their minds. Let us consider them.

1. "OUR WORKERS CANNOT COMPETE WITH LOW-WAGE WORKERS OVERSEAS." This is an argument one hears not only in Nova Jersia, but in every nation in the world, save only those with the very lowest wage rates. Swedish workers complain about "cheap" American labor; American workers complain about sweatshop labor in Hong Kong. And indeed it is true that American labor is paid less than Swedish and that Hong Kong labor is paid a great deal less than American. Does that not mean that American labor will be seriously injured if we import goods made under "sweatshop" conditions, or that Swedish labor is right in complaining that its standard of living is undermined by importing goods from "exploited" American workers?

Like the answers to so many questions in economics, this one is not a simple yes or no. The American textile worker who loses his job because of low-priced textile imports *is* hurt; and so is the Swedish worker in an electronics company who loses his job because of American competition. We will come back to their legitimate grievances later. But we must note that both workers would also be injured if they lost their jobs as a result of domestic competition. Why do we feel so threatened when the competition comes from abroad?

Because, the answer goes, foreign competition isn't based on American efficiency. It is based on exploited labor. Hence it pulls down the standards of American labor to its own low level.

There is an easy reply to this argument. The reason Hong Kong textile labor is paid so much less than American textile labor is that *average* productivity in Hong Kong is so much lower than *average* productivity in America. **To put it differently, the reason that American wages are high is that we use our workers in industries where their productivity is very high. If Hong Kong, with its very low productivity, can undersell us in textiles, then this is a clear signal that we must move our factors of production out of textiles into other areas where their contribution will be greater; for example, in the production of machinery.** It is no coincidence that machinery — one of the highest wage industries in America — is one of our leading exports, or that more than 75 percent of our manufactured exports are produced by industries paying hourly wage rates above the national average for all manufacturing industries. In fact, all nations tend to export the goods that are produced at the highest, not lowest, local wages! Why? Because those industries employ their labor most effectively.

But suppose Hong Kong accumulated large amounts of capital and became a center for the manufacture of heavy equipment, so that it sold *both* garments and electrical generators more cheaply than we sold them. We are back to Supraville and Infraville. There would still be a *comparative* advantage in one

or more of these products in which we would be wise to specialize, afterward trading with Hong Kong for our supplies of the other good.*

Many readers may say, "That is exactly the situation that faces us today! Are you telling us there is no problem in facing low-wage competition from Asia?" No, we are not saying that. But the problem involves helping displaced workers and businesses find alternative employments. The idea of comparative advantage tells us only that there is *some form* of employment in which our *comparative* productivity will be greater than that of Hong Kong, simply because our resources and opportunity costs are different. Perhaps it lies in developing new technologies. But just suppose that there were no such opportunities. Could Hong Kong then wipe out all American industry? Doubtful. What would they get paid with? How would we earn Hong Kong dollars to buy their goods unless we sold goods to the East for American dollars?

2. "TARIFFS ARE PAINLESS TAXES BECAUSE THEY ARE BORNE BY FOREIGNERS." This is a convincing-sounding argument advanced by the prime minister of Nova Jersia (and by some other prime ministers in their time). But is it true? Let us take the case of hothouse grapefruit, which can be produced in Nova Jersia only at a cost of 50 cents each, whereas foreign grapefruit (no doubt produced by sweated labor) can be unloaded at its ports at 25 cents. To prevent his home industry from being destroyed, the prime minister imposes a tariff of 25 cents on foreign grapefruit — which, he tells the newspapers, will be entirely paid by foreigners.

This is not, however, the way his political opponent (who has had a course in economics) sees it. "Without the tariff," she tells her constituency, "you could buy grapefruit for 25 cents. Now you have to pay 50 cents for it. Who is paying the extra 25 cents — the foreign grower or you? Even if not a single grapefruit entered the country, you would still be paying 25 cents more than you have to. **In fact, you are being asked to subsidize an inefficient domestic industry.** Not only that, but the tariff wall means they won't ever become efficient because there is no pressure of competition on them."

Whether or not our economic candidate will win the electoral battle, she surely has the better of the argument. Or does she? For the prime minister, stung by these unkind remarks, replies:

3. "BUT AT LEAST THE TARIFF KEEPS SPENDING POWER AT HOME. OUR OWN GRAPEFRUIT GROWERS, NOT FOREIGNERS, HAVE OUR MONEY." There are two answers to this argument. First, the puchasing power acquired by foreigners can be used to buy goods from efficient Nova Jersia producers and will thus return to Nova Jersia's economy. Second, if productive resources are used in inefficient, low-productivity industries, then the resources available for use in efficient, high-productivity industries are less than they otherwise would be, and the total output

---

* Newspapers in Southeast Asia carry editorials seeking protection from American imports because, they say, we do not use labor in our production, and it is unfair to ask its citizens to compete with our machines that do not have to be paid wages.

HIGH WAGES?

How do you tell whether a country is a high-wage country or a low-wage country? If German workers are paid 8 marks per hour, are their wages high or low compared to ours? Clearly, you cannot tell without knowing the exchange rate. If 8 marks can be traded for $1, then German workers are paid the equivalent of $1 per hour. We can then compare the German rates relative to the American. Given the average American wage of $4 per hour, we would conclude that Geman wages are low. If, however, 1 mark can be traded for 1 dollar, then German workers earn the equivalent of $8 per hour. In this case, German workers are highly paid *relative* to American workers. As a result we cannot really tell whether a country is high-wage or low-wage until we understand exchange rates and what determines them.

of the country falls. To keep out foreign grapefruit is to lower the country's real standard of living. The people of Nova Jersia waste time and resources doing something they do not do very well.

4. "BUT TARIFFS ARE NECESSARY TO KEEP THE WORK FORCE OF NOVA JERSIA EMPLOYED." This is the time to remember our investigation of macroeconomic policies. As we learned in macroeconomics, the governments of Nova Jersia and every other country can use fiscal and monetary policies to keep their resources fully employed. If grapefruit workers become unemployed, governments can expand aggregate demand and generate domestic job opportunities in other areas.

THE CASE FOR TARIFFS

Are *all* arguments against tariffs? No. But it is essential to recognize that these arguments take full cognizance of the inescapable costs of restricting trade. They do not contest the validity of the theory of free trade, but the difficulties of its application. Let us familiarize ourselves with them.

Mobility

The first difficulty concerns the problem of mobility. When Hong Kong textiles press hard against the garment worker in New York, higher wages in the auto plants in Detroit are scant comfort. She has a lifetime of skills and a home in New

York, and she does not want to move to another city where she will be a stranger and to a new trade in which she would be only an unskilled beginner. She certainly does not want to move to Hong Kong! Hence, the impact of foreign trade often brings serious dislocations that result in persistent local unemployment, rather than in a flow of resources from a relatively disadvantaged to a relatively advantaged industry.

In the early 1980s, some 250,000 auto workers and 247,000 steel workers were without jobs, partly because of the depression, but to a large degree because foreign goods had displaced domestic ones. Could those hundreds of thousands of persons be moved and reintegrated into communities and retrained? The answer is that perhaps they could—if we were willing to spend the money and make the effort. It is plain from our general indifference to the unemployed elsewhere that we are not willing to do either. The arguments in favor of free trade sound less convincing when we confront a large scale situation such as that, rather than the imaginary case that involves one person here and one there.

Transition Costs

Second, even if free trade increases the incomes and real living standards of each country participating in trade, **this does not mean that it increases the income and real living standards of each individual in each country.** The Michigan auto worker may find himself with a substantial reduction in income for the rest of his life. He is being economically rational when he resists "cheap" foreign imports and attempts to get his congressman to impose tariffs or quotas.

There is, it should be noted, an answer to this argument—an answer, at any rate, that applies to industrial nations. Since the gains from trade are generally spread across the nation, the real transition costs of moving from one industry, skill, or region to another should also be generally spread across the nation. This means that government (the taxpayers), rather than the worker or business, should bear the costs of relocation and retraining. In this way we spread the costs in such a manner that a few need not suffer disproportionately to win the benefits of international trade that are shared by many.

We should also be aware of the possibility that transition costs may actually exceed the short-term benefits to be derived from international trade. Transition costs thus place a new element in the system, since the standard analysis of competitive systems—national or international—ignores them. A country may be wise to limit its international trade, if it calculates that the cost of reallocating its own factors is greater than the gains to be had in higher real income. Remember, however, that transition costs tend to be short-lived and that the gains from trade tend to last. Thus it is easy to exaggerate the costs of transition and to balk at making changes that would ultimately improve conditions.

Full Employment

Third, the argument for free trade rests on the very important assumption that there will be substantially full employment.

In the days of the mid-nineteenth century when the free trade argument was first fully formulated, the idea of an underemployment equilibrium would have been considered absurd. In an economy of large enterprises and "sticky" wages and prices, we know that unemployment is a real and continuous object of concern for national policy.

Thus, it makes little sense to advocate policies to expand production via trade unless we are certain that the level of aggregate demand will be large enough to absorb that production. **Full employment policy therefore becomes an indispensable arm of a free trade policy.** Trade gives us the potential for maximizing production, but there is no point in laying the groundwork for the highest possible output unless fiscal and monetary policy are also geared to bringing about a level of aggregate demand large enough to support that output.

National Self-Sufficiency

Fourth, there is the argument of nationalism pure and simple. This argument does not impute spurious economic gains to tariffs. Rather, it says that free trade undoubtedly encourages production, but it does so at a certain cost. This is the cost of the vulnerability that comes from extensive and extreme specialization. This vulnerability is all very well within a nation where we assume that law and order will prevail, but it cannot be so easily justified among nations where the realistic assumption is just the other way. Tariffs, in other words, are defensible because they enable nations to attain a certain *self-sufficiency*—admittedly at some economic cost. Project Independence, the United States effort to gain self-sufficiency in energy, was exactly such an undertaking.

In a world always threatened by war, self-sufficiency has a value that may properly override considerations of ideal economic efficiency. The problem is to hold the arguments for national defense down to proper proportions. When tariffs are periodically adjusted in international conferences, an astonishing variety of industries (in all countries) find it possible to claim protection from foreign competition in the name of national "indispensability."

Infant Industries

Equally interesting is the nationalist argument for tariffs advanced by so-called infant industries, particularly in developing nations. These newly formed or prospective enterprises claim that they cannot possibly compete with the giants in developed countries while they are small; but that if they are protected by a tariff, they will in time become large and efficient enough no longer to need a tariff. In addition, they claim, they will provide a more diversified spectrum of employments for their own people, as well as aiding in the national transition toward a more modern economy.

The argument is a valid one if it is applied to industries that have a fair chance of achieving a comparative advantage once grown up (otherwise one will be supporting them in infancy, maturity, and senility). Certainly it is an argument that was propounded by the youthful industries of the United States in the early nineteenth century and was sufficiently persuasive to bring them a moderate degree of protection (although it is inconclusive as to how much their growth was ultimately dependent on tariff help). And it is being listened to today by some underdeveloped nations who feel that their only chance of escaping from poverty is to develop a nucleus of industrial employment at almost any cost in the short run.

Producer vs. Consumer Welfare

The policy of free trade versus the policy of protectionism ultimately resolves into a choice between the well-being of two groups. **Free trade favors the welfare of consumers. Protectionism favors the welfare of producers.**

To be sure, consumers are producers and producers are consumers, so that in a frictionless, perfect world there would be little to choose between the two. But in a world where frictions are an important part of ecnomic life, it matters very greatly whether we favor policies that benefit almost everyone to some degree, or policies that help or hurt a few people to a considerable degree. That is, in fact, the tradeoff when we weigh the gains from trade that accrue as lower prices for textiles or shoes or cars, versus the impact of protectionism on the jobs of textile workers or shoemakers or auto workers.

In a way the difficult choice that we face reminds us of the cost of inflation, felt by all, versus the cost of unemployment, borne by a few. The difference is that the political voice aroused by inflation drowns out the voice aroused by unemployment, whereas the injuries of those affected by foreign competition tend to override the murmur of consumers who would benefit from lower prices.

PROTECTIONISM

It is clear that when we add up the costs of a free trade policy, pursued in a world that is *not* prepared to undertake a full employment policy because of inflation fears, that is *not* much concerned about the costs of unemployment, and that *is* deeply interested in securing its national self-sufficiency, the classical arguments in favor of free trade lose a good deal of their force. The limitation of trade through tariffs or quota or any other form of protectionism may indeed cut down the level of production, but that loss seems much less serious in the circumstances of modern industrial competition.

Is protectionism therefore justifiable as a policy? The question is an academic one, for in fact protection is to some degree the policy in all nations. The United States, for example, limits by agreement the number of cars the Japanese ship to us; has enacted a "trigger" pricing mechanism that automatically puts on a tariff when steel imports exceed a certain level; allows industries to appeal if they can establish "unfair" competition (usually export subsidies from foreign governments); and has other protective institutions. Other countries have the same.

TRANSPORTATION COSTS

If every industry must have a comparative advantage in one country or another, how can there be steel industries (or any other) in more than one country? The answer, quite aside from considerations of nationalism, lies in *transportation costs*, which compensate for lower production costs in many products and thereby allow a relatively inefficient industry to supply a home market.

Transportation costs also explain why some industries, such as brick-making, are spread out in many localities, whereas others, such as diamond cutting, are concentrated in one place. If diamonds were very bulky or bricks very light, the first industry would become more dispersed, and the second less so.

A Changing International Order

Some degree of protection has always been the rule rather than the exception, free trade slogans notwithstanding. But this tendency has been encouraged by the intensification of international competition. In this altered setting, the ideal of unrestricted trade is much less appealing than in an imaginary world without vast and vulnerable investments, thousands of specialized workers whose jobs are at risk, and a worldwide condition of mutual military suspicion.

This does not mean that all-out protectionism can possibly serve as a workable model in place of free trade. A world of unrestrained protection would be a world of Nova Jersias, of grapefruit grown in hothouses. **But it seems that some middle way will have to be found between the advantages of an international division of labor and the disadvantages of an international disruption of economic and social life.**

We do not yet know what directions such a middle course may take. Perhaps it will involve a regionalization of trade, with large world areas "reserved" by treaty for regional producers in critical industries. Perhaps it will mean a world in which currencies (and companies!) are no longer permitted to move entirely as their owners wish.

The Special Case of the Underdeveloped World

This is sheer conjecture, and in any event a matter that will require many years to resolve. What is much more immediate is the need to find a way of improving economic relations between the advanced, industrialized world and the backward underdeveloped regions. Free trade has long been preached as a doctrine that would shed its benefits on all alike. In fact, however, it has not worked that way so far as the underdeveloped nations have been concerned. Many of these nations have been until fairly recently colonial possessions of the developed countries. As such, their economic structures were originally shaped to serve as useful adjuncts to the economy of their "home" countries. The result has been a typical attribute of underdeveloped economies—an extreme tilting toward monoculture—one crop such as bananas or coffee, or one product such as tin or copper—and the systematic discouragement of industrial sectors that might have offered competition with their colonial masters.

This has placed the underdeveloped world in a difficult economic situation for which free trade has given no remedy. As sellers of raw commodities they face a highly inelastic demand for their goods. Like the American farmer, when they produce a bumper crop, prices tend to fall precipitously and demand does not rise proportionately. At the same time, the industrial materials they buy in exchange tend to be firm or to rise in price over the years.

Terms of Trade. Thus the terms of trade—the actual *quid pro quo* of goods received against goods offered—have tended to move against the poorer nations, who have given more and more coffee for the same amount of machinery. In some years, when commodity prices have taken a particularly bad tumble, the poor nations have actually lost more in purchasing power than the total amount of all foreign aid they received. In effect, they subsidized the advanced nations! As an example, it has been estimated that falling prices cost the African nations more, in the first two decades after World War II, than all foreign funds given, loaned, or invested there.

It is possible—we do not yet know—that tightening markets in resources may reverse this trend. The last decade saw enormous sums flowing into the coffers of Middle Eastern governments, until an oil glut overtook the world, perhaps only temporarily. This has vastly aided the financial position of a few erstwhile poor lands. In addition, the internationalization of finance and production has created centers of rapid industrial growth in selected places, such as Singapore and South Korea. This has greatly improved the economic condition of these newly industrializing countries and indeed has made them threats to the economic security of many Western manufacturing centers.

Nevertheless, looking at the globe as a whole, where the poorest nations, with 70 percent of the world's population, still enjoy only 10 percent of its annual production, it is likely that a vast chasm will continue to separate the rich nations from the poor ones. In this situation of vastly unequal power, an insistence on free trade is more apt to reproduce the existing, tension-ridden relationships of inequality than to lead toward a more equitable and mutually rewarding division of the world's production and distribution.

As a consequence, most of the underdeveloped countries have sought to arrange commodity agreements—the international counterparts of the arrangements that support agricultural (and sometimes mining) prices and that regularize marketing in the developed, capitalist world. The developed world has not, however, been quick to respond to the plight of the poorer world. Here lies a source of serious economic and political friction for the future.

The Future of International Trade

This and the next chapter can do no more than hint at the complexities of the binding relationships of the world economy. It may be that in the textbooks of the future, the currents and connections of international economic life will be presented up front, in the first pages of an economic text. In our day, however, they must be tucked away at the back, more likely than not ignored by the harried instructor fighting against the constraints of time and by the student, overburdened with the complexities of learning about his or her own nation's economic problems. We cannot change these facts of life, but at least we must register in print the warning that economic life no longer stops at national borders (if it ever did), and that international trade and finance may very well be the most important areas of economic change in the coming decades.

looking back

KEY CONCEPTS

Bias of nationalism

1 The bias of nationalism is deep and pervasive. It leads us to assume that gains from trade, which we take for granted within a country, do not apply between countries.

Gains from trade stem from the specialization of labor

2 The gains from trade essentially stem from the improvement in productivity that results from specialization or a better division of labor. Trade is an indirect means of enhancing productivity.

Principle of comparative advantage gives gains to trading partners even when one is more productive in all activities

3 The principle of comparative advantage shows that trade is profitable even when one trading partner is more productive in all lines of endeavor than another. This is because it is possible for the superior partner to increase production in the activity that is comparatively best for itself, thus more than making up any loss from shifting resources out of the activity that is comparatively less advantageous.

Specialization allows countries to go beyond their former *PP* curves

4 By specializing production, the two trading partners gain a combined output that is larger than they could get by producing without specialization and trade. This is true as long as opportunity costs are not the same in both countries, which is almost always the case. Then specialization allows both countries to go beyond their former *PP* curves.

Prices, or exchange ratios, must lie within the ratios of tradeoff	**5** Exchange ratios, or prices, must lie within the tradeoff ratios of actual output. Otherwise the comparative advantages of the two nations would be lost.
The case for free trade is a case for maximizing productivity and consumer well-being	**6** The case for free trade stresses the gains for the entire society that come from maximizing production. By allowing "cheap" imports to come in without tariffs, we force labor to move away from low-productivity to high-productivity industry, and we benefit consumers.
Free trade also imposes costs	**7** The case for free trade hinges on a willingness to pursue full employment and to compensate the damages of competition. This seems unlikely to be realized.
Protectionism, in some degree, appears in all industrial nations exposed to modern intensified international competition	**8** Some degree of protectionism appears inescapable in a world of greatly intensified international production and competition. All industrial nations practice some degree of protectionist policy. The goal is to steer between the division of labor and the disruptions of unmanageable competition.
Free trade does not shed its benefits equitably when the structure of trade is distorted, as is the case with the underdeveloped world	**9** The arguments for free trade do not take into account the historical circumstances under which the underdeveloped nations' economies were formed. These tend to be monocultures of agriculture or mining, selling products that are highly price inelastic. Most of these nations seek commodity agreements that are the international counterpart of U.S. (or European) farm subsidies or marketing arangements.

ECONOMIC VOCABULARY

Tradeoff relationships   663
Comparative advantage   665
Opportunity cost   666
Mobility   671
Transition costs   672

Self-sufficiency   673
Infant industries   673
Producer vs. consumer welfare   674
Protectionism   674
Terms of trade   676

QUESTIONS

1. What do we mean when we say that trade is "indirect production"?
2. Suppose that two towns, Coaltown and Irontown, have equal populations but differing resources. If Coaltown applies its whole population to coal produc-

tion, it will produce 10,000 tons of coal; if it applies them to iron production, it will produce 5,000 tons of iron. If Irontown concentrates on iron, it will turn out 18,000 tons of iron; if it shifts to coal, it will produce 12,000 tons of coal. Is trade possible between these towns?

3. In which product does Coaltown have a comparative advantage? How many tons of iron does a ton of coal cost her? How many does it cost Irontown? What is the cost of iron in Coaltown and Irontown? Draw a production possibility diagram for each town. Show where the frontier lies before and after trade.

4. If iron sells for $10 a ton, what must be the price range of coal? Show that trade cannot be profitable if coal sells on either side of this range. What is the opportunity cost of coal to Irontown? Of iron to Irontown?

5. Is it possible that American watchmakers face unfair competition from Swiss watchmakers because wages are lower in Switzerland? If American watch workers are rendered unemployed by the low-paid Swiss, what might be done to help them — impose a tariff?

6. Is it possible that mass-produced, low-cost American watches are a source of unfair competition for Switzerland? If Swiss watchmakers are unemployed as a result, what could be done to help them — impose a tariff? Is it possible that a mutually profitable trade in watches might take place between the two countries? What kinds of watches would each probably produce?

7. Are the duties on French wines borne by foreigners or by domestic consumers? Both? What, if any, is the rationale for these duties? How would you go about estimating the transition costs if we were to abolish the tariff on all wines and spirits? Who would be affected? What alternative employment would you suggest for the displaced labor? The displaced land?

8. Let us suppose that the Japanese perfect a new model of car that will do a hundred miles on the gallon. The car threatens to wipe out General Motors and to deprive 500,000 auto workers of their jobs. What measures, if any, would you advocate with respect to importing the new vehicle? Suppose the Japanese agreed to buy GM's main plants and produce it here. Would you object to that?

CHAPTER 37
Buying and Selling Abroad

a look ahead

Our focus shifts from problems at home to problems in the international arena. This chapter

1 Clarifies what we mean when we say that the dollar is falling or rising.

2 Teaches us the basic elements of international exchange.

3 Introduces us to the problems of fixed and flexible exchange rates.

W e have already come to grips with some of the problems of international trade and finance. We have not yet, however, systematically investigated the mechanisms by which foreign trade is carried out in a world of many currencies. That is what we will do in this chapter.

A word before we begin. As we write these pages, the absorbing problem of international exchange is the problem of the high dollar—a problem we first looked into in Chapter 6, and have encountered more than once since then. But only a few years ago, the burning problem was quite the reverse. The dollar was taking a terrible battering in the foreign exchange markets. Millions of Americans who once thought that the dollar was "as good as gold" learned in the 1970s that it was not, as gold soared in price and the dollar correspondingly fell.

So the mechanisms of foreign exchange are two-sided and the problems of international exchange are two-directional. We shall mainly talk about a high dollar in the pages ahead, but with plenty of references to the possibility that the dollar may again become low. The task is to learn the way in which the foreign exchange markets work, so that no matter how the dollar goes, you will understand what is going on.

The Foreign Value of the Dollar

When the dollar rises or falls in the international money markets, it does not mean that a dollar will buy more or less American goods. That is a very important point to bear in mind. **When we speak of the dollar in foreign trade, it means only one thing: A dollar will buy more or less foreign money** — German marks, French or Swiss francs, Swedish krona, or whatever. As a result, it becomes cheaper or dearer for us to buy foreign goods and services.

The Rate of Exchange

Let us review what we mean by this. Suppose you enjoy French wine. French wine is sold by its producers for francs, the currency in which French producers pay their bills and want their receipts. Let us suppose they price their wine at 20 francs the bottle.

How much would 20 franc wine cost in America? The answer depends on the rate at which we can exchange dollars for francs — that is, it depends on the price of francs. We discover this price by going to banks, who are the main dealers in foreign currencies of all kinds, and inquiring what the dollar-franc *exchange rate* is. Let us say we are told it is five francs to the dollar. To buy a bottle of French wine, then, (ignoring transportation, insurance, and other costs) will cost us $4.00 (20 francs ÷ 5 = $4.00).

Now suppose that the dollar rises. This means that the dollar becomes dearer on the market for foreign money. It follows, of course, that francs will become cheaper in terms of dollars. Instead of getting 5 francs for a dollar, we now get 10. Meanwhile, the price of wine hasn't changed—it still costs 20 francs. But it now costs us $2, not $4, to purchase 20 francs. **A rising dollar therefore lowers the price of foreign goods in terms of American money.**

Conversely, a falling exchange rate would raise it. Imagine we were contemplating a trip to Germany. We inquire into the prices of German hotels, German meals, and the like, and we are told that we can do it comfortably for (let us say) 100 marks per day. "How much is that in American money?" we ask. The answer depends, of course, on the exchange rate. Suppose the rate is 3 marks to the dollar. Then 100 marks would be the equivalent of $33 a day. But if the dollar happened to be falling, we could be in for an unpleasant surprise. Perhaps by the time we were ready to leave, it would have fallen to 2 marks to the dollar. It still costs 100 marks a day to travel in Germany, but it now costs $50 to buy 100 marks, not $33.

We must remember, however, that international economics must always be viewed from both sides of the ocean. When the dollar rises, foreign goods or services become less expensive for us. But for a German, just the opposite is true. A German tourist coming to America might be told that he should allow $50 a day for expenses. "How much will that cost me in marks?" he asks his bank. The answer, again, hangs on the exchange rate. If it costs only 2 marks to buy a dollar, it will obviously be cheaper for the German tourist than if it costs 3 marks. Notice that this is exactly the opposite of the American tourist's position.

THE MARKET FOR DOLLARS

International economics entered our consciousness at a time when the dollar was very high. We know now that this means that the price of dollars, on the market for foreign currencies, must have been rising. Why did the dollar rise? As with all price changes, our first task is to look at the supply and demand situation. And that requires us to investigate the nature of the market for dollars and other currencies.

Here we can best begin by mentally grouping all the kinds of dealings in which dollars and other currencies change hands into two basic markets. **One is the market for currencies to carry on current transactions. The other is the market for currencies to carry on capital transactions.** You will have no trouble following the story if you bear these two markets in mind.

Current Transactions

The first market in which currencies are bought and sold is that in which the current transactions between firms, individuals, or governments are carried out. Here *the demand for dollars* comes from such groups as foreigners who want to import U.S. goods and services, and who must acquire dollars to purchase them; or from foreign tourists who need dollars to travel in the U.S.; or from foreign governments who must buy dollars to maintain embassies or consulates in America; or from firms abroad (American or foreign) that want to send dividends or

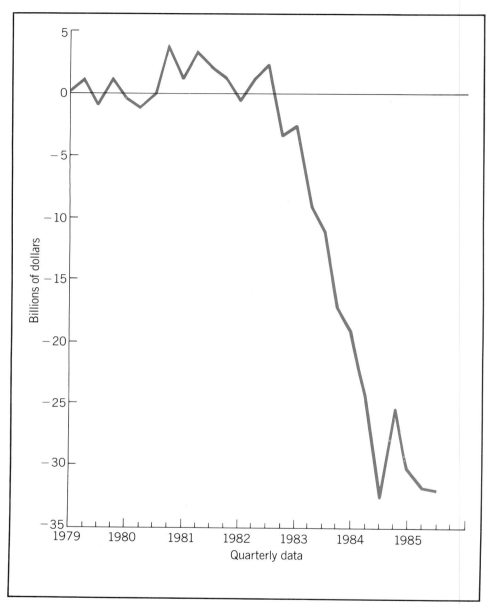

Figure 1
BALANCE ON CURRENT ACCOUNT 1978–1985

The balance on current account sums up all the supplies and demands for dollars needed for trade, travel, remittances of profits, government expenses, and the like. Until recent years, the market for current account almost always showed a favorable balance. This is no longer the case. **Source:** *Department of Commerce.*

profits to the United States in dollars. All these kinds of transactions require that holders of marks or francs or yen offer their currencies on the foreign exchange market in order to buy U.S. dollars.

And, of course, there are similar groups of Americans who *supply dollars* to the foreign exchange market for exactly the opposite reasons. Here we find American importers who want to bring in Japanese cameras and must offer dollars in order to acquire the yen to make their purchases; American or foreign firms that are sending dividends or profits earned in the U.S. to a foreign branch or headquarters; Americans or foreign residents who sell dollars in order to buy lire or drachmas or kronor to send money to friends or relatives abroad; or the American government which uses dollars to buy foreign currencies to pay diplomatic living expenses or to make military expenditures abroad.

Taken all together, these supplies and demands for dollars establish what we call our balance on current account. As Figure 1 shows, this balance took a substantial fall after 1982.

Behind the Trade Deficit

What happened to turn the balance from black to red? The answer, as we know from Chapter 6, involves two quite separate reasons. The first is that the dollar rose very sharply on the international money markets, beginning in the early 1980s. We will look very shortly into the causes for this rise, but for the moment we can simply take the rise itself as an important element behind our falling balance of trade.

We have just seen what happens to trade when a currency rises: The high-currency country finds it cheap to buy abroad and low-currency countries find it expensive to buy in the high-currency nation. This is exactly what happened to the United States. Between 1979 and 1985, the French franc fell from 4 francs to a dollar to 10; the German mark from 1.8 to a dollar to 3.3; the British pound from $2.08 to $1.09. Tourists went on specially arranged charter flights to London to pick up tweeds and woollens at half their normal prices. Our imports began to rise sharply — from a level of over $300 billion in the early 1980s to a level of nearly $450 billion in 1985. (The exact figures are in Table 2 on page 109). Imports also rose because our domestic recovery provided U.S. citizens with more dollar incomes, a considerable portion of which they devoted to buying foreign goods — the propensity to import at work.

THE MARKET FOR CAPITAL

If we think about it, we have now deepened the mystery. Americans were eagerly buying foreign currencies (and selling dollars to get them) to finance the great import boom. Foreigners were unwilling or unable to buy American exports because they were so expensive. One would think that the large supply of dollars offered by Americans and the small demand for dollars stemming from foreigners would lead the dollar to *fall* in price, not rise.

And that is, in fact, exactly what would have happened, if the only source of supply and demand in the exchange market were the needs of traders of commodities, tourists, and the like. But there is another source of supply and demand that arises to fulfill a set of needs different from those of current transactions. This is the supply and demand for dollars that arises for *capital purposes* — building or buying plants and equipment in another country, or buying stocks and bonds denominated in another country's currency.

The first of these capital flows is called **direct investment.** It arises from the efforts of American firms (mainly multinationals) to expand their ownership of plants and equipment abroad, and from the corresponding efforts of foreign companies to do the same thing here.

The second part of the capital market is made up of American or foreign individuals or firms who want to add to their overseas **portfolio investments** of stocks and bonds. Here we have Americans who buy stock in a Swedish firm or who buy German government bonds, and foreign investors who buy General Motors stock or U.S. Treasury bonds.

The Capital Inflow

If the dollar has been high despite the excess of imports over exports, the net demand for dollars on capital account must have been larger than the net supply of dollars on current account. Why should that demand have been so large? The answer lies in the relatively high rate of real return offered by United States financial assets — such as Treasury bonds — compared with their equivalents abroad.

In 1985, American nominal interest rates, although well beneath their 1980 peaks, were still very high by historical standards: One could buy 10-year Treasury bonds that paid 10 percent interest (in 1960 they paid only 4 percent!). From this yield, an investor would mentally subtract the inflation rate in 1985 of roughly 3.5 percent. The result was a real return of over 6 percent — perhaps half again as much as that obtainable in comparable bonds abroad. As a consequence, foreign capital poured into the United States in such vast quantities that the dollar — despite the worsening trade balance — rose by 47 percent from 1980 to 1985.*

This inflow of dollars could not go on indefinitely. At some point investors would hesitate before putting their funds in a nation whose ability to earn foreign exchange was in question. And even before that point, the damage caused by the high rates to our ability to earn foreign exchange was a powerful incentive for the

---

* The inflow of foreign funds helped finance our domestic budgetary deficit by buying 13 percent of Treasury bonds issued that year. We have seen that this enabled us to finance the deficit without the "crowding out" that had been anticipated and feared. It also saddled us with a substantial external debt for the first time in a century.

United States government to act. Act it did, in September 1985, by convening the major economic powers in a five-nation conference. There it was announced that measures would be taken by *all* the central banks to bring the dollar into a more sustainable relation to other currencies. This meant that the Federal Reserve would add to its reserves of foreign currencies and that other central banks would sell dollars to reduce their reserves. Presumably this determination to bring the dollar down would discourage investors from continuing to build up portfolio investments in the United States, without prompting a panicky flight from American bonds and bank accounts.

Finding a Balancing Rate

What does this imply for American policy with respect to the exchange rate? The main objective of that policy is not difficult to explain. Essentially the United States — like all other nations — must try to find a rate of exchange that will balance out the supplies and demands for its currency. The aims of our foreign economic policy can therefore be very simply stated. It is to establish a price for American dollars that will result in an "equilibrium" between America's needs for foreign currencies and foreigners' needs for our own.

Consider what happens if a country does not have such an equilibrium relationship. If the rate is too high, there will be a stimulus for the country to buy imports and a deterrent to its exports. The result will be unemployment in its export industries and as a consequence of the multiplier, unemployment elsewhere. That has been the American problem in the early 1980s, when our overvalued dollar was a major cause of a loss of 1.6 million jobs in exporting industries.

But an undervalued exchange rate also brings problems. Now there is an incentive for foreigners to buy the cheap exports or assets of country A. Foreign money will flow into A's banks, raising the money supply. (Foreign deposits increase *M* because the new deposits do not come from another domestic bank.) As the money supply increases, inflationary pressures also increase. The country will suffer from rising prices.

Thus we can present the problem of exchange rates that are too high or too low in this fashion:

Undervalued (too low) exchange rates lead to inflation.

Overvalued (too high) exchange rates lead to unemployment.

WHAT CAN BE DONE?

What can we do to bring about a better balance between the supply of and the demand for dollars? What can any nation that finds itself in a balance of payments squeeze do to right the balance?

Flexible Rates

Here we must first ask whether a nation in balance of payments difficulties need do anything. For let us not forget that a powerful force exists to right the imbalance by itself. This is the force of the marketplace — the pressure of buying and selling that arises spontaneously from the advantages and disadvantages open to traders on the international marketplace.

Imagine for a moment that we did not have a massive inflow of capital on portfolio account. In that case, as we have already noted, the excess of American demands for foreign currency (to finance imports) over the foreign demand for American dollars (to finance imports into *their* countries) would result in a fall in the price of dollars, exactly as if the dollar were a commodity such as shoes, for which the supply were greater than the demand. As the dollar fell, American goods would become cheaper for foreign buyers; conversely, foreign goods would become dearer. In this way, a system of "flexible" (changeable) exchange rates automatically tends to establish a balance in the supplies of and demands for currencies.

Speculative Flows

As we have seen, the difficulty arises from flows of portfolio capital that enter and leave countries for reasons quite unconnected with the prices of imports or exports. The treasurer of a multinational corporation is not interested in the foreign trade balance of a nation, but in the expected future price of its currency. If he thinks its price will appreciate (go up), it will be to his advantage to buy that nation's currency and wait for gain. If he expects it to fall, he will draw his funds out before the decline in exchange rates costs him money.

Two bad effects follow from this state of affairs. First, the flows of speculative capital prevent currencies from responding to market pressures and reaching prices that will "clear" the market. Second, the key importance of expectations makes capital flows highly unstable, and capable of reversing themselves overnight. Under conditions of a panicky flight, a currency can descend in a matter of weeks or days from "too high" to "too low." This is as disruptive for international trade as it would be if the value of domestic currency were arbitrarily changed from one city to the next, so that we never knew what the purchasing power of New York dollars was going to be in Chicago.

Exchange Controls

Is there not some way of preventing these speculative capital movements? One way that has been used many times is to institute an elaborate system of *exchange controls*. Under such a system, anyone who seeks to buy foreign currency must specify the reason for doing so. An importer of machinery is likely to get all the foreign exchange he or she wants, but an importer of luxury cars, or a would-be tourist is not. Similarly, a foreign corporation seeking dollars to build or buy a plant abroad will have no trouble with the authorities, whereas a corporation seeking only to park excess funds may not get permission to do so.

Most economists regard exchange controls as a poor way to prevent speculative disruptions. By their nature, controls are cumbersome, bureaucratic, and arbitrary. They require decisions as to what kinds of imports are useful and what kinds are not—decisions in which private opinion takes priority over market preferences. They must differentiate between liquid capital that will be used in the receiving country for the financing of new investment and liquid balances that are here only for speculative purposes. These are difficult, perhaps impossible decisions to make rationally. Thus exchange controls are always regarded as a last resort, never a first one. We mention them because many nations, hard pressed to achieve a healthy balance of payments, have been forced to institute such controls.

Fixed Exchange Rates

How else can we achieve the equilibrium rate of exchange we seek? Many economists have begun to ask whether there should not be a return to a different system of international currency exchange—*fixed,* not flexible, rates.

We had such a system of fixed rates for many years after World War II under the Bretton Woods Agreement, signed in 1945 among the major powers. Under this agreement, all major countries announced the value of their currencies with respect to gold (or to other key currencies, such as the dollar.) The dollar, for example, was officially valued at one thirty-fifth of an ounce of gold, or $35 per ounce. These announced rates thereupon regulated the price at which all countries bought or sold foreign exchange. Under special circumstances a nation in international economic difficulties could alter its fixed rate with the permission of the International Monetary Fund (a branch of the United Nations established by the Bretton Woods Agreement to serve as a kind of world central banker), but this was the exception, not the rule.

The Trouble with Fixed Rates

Why did not fixed rates last? The reason must be apparent. Although flows of speculative capital were much less unsettling under the fixed rates system, because they did not affect exchange rates, **there was no automatic self-corrective market mechanism to help keep the balance of payments in equilibrium.**

In those days, the United States was still a major world exporter, and ran a large surplus on its current account. As a result, the dollar should have risen, helping to bring the export surplus to an end. But since the dollar was fixed and could not rise, other countries were forced to devalue—lower their exchange rates—to achieve a viable balance with the United States. These devaluations were unsettling and demoralizing. Thus the system of fixed exchange rates became unpopular precisely because it was fixed and inflexible. Economists welcomed the eventual end of the fixed exchange system, because very few of them foresaw the destabilizing effects that would follow from a system of flexible rates.

International Currency Reform

Is there some manner of having the best of both worlds—a system that permits market pressures to keep exchange rates in some sort of balance, while preventing disruptive capital flows? In the air today are many plans to attempt to do just that. Most of them envisage a new form of international agreement under which exchange rates will be fixed *within a reasonably wide band,* allowing them to respond to normal market pressures but preventing the wild swings that have proved so destructive.

These plans are not easy to devise, for a new fixed-flexible system must allow the limits of the band to change if a nation's international situation changes—for example, if its productivity lags behind or races ahead of that of its competitors. With all its difficulties, however, some such general reform seems likely to come onto the agenda within the coming years. It is not only our own serious position of disequilibrium that must be put to rights, but the general economic stability of the world economy.

looking back

KEY CONCEPTS

A rising or falling dollar means that dollars buy more or less foreign currency, not more or less U.S. goods

1 A rising or falling dollar has a different meaning in international trade than in a domestic economy. Domestically, a rising or falling dollar means that prices have changed, so that a dollar can buy more or less goods. In international exchange, it means only that a dollar can buy more foreign currencies. From the international point of view, when the dollar rises, the exchange value of the currency it is traded against must fall.

Two markets for foreign exchange: current and capital

2 There are two separate markets for dollars (or any other currency). One is made up of the supplies and demands for current transactions—mainly imports and exports—and the other is comprised of supplies and demands for dollars (or other currencies) wanted for capital purposes, whether direct or portfolio investment.

The adverse balance on current account arises mainly from high exchange rates	**3** The U.S. trade deficit reflects an excess of supply over demand in the current market. This is the result of our import surplus. In turn this can be traced to the effects of the high dollar and to the loss of international competitiveness.
The demand for portfolio investment has dominated the market, as foreign funds have sought high U.S. real interest rates	**4** The demand for dollars for capital purposes has been sufficiently large as to overbalance the trade deficit. This demand for foreign capital does not so much reflect an influx of direct investment as portfolio investment, taking advantage of very high U.S. real rates of interest.
Dangers of an exchange rate that is too low—and too high. The ideal rate balances total supplies and demands	**5** We can generalize the international exchange rate problem in this way: A rate that is too high (like the U.S. rate in the mid-1980s) brings an excess of imports and unemployment. A rate that is too low brings an excess of exports and an impetus toward inflation. The ideal of foreign economic policy is therefore to find a price for one's currency that equilibrates the demand for it for all purposes with its supply for all purposes.
Flexible rates balance current accounts but allow speculative inflows to interfere with equilibrium	**6** Under a flexible exchange rate system such as we now have, the excess of demand over supply (or vice versa) tends to bring about an equilibrium exchange rate in the balance on current account. But flexible rates are the source of much trouble from speculative capital flows. There is a strong temptation to control speculative flows with exchange controls—a bureaucratic and inefficient measure of last resort.
Fixed exchange rates avoid speculative problems but bring problems of their own	**7** Fixed exchange rates establish durable exchange rates that greatly reduce the damage from speculative inflows. These fixed rates are changeable downward (devaluation) or upward (revaluation) only through international agreement. Devaluations have also been disruptive of foreign trade.
International currency reform will probably try to gain the advantages of both systems	**8** Many economists today hope for a new currency system that will keep rates flexible within bounds but prevent wide swings as a consequence of capital movements.

ECONOMIC VOCABULARY

QUESTIONS

1. If the rate of exchange falls, does this make traveling abroad cheaper or more expensive? Does it make American exports more or less attractive to a foreign buyer? U.S. Treasury bonds more or less attractive to a German investor?

2. Explain why a fall in the exchange rate of the dollar against francs must be exactly the same as a rise in the exchange rate of francs against dollars.

3. If you were the treasurer of an international corporation, would you seek to find the place of highest return for your liquid capital? Why would the inflation rate enter into your calculations? Would you be concerned about the possible wider repercussions of your business decision? Do you think you could be — and still be an effective treasurer?

CHAPTER 38
Where Are We Headed?

a look ahead

At the end of our book, we step back for a long historic overview.

1 This leads us to consider the relationship of the market system to societies in different stages of historic evolution.

2 From here we look to the development of the system of planning—first in a centrally planned system such as the USSR, then as a direction in which market societies themselves seem to be slowly moving.

3 Last, we try to take the measure of the strengths and weaknesses of market and planned economic societies, and to identify the problems shared by both.

At the end of our book we come back to the theme of the beginning — the trajectory of economic history. In fact, we now face for the first time those commanding but obscure questions we touched on in our opening pages: Where is capitalism headed? What are the signs and omens for the future of our kind of society? What, if anything, can be hazarded about the years ahead?

These are questions that go far beyond the competence of economists. In the end it will be considerations of political morale and belief, of social cohesion, of ideology and conviction that determine the future of the United States or Japan or France or Sweden just as much as, or more than, their common economic mechanisms. Nevertheless, there are some things an economist can say about the future, for there are a few lessons we have learned about the workings of capitalism and of socialism that bear on, even if they do not determine, the shape of things to come.

STAGES OF ECONOMIC DEVELOPMENT

We might well begin an appraisal by taking a last survey of the array of economic systems that mark our times. It is, at first glance, an extraordinary assortment: We find, in this fourth quarter of the twentieth century, a spectrum of economic organization that represents virtually every stage in economic history, from the earliest and most primitive. But at second look, a significant pattern can be seen within this seemingly disordered assemblage. The few remaining wholly traditional economies, such as those of the South Seas, have not yet begun to move into the mainstream of economic development. A much larger group of underdeveloped nations have just commenced their development efforts and are now coping with the problems preparatory to industrialization. Going yet further along we find the economies of full command, such as China and Russia. Here we find national communities that are (or recently were) wrestling with the gigantic task of rapid massive modernization. Finally, we pass to the market economies of the West, to encounter societies with their developmental days behind them, now concerned with the operation of high-consumption economic systems.

The categorization suggests a very important general conclusion. The economic structures of nations today bear an integral relation with their stage of economic development. Acts of foreign intervention aside, the choice of command or market systems is not just the outcome of political considerations or ideologies and preferences. It is also, and perhaps primarily, the result of functional requirements that are very different at different levels of economic achievement.

Inception of Growth

We have already noted this connection in our discussion of the underdeveloped areas. Now, however, we can place what we have learned into a wider frame of reference. For if we compare the trend of events in the underdeveloped economies with the equivalent stage of development in Western history, we see a significant

694

point of resemblance between the two. The emergence of command in the development-minded countries today has a parallel in the mercantile era, when the Western nations also received a powerful impetus toward industrialization under the organizing influence of the "industry-minded" governments of the seventeenth and early eighteenth centuries.

Thereafter, to be sure, the resemblance ceases. In the West, following the first push of mercantilism, it was the market mechanism that provided the main directive force for growth; in the underdeveloped lands, as we have seen, this influence is likely to be preempted to a much larger extent by political and economic command.

Present vs. Past

Three main reasons lie behind his divergence of paths. **First, the underdeveloped areas today start from a different level than did the West in the seventeenth and eighteenth centuries.** Not only have the actual institutions of the market not yet appeared in many backward lands, but the whole process of acculturation has failed to duplicate that of the West. In many ways — not all of them economic — the West was ready for industrial development. A similar readiness is not in evidence in the majority of the backward lands today, with the result that development, far from evincing itself as a spontaneous process, comes about as the result of enforced and imposed change.

Second, the West was able to mount its development effort in leisurely tempo. This is not to say that its rate of growth was slow or that strong pressures did not weigh upon many Western countries, arousing within them feelings of dissatisfaction with their progress. Yet the situation was unlike that of the backward areas today. Here immense pressures, both of population growth and of political impatience, create an overwhelming need and desire for speed. As a result, the process of growth is not allowed to mature quietly in the background of history, as it did for much of the West, but has been placed at the very center of political and social attention.

Finally, in a manner denied to the West, underdeveloped countries can see ahead of them the goal they seek to reach. Suffering from so many handicaps, they enjoy one not inconsiderable advantage. Because they are the rearguard rather than the vanguard, they know where they are going. They do not wish to reach this goal, however, by retreading the painful and laborious path marked out by the West. Rather, they intend to shortcut it, to move directly to their chosen destination by utilizing the mechanisms of command to bring about the great alterations that must be made.

Is Command Successful?

Can economic command significantly compress and accelerate the growth process? The remarkable performance of the Soviet Union suggests that it can. In 1920 Russia was but a minor figure in the economic councils of the world. Today it is a country whose economic achievements bear comparison with those of the United States. Russia has many economic problems that we will examine shortly. But no one can deny that it has made tremendous economic progress. According to a report released by the Central Intelligence Agency in late 1982, Soviet per capita GNP has grown at an average annual rate of 4.8 percent over the last three decades, considerably faster than most of the Western capitalist nations. Soviet living standards remain drab and cramped compared with those of capitalist nations, but the improvement in average well-being has been sustained and marked.*

The case of China is less clear-cut. Until the famine disaster of 1959–60, Chinese economic growth was double or triple that of India. During the turbulent years of the Cultural Revolution, economic growth was seriously set back as a consequence of a zealous pursuit of ideological purity that paid scant attention to hard realities. Since then China has embarked on a remarkable experiment in which socialist goals are combined with a high degree of capitalistic enterprise, and with a welcoming policy toward Western direct investment. It is still much too early to know how this tremendous experiment will turn out. Initial reports seem to indicate that a new burst of energy and enthusiasm has been introduced into the Chinese economy as the profit motive has been allowed to find much freer expression. Whether in the end there will be a new amalgam of capitalist motives and socialist objectives, we will have to wait to find out.

It is certainly wise not to exaggerate the advantages of a command system. If it holds the potential for an all-out attack on backwardness, it also contains the possibilities of substantial failure, as in the disaster of the planned Polish economy. The mere existence of a will to plan is no guarantee that the plans will be well drawn or well carried out or reasonably well obeyed.

In addition, the striking economic success demonstrated by some market-run systems makes it impossible to assert categorically that only a command system can move a traditional society off dead center. Thus there may be more South Koreas and Singapores in the future, as well as more Soviet Unions. But looking at the very low level of development in much of the fourth world and the antipathy of many African, Asian, and Latin American countries for Western capitalist nations, it seems likely that command systems of one kind or another will play a continuing role in bringing development to the still lagging areas of the world.

PLANNING AND ITS PROBLEMS

What are the advantages, what are the problems of planning? The subject is large enough to fill many books, and this short chapter will not attempt to discuss the full economics of planning. But a few general remarks may serve as an introduction to the subject.

How is planning carried out? This question goes to the heart of the matter, for all

* *New York Times,* December 26, 1982.

planned economies have found their central difficulty in going from the vision of a general objective to the actual attainment of that objective in fact. It is one thing to plan for 6 percent growth, another to issue the directives to bring forth just the right amounts of (quite literally) hundreds of thousands of items, so that 6 percent growth will result.

Soviet Planning

In the Soviet Union this complicated planning mechanism is carried out in successive stages. The overall objectives are originally formulated by the Gosplan, the state planning agency. The long-term overall plan is then broken down into shorter one-year plans. These one-year plans, specifying the output of major sectors of industry, are then transmitted to various governmental ministries concerned with, for example, steel production, transportation, lumbering, and so forth. In turn, the ministries refer the one-year plans further down the line to the heads of large industrial plants, to experts and advisers, and so on. At each stage, the overall plan is thus unraveled into its subsidiary components, until finally the threads have been traced as far back as is feasible along the productive process — typically, to the officials in charge of actual factory operations.

The factory manager, of, for instance, a coking operation is given a planned objective for the next year, specifying the output needed from his plant. He confers with his production engineers, considers the condition of his machinery, the availability of his labor force, and then transmits his requirements for meeting the objective back upward along the hierarchy. In this way, just as "demand" is transmitted downward along the chain of command, the exigencies of "supply" flow back upward, finally reaching the top command of the planning authority, the Gosplan itself.

Success Indicators

The coordination and integration of these plans is a tremendously complicated task. Recently the Soviets adopted techniques of computer analysis which have considerably simplified the problem. Even with sophisticated planning techniques, however, the process is bureaucratic, cumbersome, slow, and mistake-prone. A Russian factory manager has very little leeway in what he produces or in the combination of factors that he uses for production. Both inputs and outputs are carefully specified for him in his plan. What the manager *is* supposed to do is to beat the plan, by overproducing the items that have been assigned to his plant. Indeed, from 30 to 50 percent of a manager's pay will depend on bonuses tied directly to his overfulfillment of the plan, so that he has a very great personal incentive to exceed the output "success indicators" set for him.

All this seems sensible enough. Trouble comes, however, because the manager's drive to exceed his factory's quota tends to distort the productive effort from the receivers' point of view. For example, if the target for a textile factory is set in terms of yards of cloth, there is every temptation to weave the cloth as loosely as possible, to get the maximum yardage out of a given amount of thread. Or if the plan merely calls for tonnages of output, there is every incentive to skimp on design or finish or quality, in order to concentrate on sheer weight. A cartoon in the Russian satirical magazine *Krokodil* shows a nail factory proudly displaying its record output: one gigantic nail suspended from an immense gantry crane. On the other hand, if a nail factory has its output specified in terms of the *numbers* of nails it produces, its incentive to overfulfill this "success indicator" is apt to result in the production of very small or thin nails.

Profit as a "Success Indicator"

For a time, the wind for reform in the Soviet Union blew from quite another quarter. Led by economist E. G. Liberman, there was a growing demand that the misleading plan directives of weight, length, etc., be subordinated to a new

SOCIALISM AND COMMUNISM

What is the difference between *socialism* and *communism?* In the West, *socialism* implies an adherence to democratic political mechanisms, whereas *communism* does not. But within the socialist bloc there is another interesting difference of definition. Socialism there represents a stage of development in which it is still necessary to use "bourgeois" incentives in order to make the economy function; that is, people must be paid in proportion to the "value" of their work. Under communism, a new form of human society will presumably have been achieved in which these selfish incentives will no longer be needed. Then will come the time when society will be able to put into effect Karl Marx's famous description of communism: "From each according to his ability; to each according to his need."

In a true communist economy—the final terminus of economic evolution according to Marx—there were hints that the necessary but humdrum tasks of production and distribution would take place by the voluntary cooperation of all citizens, and society would turn its serious attention to matters of cultural and humanistic importance. Indeed, in a famous passage in *State and Revolution*, Lenin described the activities of administering a socialist state as having been simplified by the previous stage of capitalism "to the utmost, till they have become the extraordinarily simple operations of watching, recording, and issuing receipts, within the reach of anybody who can read and who knows the first four rules of arithmetic."

"success indicator" independently capable of guiding the manager to results that will make sense from the overall point of view. And what is that overriding indicator? It was the *profit* that a factory manager could make for the enterprise!

We should note several things about this profit. To begin with, it was not supposed to arise from price manipulations. Factory managers were to continue to operate with the prices established by planners; but they were to *sell* their output and *buy* their input, rather than merely deliver or accept them. This meant that each factory was to be responsive to the particular needs of its customers if it wished to dispose of its output. In the same way, of course, its own suppliers would have to be responsive to the factory's needs if the suppliers were to get the factory's business.

Second, the profit would belong not to the factory or its managers; but to the state. A portion of the profit would indeed be allocated for bonuses and other rewards, so that there would be a direct incentive to run the plant efficiently, but the bulk of the earnings would be transferred to the state.

The Market as a Planning Tool

Thus profits were to be used as an efficiency-maximizing indicator, just as we saw them used in our study of microeconomics.

Indeed, to view the change even more broadly, we can see that the reintroduction of the use of profits implied a deliberate return to the use of the *market mechanism* as a means of achieving economic efficiency. Not only profits but also interest charges—a capitalist term it would have been heresy to mention in the days of Stalin—were to be introduced into the planning mechanism to allow factory managers to determine for themselves what was the most efficient thing to do, both for their enterprises and for the economy as a whole.

This drift toward a market mechanism is still officially resisted in the Soviet Union at least up to the new leadership of Gorbachev, and we do not know how far it will ultimately progress. The objectives of the most recent plans have called for a much greater emphasis on consumer goods, and speak of "an extensive use of economic-mathematical methods," which implies a continuing reliance on the computer rather than a rapid movement in the direction of freer trade. Nonetheless, economists talk of *torgovot* (trading) instead of *snabzhat* (allocating). Gradually, market mechanisms seem to be insinuating themselves into the Soviet economic system. It is still not a market society—far from it—but that is the direction of change.

Market Socialism

Meanwhile, the trend toward the market has proceeded much further in a large part of Eastern Europe—above all in Hungary and Yugoslavia. There, the market rules very nearly as supreme as it does in Western capitalist countries. Yet both

PLANNING UNDER LENIN AND STALIN

Official literature of the Communist movement gives little guidance for running a socialist society. Marx's *Das Kapital,* the seminal work of communism, was entirely devoted to a study of capitalism; and in those few essays in which Marx looked to the future, his gaze rarely traveled beyond the watershed of the revolutionary act itself. With the achievement of the revolution, Marx thought, a temporary regime known as "the dictatorship of the proletariat" would take over the transition from capitalism to socialism, and thereafter a "planned socialist economy" would emerge as the first step toward a still less specified "communism."

Many of the problems of early Soviet history sprang from the total absence, on the part of its rulers, of any comprehension of the staggering difficulties of planning in fact rather than in thought. The initial Soviet attempt to run the economy was a disastrous failure. Under inept management (and often cavalier disregard of "bourgeois" concerns with factory management), industrial output declined precipitously; by 1920 it had fallen to *14 percent* of prewar levels. As goods available to the peasants became scarcer, the peasants themselves were less and less willing to acquiesce in giving up food to the cities. The result was a wild inflation followed by a degeneration into an economy of semibarter. For a while, toward the end of 1920, the system threatened to break down completely.

To forestall the impending collapse, in 1921 Lenin instituted a New Economic Policy, the so-called NEP. This was a return toward a market system and a partial reconstitution of actual capitalism. Retail trade, for instance, was opened again to private ownership and operation. Small-scale industry also reverted to private direction. Most important, the farms were no longer requisitioned but operated as profit-making units. Only the "commanding heights" of industry and finance were retained in government hands.

There ensued for several years a bitter debate about the course of action to follow next. While the basic aim of the Soviet government was still to industrialize and to socialize (i.e., to replace the private ownership of the means of production by state ownership), the question was how fast to move ahead—and, indeed, *how* to move ahead. The pace of industrialization hinged critically on one highly uncertain factor; the willingness of the large, private peasant sector to deliver food for sustaining city workers. To what extent, therefore, should the need for additional capital goods be sacrificed in order to turn out the consumption goods that could be used as an inducement for peasant cooperation?

The argument was never truly resolved. In 1927 Stalin moved into command and the difficult question of how much to appease the unwilling peasant disappeared. Stalin simply made the ruthless decision to appease him not at all, but to *coerce* him by collectivizing his holdings.

The collectivization process solved in one swoop the problem of securing the essential transfer of food from the farm to the city, but it did so at a frightful social (and economic) cost. Many peasants slaughtered their livestock rather than hand it over to the new collective farms; others waged outright war of practiced sabotage. In reprisal, the authorities acted with brutal force. An estimated five million "kulaks" (rich peasants) were executed or put in labor camps, while in the cities an equally relentless policy showed itself vis-à-vis labor. Workers were summarily ordered to the tasks required by the central authorities. The right to strike was forbidden, and the trade unions were reduced to impotence. Speedups were widely applied, and living conditions were allowed to deteriorate to very low levels.

The history of this period of forced industrialization has left abiding scars on Russian society. It is well for us, nonetheless, to attempt to view it with some objectivity. If the extremes to which the Stalinist authorities went were extraordinary, often unpardonable, and perhaps self-defeating, we must bear in mind that industrialization on the grand scale has always been wrenching, always accompanied by economic sacrifice, and always carried out by the more or less authoritarian use of power.

We might note in passing that universal male suffrage was not gained in England until the late 1860s and 1870s; Gunnar Myrdal, in *Rich Lands and Poor,* quotes Aneurin Bevan: "It is highly doubtful whether the achievements of the Industrial Revolution would have been permitted if the franchise had been universal. It is very doubtful because a great deal of the capital aggregations that we are at present enjoying are the results of the wages that our fathers went without."

countries certainly consider themselves socialist economies. As in the USSR, enterprise profits do not go to the "owners" of the business, but are distributed as incentive bonuses or used for investment or other purposes under the overall guidance of the state. And again as in the USSR, the market is used as a deliberate instrument of social control, rather than as an institution that is above question.

Thus, the main determination of investment, the direction of development of consumer goods, the basic distribution of income — all continue to be matters established at the center as part of a planned economy. More and more, however, this central plan is allowed to realize itself through the profit-seeking operations of semi-autonomous firms, rather than through being imposed in full detail upon the economy.*

* One of the important, truly socialist aspects of the Yugoslav economy is that factory managers are formally hired and fired and supervised by workers' councils elected from within the factory. To what degree these councils represent a true democratization of factory life, or to what extent they are only vehicles for political control, we do not yet know.

Market vs. Plan

The drift of planning toward markets raises a question of fundamental importance. Why plan at all? Why not let the market take over the task of coordination that has proved such a formidable hurdle for industrial planners, for is not the market itself a planning mechanism?

After all, in the market the signal of profitability serves as the guide for allocation of resources and labor. Entrepreneurs, anticipating or following demand, risk private funds in the construction of the facilities that they hope the future will require. Meanwhile, as these industrial salients grow, smaller satellite industries grow along with them to cater to their needs.

The flow of materials is thus regulated in every sector by the forces of private demand making themselves known by the signal of rising or falling prices. At every moment there emanates from the growing industries a magnetic pull of demand on secondary industries, while in turn, the growth salients themselves are guided, spurred or slowed down by the pressure of demand from the ultimate buying public. And all the while, counterposed to these pulls of demand, are the obduracies of supply — the cost schedules of the producers themselves. In the crossfire of demand and supply exists a marvelously sensitive social instrument for the integration of the overall economic effort of expansion.

Economies in Mid-Development

This extraordinary integrative capacity of market systems returns us to the consideration of the suitability of various economic control mechanisms to different stages of development. We have seen that central planning is likely to be necessary to move stagnant, traditional economies off dead center. Once the development process is well under way, however, the relative functional merits of the market and the command mechanisms begin to change. After planning has done its massive tasks — enforcing economic and social change, creating an industrial sector, rationalizing agriculture — another problem begins to assume ever more importance. This is *the problem of efficiency*, of dovetailing the innumerable productive efforts of society into a single coherent and smoothly functioning whole.

In the flush period of mid-development the market mechanism easily outperforms the command apparatus as a means of carrying out this complex coordinating task. Every profit-seeking entrepreneur, every industrial salesman, every cost-conscious purchasing agent becomes in effect part of a gigantic and continuously alert planning system within the market economy. Command systems do not easily duplicate their efforts. Bottlenecks, unusable output, shortages, waste, and a cumbersome hierarchy of bureaucratic forms and officials typically interfere with the maximum efficiency of the planned economy in midgrowth.

What we see here is not just a passing problem, easily ironed out. One of the critical lessons of the twentieth century is that the word *planning* is exceedingly easy to pronounce and exceedingly difficult to spell out. When targets are still relatively simple, and the priorities of action beyond dispute — as in the case of a nation wrenching itself from the stagnation of an ineffective regime — planning can produce miracles. **But when the economy reaches a certain degree of complexity, in which the coordination of ten activities gives way to the coordination of ten thousand, innumerable problems arise, because planned economies enjoy no natural congruence between private action and public necessity.**

Here is where the market comes into its own. As we know from our study of micro theory, each firm must combine its factors of production with one eye on their relative costs and the other on their respective productivities, finally bringing about a mix in which each factor is used as effectively as possible, given its cost. Thus in seeking only to maximize their own profits, the units in a market system inadvertently tend also to maximize the efficiency of the system as a whole.

Private Aims, Public Goals

Even more remarkable: One operating rule alone suffices to bring about this extraordinary conjunction of private aims and public goals. *That single rule is to maximize profits.* By concentrating on that one criterion of success and not by trying to maximize output in physical terms or by trying to live by a complicated book of regulations, entrepreneurs in a competitive environment do in fact bring the system toward efficiency. In other words, **profits are not only a source of privileged income, but also an enormously versatile and useful "success indicator" for a system that is trying to squeeze as much output as possible from its given inputs.**

Furthermore, the market mechanism solves the economic problem with a minimum of social and political controls. Impelled by the drives inherent in a market society, the individual marketer fulfills his public economic function without constant attention from the authorities. In contradistinction to his counterpart in a centralized command society, who is often prodded, cajoled, or even threatened to act in ways that do not appeal to his self-interest, the classical marketer obeys the peremptory demands of the market as a voluntary exercise of his own economic "freedom."

Thus it is not surprising that we find many of the motivating principles of the market being introduced into command societies. For as these societies settle into more or less established routines, they too can utilize the pressure of want and the pull of pecuniary desire to facilitate the fulfillment of their basic plans.

Economic freedom, as we know it in the West, is not yet a reality or even an official objective in any of these countries. The right to strike, for example, is not recognized, and nothing like the fluid consumer-responsive market system is allowed to exert its unimpeded influence on the general direction of economic development. But the introduction of more and more discretion at the factory level argues strongly that some principles of the market society are apt to find their place in planned societies at an appropriate stage of economic development.

High Consumption Economies

Thus our survey of successive stages of development brings us to a consideration of Western economic society; that is, to the advanced economies that have progressed beyond the need for forced industrialization and now enter the stage of high consumption.

From our foregoing discussion, it is clear that the market mechanism finds its most natural application in this fortunate period of economic evolution. Insofar as the advanced Western societies have reached a stage in which the consumer is not only permitted but encouraged to impose personal wants on the direction of economic activity, there is little doubt that the market mechanism fulfills the prevailing social purpose more effectively than any other.

1. PUBLIC GOODS. Nonetheless, as we have already noted, the market is not without its own grave problems, even in this regard. **First, the market is an inefficient instrument for provisioning societies — even rich societies — with those goods and services for which no price tag exists, such as education or local government services or public health facilities.**

A market society buys such public goods by allocating a certain amount of taxes for these purposes. Its citizens, however, tend to feel these taxes as an exaction in contrast with the items they voluntarily buy. Typically, therefore, a market society underallocates resources to education, city government, public health or recreation, since it has no means of bidding funds into these areas, in competition with the powerful means of bidding them into autos or clothes or personal insurance.

2. INCOME DISTRIBUTION. A second and perhaps even deeper-seated failing of the market system is its application of a strictly economic calculus to the satisfaction of human wants and needs. As we said before, the market is an assiduous servant of the wealthy, but an indifferent servant of the poor. Thus it presents us with the anomaly of a surplus of luxury housing existing side by side with a shortage of inexpensive housing, although the social need for the latter is incontestably greater than for the former. Or it pours energy and resources into the multiplication of luxuries for which the wealthier classes offer a market, while allowing more basic needs of the poor to go unheeded and unmet.

3. EXTERNALITIES. These shortcomings are aggravated by the tendency of market systems to ignore externalities. **The failure to capture social costs within the calculus of private benefits leads to patterns of production that are often freighted with serious consequences.** These externalities can be corrected within the market framework, but only by the imposition of an element of command — of political decision — over the workings of the market, whether by taxes, subsidies, or outright regulation.

In considering the side effects of market systems, we should not forget that elusive but very important externality we call "the quality of life." We count as gains the increases in GNP that result from the market system, but we do not give much heed to the commercialism, the trivialization, the psychological frustration and dissatisfaction that also accompany so much market activity.

4. MALFUNCTIONS. This recital of the failings of a market system ends with the micro and macro ills that spring up as a consequence of its operations. We know the severity and extent of these maladies, having just finished an examination of micro and macro economics. But it is well to remember that inflation and unemployment, the urban plight and the threat to the environment are all to some degree the products of the hugely vital, but careless and even dangerous momentum that the market imparts to the social process. We must beware of linking every social ill with the economic system in which it appears, but it would be equally foolish to absolve the market from all responsibility for the malfunctions that threaten our well-being.

The Rise of Planning

There is no need to dwell further on the deficiencies of the market system. In one way or another, all its difficulties are indicative of one central weakness. This is the inability of the market system to formulate stimuli or restraints other than those that arise from the marketplace itself.

So long as the public need roughly coincides with the sum of the private interests to which the market automatically attends, this failing of the market system is a minor one. But in an advanced economic society, it tends to become ever more important. As primary wants become satisfied, the public aim turns toward stability and security, objectives not attainable without a degree of public control. As technological organization becomes more complex and massive, again a public need arises to contain the new agglomerations of economic power. So, too, as wealth increases, pressure for education, urban improvement, welfare and the like comes to the fore, not only as an indication of the public conscience, but as a functioning requirement of a mature society. And finally, the public stimulus and management of continued growth take on increased political urgency as the ecological problems of industrial societies multiply.

We have already paid much attention to the rise of planning in the advanced market societies as a corrective force to deal with just such problems. Now we can generalize the economic meaning of this trend. Planning arises in the advanced market societies to offset their inherent goal-setting weaknesses, just as the market mechanism arises in advanced command societies to offset their inherent motivational weaknesses. In other words, planning and market mechanisms, in those societies which have begun to enter the stage of high consumption, are not mutually incompatible. On the contrary, they powerfully supplement and support one another.

Common Problems

What we see today is the appearance of similar problems in advanced industrial societies.

When we examine capitalism and socialism, we usually pay special attention to the problems that separate and distinguish these two kinds of societies. Here it is important to realize that they are also bound together by certain common difficulties.

What is the nature of these overarching problems? As we would expect, they stem from the very technical capability and social organization that bring similar economic mechanisms into being. Three problems in particular seem of major importance.

1. CONTROL OVER TECHNOLOGY. One of the most important attributes of modern history is lodged in a striking difference between two kinds of knowledge: the knowledge we acquire in physics, chemistry, engineering, and other sciences, and that which we gain in the sphere of social or political or moral activity. The difference is that knowledge in some sciences is cumulative and builds on itself, whereas knowledge in the social sphere does not. The merest beginner in biology soon knows more than the greatest biologist of a century ago. By way of contrast, the veteran student (or practitioner) of government, of social relations, of moral philosophy is aware of his modest stature in comparison with the great social and moral philosophers of the past.

The result is that all modern societies tend to find that their technological capabilities are constantly increasing, while the social, political, and moral institutions by which those capabilities are controlled cannot match the challenges with which they are faced. Television, for example, is an immense force for cultural homogenization; medical technology changes the composition of society by altering its age groups and life expectancy; rapid transportation vastly increases mobility and social horizons; and the obliterative power of nuclear arms casts a pervasive anxiety over all of life. All these technologically rooted developments fundamentally alter the conditions and problems of life, but we do not know what social, political, and moral responses are appropriate to them. As a result, all modern societies — socialist and capitalist — experience the feeling of being at the mercy of a technological and scientific impetus that shapes the lives of their citizens in ways that cannot be accurately foreseen nor adequately controlled.

2. THE PROBLEM OF PARTICIPATION. The second problem derives from the first. Because advanced societies are characterized by high levels of technology, they are necessarily marked by a high degree of organization. The technology of our era depends on the cooperation of vast masses of men, some at the levels of production, some at the levels of administration. The common undergirding of all advanced industrial societies lies not alone in their gigantic instrumentalities of production, but in their equally essential and vast instrumentalities of administration, whether these be called corporations, production ministries, or government agencies.

The problem is then how the citizen is to find a place for his or her individuality in the midst of so much organization; how he or she is to express his or her voice in the direction of affairs, when so much bureaucratic management is inescapable; how he or she is to participate in a world whose technological structure calls for ever more order and coordination. This is a matter which, like the sweeping imperative of technology, affects both capitalism and socialism. In both kinds of societies, individuals feel overwhelmed by the impersonality of the

A PERSONAL VIEW ABOUT PLANNING

For reasons that are strewn throughout these pages, we expect that the long-term trend in most capitalist nations will be toward some kind of planning. There are many such kinds, and that which works in one capitalist nation, such as Japan, may be totally inapplicable to another, like Italy or Canada or ourselves. Each nation must find its own way of devising macro and micro policies.

Thus we do not predict any particular direction of kind of planning for the United States. What we do expect is that the problems and market forces and technological capabilities of our age will blur the present distinction between "public" and "private" spheres, moving us, together with other capitalisms, in a direction that will have more business-government integration, more labor-management coordination, perhaps more national insulation against international competition.

This is a view which is deplored by the Left and denounced by the Right. Beyond that, both declare that planning does not work. They are certainly correct that planning does not work very well. What clearer evidence could there be for that than the universal presence of a crisis in all capitalist nations, despite the drift into planning of various kinds? But this objection misses a key consideration. It is that no manner of guiding society, from the most centralized to the most laissez-faire, can be expected to produce a smoothly working system in the face of today's social, political, and technological forces. The very elements that underlie our contemporary troubles — the tensions that divide the rich and poor nations, the impact of technologies of awesome power, the narrowing of ecological tolerances, the disappearance of the public fatalism of the past — must trouble any kind of economic system and any kind of government. It is not capitalism alone that is in crisis, but all modern industrial society. A realistic attitude toward planning is not that it should work well, but that it should work *well enough.* That seems a goal within reach.

work process, impotent before the power of huge enterprises — above all, the state itself — and frustrated at an inability to participate in decisions that seem more and more beyond any possibility of personal influence.

No doubt much can be done to increase the feeling of individual participation in the making of the future, especially in those nations that still deny elementary political freedoms. But there remains a recalcitrant problem of how the quest for increased individual decision-making and participation can be reconciled with the organizational demands imposed by the technology on which all advanced societies depend. This is a problem that is likely to trouble societies — capitalist or socialist

— as long as technology itself rests on integrated processes of production and requires centralized organs of administration and control.

3. THE PROBLEM OF THE ENVIRONMENT. All industrial nations may face an era in which economic growth begins to absorb resources at rates faster than we are able to provide them with new technologies; **and all industrialized societies — indeed, the whole world — may soon enter an era in which environmental limitations come into apparent conflict with expectations of growth.**

In this period, industrial socialist and capitalist nations again seem likely to share common problems — not only in overcoming environmental limits to growth, but in achieving social harmony under conditions of increasing resource diversion toward public rather than private goods.* Here too, similar social and political problems may override differences in economic institutions and ideologies.

Envoi

In a larger sense, then, we go beyond economics to the common human adventure in which economic systems are only alternate routes conducting humanity toward a common destination. Perhaps it is well that we end our survey of economics with the recognition that the long history of the market system does not project us onto a final stage in social history. Rather, we arrive at a state in which some kinds of problems — the pitifully simple problems of producing and distributing goods — find resolution, only to reveal vastly larger problems springing from the very technology and organization that supplied the earlier answers.

* Are there absolute resource limits to growth in the very long run? That would take us into a discussion of such topics as the greenhouse effect, about which neither science nor economics can yet give definite answers.

looking back

KEY CONCEPTS

The stages of economic development in the West

1 The economic structures of nations, especially with respect to market, tradition, and command, seem to bear a relation to their stages of economic development. In the West, we have begun with traditional societies, used command to mobilize ourselves for growth, and then developed full market mechanisms.

Underdeveloped countries will probably rely less on the market

2 We do not know if the underdeveloped nations will follow this pattern, but their late start, their extreme needs, and their ability to "foresee" the future suggest that the market will play a lesser role.

The problem of planning is the coordination of the economy. This is difficult to achieve without the "success indicator" of profit

3 Planning is a complex and difficult means of running an industrial society. The main task is to coordinate the myriad activities of society into a consistent whole. This is the task that the market performs easily through the "success indicator" of profit. The challenge for centrally planned systems has been to devise other success indicators. So far this has not been very successful, and centrally planned systems have been extremely inefficient, once their initial days of easy growth are over.

Many socialist economies are experimenting with limited market mechanisms

4 As a result many socialist economists are cautiously introducing aspects of the market to remedy the frictions and inefficiencies of planning. Profit maximization provides a self-enforcing "success indicator" that works to direct private action into the channels directed by market preference.

Market systems have their own failures. Hence high consumption market systems drift toward planning

5 Nevertheless, market systems develop their own problems. They do not provide for public goods. They distribute income in ways that fail to satisfy moral criteria. They cannot reflect externalities. And they have their particular malfunctions, such as instability. All these difficulties lie at the heart of the global drift of high-consumption market systems toward a greater degree of policy and planning.

Certain problems seem to transcend the market/planning division: controlling technology, assuring economic and political participation, and safeguarding the environment.

6 Looking beyond the present we can discern three problems that high-consumption economies seem to share, whether market or planned. They are: controlling their technologies; arranging for the participation of workers and citizens in the administration of economic as well as political affairs; and maintaining satisfactory economic performance within an increasingly fragile and restrictive ecological environment.

ECONOMIC VOCABULARY

Success indicator   697
Socialism and communism   698

Market socialism   699

QUESTIONS

1. How do you account for the presence in the world today of such radically different forms of economic organization as Switzerland and Saudi Arabia, Canada and China?

2. What is meant by the congruence between self-interest and public requirement in a market economy? Is this the same as the Invisible Hand? Does it mean that whatever is good for General Motors is good for America? That General Motors will automatically do whatever is good for America?

3. Do you think that a capitalist system is essential for economic freedom? If so, how do you explain the fact that many people think that Yugoslavia is "freer" than South Africa? Is it possible to make precise statements about this issue? General statements?

4. What technological process seems to you to require control? Arms? Urbanization? Genetic experimentation?

5. Take a moment to think about how you think modern society ought to be organized. If you were president, what three things would you put at the top of your economic agenda?

Glossary

Accelerator effect The effect — sometimes stimulating, sometimes depressing — exerted on investment by changes in consumption expenditure. Also *acceleration principle.*

Allocation The act of apportioning or distributing resources or incomes.

Antitrust legislation Legislation designed to minimize or prevent monopolistic behavior or monopolistic market structures.

Appreciation of exchange A rise in the ability of one nation's currency to buy the currency of another nation.

Average productivity The contribution to output of the average unit of any input. This is obtained by dividing total output by the number of units of the input. It is not the same as the contribution of the last, or marginal unit.

Average propensity to consume The relation between consumption and income, C/Y. It differs from the marginal propensity $\Delta C/\Delta Y$ because the latter is concerned only with spending out of marginal incomes.

Average propensity to save The relation between saving and income S/Y. It differs from the marginal propensity $\Delta S/\Delta Y$ because the latter is concerned only with saving out of marginal income.

Automatic stabilizers Institutional provisions that result in automatic stimulation of the economy in recession times and dampening of it in boom times. The counter-cyclical flows of unemployment insurance or farm subsidies, and the effect on consumption of the graduated income tax are key elements in these stabilizers.

Backward-bending supply curve A supply curve of labor services that displays a preference for fewer hours of labor (more leisure) when the price of labor rises above a certain level.

Balance of payments A set of accounts that records transactions between two countries. See *balance on capital* and *current accounts.*

Balance on capital account The net sum of demands and supplies for foreign exchange for all items on capital account, mainly direct and portfolio investment.

Balance on current account The net sum of demands for and supplies of foreign exchange for all items on current account, mainly merchandise exports and imports and similar transactions.

Bonds Obligations issued by private or public institutions with fixed dates of repayment and stated interest rates or coupons. See *yields.*

"Bottom" The level of GNP when income is entirely used for consumption, and investment is therefore zero.

Budget The amount of spending power possessed by an economic actor.

Business cycles The more or less regular recurrence of recession and prosperity.

Capital Wealth in an abstract form produced by capitalism. Also often used to refer to a financial sum of wealth.

Capital goods Final output used for production, not consumption. See *investment*.

Capitalism An economic system oriented toward the accumulation of capital (or generalized, abstract wealth), coordinated by a market system in which land, labor, and capital have become "factors of production."

Capitalization Calculation of a sum of wealth by dividing a flow of income by a rate of interest. A piece of land that yields an income of $100 is capitalized at $1,000 if interest rates are 10 percent ($1,000 ÷ 0.10 = $100) or at $500 if interest rates are 20 percent.

Capital/output ratio Relationship between the values of the capital stock and the flow of output of a firm, industry, or nation. Marginal capital/output ratios relate increases in output to increases in the capital stock.

Ceteris paribus Latin phrase meaning "other things being equal." The phrase refers to the need to allow for variations in the conditions that affect an experiment or an observation. For example, *ceteris paribus* requires us to make allowance for changes in income or taste when we are seeking to establish the relation of quantity demanded and price.

Circular flow The continuous circuit of spending, from households to firms and from firms back to households.

Claims Legal rights on income or wealth.

Clearing markets A market condition in which quantities demanded just balance quantities supplied.

Cobwebs Erratic jumps in prices that characterize markets which do not constantly adjust over time. Cobwebs may describe a sequence of prices that "explode" or oscillate or gradually converge to equilibrium.

Comparative advantage The relative edge enjoyed by one nation (or region or economic actor) in producing one commodity compared to another. A country can have a comparative advantage in producing a commodity even if its absolute productivity in that commodity is less than that of its trading partner.

Competition The vying of buyers and sellers in a marketplace. Competition has two aspects: (1) the contest of buyers against sellers, (2) the mutual rivalry of sellers against sellers and buyers against buyers.

Complement The technical linkage of commodities, such as cars and gasoline. Increases in the demand for a commodity automatically raise the demand for its complement.

Concentration The degree of market control enjoyed by the largest firms in an industry. Concentration ratios often measure the percentage of industry sales enjoyed by the largest four or eight firms.

Conglomerates Large corporations, usually formed by merger, that operate in widely different markets.

Constraints Barriers or boundaries to desired behavior.

Consumer sovereignty The power exerted by consumer demand over the allocation of resources.

Consumption Use of output for purposes of private enjoyment.

Cost Cost in everyday speech refers to the expenses incurred in production. In economics it refers to missed opportunities—opportunities foregone because resources are committed to a given use. This is called opportunity cost. (See also *Sunk cost*.)

Cost-benefit analysis The attempt to calculate the direct and indirect costs and benefits, whether paid or not, of any economic action.

Cost push An explanation of inflation that stresses increases in factor prices such as higher real wages, or the increase in cost of resources or other inputs. (See *Demand pull*.)

Credit crunch A severe restriction of bank credit, forcing the drastic curtailment of bank lending to businesses or consumers.

Crowding out The effect of government borrowing on the ability of the private sector to obtain funds on the loan markets.

Deepening capital Increasing the value of capital per worker.

Deficit spending Spending financed not by current tax receipts, but by borrowing or by drawing on past reserves.

Demand Willingness and ability to buy. Demand is a schedule that relates the quantities demanded with differing prices. (See also *Quantity demanded.*)

Demand gap The shortfall in demand that arises when the spending of the combined sectors is not enough to maintain a given level of GNP, or a necessary rate of growth of GNP.

Demand pull An explanation of inflation that stresses the effect of spending on the price level. Demand pull is usually focused on the effects of government or business spending. (See *Cost push.*)

Dependent variables Quantities whose value is determined by the value of another "independent" variable, contained in the equation.

Depreciation The decline in the value of capital goods over time. The term is also used to designate funds set aside to replace the worn-out capital.

Depreciation of exchange A fall in the ability of one nation's currency to buy the currency of a foreign nation.

Derived demand Demand for factors of production that results from the demand for goods and services.

Devaluation A policy deliberately intended to cheapen the exchange value of a currency in order to encourage exports. (Technically, devaluation means cheapening a currency in terms of gold.)

Diminishing returns The eventual tendency of outputs to rise more slowly than input as more and more of one factor is added to fixed amounts of other factors. Also known as the *law of variable proportions.*

Direct investment Investment in plant and equipment, as contrasted with financial investment.

Direct taxes Taxes levied by local, state, or federal governments on incomes.

Discounting Application of an interest rate to calculate the present value of a sum of money expected to be received or held in the future. At a rate of discount of 10 percent, $100 due a year hence is worth $90 today.

Discount rate The term applied to the interest rate charged by the Federal Reserve banks or loans made to their member banks.

Diseconomies of scale Increases in unit cost resulting from inefficiencies of technology or organization at rising levels (scales) of output.

Disinvestment A failure to create investment equal to the wear and tear on existing capital. Disinvestment means a diminution of capital wealth.

Disposable personal income Factor earnings plus transfers less direct taxes. Disposable personal income therefore defines aggregate household spending power.

Dissaving Expenditure that exceeds income. Dissaving requires that a dissaver use past savings, or borrowing, to finance the additional expenditure.

Distribution The process of allocating output or income among the population. Also used to refer to the results of this process, for example when we say that "income distribution is very unequal."

Economic profit Profit after the deduction of interest on capital. Profit is any residual after all factors have been paid their full values.

Economic rent See *Quasi rent.*

Economies of scale   Reductions of cost resulting from improved technology or organization at rising levels (scales) of output.

Efficiency   Relation of output to input.

Elasticity   A measure of the relation between price and quantity, or between income and quantity. If the percentage change in quantity demanded is greater than the percent change in price or income, we speak of elastic demand; if it is less, of inelastic demand.

Endogenous   Influences internal to a system. The rise in income that results from the multiplier effect is endogenous to the determination of GNP.

Entrepreneur   The person whose economic task is to direct the enterprise. His or her main task is to choose the proper scale, to make the best combination of factors, and to establish the best level of output. The entrepreneur may or may not own the enterprise, and therefore may or may not receive profits.

Entry   The ability to move into a market or line of production.

Equations   Mathematical statements usually involving dependent and independent variables in a functional relationship.

Equilibrium   A self-correcting and self-perpetuating level of prices or economic activity. Equilibrium prices equate quantities demanded and supplied, and thereby "clear" markets. Equilibrium flows of output, such as GNP, balance opposing tendencies of savings and investment to create a self-perpetuating flow.

Equimarginal rule   The general guide to optimization through equalizing the marginal returns of all factors.

Equity   Ownership, usually stock ownership.

Eurodollars   Supplies of dollars held by foreign or American banks outside the U.S.

Ex ante   The view looking forward. Ex ante refers to economic activity that has not yet taken place. Ex ante quantities or values may therefore differ from ex post figures, after the event.

Excess capacity   A market situation in which the capacity to produce is larger than the output desired by the market. Excess capacity is typical of oligopolistic industries.

Excess reserves   Bank reserves (cash or deposits at the Federal Reserve) over the required amount.

Exchange rate   The price of foreign currencies in terms of one's own currency.

Exogenous   Influences originating outside the system. An exogenous influence on GNP would be a change in the weather, or a war.

Exploitation   Payment to a factor of less than the value of the output it produces.

Ex post   The view looking backward. Ex post refers to economic activity that has already happened. (See *Ex ante*.)

External debts   Debts owed by members of one community, usually a nation, to another community or nation. (See *Internal debts*.)

Externalities   Effects (good or bad) imposed by the act of production, or consumption, for which no price is charged. A typical bad or negative externality is the pollution imposed on the public by smoke from a factory.

Factor market   The market in which the services of labor, land, or capital are sold. Factor markets regulate wages, rents, and interest rates.

Factor of production   The name given to the main kinds of inputs, land, labor, and capital, in a market society.

Federal Reserve banks   One of the 12 federally created central banks. Commercial banks may become members of the Federal Reserve System, but are not themselves Federal Reserve banks.

Federal Reserve system   The formal institution of central banking in the United States, structured around 12 Reserve banks and governed by a Board of Governors.

Final goods Goods that have reached the end of the production process. Typically these are of four kinds: consumption goods, investment or capital goods, government or public goods, and exports.

Fiscal policy Government efforts to control the level of employment or prices by spending and taxing, rather than by monetary policy.

Fixed costs Costs that do not change with the level of output. These are usually contractual costs such as rent, depreciation, etc.

Fixed exchange rates Exchange relationships between currencies fixed by government agreement and maintained by the action of central banks.

Foreign exchange Supplies of foreign currencies held by the banks or government of any nation.

Fractional reserves The legal permission to hold reserves equal to less than 100 percent of bank deposits. Fractional reserves multiply the effect of new deposits on the money supply.

Free riding The ability of economic actors to enjoy the utilities of certain outputs without paying for them.

Full employment budgets Calculation of the impact on GNP of government receipts and expenditure flows assuming that receipts and expenditures are at the levels corresponding to full employment.

Functional relationships Relationships in which the value of one variable is determined by another.

GNP (gross national product) The dollar value of the final output of the economy for a fixed period, usually a year. GNP is the sum of consumption, gross domestic investment, government purchases, and net exports.

Graphs Visual representations of functional relationships or of the movements of variables through time.

Gross investment The use of resources to create capital, whether as an addition to existing wealth or as a replacement for worn-out capital.

Gross national income The sum of factor incomes, tax receipts, and depreciation accruals. GNI is always identical with GNP.

Growth Increase in output. See nominal growth and real growth.

Horizontal equity A pattern of tax incidence that results in equal payments of tax among all members of the same income level.

Human capital The money value of skills or education.

Identities Mathematical statements of definition.

Imperialism Domination by a highly developed, powerful nation. Specifically used to describe the penetration of capitalist nations into the underdeveloped world.

Incidence of taxation The pattern of impact of taxation. The incidence of taxation attempts to discover where the burden of a tax ultimately falls.

Incomes policy Anti-inflation measures that depend on voluntary acceptance of income limitations, such as moderated wage demands.

Increasing cost The tendency of cost per unit to rise as the volume of output exceeds the point of greatest efficiency. (See *Law of increasing cost.*)

Increasing returns The initial tendency of output to rise faster than input, as one factor is added to fixed amounts of other factors.

Independent variables Quantities whose value is determined independently—that is, outside the equation.

Indexing Adjustment of nominal payments in accordance with a price index.

Indirect taxes Taxes levied by local, state, or federal government on the value of output. Cigarette or gas taxes are instances of indirect taxes.

Industrial policy The use of government policies to encourage (or discourage) industries, especially in international trade.

Infant industries Newly founded industries, especially in developing nations, that require tariff protection in order to achieve competitive scale.

Inflation A process in which prices in nearly all markets display a chronic upward tendency.

Inflation tax The effect of inflation in lessening the cost of a national debt.

Injections Any expenditures that raise the flow of income. The main injections are net investment, deficit spending, an excess of exports over imports, or a consumer spending wave, financed by drawing on past saving or on credit.

Interest The price of the factor capital.

Intermediate goods Goods or services that enter into final goods. For example, wheat is an intermediate good entering into bread.

Internal debts Debts owed by members of a community, usually a nation, to one another.

Intersectoral offsets Spending by one sector, usually business or government, used to offset the insufficient spending of another sector.

Inventories Goods on raw materials that have been produced but not yet sold to final purchasers. All increases in inventories are counted in the national accounts as net investment.

Investment The act of building capital. (See *Real vs. financial investment.*)

Invisible hand A famous phrase used by Adam Smith to indicate that individuals who followed their private self-interest would in fact fulfill a larger purpose, as if "led by an Invisible Hand."

Kondratieff cycle A cyclical pattern of roughly 25 buoyant and 25 stagnant years that may describe capitalist history. Its mechanism and even its existence are uncertain.

Law of increasing cost Eventual tendency of costs of a given output to rise as additional inputs of all factors (not just one) are used to produce it.

Law of variable proportions The tendency of output first to rise more rapidly than input, then more slowly, as one factor is added to fixed amounts of other factors.

Leakages Channels through which additional income is diverted from respending by households. The four main leakages are private saving, business profits, taxes, and imports.

Liquidity Condition of having immediately spendable resources, such as cash or very easily salable securities, such as very short-term government notes.

Liquidity preference The differing proportions of one's wealth that one seeks to hold in liquid form at differing interest rates. High interest rates impose high opportunity costs on holding cash. Therefore, usually we prefer to be less liquid when we can use our cash to earn high interest. Conversely, we seek more liquidity when the opportunity cost is low. Risk also plays an important part in determining our willingness to be liquid or illiquid.

M1 See *Money supply.*

Macroeconomics That portion of economics concerned with large-scale movements of the economy, such as growth or decline, inflation or deflation.

Marginal Additional, incremental (plus or minus).

Marginal cost The change in the cost of a firm resulting from a change in its output.

Marginal efficiency of investment The value of the expected returns of new investment discounted to the present.

Marginal productivity The change in output that can be ascribed to the addition or subtraction of any factor.

Marginal propensity to consume The relation between additional income and additional spending: $\Delta C/\Delta Y$. (See *Average propensity to consume.*)

Marginal propensity to save The relation between additional income and additional saving: $\Delta S/\Delta Y$. (See *Average propensity to save.*)

Marginal revenue   The change in the revenue of a firm resulting from a change in its output.

Market share   Proportion of an industry's sales enjoyed by a firm.

Market socialism   Socialist economies that continue to use markets as allocation mechanisms or as incentive systems, in addition to central planning of major elements such as investment.

Market system   The structure of exchange relations of buying and selling that sustains the economic process of capitalism.

Maximizing   The driving force of economic activity described as the pursuit of the largest possible amount of pleasurable wealth.

Mercantilism   The prevailing mode of economic organization in the period between late feudalism and early capitalism, characterized by a highly regulated domestic economy and an effort to achieve a surplus of exports over imports.

Microeconomics   That portion of economics concerned with the activity of individuals and firms, mainly with regard to the allocation of resources.

Mixed economies   Economies that combine attributes of capitalism, such as private property and market mechanisms, with elements of socialism, in particular welfare structures and some degree of government control over economic activity.

Mobility   The capacity to change economic location or function.

Monetarism   The body of theory that stresses the importance of the quantity of money in determining the rate of inflation and the level of activity.

Money stock   See *Money supply.*

Money supply   There are many ways of calculating the money supply. Perhaps the most common is cash held by the public, plus demand deposits at commercial banks. This is designated M1. Various other definitions (M1, M2, M3) expand the basic definition by adding other liquid assets.

Monopolistic competition   Market structures in which there are large numbers of sellers of differentiated products.

Monopoly   A single seller who supplies the entire output of a given market.

Multinational corporations   Corporations that derive a substantial proportion of their income or sales from overseas production, as contrasted with exports.

Multiplier-accelerator   The joint interaction of the multiplier effect, which creates additional income from an injection, and the accelerator effect, which creates additional investment from a rise in consumption.

Multiplier effect   The tendency of injections to create increases in income larger than the original injections. The multiplier effect results from the marginal propensity to consume.

National income   The total amount of factor incomes earned over a period of time. National income does not include transfer payments.

Nationalization   Purchase or seizure by the government of a privately owned firm.

Net investment   The use of resources to create additional capital goods.

Net national product   Gross national product minus depreciation. Net national product is also national income (factor earnings) plus the value of indirect taxes.

Nominal growth   Increase in output measured in current dollars, without allowance for changes in the purchasing power of dollars. If we compare the GNPs of two years, without deflating the dollar amounts, we are comparing nominal growth.

Nominal values   The values or prices of objects in current terms with no adjustment for changes in the value of the monetary unit.

Oligopoly   A market structure in which output is provided by a small enough number of sellers so that one seller can anticipate that others will react to changes in his strategy. In a competitive market there are so many participants that no firm can expect its own actions to disturb the workings of the market.

Open-market operations   The buying or selling of government bonds by the Federal Reserve, as a means of expanding or contracting the reserves of commercial banks.

Opportunity cost   The wealth or enjoyments that cannot be obtained because resources or inputs are already committed to a given purpose. All economic activities entail opportunity cost. Every act of consumption or production rules out the possibility of some alternative action.

Optimization   The search for the most efficient allocation of wealth or resources.

Overhead costs   Costs associated with administration or sales, rather than with direct factory-floor production.

Participation rate   The proportion of the population of working age that is actively seeking work.

Per capita GNP   Gross national product divided by the population.

Phillips curve   The presumed statistical correlation between unemployment and inflation first pointed out by A. W. Phillips.

Physiocracy   A school of economic thought developed by Francois Quesnay (1694–1774) that stressed the productive power of the land.

Portfolio investment   Financial investment, as opposed to real investment in plant and equipment.

Price index   A statistical measure of price levels in which one year is chosen as a base, and the other years expressed as a percentage of that base.

Price leadership   Role played by an industry leader that is the first to change prices in an oligopolistic market.

Production   The use of labor and resources to create wealth.

Production possibility curve   A graphic depiction of the total outputs available to a society. Production possibility curves are usually bowed outward because of the law of increasing cost.

Production possibility frontier   The outer limit of production possibilities as we move resources from one use to another. (See *Production possibility curve.*)

Productivity   A measure of output per unit of input over a given period of time, such as yearly or hourly output per worker or per machine.

Progressive incidence   A pattern of taxation that imposes proportionally heavier burdens on high income groups than on low income groups.

Propensity to consume   The relation between consumption and income: C/Y. (See also *Marginal propensity to consume.*)

Propensity to save   The relation between saving and income: S/Y. (See also *Marginal propensity to consume.*)

Proportional incidence   A pattern of taxation that imposes equal percentage burdens on all income levels.

Psychic income   The value of nonmonetary income in terms of utilities.

Public goods   Outputs provided by the public sector and not allocated by the price mechanism.

Purchasing power   The ability to buy.

Pure competition   A market structure characterized by large numbers of actors, easy entry and exit, undifferentiated products, and widespread information about market conditions.

Quantity demanded   The amount of a commodity or service that we are willing and able to buy at a given price. (See also *Demand.*)

Quantity equation $MV = PT$. (See *Quantity theory.*)

Quantity supplied   The amount of a commodity or service that we are willing and able to supply at a given price. (See also *Supply.*)

Quantity theory   The theory that relates the level of prices solely to the quantity of money.

Quasi rent Returns to a factor that derive solely from its scarcity, above the returns needed to induce the factor into production. Also called economic rent.

R&D Research and development. Research can be basic — inquiry that has no immediate commercial or economic orientation, or applied — inquiry directed at shaping knowledge for a given purpose. Development refers to commercial readying of goods or processes.

Rational expectations The tendency of markets to foresee and anticipate actions intended to alter market outcomes.

Rationality The assumption that people can intelligently adapt their actions (means) to their purposes (ends).

Rationing The distribution of resources according to some allocation mechanism. The mechanism may be the price system, or it may be a nonmarket system, such as coupons.

Real growth Increases in output corrected for changes in the purchasing power of the currency.

Real vs. financial investment Real investment is the act of devoting resources to capital formation. Financial investment denotes the purchase of equities, claims, or other instruments that channel personal savings into banks or businesses.

Regressive incidence A pattern of taxation that imposes proportionally larger burdens on low income groups than on high ones.

Rent Rent is the return paid to the owner of land or any resource for the use of his property. It is a payment necessary to bring that resource into production, and therefore differs from a quasi rent, which is a payment that results only from scarcity and is larger than that needed to bring the factor into use.

Replacement investment Investment that is designed to renew worn-out capital. Replacement investment plus net investment equals gross investment.

Reserve requirement The proportion of deposits that must be kept in vault cash or at a Federal Reserve bank. Reserve requirements are set by the Board of Governors of the Federal Reserve System.

Reserves Deposits that may not be loaned or invested. Reserves must be held in cash or at a Federal Reserve bank.

Saving The act of not using income for consumption. Saving is a financial act when we put money in a bank, but its real meaning is to relinquish a claim on resources.

Scale The size of operations, mainly of a plant. Scale is usually determined by the physical characteristics of the capital equipment used, although land or labor may be the determining elements.

Scatter diagram Graphic representation of two variables showing their associated pairs.

Schedule A list of different values of a variable, such as quantities or prices.

Sector A division of the economy with common characteristics. Usually we speak of the public and the private sector; of the consumption, investment, and government sectors; or of the agricultural, industrial, and service sectors.

Shortage The failure of a market to clear when the price is below equilibrium levels and there are unsatisfied buyers at the going price.

Stagflation An economic condition of simultaneous inflation and stagnation — that is, rising prices and inadequate growth.

Sticky prices The tendency of many prices to remain unchanged despite changes in demand and supply. This may be the consequence of contracts (a wage or rent contract) or of institutional inertia.

Stocks Legal instruments of ownership in corporations.

Substitution The capacity of one commodity to provide the utilities of another. Increases in the price of a commodity result in increases in the demand for its substitutes.

Sunk cost The cost, either in money or in foregone opportunities, that has been incurred up to the present with respect to any economic act of production.

Supply Willingness and ability to sell. Supply is a schedule that relates the quantities offered with differing prices. (See also *Quantity supplied*.)

Supply-side economics Policies seeking to use taxes or deregulation to impart a strong momentum to the economy.

Surplus The failure of a market to clear when the price is above equilibrium levels and there are unsatisfied sellers at the going price.

Terms of trade A comparison of the quantities of goods that are required to gain a given amount of goods in return. For example, the Brazilian terms of trade could measure the number of sacks of coffee needed to "buy" a computer.

Tight money A condition, associated with restrictive monetary policy, that makes it difficult for borrowers to obtain bank loans.

Tradeoff An exchange relationship denoting how much of A is needed to obtain a unit of B.

Transactions demand The amount of cash we need to carry on normal economic transactions. At higher levels of economic activity there is normally a higher demand for transactions balances, for such purposes as meeting payrolls or financing ordinary expenditures.

Transfers Any payment from one person or institution to another made for purposes other than to remunerate work. Social security is a transfer payment; so is the payment of an allowance to a minor, or a charity payment.

Unemployment Inability to find acceptable work at the going wage level.

Utility Pleasure or well-being.

Variable costs Costs that change directly with output, such as wages, or materials costs.

Variable proportions See *Law of variable proportions*.

Velocity of circulation The number of times a unit of currency is used during a period of time, usually a year. The velocity of circulation is calculated by dividing output (GNP) by the money supply.

Wealth Production that yields utilities.

Widening capital Matching additional workers with amounts of capital equal to those used by previously employed workers.

Yields The income paid by a bond compared with its market value. A bond issued at a price of $1,000 with a "coupon" of $100 (interest payable annually) will have a yield of 20 percent if the bond can be bought on the market at $500. It will have a 10 percent yield if its price is the original issue price. Its yield will fall to 5 percent if the market price of the bond rises to $2,000.

Zero-sum game A contest in which every gain is matched by an exactly equivalent loss.

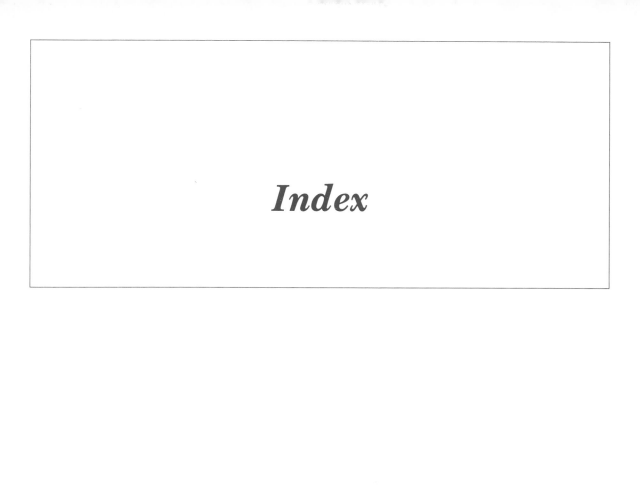

Index

Colloquy on the Anatomy of Economic Man

Present at the colloquy (left to right): Adam Smith, Thomas Malthus, David Ricardo, Jeremy Bentham, John Stuart Mill, Francois Marie Charles Fourier, Claude Henri Saint-Simon, Auguste Comte, Karl Marx, and Pierre Joseph Proudhon.